Contents

The great Welsh outdoors colour section following p.184

Festivals colour section following p.344

3

© Crown copyright

Introduction to
Wales

Perched on the rocky fringe of western Europe, Wales often gets short shrift in comparison to its Celtic cousins of Ireland and Scotland. Neither so internationally renowned nor so romantically perceived, the country is usually defined – if it is known at all – by its male voice choirs and tightly packed pit villages. But there's far more to the place than the hackneyed stereotypes and, at its best, Wales is the most beguiling part of the British Isles. Even its comparative anonymity serves it well: where the tourist dollar has swept away some of the more gritty aspects of local life in parts of Ireland and Scotland, reducing ancient cultures to misty Celtic pastiche, Wales remains brittle and brutal enough to be real, and diverse enough to remain endlessly interesting.

Within its small mass of land, Wales boasts some stunning physical attributes. Its **mountain ranges**, **ragged coastline**, **lush valleys** and old-fashioned **market towns** all invite long and repeated visits. The culture, too, is compelling, whether in its Welsh- or English-language manifestations, its Celtic or its industrial traditions, its ancient cornerstones of belief or its contemporary chutzpah. Recent years have seen a huge and dizzying upsurge in Welsh self-confidence, a commodity no longer so dependent upon comparison with its big and powerful neighbour of England. Popular culture – especially music and film – has contributed much to this revival, as has the arrival of a **National Assembly** in 1999, the first all-Wales tier of government for six hundred years. After centuries of enforced subjugation, the national spirit is undergoing a remarkable renaissance. The ancient symbol of the country, *y ddraig goch* or the **red dragon**, seen fluttering on flags everywhere in Wales, is waking up from what seems like a very long slumber.

Once you've crossed the border from England into Wales, the differences in appearance, attitude and culture between the two countries are immediately obvious. Wales shares many physical and emotional similarities with the other Celtic lands – Scotland, Ireland, Cornwall, Brittany, and even Asturias and Galicia in northwest Spain. A rocky and mountainous landscape, whose colours are predominantly grey and green, a thinly scattered, largely rural population, a culture rooted

> **Recent years have seen a huge upsurge in Welsh self-confidence.**

deeply in folklore and legend and the survival of a distinct, ancient language are all hallmarks of Wales and its sister countries. To the visitor, it is perhaps the **Welsh language**, the strongest survivor of the Celtic tongues, that most obviously marks out the country. Tongue-twisting village names and vast bilingual signposts point to a glorious tale of endurance against the odds, slap next to the heartland of English language and culture, the most expansionist in history. Everyone in Wales speaks English, but a quarter of the population also speak Welsh: TV and radio stations broadcast in it, all children learn it at school and visitors too are encouraged to try speaking at least a fragment of the rich, earthy tones of one of Europe's oldest living languages.

Although it's often the older aspects of Welsh and Celtic culture, from stone circles to crumbling castles, that bring visitors here in the first place, **contemporary Wales** is also a draw. The cities and university towns throughout the country are buzzing with an understated youthful confidence and sense of cultural optimism, while a generation or two of so-called "New Age" migrants have brought a curious cosmopolitanism to the small

▼ Millennium Stadium, Cardiff

Fact file

• Wales is the smallest of the three countries of mainland Britain, with an **area** of approximately 8000 square miles (20,800 square km). Constitutionally, it is part of the United Kingdom of Great Britain and Northern Ireland and a member state of the European Union. While it elects members of parliament to the UK government in Westminster (London), Wales also has its own devolved **National Assembly**, responsible for certain local affairs.

• The total **population** of Wales is around three million, sixty percent of whom live in the southeastern corner of the country. One quarter of the population of Wales was born out of the country, the vast majority being migrants from England. Cardiff, the capital city, has a population of 300,000, the second city of Swansea has 190,000.

• Historically, Wales has been largely an **Anglican** nation, although the British establishment church (here named the Church in Wales) has never had such deep roots as in neighbouring England. Nonconformism swept Wales between the seventeenth and nineteenth centuries, spawning many different divisions of Methodists, Baptists and Calvinists, as can be seen in the legacy of chapels everywhere in the country.

• Wales is officially a **bilingual** nation. Around one quarter of the population speak Welsh, the strongest survivor of the Celtic languages. The vast majority of Welsh speakers are concentrated in the north and west of the country. Everyone also speaks English.

market towns of mid-Wales and the west. Although conservative and traditional forces still sporadically clash with these more liberal and anarchic strands of thought, there's an unquestionable feeling that Wales is big enough, both physically and emotionally, to embrace such diverse influences. Perhaps most importantly of all, Welsh culture is underpinned by an iconoclastic democracy that contrasts starkly with the establishment-obsessed divisions of England, or even, to some extent, of Scotland or Ireland. Wales is not – and never has been – so absorbed by matters of class and status as its near neighbours. Instead, the Welsh character is famously endowed with a **musicality**, lyricism, introspection and sentimentality that produces far better bards and singers

Prehistoric and legendary Wales

Whether trudging through a dew-soaked field to some mysteriously inscribed standing stone, or catching the afternoon sun as it illumines the entrance to a cliff-top burial chamber, exploring Wales' prehistoric sites is thoroughly rewarding. At all but a few of the most popular, the bleating of sheep will be the only sound to break the contemplative silence of these spiritual places.

Prehistoric sites litter Wales. Hut circles defensively set atop windswept hills attest to a rugged hand-to-mouth pre-Celtic existence dating back four or five thousand years, while stone circles, intricately carved monoliths and finely balanced capstones set at crucial points on ancient pathways suggest the more spiritual life led by the priestly druids. Britain's greatest druidic centre was Anglesey, and the island is still home to many of Wales' best prehistoric sites, including the splendid chambers of Barclodiad y Gawres (see p.453) and Bryn Celli Ddu (see p.451). Elsewhere, numerous standing stones and circles can be found on the mysterious slopes of the Mynydd Preseli in Pembrokeshire (see p.208) and throughout Ardudwy in Gwynedd (see p.315). Many sites take their names from great figures in Celtic history and folklore, such as Arthur and Merlin (Myrddin in Welsh); legends abound to connect much of the landscape with ancient tales – details are scattered throughout the Guide and in boxes on p.90 and p.162.

than it does lords and masters. And Welsh culture is undeniably popular, arising from an inherently democratic impulse. Anything from a sing-song in the pub to the grandiose theatricality of an eisteddfod involves everyone – including any visitor eager to learn and join in.

◀ Porth Dinllaen, Llŷn Peninsula

Where to go

Only 160 miles from north to south and 50 miles from east to west, Wales is smaller than Massachusetts and only half the size of the Netherlands. Most of its inhabitants are packed into the southern quarter of the country, a fact which will largely dictate where you travel and what you do. Like all capital cities, **Cardiff** is atypical of the rest of the country, but as the first major stop on both rail and road routes from England into south Wales, it's a good place to start. Most national institutions are based here, not least the infant National Assembly, housed in brand-new splendour amidst the massive regeneration projects of Cardiff Bay. The city is also home to the National Museum and St Fagans National History Museum – both are excellent introductions to the character of the rest of Wales – and the superb Millennium Stadium, the home of huge sporting events and blockbuster gigs. The only other centres of appreciable size are loud-and-lairy **Newport** and breezy, resurgent **Swansea**, lying respectively to the east and west of the capital. All three cities grew as ports, mainly exporting millions of tons of coal and iron from the **Valleys**, where fiercely proud industrial communities were built up in the thin strips of land between the mountains.

Much of Wales' appeal lies outside the towns, where there is ample

Land of song

"Praise the Lord! We are a musical nation," intones the Rev. Eli Jenkins in Dylan Thomas' masterpiece, *Under Milk Wood*. It's a reputation of which the Welsh feel deservedly proud, and is squarely based on some considerable truth. Although plucky miners singing their way to the pithead was the dewy-eyed fabrication of Hollywood (*How Green Was My Valley*), Wales does make a great deal more noise, and make it a great deal more tunefully, than most other small countries.

The country's male voice choirs, many struggling to survive in the aftermath of the decimation of the coal industry that spawned them, are the best-known exemplars of Welsh singing, but traditions go much further back, to the bards and minstrels of the Celtic age. And although the choirs may be a shadow of their former selves, Wales continues to nurture big voices and big talent: from the hip-swivelling Sir Tom Jones and show-stopping Dame Shirley Bassey to anarchistic rockers the Manic Street Preachers and young divas like Charlotte Church, Katherine Jenkins and Duffy (below).

Wales and England

Like most countries that border each other, a distinct air of mutual suspicion hovers between Wales and its bigger, better-known neighbour, England. It's not really a battle of equals: Wales occupies a small, rocky part of the island of Britain and is home to just short of three million people. England, with fifty million inhabitants and far greater wealth, is used to having the upper hand, having welded its smaller sibling to it by force over seven hundred years ago. Memories are long hereabouts though, and those seven centuries sound like mere seconds when you listen to some of the more passionate Welsh nationalists calling for, if not outright divorce from England, at least a trial separation.

The mutual antipathy is almost all good-natured and perhaps best seen on the sporting field. But it shouldn't be underestimated. Wales and England are two different countries, and they look, sound and feel like it. Often the greatest offence to Welsh people is when those very obvious differences are blatantly disregarded or patronized. And like calling a Kiwi an Aussie or a Canadian an American, the worst thing you can possibly do is to call a Welsh person English. You have been warned.

evidence of the warmongering which has shaped the country's development. Castles are everywhere, from the hard little stone keeps of the early Welsh princes to Edward I's incomparable series of thirteenth-century fortresses at **Flint**, **Conwy**, **Beaumaris**, **Caernarfon**, **Harlech** and **Rhuddlan**, and grandiose Victorian piles where grouse were the only enemy. Fortified residences served as the foundation for a number of the stately homes that dot the country, but many castles were deserted and remain dramatically isolated on rocky knolls, most likely on spots previously occupied by prehistoric communities. Passage graves and stone circles offer a more tangible link to the pre-Roman era when the priestly order of Druids ruled over early Celtic peoples, and later religious monuments such as the great ruined abbeys of **Valle Crucis**, **Tintern** and **Strata Florida** lend a gaunt grandeur to their surroundings.

Whether you're admiring castles, megaliths or Dylan Thomas's home at **Laugharne**, almost everything in Wales is enhanced by the beauty of the countryside, from the lowland greenery of meadows and river valleys to the inhospitable heights of the moors and mountains. The rigid backbone of the **Cambrian Mountains** terminates in the soaring peaks of **Snowdonia** and the angular ridges of the **Brecon Beacons**, both superb walking country and both national parks. A third national park follows the

> **Much of the coast remains unspoilt, though seldom visited.**

Pembrokeshire Coast, where golden strands are separated by rocky bluffs overlooking offshore bird colonies. Much of the rest of the coast remains unspoilt, though seldom visited, with long sweeps of sand often backed by traditional British seaside resorts: the **north Wales coast**, the **Cambrian coast** and the **Gower peninsula** have a notable abundance.

▶ Kitesurfing, Rhossili beach, Gower peninsula

When to go

The English preoccupation with the weather holds equally for the Welsh. The **climate** here is temperate, with Welsh summers rarely getting hot and nowhere but the tops of mountain ranges ever getting very cold, even in midwinter. Temperatures vary little from Cardiff in the south to Llandudno in the north, but proximity to the mountains is a different matter: Llanberis, at the foot of Snowdon, gets doused with more than twice as much rainfall as Caernarfon, seven miles away, and is always a few degrees cooler. With rain never too far from the mind of any resident or visitor, it is easy to forget that throughout much of the summer, Wales – particularly the coast – can be bathed in sun. Between June and September, the Pembrokeshire coast, washed by the Gulf Stream, can be as warm as anywhere in Britain. The bottom line is that it's impossible to say with any degree of certainty that the weather will be pleasant in any given month. May might be wet and grey one year and gloriously sunny the next, and the same goes for the autumnal months – November stands an equal chance of being crisp and clear or foggy and grim. Obviously, if you're planning to lie on a beach, or camp in the dry, you'll want to go

Sheep in the Brecon Beacons

between June and September – a period when you should book your accommodation as far in advance as possible. Otherwise, if you're balancing the likely fairness of the weather against the density of the **crowds**, the best time to get into the countryside or the towns is between April and May, or September and October. If **outdoor pursuits** are your objective, these are the best months for walking, June to October are warmest and driest for climbing, and December to March the only times you'll find enough water for kayaking.

Wales' climate

Average daily temperatures and monthly rainfall.

	Jan	Feb	Mar	Apr	May	Jun	Jul	Aug	Sept	Oct	Nov	Dec
Aberystwyth												
max (°C)	8.0	7.9	9.8	12.2	15.7	17.7	19.8	19.5	17.5	14.2	10.6	8.9
max (°F)	46	46	50	54	60	64	68	67	64	58	51	48
min (°C)	2.0	2.0	2.8	3.4	6.2	8.5	11.4	11.0	9.2	7.1	4.2	2.9
min (°F)	36	36	37	38	43	47	53	52	49	45	40	37
rainfall (mm)	126	92	99	71	66	79	72	91	104	134	140	140
rainfall (in)	5.0	3.6	3.9	2.8	2.6	3.1	2.8	3.6	4.1	5.3	5.5	5.5
Cardiff												
max (°C)	7.9	8.2	10.6	13.1	16.7	19.2	21.5	21.3	18.4	14.6	10.9	8.9
max (°F)	46	47	51	56	62	67	71	70	65	58	52	48
min (°C)	2.1	2.1	3.7	4.8	7.8	10.5	12.8	12.5	10.0	7.5	4.3	3.2
min (°F)	36	36	39	41	46	51	55	55	50	46	40	38
rainfall (mm)	119	91	89	65	65	66	61	90	104	117	117	128
rainfall (in)	4.7	3.6	3.5	2.6	2.6	2.6	2.4	3.5	4.1	4.6	4.6	5.0
Llandudno												
max (°C)	8.2	8.2	9.9	11.5	14.8	17.0	19.3	19.2	17.0	14.1	10.8	9.1
max (°F)	47	47	50	53	59	63	67	67	63	57	51	48
min (°C)	2.8	2.6	3.9	5.0	7.3	10.0	12.1	12.1	10.2	7.9	5.3	3.7
min (°F)	37	37	39	41	45	50	54	54	50	46	42	39
rainfall (mm)	77	48	58	47	54	59	44	63	67	91	89	92
rainfall (in)	3.0	1.9	2.3	1.9	2.1	2.3	1.7	2.5	2.6	3.6	3.5	3.6
Tenby												
max (°C)	8.5	8.0	9.7	11.7	14.8	17.3	19.5	19.3	17.1	14.2	11.2	9.5
max (°F)	47	46	49	53	59	63	67	67	63	58	52	49
min (°C)	3.1	2.8	3.8	4.7	7.4	9.9	12.0	11.8	10.3	8.3	5.3	4.0
min (°F)	38	37	39	40	45	50	54	53	51	47	42	39
rainfall (mm)	115	90	87	61	52	67	53	93	102	131	130	126
rainfall (in)	4.5	3.5	3.4	2.4	2.0	2.6	2.1	3.7	4.0	5.2	5.1	5.0

things not to miss

It's not possible to see everything that Wales has to offer in one trip – and we don't suggest you try. What follows is a selective taste of the country's highlights: outstanding buildings and natural wonders, plus the best festivals and outdoor activities. They're arranged in five colour-coded categories, which you can browse through to find the very best things to see and experience. All highlights have a page reference to take you straight into the Guide, where you can find out more.

01 **Pembrokeshire Coast Path** Page **183** ● Break up this path around some of Wales' wildest coastal scenery into a series of day walks, or tackle the full 187 miles in one big push.

03 **Tryfan** Page **370** • Jumping the gap between the Adam and Eve rocks, on the top of Tryfan mountain in Snowdonia, is the traditional encore for any climber who's made it to the summit.

02 **A Welsh oak wood** Page **489** • Once the sacred place of the druids, the twisty oak woods of Wales, often with lively streams burbling through, clear the mind and soul.

04 **Portmeirion** Page **396** • The grandest folly of them all, Portmeirion is a gorgeous visual poem that will melt the hardest heart.

05 Aberystwyth Page **287** • The capital of sparsely populated mid-Wales, Aberystwyth is a breezy and bright university and seaside town surrounded by luscious countryside.

06 Harlech Castle Page **319** • Of all of Edward I's mighty fortresses, Harlech Castle is the finest, its setting as impressive as the medieval building itself.

07 **Llandudno** Page **425** • North Wales' most genteel seaside resort, Llandudno spreads languidly around the bay beneath the ancient rock plug of the Great Orme.

08 **National Waterfront Museum, Swansea** Page **143** • The newest addition to the country's string of national museums, using the latest in technical wizardry to explore the mysteries of the past.

09 **Dyffryn Arms (aka Bessie's)** Page **211** • Head for a pint and a chinwag at perhaps Wales' finest old-fashioned pub. There's no food and only middling beer, but places like this surely won't be around for much longer.

17

10 Surfing Page **55** • Sure, the water isn't warm but don't let that deter you. Suit up and surf some of the UK's finest waves.

12 Ffestiniog Railway Page **396** • Of Wales' many "great little trains", the Ffestiniog Railway, winding down through the Snowdonia mountains, is by far the best.

11 Brains beer Page **47** • Cardiff's famous pint can be supped in any number of traditional pubs.

13 Rugby Page **56** • Although Wales' standing in international rugby fluctuates wildly, the game remains nearly a religion here, never more so than when the national team are playing at Cardiff's awesome Millennium Stadium.

14 Pistyll Rhaeadr Page **266** • Narrow lanes thread their way through the border country of mid-Wales to what, at 240ft, is the country's highest waterfall.

15 A night out in Swansea Page **144** • For sheer boisterous, boozy fun it's hard to beat Swansea's Wind Street.

16 Machynlleth market Page **299** • Old boys in flat caps mingle with rosy-cheeked hippies in the lively weekly market of Machynlleth, good for everything from fresh produce to second-hand tat.

17 Cadair Idris

Page **298** • The dominant mountain of southern Snowdonia, Cadair Idris is a magnificent beast chock-full of classic glacial features.

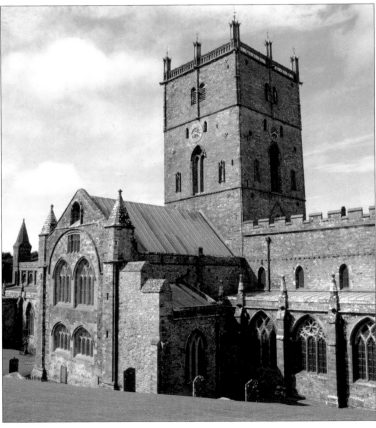

18 St Davids Cathedral Page **199** • The heart of Welsh spirituality, St Davids Cathedral is at Wales' westerly extremity and has drawn pilgrims for a millennium and a half.

19 Aberglasney Page **165** • Rescued from near-terminal decay, these formal gardens in the Tywi Valley are a perfect counterpoint to the nearby National Botanic Garden of Wales.

20 Male voice choirs Page **106** • Burly miners singing their hearts out at eisteddfodau may be a thing of the past, but Welsh male voice choirs still survive and thrive.

21 Carreg Cennen Castell Page **167** • The most romantic ruin in Wales, Carreg Cennen Castell sits in glorious isolation amidst the velvet green of Carmarthenshire.

22 Conwy Page **431** • One of north Wales' finest walled medieval towns, Conwy contains over two hundred listed buildings within its tight grid.

23 Transporter Bridge Page **88** • "A giant with the might of Hercules and the grace of Apollo", as Newport's Transporter Bridge was described when it opened in 1906.

24 Glamorgan sausages Page **46** • Even hardened carnivores will enjoy this leek and cheese sausage, regularly served with a cooked breakfast.

25 The Valleys Page **92** • Colourful terraces of housing, hunkered down under the hills, are the hallmark of Wales' world-famous Valleys, the old mining area in the south.

26 **Cardiff Bay architecture** Page **121** • The wonderful National Assembly Building is one of many striking modern structures around the rejuvenated Cardiff Bay.

27 **Mawddach Estuary** Page **308** • Wales' finest estuary, the Mawddach, is best seen from the 2253-foot rail and foot bridge into Barmouth.

28 Soar-y-Mynydd chapel Page **248** • Duw cariad yw (God Loves You) at Wales' most remote chapel, in the wild countryside of Mynydd Eppynt.

30 St Fagans National History Museum Page **130** • An unmissable chronicle of Welsh life, featuring period buildings from all over the country.

29 National Museum and Gallery, Cardiff Page **119** • One of Britain's finest collections, with archeological treasures, stunning Impressionist paintings and some fabulous sculptures.

Basics

Basics

Getting there

Wales is easily reached from the rest of the UK, Ireland and continental Europe. There are no direct flights to Wales from outside Europe, so you're best off flying to London (or perhaps Manchester) and continuing overland from there. The range of options is greatest – and the fares usually lowest – flying into London, Britain's busiest gateway city. Two of London's airports – Heathrow and Gatwick – handle long-haul flights, and in terms of convenience for onward travel they're about equal. For quicker access to mid- or north Wales, you might consider one of the limited number of direct flights into Manchester or Birmingham airports. An alternative to transiting through England is to arrive at Cardiff International Airport, which is served by flights from Belfast, Cork, Dublin, Edinburgh, Glasgow, Paris and many other European cities (see p.28 for full details).

Long-haul **airfares** depend on the season, with the highest being around May to August, when the weather is best; fares drop during the "shoulder" seasons (Sept and April) and drop further during the low season (Oct–March, excluding Christmas and New Year, when prices jump and seats are at a premium). Note also that flying on weekends ordinarily adds five or ten percent to the round-trip fare; price ranges quoted below assume midweek travel.

Booking flights online

Booking online via airlines' own websites or discount travel sites invariably works out cheaper than booking by phone. You can also often cut costs by going through a specialist flight agent – either a consolidator, who buys up blocks of tickets from the airlines and sells them at a discount, or a discount agent, who in addition to dealing with discounted flights may also offer special student and youth fares and a range of other travel-related services such as travel insurance, rail passes, car rentals, tours and the like. Some agents specialize in charter flights, which may be cheaper than anything available on a scheduled flight, but again departure dates are fixed and withdrawal penalties are high.

Online booking agents

ⓦ **www.cheapflights.com** Good links to travel agents and other travel sites.

ⓦ **www.cheaptickets.com** Discount flight specialist.

ⓦ **www.etn.nl/discount.htm** A hub of consolidator and discount agent weblinks, maintained by the non-profit European Travel Network.

ⓦ **www.expedia.com** Discount airfares, all-airline search engine and daily deals.

ⓦ **www.flyaow.com** Online air travel info and reservations site.

ⓦ **www.gaytravel.com** Gay online travel agent, concentrating mostly on accommodation.

ⓦ **www.hotwire.com** Bookings from the US only. Last-minute savings of up to forty percent on regular published fares. Travellers must be at least 18 and there are no refunds, transfers or changes allowed. Log-in required.

ⓦ **www.lastminute.com** Offers good last-minute holiday package and flight-only deals.

ⓦ **www.skyauction.com** Bookings from the US only. Auctions tickets and travel packages using a "second bid" scheme. The best strategy is to bid the maximum you're willing to pay, since if you win you'll pay just enough to beat the runner-up regardless of your maximum bid.

ⓦ **www.travelocity.com** Destination guides, web fares and deals on car rental, accommodation and lodging.

Getting there from the UK and Europe

Crossing the border **from England** into Wales is straightforward, with train and bus services forming part of the British national network. Minimal time savings mean that flights within Britain are of little use, with the exception of those from Scotland. If you're driving from England, the two roads providing the quickest access into the heart of the country run along opposite coasts: the **M4 motorway** in the south, and the **A55 expressway** in the north. Both are fast and busy; minor routes are more appealing if you aren't in too much of a hurry.

From Ireland, ferries are by far the cheapest and easiest (if not necessarily fastest) way of getting to Wales. **From the rest of Europe**, alternatives to air travel are the traditional cross-Channel ferry services or the Channel Tunnel.

The website The Man in Seat 61 (ⓦwww .seat61.com) is an independent and invaluable source of information for sea and train travel.

By plane

The only airport of any size in Wales is **Cardiff International Airport** (ⓦwww.cwlfly .com), ten miles southwest of the capital, which has scheduled flights from Canada, selected European cities and a few British and Irish destinations. The main international carriers are KLM (UK information on ☏0870/5074074, ⓦwww.klm.com), which flies into Cardiff from Amsterdam; and bmibaby (☏0870/2642229, ⓦwww .bmibaby.com) for services from Alicante, Amsterdam, Barcelona, Belfast, Edinburgh, Faro, Geneva, Glasgow, Jersey, Malaga, Murchia, Palma Mallorca and Warsaw. Other airlines flying into Cardiff are Thomsonfly (ⓦwww.thomsonfly.com), Aer Arann (ⓦwww .aerarann.com), Flybe (ⓦwww.flybe.com), Eastern Airways (ⓦwww.easternairways .com), and a Skybus service to Newquay in Cornwall, England (ⓦwww.skybus.co.uk). Many of the most useful routes run mostly business flights, timed and priced accordingly, and often not operating at weekends.

Within Wales, the sole scheduled **domestic flights** are between Cardiff Airport and Valley airfield on Anglesey with Highland Airways (ⓦwww.highlandairways.co.uk).

By train

Britain's **rail network** is split between different companies, although through-ticketing is always available: the national rail enquiries line (☏08457/484950, from outside the UK ☏+44 20 7278 5240; ⓦwww.nationalrail .co.uk) should be your first port of call for all queries regarding train travel. The website ⓦwww.thetrainline.com offers some good deals on fares. For more details on ticket types and booking, see the box on p.36.

From France and Belgium

England has direct passenger trains to France and Belgium via the twenty-mile-long Channel Tunnel with **Eurostar** (☏0870/1606600, ⓦwww.eurostar.com), which runs hourly between London (St Pancras), Stratford (east London), Ebbsfleet (Dartford, near the M25) and Paris, Lille, and Brussels, plus a direct service between London and Avignon from December to April. The least expensive return fares to London, which are nonexchangeable and nonrefundable, are €77 from Paris or Lille and €80 from Brussels. Full fares with no restrictions are €435 from Paris, €370 from Brussels and €335 from Lille. Nonexchangeable, nonrefundable youth tickets (for under-26s) cost from €75 from Paris or Brussels and from €60 from Lille. Eurostar also offers frequent promotional fares, particularly for advance bookings, so it's always worth checking the website.

A 35-minute bus, motorbike and car-carrying train service through the Channel tunnel known as "**Le Shuttle**" is operated by Eurotunnel (from the UK ☏08705/353535, from other countries ☏+33 (0)321002061, ⓦwww.eurotunnel.com). You can just turn up on the day you want to travel, but booking is advised, especially at weekends. The standard one-way fare for a car and all its passengers starts from £49, with various flexi and short-stay discount return fares available.

Despite the tunnel, **car ferries** remain well and truly in business, often undercutting the tunnel prices and, in the case of the Calais–Dover service, not taking much longer (see p.33 for contacts).

From England and Scotland

While services in Wales and the Borders are operated by Arriva Trains Wales (see "Getting Around", p.35), those into Wales are operated by other groups. Fast, frequent services from London Paddington to **Newport**, **Cardiff and Swansea**

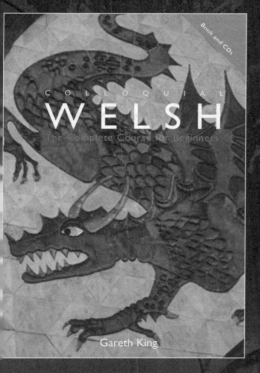

Train fares and savings

Ordinary standard-class fares on UK trains are high, and first-class costs an extra 33 percent, but there are various types of reduced-fare ticket.

Savers are return tickets that can be used on all trains on Saturdays, Sundays and bank holidays, on most weekday trains outside the morning rush hour for the outward journey; there may also be restrictions for travel times for the return leg, and for the length of validity during which the return journey must take place. If you buy a return ticket at any station outside the morning rush hour, you'll routinely be issued with a Saver ticket. **SuperSavers** are cheaper, but may have greater restrictions on outward and return journey times you can travel. Check conditions when you're purchasing tickets.

Considerable savings can be made with **Advance fares** – single fares that are booked in advance, subject to availability. Generally, the earlier you book, the greater the savings.

Rover and **Ranger** tickets can be particularly useful for travellers, allowing unlimited travel throughout a particular area. Some travel time restrictions may apply. Rover Tickets are usually available for a certain number of days (eg seven consecutive days, or any three days within fifteen consecutive days). Ranger Tickets offer the same flexibility, but are generally valid for just one day. For more information, see p.36.

Up to two **children** under 5 per adult-fare-paying passenger travel free, while those aged 5–15 inclusive pay half the adult fare on most journeys. Awkward pieces of luggage – skis, for example, etc – usually incur a fee, but **bicycles** are carried free, though cyclists must reserve in advance.

As a guide to **prices**, a standard-class one-way ticket on the London–Cardiff route can cost anything between £11.50 (Advance) and £79 (standard open single ticket), with a saver ticket (£56) in between.

---

are operated by First Great Western (ⓦ www.firstgreatwestern.co.uk; sales ☏08457/000125). Very few direct trains from England go beyond Swansea, although connections at either Cardiff or Swansea link up with services to Carmarthen and stations in Pembrokeshire. The **north coast service**, from London Euston to Chester, Llandudno Junction, Bangor and Holyhead is operated by Virgin Trains (ⓦ www.virgintrains.co.uk; sales ☏08457/222333). From other cities in England and Scotland, you'll probably need to change en route – at Bristol or Bath for the south coast line, at Crewe for the north coast.

Mid-Wales is best reached via Birmingham and Shrewsbury, with two lines plunging deep into the heart of the country. The faster route heads through Welshpool, Newtown and Machynlleth, beyond which it divides at Dyfi Junction. The southern spur goes a few miles to Borth and Aberystwyth, the northern one crawls up the coast through Tywyn, Barmouth, Harlech and Porthmadog to Pwllheli. Even slower (but very picturesque) is the second route from Shrewsbury, the **Heart of Wales** line, which runs through Knighton, Llandrindod Wells, Llanwrtyd Wells, Llandovery, Llandeilo and a host of tiny halts on the way to Llanelli and Swansea.

Journey times between main centres are short: London–Cardiff takes around two- and a- quarter hours and London–Swansea around three hours. Heading for the north coast, the London–Holyhead service takes just over four hours.

By bus

Inter-town bus services duplicate a few of the major rail routes, often at half the price of the train or less, but taking considerably longer. Buses are reasonably comfortable and often have on-board drinks and sandwiches available on longer routes. By far the biggest national operator is **National Express** (☏08717/818181, ⓦ www.nationalexpress.com), whose network covers

England and sends half a dozen tendrils into Wales. The chief routes are from London to Cardiff, Swansea and on to Pembroke and Milford Haven; London to Wrexham; London to Aberystwyth; London along the north Welsh coast to Holyhead and Pwllheli, both via Birmingham; Birmingham to Cardiff and Swansea; Birmingham to Haverfordwest; Chester along the north coast to Llandudno, Bangor and Holyhead; and Cardiff to both Glasgow and Edinburgh. National Express services are so popular that for busy routes and services during weekends and holidays, it's a good idea to buy a reserved journey ticket, which guarantees a seat.

One-way **fares** to Cardiff can be as little as £5 from London (£21.30 for a refundable, amendable fare), subject to availability. If you're planning to travel extensively throughout Britain by bus, the various **National Express discount passes** may save you a lot of money. UK residents aged 16–26 or in full-time education or can buy a National Express Coachcard discount card (£10), which is valid for one year and entitles the holder to up to thirty percent off many fares. If you're over 60 you automatically qualify for concessionary fares (upto 50 percent discount) All foreign passengers are entitled to buy a **Brit Xplorer pass**, which offers unlimited travel on the National Express network. Choose between seven days (£79), fourteen days (£139) or 28 days (£219). You can buy these passes online or in Britain from major travel agents and at major National Express offices. In North America, these passes should be available through travel agents.

For more on bus passes for Wales and the rest of Britain, see "Getting around", pp.35–41.

By road: driving

Travelling to Wales by car from England, the main roads into the north are the coastal **A55** expressway (from Chester to the Irish ferries at Holyhead), and the **A5** through Llangollen (the major road into north Wales from the Midlands and the south of England, best approached from the M6 just north of Wolverhampton, via the fast M54 and Shrewsbury bypass). Much of the A5 has been improved in recent decades, although there are still bottlenecks at Llangollen and Betws-y-Coed.

The best route into mid-Wales as far south as Newtown and Aberystwyth is via the **A458** to Welshpool from the Shrewsbury bypass. Further south, the **A456** from Birmingham, via Kidderminster and Leominster, is occasionally slow when passing through towns, but generally easier than the route through Worcester and Hereford to reach the A44 in Radnorshire and, to the south, the A438/470 to Brecon. This road connects with the swift westbound **A40** at the Brecon bypass, best for routes from the Midlands and north of England to southern Cardiganshire and northern Carmarthenshire. An alternative route from the Midlands is via the **M50** "Ross Spur", a quiet motorway off the M5 south of Worcester, meeting the A449 dual carriageway at Ross-on-Wye. The road continues south, dividing at Raglan into the quick A40 for Brecon and the A449 down to Newport, the M4 and all destinations west.

The **M4** from London makes the most dramatic entry into Wales, across the twin River Severn Bridges. Stay on the M4 and you'll be ushered into Wales across the Second Severn Crossing (£5.30 toll westbound only; no footpath or cycle lane), a graceful bridge a few miles south of the M48 and the original Severn Bridge (same toll; footpath and cycle lane available), rising high over the mud flats as it descends towards Chepstow. Neither bridge accepts credit cards; check conditions and closures at ⑩ www.severnbridge.co.uk. Both motorways reconnect just west of Caldicot. The M4 coasts quickly westwards, although tailbacks are frequent around Cardiff and Newport. At Pont Abraham, a few miles north, the M4 mutates into the **A48** dual carriageway, connecting with the excellent A40 at Carmarthen and coursing west to Haverfordwest for connections to Pembrokeshire and southern Ceredigion.

Hitching and lift-sharing

The extensive motorway network and the density of traffic makes long-distance **hitching** through England and Scotland to the Welsh border and along the M4 to Cardiff and Swansea relatively easy. Key junctions on the edge of metropolitan areas and motorway service stations are the favoured hitching spots, and standing with a sign at the exit produces the best results.

However, for safety reasons, hitching is not generally advised, especially for women travelling alone. A good alternative is **lift-sharing**, whereby you share the travel costs with someone already going in your direction. One of the best ways is through web-based agencies such as Liftshare (ⓦwww.liftshare.org) and Freewheelers (ⓦwww.freewheelers.co.uk), where you register (free) and enter your desired route so that the database can come up with suitable matches. You then contact the resulting matches by email and make arrangements. It's also worth checking noticeboards in hostels, health food shops and other like-minded establishments to see if anyone's going your way.

By ferry

Wales has three main **ferry ports** all serving boats from Ireland (see box opposite). Ferries and high-speed catamarans from Dublin, and catamarans from Dun Laoghaire (six miles south of Dublin), arrive at **Holyhead** on the northwest tip of Wales, while Rosslare,

just outside Wexford, is the departure point for ferries and catamarans to **Fishguard**, and ferries to **Pembroke Dock**, both in southwest Wales.

Stena Line operates ferries from Dublin to Holyhead, fast cats from Dun Laoghaire to Holyhead, and both ferries and cats between Rosslare and Fishguard; Irish Ferries runs ferries and cats from Dublin to Holyhead, and ferries between Rosslare and Pembroke Dock. Ferry prices for the two companies are almost identical, whichever ports you travel between. One-way foot passenger fares are €35, while the one-way fare for a car and driver ranges from €89 to €148, depending on the season. Huge savings are available by maximizing various midweek and advance purchase offers.

There's a much greater choice of ferries from Europe to **ports in England**. Competitive pricing means that unless you're in a hurry, lower prices may lure you onto a boat rather than into the Channel Tunnel. There are regular crossings with SeaFrance and P&O from Calais to Dover, the shortest route, for which the lowest fare for a small car and driver is around £117, though there are frequent specials. For full details of ferry

Fly less – stay longer! Travel and climate change

Climate change is perhaps the single biggest issue facing our planet. It is caused by a build-up in the atmosphere of carbon dioxide and other greenhouse gases, which are emitted by many sources – including planes. Already, **flights** account for three to four percent of human-induced global warming: that figure may sound small, but it is rising year on year and threatens to counteract the progress made by reducing greenhouse emissions in other areas.

Rough Guides regard travel as a **global benefit**, and feel strongly that the advantages to developing economies are important, as are the opportunities for greater contact and awareness among peoples. But we also believe in travelling responsibly, which includes giving thought to how often we fly and what we can do to redress any harm that our trips may create.

We can travel less or simply reduce the amount we travel by air (taking fewer trips and staying longer, or taking the train if there is one); we can avoid night flights (which are more damaging); and we can make the trips we do take "climate neutral" via a carbon offset scheme. **Offset schemes** run by climatecare.org, carbonneutral.com and others allow you to "neutralize" the greenhouse gases that you are responsible for releasing. Their websites have simple calculators that let you work out the impact of any flight – as does our own. Once that's done, you can pay to fund projects that will reduce future emissions by an equivalent amount. Please take the time to visit our website and make your trip climate neutral, or get a copy of the Rough Guide to Climate Change for more detail on the subject.

www.roughguides.com/climatechange

Ferry connections from Ireland to Wales

Route	Company	Frequency	Duration
Dublin–Holyhead	Stena/Irish Ferries	2–6 daily	1hr 40min/3hr 15min
Dublin–Liverpool	P&O Irish Sea	1–2 daily	7hr 30min
Dun Laoghaire–Holyhead	Stena	2 daily	1hr 40min
Rosslare–Fishguard	Stena	2–6 daily	1hr 35min–3hr 30min
Rosslare–Pembroke	Irish Ferries	2 daily	3hr 45min

routes and prices, contact the ferry companies direct. The websites Seaview ferry (www.seaview.co.uk/ferries.html) and Direct Ferries (www.directferries.co.uk) are particularly handy resources with links to all the following companies:

Brittany Ferries 0871/2440744, www.brittanyferries.co.uk.

Condor Ferries 0845/6091024, www.condorferries.co.uk.

Irish Ferries 08705/171717, www.irishferries.com.

P&O Ferries 08716/645645, www.poferries.com.

Sea France 0871/4237119, www.seafrance.com.

Stena Line 08705/707070, www.stenaline.com.

Transmanche Ferries 0800/9171201, www.transmancheferries.com.

Flights from North America

The enormous volume of air traffic crossing the Atlantic keeps prices relatively low and virtually guarantees you'll find a seat at all but the busiest times. There are no direct flights from North America to Wales, but numerous airlines fly from the **eastern seaboard** and the **Midwest** to London, the principal British gateway for visitors to Wales. You'll also come across direct flights to regional airports with good links to Wales, such as Manchester and Birmingham. Fares are usually higher than those to London, but deals can be found. Several airlines – American, British Airways, United, Virgin and others – fly nonstop from **Los Angeles**. British Airways and others also fly direct to London from **San Francisco** and **Seattle**, and other airlines offer easy connections.

Low-season round-trip **fares** from New York, Boston and Washington to London start at around US$450, though US$500–550 is more normal, and through the summer you can expect to pay US$550–800. Add US$100–200 from other eastern cities. Low-season fares from the West Coast start at a little under US$700, though expect more like US$1300 in peak summer and around Christmas.

In **Canada**, you'll get the best deal flying to London from the big gateway cities of Toronto and Montreal, where low-season fares start at around CAN$600 round-trip, and high-season round-trips cost just over CAN$1000. Flights from almost all other eastern Canadian cities travel via one of these two hubs, with those from Ottawa costing about the same and those from elsewhere CAN$100–200 more. From the west, flights from Vancouver, Edmonton and Calgary start around CAN$800 in the low season and CAN$1300 at peak times.

Airlines

Aer Lingus 1-800/IRISH-AIR, www.aerlingus.com.
Air Canada 1-888/247-2262, www.aircanada.com.
American Airlines 1-800/433-7300, www.aa.com.
British Airways 1-800/AIRWAYS, www.ba.com.
British Midland 1-800/788-0555, www.flybmi.com.
Continental Airlines 1-800/231-0856, www.continental.com.
Delta Air Lines 1-800/241-4141, www.delta.com.
Lufthansa US 1-800/645-3880, Canada 1-800/563-5954; www.lufthansa.com.
Northwest/KLM Airlines 1-800/225-2525, www.nwa.com.
United Airlines 1-800/538-2929, www.united.com.
Virgin Atlantic 1-800/821-5438, www.virgin-atlantic.com.

Discount travel companies

Air Brokers International ☎1-800/883-3273, ⓦwww.airbrokers.com. Consolidator and specialist in round-the-world tickets.

Airtech ☎212/219-7000, ⓦwww.airtech.com. Standby seat broker and dealer in consolidator fares.

Educational Travel Center ☎1-800/747-5551 or 608/256-5551, ⓦwww.edtrav.com. Student/youth discount agent.

STA Travel ☎1-800/781-4040, ⓦwww.statravel .com. Worldwide specialist in independent travel; also student IDs, travel insurance, car rental, rail passes, etc.

TFI Tours ☎1-800/745-8000 or 212/736-1140, ⓦwww.tfitours.com. Consolidator.

The Travel Site ⓦwww.thetravelsite.com. Consolidator and charter broker.

Travelers Advantage ☎1-800/835-8747, ⓦwww.travelersadvantage.com. Discount travel club; annual membership fee required (currently US$1 for a month-long trial).

Travel Cuts US ☎1-800/592-2887, Canada ☎1-866/246-9762; ⓦwww.travelcuts.com. Canadian student-travel organization.

Worldtek Travel ☎1-800/243-1723, ⓦwww .worldtek.com. Discount travel agency for worldwide travel.

Packages and organized tours

Although you may want to see Wales at your own speed, you shouldn't dismiss the idea of a **package deal**. Many agents and airlines put together very flexible deals, sometimes amounting to nothing more restrictive than a flight plus accommodation and car or rail pass, and these can actually work out cheaper than making the same arrange-ments yourself on arrival. A package can also be great for your peace of mind, if only to ensure a worry-free first week while you're finding your feet for a longer tour.

There are hundreds of tour operators specializing in travel to the British Isles. Most can do packages of the standard highlights, but of greater interest are the outfits that help you explore Britain's unique points: many organize walking or cycling trips through the countryside, boat trips along canals, and any number of theme tours based around Britain's literary heritage, history, pubs, gardens, theatre, golf – you name it. A few of the possi-bilities are listed below, and a travel agent will be able to point out others. For a full listing, contact **Visit Wales** directly (see p.67).

Be sure to examine the fine print of any deal, and bear in mind that everything in brochures always sounds great. Choose only an operator that is a member of the United States Tour Operator Association (USTOA) or has been approved by the American Society of Travel Agents (ASTA).

Contiki Tours ⓦwww.contiki.com. Organized tours with a party-like atmosphere geared toward 18–35-year-olds. Book through a travel agent.

Home at First ☎1-800/523-5842, ⓦwww .homeatfirst.com. Independent travel packages including airfare, ground transportation and cottage, house or apartment rental.

Select Travel Service ☎1-800/752-6787, ⓦwww .selecttravel.com. Customized history, literature, theatre, horticulture and other specialized tours.

Flights from Australia and New Zealand

To get to Wales from Australia or New Zealand you'll need to fly through London, though there are also a few direct flights from Australia or New Zealand to Manchester in northern England. For all onward details, see "Getting there from the UK and Europe" (see pp.27–33). The route from Australasia to London is a highly competitive one, with flights via Southeast Asia generally being the cheapest option.

Fares from Australia's **eastern cities** are generally common rated, while flights from Perth via Asia and Africa are around A$200 less, and via the Americas about A$400 more. The cheapest **scheduled flights** are around A$1400 with Korean Air, Japan Airlines (JAL) and Royal Brunei, usually involving a transfer (and perhaps an overnight stay) in the carrier's hub city. For a little more, Emirates, Malaysian Airlines or Qantas can get you to London via Kuala Lumpur from A$1600, though in high season rates start at closer to A$2000.

From New Zealand low-season fares start as low as NZ$2000 with Air New Zealand and Lufthansa via LA and Frankfurt, though flights with Asian carriers such as Emirates are also very competitive. High-season fares start at around NZ$2600.

Airlines

Air New Zealand Australia ☎13 24 76, NZ ☎0800/737 000; ⓦwww.airnewzealand.com.

British Airways Australia ☏ 1300/767 177, NZ
☏ 09/966 9777; ⊛ www.britishairways.com.
Cathay Pacific Australia ☏ 13 17 47, NZ
☏ 0508/800 454; ⊛ www.cathaypacific.com.
China Airlines Australia ☏ 02/9231 5588,
⊛ www.china-airlines.com.
Emirates Australia ☏ 1300/303 777, NZ
☏ 0508/364 728; ⊛ www.emirates.com.
JAL (Japan Airlines) Australia ☏ 1300/525 287,
NZ ☏ 09/379 9906; ⊛ www.jal.com.
KLM Australia ☏ 1300/392 192, NZ ☏ 09/921
6040; ⊛ www.klm.com.
Korean Air Australia ☏ 02/9262 6000, NZ
☏ 09/914 2000; ⊛ www.koreanair.com.au.
Lufthansa Australia ☏ 1300/655 727, NZ
☏ 0800/945 220; ⊛ www.lufthansa.com.
Malaysia Airlines Australia ☏ 13 26 27, NZ
☏ 0800/777 747; ⊛ www.malaysiaairlines.com.
Qantas Australia ☏ 13 13 13, NZ ☏ 0800/808 767
or 09/357 8900; ⊛ www.qantas.com.
Royal Brunei Australia ☏ 1300/721 271, NZ
☏ 09/977 2209; ⊛ www.bruneiair.com.
Singapore Airlines Australia ☏ 13 10 11, NZ
☏ 0800/808 909; ⊛ www.singaporeair.com.
Thai Airways Australia ☏ 1300/651 960, NZ
☏ 09/377 3886; ⊛ www.thaiair.com.
United Airlines Australia ☏ 13 17 77, ⊛ www
.united.com.

Discount and specialist travel agents

Adventure World ⊛ www.adventureworld
.com.au and www.adventureworld.co.nz. Various
tours around Wales and the rest of Britain. Book
through major travel agents.

Explore Holidays Australia ⊛ www
.exploreholidays.com.au. Organized tours of Britain
plus bus and coach passes and accommodation
vouchers. Book through travel agents.
Flight Centre Australia ☏ 13 31 33, ⊛ www
.flightcentre.com.au; NZ ☏ 0800/243 544, ⊛ www
.flightcentre.co.nz. Discount flights.
STA Travel Australia ☏ 13 47 82, ⊛ www
.statravel.com.au; NZ ☏ 0800/474 400, ⊛ www
.statravel.co.nz. General travel agent specializing in
student and youth fares.
Trailfinders Australia ☏ 1300/780 212, ⊛ www
.trailfinders.com.au. One of the best-informed and
most efficient agents for independent travellers.
travel.com.au Australia ☏ 1300/130 481, ⊛ www
.travel.com.au. Comprehensive online travel company.

Flights from South Africa

South African Airways fly direct to London
from Johannesburg for around ZAR4000 in
the off season, rising to at least ZAR6500 in
the northern summer. Similar prices are
offered by British Airways, who fly to London
from Jo'burg and Cape Town. Other
competitive carriers include Virgin and
United, who both fly direct between Jo'burg
and London Heathrow, and Iberia and KLM,
who require a change in either Madrid or
Amsterdam.

Airlines

South African Airways ☏ 0861/359722, ⊛ www
.flysaa.com.

Getting around

The large cities and densely populated valleys of south Wales support comprehensive train and bus networks, but the more thinly populated areas of mid- and north
Wales have to make do with skeletal services. That said, it's rare to find somewhere
that isn't reached by an occasional bus. Getting about by car is easy and, outside
the cities, sheep and agricultural equipment are likely to be a more persistent
problem than other road users. Take the more scenic backroads unless you're in a
real hurry. Information for cyclists is listed in the outdoor activities section, p.53.

Trains

Following the confusion of rail privatization in
the 1990s, things are slowly getting better on

Britain's train network. In Wales, all but the
major inter-city services from England (see
"Getting there", p.28) are run by one company:

Arriva Trains Wales (@www.arrivatrainswales.co.uk; train information on ☏0845/748 4950, bookings ☏0870/900 0773). For very efficient **public transport information** about trains and buses, contact **Traveline Cymru** (☏01871/2002233, @www.traveline-cymru.org.uk): its website is particularly useful for planning integrated journeys. You can also pick up the very useful **Wales Bus, Rail & Tourist Map & Guide** for free from tourist offices. For more information on UK train services, including online booking, go to @www.nationalrail.co.uk, @www.thetrainline.com or @www.qjump.co.uk.

The train is one of the best ways to get around Wales: the views are superb and the engineering often impressive. In addition to the main-line network, there are over a dozen volunteer-run train lines (see pp.37–38), all of which run steam trains, most on narrow-gauge tracks, and predominantly as tourist attractions.

Services in Wales cover all the main cities and a seemingly random selection of rural towns and wayside halts. The two **major lines** run along the **north** (Chester–Llandudno Junction–Bangor–Holyhead) and **south** (Newport–Cardiff–Swansea) coasts, although there is plenty of stopping local traffic along each line too. Services on the remainder of Wales' train lines are infrequent, and are occasionally replaced by buses on Sunday: quieter lines include the Heart of Wales from Swansea to Shrewsbury, and the mid-Wales line from Shrewsbury to Aberystwyth and Pwllheli.

At many smaller stations, ticket offices close on weekends, and in a lot of minor

Train and bus passes and discounts

In addition to the passes listed below, savings can be made by obtaining a discount Railcard (@www.railcard.co.uk): available to full-time students and those aged 16–25, the Young Persons Railcard costs £24, is valid for a year and gives 33 percent reductions on most rail fares. A Seniors Railcard, also £24 and offering 33 percent reductions, is available to those aged 60 or over. The Family Railcard also costs £24, and gives discounts for up to four adults travelling with up to four children (aged 5–15); adults get 33 percent off, and kids get sixty percent off. Note that children aged under 5 travel free at all times.

Britain and Wales

All-Line Rail Rover @www.nationalrail.co.uk. Unlimited travel on the entire network throughout England, Scotland and Wales for seven (£375) or fourteen (£565) consecutive days. Available within Britain from larger train stations.

BritRail Pass Foreign visitors planning on travelling through other parts of Britain might consider investing in a BritRail Pass, which must be bought before you enter the country. A huge range of passes are available for unlimited travel in England, Scotland and Wales over various combinations of consecutive days or a certain number of days within various timeframes, plus further Youth (under 26), and Senior (over 60) discounts of 20–40 percent. One child can travel free on each adult pass (other children aged 5–15 travel at half price). All these passes can be booked online at @www.britrail.com.

Alternatively, **North Americans** can visit the British Travel Shop in New York City (551 Fifth Ave, fl. 7, Midtown, ☏212/490-6688), or go to @www.raileurope.com or @www.europrail.net. **Australians and New Zealanders** can buy BritRail passes from most travel agents at equivalent prices and get information at @www.railplus.com.au or @www.railplus.co.nz.

Freedom of Wales Flexi Pass ☏0845/606 1660, @www.walesflexipass.co.uk. Comprehensive ticket allowing both bus and train travel throughout Wales, and on connecting services through England. The "4 in 8 Day All Wales Pass" (£69) gives eight days' bus travel plus four days' rail travel within that period. If your travel is concentrated in one area, you can opt for the "South Wales Flexi Rover" or "North & Mid-Wales Flexi Rover" (see opposite), which again also gives free bus travel.

towns they've shut for good. In these instances, there's sometimes a vending machine on the platform. If there isn't a machine, you can buy your ticket on board – but if you've boarded at a station with a machine or ticket office and haven't bought a ticket, you're liable for an on-the-spot fine.

Steam railways

With the rising demand for quarried stone in the nineteenth century, quarry and mine owners had to find more economical ways than packhorses to get their products to market, but in the steep, tortuous valleys of Snowdonia, standard-gauge train tracks proved too unwieldy. The solution was rails, sometimes less than a foot apart, plied by steam engines and dinky rolling stock. The charm of these railways was recognized by train enthusiasts, and long after the decline of the quarries, they banded together to restore abandoned lines and locos. Most lines are still largely run by volunteers, who have also started up new services along unused sections of standard-gauge bed.

Although run primarily as tourist attractions, several of the **steam railways** operate as public transport. Note, though, that most are seasonal in their operation, with few, if any, winter services. Tickets are generally sold separately, but nine railways – under the umbrella name of **The Great Little Trains of Wales** (designated by "GLT" in the following list; ⓦwww.greatlittletrainsofwales .co.uk) – offer a Discount Card (£10), giving you 20 percent off the cost of the return journey on each of the GLT railways during a twelve-month period.

Additional benefits for all these passes include free travel on the Ffestiniog and Welsh Highland (Caernarfon) railways, twenty percent discounts on many other narrow-gauge railways, and reduced entry to CADW and National Trust properties. Tickets can be bought at most staffed train stations, major tourist offices and travel agents, larger YHAs, online and by phone.

North and mid-Wales
North and Mid-Wales Flexi Rover Bus and train travel in the northern half of Wales; allows four days' train travel in an eight-day period, plus eight days' bus travel on Bus Gwynedd and Arriva bus services (£47).

North and Mid-Wales Day Ranger One day's regional train and bus travel after 9.15am (and all weekend) for £22.

Red Rover All-day bus travel throughout northwest Wales for £4.95. Buy on the bus.

Snowdon Sherpa Day Ticket All-day travel on the routes immediately surrounding Snowdon for £4. Buy on the bus.

West and mid-Wales
Cambrian Coaster Day Ranger One day's train travel between Aberystwyth and Pwllheli (£7.70), valid after 9.15am and all weekend. There's also a bargain Evening Ranger (£4.50; valid after 6.30pm).

Mid-Wales Day Ranger One day's regional train travel after 9.15am Mon–Fri and all weekend (£22).

West Wales Rover Ticket All-day bus travel in West Wales south of Aberysytwyth for £6.30. Buy on the bus.

South Wales
Freedom of South Wales Flexi Rover Eight days' bus travel and four days' rail travel within the same period (£47).

Valley Lines Day Explorer One day's Cardiff and Valleys bus and train travel (£7.70).

Swansea First Day Ticket All-day bus travel in the Swansea Bay area for £3. Buy on the bus. Route map downloadable at ⓦwww.firstgroup.com/ukbus/wales/swwales/map/swansea.pdf.

The railways below are listed north to south:

Welsh Highland Railway: Caernarfon Branch
☏01766/516000, ⓦwww.welshhighlandrailway.net. Caernarfon to Rhyd-Ddu, gradually being extended to Beddgelert and ultimately to the West Highland Railway in Porthmadog. 24-inch gauge. GLT. See p.395 & p.412 for further information.

Llanberis Lake Railway Llanberis
☏01286/870549, ⓦwww.lake-railway.co.uk. 24-inch gauge. GLT. See p.376.

Snowdon Mountain Railway Llanberis
☏0870/458 0033, ⓦwww.snowdonrailway.co.uk. Climbs Wales' highest peak. 31.5-inch gauge. See p.374.

Ffestiniog Railway Porthmadog
☏01766/516073, ⓦwww.festrail.co.uk. The best railway of them all: Porthmadog to Blaenau Ffestiniog. Links two standard gauge lines. 13 miles. 23.5-inch gauge. GLT. See p.396.

Welsh Highland Railway: Porthmadog
☏0870/321 2402, ⓦwww.whr.co.uk. Tiny line. 24-inch gauge. GLT. See p.395 & p.412.

Llangollen Railway Llangollen
☏01978/860951, ⓦwww.llangollen-railway .co.uk. Llangollen to Carrog. Standard 56.5-inch gauge. See p.335.

Bala Lake Railway Bala ☏01678/540666, ⓦwww.bala-lake-railway.co.uk. Four-mile lakeside run. 24-inch gauge. GLT. See p.388.

Fairbourne Railway Fairbourne ☏01341/250362, ⓦwww.fairbourne-railway.co.uk. Short seafront shuttle. 12-inch gauge. See p.308.

Welshpool and Llanfair Railway Llanfair Caereinion ☏01938/810441, ⓦwww.wllr.org.uk. An eight-mile shuttle to Welshpool. 30-inch gauge. GLT. See p.264.

Corris Railway near Machynlleth
☏01654/761303, ⓦwww.corris.co.uk. Tiny line. 27-inch gauge. See p.303.

Talyllyn Railway Tywyn ☏01654/710472, ⓦwww.talyllyn.co.uk. Lovely seven-mile run to Abergynolwyn. 27-inch gauge. GLT. See p.305.

Cambrian Steam Train ☏01524/732100, ⓦwww.westcoastrailways.co.uk. Late July and late Aug weekday service from Machynlleth to Porthmadog via Tywyn and Barmouth, plus Wed and Fri services on to Pwllheli. See p.301.

Vale of Rheidol Railway Aberystwyth
☏01970/625819, ⓦwww.rheidolrailway.co.uk. Stunning twelve-mile run to Devil's Bridge. 13.5-inch gauge. GLT. See p.294.

Brecon Mountain Railway Pant, near Merthyr Tydfil ☏01685/722988, ⓦwww .breconmountainrailway.co.uk. Two-mile lakeside line. 24-inch gauge. GLT. See p.231.

Pontypool and Blaenavon Railway near Blaenafon ☏01495/792263, ⓦwww .pontypool-and-blaenavon.co.uk. Currently a mere 17min round-trip from Furnace Sidings (signposted just off the B4248 between Blaenafon and Brynmawr), but will ultimately extend to Blaenafon. Standard gauge. See p.96.

Buses and coaches

The limited train network in Wales is supplemented by **buses**, which penetrate much deeper into the countryside. There are a few inter-town buses (aka "**coaches**") run by **National Express** (☏08705/808080, ⓦwww.nationalexpress.com; see p.30), but travel within Wales is provided by **local bus services** run by a bewildering array of companies. Integration is improving: check with **Traveline Cymru** (☏01871/2002233, ⓦwww.traveline-cymru.org.uk) for all details. Though services are more expensive and less frequent in rural areas, there are very few places without any service, even if it's only a private minibus on market day or one of the "**postbuses**" (see opposite) that also pick up mail. An invaluable resource for planning bus travel nationwide is the website http://timetables.showbus.co.uk/wales.htm, with links to all the major bus companies.

For occasional bus journeys, just pay as you get on, but good savings can be made with one of the various **bus passes** and combined bus and rail passes (see box, p.37).

In the **northern** half of Wales, Llandudno-based Arriva Cymru (☏01248/750444, ⓦwww.arrivabus.co.uk) runs the majority of local services as well as the handy #X32 TrawsCambria from Llandudno to Bristol via Aberystwyth and Cardiff.

In the **southern** half of the country, the system is far less unified, though most services west of Cardiff and south of Carmarthen are run by the Swansea-based First Cymru (☏01792/572255, ⓦwww .firstcymru.co.uk). Cardiff Bus (Bws Caerdydd; ☏0870/6082608; ⓦwww.cardiffbus.com) is the major company serving Cardiff and the Vale of Glamorgan. Various day, weekly and monthly passes are available, all of which can be bought aboard the bus.

All regions have their own detailed local **timetables**, easily obtained from tourist offices, libraries and bus and/or train stations.

Guided bus tours

If you're short on time or want to see the sights in the company of like-minded travellers, various operators offer guided bus tours. Some of the best include:

Bus Wales ℡0800/328 0284, ⓦwww.buswales.co.uk. Wide range of backpacker and smarter tours, from daytrips (£50) to six- and ten-day trips (from £235/400 staying in hostel dorms; pricier, more luxurious accommodation options also available).

Dragon Backpacker Tours ℡01878/658124, ⓦwww.dragonbackpackertours .co.uk. Great selection of tours, from two-day mountain breaks (£150 including hostel accommodation) to five-day all-Wales trips (£299 including hostel accommodation).

Road Trip ℡0845/200 6791, ⓦwww.roadtrip.co.uk. London-based outfit running all-inclusive minibus trips: the weekend "Wales Coast & Mountains" tour (£159) visits Chester in England, along with the North Wales Coast, Conwy Castle, Snowdonia and a steam train ride, while the "Horseriding in Wild Wales" trip (£115) includes trekking in the Brecon Beacons.

Shaggy Sheep Tours ℡01267/281202, ⓦwww.shaggysheep.com. Great fun and hugely enthusiastic, the booziest backpacker tours around leave twice-weekly from London. Choose between a long weekend (£108) or a four-day (£138) trip – both cheaper if you join at Cardiff. For independent travellers, there's also a handy jump-on, jump-off return bus service from London (£79) stopping at key destinations in Wales.

Backpackers might want to consider Shaggy Sheep's **hop-on**, **hop-off** bus service (see above).

Postbuses

In parts of west and mid-Wales, bus services and mail delivery are combined in a network of **postbuses** which cover some of the most remote and beautiful Welsh regions, while offering an insight into life in rural Wales. These services are decreasing, however – for latest information, check ⓦwww.royalmail .com/portal/rm/postbus, which has a handy route-finder service, or, alternatively, ask at a post office. Prices are comparable with other bus fares for similar distances, with most tickets around £2–5.

Driving

If you want to cover a lot of the countryside in a short time, or just want more flexibility, you'll need your own transport. Within Wales, the only really fast roads are the A55 expressway along the north Wales coast to Holyhead and the M4 **motorway** in south Wales. The latter is the main westbound route into the country from London. An extensive network of dual carriageways and good-quality "A" roads link all major

centres, but in rural areas you'll often find yourself on winding, sometimes hair-raisingly narrow single-track lanes (though usually sealed) with slightly broader sections ("passing places") where two vehicles can squeeze by – with this in mind, you might want to select a compact rental car. In very remote areas, you may still occasionally have to open gates designed to keep sheep from straying (make sure you close them again afterwards).

In order to **drive in Britain**, you must have a current **driving licence**; most foreign nationals will get by with their licence from home, but if you're in any doubt, you can supplement this with an **international driving permit**, available from national motoring organizations for a small fee. If you're bringing your own vehicle into the country, you should also carry vehicle registration or ownership documents at all times. By law, you must be adequately **insured**, so be sure to check your existing policy.

As in the rest of the UK, you **drive on the left** in Wales. **Speed limits** are 30–40mph (50–65km/h) in built-up areas, 70mph (110km/h) on motorways (freeways) and dual carriageways, and 50mph (80km/h) on most other roads. As a rule, assume

Pay-and-display

Wherever you go in Wales, you almost always have to pay for parking. Towns, beaches and tourist attractions are often tucked into folds in the mountains or wedged below cliffs, giving little space for parking.

At most pay-and-display car parks, tickets are issued by machine (you may have to type in your car registration number, a system designed to prevent people passing on their partially used tickets to other drivers). Even car parks attached to large stores and shopping centres sometimes require you to pay for parking, though you can sometimes get your parking costs redeemed at the check-out if you make a purchase.

Parking prices can be as little as 20p for 4hr in less popular areas, but 50p to £1 an hour is more common, and some places charge a flat fee of up to £4. It's definitely an incentive to use public transport – some eco-oriented attractions even give discounted entry to those arriving without a car.

that in any area with street lighting, the speed limit is 30mph (50km/h) unless stated otherwise. Road signs are pretty much international ("Give Way" means "Yield"), and road rules are largely common sense. North American drivers should note that in the UK, you are not permitted to make a kerbside turn against a red light; and to always give way to traffic (circulating clockwise) that has already entered a **roundabout**. This applies even for so-called "mini-roundabouts", which may be no more than a white circle painted on the road.

Petrol (gas) is sold in litres (a UK gallon = 4.56 litres, a US gallon = 3.8 litres), and is expensive – at the time of writing unleaded petrol cost in the region of £1.40 per litre, four-star and diesel both slightly more, though may have increased by the time you read this. Prices are generally lowest in the suburbs of cities, where competition is fiercest, and highest at motorway service stations and in remote rural areas.

Motoring organizations including the Automobile Association (AA; general enquiries ☎0800/444500, breakdowns ☎0800/887766, ⊛www.theaa.co.uk), the Royal Automobile Club (RAC; general enquiries ☎0800/550055, breakdowns ☎0800/828282, ⊛www.rac.co.uk) and Green Flag (general enquiries ☎0800/3288772, breakdowns ☎0800/400600, ⊛www .greenflag.com) all operate 24-hour emergency **breakdown** services. The AA and RAC also provide many other motoring services, as well as a reciprocal arrangement for free assistance through many overseas

motoring organizations – check the situation with yours before setting out. On motorways, the AA and RAC can be called from roadside booths (though these are diminishing due to increasingly wide mobile phone coverage); otherwise ring the breakdown numbers listed above. You can ring these emergency numbers even if you are not a member, although you'll be charged a substantial fee.

Car rental

It invariably works out cheaper to book **car rental** online rather than over the phone, or alternatively, to opt for a fly-drive deal. Generally, the least you can expect to pay is around £85 a week for a small hatchback. Rental agencies expect you to pay with a credit card; if you don't have one you'll have to leave a substantial deposit, or they may not rent you a vehicle at all. There are very few **automatics** at the lower end of the price scale – if you want one, you should book well ahead and expect to pay at least £140 a week for a slightly bigger model. You'll also need to show your driving licence: few companies will rent to drivers with less than one year's experience, and most will only rent to people between 21 and 70 years of age.

In addition to the car rental companies listed below, North Americans might want to contact the independently owned Europe by Car (US ☎1-800/223-1516, ⊛www .europebycar.com), which has good deals on short and longer-term rentals.

Car rental agencies

1car1 ☎ 0113 387 5866, ⓦ www.1car1.com
Avis ☎ 0844/581 0147, ⓦ www.avis.co.uk.
Budget ☎ 0844/581 9998, ⓦ www.budget.co.uk.
Enterprise ☎ 0870/350 3000, ⓦ www.enterprise
.co.uk
Europcar ☎ 0845/7585375, ⓦ www.europcar.co.uk.
Hertz ☎ 01446/711722, ⓦ www.hertz.co.uk.
National ☎ 029/2049 6296, ⓦ www.nationalcar
.co.uk.
Suncars ☎ 0870/902 8021, ⓦ www.suncars.co.uk.
Thrifty ☎ 01494/751500, ⓦ www.thrifty.co.uk.

Motorbike rental

A motorbike is a pleasurable way to see the Welsh countryside, but unfortunately there are hardly any **motorbike rental** outlets in the UK, and those that do exist are forced to charge high prices on account of the ludicrous insurance premiums. London-based HGB Motorcycles (☎ 01895/676451, ⓦ www.hgbmotorcycles .co.uk) rents Honda ER500s (£60 a day; comprehensive insurance £10) right up through the range to a GL1800 (£110). Rentals require a hefty security deposit.

Accommodation

Tourist accommodation in Wales is constantly improving, with top-rank international hotels, farmhouse accommodation, hostels, restaurants-with-rooms, and ubiquitous bed and breakfast (B&B) establishments. If you want to ensure you're staying in places where Welsh is spoken, check out the website ⓦ www .gwyliaucymraeg.co.uk, covering accommodation and pubs/restaurants.

Hotels and B&Bs

The distinction between hotels, B&Bs and most other forms of serviced accommodation is blurring all the time. A bad, fully fledged hotel (so called because of its licensed status) can be vastly inferior to a similarly priced or even cheaper B&B or guesthouse. This is especially the case amongst the growing army of farmhouse B&Bs and country houses, which quite often outstrip any hotel for the sheer warmth of welcome, informal hospitality and quality of home cooking.

B&Bs may be anything from a private house with a couple of bedrooms set aside for paying guests to a small, stylish boutique establishment. **Guesthouses** tend to be larger, usually with around half a dozen rooms plus a guests' lounge, and can also vary from homely to very flash. In both places

you'll get a room with TV, tea- and coffee-making facilities and, usually, your own en-suite bathroom, for £25–45 per person, sometimes a little less out of season or in less popular areas. A few places still have rooms without a private bathroom (though usually with a sink in the room) for which you'll pay slightly less. Rooms in all the places to stay listed in the Guide have private bathrooms unless specifically stated otherwise.

In the countryside you're more likely to find places described as a **farm** (essentially a B&B on a working farm) or an **inn** (usually village pub with rooms above). As visitor expectations and the demand for weekend breaks increase, some places in all the above categories are ramping up the standards, with sumptuous furnishings, better food and those little touches which

Accommodation price codes

Throughout this guide, hotel and B&B accommodation has been coded on a scale of ① to ⑨, the number indicating the lowest price you could expect to pay per night in that establishment for a double room in high season. For backpacker hostels and camping barns we've listed the price of a dorm bed, and added a price code when double or twin rooms are also available. Campsite prices are either listed per person, or per pitch based on two people in one tent.

The prices indicated by the codes are as follows:

① £50 and under	④ £71–80	⑦ £121–150
② £51–60	⑤ £81–100	⑧ £151–200
③ £61–70	⑥ £101–120	⑨ £201 and over

make your stay special. Of course, you pay considerably more for such pampering. In all except the more expensive places you should expect to **pay in cash**, though bottom-end B&Bs are gradually accepting credit and debit cards.

In town centres, B&Bs and guesthouses are supplemented by **hotels**, often just rooms above a noisy bar, but also larger places that are often the grandest in town. Once the staple of travelling salespeople, these have now largely been supplanted by town-fringe business hotels with all the facilities but little character.

Wherever you stay, **breakfast** will almost certainly be included in the price. This may just be continental (orange juice, cereal, toast and tea or coffee) but more often will also include a full cooked breakfast of eggs (normally fried, but often poached or scrambled if you prefer), bacon, sausage, fried tomato and perhaps baked beans and hash browns. In fancier places there'll be a choice of juices, preserved fruit, yogurt, and the like.

A couple of free **publications** are well worth looking out for: the *Great Little Places* booklet (available online at ⓦwww .little-places.co.uk) which lists around fifty of the best small hotels, country inns, and farmhouse B&Bs in Wales; and *Welsh Rarebits* (ⓦwww.welsh.rarebits.co.uk), a similarly select listing of more substantial hotels and country mansions. Both websites give full coverage of all listed establishments, and you can pick up the booklets at tourist offices. There are also Visit Wales' comprehensive *Where to Stay* and *Farm Holidays* brochures, which can be ordered through its website.

Reservations can be made directly by phone and sometimes online. Alternatively, you can book though the local **tourist office**, though they will only provide information on "verified" accommodation (see box opposite), and can sometimes be reluctant to divulge details of places that don't advertise in the official local guide: if you don't see something suitable in the guide itself, don't be afraid to ask if there's anywhere else that matches your requirements for price and location.

When you book, you'll have to pay the tourist office ten percent of the cost on the spot, which will then be knocked off your bill at the hotel, plus a £2 booking fee. Especially in busy periods, this booking fee quickly pays for itself by saving you phone calls or driving around.

Hostels

There are around forty **YHA hostels** (see opposite for contact details) in Wales, offering bunk-bed accommodation in single-sex dormitories or smaller rooms. A few of these places are spartan establishments of the sort traditionally associated with the wholesome, fresh-air ethic of the first hostels, but many have moved well away from this institutional ambience. Welsh hostels range from some remote, unheated barns in the wilds of mid-Wales and Snowdonia to relatively swanky centres in places such as Cardiff and Conwy. By far the greatest concentration of hostels is in Snowdonia, with smaller clusters around the Pembrokeshire coast and in the Brecon Beacons. Prices range from £9.95 to £24 per night per person. Most hostels have self-catering facilities, and many also serve breakfast (around £4) and a three-course dinner (around £10), as well as offering packed lunches (around £5). Some hostels close from 10am to 5pm and have an 11pm curfew.

Bed prices quoted in this book are for members: non-members are welcome but you'll be charged an extra £3 a night. One year's membership of the England and Wales YHA, which is open only to residents of the EU, costs £15.95 per year (£9.95 for under-26s; £22.95 for two adults living at the same address), and can be obtained online, by calling the YHA (see below) or in person at any YHA hostel. Members are issued with a directory of all YHA hostels and gain automatic membership of the hostelling associations of the eighty-odd countries affiliated to Hostelling International (HI). Visitors from outside the EU should join their home country's hostelling association before setting out.

At any time of year it's best to **book** well in advance, and it's pretty much essential at Easter, Christmas and from May to August. Some hostels offer online reservations through ⓦwww.yha.org.uk, and all accept phone bookings with payment by Master-Card or Visa. If you're tempted to turn up on the spur of the moment, bear in mind that very few hostels are open year-round, many are closed at least one day a week even in high season, and several have periods during which they take group bookings only – always check ahead.

YHA hostels still outnumber **independent hostels**, though there are a growing number of non-affiliated places offering similar facilities to YHAs, though often with a less regimented regime and no curfews or lockouts. We've mentioned almost all independent hostels in this book but it is worth consulting *The Independent Hostel Guide: Britain & Europe* (£5.95 including postage) published by The Backpackers Press (ⓦwww.backpackerspress.com), or having a look at ⓦwww.hostels.com.

Both these resources also list **bunkhouses**, typically more primitive affairs close to the mountains designed for hikers, climbers, mountain bikers and the like. The flashest are up to hostel standards, but many are little more than barns with toilet, shower and basic cooking facilities, starting from around £10. Bunkhouses may give preference to group bookings, and some purely cater to groups.

Youth Hostel Associations

England and Wales Youth Hostel Association (YHA). Membership ☎01629/592700, reservations ☎01629/592700, ⓦwww.yha.org.uk.
Australia YHA Australia ☎02/9261 1111, ⓦwww .yha.com.au.
Canada Canadian Hostelling Association ☎613/237-7884, ⓦwww.hihostels.ca.
New Zealand New Zealand Youth Hostels Association ☎0800/278299 or 03/379 9970, ⓦwww.stayyha.com.
Northern Ireland Hostelling International Northern Ireland ☎028/9032 4733, ⓦwww.hini.org.uk.
Republic of Ireland An Óige ☎01/830 4555, ⓦwww.anoige.ie.
Scotland Scottish Youth Hostel Association ☎01786/891400, ⓦwww.syha.org.uk.
USA HI National Office ☎301/495-1240, ⓦwww .hiusa.org.

The accommodation grading system

Wales' tourist board, Visit Wales, operates a grading system for accommodation, assigning them a minimum of one star (seldom used) to a maximum of five stars, ranking an establishment's quality and the condition of its facilities and services. These ratings tend to favour objective facts (such as a check list of amenities) over subjective impressions, including indefinable but nevertheless important qualities such as the general atmosphere of the place or the friendliness of its owners.

Hotels are subdivided into four categories: country house hotel, small hotel, town house hotel and metro hotel. The term "Guest Accommodation" covers B&Bs, guesthouses, farmhouses, inns and restaurants-with-rooms.

To achieve a star rating, an establishment must be "verified" by Visit Wales inspectors, which ensures that you shouldn't be short-changed. For various reasons, some wonderful establishments choose to remain outside the official verification system, so the absence of a rating alone needn't be a deterrent.

StayinWales
.co.uk

Visit Wales' biggest and busiest holiday guide to find what you're looking for, fast! We list all types of accommodation, from campsites and bunkhouses to cottages and luxury hotels, in all areas. Book direct with owners, or online.

start your holiday today at **www.stayinwales.co.uk**

Camping, caravanning and self-catering

There are hundreds of **campsites** in Wales, charging from around £3 per person per night for a spot in a field with a tap and a toilet to upwards of £20 for a two-person tent at the plushest sites, where you'll find amenities such as laundries, shops and sports facilities. Such places are used both by campers and **caravans**.

Some hostels have small campsites on their property, for which you'll pay half the indoor fee. Farmers without a reserved camping area may let you pitch in a field if you ask first, and may charge you nothing for the privilege; setting up a tent without asking is an act of trespass and won't be well received. Note that wild camping is illegal in national parks and nature reserves. That said, there are a growing number of informal sites in some of Wales' most beautiful spots. These are free to use and have no facilities; details are given throughout the Guide.

As a hangover from the days when thousands of holiday-makers from northern England and the Midlands decamped to the Welsh coast for a fortnight, many of the traditional seaside resorts are enveloped by camp upon camp of **permanently sited caravans**, rented out for self-catering holidays. Although these can certainly be cost-effective, with facilities such as bars, shops and discos thrown in, many people prefer to take more robust self-catering holidays in self-contained **cottages**, **farms**, **town houses**, **apartments** or even purpose-built estates. The usual minimum rental period is a week, though long-weekend breaks can often be arranged out of season. In midsummer or over Christmas and New Year, prices start at around £400 for a place sleeping four, although in winter, spring or autumn they can dip towards £250 for the same property. Some companies specializing in Welsh holiday cottages are listed below; tourist offices throughout Wales also have lists of self-catering holiday options.

Detailed, annually revised **directories** of Wales' camping and caravan sites include the AA's *Camping and Caravanning in Britain and Ireland*, which lists their inspected and graded sites, and *Cade's Camping*, *Touring and Motor Caravan Site Guide*, published by Marwain (Ⓦ www.cades.co.uk). Visit Wales (see p.67) produces a *Wales – Where to Stay* brochure, which includes campsites. Alternatively, the excellent independent guide *Cool Camping: Wales* (Ⓦ www.coolcamping .co.uk) has in-depth reviews of some superbly situated tent-only campsites, and is available in bookshops or can be ordered online.

Self-catering accommodation companies

Brecon Beacons Holiday Cottages ☏01874/676446, Ⓦ www.breconcottages .com. Over 300 cottages and other buildings, some decidedly quirky, in the Brecon Beacons National Park and Wye Valley.

Coastal Cottages of Pembrokeshire ☏01437/765765, Ⓦ www.coastalcottages.co.uk. Hundreds of cottages, chalets, flats and houses – some with impressive leisure and activity facilities – around or near the Pembrokeshire coast.

North Wales Holiday Cottages & Farmhouses ☏0844/582 1492, Ⓦ www .northwalesholidaycottages.co.uk. Extensive array of cottages in the Snowdonia National Park and throughout north Wales, both on the coast and in the countryside.

Powell's Cottage Holidays ☏01834/812791, Ⓦ www.powells.co.uk. Concentrates on properties in Pembrokeshire and the Gower.

Quality Cottages ☏0800/007 5299, Ⓦ www .qualitycottages.co.uk. Over 250 coastal cottages throughout Wales.

Under the Thatch (pp.284–285) Atmospheric cottages and cabins along the Cambrian coast.

Wales Cottage Holidays ☏01686/628200, Ⓦ www.wales-holidays.co.uk. A varied selection of over 500 properties all over Wales.

Food and drink

Wales is now home to some truly world-class food festivals, restaurants, farmers' markets and producers – part of the general renaissance of British cuisine combined with an increasing focus on fresh local produce. The country's natural larder includes freshly caught fish, tender local lamb and a smorgasbord of cheeses. These staple ingredients are used in everything from traditional dishes to fusion creations in some of the cities' most cosmopolitan restaurants.

Eating

Native **Welsh cuisine** is frequently rooted in economical ingredients, although this does not mean that it is of a poor quality. Traditional dishes, such as the salt-marsh lamb (best served minted or with thyme or rosemary), fresh salmon, sewin (sea trout) and other trout can be found on an increasing number of menus, frequently combined with the national vegetable, the leek. Specialities include **laverbread** (*bara lawr*), a tasty seaweed and oatmeal cake, often fried with a traditional breakfast of pork sausages, egg and bacon. Other dishes well worth investigating include **Glamorgan sausages** (a vegetarian combination of local cheese and spices), cawl (a chunky mutton broth), and cockles, trawled from the estuary north of the Gower.

The best-known of Wales' famed **cheeses** is Caerphilly, a soft, crumbly, white cheese that forms the basis of a true Welsh Rarebit when mixed with beer and toasted on bread. Creamy goat's cheeses can be found all over the country, such as the superb Cothi Valley goat's cheese, as well as delicacies like organic Per Las blue cheese, and Colliers mature cheddar. Other dairy products include ice cream, which, despite the climate, is exceptionally popular, with numerous companies creating home-made ices such as the Swansea area's Joe's Ice Cream (p.149).

Also stemming from the cheapness of their ingredients are some traditional **sweets and cakes**: Welsh Cakes are flat, crumbling pancakes of sugared dough (a little like a flattened scone), while *bara brith*, a popular accompaniment to afternoon tea, literally translates as "speckled (with dried fruit) bread".

Menus featuring Welsh dishes can be found in numerous restaurants, hotels and pubs, many of which are part of the **Taste of Wales** (Blas ar Gymru; ⓦ www.walesthetruetaste.com) scheme to encourage local cuisine. Such establishments generally display a sticker in their windows.

Where to eat

If you're staying in a hotel, guesthouse or B&B, a cooked breakfast (generally served 8–9am) will usually be offered as part of the deal. A hearty breakfast is usually enough to see most people through the day, with maybe a snack in the middle of the day. Evening meals are served from 6 to 10pm, though in rural areas, especially early in the week, you may find it difficult to get served after 9pm.

Cafés and **tearooms** (the terms are used pretty much interchangeably) can be found absolutely everywhere, and are generally the cheapest places to eat, providing hearty, if cholesterol-laden, breakfasts, a solid range of snacks and full meals for lunch and, in a few instances, evening meals as well. Wales' steady influx of New Agers over the past forty or so years has seen the **wholefood café** become a standard feature of many mid- and west Welsh towns. Cheap and usually vegetarian, these rely extensively on fresh local produce. Throughout the land, cafés and restaurants are also increasingly equipped with **espresso** machines.

Food in **pubs** varies as much as the establishments themselves. In recent years intense competition has seen a lot of places sharpen up their act, and many pubs now offer more imaginative dishes than microwaved lasagne and chips. Most serve food at lunchtime and in the evening (usually until 8.30 or 9pm), and in many towns, the local pub is the most economical place (and, in smaller towns, sometimes the only place) to grab a filling evening meal.

People of all nationalities call Wales home and few towns of any decent size are without Indian and Chinese **restaurants**, joined in recent years by Japanese, French, Thai, American, Mexican, Belgian and more. In the more cosmopolitan centres, **bistros** and **brasseries** have sprung up, many offering superb Welsh and international cuisine at affordable prices.

Our restaurant listings include a mix of high-quality and good-value establishments, but if you're intent on a culinary pilgrimage, you'd do well to arm yourself with a copy of the annual *Good Food Guide* (Which? Books), which includes detailed recommendations. Throughout this book, we've supplied the phone number for all restaurants where you may need to book a table. Generally speaking, excluding drinks, in pubs and cafés you can expect to pay under £10 per head; in most restaurants and bistros it should be between £10 and £30; rarely will you pay over £30.

Drinking

Daytime cafés are not usually licensed to sell alcohol, and though restaurants invariably are, **pubs** remain the centre of social activity, as in others part of the British Isles. The **legal drinking age** is 18, though those aged 16 and over can enter a pub unaccompanied, subject to management discretion. Some places offer special family rooms for people with children, and beer gardens where younger kids can run free.

Pubs

Pubs in Wales vary as much as the landscape, from opulent Edwardian palaces of smoked glass, gleaming brass and polished mahogany in the larger towns and cities, to thick-set stone barns in wild, remote countryside. Where the church has faltered as a community focal point, the pub still holds sway, with those in smaller towns and villages, in particular, functioning as community centres as much as places in which to drink alcohol. Live music – and, this being Wales, singing – frequently round off an evening. As a rule of thumb, if a pub has both a **bar** and a **lounge**, the bar will be more basic and frequently very male-dominated, while the lounge will tend to be plusher, more mixed and probably a better bet for a passing visitor.

Opening times are fairly standard: Monday to Saturday 11am to 11pm, Sunday noon to 10.30pm (with many quieter places closed between 3 and 6pm throughout the week), with "last orders" called by the bar staff about fifteen minutes before closing time. Gradual liberalization of licensing laws has allowed pubs to stay open later, but with the exception of city centres most places are so far sticking close to the standard hours. Even puritanical areas which once observed the "dry" Welsh Sunday turned "wet" well over a decade ago, so all over Wales you can drink any day of the week.

What to drink

Beer, sold by the pint (£2–3) and half pint (half the price), is the staple drink in Wales, as it is throughout the British Isles. Traditionalists drink **bitter**, an uncarbonated, deep-flavoured beer, best when hand-pumped from the cellar. **Lager**, a chilled, fizzy and light drink that corresponds with European and American ideas of beer, is also stocked everywhere. Despite being hard to find in England, mild, or **dark** as it is usually known in Wales, is quite common. Even stronger, sweeter and darker than "dark" is **porter**. Irish **stout** (Guinness, Murphy's or Beamish), although never as good as it is in Ireland, is widely available.

Many pubs are owned by large, UK-wide breweries who sell only their own products, so it's worth choosing your pub carefully. Among beers worth looking out for are the heady brews produced by Cardiff-based **Brains**, mainly found in the southeastern corner of Wales. Llanelli-based **Felinfoel** covers the whole southern half of Wales, with Double Dragon Premium bitter the aromatic ace in their pack. **Crown Buckley**, also based in Llanelli, produces three excellent bitters and a distinctive mild. The best resource for any serious hophead is the annual *Good Beer Guide* produced by

CAMRA (the Campaign for Real Ale; Ⓦwww .camra.org.uk), which should steer you around the best pubs. If you see a recent CAMRA sticker in a pub window, chances are the beer will be well worth sampling.

As in other Celtic regions, **cider** has a huge following; look out for Orchard Gold (a traditional farmhouse apple cider), and Perry Vale (pear cider), both made by the Welsh Cider and Perry Company (Gwynt y Ddraig).

Pubs and off-licences (liquor stores) increasingly stock a growing range of Welsh

spirits, such as Merlyn (cream liquor, similar to Baileys), Taffoc (toffee spirit), Five (vodka), and Penderyn (single malt whisky). There are also a number of Welsh **wines**, the best being the dry whites from Llanerch Vineyard (see p.134, Llanerch Vineyard), near Cardiff. Be warned that wine sold in pubs tends to scrape the bottom of the barrel when it comes to quality, with the notable exception of pubs serving decent food. Even so, in these establishments and in dedicated **wine bars**, the cost of a bottle can be outrageous.

The media

The media that you will encounter in Wales is a predictable hybrid of Welsh and Britain-wide information. Although the London-based UK media attempts to cover life in the other corners of Britain, few people would agree that Wales receives a fair share of coverage in any medium. Of all the solely Welsh media, newspapers are probably the weakest area, and periodicals and TV coverage the strongest and most interesting.

Newspapers and magazines

The **British daily newspapers** are all available in Wales, but news of Wales is not terribly well covered – even the Welsh Assembly in Cardiff is poorly covered, let alone any other area of Welsh life. As devolution bites there is the likelihood that an increasing number of English papers will produce targeted Welsh editions, although this may amount to little more than them displaying a special dragon or daffodil masthead and the odd football report on Cardiff or Swansea City. The London-based **tabloid newspapers** – known otherwise, and with good reason, as the "gutter press" – are the papers you are most likely to see read in any part of Britain. Specializing in prurient gossip and scandal, the two leaders in this field are Rupert Murdoch's boisterous *Sun* and the damply leftish *Daily Mirror*, which does at least manage some hard-hitting investigation and comment on occasion. Slightly more upmarket, adding in a bit more news but always filtered through a severely

right-wing analysis, are the *Daily Mail* and *Daily Express*. Best of the quality broadsheet papers are the vaguely left-leaning *Guardian*, the right-wing *Daily Telegraph*, the centre-right *Times* and the generally robust *Independent*. The only quality **Welsh daily** is the *Western Mail* (Ⓦwww.walesonline.co.uk) a sometimes uneasy mix of local, Welsh, British and a token smattering of international news coupled with an increasing amount of populist lifestyle pap and features on TV stars. The arrival of the National Assembly has at last given some purpose to the paper, though with a few honourable exceptions, the quality of writing and analysis is lightweight. What the *Western Mail* is to south Wales, the *Daily Post* (Ⓦwww.dailypost.co.uk) is to the north of the country, with an ever-expanding catchment area and a fairly decent spectrum of news and features that marks it out from other local dailies. All areas have their own long-standing **weekly papers**, generally an entertaining mix of local news, parish gossip and events listings. Wales' national **Sunday paper**, *Wales* on Sunday, from the same family as the *Western Mail*, has descended somewhat into tabloid trivia, but it's still worth buying for its bright, colourful take on Welsh life and occasional hard-hitting exposés and campaigning journalism. It's also very good on Welsh sport.

Go into any bookshop in Wales, and you'll be surprised by the profusion of Welsh **magazines**, in both English and Welsh. For a broad overview of the arts, history and politics, it's hard to beat *Planet* (@www .planetmagazine.org.uk), an English-language bimonthly that takes a politically irreverent line, combining Welsh interest with a wider cultural and international outlook. The more serious English-language monthly *New Welsh Review* (@www.newwelshreview .com) is steeped in Wales' political, literary and economic developments, while *Poetry Wales* is an excellent publication of new writing. The bimonthly glossy *Cambria* (@www.cambriamagazine.com) subtitles itself as "Wales's Magazine", an epithet that it's doing its best to fulfil with sparky writing on all matters Cymric, together with superb photography. For a wider view of Welsh social issues, with insights into "alternative" culture and news untouched by the papers, together with creative writing and a hearty infusion of cynical humour, pick up the weekly *Big Issue Cymru*, sold by homeless vendors on the streets of major towns and cities. If you're half-proficient in Welsh, the weekly news digest *Y Cymro* is an essential read, although younger, funkier features can be found in the weekly glossy *Golwg*, and more political topics are chewed over in the monthly *Barn*. If you're attempting to master the language, try *Lingo Newydd* magazine, aimed at learners at all levels.

Television and radio

In marked contrast to the London-centric print media, **TV and radio** are wholeheartedly moving out of southeast England. Cardiff is home to the Welsh branches of devolved broadcasting organizations including the mighty BBC, ITV, and indigenous Welsh operators such as S4C.

On terrestrial television, the state-funded British Broadcasting Corporation (@www .bbc.co.uk/wales) operates two **TV** channels in Wales – the mainstream **BBC 1 Wales** and the more esoteric **BBC 2 Wales**. Although these official titles make the stations sound avowedly Welsh, the vast majority of programming is UK-wide, with Welsh programmes, principally news and sport, but also features, political and education programmes, slotted into the regular schedules of documentaries, soaps, arts and music shows, quizzes, quality drama and imports. This is even more the case with **ITV1 Wales** (@www.itvlocal.com /wales), the Welsh holder of the licence to broadcast on the commercial, and determinedly populist, ITV network.

The principal **Welsh channel** is **S4C** (*Sianel Pedwar Cymru*, verbally "ess pedwar eck"; @www.s4c.co.uk), whose existence is owed to the protesters (including the Plaid Cymru president) who refused to allow the government to renege on its commitment to a Welsh fourth channel alongside the planned UK-wide Channel 4. The station has grown from shaky beginnings in the early 1980s to become a major player, sponsoring diverse projects including Welsh animation and feature films, notably the Oscar-nominated movies *Hedd Wyn* and *Solomon a Gaenor* and the terrifically tasteless prehistoric cartoon *Gogs*. S4C's programming is slick, confident and occasionally controversial, and includes a nightly dose of the BBC's longest-running TV soap, *Pobol y Cwm* (*People of the Valley*). From 2009 it will become a solely digital channel broadcasting wholly in Welsh. The sister English-language Channel 4 will also be available all over Wales for the first time.

Augmenting the terrestrial stations, **satellite** and **cable** systems tune into a vast array of European pap networks and Rupert Murdoch's **Sky** – consisting of numerous channels of consumer-oriented dross interspersed with expensive sports programming and a surprisingly good 24-hour news service. **Digital television** services are gaining strength too: the BBC operates a number of channels, including the innovative **2W** service just for Wales.

The BBC is also a major player in **radio**, with five UK terrestrial networks, all broadcasting in Wales: Radio One combines pop with a slick interpretation of youth and dance culture; Two is pop and rock skewed to those in their 30s and 40s; Three is classical, Four offers a passionately loved ragbag of magazine shows, current affairs, drama, arts and highbrow quizzes; and Five Live broadcasts a constant, entertaining mix of news and sport. It also operates two stations in Wales alone: **BBC Radio Wales**, a competent, if gentle, English-language service of news, features and music, with occasional dashes of élan, and **BBC Radio Cymru**, a similarly easy-going mix in the Welsh language. Radio Wales and Radio Cymru alike can often be a more entertaining option in the evening or at weekends, away from the daytime tyranny of rolling news, sport, weather and traffic congestion.

Of the commercial stations, the brashest is Radio One soundalike **Red Dragon FM**, serving Cardiff and around, together with **Capital Gold**, its twin for news, features and greatest hits and oldies music. Also in the capital and along the south coast are **Real Radio**, for music, sport and phone-ins and **Kiss 101** for dance, hip hop and drum n' bass. **Swansea Sound**, whose reception extends west towards Pembrokeshire, is solid and frequently interesting; its local twin **The Wave 96.4** isn't. There are bilingual services from **Radio Ceredigion** and **Radio Pembrokeshire** on the west coast, **Radio Carmarthenshire** inland 'and **Champion FM** around Caernarfon and Bangor.

Festivals and events

Wales' wealth of festivals today builds on its ancient pedigree. Most notable are the eisteddfodau – age-old competitions in poetry and music – that still form the backbone of national culture. The colour section goes into more detail on this and some of the country's other big annual jamborees.

Many towns and cities now have annual **arts festivals** of some kind, mentioned throughout the Guide and, in the case of the major events, in the list below. There are numerous other more offbeat events, ranging from the annual Cilgerran **coracle races** (see p.282) to bizarre happenings like peat-bog snorkelling competitions. **Rock festivals**, **DJ-led events** and New Age **fairs** and **festivals** are another common feature of summer throughout Wales; these are usually publicized by handbills, posters in wholefood shops and cafés, and by word of mouth. For more on music festivals, see p.496.

Events calendar

Visit Wales maintains a fairly comprehensive events list on its website (⊛www.visitwales .com).

January 1 Mari Lwyd, Llangynwyd, near Maesteg ⊛www.folkwales.org.uk. Most authentic survivor of the ancient Welsh custom of parading a horse's skull through the village streets.

February to March Six Nations rugby championship. Recently won by Wales, with a tremendous Grand Slam, in 2008.
March 1 St David's Day. Wales' national day, with hwyrnos and celebrations nationwide.
Late April Wonderwool Wales, Builth Wells ⊛www .wonderwoolwales.co.uk. Two-day showcase of Welsh wool and wool products, from raw materials to designer fashion, with plenty of sheep. Held concurrently with the Mid-Wales Mouthful Food Festival, with over 60 stalls.
Mid-May Tredegar House Folk Festival ⊛www .tredegarhousefolk.ik.com. A weekend of international dance, music and song at this grand seventeenth-century mansion.
Late May to early June Guardian Hay-on-Wye Festival ⊛www.hayfestival.com. One of the most feted literary festivals in the world.
End of May to first week in June St Davids Cathedral Festival ⊛www.stdavidscathedral.org.uk. Superb setting for classical concerts and recitals.
End of May to first week in June Eisteddfod Genedlaethol yr Urdd ⊛www.urdd.org. Vast and enjoyable youth eisteddfod – the largest youth festival in Europe – alternating between north and south Wales.

Mid-June Cardiff Singer of the World competition Ⓦwww.bbc.co.uk/cardiffsinger. Huge, televised week-long festival of music and song held in odd-numbered years, with a star-studded list of international competitors.

Mid-June Man Versus Horse Marathon, Llanwrtyd Wells, Powys Ⓦwww.green-events.co.uk. A 22-mile race between runners, cyclists and horses.

Late June Gwyl Ifan Ⓦwww.gwylifan.org. A weekend of folk-dancing workshops, displays and processions in various locations in and around Cardiff.

Late June Criccieth Festival Ⓦwww.cricciethfestival.co.uk. Music, theatre and art.

Last week in June Gregynog Festival, near Newtown, Powys Ⓦwww.gwylgregynogfestival.org. Classical music festival in the superb country house surroundings of Gregynog Hall.

Early July Beyond the Border, St Donat's Castle, Vale of Glamorgan Ⓣ01446/799100, Ⓦwww.beyondtheborder.com. Three-day international storytelling festival in a fairy-tale castle setting, held every odd-numbered year.

First Friday in July Fancy Dress Night, Llanidloes, Powys Ⓦwww.llanidloes.org.uk. Pubs open late, streets are cordoned off and virtually the whole town dresses up.

First or second week in July Llangollen International Music Eisteddfod Ⓦwww.international-eisteddfod.co.uk. Over twelve thousand participants from all over the world, including choirs, dancers, folk singers, groups and instrumentalists.

Mid-July Gower Festival Ⓦwww.gowerfestival.org. Mostly classical music.

Mid-July Sesiwn Fawr (Big Session), Dolgellau Ⓦwww.sesiwnfawr.co.uk. A superb weekend of Celtic bands all over the town.

Mid-July Wakestock, Abersoch, Gwynedd Ⓦwww.wakestock.co.uk. Big, bold wakeboarding and music festival with some huge headline acts, held over a long weekend with camping. One of Wales's hippest events.

Late July Royal Welsh Show, Builth Wells, Powys Ⓦwww.rwas.co.uk. Europe's largest agricultural show and sales fair; an absolute Welsh institution.

Late July Ras yr Wyddfa Ⓦwww.snowdonrace.com. A one-day race from Llanberis up Snowdon, attracting masochists from across the world.

Last week in July to first week in August Cardiff Street Festival Ⓦwww.cardiff-festival.com. Includes the MAS Carnival, with outrageously colourful costumes.

First week in August Royal National Eisteddfod Ⓦwww.eisteddfod.org.uk. Wales' biggest single annual event: fun, very impressive and worth seeing if only for the overblown pageantry. Bardic competitions,

readings, theatre, TV, debates and copious help for the Welsh language learner.

Mid-August Brecon Jazz Festival, Powys Ⓦwww.breconjazz.co.uk. Widely regarded as one of the best jazz festivals in Britain.

Late August Green Man Festival, near Abergavenny Ⓦwww.thegreenmanfestival.co.uk. Three days of folk and folktronica with real food, proper ales, a relaxed atmosphere and acts like Badly Drawn Boy, Martha Wainwright and Iron and Wine.

Late August Pontardawe Music Festival, West Glamorgan Ⓦwww.pontardawefestival.org.uk. Folk, ceilidhs, international music and dance.

Late August Cilgerran Coracle Races, Dyfed Ⓦwww.coracle-fishing.net. Coracle boat races.

Late August Faenol Festival, near Caernarfon Ⓦwww.brynfest.com. Originated by opera megastar Bryn Terfel, this three-day event now encompasses all kinds of music, including one night of Welsh pop and rock.

Late August Llandrindod Wells Victorian Festival, Powys Ⓦwww.victorianfestival.co.uk. A week of family fun, street entertainment and Victorian costumes rounded off with a fireworks display and torchlit procession.

Last week in August Gwyl Machynlleth Ⓦwww.tourism.powys.gov.uk. Wide-ranging arts festival, with a solid programme of chamber music at its core.

August Bank Holiday Monday World Bog Snorkelling Championships, Llanwrtyd Wells, Powys Ⓦwww.green-events.co.uk. Incorporates a mountain bike bog-leaping contest.

First Saturday in September Cardiff Mardi Gras Ⓦwww.cardiffmardigras.co.uk. Cardiff's lesbian and gay festival first took place in 1999 with live acts, dance tents and stalls in the grounds of the castle. It was cancelled in 2008 due to lack of funding and volunteers, but was expected to be back as of 2009.

Mid-September Abergavenny Food Festival Ⓦwww.abergavennyfoodfestival.com. Wales' premier gastronomic event, held over a long weekend.

Late September Tenby Arts Festival Ⓦwww.tenbyartsfest.co.uk. Long-established arts romp in Tenby, with a lively fringe too.

October Swansea Festival of Music and the Arts Ⓦwww.swanseafestival.com. Three weeks of concerts, jazz, drama, opera, ballet and art events throughout the city.

Early November Bonfire Night and Lantern Parade, Machynlleth Ⓦwww.tourism.powys.gov.uk. Superb procession culminating in fireworks and performance.

Early November Dylan Thomas Festival, Swansea Ⓦwww.dylanthomas.com. Talks, performances, exhibitions, readings and music with a DT theme.

Late November Great Welsh Beer and Cider Festival ⊛ www.gwbcf.org.uk. Three days to sample 120 brews, many of them Welsh.

December 31 New Quay ⊛ www.tourism .ceredigion.gov.uk. Seaside New Quay is *the* place to party on New Year's Eve, followed by a three-legged race around the pubs on New Year's Day.

Sport and outdoor activities

No matter where you are in Wales – even in the more populated valleys and along the southern coast – you're never far from a stretch of countryside where you can lose the crowds on a brief walk or cycle ride. For tougher specimens, there are long-distance footpaths and skyline ridge walks, as well as some of the best rock climbing and potholing (caving) in Britain. Along the coast and at many of the country's inland lakes, you can follow the pursuits of sailing and windsurfing, and there are plenty of fine beaches for less structured fresh-air activities.

Walking

There isn't a built-up area in Wales that's more than half an hour away from some decent walking country, but three areas are so outstanding they have been designated **national parks**. Most of Wales' northwestern corner is taken up with the **Snowdonia National Park**, comprising a dozen of the country's highest peaks separated by dramatic glaciated valleys and laced with hundreds of miles of ridge and moorland paths. From Snowdonia, the Cambrian Mountains stretch south to the **Brecon Beacons National Park**, with its striking sandstone scarp at the head of the south Wales coalfield and lush, cave-riddled limestone valleys to the south. One hundred and seventy miles of Wales' southwestern peninsula make up the third park, the **Pembrokeshire Coast National Park**, best explored along the **Pembrokeshire Coast Path**, one of Wales' increasing number of designated **Long Distance Paths** (see *The great Welsh outdoors* colour section).

Unless you're doing your walking on out-of-season weekdays, don't expect to have trails to yourself. Walking is very popular in all the national parks, and finding solitude can require some effort. Many of the best one-day walks in the country are detailed in this Guide, but for more arduous mountain treks, you'll benefit from bringing a specialist walking guidebook, which are widely available. The best are listed in Contexts (p.509), and you can get more information from The Ramblers' Association (☏020/7339 8500, ⊛ www.ramblers.org.uk), Britain's main countryside campaigning organization and self-appointed guardian of the nation's footpaths and rights of way. They maintain a Welsh office at 3 Coopers Yard, Curran Road, Cardiff CF10 5NB (☏029/2064 4308, ⊛ www.ramblers.org.uk/wales).

Rights of access

Although they are managed by committees of local and state officials, all three Welsh national parks are, in fact, predominantly privately owned. Until recently it was the goodwill of landowners that gave access to much of the land, but in 2005 the **Country-side and Rights of Way Act** (CRoW) was implemented across Wales giving open access on foot (but not generally by bike or horse) to "all land that is predominantly mountain, moor, heath or down". Such areas (which comprise almost a fifth of Wales) are marked on all new Ordnance Survey maps, and at boundaries you'll see a brown "walking man" sign. Landowners are, however, allowed to restrict access for a number of reasons, and signs will be posted locally.

Access to other land is restricted to **public rights of way: footpaths** (pedestrians only) and **bridleways** (pedestrians, horses and bicycles) that have seen continued use over the centuries. Historically, these are often over narrow mountain passes between two hamlets, or linking villages to mines or summer pastureland. Rights of way are marked on Ordnance Survey maps and are indicated with a Public Footpath (*Llwybr Cyhoeddus*) sign; any stiles and gates on the path have to be maintained by the landowner. Some less scrupulous owners have been known to block rights of way by destroying stiles – and with some walkers wilfully straying from official rights of way, some resentment is perhaps understandable. Disputes are uncommon, but your surest way of avoiding trouble is to meticulously follow the right of way on an up-to-date map.

Ordnance Survey maps also indicate routes with **concessionary path** or **courtesy path** status, where access is given over private land at the goodwill of the owner; though these are usually open for public use they can be closed at any time.

Rock climbing and scrambling

As well as being superb walking country, Snowdonia offers some of Britain's best **rock climbing** and several challenging **scrambles** – ascents that fall somewhere between walks and climbs, requiring the use of your hands. One or two of the tougher walks included in the text have sections of scrambling, but for the most part this is a specialist discipline, well covered in the walking books listed in Contexts (see p.509). We've covered the subject in more detail in the colour insert.

The best general guide for experienced climbers, *Rock Climbing in Snowdonia* by Paul Williams (Frances Lincoln), is stocked in the region's numerous climbing shops.

Beginners should contact Plas y Brenin: The National Mountain Centre (see p.66 & p.367), or the British Mountaineering Council (☎0161/445 6111, ⊛www.thebmc.co.uk), which can put you in touch with climbing guides and people running courses.

Cycling

In the last few years, Wales has positioned itself as one of Britain's premier **cycling** destinations, with a complex web of traffic-free bike paths and low-traffic cycle routes, plus some excellent mountain bike parks (see *The great Welsh outdoors* colour section). Backroad routes along river valleys and over mountain passes have a sufficient density of pubs and B&Bs to keep the days manageable, and while steep gradients can be a problem, ascents are never long, with Wales' highest pass barely reaching 1500ft. The picture isn't so rosy in most towns and cities, where cyclists are still treated with notorious disrespect by many motorized road users and by the people who plan the country's traffic systems. If you plan to ride in built-up areas, get a **helmet** and a secure **lock** – cycle theft is an organized racket.

Transporting your bike by **train** is a good way of getting to the interesting parts of Wales without a lot of stressful pedalling. With the current profusion of companies running train services, it's hard to be specific about what you'll encounter, but in general,

Safety in the Welsh hills

Welsh mountains are not high by world standards, but they should still be treated with respect. The fickle weather makes them more dangerous than you might expect, and you can easily find yourself disoriented in the low cloud and soaked by unexpected rain. If the weather looks like it's closing in, get down fast. It is essential that you are properly equipped – even for what appears to be an easy expedition in apparently settled weather – with proper warm and waterproof layered clothing, supportive footwear, adequate maps, a compass and food. Always tell someone your route and expected time of return – and call when you get back so they know you're safe.

bikes are carried free on suburban trains outside the weekday rush hours of 7.30–9.30am and 4–6pm. On most routes in Wales, there is only space for two bikes (first-come-first-served) and reservations are not accepted – not much help if you're working to a schedule. On inter-city routes, say from England into Wales, space is still very limited but free reservations are accepted. The free *Cycling by Train* brochure published by Arriva Trains Wales (download-able from Ⓦwww.arrivatrainswales.co.uk), and the *National Rail Guide: Cycling by Train* (from Ⓦwww.nationalrail.co.uk) are both useful resources.

Bike rental is available at bike shops in most large towns (outlined throughout the Guide) and many resorts, but the specimens are seldom top-quality machines – alright for a brief spin, but not for any serious touring. Expect to pay in the region of £20 per day, more for specialist off-road machines with suspension.

Finding **spare parts** might be a problem in remoter areas, but most decent-sized towns now have well-stocked bike shops: the CTC (see below) lists many on their website.

Cycle touring routes

The best of Wales' narrow lanes, disused railway lines and forest paths have been linked together to form **cycle routes** as part of the National Cycle Network created by **Sustrans** (☎0845/113 0065, Ⓦwww.sustrans.org.uk). Set up in 1977, this charity promotes sustainable transport, principally by developing cycling routes – over 10,000 miles have been created and there's more to come, much of it on traffic-free paths and trails, the rest on quiet roads. The entire network is covered in the official *Cycling in the UK* handbook (£15).

Three major cycling routes cross Wales. The main north–south **Lôn Las Cymru** (the Welsh National Route; Route 8) was opened in 1996 and covers three hundred hilly miles from Anglesey, through Snowdonia, the Brecon Beacons and the industrial valleys of the south, to the Severn Bridge. Sustrans publishes two maps of the route (£6 each), one covering Holyhead to Builth Wells and the other from Builth Wells to Chepstow and Cardiff. **Lôn Geltaidd** (the Celtic Trail; Route 4)

traverses 186 miles across the south of the country (70 percent of it traffic-free) from Fishguard to the Severn Bridge: again two £6 maps cover the route. Along the north coast the busy roads are avoided on the **North Wales Coastal Route** (Route 5). In addition there are numerous other local routes, sometimes on dedicated traffic-free paths but often directed along quiet lanes: free leaflets available locally are easy to follow. Areas worth considering are the Gower peninsula, Pembrokeshire, Anglesey and the Llŷn.

Mountain biking

Mountain biking, featured in the colour insert, is a big deal in Wales, with dedicated **bike parks** throughout the managed forests. There's no charge for using them (though there may be a small parking fee), but bike-rental facilities are rare and you are usually better off bringing your own machine or renting one from a nearby town.

Elsewhere, off-road cycling is allowed along designated bridleways, including the Snowdon Ranger, Rhyd Ddu and Llanberis paths up Snowdon (detailed on p.378), but conflict between hikers and bikers has led to the creation of the **Snowdon Voluntary Cycling Agreement**, which limits the hours riders can use them. Anytime in winter (Oct–April) is OK and you can ride before 10am and after 5pm throughout the summer. Footpaths, unless otherwise marked, are for pedestrian use only, and even on bridleways cyclists should always pass walkers at a considerate speed and with a courteous warning of your presence.

For more **information** check out: Ⓦwww.mbwales.com, a Visit Wales site concentrating on the main bike parks, or Ⓦwww.mtb-wales.com, which has excellent articles on routes and gear along with a forum and online shop. Local bookshops and bike stores stock relevant guides, but some of the best trails the country has to offer are covered by *Bikefax: The best mountain bike trails in Snowdonia* (£17).

The CTC and holidays

Britain's biggest **cycling organization**, the Cyclists' Touring Club (CTC: ☎0844/736 8450, Ⓦwww.ctc.org.uk), supplies members with touring and technical advice as well as insurance. Its website is a wealth of information, including dozens of routes through Wales.

If you want a guaranteed hassle-free **cycling holiday**, various companies offer easy-going tours where you ride from hotel to hotel, and a van carries your bags. Some give you an arranged itinerary, while others guide you. The best of the latter is Bicycle Beano, Erwood, Builth Wells, Powys LD2 3PQ (☏01981/560471, ⓦwww .bicycle-beano.co.uk), which offers long-weekend (£290–340) or week-long (£560–640) cycling holidays through the Wye Valley, the Cambrian coast and Snowdonia, with costs including all meals except lunch. They're a lot of fun, good value for money and the cooking is vegetarian. Other good operators offering fixed itineraries include PedalAway, Trereece Barn, Llangarron, Ross-on-Wye, Herefordshire HR9 6NH (☏01989/770357, ⓦwww.pedalaway.co.uk) based over the border in England but offering two-, four- and six-day itineraries into the Black Mountains, Wye Valley and the Brecon Beacons plus off-road tours; and Beics Eryri Cycle Tours (☏01286/676637, ⓦwww.beics .co.uk), which runs trips in Snowdonia.

Beaches, surfing and windsurfing

Wales is ringed by fine **beaches** and **bays**, many of which are readily accessible by public transport – though this also means that they tend to get very busy in high summer. With most of the Welsh coast influenced by the currents of the North Atlantic Drift, water temperatures are higher than you might expect for this latitude, but only the truly hardy should consider swimming outside summer. For swimming and sunbathing, the best areas to head for are the Gower peninsula, the Pembrokeshire coast, the Llŷn and the southwest coast of Anglesey. Though it has more resorts than any other section of Wales' coastline, the north coast certainly hasn't got the most attractive beaches, nor is it a place to swim.

Wales' southwest-facing beaches offer the best conditions for either board or kayak **surfing**, with decent, but by no means Hawaiian-sized, waves at several key spots. In the south, this means Rhossili, at the western tip of the Gower, Rest Bay, near Porthcawl, and Whitesands Bay (Porth-mawr), near St Davids. The surfing scene in north Wales centres on the long sweep of Porth Neigwl (Hell's Mouth), near Abersoch on the Llŷn, and Rhosneigr on Anglesey. **Windsurfers** tend to congregate at these major surf beaches and at Barmouth, Borth, around the Pembrokeshire Coast, and at Mumbles. For more information, call the Welsh Surfing Federation Surf School, Llangennith, Gower, Swansea SA3 1HU (☏01792/386426, ⓦwww.wsfsurfschool.co.uk).

If you'd rather surf indoors, the waterpark at Swansea's new state-of-the-art LC leisure complex (☏01792/466500, ⓦwww .thelcswansea.com) features the "Board Rider", the UK's only standing surfing wave machine, with beginner, intermediate and advanced surfing lessons available.

Kayaking and rafting

Board riders constantly have to compete for waves with the surf ski riders and **kayakers** who frequent the same beaches. Paddlers, however, have the additional run of miles of superb coastline, particularly around Anglesey, the Llŷn and the Pembrokeshire coast. The best general guide is the encyclopaedic *Welsh Sea Kayaking* (£20) by Jim Krawiecki and Andy Biggs. Inland, short, steep bedrock rivers come alive after rain. The best of these are detailed in Chris Sladden's *The Welsh Rivers* (£17.50), which contains maps and paddling notes.

As equipment improves, paddlers have become more daring, and Victorian tourist attractions such as Swallow and Conwy falls, both near Betws-y-Coed, are now fair game for a descent. Most of the kayaking is non-competitive, but on summer weekends you might catch a slalom event at Canolfan Tryweryn National Whitewater Centre, outside Bala (☏01678/521083, ⓦwww .ukrafting.co.uk), where you can also ride the rapids in rubber rafts.

Without your own kayak or canoe, it's still possible to get on the water with tour companies, who can be contacted through the Welsh Canoeing Association (ⓦwww .welsh-canoeing.org.uk) and via ⓦwww .canoewales.com.

Pony trekking

Wales' scattered population and large tracts of open land are ideal for **pony trekking**, now a major business, with almost a hundred approved riding centres and many smaller operations. Don't expect too much cantering over unfenced land: rides tend to be geared towards unhurried appreciation of the scenery from horseback, and are often combined with accommodation on farms. Rates are typically around £15–20 for the first hour and £10–15 for each subsequent hour.

Mid-Wales has the greatest concentration of stables, but there are places all over the country, amply detailed in the brochures supplied by the Wales Trekking and Riding Association (☎01497/847454, ⊛www.ridingwales.com). There's also a stack of information on Visit Wales' extensive riding site at ⊛www.horsebackwales.com.

Rugby

Rugby (or, more precisely, Rugby Union – not to be confused with the different form of the game known as Rugby League) is a passion with the Welsh, and their national game. Support is strongest in the working-class valleys of south Wales, where the fanaticism has traditionally been fuelled by the national side's success. Welsh rugby saw its glory days in the 1970s, when Wales turned out some of the best sides ever seen. The scarlet jerseys struck fear into their opponents in the **Five Nations Championship** – an annual tournament where Wales, England, Scotland, Ireland and France all played each other (now superseded by the Six Nations Championship, with the addition of Italy). That 1970s side won six out of the ten championships – three of them **Grand Slams**, where all four of the Five Nations opponents were beaten individually. The players that made Wales so formidable included fearless fullback J.P.R. Williams, the elusive and magical outside-halves Barry John and Phil Bennett, and the prolific scrum-half, Gareth Edwards.

But victories were harder to come by in the 1980s, and by 1991, the national side reached its nadir with its worst-ever international loss of 63–6 at the hands of Australia. When rugby turned professional in 1995 it was able to coax back players who had defected to the rival code, rugby league, but Wales generally struggled to keep up with the standards of arch adversary England throughout the 1990s, let alone match the power and attacking panache of the all-conquering southern hemisphere sides of the era, Australia, New Zealand and South Africa. Recognizing this southern dominance, the Welsh Rugby Union (⊛www.wru.co.uk) enlisted the help of New Zealander, Graham Henry. After taking over in 1998, he oversaw an astonishing string of victories including one over South Africa in the first game to be played at the brand-new 72,500-seater **Millennium Stadium**, built on the site of the legendary Cardiff Arms Park. All this raised hopes of success in the 1999 Rugby World Cup, hosted by Wales. They stumbled at the quarter-final stage, but in the process, Neil Jenkins overtook Australian Michael Lynagh's record for the greatest number of international points scored. A subsequent string of poor results (including an embarrassing loss to Argentina and a drubbing by Ireland) put an end to Henry's reign. His successor, fellow Kiwi Steve Hansen, only managed to get them to the quarter-finals of the 2003 Rugby World Cup in Australia, but under Mike Ruddock in 2005 Wales saw a massive turnaround, with the national team lifting the Six Nations trophy with a Grand Slam. A few months later they were brought back to earth when thumped 41–3 by the All Blacks and the next couple of years saw poor results culminating in an abominable 2007 Rugby World Cup when the national team came third in their pool (behind Australia and Fiji) and failed to progress to the quarter-finals. Under another Kiwi coach, Warren Gatland, the national side rebounded in 2008 with a massive Grand Slam in the 2008 Six Nations, conceding just two tries in the process.

To see an international game, you'll have to be affiliated to one of the Rugby Union clubs or be prepared to pay well over the odds at one of the ticket agencies. Most tickets are allocated months before a match, and touts will often be found selling tickets for hundreds of pounds outside the gates on the day. Away from the international arena, a thriving rugby scene exists at club level, with upwards of a hundred clubs and 40,000 players taking to the field most Saturdays throughout the season (Sept to just after Easter). The upper tier is known as the Welsh Premiership though the top teams – the Cardiff Blues, Scarlets (formerly the Llanelli Scarlets), Newport Gwent Dragons and Swansea Ospreys – play in the Celtic League (aka Magners League) against teams from Scotland and Ireland.

It's often worth going to a match purely for the light-hearted crowd banter – if you can understand the accents. Check with individual clubs for fixtures and ticket prices, which start at under £10 (though £15–25 is typical).

Football

Compared to rugby, **Welsh football** (soccer) is seen as a minority sport, but in fact there are just as many Welsh footballers who prefer not to pick up the ball and run with it as those who do. The three top sides in the country have traditionally been Cardiff City, Swansea City and Wrexham, all of whom were long-standing members of the English Football League. Wrexham were relegated from the fourth division of the Football league at the end of the 2007/08 season, but the other two teams are both competing in the second division, known as the Championship. Swansea are currently enjoying their highest league position since the 1980s, and in 2008 Cardiff reached the final of the FA Cup for the first time since 1927.

The rest of the clubs play in the lacklustre (but improving) **Welsh Premier League** (Ⓦ www.welshpremier.com). For more on the Welsh game, check the website of the Football Association of Wales (Ⓦ www.faw .org.uk).

Under the stewardship of former player Mark Hughes, the national side experienced a brief spell of success between 2002 and 2004. Wales remained unbeaten during Hughes' first eight games in charge, often thanks to the mercurial brilliance of Ryan Giggs, with a morale-boosting win over Finland in Helsinki followed by a shock 2–1 victory over Italy.

In the end, Wales narrowly missed out on reaching the finals of Euro 2004, which would have been their first major finals since the 1958 World Cup, when they lost to eventual winners Brazil in the quarter-finals.

Recent results haven't been great, with few wins in the team's unsuccessful campaigns to reach the finals of either the 2006 World Cup in Germany or Euro 2008. They are currently ranked around 60th in the world.

Alternative, New Age and green Wales

Possibly more than any other part of Britain, Wales – the mid and west in particular – has become something of a haven for those searching for alternative lifestyles. The 1960s saw mass migration west, something that has continued unabated since. Permanent testimonials to this include the Centre for Alternative Technology (CAT), near Machynlleth, now one of the area's most visited attractions, and Tipi Valley, near Talley, a permanent community living in Native American tepees who run a regular public sweat lodge. Both institutions were founded in the idealistic mid-1970s and have prospered through less happy times. For the most part, it's been a fairly smooth process, although antagonism between New Agers and local, established families does break out on occasion, usually stoked by the sometimes liberal smugness of some incomers.

For visitors, the legacy of this "green" influx is evident throughout Wales. Even in some of the smallest rural towns, you'll often find a health-food shop, wholefood café, somewhere flogging esoteric ephemera or an alternative resource centre. Any of these will give you further ideas and contacts for local happenings, places, groups and individuals. We've tried to give details of such places throughout the Guide.

Other manifestations of such prolific non-mainstream activity include a robust **free party scene** in the rural parts of north, mid- and west Wales. These are often held in spectacularly beautiful settings – by lakes, on beaches – and take place virtually every weekend throughout the summer. There's also a plethora of good **festivals** from spring to autumn, ranging from big folk and blues bashes to smaller gatherings in remote fields, with little more than a couple of banging sound systems. Information travels best by word of mouth, so keep your eyes and ears peeled for information and don't hesitate to ask around. For more organized and larger events, you'll see adverts and fliers months in advance.

For ecologically minded tourists, there are now numerous package deals that include walking, cycling, dancing and healing holidays and retreats in remote centres, usually with vegetarian and vegan food as part of the deal. Some of these are static, many are in temporary sites, while others keep you on the move. Again, we have included many of these within the body of the Guide, and some further ones are listed below.

Retreats and holidays

Buckland Hall Bwlch, near Brecon ℡01874/730330, ⊛www.bucklandhall.co.uk. Beautiful hall and gardens hosting holistic lifestyle courses and workshops.

Cae Mabon near Llanberis, Gwynedd ℡01286/871542, ⊛www.caemabon.co.uk. Stunning Snowdonia setting for residential courses, storytelling and arts events, with accommodation in barns, bothies and benders.

Centre for Alternative Technology Llwyngwern, near Machynlleth, Powys ℡01654/705950, ⊛www.cat.org.uk. Residential courses on green themes such as self-build homes and organic gardening.

Dance Camp Wales Pembrokeshire ⊛www .dancecampwales.org. Ten-day dance festival held in August in a beautiful location, with about 500 participants.

Healing Tao Britain 7 Miners Lane, Old Colwyn, Conwy ℡01492/515776. Residential weekend workshops on meditation and Chi Kung.

Heartspring Llansteffan, Carmarthenshire ℡01267/241999, ⊛www.heartspring.co.uk. Three- or five-day retreats in a beautiful house, with holistic therapies and great veggie food.

Spirit Horse Camp Powys ⊛www.spirithorse .co.uk. Camps to celebrate ancient ceremonial and cultural traditions in a stunning, secluded setting.

Vajraloka Buddhist Meditation Centre Corwen, Denbighshire ℡01490/460406. Regular retreats for men.

Travel essentials

Costs

Prices in Wales are generally lower than in many parts of England, particularly London. For foreign visitors, however, the current strength of the pound (certainly in relation to the US dollar), means that Wales may seem a relatively expensive destination.

The **minimum expenditure**, if you're camping and preparing most of your own food, would be in the region of £20 per day, rising to around £30 per day if you're using the hostelling network, some public transport and grabbing the odd takeaway or meal out. Couples staying at budget B&Bs, eating at unpretentious restaurants and visiting a fair number of tourist attractions are looking at £50–60 each per day – if you're renting a car, staying in comfortable B&Bs or hotels and eating well, you should reckon on at least £80 a day. Single travellers should budget on spending around sixty percent of what a couple would spend, mainly because single rooms tend to cost more than half the price of a double. For more detail on the cost of accommodation, transport and eating, see the relevant sections.

VAT

Most goods in Britain, with the chief exceptions of books and groceries, are subject to a 17.5 percent **Value Added Tax (VAT)**, which is almost always included in the quoted price. Visitors from non-EU countries can save money through the **Retail Export Scheme**, which allows a refund of VAT on goods to be taken out of the country. Shops participating in this scheme will have a sign in their window and can provide you with the documentation necessary to claim your refund when leaving the country. Note that you cannot reclaim VAT charged on hotel bills or other services.

Student and youth cards

The various official and quasi-official **youth/ student ID cards** are of relatively minor use in Wales, saving only a few pence for entry to some museums and maybe discounts at national movie chains and fast-food outlets. If you already have one then bring it, but if you don't, it's barely worth making a special effort to get one.

Full-time students are eligible for the International Student ID Card (ISIC, ⓦwww .isiccard.com), while anyone under 26 can apply for an International Youth Travel Card, which carries the same benefits. Both cost £9 or equivalent.

Several other travel organizations and accommodation groups also sell their own cards, good for various discounts. A university photo ID might open some doors, but is not as easily recognizable as the ISIC cards.

Tipping and service charges

In restaurants a service charge is sometimes included in the bill; if it isn't, leave a tip of 10–15 percent unless the service is unforgivably bad. Some restaurants are in the habit of leaving the "total" box blank on credit-card counterfoils, to encourage customers to add another few percent on top of the service charge – if you're paying by credit card, check that the "total" box is filled in before you sign. Taxi drivers expect a tip in the region of ten percent. You do not generally tip bar staff – if you want to show your appreciation, offer to buy them a drink.

Tourist attractions

Many of Wales' most treasured sites – from castles, abbeys and great houses to tracts of protected landscape – come under the control of the privately run UK-wide National Trust or the state-run CADW, Welsh Historic Monuments whose properties are denoted in the Guide by "NT" and "CADW".

Both organizations charge an entry fee for most places, and these can be quite high, especially for the more grandiose NT estates. When entering such places you are often encouraged to pay the gift aid price, which adds around ten percent to the normal adult price, but through tax benefits gives the NT considerable benefit.

If you think you'll be visiting more than half a dozen NT places or a similar number of major CADW sites, it's worth buying an annual pass. Membership of the National Trust (℡0844/800 1895, ⊛www.nationaltrust.org.uk; £46, under-26s £21) allows free entry to its properties throughout Britain. Sites operated by CADW (℡01443/336000, ⊛www.cadw.wales.gov.uk; £35, seniors £22, ages 16–20 £20, under-16s £16) are restricted to Wales, but membership also grants you half-price entry to sites owned by English Heritage and Historic Scotland. In addition, CADW offers the World Heritage Explorer Pass, which allows free entry into all five CADW World Heritage sites over three consecutive days (adult £11, family £25), or seven days (£16/£34).

A few Welsh **stately homes** remain in the hands of the landed gentry, who tend to charge in the region of £5 for edited highlights of their domain. Many other old buildings, albeit rarely the most momentous, are owned by the local authorities, and admission is often cheaper. Municipal **art galleries** and **museums** are usually free, and as part of the Welsh Assembly's drive to popularize the nation's cultural heritage, so are sites run by the National Museums and Galleries of Wales (⊛www.museumwales.ac.uk), including the National Museum and Gallery and St Fagans National History Museum, both in Cardiff. Although a donation is usually requested, **cathedrals** tend to be free, except for perhaps the tower, crypt or other such highlight, for which a small charge is made. Increasingly, **churches** are kept locked except during services; when they are open, entry is free. (You'll normally be able to find a notice in the porch or on a board telling you where to get a key if the church is locked.) Wales also has a number of ventures exploiting the country's **industrial heritage**, mostly concerned with mining for coal, slate, copper or gold. A short tour supplemented by a video should cost a couple of pounds, while the full underground interactive "experience" can be up to £10. Keen birders might consider joining the **RSPB**, where membership (⊛www.rspb.org.uk; £34 a year) gives you free entry to its reserves throughout Britain.

Entry charges given in the Guide are the full adult rates, but the majority of the fee-charging attractions located in Wales have 25–35 percent **reductions** for senior citizens, the unemployed and full-time students, and 50 percent reductions for under-16s – under-5s are admitted free almost everywhere. Proof of eligibility is required in most cases. Family tickets are also common, usually priced just under the rate for two adults and a child and valid for up to three kids.

Finally, foreign visitors planning on seeing more than a dozen stately homes, monuments, castles or gardens might find it worthwhile to buy a Great British Heritage Pass (⊛www.britishheritagepass.com), which gives free admission to around six hundred sites throughout the UK. Over sixty of these are in Wales, including the Bishop's Palace in St Davids, Tredegar House at Newport and Cardiff Castle, as well as all National Trust and CADW properties. The pass can be purchased for periods of four days (£30), seven days (£44), fifteen days (£59) or a month (£79) either online or from the main air-and sea ports, and tourist offices in the largest cities.

Electricity

In Britain, the current is 240V AC at 50Hz. North American appliances will need a transformer, though most laptops, phone and MP3 player chargers are designed to automatically detect and adapt to the electricity supply and don't need any modification. Almost all foreign appliances will require an adapter for the chunky British three-pin electrical sockets.

For details of how to plug your **laptop** in when abroad, phone country codes around the world, and information about electrical systems in different countries look at ⊛www.kropla.com.

Emergencies and police

As in any other country, Wales' major towns have their dangerous spots, but these tend to be inner-city housing estates where you're unlikely to find yourself. The chief risk on the streets – though still minimal – is pickpocketing, so carry only as much money as you need, and keep all bags and pockets fastened. Should you have anything stolen or be involved in an incident that requires reporting, go to the local police station. The ☎999 or 112 numbers for police, fire and ambulance services should only be used in emergencies.

Entry requirements

Citizens of all European countries – other than Albania, Bosnia Herzegovina and most republics of the former Soviet Union – can enter Britain with just a passport, generally for up to three months. US, Canadian, Australian and New Zealand citizens can travel in Britain for up to six months with just a passport. All other nationalities require a visa, available from the British Consular office in the country of application.

For stays longer than six months, **US, Canadian, Australian and New Zealand citizens** should apply to the British Embassy or High Commission (see below). If you want to extend your stay, you should visit the UK Border Agency website (ⓦwww .ind.homeoffice.gov.uk), where you can download the appropriate form. Do this before the expiry date given on the endorsement in your passport.

Embassy contact details are listed on the website of the Foreign and Commonwealth Office (ⓦwww.fco.gov.uk): look for links to "UK Embassies abroad" and "Foreign Embassies in the UK".

Overseas representation in Britain

Except for the Irish consulate in Cardiff, foreign embassies are all found in London.
Australia ☎020/7379 4334, ⓦwww.australia .org.uk
Canada ⓦwww.canada.org.uk.
Ireland ☎020/7235 2171, ⓦireland .embassyhomepage.com; Consulate, Brunel House, 2 Fitzalan Rd, Cardiff CF24 0EB ☎029/2066 2000.
Netherlands ☎020/7590 3200, ⓦwww .netherlands-embassy.org.uk.
New Zealand ☎020/7930 8422, ⓦwww .nzembassy.com.
RSA ☎020/7451 7299, ⓦwww.southafricahouse .com.
USA ☎020/7499 9000, ⓦwww.usembassy.org.uk.

Customs and biosecurity

Travellers entering Britain directly from another EU country do not have to make a declaration to **customs** at their place of entry, and can effectively bring almost as much wine or beer as they like. The guidance levels are 90 litres of wine and 110 of beer, which should be enough for anyone – any more than this, and you're supposed to have proof that it's for personal use only, though even that is seldom checked. If you're travelling to or from a non-EU country, you can still buy duty-free goods, but within the EU, this perk no longer exists. The duty-free allowances are as follows:

Tobacco: 200 cigarettes; or 100 cigarillos; or 50 cigars; or 250g of loose tobacco.

Alcohol: Two litres of still wine, **plus** one litre of drink over 22 percent alcohol, or two litres of alcoholic drink not over 22 percent, or another two litres of still wine.

Perfumes: 60ml of perfume plus 250ml of toilet water.

You're also allowed other goods to the value of £145.

There are import restrictions on a variety of articles and substances, from firearms to furs derived from endangered species, none of which should bother the normal tourist. However, if you need any clarification on British import regulations, contact HM Revenue & Customs (☎0845/010 9000, international ☎44 2920/501261, ⓦwww .hmrc.gov.uk).

Biosecurity is also an issue, especially after the disastrous 2001 outbreak of Foot and Mouth disease, and it is now illegal to import meat, milk and other animal products from outside the EU: see ⓦwww.defra.gov .uk for more details. For similar reasons you are not allowed to bring **pets** into Britain without subjecting them to prohibitively long periods of quarantine.

Gay and lesbian Wales

Homosexual acts between consenting males were legalized in Britain in 1967, but it wasn't until 2000 that the age of consent for gay men was made equal to that of straight men at sixteen. Lesbianism has never specifically been outlawed, apocryphally owing to the fact that Queen Victoria refused to believe it existed. In December 2005, civil partnerships between same sex-couples were legalized – marriage in all but name.

With such a rural culture, it's perhaps not surprising that Wales is less used to the lesbian and gay lifestyle than its more cosmopolitan English neighbour. That said, there's little real hostility, with the traditional Welsh "live and let live" attitude applying as much in this area as any other. Several Welsh musicians, academics, TV stars and politicians have come out in recent years, and no one's really batted an eyelid.

The organized gay scene in Wales, however, is fairly muted. The main cities – Cardiff, Newport and Swansea – have a number of pubs and clubs, with Cardiff especially beginning to see a worthy and confident gay scene – a Mardi Gras festival in early September included (see p.51) – more in keeping with the capital's size and status. Details are given in the text of the Guide. Out of the southern cities, however, gay life becomes distinctly discreet, although university towns such as Lampeter, Bangor and Wrexham manage support groups and the odd weekly night in a local bar, while Aberystwyth is a significantly homo-friendly milieu. Cardiff's lesbian and gay telephone lines (see p.127) are the most up-to-date source of information on places, events, accommodation and contacts throughout Wales. Alternatively, there are some informal but well-established networks, especially amongst the sometimes reclusive alternative lifestylers found in mid- and west Wales. **Border Women** (who should surely have called themselves Offa's Dykes; Ⓦwww.borderwomen.org.uk) is a well-organized lesbian network for mid-Wales and the Marches, with walks and monthly lunches. For groups, events, pubs, clubs and **gay-friendly tourist accommodation** in all corners of Wales, by far the best resource is the excellent **Gay Wales website** (Ⓦwww .gaywales.co.uk).

Health

No vaccinations are required for entry into Britain. Citizens of all EU countries are entitled to free medical **treatment** at National Health Service hospitals; citizens of other countries are charged for all medical services except those administered by accident and emergency units at National Health Service hospitals. Thus a US citizen who has been hit by a car would not be charged if the injuries simply required stitching and setting in the emergency unit, but would be if admission

to a hospital ward were necessary. Health insurance is therefore strongly advised for all non-EU nationals.

Pharmacies (known generally as chemists in Britain) can dispense only a limited range of drugs without a doctor's prescription. Most pharmacies are open during standard shop hours, though in large towns some may stay open as late as 10pm – local newspapers carry lists of late-opening pharmacies. Doctors' surgeries tend to be open from about 9am until early evening; outside surgery hours, you can turn up at the casualty department of the local hospital for problems that require immediate attention – unless it's a real **emergency**, in which case ring for an ambulance on ℡999.

Insurance

Wherever you're travelling from, it's a good idea to have some kind of travel insurance to cover you for loss of possessions and money, as well as the cost of any medical and dental treatment. Before paying for a new policy, however, it's worth checking whether you are already covered: some all-risks home insurance policies may cover your possessions when overseas, and many private medical schemes include cover when abroad. Students will often find that their student health coverage extends during the vacations and for one term beyond the date of last enrolment.

After exhausting the possibilities above, you might want to contact a specialist travel insurance company, or consider the travel insurance deal we offer (see box opposite). A typical travel insurance policy usually provides cover for the loss of baggage, tickets and – up to a certain limit – cash or cheques, as well as cancellation or curtailment of your journey. Most of them exclude so-called dangerous sports unless an extra premium is paid: in Wales this can mean whitewater rafting, windsurfing and coasteering, though probably not ordinary hiking. Many policies can be chopped and changed to exclude coverage you don't need – for example, sickness and accident benefits can often be excluded or included at will. If you do take medical coverage, ascertain whether benefits will be paid as

Rough Guides travel insurance

Rough Guides has teamed up with Columbus Direct to offer you tailor-made **travel insurance**. Products include a low-cost **backpacker** option for long stays; a **short break** option for city getaways; a typical **holiday package** option; and others. There are also annual **multi-trip** policies for those who travel regularly. Different sports and activities (trekking, skiing, etc) can usually be included.

See our website (ⓦ www.roughguides.com/website/shop) for eligibility and purchasing options. Alternatively, UK residents can call ☏ 0870/033 9988, Australians ☏ 1300/669 999 and New Zealanders ☏ 0800/559 911. All other nationalities should call ☏ +44 870/890 2843.

treatment proceeds or only after return home, and whether there is a 24-hour medical emergency number. When securing baggage cover, make sure that the per-article limit – typically under £500 – will cover your most valuable possession. If you need to make a claim, you should keep receipts for medicines and medical treatment, and in the event you have anything stolen, you must obtain an official statement from the police.

Internet

Throughout Wales, almost all public libraries now have **internet access**, usually with several speedy machines loaded with word-processing, spreadsheet and database software. Typically you just front up, and sign in for the next available half-hour or hour-long slot. The service is usually free to visitors, but even in the rare cases where a fee is charged it usually works out cheaper than visiting one of the relatively abundant cybercafés dotted around the country (where you can expect to pay £2–4 an hour). At more expensive accommodation, there'll often be a free-use computer.

Wi-fi coverage is fairly widespread. You'll often have free access at better B&Bs and hotels, and there's always the chance you'll stumble across unsecured access (though this isn't that common). Free access can also be found at McDonalds and at Wetherspoon pubs which are found in all the larger towns.

Mail

Virtually all **post offices** (*swyddfa'r post*) are open Monday to Friday 9am to 5.30pm, Saturday 9am to 12.30/1pm. In small communities, you'll find sub-post offices operating out of a shop, but these work to the same hours even if the shop itself is open for longer. Stamps can be bought at post office counters and from a large number of newsagents and other shops, although often these sell only books of four or ten stamps. A first-class letter to anywhere in Britain (up to 100g) costs 36p and should arrive the next day; second-class letters cost 27p, taking two to four days to arrive. Postcards cost 50p to EU countries, and 56p to everywhere else. For parcel rates visit ⓦ www.royalmail.com.

Maps

Most bookshops will have a good selection of **maps of Wales** and Britain, though the best can be found in specialist travel bookshops. Virtually every petrol station in Britain stocks one or more of the large-format **road atlases** produced by the AA, RAC, Collins, Ordnance Survey (OS) and others, which cover all of Britain at a scale of around three miles to one inch and include larger-scale plans of major towns. The best of these is the Ordnance Survey road atlas, which handily uses the same grid reference system as their accurate and detailed folding maps.

If you want more detail, the most comprehensive maps are again produced by the **Ordnance Survey** (ⓦ www.ordnancesurvey .co.uk), a series renowned for its accuracy and clarity. The 204 maps in its 1:50,000 (a little over one inch: one mile) Landranger series (£7 each) cover the whole of Britain in enough detail to be useful for most walkers. The 1:25,000 Explorer series (£8 each) is more detailed, but most serious hikers favour the same-scale Explorer OL maps, which cover only the most frequently walked areas. Each is sensibly designed to take in a specific area, and even shows fencelines and field boundaries to aid navigation. There are eight Explorer OL maps for Wales, three covering Snowdonia from the north coast down to Cadair Idris, three large double-sided ones spanning the Brecon Beacons, Black Mountains and Wye Valley, and another two charting Pembrokeshire. OS maps are widely available in bookshops, and you can be sure to find the relevant maps on sale locally in any popular walking district in Wales.

Money

The British **pound sterling** (£; *punt* in Welsh, and widely referred to as a "quid") is divided into 100 pence (p; in Welsh, c for *ceiniogau*). Coins come in denominations of 1p, 2p, 5p, 10p, 20p, 50p, £1 and £2. Notes come in denominations of £5, £10, £20 and £50. Shopkeepers will carefully scrutinize any £20 and £50 notes tendered, as forgeries are not uncommon.

You may also come across Scottish bank-notes which are legal tender in England and Wales, though often refused by traders. They come in the same denominations and have the same value as the British notes but are issued by three different banks; the Bank of Scotland, the Royal Bank of Scotland and the Clydesdale Bank.

Cards, cheques and ATMs

Most hotels, shops and restaurants in Wales are happy to accept the major **credit, charge and debit cards**, **particularly** Access/MasterCard and Visa/Barclaycard. American Express and Diners' Club are less widely accepted. Cards generally are less useful in rural areas, and smaller establishments all over the country, such as B&B accommodation, will often accept cash only. Some places that do accept cards require a £10 minimum purchase. With a suitable PIN (ask at your bank before leaving home) your card will also enable you to get cash advances from most ATMs, though there may be a standard fee which makes it more cost effective to withdraw larger sums. In addition, you may be able to make withdrawals from your home

bank account using your ATM cash card via the international Cirrus and Plus networks – check before leaving home.

The safest way to carry your money is in **traveller's cheques**, available for a small commission (normally one percent) from any major bank. These can be exchanged at banks and bureaux de change and replaced if lost of stolen. Recognized brands – American Express, Thomas Cook, Mastercard and Visa – are accepted in all major currencies, but traveller's cheques (even in sterling) aren't accepted as cash.

There are no exchange controls in Britain, so you can bring in as much cash as you like and change traveller's cheques up to any amount.

Banks

Banks are almost always the best places to **change money and cheques**, and in every sizeable town in Wales you'll find a branch of at least one of the big five: NatWest, Halifax, HSBC, Barclays and Lloyds TSB. As a general rule, **opening hours** are Monday to Friday 9 or 9.30am to 4.30pm or 5pm, and branches in larger towns are often open on Saturday from 9am to 1pm. In the larger towns you may be able to find a **bureau de change** (often the post office), which will be open longer hours but may charge high commission. Hotels are expensive places to change money.

Opening hours and public holidays

General **shop hours** are Monday to Saturday 9am to 5.30/6pm, although there's an increasing amount of Sunday and late-night shopping in the larger towns, with Thursday or Friday being the favoured evenings. The big supermarkets also tend to stay open until 8 or 9pm from Monday to Saturday, and open on Sunday from 10am to 4pm, as do many of the stores in the shopping complexes springing up on the outskirts of major towns. Many provincial towns still retain an "early closing day" when shops shut at 1pm – Wednesday is the favourite. Note that not all **service stations** are open 24 hours, although you can usually get fuel around the clock in the larger towns and cities. Also, most fee-charging sites are open

Public holidays

New Year's Day January 1

Good Friday late March to mid-April

Easter Monday late March to mid-April

May Bank Holiday first Monday in May

Spring Bank Holiday (sometimes referred to as Whitsun) last Monday in May

Summer Bank Holiday last Monday in August

Christmas Day December 25

Boxing Day December 26

Note that if January 1, December 25 or December 26 falls on a Saturday or Sunday, the next weekday becomes a public holiday.

on bank holidays, when Sunday hours usually apply.

In addition to the public holidays (see box above) your travels around Wales may be disrupted by **school holidays**, when accommodation in popular areas (especially near beaches) is stretched by holidaying families. The main school holidays are two weeks around Christmas and New Year, two weeks around Easter, and six weeks from mid-July to early September. There is also a one-week break in the middle of each term, one usually falling in late May.

Phones

Given the near-ubiquity of mobile phones, most people don't have much need for public **payphones** (*teleffon*), which are operated by BT (⑩www.bt.co.uk), and still found all over the place. Calls to anywhere in the UK (except to mobiles and premium numbers) **cost** 40p for the first 20 minutes then 10p for every 10 minutes thereafter. Most payphones in out-of-the-way places no longer take coins, forcing you to use credit and debit cards (UK calls 20p/min, minimum £1.20), or account-based phonecards available from post offices and some shops. When buying such cards, read the small print, as there are often all manner of extra charges and penalties.

Phone numbers

Numbers with the prefix ☎0800 and ☎0808, are free to the caller; ☎0845 numbers are charged at the local call rate (daytime 3p/min; evenings and weekend 1p/min); and ☎0870 numbers are charged at the national call rate (daytime 8p/min; evenings and weekends 4p/min). Numbers starting with ☎090 are all premium rated, generally costing 60p–£1 per minute, though ☎0905/6xxxxxx calls can be any price, as can the salacious ☎0909 numbers. Calling a mobile phone (all prefixed ☎07) costs far more than dialling a land line.

To **call Wales** from outside the UK, dial the international access code (☎011 from the US and Canada, ☎0011 from Australia and ☎00 from New Zealand), followed in all cases by 44, then the area code minus its initial zero, and finally the number.

National operator (freecall) ☎100

International operator (freecall) ☎155

National Directory Enquiry Several services are available including ☎118 500 (64p per minute plus 23p connection charge).

International Directory Enquiry ☎118 505 (£2 per minute plus 69p minimum charge).

Mobile phones

For sheer convenience you can't do better than a **mobile phone**, and it needn't cost the earth. If you want to use your own phone, you'll need to check with your phone provider whether it will work in Britain, and what the call charges are. The GSM system used in Britain is compatible with other European systems, Australian systems and some in New Zealand, though most North American single-band phones don't work here. A better bet might be to bring your phone and buy a new pre-pay SIM card for it (about £5). With no contract you simply top up your account as you need to. Of course you'll have to tell your friends and colleagues your new number but you'll save on call costs. If your phone doesn't work on UK frequency bands you may need one that does. These are available from the numerous high street outlets from as little as £20.

There's frenetic competition between the main operators – Vodafone (⑩online .vodafone.co.uk), O2 (⑩www.o2.co.uk), Orange (⑩www.orange.co.uk) and T-mobile

Note that the initial zero is omitted from the area code when dialling the **UK**, Ireland and Australia.
Australia 00 + 61 + city code.
NZ 00 + 64 + city code.
Republic of Ireland 00 + 353 + city code.
South Africa 00 + 27 + city code.
US and **Canada** 00 + 1 + area code.

(ⓦ www.t-mobile.co.uk) – so shop around for a package that suits you.

Shopping

The quintessential Welsh memento is a **lovespoon** – an intricately carved wooden spoon that in centuries gone by was offered by suitors when courting. The meanings of the various designs range from a Celtic cross (symbolizing faith/marriage) to vines (growing love) and a double spoon (commitment), with dozens of others available. Prices range from a few pounds for a small version, to several hundred pounds for a large, elaborate spoon by a well-known carver. You'll find them in craft shops all over the country, including some dedicated solely to these ornaments.

Other unique items include some superb paintings, jewellery, leatherwork and screen-printing from **arts and crafts** galleries throughout Wales; some are run by the artists themselves, and you can watch them at work. Given that Wales has an estimated three to four times as many sheep as humans, it's not surprising that there are some wonderful **woollen products** available.

Smoking

Wales banned smoking in almost all enclosed public areas in April 2007 (a few months before similar legislation came into effect in England). This effectively prohibits smoking on public transport and in all restaurants, bars and clubs. You'll now see clusters of die-hard smokers outside pubs and occupying café pavement tables in all weathers. The legislation is in line with a dramatic change in attitudes towards smoking and a significant reduction in the consumption of cigarettes.

Studying in Wales

There are numerous places around Wales where you might attend full-day or multi-day courses (residential or otherwise) to pursue all manner of interests. Some of the most interesting are:

Nant Gwrtheyrn: The Welsh Language and Heritage Centre 10 miles north of Pwllheli ☏ 01758/750334, ⓦ nantgwrtheyrn.org. If you're keen on acquiring some Welsh beyond the basics, this is about the best bet there is. Residential courses are run for everyone from complete beginners to near-fluent speakers: either weekend (non-residential £115/full board £180); three-day (£165/230) or five-day (£275/395). See p.407.

Plas y Brenin: The National Mountain Centre Capel Curig ☏ 01690/720214, ⓦ www.pyb.co.uk. This internationally recognized outdoor training centre runs a huge range of residential courses and two-hour samplers at all levels up to expert, plus expedition training. Examples of beginner courses include: the two-day Navigation Skills course for hill-walkers (£205), the five-day Scrambling Week (£480), the weekend Introduction to Climbing (£240), five days of White Water Sea and Surf (£415) aimed at those with basic kayaking skills, a multi-activity weekend (£150), and many more. Also offers qualification courses for all levels of instructors. See p.367.

Plas Menai: The National Watersports Centre near Caernarfon ☏ 01248/670964, ⓦ www.plasmenai.co.uk. All manner of predominantly two- and five-day courses covering sailing, windsurfing, kayaking and jet skiing in a beautiful location on the Menai Strait. For two-day courses expect to pay £175 (£135 non-resident), for five-day budget on £415 (£315).

Plas Tan y Bwlch near Porthmadog ☏ 01766/772 600, ⓦ www.plastanybwlch.com. Snowdonia National Park Study Centre which runs residential courses focusing mainly on the environment and appreciation of the countryside. They extend to digital landscape photography (3 days, £230), botanical watercolour painting (5 days, £270), mushrooms and toadstools (2 days, £150), drovers and drovers' roads (4 days, £270), fly-fishing (5 days, £400), preserved railways (6 days, £510) and much more. See p.387

Time

Greenwich Mean Time (GMT) is in force from late October to late March, when the clocks go forward an hour for British Summer Time (BST). GMT is five hours ahead of New York, ten hours behind Sydney, and twelve hours behind New Zealand.

Tourist information

Wales promotes itself enthusiastically, broadly through **Visit Britain** and more specifically through **Visit Wales** – addresses for both agencies are listed below. Both have extensive websites offering a wealth of free literature, some of it just rose-tinted advertising copy, but much of it extremely useful – especially the maps, city guides and event calendars.

Visit Wales and tourist offices

Visit Wales (aka Croeso Cymru; ☏0870/830 0306, ⓦwww.visitwales.com) operates a central information service that's excellent for pre-trip planning, with a detailed website and plenty of free brochures which can either be downloaded or sent by mail. There is also representation at Visit Britain, 1 Regent St, London SW1Y 4XT (☏020/8846 9000, ⓦwww.visitbritain.com).

Tourist offices (usually called Tourist Information Centres) exist in virtually every Welsh town – you'll find their contact details and opening hours in the relevant sections of the Guide. The average opening hours are much the same as standard shop hours, with the difference that in summer they'll often be open on a Sunday and for a couple of hours after the shops have closed on weekdays; opening hours are generally shorter in winter, and in more remote areas the office may well be closed altogether. All centres offer information on accommodation (which they can often book – see p.42), local public transport, attractions and restaurants, as well as town and regional maps. In many cases all of this is free, though some offices make a small charge for their accommodation list or the town guide with accompanying street plan.

Areas designated as national parks (the Brecon Beacons, Pembrokeshire coast and Snowdonia) also have a fair sprinkling of **National Park Information Centres**, which are generally more expert in giving guidance on local walks and outdoor pursuits.

Travellers with disabilities

Visitors with disabilities will find travelling in Wales easier than in much of the world, though many older buildings (and especially cheaper places to stay) are difficult or impossible to adapt and it always pays to call ahead to check the situation. Disabled parking spaces are common, new buildings (including accommodation) are required to make appropriate provision, and a fair number of existing hotels, B&Bs and restaurants are retrofitting accessible bathrooms and ramps. Some YHAs (see p.42) also incorporate disabled facilities.

Public transport companies are beginning to make more of an effort to accommodate passengers with mobility problems. Some rail services now accommodate wheelchair users in relative comfort, and some assistance is available at stations if you call in advance, preferably 48 hours ahead; call National Rail Enquiries (☏0845/484950, textphone 0845/6050600) to get the number of the appropriate rail company. People with other disabilities are eligible for the Disabled Persons Railcard (£18 per year), which gives a third off most tickets. The link for "disabled passengers" at ⓦwww.nationalrail.co.uk has reams of information for journey planning, including maps identifying stations that have access to platforms without steps. There are no bus discounts for disabled passengers who are not Welsh citizens. Rental cars with hand controls are rare and expensive; Hertz offers models at the same rate as conventional vehicles, though in the more expensive categories.

Access to **monuments and museums** is improving all the time. The National Trust produces a sheet detailing accessibility to NT sites throughout England and Wales (downloadable from ⓦwww.nationaltrust .org.uk or by calling its Access For All office on ☏01793 817400); disabled visitors must pay entry fees, but they can bring a friend or carer in to assist them free of charge. CADW allows wheelchair users and the visually handicapped, along with their assisting companion, free entry to all monuments. Access to theatres, cinemas and other public places is slowly improving.

In some areas of Wales where **public toilets** need to be locked to avoid vandalism, local authorities have joined the National Key System (NKS) administered by British charity RADAR (see p.68 for details), in which disabled people are able to gain access to facilities via a standard key (£3.50) which comes with a booklet detailing locations. Some tourist offices also hold a key which you can borrow.

There's no shortage of contact points for information, the best being RADAR and Disability Wales. The AA publishes the annual *Disabled Traveller's Guide* (free to members; and downloadable at ⓦwww.theaa.com /staticdocs/pdf/services/disabled_travellers_ guide.pdf), and there's a helpful website at ⓦwww.youreable.com.

Contacts for travellers with disabilities

UK and Ireland

All Go Here ⓦwww.everybody.co.uk. Provides information on accommodation suitable for disabled travellers throughout the UK.
Disability Wales ☏029/2088 7325, ⓦwww .disabilitywales.org. Welsh equivalent of RADAR (see below).
Irish Wheelchair Association ☏01/818 6400, ⓦwww.iwa.ie. Useful information provided about travelling abroad.
RADAR: the disability network ☏020/7250 3222, TTY 7250 4119, ⓦwww.radar.org.uk. A good source of advice on holidays and travel in the UK. Produces an annual holiday guide called *Holidays in Britain and Ireland* for £13.50.
Tourism For All UK ☏0845/124 9971, ⓦwww .tourismforall.org.uk. Previously "Holiday Care";

offers various guides and advice for access throughout Britain.
Wales Council for the Blind ☏029/20473954, ⓦwww.wcb-ccd.org.uk. Though not specifically set up with visitors in mind, it does provide a good contact point.
Wales Council for the Deaf ☏01443/485687, minicom 01443/485686, ⓦwww.wcdeaf.org.uk. Also not specifically set up with visitors in mind but provides a good contact point.

North America

Access-Able ⓦwww.access-able.com. Online resource for travellers with disabilities.
Mobility International USA ☏ & TTY 541/343- 1284, ⓦwww.miusa.org. Information and referral services, access guides, tours and exchange programmes.
Society for the Accessible Travel and Hospitality (SATH) ☏212-447-7284, ⓦwww .sath.org. Longstanding non-profit educational organization with useful travel tips and access information on its website.

Australia and New Zealand

Disabled Persons Assembly ☏ & TTY 04/801 9100, ⓦwww.dpa.org.nz. Resource centre with lists of travel agencies and tour operators for people with disabilities.
National Disability Services ☏ & TTY 02/6283 3200, ⓦwww.nds.org.au. Formerly "ACROD"; provides lists of travel agencies and tour operators for people with disabilities.

Guide

Guide

1

Southeast Wales

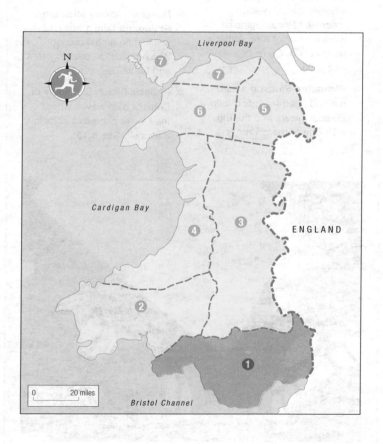

CHAPTER 1 # Highlights

* **Tintern Abbey** Get your poetic juices flowing at Tintern's towering, ivy-clad ruins, romantically situated in the Wye Valley. See p.78

* **Caerleon** Contemplate whether Wales' best-preserved Roman remains were the site of King Arthur's fabled court, Camelot. See p.90

* **Blaenafon** Strap on a hard-hat and head-lamp and follow ex-coal miners into the Big Pit – one of the country's most poignant and powerful museums. See p.95

* **Cardiff** Catch a waterbus from the city centre along the River Taff to the revitalized Bay. See p.109

* **National History Museum, St Fagans** Take a free and fascinating amble around Welsh buildings, past, present and future. See p.130

* **Rhossili beach** Surf some of Britain's best waves where the Gower peninsula ends in a flourish. See p.151

▲ Tintern Abbey

Southeast Wales

Home to some sixty percent of the country's population, the southeastern corner of Wales is one of Britain's most industrialized regions. Both people and industry are most heavily concentrated around the sea ports and former mining valleys, though quiet hills and beaches are only ever a few miles away.

Wales unfolds from the English border in a beguilingly rural manner. The **River Wye** flows forth from its mouth at the fortress town of **Chepstow**, where you'll find one of the most impressive castles in a land where few towns are without one. In the Wye's beautiful valley lie the spectacularly placed ruins of **Tintern Abbey**, downstream from the old county town of **Monmouth**, which makes a fine base for visiting the craggy ruins of the Three Castles, and even the fringes of the Brecon Beacons National Park.

Industrialization intensifies as you travel west to the **River Usk** which spills out into the Bristol Channel at **Newport**, Wales' newest city and third-largest conurbation, and home to the remains of an extensive Roman settlement in adjacent **Caerleon**.

To the west and north are the world-famous **Valleys**, once the coal- and iron-rich powerhouse of the British Empire. This is the Wales of popular imagination: hemmed-in valley floors packed with seemingly never-ending lines of red-brick terraced houses, slanted towards the pithead. Although all the deep mines have closed, the area is still one of tight-knit towns, with a rich working-class heritage displayed in some illuminating museums and colliery tours, such as the **Big Pit** at Blaenafon and the **Rhondda Heritage Park** in Trehafod. The valleys follow rivers coursing down towards the coast, where great ports shipped their products all over the world. The greatest of them all was **Cardiff**, once the world's busiest coal port, now Wales' upbeat capital. Stellar museums, a storybook castle, exciting rejuvenation projects and Wales' best cultural pursuits make the city an essential stop.

Immediately west of the capital, and a world away from the industrial hangover of the city and Valleys, is the lush **Vale of Glamorgan** and **Glamorgan Heritage Coast**, which stretches twenty-eight miles westwards to include the neighbouring county of Bridgend. The entire area is dotted with stoic little market towns and chirpy seaside resorts – most notably **Barry** in the east and **Porthcawl** in the west.

West again is Wales' second city, **Swansea**. Bright, breezy and brash, Swansea is renowned for its nightlife and is undergoing rapid development, particularly along its historic waterfront. Like Cardiff, Swansea grew principally on the strength of its now revitalized docks, from where the coast arcs round from the **Port Talbot** steelworks in the east to the elegant holiday town of **Mumbles**

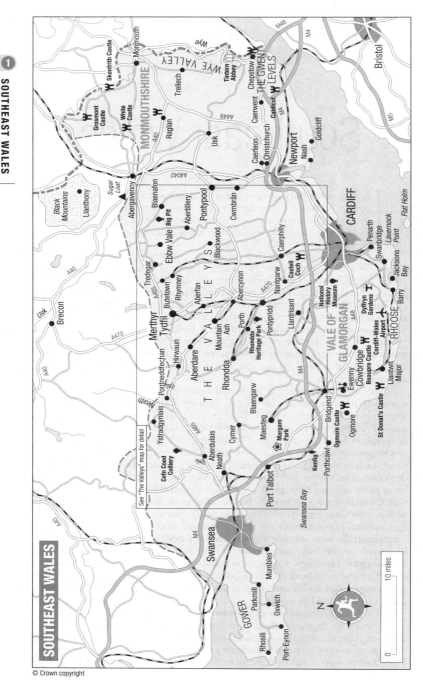

SOUTHEAST WALES

Monmouth
Skenfrith Castle
Grosmont Castle
White Castle
Raglan
Trellech
WYE VALLEY
Wye
Tintern Abbey
Chepstow
THE GWENT LEVELS
Caerwent
Caldicot
MONMOUTHSHIRE
Usk
Caerleon
Christchurch
Newport
Nash
Goldcliff
M48
M4
Bristol
M5

Black Mountains
Llanthony
Sugar Loaf
Abergavenny
Blaenafon
Big Pit
Abertillery
Pontypool
Cwmbrân
Blackwood
Caerphilly
Castell Coch
National History Museum
CARDIFF
Penarth
Swanbridge
Lavernock Point
Flat Holm

Brecon
Usk
A40
A470
A40
Tredegar
Butetown
Rhymney
Merthyr Tydfil
Aberfan
Abercynon
Nantgarw
Dyffryn Gardens
Jacksons Bay
Barry
RHOOSE
Cardiff-Wales Airport

Neath
Pontneddfechan
Hirwaun
Aberdare
Mountain Ash
Porth
Pontypridd
Rhondda Heritage Park
Llantrisant
VALE OF GLAMORGAN
Cowbridge
Beaupre Castle
Llantwit Major
St Donat's Castle

THE VALLEYS

Ystradgynlais
See "The Valleys" map for detail
Cefn Coed Colliery
Aberdulais
Neath
Rhondda
Blaengarw
Cymer
Maesteg
Margam Park
Kenfig
Porthcawl
Blaengarw
Ewenny
Bridgend
Ogmore Castle
Ogmore

Port Talbot
Swansea Bay
Swansea
GOWER
Mumbles
Parkmill
Oxwich
Rhosili
Port-Eynon

N

0   10 miles

© Crown copyright

on the jaw of the magnificent **Gower peninsula** in the west. The Gower was Britain's first-ever designated Area of Outstanding Natural Beauty, and remains a microcosm of rural Wales, with its grand beaches, rocky headlands, ruined castles and bracken heaths roamed by wild horses.

Getting around

Southeast Wales is by far the easiest part of the country to travel around. Swift dual carriageways connect with the M4, bringing all corners of the region into close proximity. **Public transport** is similarly thorough: this is the only part of Wales with a half-decent train service, and most suburban and rural services interconnect with Cardiff, Newport or Swansea. Bus services fill in virtually all of the gaps, though often rather slowly.

The Wye Valley

The **Wye Valley** was only finally recognized as part of Wales in the local government reorganization of 1974; before this, the county was officially included as part of neither England nor Wales, so that maps were frequently headlined "Wales and Monmouthshire" (the county name). In this easterly corner, the two main towns are decidedly English in flavour: **Chepstow**, at the mouth of the Wye, with its massive castle radiating an awesome strength; and **Monmouth**, sixteen miles upstream, a spruce, old-fashioned town with the lingering air of an ancient seat of authority.

Six miles north of Chepstow, on the banks of the Wye, stand the inspirational ruins of the Cistercian **Tintern Abbey**, while across the river the southern segments of the **Offa's Dyke** earthworks are shadowed by a long-distance footpath (see box, p.257).

Chepstow

Of all the places that call themselves "the gateway to Wales", **CHEPSTOW** (Cas-Gwent) – the first Welsh town on the main road into the country – has probably the strongest claim. Situated on the western bank of the River Wye, just over a mile from where its tidal waters recede into the Severn estuary, Chepstow is an easy-going and engaging place, and worth a stop to visit its ancient castle.

Arrival, information and accommodation

Trains between Cardiff and Birmingham stop at Chepstow's **train station**, five minutes' walk south of the High Street. The town's **bus station** is on Thomas Street on the other side of the West Gate, and has frequent services to Newport but only one every couple of hours to Tintern and Monmouth. The extremely efficient **tourist office** is located in the castle car park, off Bridge Street (daily: Nov–Easter 10am–3.30pm; Easter–Oct 10am–5.30pm; ☏01291/623772, ✉chepstow.tic@monmouthshire.gov.uk). **Accommodation** is not especially abundant, though there are a few good places.

Afon Gwy 28 Bridge St ☏01291/620158, ⓦwww .afongwy.co.uk. Pleasant "restaurant with rooms" – some of the which have river views. ❸
Castle View Hotel 16 Bridge St ☏01291/620349, ⓦwww.hotelchepstow.co.uk. Thirteen spacious,

unfussy rooms in a central location; some have views of the castle, and all are en suite. ❺
First Hurdle Guesthouse 9 Upper Church St ☏01291/622189, ⓦwww.thefirsthurdle.com. Rooms in this large, central B&B have bathrooms,

firm beds and attractive decor; "English" breakfast is included. ❸

Smith & Jones (George Hotel) Moor St, next to the West Gate ☎01291/625363, ⓦwww .thegeorgechepstow.com. Extensively modernized yet still stately old place, with a ground-floor bar and restaurant. ❺

The Town

Chepstow's position as a former river port is evident in the thirteenth-century **Port Wall**, encasing the castle precincts and the town centre in their loop of the river. The fifteenth-century **West Gate** marks the southern end of the **High Street**, a handsome thoroughfare sided by Georgian and Victorian buildings and sloping down from the gate towards the river. Here, an elegant five-arch cast-iron **Old Bridge**, built in 1816, is still in use for cross-border traffic into England. This section of the Wye is tremendously tidal, with a mighty 49-foot difference in the water level between high and low tides – the second highest tidal drop in the world, after the Bay of Fundy on the US/Canadian border. A short street with a riverside esplanade, The Back, runs southeast from the bridge; a plaque at the beginning of the road commemorates the quay as the site from which the three leaders of Newport's Chartist March of 1839 were dispatched to Van Diemen's Land (now Tasmania), in Australia.

Bridge Street leads from the old bridge up towards the main entrance of **Chepstow Castle** (April–Sept daily 9am–5pm; Nov–March Mon–Sat 9.30am–4pm, Sun 11am–4pm; £3.70; CADW). The castle's strategic location could scarcely be bettered. Built tight into a loop of the River Wye, it guards one of the most important routes into Wales. Chepstow was the first stone castle to be built in Britain, with its first Norman incarnation, the Great Tower keep, rising

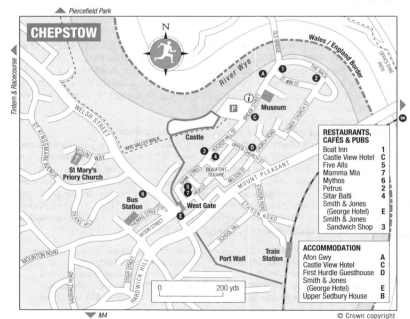

© Crown copyright

▲ Chepstow Castle

in 1067, just one year after William the Conqueror's victory at Hastings. William had realized the importance of subduing the restless Welsh, creating borderland Marcher Lordships and encouraging the title holders to expand into Welsh territory: a succession of Chepstow's lords attempted this, necessitating the renewed and increasingly powerful fortification of their castles over the next two hundred years. Ownership of both title and castle passed to the earls of Norfolk and then Pembroke, who retain the fortress to this day.

The walled castle comprises three separate enclosures. The Lower Ward, dating mainly from the thirteenth century, is the largest. Here, you'll find the **Great Hall**, home to a wide-ranging exhibition on the history of the castle.

Twelfth-century defences separate the Lower Ward from the Middle Ward, which is dominated by the still-imposing ruins of the **Great Tower**, whose lower floors include the original Norman keep. Beyond the Great Tower is the far narrower Upper Ward which leads up to the Barbican **watchtower**, from where there are superlative views back over the castle and down the cliff to the mud flats of the river estuary.

Opposite the castle, a cream-painted Georgian town house contains the **Chepstow Museum** (July–Sept Mon–Sat 10.30am–5.30pm, Sun 2–5.30pm; Oct–June Mon–Sat 11am–5pm, Sun 2–5pm; free). The displays cover aspects of local life, with nostalgic photographs and paintings of the trades supported in the past by the River Wye, and records of Chepstow's brief spell as a shipbuilding centre in the early part of the twentieth century.

Across town, on Mount Way, Chepstow's **St Mary's Priory Church** was founded at the same time as the castle, in around 1072, as a Benedictine priory by William FitzOsbern, who also instigated the castle's construction and who had been granted the Lordship of Striguil by his second cousin, William the Conqueror, in gratitude for his support in the Norman conquest of England. Large sections were destroyed during the 1536 Dissolution of the Monasteries, and much of what survived has been modernized over the centuries, but today you can still see its Norman origins, including an intricate arched eleventh-century doorway.

From Chepstow, you can follow the fairly challenging, two-and-a-half-hour **Wye Valley Walk** to Tintern Abbey, which starts from the castle car park. A map – or the official route guide (£7.95), available from the tourist office – is advisable, as the path tucks and meanders around and above the twisting Wye. The walk brushes past the picturesque old estate of **Piercefield Park**, a mile north of town, part of which has metamorphosed into **Chepstow Racecourse** (☎01291/622260, ⓦwww.chepstow-racecourse.co.uk), one of the country's premier racing venues, with regular, year-round meets. The entrance is off the A466 north of town. You could return along the other side of the river on the Offa's Dyke Path (see p.257), which passes the dramatic viewpoint of Devil's Pulpit (just off the B4228) and reaches its southern end at Sedbury Cliffs, a mile or so east of town on the English side of the border.

Eating and drinking

Chepstow has a handful of decent **restaurants** and a few good **pubs**, some by the river.

Boat Inn The Back. An enormously convivial waterside pub with a good, vegetarian-friendly menu.

Castle View Hotel 16 Bridge St ☎01291/620349, ⓦwww.hotelchepstow.co.uk. Highly rated hotel restaurant serving succulent meals such as pan-fried red snapper, and also offering lighter lunches.

Five Alls High St. Genuine local inn with a friendly atmosphere, a wicked jukebox and occasional live music.

Mamma Mia 29 High St ☎01291/630572. Consistently good Italian restaurant with extremely reasonably priced fare including plenty of vegetarian options.

Mythos Welsh St ☎01291/627222. Lively young bar serving delicious and inexpensive Greek food. Closed Sun lunch.

Petrus The Back ☎01291/622929. Chepstow's finest dining, serving Spanish tapas and modern Mediterranean cuisine, plus a bargain two-course lunch menu. Closed Mon.

Sitar Balti The Cellar, Beaufort Square ☎01291/627351. Quality Indian restaurant, specializing in balti lamb and chicken dishes, in the basement of a town house. Open evenings only; daily.

Smith & Jones (George Hotel) Moor St, next to the West Gate. Funky contemporary pub attracting a fun younger crowd.

Smith & Jones Sandwich Shop Hocker Hill St. Excellent independent sandwich shop; great for a castle or riverside picnic.

Tintern Abbey

Six miles north of Chepstow, the roofless ruins of **Tintern Abbey** (April–Oct daily 9am–5pm; Nov–March Mon–Sat 9.30am–4pm, Sun 11am–4pm; £3.70; CADW) are spectacularly sited on one of the most scenic stretches of the River Wye. The abbey and its valley have inspired writers and painters ever since the Reverend William Gilpin published a book in 1782 extolling their picturesque qualities, and the "tall rock/The mountain, and the deep and gloomy wood" written about by Wordsworth are still evident today. Such is the abbey's enormous popularity, however, that in the middle of a summer's day, the magic can all but evaporate: ideally go out of season or at the beginning or end of the day when the crowds have thinned out.

The abbey lasted as a monastic settlement from its foundation by the Cistercian order in 1131 until its dissolution in 1536, and the original order of monks was brought wholesale from Normandy, its members establishing themselves as major local landholders and agriculturalists. This increased the power and wealth of the abbey, attracting more monks and necessitating a massive rebuilding and expansion plan in the fourteenth century, when Tintern was at its mightiest. Most of the remaining buildings date from this time, after which the influence of the abbey and its order began to wane. Upon dissolution, many of the buildings were plundered and stripped, leaving the abbey to crumble. The fact that the ruins have survived at all is largely thanks to their remoteness, as there were no nearby villages to use the stone for rebuilding.

The centrepiece of the complex was the magnificent Gothic **church**, built at the turn of the fourteenth century to encase its more modest predecessor. Much of the building remains intact, including the remarkable tracery in the west window and intricate stonework of the capitals and columns.

Around the church are the less substantial ruins of the **monks' domestic quarters**, mostly reduced to one-storey rubble. Rooms are easily distinguishable, however, including an intact serving hatch in the kitchen and the square of the monks' **cloister**. The course of the abbey's waste disposal system can be seen in the **Great Drain**, an irregular channel that links kitchens, toilets and the infirmary with the nearby Wye. The **Novices' Hall** lies close to the Warming House, which, together with the kitchen and infirmary, would have been the only heated parts of the abbey, suggesting that novices might have gained a falsely favourable impression of monastic life before taking their final vows. In the dining hall, you can still see the **pulpit door** that would once have led to the wall-mounted pulpit, from which a monk would read the scriptures throughout each meal.

The best way to appreciate the scale and splendour of the abbey ruins is walking along the opposite bank of the Wye. Just upstream from the abbey, a bridge crosses the river, from where a path climbs a wooded hillside. Views along the way and from the top are magnificent.

Four miles northwest of the ruins, the sleepy hilltop settlement of **TRELLECH** (literally "three stones") was one of the largest boroughs in the vicinity. Reminders of its ancient status abound: there's a thirteenth-century steepled church on a seventh-century site, and, nearby, the curious **Tump**, an ancient mound that, legend has it, cannot be disturbed without deadly reprisal. A few hundred yards further south, by the B4293 Llanishen road, are the three **stones** of the village's name. Also known as Harold Stones, the straining fingers of rock, around 3500 years old and thrusting up in the middle of a sheep-filled field, are thought to be aligned with The Skirrid mountain, Monmouthshire's holiest. Off the lane to Tintern, you'll find the **Virtuous Well**, long a place of pilgrimage, with reputed healing qualities that probably stem from the water's high iron content.

Practicalities

Now cluttered with teashops and overpriced hotels, the tiny village of **TINTERN** (Tyndyrn), immediately north of the abbey, is strung along a mile or so of the A466 around a loop of the river. The principal **visitor centre** (April–Oct daily 10.30am–5.30pm; ℡01291/689566) is located another few hundred yards towards Monmouth at the **Old Station** complex, where there's an interesting exhibition on the old Wye Valley railway and a good selection of leaflets on local walks, including sections of the Offa's Dyke path (see p.257) and cliff rambles above the meandering river. Bibliophiles will want to browse through the rare and out-of-print titles at Tintern's wonderful independent **bookshop**, Stella Books, on Monmouth Road.

B&B **accommodation** is available locally at *Parva Farmhouse*, north of the abbey off the main road (℡01291/689411, Ⓦwww.parvafarmhouse.co.uk; ❹), with all-en suite, mostly river-view rooms and a cosy restaurant warmed by a beamed fireplace and serving British cuisine with a few French twists, as well as vegetarian options such as veggie sausages with leeks. For the best pint locally, go to the charming 🌳 *Cherry Tree* (half a mile up the road that forks off by the Best Western *Royal George Hotel* in Tintern). As well as beer, the *Cherry Tree* also does great food (lamb shanks in rosemary and raspberry sauce and the like) and has four cherry-toned B&B rooms (℡01291/689292, ⓦwww.thecherry .co.uk; ❸). Those looking to pitch a **tent** can do so in the paddock behind the Old Station in Tintern (£3 per person); facilities extend as far as a water pipe and toilets.

Monmouth

Bordered on three sides by the rivers Wye and Monnow, elegant **MONMOUTH** (Trefynwy) retains the quiet charm of its days as an important border post and one-time county town.

The centre of the town is **Agincourt Square**, a large and handsome open space at the top of the wide, shop-lined Monnow Street, gently descending to a distinctive thirteenth-century bridge over the River Monnow. The cobbled square is dominated by old coaching inns, flanking the arched Georgian **Shire Hall** – its facade includes an eighteenth-century statue of the Monmouth-born King Henry V, victor at the 1415 Battle of Agincourt, which brought Normandy (and soon afterwards France) under the rule of the English crown. (The hall was closed to the public at the time of writing, but is scheduled to reopen in 2010 with a new visitor centre – check with the tourist office for latest information.) In front of the Shire Hall is a florid statue of another local, the Honourable Charles Stewart Rolls, who in 1910 became the first man to pilot a double-flight over the English Channel, and also co-founded the Rolls-Royce empire.

Almost opposite Shire Hall is **Castle Hill**. Walk up it to glimpse some of the ruins of the **castle**, founded in 1068, rebuilt in stone in the twelfth century and almost annihilated in the Civil War. The only notable part of the castle that remains is the Great Tower, in which Henry V is thought to have been born in 1387. Next to the castle, the gracious seventeenth-century **Great Castle House**, built from castle bricks, now serves as the headquarters of the Royal Monmouthshire regiment. Their history is celebrated in the **Regimental Museum** (April–Oct daily 2–5pm; Nov–March Sat & Sun 2–4pm; free) along with intriguing finds from archeological digs such as oddly shaped twelfth-century bone dice.

Priory Street leads north from Agincourt Square to the market hall complex, which contains the **Nelson Museum and Local History Centre** (Mon–Sat 11am–1pm & 2–5pm, Sun 2–5pm, Nov–Feb until 4pm; free), an attempt to portray the life of the great admiral through his personal artefacts – sword, medals, intimate letters and china – together with pictures, prints and naval equipment of the day. Charles Rolls' mother, Lady Llangattock, was an ardent admirer of Nelson and a voracious collector of related memorabilia, and it is her collection now on display in the museum.

At the bottom of Monnow Street, a couple of hundred yards from Agincourt Square, the road narrows to squeeze into the confines of the fortified **Monnow Bridge** and its hulking stone gate, dating from 1262. This served both as a means of defence for the town and a toll collection point and is now the sole remaining medieval fortified river bridge in Britain where the gate tower actually stands on the bridge

Just over a mile east of Monmouth, a steep road climbs up to **The Kymin** (daily dawn–dusk; free; NT), a fine viewpoint over the town and the Wye Valley. It's crowned by the crenellated Georgian **Round House** (Easter–Oct Sat

11am–4pm; £2.30; NT), built as a banqueting hall, and a Neoclassical **Naval Temple**, constructed in 1801 to cheer Britain's victories at sea.

Practicalities

Buses operate from the **bus station** at the bottom of Monnow Street. Monmouth's **tourist office** is in the Market Hall, Priory Street (daily: April–Oct 10am–5.30pm, Nov–March Mon–Sat 10am–4pm; ☎01600/713899, ⓔmonmouth.tic@monmouthshire.gov.uk). **Bike rental** is available over the border at Pedalaway in Llangarron near Ross-on-Wye (☎01989/770357, ⓦwww.pedalaway.co.uk); they'll deliver locally. The Monmouth Canoe & Activity Centre (☎01600/713461, ⓦwww.monmouthcanoe.co.uk), right by the Wye in Castle Yard, offers **canoe rental**, plus instruction if needed. Book in advance.

For **accommodation**, good B&Bs include *Tŷ Mawr* at 7 Monk St (☎01600/714261; ❷); *Hotel Prego* at 7 Church St (☎01600/712600, ⓦwww.pregomonmouth.co.uk; ❸), with eight crisp en-suite rooms and a great bistro (see below); and the simple but agreeable *Burton House* on St James Square (☎01600/714958; ❷). The tent-friendly *Monnow Bridge* **campsite** is on Drybridge Street (over Monnow Bridge then right; ☎01600/714004; £10 per pitch) behind the *Three Horseshoes* pub.

The best place to **eat** in town is the welcoming ☺ *Bistro Prego*, at the *Hotel Prego* (see above; generally closed Sun & Mon), serving tasty Italian cuisine like potato gnocchi in duck sauce, plus some British staples such as venison pie. Alternatively, it's well worth the trip out to ☺ *Stonemill at Rockfield* (restaurant closed all-day Mon & dinner Sun; ☎01600/716273), two miles west of town on the B4233, which has exceptional, locally sourced fare along the lines of rack of new season lamb with mustard mash topped off with hot chocolate soup, plus home-made ice cream for dessert.

Monmouth is home to a staggering number of **pubs**: worth trying are the lively *Queen's Head* on St James Street, with better-than-average pub grub; the reputedly haunted *Punch House* on Agincourt Square, which also does good food; the *Green Dragon* on St Thomas Square, where you'll often get live music; and the *Robin Hood*, on Monnow Street near the bridge, where Shakespeare is said to have drunk.

The Three Castles

The fertile, low-lying land north of Monmouth, between the Monnow and the River Usk, was important as an easy access route into the agricultural lands of south Wales, and in the eleventh century the Norman invaders built a trio of strongholds here – **Skenfrith**, **Grosmont** and **White castles** – within an eight-mile radius of each other.

The castles' size and splendour demonstrates their significance in protecting the borderlands from the restless English, as well as the disgruntled Welsh, who first attacked nearby Abergavenny Castle in 1182, prompting King Ralph of Grosmont to rebuild the three castles in stone. In July 1201, all three were presented by King John to Hubert de Burgh, who fought extensively on the Continent and brought back sophisticated new ideas on castle design to replace earlier models with square keeps. He rebuilt Skenfrith and Grosmont, and his successor as overlord, Walerund Teutonicus ("the German"), worked on White Castle. In 1260, the advancing army of Llywelyn ap Gruffydd threatened the king's supremacy in south Wales, and the three castles were refortified in readiness.

Gradually, the castles were used more as living quarters and royal administrative centres rather than military bases, as the Welsh began to adapt to English rule. The only return to military usage came in 1404–05, when Owain Glyndŵr's army pressed down to Grosmont, only to be defeated by the future King Henry V. The castles fell into disrepair, and were finally sold by the Duchy of Lancaster to the Duke of Beaufort in 1825. The Beauforts sold the castles off separately in 1902, the first time since 1138 that the three had fallen out of single ownership.

White Castle

Named for its white rendering (a few patches remain on the exterior walls), **White Castle** (Castell Gwyn; Easter–Sept Wed–Sun 10am–5pm; £2.70; all other times – generally daily 10am–4pm and free access; CADW) lies about eight miles west of Monmouth, just north of the village of Llantilio Crossenny. The most dramatic of the three castles, it's situated in open, rolling countryside with some superb views over to The Skirrid mountain (see Chapter 3, p.239). From the grassy Outer Ward, a bridge leads over the moat into the dual-towered Inner Gatehouse, where the western tower, on the right, can be climbed for its vantage point. Here, you can appreciate the scale of the tall twelfth-century curtain walls in the Inner Ward. Of the domestic buildings within the walls, only the foundations and a few inches of wall remain. At the back of the ward, there are massive foundations of the Norman keep, demolished in about 1260 and unearthed in the early part of the twentieth century. The southern wall that took the place of the keep was once the main entrance to the castle, as can be seen in the postern gate in the centre, on the other side of which a bridge leads over to the Hornwork, one of the castle's three original enclosures, although now no more than a grass-covered mound.

Skenfrith Castle

Seven miles northeast of White Castle, alongside the River Monnow, the thirteenth-century **Skenfrith Castle** (unrestricted access; free; NT), on the main street of the tiny, pretty border village of **SKENFRITH** (Ynysgyn-wraidd), is dominated by the circular keep that replaced an earlier Norman incarnation.

The castle's walls are built of sturdy red sandstone in an irregular rectangle. In the centre of the ward is the 21-foot-high round keep, raised slightly on an earth mound to give archers a greater firing range, and containing the vestiges of the private apartments of the castle's lord on the upper floors. The Hall Range of domestic buildings includes an intact thirteenth-century window, complete with its original iron bars.

Grosmont Castle

Five miles upstream of Skenfrith, right on the English border, the most dilapidated of the Three Castles, **Grosmont Castle** (Castell y Grysmwnt; unrestricted access; free; CADW) sits on a small hill above the village of **GROSMONT**. Entering over the wooden bridge above the dry moat, you first pass through the ruins of the two-stage gatehouse. This leads into the small central courtyard, dominated on the right-hand side by the ruins of a large Great Hall, dating from the first decade of the thirteenth century. The village **church** is also worth a look, with some impressive Norman features, most notably the nave arches and the font. A memorial in the nave is popularly believed to be of John Kent, a fifteenth-century bard and magician sometimes believed to have been Owain Glyndŵr in hiding.

Practicalities

Though you can drive around all three castles in a couple of hours, the nature of this peaceful countryside makes a more sedate mode of transport preferable. Bikes can be rented locally (see p.81 & Chapter 3, p.236 for Abergavenny) for a pleasant day-long outing, or you can hike the nineteen-mile circuit of paths detailed in a **booklet** (£3.95 from the tourist offices).

Accommodation and eating options in the area, though sparse, are good: half a mile north of White Castle, in a fifteenth-century farmhouse near the village of **LLANVETHERINE** (Llanwytherin), is the very friendly *Great Tre-Rhew Farm* (℡01873/821268, ✉trerhew@btopenworld.com; ❷), on what is still a working 165-acre farm. In the nearby village of **LLANGATTOCK LINGOED**, there's a wonderful foodie pub, the ⚇ *Hunter's Moon Inn* (℡01873/821499, ⓦwww .hunters-moon-inn.co.uk; ❶–❷), which also has four floral (but not too floral) en-suite rooms. Yards away, the *Old Rectory* (℡01873/821326; ❶–❷) offers great B&B accommodation, though the plushest option hereabouts is at the *The Bell* gastropub in Skenfrith (℡01600/750235, ⓦwww.skenfrith.com; ❻–❾), with countrified yet contemporary rooms, some with river views. If you're just after a taster of the pub's fabulous atmosphere, you could always pop in for a pricey but worthwhile lunch or dinner.

Mid-Monmouthshire

The disputed past of mid-Monmouthshire, between Chepstow and Newport, is obvious from the yet more castles that dot the landscape, such as that at **Caldicot**, just off the M4 near the southern Severn Bridge. Nearby **Caerwent** is now a quiet village which was once a great Roman town.

To the north is an undulating land of forests and tiny villages, crisscrossed by winding lanes that offer unexpectedly delightful views – and quaint pubs – around each corner. The contours shelve down in the west to the valley of the **River Usk**, the former border of Wales as decreed in the sixteenth century by Henry VIII. Today, the A449 road roars through the valley, bypassing lanes, villages and the peaceful small town of **Usk** before joining the A40 near the spectacular ruins of **Raglan** castle.

Caldicot and the Gwent Levels

CALDICOT (Cil-y-coed) is the first sight of Wales for train travellers using the main line from London and drivers using the second Severn bridge crossing from Bristol. Wedged between this road and railway, Caldicot is a sprawling, overgrown village of modern housing, though its heavily restored **castle** (Easter–Oct daily 11am–5pm; £3.75), on the eastern side of the village, dates from the twelfth century – one of the Norman Marcher castles built to keep a wary eye on the Welsh. The castle crumbled in the years leading up to the 1800s, before being rebuilt by a wealthy Victorian barrister, Joseph Cobb. The only original parts are a large fourteenth-century round tower and elaborate gatehouse, situated either side of a grassy courtyard, whose centrepiece is one of Nelson's battle cannons from his *Foudroyant* flagship. The castle buildings contain an impressive furniture collection, with items from the seventeenth to the nineteenth centuries.

The Gwent Levels

Recently constructed access roads have, to some degree, eaten into one of Wales' most unexpected landscapes: the lush, low-lying **Gwent Levels**, southwest of Caldicot, which are great for gentle cycling, walking and poking around tiny villages and ancient churches. The best place to appreciate the area's tranquillity is at **Goldcliff**, a straggle of houses petering out by the mud flats of the estuary. Here, you can walk along the sea walls and watch diving sea birds and fishermen competing for the same catch. A new **wildlife and wetland centre** (unrestricted access) can be found just to the west of the village of **Nash**. Built as a compensatory gesture by the developers of the Cardiff Bay barrage scheme to help offset the loss of wading birds' habitats, the pools, reed beds and hides make for a surprisingly lovely spot, considering the whole site is the old dumping ground for the neighbouring Uskmouth power station. The community-run *Waterloo* pub in Nash village, beside the spired church, is a great stop for a good-value lunch or dinner.

Caerwent

Two miles northwest of Caldicot lies the historic village of **CAERWENT**. Almost two thousand years ago, the village was known by the Romans as Venta Silurum, the "market town of the Silures", a local tribe forcibly relocated here from a nearby hillfort by the conquering Romans in around 75 AD, after 25 years of battle.

The most notable remnants of the Roman town are the crumbling **walls** which form a large rectangle around the modern village. Access is easiest from the steps next to the *Coach and Horses* pub, leading you up onto stone ramparts that command melancholic views around the quiet valley. The South Wall is the most complete, still maintaining its fourth-century bastions. Follow the South Wall as it continues around to the old West Gate. Halfway along, a lane cuts up towards the village **church**: maps and diagrams in the porch explain the site of the village, and you can also see two inscribed stones, one a dedication from the Siluri tribe to their Roman overlord, Paulinus, and another, dedicated to Ocelus Mars, demonstrating the odd merging of Roman and Celtic gods for worship. Opposite the church, on the village's main street, the shin-high, rectangular outline of a Roman temple has been excavated.

Usk

Bypassed by the main A449, the quaint town of **USK** (Brynbuga) straddles the river of the same name. Pastel-painted houses, shops and some great pubs and restaurants line narrow Bridge Street, which leads up from the river and crosses towards the **castle** (free access; donation requested), looming up on a hilltop to the left. Opposite the ivy-clad ruins is the town's hub, **Twyn Square**, where buses stop amongst the copious flower boxes that surround the restored clock tower. At the top of the square is a thirteenth-century **gatehouse**, once part of a Benedictine nunnery, and now guarding the passage to the impressive twelfth- and thirteenth-century church. Surviving features from its days as a nunnery in the 1200s include the nave and tower.

Forking to the right off Bridge Street near the river is New Market Street, which runs past the fascinating **Usk Rural Life Museum** (Easter–Oct Mon–Fri 10am–5pm, Sat & Sun 2–5pm; free), housed in a converted eighteenth-century malt barn with collections put together over many decades by hundreds of local residents. Aspects of farming are explained in a pleasantly haphazard way, and everything from animal-castrating implements to re-creations of domestic and farming interiors (including a dairy, brewery, laundry, thatcher's and carpentry workshop) are packed into every available corner, while outdoor barns continue the exhibition with farm carts, stagecoaches and an exhibition about the Great Western Railway. Give yourself a good few hours to take it all in.

Practicalities

Usk is a relaxed and enjoyable place to **stay**, with good pubs for evening entertainment. The cosy old *Cross Keys Inn* at 24 Bridge St (℡01291/672535; ④) is a good bet. Alternatively, for a bit more money, try the landmark *Three Salmons Hotel*, Bridge Street (℡01291/672133; ⑥); rates often fall significantly outside peak season – check when you book. The good attached restaurant serves quality local fish, specializing, of course, in salmon. For something more rarefied try *Glen-yr-Afon House Hotel* on Pontypool Road (℡01291/672302, ⓦwww .glen-yr-afon.co.uk; ⑦), an elegant and gracious country house five-minutes' walk west of town, with an equally refined restaurant.

Most of the town's pubs also serve **food**, of which the best is the *King's Head* on Old Market Street, closely followed by the *Nag's Head* in Twyn Square. In addition, Bridge Street is lined with small cafés, delis and restaurants.

Raglan Castle

Seven miles north of Usk is the village of **RAGLAN** (Rhaglan), lorded over by its glorious **castle** (April–Oct daily 9am–5pm; Nov–March Mon–Sat 9.30am–4pm, Sun 11am–4pm; £3.10; CADW). Unlike so many crumbling Welsh fortresses, the castle's ornate style and comparative intactness set it apart. The late-medieval castle was constructed on the site of a Norman motte in 1435 by Sir William ap Thomas. Various descendants added to the castle after his death, and building carried on into the late sixteenth century.

The **gatehouse** is still used as the main entrance, and the finest examples of the castle's showy decoration appear in its heraldic shields, intricate stonework edging and gargoyles. Inside, stonemasons' marks, used to identify how much work each man had done, can be seen on the walls. Ap Thomas' grandson, William Herbert II, was responsible for the two inner courts, built in the mid-fifteenth century around his grandfather's original gatehouse, hall and keep. The first is the cobbled **Pitched Stone Court**, designed to house the kitchen and servants' quarters. To the left is **Fountain Court**, once surrounded by opulent residences that included grand apartments and state rooms. Separating the two are the original 1435 **hall**, the **buttery**, the remains of the **chapel** and the **cellars** below.

Off Fountain Court, through the South Gate, is the pristine **bowling green**, standing on twelve-foot-high walls above the Moat Walk, and reached by a flight of stone steps from the green. The moated yellow ashlar **Great Tower**, off Fountain Court, manifests Continental influences in its construction, and has a surprisingly contemporary appearance. Two sides of the hexagonal tower were blown up by Cromwell's henchman, Fairfax, after an eleven-week onslaught against the Royalist castle in 1646. The tower can still be climbed, however.

Raglan is served by numerous **buses** daily from Usk, and is also easily reached from Monmouth.

Newport and around

Wales' third-largest urban area, lively, gritty **NEWPORT** (Casnewydd-ar-Wysg) grew up around the docks at the mouth of the Usk and was finally granted city status in 2002. Evidence of Newport's rich history was largely

Caerleon

CAERLEON ROAD
CHURCH ROAD

QUEEN'S HILL CRESCENT
QUEEN'S HILL

CLARENCE PLACE
CHEPSTOW ROAD

Castle

FIELDS ROAD
MILL STREET

RODNEY ROAD

①

CORPORATION ROAD

Ⓐ

Chepstow, M4 & Celtic Manor Resort

Train Station

DEVON PLACE
GODFREY ROAD

Steel Wave

②

③

HIGH ST

Market

Riverfront Arts Centre

QUEENSWAY

SKINNER ST

KINGSWAY

Civic Centre

CLYTHA PARK ROAD
BRIDGE STREET

Ⓑ

⑤

④

Westgate Hotel

Bus Station

Footbridge

Ⓒ

⑥

BLEWITT STREET
ST MARY STREET

NORTH STREET

STOW HILL

COMMERCIAL STREET

CHARLES STREET

JOHN FROST SQUARE

River Usk

M4

CAERAU ROAD

YORK PLACE

S WOOLOS RD

CLIFTON ROAD

HILL ST

ⓘ⑦ Newport Centre, Art Gallery & Museum

KINGSWAY

LOWER DOCK STREET

George Street Bridge

Ⓒ

STOW HILL

✚ Newport Cathedral

KEYNSHAM AVE

⑧

GEORGE STREET

⑨

Cardiff, Ⓓ & Ⓔ

STOW PARK AVE

St Woolos' Hospital

DEWSLAND PARK ROAD

RUPERRA STREET

COMMERCIAL ROAD

EAST DOCK ROAD

FRIARS ROAD

BELLEVUE LANE

Royal Gwent Hospital

DOLPHIN STREET

BOLT STREET

USK WAY

Bellevue Park

WATERLOO ROAD

CARDIFF ROAD

ALMA STREET

FREDERICK STREET

CAPEL CRESCENT

PORTLAND ST

COURTYBELLA TERRACE

CHURCH STREET

MENDALGIEF ROAD

LIME STREET

POTTER TERRACE

ADELINE STREET

ADELAIDE STREET

ALEXANDRA ROAD

MILL PARADE

USK WAY

ACCOMMODATION

Craignair	A
Hotel@Walkabout	B
Olive Tree Guest House	E
St Etienne	C
Tredegar House Campsite	D
Waterloo Hotel	F
West Usk Lighthouse	G

RESTAURANTS, CAFÉS & PUBS

Bassment	4
The Chandlery	9
Gemelli's	6
The Lamb	5
Meze Lounge	2
Olde Murenger House	3
Oriel Café	7
TJ's	1
Tom Toya Lewis	8
Waterloo Hotel	G

BRUNEL ST

Ⓕ

Visitor Centre

DOCKS WAY

USK WAY

STEPHENSON ST

Transporter Bridge

N

0   300 yds

Ⓖ

NEWPORT

© Crown copyright

erased by unfortunate twentieth-century development, but the city is currently in the throes of a massive regeneration project, replacing some of the offending concrete monstrosities with contemporary glass-and-steel buildings. And, though it may not be immediately apparent, Newport is ranked by the WWF as the UK's greenest city, using fewer natural resources than any other urban centre.

Vestiges of the city's history remain, however, particularly along the river by the monumental **Transporter Bridge**, while there are also the scant ruins of a riverside **castle** and, high on a hill above town, the **Newport Cathedral** of St Woolos, King & Confessor. The superb civic **museum** explores the town's vibrant past, including a memorable section on the nineteenth-century **Chartist movement**, formed to fight for universal franchise.

Predating Newport by at least a thousand years is **Caerleon** – the "old port" on the River Usk – which is now essentially a northern suburb of the city. Its well-preserved remains constitute one of the most important Roman military stations in Britain, but it's best known for its reputed association with King Arthur.

Note that continuing urban regeneration works mean that there are ongoing changes to the city's road layout and traffic routing – check for updates at the tourist office or online at ⓦwww.newport.gov.uk, which has downloadable maps.

The City

Scything the city in two is the River Usk, whose tidal waters flow to the Severn estuary, three miles away. Between the rail and main road bridges are the risible remains of the town's **castle**, first built in 1191, rebuilt in the fourteenth century, sacked by Owain Glyndŵr in 1402 and refortified later in the same century.

On the other side of the Newport Bridge, a walkway leads along the riverbank past Peter Fink's giant red sculpture, **Steel Wave**, a nod to one of Newport's great industries. Nearby, building work in 2002 on the new Riverfront arts centre revealed the remains of a medieval ship, built in the mid-fifteenth century and currently being restored (see latest plans on ⓦwww.thenewportship.com). The pedestrianized High Street leads from here up to Westgate Square, overlooked by the **Westgate Hotel**, an ornate Victorian successor to the hotel where soldiers sprayed a crowd of Chartist protesters (see box, p.88) with gunfire in 1839, killing nearly two dozen – the hotel's original pillars still show bullet marks.

Commercial Street, leading south from Westgate Square, is Newport's chief shopping thoroughfare, framing the famous Transporter Bridge. One hundred yards along Commercial Street, the pedestrianized **John Frost Square** (named after a former mayor and one of the 1839 Chartist leaders) is being remodelled as a landscaped open space leading down to the river and new **footbridge** – made up of four crane-like masts which reflect the city's maritime and industrial heritage – linking the river's east and west banks. The square is also home to the town's library, tourist office and imaginative civic **museum** (Mon–Thurs 9.30am–5pm, Fri 9.30am–4.30pm, Sat 9.30am–4pm; free). Starting with the origins of Gwent, displays examine the county's original occupants and their lifestyles, and include a section on mining with a roll call of those killed in local pit accidents – 3508 men between 1837 and 1927. Newport's spectacular growth from a small Uskside dock in 1801 with a population of 1000 to a grimy port town of 70,000 people by the early twentieth century is well charted through photographs, paintings and contemporary documents. The two most interesting sections deal with the Chartist uprising and the Roman mosaic remains excavated at Caerwent. The top-floor art gallery contains the **Wait Collection** of Edwardian kitsch, including three-hundred-plus teapots.

The other road heading south from Westgate Square is **Stow Hill**, where you'll find one of Newport's few remaining rows of Victorian and Georgian town houses. A ten-minute walk up the hill leads to **Newport Cathedral**, a curious jigsaw of architectural styles and periods. The tiny, whitewashed twelfth-century Lady Chapel leads through a superb Norman arched doorway – supported by columns reputedly of Roman origin from Caerleon – into the Norman nave, notable for its clerestory windows, bounded by two fifteenth-century aisles. The cathedral's modern east end harks back to these original Norman features, sporting a circular marble east window.

Dominating the Newport skyline is the 1906 **Transporter Bridge** (April–Sept Mon–Sat 8am–9.50pm, Sun 1–9pm; Oct–March Mon–Sat 8am–5.50pm, Sun 1–5pm; car toll 50p, free for cyclists and pedestrians), built to enable cars and people to cross the river without disturbing shipping, by hoisting them high above the Usk on a dangling blue gondola. Its comical, spidery legs flare out to the ground, connecting Brunel Street on the west bank and Stephenson Street opposite. The ride is smooth and the two-minute crossing has successfully cut commuting times since the bridge was reopened in the mid-1990s. A small **visitor centre** (April–Sept Wed–Sat 10am–5pm, Sun 1–5pm; Oct–March Sat 10am–5pm, Sun 1–5pm) on the river's west bank elaborates on the bridge's history.

Tredegar House

Buses #15 and #30 go two miles out to Newport's westerly suburbs and **Tredegar House** (house: Easter–Sept Wed–Sun 11.30am–4pm; park: daily 9am–dusk; house tour & gardens £6.05, park and gardens free), just off junction 28 of the M4. The home of wealthy local landowners, the Morgan family, from 1402 until 1951, Tredegar and its ninety acres of grounds have been transformed into a park complete with boating and fishing lake and craft workshops. The seventeenth-century red-brick house replaced the Morgans' earlier home, and its interior is far more lavish than its unassuming exterior suggests. Of its thirty rooms open to the public, most memorable is the first-floor Gilt Room: an explosion of glittering fruit bosses, an intricate gilded marble fireplace, mock-walnut panelling and an elaborately painted gold stucco ceiling. The formal walled gardens behind the housekeeper's shop have been relaid in patterns culled from eighteenth-century designs.

The Chartists

In an era when wealthy landowners bought votes from the enfranchised few, the struggles of the **Chartists** were a historical inevitability. Thousands gathered around the 1838 People's Charter that called for universal male franchise, a secret (and annual) ballot for Parliament and the abolition of property qualifications for the vote. Demonstrations in support of these principles were held all over the country, with some of the most vociferous and bloodiest taking place in the radical heartlands of industrial south Wales. On November 4, 1839, Chartists from all over Monmouthshire marched on Newport and descended Stow Hill, whereupon they were fired at by soldiers hiding in the Westgate Hotel, killing around 22 protesters. The leaders of the rebellion were sentenced to death, which was commuted to transportation, by the wealthy leaders of the town. Queen Victoria even knighted the mayor who ordered the arbitrary shooting.

Practicalities

Newport's **tourist office** (Mon–Sat 9.30am–5pm; ☎01633/842962, ©newport.tic@newport.gov.uk) is in the museum complex on John Frost Square, a hundred yards from the **bus station** on Kingsway and a quarter-mile from the **train station** on Queensway.

Accommodation

The range of **accommodation** in Newport is improving thanks to the **Ryder Cup** – due to be held in 2010 at Newport's ritzy *Celtic Manor Resort* (☎01633/413000, ⓦwww.celtic-manor.com; ⑧–⑨) and its three on-site championship golf courses, which is slated to attract 50,000 visitors per day. For B&B, there's the cheap and fairly cheerful *Craignair* at 44 Corporation Rd (☎01633/259903, ©ruthuen-craignair@ntlworld.com; ①), and the genteel *St Etienne*, 162 Stow Hill (☎01633/262341, ©marilynfanner@yahoo.co.uk; ③). Peaceful accommodation options can also be found in nearby Caerleon (p.90).

Hotel@Walkabout 19 Bridge St ☎01633/235990, ⓦwww.walkabout.eu.com. Modern, reasonably priced and central, although it can get noisy at times, especially when there's a televised Aussie sporting event in the bar. ③

Olive Tree Guest House 3.4 miles west of town on Church Lane in Coedkernew ☎ 01633/681121, ⓦwww.olivetreeguesthouse.co.uk. Beautifully furnished rooms, Italian-style evening meals on request and fishing nearby. ④–⑤

Waterloo Hotel 113 Alexandra Rd ☎01633/264266, ⓦwww.thewaterloohotel.co.uk. Opposite the Transporter Bridge, this stylishly refurbished hotel occupies a landmark turreted red-brick building. Rooms in the tower have four-poster beds, and many have dramatic views of the floodlit bridge by night. Mod cons include underfloor heating in the bathrooms. ⑤

🏃 **West Usk Lighthouse** ☎01633/810126, ⓦwww.westusklighthouse.co.uk. Beyond the suburb of Duffryn, this place is set inside an 1821 lighthouse (decommissioned in 1922) at the mouth of the Usk on its western bank, with exquisite nautical-style rooms, holistic therapies including a flotation tank, and a life-size Dalek at the entrance signed by the third Dr Who, John Pertwee. ⑥–⑦

Campsite

Tredegar House ☎01633/815600. Well-equipped campsite within the grounds of Tredegar House (see p.88); £8.25–12.60 per pitch.

Eating

Quick-fix **food** outlets proliferate along Bridge and Commercial streets, but to date downtown Newport is pretty much a culinary desert.

The Chandlery 77–79 Lower Dock St ☎01633/256622. Occupying a converted nineteenth-century ship's chandlery on the edge of the city centre, this place excels in seafood such as grilled organic salmon, and also has a robust turf-based menu.

🏃 **Gemelli's** 42 Bridge St ☎01633/251831. *Gemelli* is Italian for "twins", and this restaurant – founded by Italian twin brothers Pasquale and Sergio – is both inviting and authentic. Specialties include home-made tagliatelle with Welsh lamb sauce or with lobster and scallops. Closed Sun & Mon.

Meze Lounge 6 Market St. Stylish snacks are available throughout the day at this trendy bar, which becomes a venue for live music and DJs in the evening.

Oriel Café Top floor of the museum, John Frost Square. Good place for coffee and a light snack.

Waterloo Hotel 113 Alexandra Rd ☎01633/264266, ⓦwww.thewaterloohotel.co.uk. This excellent restaurant (closed Sun) serves a seasonally changing Mediterranean-accented modern British menu featuring creations such as blackcurrant and honey-glazed duck breast with black pudding, and an impressive stand-alone vegetarian menu.

Drinking and entertainment

Of the profusion of **pubs** (many of which can be rough), the best are the 1530 *Olde Murenger House*, on the High Street, with a beautiful Tudor frontage and lamplit interior; the enormous *Tom Toya Lewis* at 108–112 Commercial St; and the cosy *Lamb* at 6 Bridge St.

Newport is one of the centres of the buoyant Welsh **rock and dance music** scene – this is, after all, the city that produced gloriously daft hip-hop outfit Goldie Lookin' Chain. The legendary try-out pub venue, *TJ's*, over the river from the castle at 14 Clarence Place (☎01633/216608, ⓦ www.tjsnewport .com), is where some of the UK's biggest bands (Oasis et al) played in their early days, and still attracts up-and-comers. The *Bassment*, at the bottom of Stow Hill, while not the poshest of venues, is the best bet for indie and studenty-type music, with great character and a laid-back crowd. For late-night dancing try the chilled-out *Meze Lounge* (see p.89).

Caerleon

Frequent buses make the three-mile journey north of Newport to **CAERLEON** (Caerllion), whose compact town centre is situated to the northwest of the town bridge over the River Usk. The remnants of the Roman town lie scattered throughout the present-day centre.

It was the Usk (Wysg) that gave Caerleon its old Roman name of Isca, a major administrative and legionary centre built by the Romans to provide ancillary and military services for smaller, outlying camps in the rest of south Wales. Its only near equivalents in Roman Britain were Chester, servicing north Wales and northwest England, and York, dealing with the Roman outposts up towards Hadrian's Wall and beyond.

Founded in 74 AD and lasting until its abandonment late in the fourth century, Isca was a garrison housing up to five thousand members of the Second Augustan Legion in a neat, rectangular walled town. Although the settlement gradually decayed after the Romans left, there were still some massive remains standing when itinerant churchman Giraldus Cambrensis

King Arthur

The name King Arthur is ubiquitous in Wales – in history, folklore books and dozens of place names on the map (only the Devil has more places named after him across Britain). He has become one of the greatest Celtic allegories, a figure to be invoked for all manner of causes and one claimed by almost every part of the British Isles, but the earliest and strongest evidence for the reality of Arthur comes indisputably from Wales.

The first mention of King Arthur was around 800 AD in the *Historia Britonum* (History of the British), by the Welsh monk Nennius. Three centuries later, his compatriot Geoffrey of Monmouth used this work, amongst others, as the source material for his magisterial twelve-volume *Historia Regum Britanniae* (History of the Kings of Britain), in which he writes that Arthur was a sixth-century Celtic British king who defeated the invading Saxon army in the turbulent decades after the departure of the Romans. From sparse, semi-factual beginnings, epic stories developed. Arthur became an idealized medieval European knight, a totem of Celtic resistance and supernatural powers.

Caerleon is widely believed to be the location of Arthur's court, **Camelot**, although other claims place Camelot near Llangollen, in England at Glastonbury and in Cornwall, and in Brittany in France. Wales, however, remains perhaps the strongest contender, mentioned by Geoffrey in the twelfth century. Dozens of areas throughout Wales have Arthurian associations, and there are a plethora of books on the subject, such as Laurence Main's *In the Footsteps of King Arthur* (Western Mail Publications), which has some great walks to get you to remote spots of Arthurian significance.

▲ King Arthur at Guinevere's Throne at Ffwrrwm

visited in 1188, chronicling the "immense palaces, which, with the gilded gables of their roofs, once rivalled the magnificence of ancient Rome". Today, the excavated bathhouse and preserved amphitheatre still retain a powerful sense of ancient history.

At the back of the *Bull Inn* car park are the Roman **fortress baths** (Easter–Oct daily 9.30am–5pm; Nov–Easter Mon–Sat 9.30am–5pm, Sun 11am–4pm; £3.10; CADW). The bathing houses, cold hall, drain (in which teeth, buttons and food remnants were found) and communal pool area are all remarkably intact.

A few steps along the High Street, a Victorian Neoclassical portico is the sole survivor of the original **National Roman Legion Museum** (Mon–Sat 10am–5pm, Sun 2–5pm; free), now housed in the modern building behind. There are hundreds of artefacts dug from the remains of Isca and a smaller fortress at nearby Burrium (Usk): intricately carved gemstones, lamps, tools, dental equipment, belt buckles, soldiers' amulets, dice, game counters, personal hygiene items such as tweezers and nail cleaners, and much more. The museum's new **Capricorn Centre**, although aimed squarely at school parties, is interesting for the re-created Roman barracks where you can try on a typical soldier's armour.

Opposite the museum, Fosse Lane leads down to the Roman **amphitheatre** (unrestricted access), the only one of its kind in Britain. Hidden under a grassy mound called King Arthur's Round Table until excavation work brought it to light in the 1920s, the amphitheatre was built around 80 AD, the same time as the Colosseum in Rome; legions of up to six thousand would watch the gory combat of gladiators, animal baiting or military exercises. The amphitheatre is backed by grassy stepped walls, on which the members of the legion would sit, tightly packed in, to watch activities in the middle. Over the road, alongside the school playing fields, are the scant foundations of the legion's **barracks**, the only Roman barrack blocks still visible in Europe.

Lord Tennyson came here to investigate rumours that Caerleon was the seat of King Arthur's court (see p.90); traders at the **Ffwrrwm Centre** (most shops daily 9.30am–5.30pm) do their best to attempt to convince visitors of the truth of the legends. Stunning courtyard sculptures here are inspired by ancient Celtic and Arthurian lore, surrounded by some great craft and New Age shops and a wonderful bistro (see below). Near the entrance to the complex, you can clasp the gold horns of a Welsh fertility bull, an act that is supposed to lend you untold powers of procreation. It is also now home to the largest-ever Welsh lovespoon (see p.66), carved from a 44ft cedar trunk.

Practicalities

Caerleon's **tourist office** (daily: April–Oct 10am–6pm, Nov–March 10am–4pm; ℡01633/422656, ℮caerleon.tic@newport.gov.uk) is beside the Legionary Museum on the High Street.

Accommodation

Caerleon has some really beautiful **places to stay**. In addition to the places listed below, between late June to mid-September you can get a cheap room at the Caerleon campus of University Wales College Newport (℡01633/432800; ❶), fifteen minutes' west along High Street (past the museum).

Great House Isca Rd ℡01633/420216, ☻www .greathousebb.co.uk. Not as large as its name suggests, but a great B&B option nonetheless, set in a sixteenth-century stone cottage filled with antiques, with friendly service and lovely views from the riverside garden. ❹

The Old Rectory B&B In the village of Christchurch, between Caerleon and Newport ℡01633/430700, ☻www.the-oldrectory.co.uk. Two rooms, each with rolltop bath, uncluttered neutral decor and views across the Bristol Channel. ❹

Pendragon House 18 Cross St ℡01633/430871, ☻www.pendragonhouse .co.uk. Central freshly refurbished B&B with cool white-on-white rooms. ❸

Priory Hotel Main St ℡01633/421241, ☻www.thepriorycaerleon.co.uk. In a grand old twelfth-century building opposite the baths, steeped in atmosphere, and with spacious rooms. There's also a good restaurant (closed dinner Sun) specializing in seafood. ❹

Radford House Broadway ℡01633/430101, ☻www.radfordhouse.co.uk. Opposite the museum, this award-winning guesthouse has two richly decorated rooms and a grand communal drawing room with plenty of books and a log fire. ❻

Sarum House 13a Mill St ℡01633/431225, ☻www.sarumhouse.co.uk. Two blocks northeast of the museum, with a pair of charming rooms, one of which has its own balcony with Usk Valley views. ❸–❹

Eating and drinking

During the day, the best place to **eat** is the *Oriel* bistro (℡01633/430238) in the Ffwrrwm courtyard, with outdoor seating in summer and a roaring fire in winter. For lunch or dinner, try ⚲ *Kemeys Manor* (℡01633/450143; bookings essential), a stunning sixteenth-century manor house in private gardens just off the Catsash Road, between Langstone and the *Celtic Manor Resort*, serving modern British cuisine with an Italian slant; or the *Priory Hotel* (see above).

Caerleon is Newport's most chic **drinking** zone. Most enjoyable are the *Olde Bull Inn* on the High Street, good for food, drink and live entertainment; and the *Hanbury Arms*, at the bottom of the road above the river, which was Lord Tennyson's base in Caerleon.

The Valleys

No other part of Wales is as instantly recognizable as **the Valleys**, a generic name for the string of settlements packed into the narrow cracks in the mountainous terrain to the north of Newport, Cardiff and Swansea. Coming

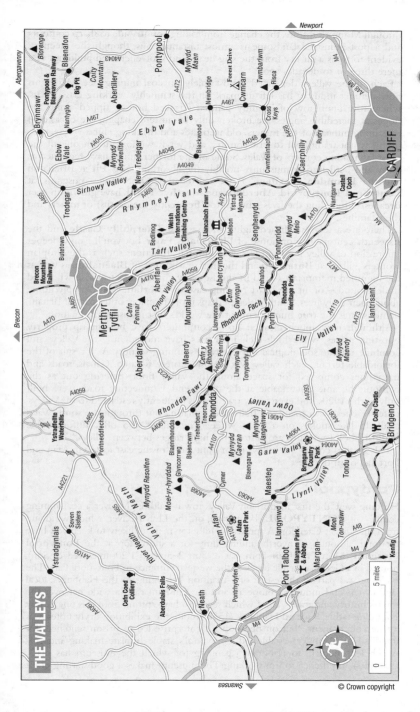

THE VALLEYS

Newport ▲

Swansea ▲

Brecon ▲

Abergavenny ▲

CARDIFF

N

0   5 miles

© Crown copyright

through Monmouthshire, the change from rolling countryside to sharp contours and a post-industrial landscape is almost instantaneous, though the greenery evident today is a far cry from the slag heaps and soot-encrusted buildings of a mere three or so decades ago.

Each of the valleys depended almost solely on coal mining (see p.97). This now-defunct industry has left its mark on the staunchly working-class towns, where row upon row of brightly painted terraced houses, tipped along the slopes at incredible angles, are broken only by austere chapels, the occasional remaining pithead or the miners' old institutes and drinking clubs.

This is not traditional tourist country, and yet is without doubt one of the most fascinating corners of Wales. Some of the former mines have reopened as gutsy and hard-hitting museums, notably the absorbing **Big Pit** at Blaenafon and the **Rhondda Heritage Park** at Trehafod. Other civic museums, at **Pontypool**, **Pontypridd**, **Aberdare** and **Merthyr Tydfil**, have grown up over decades, chronicling the lives (and, all too frequently, the deaths) of miners and their families.

There are a few established sights, such as vast **Caerphilly Castle** and the sixteenth-century manor house of **Llancaiach Fawr**, but you'll gain a deeper impression of valley life from less conventional attractions such as the Utopian workers' village at **Butetown** and the iron gravestones of **Blaenafon**, as well as the dignified memorials, found in almost every community, to those who died underground – or, in the heart-rending case of **Aberfan**, whilst simply going about their daily lives. South Wales, perhaps more than any other part of Britain, demonstrates the true human cost of the world's first industrialized nation.

Although now much cleaned up – commuters have bought up property, boosting prices, while high-tech industries have moved in – the Valleys still combine unique sociological interest with stunning scenery. As a result of the formidable terrain, each valley was almost entirely isolated. Canals, roads and train lines competed for space along the valley floor, petering out as the contours became untameable at the upper end. Connecting roads were built only in the 1920s, and even today transport is frequently restricted to the Valleys' outer reaches, with roads and train lines radiating out through the south Wales coalfield like spokes on a giant wheel. The Valleys also offer unforgettable **walking** holidays; paths are best on the high ridges between valleys.

This section covers the valleys from Pontypool in the east to Cwm Afan and Port Talbot in the west.

Pontypool

Heading west, the first identifiably Valleys town – although never a coal-mining centre – is **PONTYPOOL** (Pontypŵl), on the Llwyd River, which winds up from the Usk at Caerleon. A sprawling, hilly town, it's unlikely to keep you busy for long, although it's worth finding time for a short stop at the **Pontypool Museum** (Mon–Fri 10am–5pm, Sat & Sun 2–5pm; £1.20, free Wed & Sun), housed in a Georgian stable block at the western entrance to Pontypool Park. The building was part of the estate of a mansion belonging to the Hanburys, local landowners and industrial pioneers, and the museum casts a wide net over the town's history and trades, all of which seems to have sprung from this one family. Founding father Richard Hanbury (1538–1608), the exhibition dryly notes, was a true entrepreneur, "but on occasion his enterprise led to prison sentences for fraud". The Hanburys established Pontypool's staple tinplate-making industry, which led, in turn, to elaborate japanning (of which the museum has many examples) and thence to ironworking. The museum makes a good starting point for a stiff hike up through the park to a couple of products of Victorian whimsy: the **Shell Grotto** (May to early Sept Sat, Sun & bank holidays 2–5pm; free), a thirty-minute walk from the museum, boasts an interior completely plastered in molluscs, while twenty minutes further on lies the traditional **Folly Tower** (Mon–Thurs 8.30am–5.30pm, Fri 8.30am–4.30pm; free). Just across the river from the museum, the **market hall** in Pontypool's handsome town centre is great for fresh food and some oddball stalls.

The **train station** is inconveniently situated over a mile to the east of the town centre, making **buses**, which stop by the handsome Victorian town hall, a far better option. The frequent #X24 service (Mon–Sat; up to 6 hourly) will take you to **Griffithstown**, a mile south of the town centre, home of a superb **railway museum** (daily 10am–5pm; £1) on Station Road. Housed in an old goods shed, the museum is one man's life-collection of memorabilia, mainly from the extensive local network, most of which has long gone. Together with his own model railway upstairs, it's fascinating stuff.

If you want to stay round these parts, the village of **MAMHILAD**, a couple of miles north of Pontypool by the Monmouth & Brecon Canal, is home to a lovely farmhouse B&B, *Tŷ Cooke Farm* (☎01873/880382, ⓦ www .downourlane.co.uk; ❸), a working sheep and beef property which is also handy for the village's atmospheric *Star Inn*.

Blaenafon and around

Road and river continue six miles north from Pontypool to the iron and coal town of **BLAENAFON** (sometimes referred to by its English spelling, Blaenavon), the source of the River Llwyd. Blaenafon's lofty hillside position makes it feel less claustrophobic than many valley towns, but its decline is testified by a population of little more than 5000, a third of its nineteenth-century size. It remains a spirited and evocative place, a fact recognized when it gained UNESCO World Heritage Site status in 2000.

Blaenafon is perhaps best known for its **Big Pit** (see p.96), a old coal mine-turned-museum. It's also where the hit BBC docu-drama *Coal House* is filmed, with families trading twenty-first-century life for the conditions of the 1920s. Visits to the cottages featured in the TV series can be arranged by contacting the Heritage Centre.

The Town

The town's Victorian boom can be seen in its architecture, most notably the florid **Working Men's Hall**, dominating the town centre, where miners used to pay a halfpenny a week for the use of the library and other recreational and educational facilities; it's now a **cinema**, screening current-release films (Mon–Thurs 6.30–10.30pm). The parish **church of St Peter** is a good example of what became known as Enginehouse Churches – an engine house being the sole type of building familiar to local masons. Contact the reverend on ☎01495/790292 if you'd like to see the interior with its tomb covers, pillars and font, all fashioned out of iron.

Blaenafon's brand new **Heritage Centre** is on Church Road, and doubles as the town's **tourist office** (April–Sept daily 9am–5pm; Oct–March Tues–Sun 9am–4pm; ☎01495/742333). There are also some exhibits relating to the history of the coal-mining and ironworking industries here, plus an excellent daytime café.

About 700 yards up the hill on North Street are the town's **ironworks** (Easter–Oct: Mon–Fri 9.30am–4.30pm, Sat 10am–5pm, Sun 10am–4.30pm;

same contact details as Heritage Centre; free; CADW). Though the works were founded in 1788, iron smelting in the area dates back to the sixteenth century. Limestone, coal and iron ore – ingredients for successful smelting – were locally abundant, and during the early nineteenth century the Blaenafon works grew to become one of the largest in Britain, finally closing in 1900. The remains of the site offer a thorough picture both of the process used to produce iron and the workers' lifestyles that went with it. The ironworks' **museum**, housed in the Stack Square cottages (built for the foremen and craftsmen between 1789 and 1792), contains exhibitions on the history of iron- and steel-making in the Llwyd Valley.

Within the library, on Lion Street, the **Blaenafon Community Heritage & Cordell Museum** (April–Sept Mon–Thurs 10am–4pm, Sat 10am–1pm; Oct & Nov Mon, Tues & Thurs 10am–1pm & 2–4pm, Sat 10am–1pm; £1) has fascinating exhibits on the life and works of author Alexander Cordell (1914–97), including his typewriter and desk. Born in Ceylon (now Sri Lanka), Cordell developed a deep affinity for Wales and its industrial past during the many years he spent living in the area, and is regarded as one of Wales' foremost writers. Also available here are details of four local driving tours around "Cordell Country", taking you through areas evoked in Cordell's books.

On Sundays and most Saturdays between Easter and September, steam train buffs can ride on the **Pontypool and Blaenavon Railway** (℡01495/792263, ⓦwww.pontypool-and-blaenavon.co.uk; £2.50 return), which shunts between the *Whistle Inn* (see opposite) and Furnace Sidings (signposted just off the B4248 between Blaenafon and Brynmawr), taking seventeen minutes round-trip; tickets can be booked at the Railway Shop in Blaenafon at 13a Broad St.

Big Pit

Three-quarters of a mile west of the town (and connected to Blaenafon by a half-hourly shuttle bus) lies one of Wales' best tourist attractions, the **Big Pit National Coal Museum** (Feb–Nov; frequent one-hour tours daily 10am–3.30pm; Dec & Jan call for tour times and availability; free), occupying a former colliery which opened in 1880 and closed exactly a century later. Of all the mining museums in south Wales, Big Pit brings you closest to the experience of a miner's work and life, as you descend 300ft, kitted out with lamp, helmet and heavy battery pack into a labyrinth of shafts and coal faces. The guides are ex-miners, who give you a personal insight into mining life as they lead you through examples of the different types of coal mining, from the old stack-and-pillar operation, where miners would manually hack into the coalface before propping up the ceiling with a wooden beam, to more modern mechanically worked seams. Constant streams of rust-coloured water flow by, adding to the dank and chilly atmosphere (bring a jacket) that terrified the small children who were once paid twopence for a six-day week (of which one penny was subtracted for the cost of their candles) pulling the coal wagons along the tracks.

Back on the surface, the old pithead baths, blacksmith's, miners' canteen and winding engine house have all been preserved and filled with some fascinating displays about the local and south Wales mining industries, including a series of feisty testimonies from the miners made redundant here.

Accommodation and eating

Blaenafon has some smart B&B **accommodation** attached to the friendly *Rifleman's Arms* on Rifle Street (℡01495/792297; ❷–❸), off the Abergavenny road, which is also great for **food**. Other **pubs** serving good food include the

The Welsh coal industry

The land beneath the inhospitable hills of the south Wales valleys had some of the world's most abundant and accessible natural seams of **coal**, as well as iron ore. During the boom years of the nineteenth and early twentieth centuries, wealthy English capitalists came to Wales and ruthlessly stripped the land of its natural assets, while paying paltry amounts to those who risked life and limb in the mines. The mine owners were in a formidably strong position – thousands of Welsh working class, bolstered by their Irish, Scottish and Italian peers, flocked to the Valleys in search of work and some sort of sustainable life. The Valleys – virtually unpopulated at the start of the nineteenth century – became blackened with soot and packed with people, pits and chapels by the beginning of the twentieth.

By 1920, there were 256,000 men working in the 620 mines of the south Wales coalfield, providing one third of the world's coal resources. Vast **miners' institutes**, paid for by a wages' levy, jostled for position with the Nonconformist chapels, whose muscular brand of Christianity was matched by the zeal of the region's politics, trade-union-led and avowedly left-wing. Great socialist orators rose to national prominence, and even Britain's pioneering **National Health Service**, founded by a radical Labour government in the years following World War II, was based on a Valleys community scheme by locally born Aneurin Bevan.

Over half of the original pits closed in the harsh economic climate of the 1930s. World War II saw a brief respite in the closure programme, which continued even more swiftly in the years immediately after. As coal seams became less economical (due to the additional distance to reach the coalface from the pitheads), and the political climate shifted, the number of people employed in the industry dipped down into four figures in the aftermath of the 1984–85 miners' strike. No coalfields were as solidly behind the strike as south Wales, whose workers and families responded wholeheartedly to the call to defend the industry, which their trade union, the **National Union of Mineworkers** (NUM), claimed was on the brink of being decimated. The year-long war of attrition between the Thatcher government and Arthur Scargill's NUM was bitter, finally seeing the government victorious as the number of miners returning to work outnumbered those staying out on strike. Over a quarter of a century on, all of the south Wales pits have now closed.

Today, powerful museums such as the **Big Pit National Coal Museum** (see p.96) provide an illuminating insight into the coal industry, and the comradeship forged between the miners, something that's missed by many ex-miners today, although not the risks and all-too-frequent accidents.

Interestingly, there is still coal in parts of the Valleys. While it would be a massive undertaking to reopen the mines and make them safer, greener and economically viable, coal mining could yet be revived in addressing energy shortfalls in the future.

central *Queen Victoria* on Prince Street (which also has regular live music), plus a couple of miles or so out of town, the mining memorabilia-filled *Whistle Inn*, off the road to Brynmawr; and the atmospheric *Lamb & Fox*, sole survivor of the demolished pit village of Pwll-du, down the lane off the Abergavenny road to the north (on the Blorenge mountain).

Ebbw Vale

West of Pontypool and Blaenafon, the settlements of the **Ebbw Vale** are hemmed in by forest, best seen along the **Cwmcarn Forest Drive** (Easter–Aug daily 11am–7pm; July & Aug weekends until 9pm; Sept daily 11am–6pm; March & Oct daily 11am–5pm; Nov Sat & Sun 11am–4pm; £3 per car), off the main A467 in Cwmcarn village, two miles north of Risca. Setting out from the

Visitor Centre, the seven-mile figure-of-eight drive takes in superb scenery, as well as kids' play areas, a decent visitor centre, an Iron Age hillfort, mountain bike trails and a good, grassy **campsite** (℡01495/272001; £7–13). The visitor centre also has information about some challenging downhill **mountain biking** trails. Bikes can be rented in Cwmcarn village from Ryders, at 13 Park St (℡01495/270623).

Caerphilly and the Rhymney Valley

Now almost a suburb of Cardiff, just seven miles north of the capital at the foot of the **Rhymney Valley**, the town of **CAERPHILLY** (Caerffili) is wrapped around its staggering moated **castle** (April, May & Oct daily 9am–5pm; June–Sept daily 9.30am–6pm; Nov–March Mon–Sat 9.30am–4pm, Sun 11am–4pm; £3.70; CADW). Built on the site of a Roman fort and an earlier Norman fortification, construction began on the castle in 1268 under Gilbert de Clare, who wanted to protect the vulnerable coastal plains around Cardiff from Llywelyn ein Llyw Olaf (Llywelyn the Last).

For the next few hundred years, Caerphilly was given at whim by various kings to their favourites – most notably by Edward II to his minion, and some say lover, Hugh le Despenser, in 1317. The Civil War necessitated the building of an armoury, which prompted Cromwell to seize it, drain the moat and blow up the towers. By the early twentieth century, the castle was in a sorry state, sitting amidst a growing industrial town that saw fit to build in the moat and the castle precincts. Houses and shops were demolished and the moat reflooded in 1958, and the thirty-acre site is now one of Wales' most visited tourist attractions.

You enter the castle through the great **gatehouse** that punctuates the barbican wall by a lake, much restored and now housing an exhibition about the castle's history. A platform behind the barbican wall exhibits medieval war and siege engines, pointing ominously across the lake. From here, a bridge crosses the moat, part of the wider lake, to the outer wall of the castle itself, behind which sits the hulking inner ward. On the left is the southeastern **leaning tower**, with a great cleft in its walls where Cromwell's men are said to have attempted to blow it sky-high (though the tilt is more likely due to simple subsidence). With the exception of the ruined northeastern tower, the other corner turrets have been blandly restored since the Civil War, with the northwestern tower housing a reasonably interesting exhibition on Welsh castles, their methods of construction and some speculative facts and figures about the day-to-day life of their medieval inhabitants. More interesting is the massive **eastern gatehouse**, which includes an impressive upper hall and oratory and, to its left, the wholly restored and reroofed **Great Hall**, largely built around 1317 by Hugh le Despenser.

In addition to its castle, Caerphilly is also synonymous with its crumbly white **cheese**, but the only place in town to buy actual Welsh Farmhouse Caerphilly cheese (rather than those made elsewhere but still carrying the Caerphilly label) is the shop within the **tourist office** (daily: April–Sept 10am–6pm; Oct–March 10am–5pm; ℡029/2088 0011, ⓦwww.visitcaerphilly.com), opposite the castle entrance in Lower Twyn Square. Both the castle and the tourist office are a five-minute stroll down Cardiff Road from the **bus** and **train stations**.

Caerphilly's cheese has inspired the town's vibrant festival, **The Big Cheese** (ⓦwww.caerphilly.gov.uk/bigcheese), held over three days in late July in the shadow of the castle and encompassing everything from street theatre to concerts, a funfair, falconry, historical re-enactments and craft market, as well as a food market selling cheese along with all manner of local produce.

Caerphilly makes an easy day-trip from Cardiff, so you're unlikely to end up staying here, but there are some appealing **accommodation** options nearby at Llancaiach Fawr Manor (see p.101). As for **eating**, the view of Caerphilly's castle alone makes the *Courthouse* inn on Cardiff Road, behind the NatWest bank, worthwhile. For a real Caerphilly cheese rarebit, head to *Glanmor's Tearooms*, facing the castle on the edge of the Castle Court shopping precinct.

The Rhymney Valley

North of Caerphilly, the Rhymney Valley becomes increasingly industrialized as it steers past a seamless succession of small towns. Ten miles up the valley from Caerphilly is **NEW TREDEGAR**, where the **Winding House** (daily 10am–5pm; free), with its gleaming steam engine that once powered the colliery's high-speed lifts, is worth a visit. It's on White Rose Way, a ten-minute walk from Tir-phil station.

At the head of the valley, a mile beyond Rhymney town and just short of the A465 Heads of the Valleys road, tiny **BUTETOWN** (Drenewydd) was constructed as a model workers' estate in 1802–03 by the idealistic Marquess of Bute, a member of Wales' richest land- and minerals-owning family, although only the central grid of houses was ever built.

A mile east of Butetown, the **Bryn Bach Country Park**, on the northern edge of the little town of **TREDEGAR**, has tearooms and a visitor centre (☏01495/711816) which can provide information about its lakeside **campsite**. There's also a great independent **hostel** in the middle of Tredegar – *Hobo Backpackers* (☏01495/718422, ⓦwww.hobo-backpackers.com; dorm beds £12) on Morgan Street, just down from the town clock. On the same street is the parkland of **Bedwellty House**, a Georgian mansion built for the local ironmaster. In the grounds (unrestricted access; free) you'll find an arboretum, ice house, and the world's largest lump of coal, a fifteen-ton block exhibited as part of the 1951 Festival of Britain.

The Taff and Cynon valleys

Like the River Rhymney, the River Taff also empties into the Bristol Channel at Cardiff, after passing through a condensed 25 or so miles of industry and population that obscure the former **china works** at Nantgarw. The first town in the Taff Vale is **Pontypridd**, one of the most cheerful in the Valleys, where the Rhondda River hives off west. Continuing north, the river splits again at **Abercynon**, where the Cynon River flows in from **Aberdare**. Just outside Abercynon is the enjoyable seventeenth-century **Llancaiach Fawr** manor house, while to the north, the Taff is packed into one of the tightest of all the Valleys, passing **Aberfan** five miles short of the valley head town of **Merthyr Tydfil**.

Nantgarw

Barrelling north along the A470, you'd never suspect that the **China Works Museum** (April–Sept Tues–Sun 10am–4.15pm; Oct–March Thurs–Sun 10am–3.15pm; free) is tucked behind a thicket of trees just by the junction for **NANTGARW**. For less than five years in the 1810s, the pottery here produced some of the finest porcelain in the world, the few florid examples on display only serving to whet your appetite for the extensive collection in the National Museum and Gallery in Cardiff. Master porcelain painter William Billingsley set up the works with high ambition using Valleys coal and Cornish clay, but the extremely difficult "soft paste porcelain" process resulted in just a ten-percent firing success rate and the enterprise soon folded. One of the firing kilns has now been rebuilt and the main building contains small displays on the process and the history of the site.

Pontypridd

Hometown of crooner Tom Jones, **PONTYPRIDD** is today rapidly gentrifying as Cardiff commuters move in, but retains its own unique spirit. Arriving in Pontypridd you're greeted by the town's distinctive arched **bridge** of 1775, once the largest single-span stone bridge in Europe. Featuring three holes either side to lessen the bridge's overall weight and allow gusty winds through, it was built by local amateur stonemason William Edwards, whose previous attempts crumbled into the river below.

On the far side of the river from the town centre is **Ynysangharad Park**, where you'll find Sir W. Goscombe John's cloying allegorical statue and tomb in honour of Pontypridd weaver Evan James, who in 1856 composed the stirring *Hen Wlad Fy Nhadau* (*Land of My Fathers*) that subsequently became the Welsh national anthem.

By the bridge at the end of Taff Street, the **Pontypridd Museum** (Mon–Sat 10am–5pm; free) is housed in what was one of the town's great chapels. Built in 1861, it has been lovingly restored, and boasts unusually ornate ceiling bosses, pillars, pulpit, stained-glass window and organ that all contribute to the reverential atmosphere. The centre's contents are a real treasure trove of photographs, video, models and exhibits which succeed in painting a warm picture of the town and its outlying valleys. Tom Jones and local opera star and actor Sir Geraint Evans are also celebrated amongst the exhibitions here.

Near the elegant and impressive train station, **John Hughes' Grogg Shop**, at 159 Broadway, sells figurine caricatures of legions of rugby stars and Welsh celebrities in oddball sculpture – worth a visit even if you don't plan on buying anything. A short walk past the pubs at the bottom of Taff Street brings you out parallel to Market Street and the chaotic bustle of the old-fashioned **market** which spills out into the surrounding streets and squares on Wednesday and Saturday, the main trading days. Visitors are welcome to pop along to Tabor Hall on Vaughn Street in the Pwllgwaun neighbourhood of Pontypridd to listen to the local **male voice choir**; the tourist office has rehearsal schedules.

Practicalities

Pontypridd is well connected to bus, train and road networks. The **train station** is a ten-minute walk south of the old bridge on The Graig; the **bus station** is directly above the old bridge on the western bank. Just below is the friendly **tourist office** (Mon–Sat 10am–5pm; ☏01443/490748), in the Pontypridd Museum on Bridge Street, which can advise on **accommodation**. There are several appealing options three to four miles away close to Llancaiach Fawr Manor (see opposite).

There's decent pub **food** at *The Tumble*, near the station on Broadway. For pure **drinking**, make for the old-fashioned, stone-fronted *Llanover Arms* on Bridge Street, just over the river from the museum. Regular **live music** takes place at *Club-y-Bont*, down the narrow lane behind Boots on Taff Street; and in *Tom's Bar*, at 71 Wood Rd, renamed from the Wood Road Working Men's Club in honour of Tom Jones, who gave his first-ever performance here. Sir Tom reportedly transplanted a telephone box from Wood Road to his current Las Vegas home.

Llancaiach Fawr and the Welsh International Climbing Centre

The river divides at **Abercynon**, four miles up the Taff Valley, with the Cynon River flowing in from Aberdare in the northwest. Two miles east of Abercynon, just north of the village of **NELSON**, is **Llancaiach Fawr Manor** (Mon–Fri 10am–5pm, Sat & Sun 10am–6pm; closed Mon Nov–Feb; £5.75), a Tudor house built around 1530 which has been transformed into a living-history museum set in 1645, the time of the Civil War, with guides dressed as house servants and speaking seventeenth-century English. Although the whole experience could easily be nightmarishly tacky, it's actually very deftly done, with well-researched period authenticity and numerous fascinating anecdotes from the staff. Last admission is one hour prior to closing; special tours – candlelit, murder-mystery and seventeenth-century evenings – are also available. Regular buses from Pontypridd and Cardiff pass the entrance.

If you want to **stay**, try the friendly, well-kept *Fairmead* guesthouse (☎01443/411174; ❸), almost opposite the manor, or the traditionally styled, floral *Llechwen Hall* (☎01443/742050, ⓦwww.llechwen.co.uk; ❻), which sits high in the hills to the south of Nelson, signposted off the A470 a couple of miles north of Pontypridd. Alternatively, in Nelson itself, ⚶ *Sergeants* (☎01443/450999, ⓦwww.sergeantsrestaurant.co.uk; ❷), on Station Road, occupies an old police station which has been transformed to house three elegant en-suite rooms plus an increasingly well-known **restaurant** (open dinner Wed–Sat and lunch Sun), serving moderately priced locally sourced dishes like Welsh lamb three ways (braised shoulder, roasted cutlet and faggot on lentil casserole), or ginger-glazed salmon.

A couple of miles north of Llancaiach Fawr, just beyond the village of **Trelewis**, the old Taff Merthyr colliery has been transformed into the **Welsh International Climbing Centre** (Mon–Fri 9am–10pm, Sat & Sun 9am–6pm; ☎01443/710749, ⓦwww.e2-adventures.com). As well as vast climbing walls (from £4–7), it offers a wide range of adventure options, including caving instruction in a purpose-built artificial cave system (£30 per person), and has cheap mountain bike rental. There are also exercise rooms, a sauna, a restaurant and bar (open Mon–Fri 7–11pm, Sat & Sun 1–7pm). It's popular with groups, so it's worth booking your visit ahead.

Aberfan

North of Abercynon, the Taff Valley village of **ABERFAN** contains one sight that's impossible to forget: the two lines of arches that mark the **graves** of the 144 people killed in October 1966 when an unsecured slag heap slid down a hill and onto the Pantglas Primary School in the village. The death toll – including 116 children – is beyond comprehension. Official enquiries revealed the sorry inevitability of the disaster, given the cavalier approach to safety so often displayed by the coal bosses. Over four decades later, the tragedy lives on in the memory of the thousands of people from all over southeast Wales and beyond who came to help recover the bodies.

Aberdare

Eight miles northwest of Abercynon, towards the top of the Cynon Valley, is the sprawling town of **ABERDARE** (Aberdâr), lined with terraced houses. A short walk from the train station brings you to one of the Valleys' best museums, the **Cynon Valley Museum & Gallery** (Mon–Sat 9am–4.30pm; free), housed in an old tram depot next to the Tesco superstore. Exhibits convey the social history of the valley, from the appalling conditions of the mid-nineteenth century, when nearly half of all children born here died by the age of 5, to stirring memories of the 1926 General Strike and the 1984–85 Miners' Strike. Alongside are some videos and displays on Victorian lantern slides, teenage life through the ages, the miners' jazz bands and Aberdare's role as a prominent centre of early Welsh-language publishing.

On the western flank of town is the lovely **Dare Valley Country Park**, whose **visitor centre** (daily: April–Sept 9am–5.30pm; Oct–March 9am–4pm; ☎01685/874672) has a café and some interesting changing art exhibits, and handles enquiries for the basic on-site hotel (❶) and the inexpensive campsite (£5 per two-person pitch). The visitor centre is also the starting point of the 32-mile **Glamorgan Forest Way** to Afan Argoed and Margam Country Park (see p.108).

It's only a short walk into the town centre, where you'll find some good shops, lots of **cafés**, and tons of **pubs** such as the lively *Yr Ieuan ap Iago* on the High Street.

Merthyr Tydfil

On the cusp of the grand, windy heights of the Brecon Beacons to the north and the industrial valleys to the south, the fortunes of **MERTHYR TYDFIL** (Merthyr Tudful) have risen and fallen more than once, and its absorbing history makes it well worth a visit. Merthyr's strategic location was first exploited by the Romans as an outpost of their base at Caerleon. In 480 AD, Tydfil, Welsh princess and daughter of Brychan, Prince of Brycheiniog, was captured as she rode through the area, and murdered for her Christian beliefs. She became St Tydfil the Martyr, and her name was bestowed on the area.

In the seventeenth century, the village became a focal point for Dissenters and Radicals, movements which, through poverty and oppression, gained momentum in the eighteenth century as the town's four massive ironworks were founded to exploit locally abundant seams of iron ore and limestone. Merthyr became the largest iron-producing town in the world, and by far the most populous town in Wales: in 1831, the town had a population of 60,000, more than Cardiff, Swansea and Newport combined. Workers flocked from all over Britain and beyond, finding themselves crammed into squalid housing, whilst the ironmasters built themselves great houses and palaces nearby. Merthyr's **radicalism** bubbled furiously: it was here that the red flag was first raised, when rioters in 1831 gathered around a standard dipped in the blood of a killed calf; another martyr, union organizer Dic Penderyn, was hanged unjustly for his role in the riots. Later, the town saw the election of Britain's first-ever socialist MP, Keir Hardie, in 1900.

Merthyr's precipitous development saw it peak and trough earlier than anywhere else: of its four mighty ironworks, only one was still open at the end of World War I, and that closed in the 1930s. In 1939, a Royal Commission suggested that the town be abandoned and the inhabitants shifted to the coast. The plan was forgotten when war broke out.

Throughout the rest of the twentieth century and into the twenty-first, the town has suffered from unemployment that continues to be among the highest in the UK, but its commuting proximity to Cardiff has seen property prices skyrocket of late.

The Town

The town centre is wedged between the High Street and the River Taff, but the sights listed here are all around the Taff to the immediate northwest. The **Ynysfach**

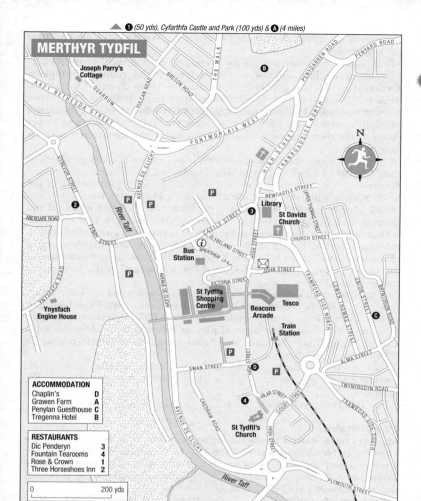

MERTHYR TYDFIL

Joseph Parry's Cottage

ACCOMMODATION
Chaplin's   D
Grawen Farm   A
Penylan Guesthouse C
Tregenna Hotel   B

RESTAURANTS
Dic Penderyn   3
Fountain Tearooms   4
Rose & Crown   1
Three Horseshoes Inn 2

0   200 yds

© Crown copyright

Engine House (Mon–Fri 10am–4pm; free) was once the powerhouse behind the mighty Cyfarthfa ironworks and has now been revitalized by the Merthyr Tydfil Heritage Trust, with displays of costumed mannequins portraying scenes from Merthyr's past as a centre of iron and steel making, and an entertaining video about the town's industrial history.

Half a mile further up the River Taff, tucked amongst modern houses just off the A4102 (Bethesda Street), is **Chapel Row**, a line of cottages built in the 1820s for skilled ironworkers. One of these is **Joseph Parry's Cottage** (April–Sept Thurs–Sun 2–5pm; free), where the composer was born, though this mini-museum is most interesting as a social record of slightly better-than-average workers' domestic conditions of the nineteenth century. Parry's music, including the national favourite *Myfanwy*, is piped between

103

rooms, and the upstairs section of the house is given over to a display of his life and music.

Back across the other side of the river, just beyond the Brecon road, is a home in absolute contrast to Parry's humble and cramped birthplace: **Cyfarthfa Castle** (April–Sept daily 10am–5pm; Oct–March Tues–Fri 10am–4pm, Sat & Sun noon–4pm; free). Built in 1825 as an ostentatious mock-Gothic castle for William Crawshay II, boss of the town's original ironworks, it's set within an attractive, 160-acre **park** that slopes down to the river and once afforded Crawshay a permanent view over his iron empire.

Cyfartha's current incarnation, however, is as a museum, and a great one at that. You start in a well-re-created Valleys traditional Welsh café on the ground floor, then go downstairs into the old wine cellars for a gutsy history of the town. Starting with tales of the martyr Tydfil, the Penydarren Roman fort and ruined Morlais Castle, the narrative soon leads into Merthyr's industrial and political heritage. Merthyr's place in working-class history is well examined, with an interesting set of panels and pamphlets on the 1831 riot. Other exhibits examine Aberfan, the 1984–85 miners' strike, pubs and the temperance movement, as well as the beleaguered 1980s Sinclair C5 car, constructed here at the Hoover plant – "built by Hoover, driven by suckers" as the local phrase memorably had it.

Upstairs, the castle's opulent main rooms, all chandeliers and acres of curtains, now house a superb collection of Welsh and international **art**. Welsh highlights include an uncharacteristically gentle study of *The Elf* by monumental sculptor Goscombe John, and works by local painters Penry Williams, Augustus John, Cedric Morris, Kyffin Williams and Alfred Jones, whose double portrait of Salome is quite mesmerizing.

The surrounding **park** contains landscaped walks, a plant nursery, café, bowling green, tennis courts, a pitch-and-putt course and a stage set next to the main lake.

The **Taff Trail cycle route** (see p.228) passes by Merthyr Tydfil.

Practicalities

Merthyr's **train station** lies east of the town centre, a minute's walk from the High Street. North from here is Wheatsheaf Lane and the **bus station**, where services depart for all parts of south and mid-Wales. The **tourist office** (Mon–Sat 9.30am–4pm; ☎01685/379884, ⓔtic@merthyr.gov.uk) is behind the bus station at 14a Glebeland St.

Accommodation options range from the plush *Tregenna Hotel* (☎01685/723627, ⓦwww.tregennahotel.co.uk; ❸), on Park Terrace, next to Penydarren Park, to the comfortable *Chaplin's*, 30–31 High St (☎01685/387272, ⓦwww.chaplinshotel.co.uk; ❸–❹), and, cheapest of all, the *Penylan* guesthouse, 12 Courtland Terrace (☎01685/723179; ❶). There's a **campsite** four miles north of town in the beautiful surroundings of *Grawen Farm*, Cwm Taf (☎01685/723740; from £8 per tent).

There are plenty of daytime **food** outlets in the main shopping area of the town centre, as well as the friendly *Fountain Tearooms* just off the bottom of the High Street. Plenty of places along the High Street open in the evening, including *Dic Penderyn* at nos. 102–103, which has reasonable beer and food. You could also try the historic *Three Horseshoes Inn* on Dynevor Street, where up to three hundred Chartists once crammed into the small bar. Either of these will also prove amenable for a night's **drinking**, as will the sporty *Rose & Crown* on Morgan Street, up towards Cyfarthfa Park.

The Rhondda

The twin valleys of the **Rhondda** – Rhondda Fach (Little Rhondda) to the east and Rhondda Fawr (Great Rhondda) to the west – are each sixteen miles long yet less than a mile wide. Between them they once formed the heart of the massive south Wales coal industry. Hollywood romanticized the area in the 1947 Oscar-winning weepie *How Green Was My Valley*, although the story was based on author Richard Llewellyn's early life in nearby Gilfach Goch, outside the valley.

Early records show that in 1841 the Rhondda had a population of under a thousand, but that exploded with the discovery of coal and, by 1924, 167,000 people had squeezed into the available land in ranks of houses packed around sixty or so pitheads. Poverty and hardship were rife, but so were pride, self-reliance, radical religion and firebrand politics. The Communist Party ran the town of Maerdy (nicknamed "Little Moscow" by Fleet Street in the 1930s) for decades. The 1984–85 miners' strike saw solidarity in the Welsh pits on a greater scale than any other part of Britain until the Rhondda's last pit closed in 1990. Today there's a range of new attractions, not least superb hillwalking, with astounding views over the densely packed houses below.

The Rhondda starts just outside **Pontypridd**, winding through the mountains alongside railway, road and river to **Trehafod** and the colliery museum of the **Rhondda Heritage Park** (daily 10am–6pm, last admission 4.30pm; closed Mon Oct–March; £5.60). Set up by locals when the Lewis Merthyr pit closed in 1983, you can explore the engine winding houses, lamp room, fan house and take a simulated "trip underground", with stunning visuals and sound effects, re-creating life (and death) in the late nineteenth century and 1950s through the eyes of colliers. The Trehafod **train station** is just a five-minute walk from the Heritage Park.

The Rhondda's two valleys divide at the bustling town of **PORTH** ("Gateway"), a mile beyond the museum, from where the Rhondda Fach (Little

▲ Pithead, Rhondda Heritage Park

Rhondda) River twists its way northwards through the smaller and frequently forgotten valley of the same name, passing endless archetypal Valleys towns like Ynyshir, Pontygwaith, Tylorstown, Ferndale and Maerdy – row after row of tiny houses clinging to sheer valley walls.

The **Rhondda Fawr** (Great Rhondda) stretches from the outskirts of Pontypridd to Blaenrhondda and is blessed with a train line, a decent road and most of the sights. The first notable settlement is **TONYPANDY**, followed a mile later by **LLWYNYPIA**, wedged in between walkable, forested hillsides. From here, a steep two-mile climb leads up to **Mynydd y Gelli**, where the remains of an Iron Age hut settlement and a Bronze Age burial chamber and stone circle can be seen.

The road, river and train line wind tortuously past an endless stream of towns to **TREORCHY** (Treorci), best known internationally for its famed **Treorchy Male Choir**, Wales' oldest. Visitors are welcome to rehearsals, which take place each Tuesday and Thursday evening; prearrange by phoning ☎01443/422935. Treorchy is also home of the splendid **Parc and Dare Hall** (☎01443/773112), a multipurpose arts venue that's always busy.

Heading west from Treorchy, the **A4601** is one of the most spectacular roads in Wales, climbing up the mountainside and twisting its way around Mynydd Maendy and Mynydd Llangeinwyr before dividing a few miles west of Treorchy to head west (as the A4017) down the Cwm Afan and south (as the A4061) for the forested Ogwr Fawr.

North of Treorchy, at the top of the Rhondda Fawr, is **TREHERBERT**, its straggle of houses continuing up the valley at **BLAENCWM** and **BLAENRHONDDA**, two communities effectively bypassed since a new road was built in the 1930s by unemployed miners, connecting Treherbert to the forests and lakes of Hirwaun Common en route to Brecon.

Spectacular **walks** abound in the Rhondda. A mildly difficult two-mile hike from Blaencwm, for instance, leads to the remarkable mound of **Penpych**, sitting sentinel over the Rhondda Fawr, while a diversion east at Ferndale in the Rhondda Fach passes the remains of a Roman marching camp, **Twyn-y-Briddallt**, and **Old Smokey** (aka the Tylorstown Tip), a huge pile of colliery spoil with excellent views, before winding up at the isolated little ridge-top village of **LLANWONNO**, with its remote glades, an ancient church and a cracking village pub, the *Brynffynon Arms*.

Male voice choirs

Although Wales' **male voice choirs** can be found all over the country, it is in the southern, industrial heartland that they are loudest and strongest. The roots of the choirs lie in the Nonconformist religious traditions of the seventeenth and eighteenth centuries, when Methodism in particular swept the country, and singing was a free and potent way of cherishing the frequently persecuted faith. Throughout the breakneck nineteenth-century industrialization in the Valleys, choirs of coal miners came together to praise God in the fervent way that was typical of the packed, poor communities. Classic hymns like *Cwm Rhondda* and the Welsh national anthem, *Hen Wlad Fy Nhadau* (*Land of My Fathers*), are synonymous with the choirs, whose full-blooded interpretations render all other efforts insipid.

Despite the collapse of coal mining in the twentieth century, most choirs continue to perform in Wales and abroad. Each small Valleys town has its own choir, most of whom happily allow visitors to sit in on rehearsals. Ask at the local tourist office or library, and take the chance to hear one of the world's most distinctive choral traditions in full, roof-raising splendour.

Practicalities

A **train** line, punctuated with stops every mile or so, runs the entire length of the Rhondda Fawr from Pontypridd to its terminus at Treherbert. **Buses** also cover the route; change in Merthyr Tydfil for connections to the Brecon Beacons.

Accommodation in the twin valleys is sparse. Decent places include the business-oriented *Heritage Park Hotel* (℡01443/687057; ❹), beside the Rhondda Heritage Park at Trehafod, which has its own pool; and *The Bertie* bar and B&B (℡01443/681688; ❷–❸) nearby at 1–3 Phillips Terrace. Nearer the top end of the Rhondda Fawr is the reasonable *Baglan Hotel* (℡01443/776111; ❷) on the main road in Treherbert.

For the most part **eating** options in the Rhondda towns consist of chippies and Chinese takeaways, though a few **pubs** offer good food – try the *Greenfield* at 13–14 William St in Ystrad, where the road from Penrhys and the Rhondda Fach joins the Rhondda Fawr, or the *Lion* at 102 Bute St in Treorchy, both on the main A4058 through the Rhondda Fawr.

The Ogwr, Garw and Llynfi valleys

To the southwest of the Rhondda, the Ogwr, Garw and Llynfi valleys are different to their bigger, better-known neighbour: the contours are slightly softer, the open spaces wider and the towns less bustling.

The **Ogwr Valley** plunges south from Treorchy in the Rhondda Fawr to the ancient settlement and now county town of **BRIDGEND** (Pen-y-bont ar Ogwr), guarding the entrance to the three valleys, which makes a useful transport interchange, with a good selection of shops and a few handsome buildings, and has regular festivals throughout the year, listed at ⓦwww .bridgend.gov.uk. Just over a mile northeast of the town are the substantial remains of **Coity Castle** (free access; CADW), built around the end of the twelfth century by one of the earliest Norman knights in the area. Bridgend is also very handy for Porthcawl, Ewenny Priory and beyond, detailed in the Vale of Glamorgan section (p.132).

The dead-end **Garw Valley** consists of a road, river and the disused railway crammed in on the valley floor, before they all peter out into wooded hillsides. Most of the scars of the valley's mining past have now been levelled and landscaped, leaving it surprisingly pretty, and, as it's well off any tourist track, very rewarding for good walks and congenial company in local pubs and shops. At the southern end of the valley, the **Bryngarw Country Park** (daily dawn–dusk; free, but charges for special events) is a pleasant diversion, with landscaped gardens, exceptional flower collections and mature woodlands gathered around the restored Bryngarw House, which now houses a bistro and conference centre.

Still hard hit economically from the closure of the collieries, the **Llynfi Valley**, stretching up from Bridgend and Tondu along the A4063, is broad-bottomed and leafy, the main settlement being **MAESTEG**, from where the main road links up with the A4107 at Cymer, for Cwm Afan (see p.108).

On top of the mountain to the south of Maesteg is the beautiful village of **LLANGYNWYD**. Birth- and burial-place of bard Wil Hopcyn, it has an ancient atmosphere in stark contrast to the ex-mining towns below. The splendid *Yr Hen Dŷ* pub is said to be the oldest inn in south Wales, where revellers traditionally congregate on New Year's Day for the hallowed Welsh custom of the **Mari Llwyd** (Grey Mare), during which a horse's skull is paraded through the village to ward off evil spirits during the forthcoming year.

The best place to **stay** in this area is south of the M4 at the Edwardian *Court Colman Manor*, amid rolling green hills at Pen-y-Fai, Bridgend (☎01656/720212, ⓦwww.court-colman-manor.com; ➍–➑), with also has an award-winning Indian restaurant. Alternatively, there are many fine wild sites to pitch a **tent**. Bridgend's tourist office, within the Bridgend Designer Outlet, The Derwen (Mon–Wed & Fri–Sat 10am–6pm, Thurs 10am–8pm, Sun 11am–5pm; ☎01656/654906) can also help with accommodation.

Cwm Afan, Port Talbot and Margam

Winding its way between the top of the Llynfi Valley and the coast at Port Talbot, the main attraction in bucolic **CWM AFAN** is the **Afan Forest Park**, 9000 acres of hilly forest fanning out from an excellent **countryside centre** (April–Sept Mon–Fri 9.30am–5pm, Sat & Sun 9.30am–6pm; Oct–March Mon–Fri 10.30am–4pm Sat & Sun 10.30am–5pm; ☎01639/850564; free), situated three miles west of little **CYMER**. The centre houses the memorabilia-filled **South Wales Miners' Museum** (same times; entrance price yet to be announced), closed for refurbishment during research, but due to re-open by the time you're reading this. The centre also organizes regular events and walks, has very basic **camping** (£2.50 per person) and a great range of **self-catering** units, from old farmhouses to log cabins, from around £360 per week. The centre and forest are best known for their waymarked **mountain biking** trails for all levels. Bikes can be rented from Afan Valley Bike Hire (☎07952/577316; ⓦwww.afan-valley-bike-hire .com) in nearby Glyncorrwg; delivery can be arranged.

The valley descends towards the sea, reaching the village of **PONTRHY-DYFEN** in a couple of miles. Actor Richard Burton was born in a house at the foot of one of the impressive viaducts that slice through the village. From here, roads either side of the river continue south to the industrial sprawl of **PORT TALBOT**, still dominated by its massive steelworks.

A couple of miles southeast of Port Talbot, on the other side of junction 38 of the M4, **MARGAM** was originally a Cistercian settlement and later the home of various industrial magnates. The first left turn after the motorway junction leads to the arcaded twelfth-century **abbey church**, the sole remaining Cistercian house of worship in Wales. The neighbouring **Margam Stones Museum** (April–Sept Wed–Sun 10.30am–4pm; Oct–March Wed & Fri only by appointment; £2; CADW) houses numerous important Roman, Celtic and medieval standing stones, as well as figures and gargoyles from destroyed Welsh churches and monasteries.

Lying just the other side of the abbey church and accessed by car along the next turn-off from the main road, the 850-acre **Margam Country Park** (castle and grounds April–Sept daily 10am–7pm; Oct–March park only Mon–Tues 1–4.30pm, Wed–Sun 10.30am–4pm; free) is centred around the nineteenth-century Gothic pile of **Margam Castle**. There's a lot to see and do within the grounds: walks go up to the ruined hilltop Capel Mair, around Mynydd-y-Castell Iron Age fort and through superb floral grounds dotted with some exciting contemporary sculpture. Tucked in by the abbey church walls are the impressive remains of the original Cistercian abbey, most notable for the vaulting of its twelve-sided chapter house, which survived the dissolution of the monasteries only to have its roof collapse under the weight of weeds in 1799. Nearby is Margam's showpiece **orangery**, a splendid Georgian outhouse, built in 1790 and 327ft long. Nestled in the same corner is a kids' "fairyland" play area. Waterfalls, sculpture and some splendid shrubbery fill the spaces around the ceremonial boardwalk, leading up to the castle. The castle-cum-mansion was gutted by fire in 1977, but you can still wander into the lobby and peer up the octagonal lantern tower and see a few models and photos. There's a café and shop in the courtyard.

The area is an easy **day-trip** from Cardiff or Swansea. You'll find decent **food** in the *Lord Caradoc* pub on Station Road in Port Talbot and many of the country pubs along the winding main roads.

Cardiff

Splendidly situated on the banks of the River Taff, **CARDIFF** (Caerdydd) continues to evolve into a true international capital. Massive developments in recent years include the shiny new buildings housing the Welsh National Assembly and Millennium Centre for the arts on the rejuvenated Cardiff Bay waterfront, and the Millennium sports stadium smack-bang in the city centre.

Up until the nineteenth century Cardiff was an insignificant fishing village – the civic charter incorporating the city dates only from 1905. These days, Cardiff is, fittingly, becoming increasingly Welsh as more young Welsh-speakers flock to the country's buoyant capital for jobs in education, government and media. The most recent census showed that over ten percent of people in this creative and cosmopolitan city now speak *Cymraeg* – more than double the figure of forty years ago.

As well as its cultural and political profile, Cardiff has a mighty reputation, in any language, as a party town, and you need only wander around the centre on a weekend night to see the proof. With some seriously good food, drinking and dancing options, and a rapidly improving selection of accommodation, it's no surprise that Cardiff continues to be one of the fastest-growing city-break destinations in Britain.

Some history

Cardiff's origins date back to Roman times, when tribes from Isca settled in Cardiff, building a small village alongside the Roman military fort. The fort was largely uninhabited from the Romans' departure until the Norman invasion, when William the Conqueror offered Welsh land to his knights if they could subdue the local tribes. In 1093, Robert FitzHamon built a simple fort on a moated hillock that still stands today in the grounds of the castle. A town grew up in the lee of the fortress, developing into a small fishing and farming community that remained a quiet backwater until the end of the eighteenth century. The **Bute family**, lords of the manor of Cardiff, instigated new developments on their land, starting with the construction of a canal from Merthyr Tydfil (then Wales' largest town) to Cardiff in 1794. The second Marquis of Bute built the first dock in 1839, opening others in swift succession. The Butes, who owned massive swathes of the rapidly industrializing south Wales valleys, insisted that all coal and iron exports used the family docks in Cardiff, and it subsequently became one of the busiest ports in the world. By the beginning of the twentieth century, Cardiff's population had soared to 170,000 from its 1801 figure of around 1000, and the ambitious new civic centre in Cathays Park was well under way.

The twentieth century saw the city's fortunes rise, plummet and rise again. The dock trade slumped in the 1930s, and the city suffered heavy bombing in World War II, but since being created capital of Wales in 1955 – a move widely felt to be long overdue – the city's optimism and confidence have blossomed. Many government and media institutions have moved here from London, especially since the inauguration of the National Assembly in 1999, and the city's entertainment and leisure sectors are unrivalled in Wales.

Arrival, information and getting around

Cardiff international **airport** (℡01446/711111, ⒲www.cwlfly.com) is ten miles southwest of the city on the other side of Barry. The cheapest way to reach the city centre is on a shuttle bus from the main terminal to Rhoose Cardiff International Airport train station and then a connecting train (Mon–Sat hourly, Sun every 2hr; £3.70 combined ticket). Alternatively, the more convenient direct AirBus Xpress service #X91, runs at least hourly every day (£3.40) and takes you from the main terminal into the city. A **taxi** from the airport to Cardiff Central will cost around £24.

The city's main **bus station** (under reconstruction at the time of writing) is next to Cardiff Central **train station**, which handles all inter-city services (including a speedy hourly shuttle to London), as well as many suburban and Valley Line services. **Queen Street Station**, at the eastern edge of the centre, is for local services only, including those to Cardiff Bay.

Cardiff's large and efficient **tourist office** at the Old Library on The Hayes (Mon–Sat 9.30am–6pm, July & Aug until 7pm, Sun 10am–4pm; ℡08701/211258, ⒲www.visitcardiff.com) is a five-minute walk from the bus and train stations. Staff can book accommodation, provide good free maps of the city and give details of walking tours and jaunts such as open-topped sightseeing bus tours (see opposite). The tourist office stocks copies of *Buzz*, a free, occasionally ribald monthly guide to arts and events in the city. For more esoteric information, including fliers for gigs and club nights, try some of the shops in the Castle and High Street arcades (see p.115).

City transport

One of the highlights of Cardiff is that it's an easy, flat and compact city to **walk** around; even the bay area is within thirty-minutes' stroll of Central station. Out of the centre, there's an extensive and reliable **bus network** operated by the Cardiff Bus (Bws Caerdydd) company. Its **sales and information kiosk** is on Wood Street (Mon–Fri 8.30am–5.30pm, Sat 9am–4.30pm; ℡029/2066 6444). The city is divided into four colour-coded **fare zones**; fares depend on the number of zones crossed and the time you travel, ranging from £1.20 in a single zone to £1.60 across all four.

Various **travel passes** offer good savings: a **City Rider** "Day to Go" ticket (£3) gives unlimited travel around Cardiff and Penarth for a day, a range which can be extended to Barry, the Vale of Glamorgan, the Caerphilly district and Newport with the Network Rider ticket (£6.50). A "Weekly to Go" ticket (£14) is good for seven days' unlimited travel around Cardiff and Penarth; for a few pounds more you can extend the ticket further. All are available from the Cardiff Bus sales office or on board buses themselves. If you want to use local trains as well as buses, the **Capital Card** is available for one day (£4.80; after 9.30am Mon–Fri, any time Sat & Sun; buy it on the first bus or train) or one week (£16.10; available from bus office or train station only).

The **last buses** generally leave the city centre at around 11.30pm, although there are four night bus services usually operating hourly from Westgate Street

Trips and tours

You can get a good introduction to Cardiff aboard an open-top double-decker **sightseeing bus tour** (every 30min: Feb–Dec daily 10am–4pm, extended hours in summer; day-ticket £8) starting from outside the castle and carving a circuit around the city and Cardiff Bay, which allows you to hop on and off at will. Alternatively, you can take a **walking tour** operated by Cardiff Bay Tours (℡029/2070 7882, ⓦwww.cardiffbaytours.com; ring for prices and schedules). A scenic **waterbus** service (hourly; £5 return; ℡07940/142409, ⓦwww.cardiffcats.com) operates daily between Mermaid Quay, Penarth and the city centre at Taff's Mead Embankment, diagonally across from the Millennium Stadium. Depending on the river flow, it also runs to Bute Park, by Cardiff Castle. For something a little more adrenaline-fuelled, **Bay Island Voyages** (℡01446/420692; ⓦwww.bayisland .co.uk) offer various boat trips out to Flat Holm island (see p.132), plus high-octane trips in a rigid-hulled inflatable boat around the Bay. They usually have a kiosk by the Pierhead Building.

until 3.30am on Friday and Saturday nights only – the Cardiff Bus sales and information kiosk (see opposite) has current timetable information. Otherwise, you'll find **taxi** ranks at Central station, Duke Street by the castle and Queen Street station. To order a taxi, call Capital Cars (℡029/2077 7777) and Dragon Metro (℡029/2033 3333). There's cheap **bike rental** from the council campsite in Pontcanna Fields (see p.118).

Accommodation

Hotels are concentrated in the city centre and the Bay, with a well-established belt of guesthouses and hotels lining the leafy Cathedral Road, in the suburb of Pontcanna, a pleasant fifteen-minute walk northwest from the city centre. Many major chains are represented in the city – from the Holiday Inn to the Marriott, and with a new Radisson SAS on the way. In addition to the places listed below, the wonderful *The Old Post Office* restaurant (see p.131), which also has rooms, is just outside the city in nearby St Fagans.

Hotels and guesthouses in the city centre

All the following places are marked on the map on p.116.

Austin's 11 Coldstream Terrace, Riverside ℡029/2037 7148, ⓦwww.hotelcardiff.com. Basic but perfectly adequate B&B a short hop across the river from – the city centre. ❷

Barceló Cardiff Angel Hotel Castle St ℡029/2064 9200, ⓦwww.barcelo-hotels.co.uk. Much-restored Victorian bauble right opposite Cardiff Castle, with smart modern amenities. ❼

Big Sleep Hotel Bute Terrace ℡029/2063 6363, ⓦwww.thebigsleephotel.com. Surprisingly snazzy budget option in the city centre occupying a former 1960s office block turned retro-designer hotel with boxy rooms in vivid shades of blue. ❷–❸

Hilton Kingsway ℡029/2064 6300, ⓦwww.hilton .co.uk/cardiff. Five-star splendour with all the trimmings, including a lap pool and gym, bang in the city centre. ❽

Park Plaza Greyfriars Rd ℡029/2011 1111, ⓦwww.parkplaza.com. Smart, stylish, contemporary hotel in the heart of the action. ❼

Royal Hotel St Mary St ℡0870/161 0807, ⓦwww.theroyalhotelcardiff.com. A central Victorian showpiece that's been given a modernist makeover, and very successfully too. ❽

Sandringham Hotel St Mary St ℡029/2023 2161, ⓦwww.sandringham-hotel.com. Established family-run hotel, great value for money, with plain but clean decor, good service and a friendly atmosphere. ❷

Sleeperz Next to Central Station ℡0800 0439035, ⓦwww.sleeperz.com. Handy new hotel, due to open by autumn 2008, with rooms for around £65 per night.

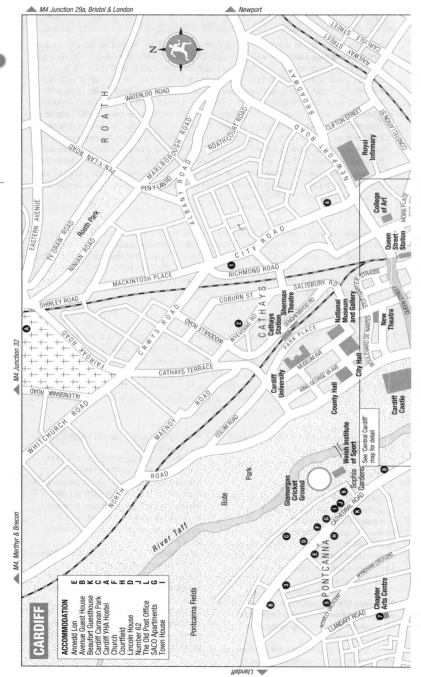

▲ M4 Junction 29a, Bristol & London

▲ Newport

N

RAILWAY STREET

CARLISLE STREET

WATERLOO ROAD

R O A T H

PEN-Y-LAN ROAD

MARLBOROUGH ROAD

ROATH COURT ROAD

CLIFTON STREET

Royal Infirmary

EASTERN AVENUE

TY-DRAW ROAD

NINIAN ROAD

Roath Park

PEN-Y-LAN RD

ALBANY ROAD

CITY ROAD

NEWPORT ROAD

CORNWALL ST

College of Art

MOIRA PLACE

Queen Street Station

MACKINTOSH PLACE

RICHMOND ROAD

1

SHIRLEY ROAD

COBURN ST

SALISBURY RD

STUTTGARTER STRASSE

QUEEN STREET

FAIROAK ROAD

ALLENSBANK ROAD

CRWYS ROAD

WOODVILLE ROAD

WYEVERNE RD

C A T H A Y S

Cathays Station

SENGHENNYDD RD

Sherman Theatre

National Museum and Gallery

BOULEVARD DE NANTES

New Theatre

2

PARK PLACE

▲ M4 Junction 32

WHITCHURCH ROAD

CATHAYS TERRACE

MAENDY ROAD

COLUM ROAD

Cardiff University

MUSEUM AVE

KING GEORGE V AVE

City Hall

County Hall

Cardiff Castle

NORTH ROAD

Bute Park

River Taff

Glamorgan Cricket Ground

Welsh Institute of Sport

Sophia Gardens

CATHEDRAL ROAD

See 'Central Cardiff' map for detail

8

A

▲ M4, Merthyr & Brecon

Pontcanna Fields

P O N T C A N N A

WYNDHAM CRESCENT

ROMILLY CRESCENT

LLANDAFF ROAD

Chapter Arts Centre

7

5

3

B

C

D

E

F

G

H

I

J

K

6

▲ Llandaff

CARDIFF

ACCOMMODATION

Anedd Lon	E
Avenue Guest House	B
Beaufort Guesthouse	K
Cardiff Caravan Park	C
Cardiff YHA Hostel	A
Church	F
Courtfield	H
Lincoln House	D
Number 62	J
The Old Post Office	L
SACO Apartments	G
Town House	I

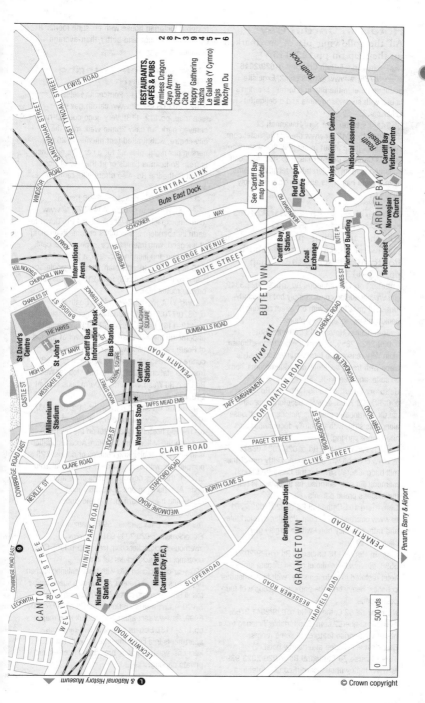

RESTAURANTS, CAFES & PUBS

Armless Dragon	2
Cayo Arms	8
Chapter	7
Cibo	3
Happy Gathering	9
Hazha	4
Le Gallois (Y Cymro)	5
Milgis	1
Mochyn Du	6

See 'Cardiff Bay' map for detail

113

© Crown copyright

Hotels in Cardiff Bay

All the following places are marked on the map on pp.122–113.

Jolyon's 5 Bute Crescent ☎029/2048 8775, ⓦwww.jolyons.co.uk. Exquisite boutique hotel in the Bay in a former seaman's house with six stylish rooms and a delightful cellar bar. **⑤–⑥**

St David's Hotel and Spa Havannah St ☎029/2045 4045, ⓦwww.thestdavidshotel.com. Looking as if it's about to set sail, this waterfront hotel is Cardiff's premier place to stay: all clean lines and elegant, understated decor. All rooms have private balconies and there's a heavenly spa. **⑧**

Hotels and guesthouses on Cathedral Road

All the following places are along Cathedral Road in the suburb of Pontcanna; see the map on pp.112–113.

Annedd Lon 157 Cathedral Rd ☎029/2022 3349, ⓦwww.anneddlon.co.uk. Simply but pleasantly furnished guesthouse with off-street parking. Bookings only accepted by phone. **②**

Avenue Guest House 163 Cathedral Rd ☎029/2023 2855, ⓦwww.theavenueguesthouse .com Very reasonable family-run Victorian-style place with fresh, tastefully decorated rooms, some en suite, and free wi-fi. **②–③**

Beaufort Guesthouse 65 Cathedral Rd ☎029/2023 7003, ⓦwww.beauforthousecardiff .co.uk. Yet another gracious Victorian guesthouse along this strip, with tastefully decorated rooms and secure parking. **④**

Church 126 Cathedral Rd ☎029/2034 0881, ⓦwww.churchtownhouse.co.uk. Fairly run-of-the-mill budget hotel, save for the Charlotte Church memorabilia – no surprise, as this place is run by the singer's proud parents. **③**

Courtfield 101 Cathedral Rd ☎029/2022 7701, ⓦwww.courtfieldhotel.com. Popular, comfortable and rather flouncy hotel with a largely gay clientele. **③**

Lincoln House 118 Cathedral Rd ☎029/2039 5558, ⓦwww.lincolnhotel.co.uk. Elegant small hotel restored in Victorian style, with button-leather couches, heavy brocade and even a couple of four-poster beds. **⑤**

Number 62 62 Cathedral Rd ☎029/2041 2765, ⓦwww.number62.com. Comfortable Victorian town house with period features in some rooms. Breakfast is included at a nearby hotel. **④**

Town House 70 Cathedral Rd ☎029/2023 9399, ⓦwww.thetownhousecardiff.co.uk. Hotel in a restored Victorian house with en-suite rooms, a comfortable lounge and better-than-average facilities. **④**

Hostels, self-catering and camping

Cardiff Caravan Park Pontcanna Fields ☎029/2039 8362, ⓦwww.cardiff.gov.uk (see map, pp.112–113). Very good council-run caravan park, an easy 25min walk from the city centre, with limited tent pitches at £5 per person per night, plus £3 for a car. The entrance is from Pontcanna Fields or at the end of Dogo St, off Cathedral Rd. Also offers bike rental to anyone.

Cardiff Backpacker 96–98 Neville St, Riverside ☎029/2034 5577, ⓦwww .cardiffbackpacker.com (see map, p.116). Down-to-earth independent hostel that's become something of a legend, with internet access, pool table, café, bar, kitchen and laundry facilities, a fab rooftop BBQ terrace and friendly staff. Bunks in single-sex and mixed dorms (max 8) from £18.50, plus some private rooms (**①**).

Cardiff YHA Hostel 2 Wedal Rd, Roath Park ☎0870/770 5750, ⓔcardiff@yha.org.uk (see map, pp.112–113). Large, purpose-built building just underneath the A48 Eastern Ave flyover at the top of Roath Park, almost two miles from the city centre and reachable via bus #28, #29 or #29B from the station (get off at the bus stop for Wedal Rd/Lake Rd West). No curfew. Dorm beds start at £10, including breakfast.

Nos Da 53–59 Despenser St ☎029/2037 8866, ⓦwww.nosda.co.uk (see map, p.116). Hip hostel/budget hotel on the riverbank opposite the Millennium Stadium. Accommodation is in en-suite singles and doubles or dorms (£25 per person), with avant-garde decor like outsized artwork that flips down and transforms into beds. Also home to one of Cardiff's most happening bars, *Tafarn* (p.127) and clubs, *Tafod* (p.128). **②**

Riverhouse Backpackers 59 Fitzhamon Embankment ☎029/2039 9810, ⓦwww .riverhousebackpackers.com (see map, p.116). Cosy, contemporary backpackers set in a 120-year-old Victorian villa with a self-catering kitchen, airy dorms and twin rooms, as well as a sunny wraparound BBQ deck and cheap bike rental. **①**

SACO Apartments 76 Cathedral Rd ☎011/7970 6999, ⓦwww.sacoapartments.co.uk (see map, pp.112–113). Elegant one- and two-bedroom apartments in a large town house with full kitchens, washer/dryers, broadband internet and private parking. **④–⑥**

University of Wales Cardiff Cathays
ⓣ029/2087 4702, ⓔgroupaccom@cardiff.ac.uk
(see map, pp.112–113). Thousands of single, en-suite student rooms near the city centre are available from June – Sept on a B&B or self-catering basis. A good, cheap option. ❶

The City

Cardiff's sights are clustered around fairly small, distinct districts. Easily navigable on foot, the **commercial centre** is bounded by the River Taff – source of the nickname of generations of expatriate Welsh – on the western side. The Taff flows past the high stone walls of Cardiff's **castle** and the **Millennium Stadium**. Near the southeastern tip of the castle walls is Cardiff's main crossroads, where the great Edwardian shopping boulevards Queen Street and High Street conceal a world of arcades, great stores and run-of-the-mill malls. North of the castle, a series of white Edwardian buildings is home to the **National Museum and Gallery**, **City Hall** and **Cardiff University**.

A mile south of the commercial centre is **Cardiff Bay**, revitalized since the construction of a barrage to form a vast freshwater lake, home to the **National Assembly** and **Wales Millennium Centre**, as well as trendsetting bars and eateries.

Two miles northwest of the city centre above the banks of the Taff, the village-like suburb of **Llandaff** is built around the city's patchwork **cathedral**.

The commercial centre

Between Central station and Castle Street is the building that dominates the city from all angles: the **Millennium Stadium** (daily tours, subject to events, hourly Mon–Sat 10am–5pm, Sun 10am–4pm,; ⓣ029/2082 2228, ⓦwww .millenniumstadium.com; £6.50). Shoehorned so tightly into its Taff-side site that the surrounding walkways had to be cantilevered out over the river, this 74,500-seat giant has become an iconic symbol not only of Cardiff, but of Wales as a whole. The location was once occupied by the legendary Cardiff Arms Park, and though the old terraces and the famous name have now gone, the turf is still the home of Welsh rugby, and when Wales have a home match – particularly against old enemy England – the stadium and surrounding streets are charged with good-natured, beery fervour. The stadium is also used for Wales' international football matches and for a host of huge rock gigs and other musical spectaculars. Stadium tours start from the **shop** at Entrance Gate 3 on Westgate Street and take you into the players' tunnel, dressing rooms, VIP areas and the on-site rugby museum. The stadium's **ticket office** is at 98 St Mary St (ⓣ08705/582582).

Running up from Central station to the castle walls is **St Mary Street**, one of the city's grandest boulevards of ornate Victorian and Edwardian shop frontages. Accessed from St Mary Street is the hip new **Brewery Quarter**, the site of the old Brains Brewery, which has been converted into a bar and restaurant complex (primarily chains), retaining the original vaults and the old clock tower, fronted by its flagship real-ale pub, *The Yard*.

St Mary Street leads north to become the **High Street**, where, at no.18, you'll find the **TSO Bookshop** (Mon–Sat 9am–5.30pm), a good stockist of Welsh-interest publications, maps and travel paraphernalia. Off the High Street is the elegant Victorian **indoor market**, **Cardiff Market**, great for fresh food and specialist bric-a-brac stalls. Along both streets, renovated Edwardian arcades, with some of the city centre's most interesting shops inside, lead off between the buildings. Of these, **High Street** and **Castle arcades**, at the top of High Street, are the most rewarding, packed with great club clothes shops,

CENTRAL CARDIFF

0   200 yds

RESTAURANTS, CAFÉS & PUBS

Bar Europa	2
Café Minuet	3
City Arms	9
The Cottage	15
Dorothy's	18
Ha-ha Bar	1
IO Feet Tall	12
Juboraj II	21
La Brasserie	13
Las Iguanas	20
Louis Restaurant	11
Madeira	6
Old Arcade	5
The Plan	14
Porto's	10
Queen's Vaults	8
Servini's	17
Tafarn	F
Topo Gigio	4
Walkabout	19
The Yard	16
Zero Degrees	7

ARCADES

Andrew's	aa
Castle	dd
Dominions	bb
Duke Street	cc
High Street	ee
Morgan	ff
Royal	gg
Wyndham	hh

ACCOMMODATION

Austin's	C
Barceló Cardiff Angel Hotel	D
Big Sleep Hotel	J
Cardiff Backpacker	G
Hilton	B
Nos Da	F
Park Plaza	A
Riverhouse Backpackers	H
Royal Hotel	I
Sandringham Hotel	E

University

Queen St Station

Cardiff International Arena

Capitol Shopping Centre

New Theatre

Central Library

Cineworld Multiplex

St David's 2 Centre

St David's Centre and Hall

Spillers Records

St John's Church

Old Library

Cardiff Market

TSO Bookshop

Cardiff Bus Information Kiosk

Bus and Coach Station

Central Station

Castle

Bute Park

Cardiff Rugby Club

Millennium Stadium

Multiplex & Jongleurs Comedy Club

River Taff

★ Waterbus Stop

Roads / labels:
FITZALAN PLACE, NEWPORT ROAD, KNOX ROAD, FITZALAN ROAD, ADAM STREET, STATION TERRACE, DUMFRIES PLACE, WINDSOR PLACE, PARK LANE, PARK PLACE, STUTTGARTER STRASSE, CROCKHERBTOWN LANE, CHURCHILL WAY, DAVID ST, MARY ANN STREET, BUTE TERRACE, BUTE STREET, CUSTOM HOUSE ST, PENARTH RD, HERBERT STREET, TYNDALL STREET, CENTRAL LINK, Bute Dock East, SANDON STREET, BRADFORD ST, CHARLES STREET, QUEEN STREET, CHURCH STREET, WORKING STREET, TRINITY ST, ST JOHN STREET, ST MARY STREET, THE HAYES, HILLS STREET, BAKERS ROW, BREWERY QUARTER, CAROLINE STREET, MILL LANE, WOOD STREET, PARK STREET, GREYFRIARS ROAD, GREYFRIARS PLACE, THE FRIARY, KINGSWAY, BOULEVARD DE NANTES, DUKE ST, CASTLE STREET, HIGH STREET, WESTGATE STREET, WOMANBY ST, QUAY ST, GOLATE, TUDOR STREET, FITZHAMON EMBANKMENT, COLDSTREAM TERRACE, PLANTAGENET STREET, DESPENSER STREET, MARK STREET, BROOK STREET, QUEEN STREET, CLARE ROAD, CARDIFF BRIDGE

▲ Cathays Park & Civic Centre
▲ Cardiff Bay
▼ Cathedral Road & Llandaff

N

© Crown copyright

quirky gift shops, fab little coffee houses and a range of esoteric emporia where you can pick up fliers for clubs and events.

Further down the High Street towards Central station, the glorious **Morgan Arcade**, with original 1896 detailing and Venetian windows, and its near neighbour, the **Royal Arcade**, run east to the bottom of **The Hayes**, a pedestrianized street of disparate restaurants and some great pubs. Bridge Street runs away to the east and into the elegant Regency part of the city centre around David and Charles streets. Slicing off south from The Hayes, opposite the *Marriott* hotel, is Mill Lane, Cardiff's colourful **café quarter**. A few paces north along The Hayes is the legendary **Spillers Records**, at 36 The Hayes, which was founded in 1894, making it the world's oldest record shop; you can easily spend a few hours browsing amongst its hard-to-find tracks of all genres including loads of local releases.

The Hayes leads north to the beautifully colonnaded frontage of the **Old Library**, home to the city's tourist office (see p.110). North of here is the fifteenth-century grey limestone parish **church of St John**. Its most notable feature – the slender tower – is difficult to appreciate with the cluster of buildings around it, although the light and graceful interior is worth seeing, especially for the floridly pompous altar in the south aisle by prolific Victorian sculptor, Goscombe John. The right turn at the Old Library is **Working Street**, a very busy shopping area, especially around the entrances to the **St David's Hall** complex (incorporating a central concert and entertainment venue), the gargantuan **St David's Centre**, with extensive work underway at the time of writing on the huge **St David's 2**, with 180 shops as well as apartments and Cardiff's new **Central Library**. Between them, the developments have succeeded in obliterating a huge section of the old city centre, but the activity and increasing number of apartments – and hence local residents – adds to the area's dynamism.

On the north side of the St David's Hall and Centre, **Queen Street** is Cardiff's most impressive shopping thoroughfare, now pedestrianized and with many of its fine nineteenth-century buildings spruced up, albeit they've now been effaced by the chain-store frontages typical of a British shopping street. That said, Queen Street is usually dependable for buskers and street theatre, making it a very easy place to while away a few hours. At the western end of the street, a statue of **Aneurin Bevan**, postwar Labour politician and classic Welsh firebrand, stands aloof from the bustle.

Cardiff Castle

The geographical and historical heart of the city is **Cardiff Castle** (daily: March–Oct 9am–6pm; Nov–Feb 9.30am–5pm; £8.95), an intriguing hotchpotch of remnants of the city's past. The fortress hides inside a vast walled yard, each side measuring well over 200 yards long and corresponding roughly to the outline of the original fort built by the Romans. A few dozen yards of **Roman wall**, the sole reminder of their presence, has been unearthed to the immediate right of the entrance in the thirteenth-century Black Tower on Castle Street, and is now lit and labelled, along with some excellent three-dimensional murals depicting life in a Roman fort. Tucked into the southeastern corner wall beyond the Roman segment are the dry **regimental museums** of the Queen's Dragoon Guards and the Welsh Regiment, filled with a starchy collection of military memorabilia. From here, walkways lead along the **battlements**, giving excellent views over the city. The castle's interior can only be seen on a guided tour; the admission price also includes a self-guided audio tour of the grounds.

Occupying the northwestern corner of the castle grounds is a neat Norman motte crowned with the eleventh-century **keep**, with views down onto the turrets and towers of the **domestic buildings**, dating in part from the fourteenth and fifteenth centuries, but much extended in Tudor times, when residential needs began to overtake military safety in terms of priority. Ultimately, it was the third Marquis of Bute (1847–1900), one of the richest men on the globe, who lavished a fortune on upgrading his pile, commissioning architect and decorator William Burges (1827–81) to aid him. With their passion for the religious art and the symbolism of the Middle Ages, they systematically overhauled the buildings, adding a spire to the octagonal tower and erecting a clock tower; but it was inside that their imaginations ran free, and they radically transformed the crumbling interiors into palaces of vivid colour and intricate design.

The tour starts in the square-cornered **clock tower**, running through the **Winter Smoking Room** at the bottom, up to the **Bachelor's Bedroom** and bathroom and, above that, the **Summer Smoking Room**. All are decorated in rich patterns of gold, maroon and cobalt, with many of the images culled from medieval myths and beliefs. From here, the tour goes through the 1878 **Nursery**, with hand-painted tiles and silhouette lanterns depicting contemporary nursery rhymes, the 1881 **Arab Room**, decorated by imported craftsmen, and into the grand **Banqueting Hall**, which dates orginally from 1428, but was transformed by Bute and Burges with the installation of a riotously kitsch fireplace. In all the rooms, fantastically rich trimmings complement the gaudy style so beloved of two nineteenth-century eccentrics, and it's worth remembering that, as one of over sixty residences owned by the Butes in Britain alone, Cardiff was only lived in for six weeks of the year.

The last point of note in Cardiff Castle can only be seen from outside the precincts. The **Animal Wall**, where stone creatures are frozen in impudent poses, was another tongue-in-cheek nineteenth-century creation, running all along the route of Castle Street west to the river bridge.

Bute Park to Pontcanna Fields

Immediately west of Cardiff Castle lies **Bute Park**, once the private estate of the castle, and now containing an **arboretum**, superb flowerbeds, a stone circle, the remains of an old priory and some pleasant walks along the Taff banks. The main road crosses over the river at Cardiff Bridge, with a right turn leading up into the coolly formal **Sophia Gardens**. A quarter of a mile along the river is the multipurpose **Welsh Institute of Sport**, the national sports centre. Beyond this is the stadium of Wales' sole first-class cricket team, Glamorgan, and the less formal open spaces of **Pontcanna Fields**, which lead along the Taff for a couple of miles to the suburb of Llandaff (see p.124).

Cathays Park and the civic centre

On the north side of the city centre, only a hundred yards from the north-eastern wall of the castle precinct, is the area known most commonly as **Cathays Park**. The park itself forms the centrepiece for the impressive Edwardian buildings of the **civic centre** – the area containing the County Hall, City Hall, National Museum and Cardiff University – although the name Cathays Park is generally used for the whole complex. Dating from the first couple of decades of the twentieth century, the gleaming white buildings arranged with pompous Edwardian precision speak volumes about Cardiff's self-confidence, a full half-century before it was officially declared capital of Wales. Fronting the complex on the city-centre side is the busy **Boulevard de**

Nantes, named after Cardiff's twin city in France. The two cities not only share a riverside setting and creative bent, but close Celtic affiliations too (until WWII Nantes was the capital of Brittany, and retains a strong Breton spirit).

The centrepiece of the civic centre is the magnificent, domed, dragon-topped **City Hall** (1905), an exercise in ostentatious civic self-glory that is open to the public in normal office hours. Note the Peace sculpture in the main entrance lobby as you go in: it depicts one of the women who marched from Cardiff in 1981 to establish the Greenham Common peace camp. The ornate interior is a riot of finery that reaches a peak in the particularly showy first-floor Marble Hall: all Sienese marble columns and statues of Welsh heroes. Amongst the figures are twelfth-century chronicler Giraldus Cambrensis, thirteenth-century native prince of Wales, Llywelyn ap Gruffydd, fifteenth-century national insurgent and perpetual hero, Owain Glyndŵr, Welsh king Henry Tudor and tenth-century architect of Wales' progressive codified laws, Hywel Dda (Howell the Good). Overseeing them all is the figure of Dewi Sant himself – the national patron saint, St David. Also in the hall is a syrupy triple portrait of the late Diana, Princess of Wales, and there are numerous other works of art throughout the building.

The low-key **Law Courts** (1906) stand to the left of the City Hall, with the **National Museum and Gallery** (see below) balancing the view on the right-hand side. Behind them, two ruler-straight boulevards, evidently designed with ceremonial splendour in mind, run through the rest of the civic centre, arranged in symmetrical precision around **Alexandra Gardens** in the middle. At the very centre of the park is the colonnaded circular **National War Memorial** (1928), a popular and surprisingly quiet place to sit and contemplate the rush of civic and governmental duty all around. At the north end of the western boulevard, **King Edward VII Avenue**, is the **Temple of Peace** (1938), dedicated just before the outbreak of World War II to Welsh men and women the world over who were fighting for peace and relief of poverty. The eastern road, **Museum Avenue**, runs past an assortment of buildings belonging to Cardiff University.

To the northeast of Cathays, **Albany Road** is great for a wander to check out its charity and one-off speciality shops selling everything from African beads to vintage vinyl – take bus #52 or #53.

National Museum and Gallery

The **National Museum and Gallery** (Tues–Sun 10am–5pm; free, audioguide £2.50) is one of Britain's finest. Housed in a massive domed Portland-stone building that was constructed in sections from 1912 through to 1992, it attempts to tell the story of Wales and reflect the nation's place in the wider, international sphere.

The most obvious crowd-pleaser, starting on the ground floor, is the epic **Evolution of Wales** gallery, a natural history exhibition packed with high-tech gizmos and a staggering amount of information. It starts with a stirring large-screen video presentation, *Dyma Gymru* (This is Wales), full of stunning aerial footage taken over mountains, waterfalls and other natural Welsh wonders. It then goes on to explain, through fossils, rocks and footage of volcanoes, earthquakes and the galaxies, the slow beginnings of life on earth. Dinosaurs and the early mammals get a good look in, such as a terrific Tyrannosaurus rex skull.

The environmental education continues in the adjacent **Natural History** galleries, with a magnificent collection of sparkling crystals, re-creations of assorted environments – mountain, wetland, seashore, dunes – and some great interactive technology and interpretive boards. It then heads upstairs with a display entitled "Man and the Environment", featuring numerous animals and their habitats, and culminates in the world's largest leatherback turtle, caught off Harlech in 1988. Displays looking at the effect of mankind on our changing environment complete the section.

The first floor also houses the excellent **archeology galleries**, whose treasures include intricate gold torques from the Bronze Age and the dazzling **Caergwrle Bowl**, a gold votive container in the shape of a boat that's more than 3000 years old. Leading off is an unusually interesting **coin** collection, with some good panels on the history of Welsh and British minting, and the **Tregwynt Treasure Trove**, found near Fishguard in 1996: an impressive cache of gold and silver coins dating back to the Civil War. At the back, there's an inspirational collection of 23 stones and 14 casts, spanning the earliest carved fragments (around the fifth century), through Celtic and early Christian standing stones to the more elaborate examples of the early medieval age.

The art collections

The "Evolution of Wales" and natural history galleries occupy the entire western and central flank of the ground and first floors. The eastern side of the building is home to the **art galleries**. Galleries One to Ten examine Wales' artistic heritage, starting with a marble altar from the first century BC and taking in works from the medieval Renaissance, including some stunning pieces from the studios of Botticelli and El Greco. There's a strong collection from the **eighteenth-century** British and Italian schools, rich in the work of Wright, Gainsborough and Reynolds. This era was perhaps the heyday of Welsh art, and the three main protagonists – Richard Wilson, William E. Parry and Thomas Jones – are well represented. Wilson's skill in capturing Wales' unique light can be seen to lustrous effect in his studies of castles at Caernarfon, Dolbadarn and Pembroke, as well as more emotionally intense pieces such as the beautiful *Pistyll Cain*. One of Wilson's protégés, William Hodges, also makes an appearance, most notably in his gentle evocation of *Llanthony Priory*.

Scattered throughout the first ten rooms is an intriguing, eclectic ragbag of British art of the last 150 years: Frank Brangwyn's teeming canvases, a typically rich and detailed collection of Pre-Raphaelites, and an astonishingly gaudy gold, silver and enamel table centrepiece given by the people of Wales to the Duke and Duchess of York (later King George V and Queen Mary) for their wedding in 1893. Welsh painters are well highlighted: you'll find cool, blanched portraits by Gwen John, and her brother Augustus' measured, intensely poetic depictions of Dylan Thomas and Newport "supertramp" W.H. Davies. There's also a superb, and growing, collection of **ceramics**, one of Wales' most prolific areas of applied art.

But the most exciting art works are contained in Galleries Eleven through Fifteen, kicking off with a fabulous **sculpture** collection, including many by the celebrated one-man Welsh Victorian statue industry, Goscombe John. Far better here than on the dreary municipal plinths they usually adorn, his male studies verge on the homoerotic and his female forms are exquisite.

Mesmerizing pieces by Rodin pepper the building, particularly in Gallery Twelve, where a copy of *The Kiss* and his original *Eve* share space with the watery landscapes of Boudin, Renoir's coquettish *The Parisienne*, and numerous works by Manet, including the intricately observed *Effect of Snow at Petit Montrouge*.

Gallery Thirteen houses what is arguably the museum's strongest suit, its collection of **Impressionists**, the bequest of two local wealthy sisters, Margaret and Gwendoline Davies. The sisters' favourite was Cézanne, whose work features alongside artists such as Sisley (including his view of Penarth), Carnière,

Degas and Pissarro. Van Gogh's stunning *Rain at Anvers* – angry slashes of rain run right across the otherwise harmonious canvas – was painted just weeks before his suicide. Gallery Fourteen includes Postimpressionists, Futurists and Surrealists such as Magritte, Sickert, Sylvia Gosse, Harold Gilman's colourful London scenes and studies by Edward Morland Lewis, including a bold depiction of *The Strand, Laugharne*. Finally, Gallery Fifteen houses a hearty collection of British **abstractionism**, with a strong Welsh bent. Highlights include some stunning and wild pieces by Welsh supremo Ceri Richards, Evan Walters' piercing 1936 portrait of a *Welsh Miner*, Josef Herman's rousing *Miners Singing* and Kyffin Williams' brooding Welsh skies and jagged landscapes. Some sculpted pieces, including some fine works by Henry Moore, among them *Upright Motif*, and Barbara Hepworth's haunting *Oval Sculpture*, complete the room.

Cardiff Bay

The most relaxing way to reach **Cardiff Bay** is by waterbus (every hour from Bute Park and Taff's Mead Embankment), train (every 15min from Queen Street station) or bus (#2, #6, #7, #8 or #35, #36 from outside Central station). Alternatively, it's an easy half-hour stroll from the city centre from Callaghan Square, just southeast of Central station via Bute Street, or, across the railway tracks, the new "ceremonial boulevard", **Lloyd George Avenue**.

In years gone by, when the docks were some of the busiest in the world, the area was better known by its evocative name of **Tiger Bay**, one that was immortalized by locally born chanteuse Shirley Bassey. The Bay area comprises three distinct parts: the swanky civic precincts around the glorious **Wales Millennium Centre**, on the eastern side of the water, the all-new, shiny **millennium waterfront** to the west, including the retail and leisure complex known as **Mermaid Quay**, and, set back from the water's edge, the increasingly gentrified Taff-side suburb of **Butetown**.

Cardiff Bay has become one of the world's biggest regeneration projects, aiming to transform the downbeat dereliction of the old docks into a designer heaven. Although it is still consolidating a life beyond the shifts of the office workers who are the main users of its bars and restaurants, it is deservedly a must-see part of any Cardiff tour.

The Wales Millennium Centre and surroundings

From Cardiff Bay station, turn left and head down towards the vast open space known as **Roald Dahls Plass**, named after the Cardiff-born children's author (1916–1990) best known for his 1964 classic, *Charlie and the Chocolate Factory*. Dominating the square is the mesmerizing new **Wales Millennium Centre** (WMC; ☎08700/402000, ⓦwww.wmc.org.uk), a vibrant performance space for theatre and music, and the resident home to many of Wales' premier arts organizations. Likened by critics to a copper-plated armadillo or aardvark, or a great snail, the WMC soars over the Bay rooftops, its exterior swathed in numerous Welsh building materials, including different slates, wood and stone, topped with a stainless steel shell tinted with a bronze oxide to resist salty air.

Pause before entering to mull over the inspirational bilingual inscription writ large across the frontage in seven-foot-high letter windows. Crafted by poet Gwyneth Lewis, the phrases read downwards – in English "In these stones, horizons sing" and in Welsh "Creu gwir fel gwydr, o ffwrnais awen" ("Creating truth like glass, from the furnace of inspiration") – but, ingeniously, they also read across each line, in two languages, and still make crystal-clear poetry.

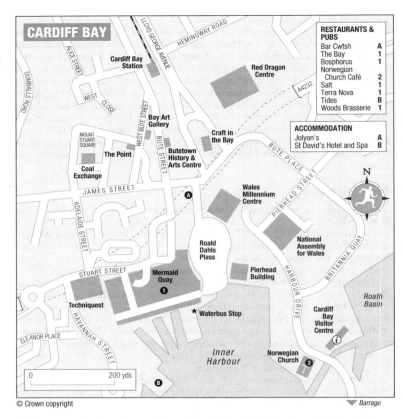

The grace and style continue throughout the interior, fashioned from materials that hark back to Wales' mineral-extracting past, from the native oak, ash, beech, sycamore, alder, birch, chestnut and cherry woods to the riveted steel and coal-like pillars. It all makes for a supremely tactile visit.

The ground floor houses the main box office, a deftly interactive exhibition about the centre, plus music shop, souvenir shop, bar and brasserie. Upstairs there's a champagne bar and entrances into the main auditorium, the acoustically sensational Donald Gordon Theatre. The best way to see all this, and other parts of the building that you won't see otherwise, is to take a **guided tour** (daily 11am & 2pm; it's best to pre-book on ☏08700/402000; £5.50). Daily **free performances** of anything from poetry to hip-hop take place in the WMC foyer, usually at lunchtime and 6pm.

At the far end of the square, down by the water's edge, is the magnificent red-brick **Pierhead Building**, which has beckoned ships into Cardiff port since its construction in 1896. A typically ornate neo-Gothic terracotta pile, it was built for the Bute Dock Company and perfectly embodies the wealth and optimism of the Bute family and their docks. It now houses a surprisingly enjoyable **exhibition** (Mon–Fri 9.30am–4.30pm, Sat & Sun 10.30am–4.30pm; free) about the workings of the nearby **National Assembly for Wales**, a striking building designed by Richard Rogers (he of Paris's Pompidou Centre fame).

Harbour Drive leads down from the Assembly building towards the startling **Cardiff Bay Visitor Centre** (Mon–Sat 9.30am–6pm, Sun 10.30am–6pm; Oct–April closes 5pm; ☎029/2046 3833), a giant tubular eye peering out over the bay. In front of the Visitor Centre is the gleaming white **Norwegian church** (Mon–Fri 10am–5pm, Sat & Sun 10am–6pm; opening hours can vary depending on special events; ☎029/2045 4899 for events), an old seamen's chapel, in which Roald Dahl – whose parents were Norwegian – was christened and which has now been converted into a charming café (see p.126) and performance and exhibition space.

Central to the whole Bay project is the kilometre-long **Cardiff Bay Barrage** (daily: April–Oct 8am–8pm; Nov–March 8am–4pm; free), built right across the Ely and Taff estuaries, which transformed a vast mud flat into a freshwater lake and created eight miles of useful waterfront. Despite its controversies, the barrage is a phenomenal bit of engineering, and it's well worth having a wander along the embankment to see the lock gates, sluices, fish path and stunning views. If mobility is a problem or you're with kids, take the daft little **road train** (daily 11am–4pm; £3) across the barrage, leaving hourly from Stuart Street, near Techniquest (see below) or join one of the **tours** detailed on p.111.

The Mermaid Quay district

Continuing west along the waterfront from the Pierhead brings you straight into **Mermaid Quay**, an airy jumble of shops, bars and restaurants that on a warm day is a fine place to hang out and watch the world amble by. The city's **waterbuses** (see p.111) leave from here, and information boards carry details of a variety of boat-rental opportunities to get you out onto the water.

Further west around the waterfront, the metal-and-glass-crowned **Techniquest**, on Stuart Street (Mon–Fri 9.30am–4.30pm, Sat & Sun 10.30am–5pm; £6.90), is one of the largest and most impressive hands-on science museums in the UK,

▲ Millennium Centre, Cardiff

packed full of exhibits, experiments and numerous chances to play like a five-year-old. It also includes a planetarium (£1.20) and science theatre.

Jutting out over the water like an ocean-going liner, the five-star **St David's Hotel** (see p.114) acts as a stylish full stop to the sweep of the bay. From its car park, a path leads a couple of hundred yards to an eight-hectare **wetland reserve**, created partly to help offset the loss of wading-bird habitats when the barrage was built and the Bay flooded. It's a surreally peaceful spot in which to have a picnic or just stop and let the world go by for a while.

Butetown

The area immediately inland from the Bay is the salty old district of **Butetown**, whose inner-city dereliction still peeps through the rampant gentrification that has taken place here over the past couple of decades. James Street, a block north of Techniquest, is the main commercial focus, while to its north are the cleaned-up old buildings around **Mount Stuart Square**. Many of these are trendy offices and bars now, but the most impressive is the mammoth **Coal Exchange Building** (☎029/2049 4917, ⊛www.coalexchange.co.uk). Built in the 1880s as Britain's central Coal Exchange, the building saw the world's first £1 million cheque signed in 1908 and is now used for conferences, exhibitions and concerts (though it was closed at the time of writing for renovations; check the website for latest updates). Close by, on the corner of West Bute Street, the old church of St Stephen has been converted into **The Point**, a superb venue for music and, occasionally, drama (see p.129).

A block further east is **Bute Street**, where the community-based **Butetown History & Arts Centre** at 5 Dock Chambers (gallery and shop Tues–Fri 10am–5pm, Sat & Sun 11am–4.30pm; ☎029/2025 6757, ⊛www.bhac.org) aims to record and celebrate the remarkable multicultural pedigree of a district that is home, for example, to one of the oldest black communities in Britain; to that end, the centre mounts exhibitions, offers guided tours and maintains a growing archive.

A few paces up the street at no. 54b, the cool, contemporary **Bay Art** gallery (Tues–Sat noon to 5pm; free) has a varied programme of exhibitions. Even more impressive is **Craft in the Bay** (daily 10.30am–5.30pm; free), an old maritime warehouse now marooned rather stylishly in the middle of the new Lloyd George Avenue, one block further east. Craft practitioners from all over Wales exhibit here, and there's a cute café. Across the road, the sweeping roofline and glass-brick curtain wall of the **Red Dragon Centre** (formerly Atlantic Wharf) make a striking front for what is essentially a big box filled with a twelve-screen multiplex, bowling alley, bars and restaurants. From here it's just a short hop across the road back to Cardiff Bay train station.

Llandaff

A small, quiet ecclesiastical village, **Llandaff** (bus #33 or #33A) lies two miles northwest of the city centre along Cathedral Road. The church that has now grown up into the city's **cathedral** is believed to have been founded in the sixth century by St Teilo, but was rebuilt in Norman style from 1120 well into the thirteenth century. From the late fourteenth century, the cathedral fell into disrepair, hurried along by the adverse attention of Cromwell's soldiers during the Civil War. In the early eighteenth century, one of the twin towers and the nave roof collapsed. Restoration only began in earnest in the early 1840s, and Pre-Raphaelite artists such as Edward Burne-Jones, Dante Gabriel Rossetti and the stained-glass firm of William Morris were commissioned to provide colourful new windows and decorative panels. In January 1941, a German landmine destroyed whole sections of it, but faithful and painstaking restoration was finally completed in 1960.

The fusion of different styles and ages is evident from outside, especially in the mismatched western towers. The northwest tower is by Jasper Tudor, a largely fifteenth-century work with modern embellishments, whilst the adjoining tower and spire were rebuilt from nineteenth-century designs.

Inside, Jacob Epstein's overwhelming *Christ in Majesty* sculpture, a concrete parabola topped with a circular organ case on which sits a soaring Christ figure, was the only entirely new feature added in the postwar reconstruction, and dominates the nave today. At the west end of the north aisle, the **St Illtyd Chapel** features Rossetti's cloying triptych *The Seed of David*, whose figures – David the shepherd boy, David the King and the Virgin Mary – are modelled on Rossetti's Pre-Raphaelite friends. Along a little further, in the south presbytery, is the tenth-century Celtic cross that is the cathedral's only pre-Norman survivor.

At the far end of the cathedral is the elegantly vaulted and beautifully painted **Lady Chapel**, notable for its gaudy fifteenth-century reredos on the back wall that contains, surrounded by golden twigs and blackthorn in each niche, bronze panels with named flowers (in Welsh) in honour of Our Lady. Over two dozen flowers take their Welsh names from the Virgin Mary.

While you're here, it's worth having a quick look at the medieval **walled garden** (open access; free) of the Llandaff Bishops' Palace on the Cathedral Green. With herbaceous plants planted according to medieval patterns, it makes a pleasant – and fragrant – place to sit for a few minutes.

Eating

The city's long-standing internationalism, particularly its Italian influence, has paid handsome dividends in its range of **restaurants** and **cafés**. Most places are within easy walking distance of the city centre, with a particular concentration in the "Café Quarter" around Mill Lane. There are also good options in the cheaper corners of Cathays and Roath (especially the curry houses along Crwys, Albany and City roads), north of the centre, while a mile west of the centre, the arty inner suburb of Canton is home to some great Indian restaurants. The redeveloped Cardiff Bay is home to increasing numbers of showpiece bars and restaurants. Note that we've only listed telephone numbers for places where a reservation is recommended.

For bargain **takeaways** in the city centre until the wee hours, your best bet is Caroline Street (aka "Chippy Lane" or "Chippy Alley"), between St Mary Street and the bottom of The Hayes (watch out when it's raining, as the grease makes the street seriously slippery). If you're packing a **picnic**, head for the **Riverside Farmers' Market**, opposite the Millennium Stadium on Fitzhamon Embankment (Sun 10am–2pm), which has great artisan produce.

City centre

All these places are marked on the map on p.116.

Café Minuet Castle Arcade ☎029/2034 1794. Cheap, tiny and delightfully odd restaurant specializing in hearty, authentic Italian regional cooking.

Dorothy's Caroline St. The best-loved of the chippies on "Chippy Lane" and an essential last stop on many a night out in Cardiff.

Juboraj II 10 Mill Lane ☎029/2045 5123. One of Cardiff's best Indian and Bangladeshi restaurants, and still moderately priced. Closed Sun.

La Brasserie 60 St Mary St ☎029/2023 4134. Popular and lively French eatery that does very tasty food and can be huge fun.

Las Iguanas 8 Mill Lane ☎029/2022 6373. Lively and enjoyable Mexican restaurant in the heart of the café quarter, with fair-priced portions of well-cooked classics.

Louis' Restaurant 32 St Mary St. Wondrously old-fashioned restaurant, serving great heapings of well-cooked, good-value traditional British comfort food, served until around 7.30pm.

Madeira 2 Guildford Crescent, off Churchill Way ☏029/2066 7705. Enjoyable Portuguese restaurant, great for skewers of meat and other carnivorous delights. Particularly good value for the set lunch menu.

The Plan 28–29 Morgan Arcade. Good for veggie café specials and a range of coffees.

Porto's 40 St Mary St ☏029/2022 0060. Authentic Portuguese restaurant in a dark wood-beamed room, serving massive portions of traditional favourites from endless variations on dried cod to the Madeiran speciality, *espetada*: skewers of tender chargrilled meat or fish doused with garlic butter.

Servini's Wyndham Arcade, off Mill Lane. Tasty sandwiches and salads to take away or eat in.

Topo Gigio 12 Church St, ☏029/2034 4300. Mid-range, ever-popular Italian eatery that throws in a few canny Welsh influences.

Cardiff Bay

All these places are marked on the map on p.122.

The Bay Mermaid Quay ☏029/2048 3388. Offers a good roll call of Thai and Cantonese classics with great-value set dinners. Surprisingly inexpensive, given the location.

Bosphorus Mermaid Quay ☏029/2048 7477. Elegantly styled Turkish restaurant on a pier in the harbour with generous portions, though often let down by poor service. Bookings essential.

Norwegian Church Café Harbour Drive. Cosy spot for Norwegian open sandwiches, salads, scrumptious cakes and good coffee.

Tides *St David's Hotel* ☏029/2045 4045. Elegant, expensive modern British dining with wonderful Cardiff Bay views and imaginative, superbly prepared dishes: try the seared scallops with a

sweet chilli dressing or the Brecon venison with glazed apples and juniper sauce.

Woods Brasserie Stuart St ☏029/2049 2400. One of Cardiff's most stylish and pricey establishments where you'll definitely need to book in advance to sample delicacies such as foie gras parfait, sea bass with egg tagliatelle, or saddle of venison in bitter chocolate sauce. Lunches are a good bet if you're watching your budget.

Out from the centre

All these places are marked on the map on pp.112–113.

Armless Dragon 97 Wyeverne Rd, Cathays ☏029/2038 2357. Unusual and enjoyable place, with an inspired range of Welsh dishes, generally served with a delicious twist. Moderate to expensive prices. Best to book.

Cibo 83 Pontcanna St, off Cathedral Rd ☏029/2023 2226. Small, moderately priced and tremendously busy but always welcoming trattoria serving ciabatta sandwiches, fragrant pastas, proper pizza and a blackboard of daily specials and desserts. Booking recommended.

Le Gallois (Y Cymro) 6–10 Romilly Crescent, Canton ☏029/2034 1264. Sophisticated and fashionable restaurant on a busy suburban road and serving delicious (and expensive) French cuisine, with a Welsh twist.

Happy Gathering 233 Cowbridge Rd East, Canton ☏029/2039 7531. A true Cardiff institution; the best and most authentic Chinese food in the city.

Hazha 42 City Rd ☏029/2049 6088. Incredibly cheap off-the-beaten-track Kurdish restaurant with specialties like a couscous and fruity lamb *kiftta*, and mixed-grill flatbread *moshakal*.

Milgis 213 City Rd. Afternoon/evening venue (from 3pm) with Welsh food, stellar coffee, amazing cocktails and a yurt in the back garden.

Drinking

Cardiff's **pub life** has expanded exponentially in recent years, with chic cosmopolitan bars jostling for space alongside the more traditional Edwardian palaces of etched smoky glass and deep-red wood. Weekend nights are legendarily raucous in Cardiff, during which time the city centre is not for the fainthearted. Good drinking spots are found all over the city: up-and-coming Westgate Street, leading down from Castle Street, is a good place to start, as is the new brewery quarter (see p.115) on the site of **Brains**' former brewery.

Brains still brews in Cardiff, making a great range of smooth and cask beers, as well as a fantastic "continental-style" golden ale, named "45", any or all of which should not be missed. Brewery tours are mooted to open in the future – check with the tourist office for updates.

For **gay bars**, see below.

City centre

All these places are marked on the map on p.116.

10 Feet Tall Church St ☎029/2022 8883, ⓦwww .thisis10feettall.co.uk. Ultra-hip new pastiche of north African and Mediterranean dining in its street-level deli and café bar, mezzanine restaurant, and top-floor, tune-spinning "bistrotheque", plus regular live music.

Bar Europa 25 Castle St. Earnest little café transforms itself into an arty little bar Wed–Sat evenings with live DJs, poetry and the like.

City Arms 10 Quay St. Opposite the Millennium Stadium, this no-nonsense boozer is always popular, especially on international match days.

The Cottage 25 St Mary St. Traditional Edwardian pub, serving up some of the best Brains in the city centre, as well as decent, cheap food.

Ha-ha Bar The Friary. Decent posing palace, with a young and funky atmosphere and great food.

Old Arcade Church St. Small, old-fashioned arcade bar next to the market, opening its lounge bar on busy nights only. Popular with rugby fans for its sporting memorabilia.

Queen's Vaults 29 Westgate St. Cavernous rugby-memorabilia pub with antique fittings, though the ear-splitting music isn't conducive to conversation.

🏃 **Tafarn** 53–59 Despenser St, Riverside. The best-located bar in Cardiff, with a heated outdoor deck overlooking the river, a cantina serving locally sourced meals and bar snacks, and an impressive range of Welsh beers, ciders and spirits.

ZeroDegrees 27 Westgate St. Shiny new microbrewery in a lino-clad converted garage with friezes made from heat-compressed Wellington boots and discarded mobile phones. The £2 beer sampler lets you taste all five of its house brews, including mango and a couple of wheat beers. Great gourmet pizzas too.

Cardiff Bay

All these places are marked on the map on p.122.

Bar Cwtsh Jolyon's Hotel, 5 Bute Crescent. Cosy bar with a wood-burning stove and terrific atmosphere.

Salt Mermaid Quay. Driftwood and sofas make this spacious bar a little more unusual than its nearby competition.

Terra Nova Mermaid Quay. Big and busy timber-filled pub with balconies overlooking the water, and good-value pub food.

Out from the centre

All these places are marked on the map on pp.112–113.

Cayo Arms Cathedral Rd. Convivial pub a 5min walk up Cathedral Rd from the city centre. Proudly Welsh, with Tomos Watkin beers and decent food every day until 8pm.

Chapter Market Rd, Canton. A trendy bar in the arts centre, with a good choice of real ale, imported lagers and whisky. Frequented by the Canton media and arts crowd.

🏃 **Mochyn Du** Sophia Close, off Cathedral Rd. Relaxed pub with tables spilling out into the greenery. Good bar menu, great beer and popular with Welsh speakers.

The lesbian and gay scene

Cardiff's scene is far from massive, but robust all the same. The best source for current information and advice is the **Mardi Gras** website (ⓦwww .cardiffmardigras.co.uk) and the **South Wales Friend** information line (Tues–Thurs 7.30–9.30pm; ☎029/2034 0101). It doesn't take too much effort to discover what's going on, as practically all of the venues are on Charles Street, just off Queen Street in the city centre. All venues are for men and women unless otherwise noted.

Bar Icon 60 Charles St. Trendy new bar, with muted, comfy decor and a tendency to get funky towards the weekend.

Club X 39 Charles St. Stylish and popular gay club which manages to span both cheesy and cutting

edge. Also has a wonderful roof garden and a great atmosphere. Open Wed till 2am, Fri 3am, Sat 4am & Sun 1am.

Golden Cross 283 Hayes Bridge Rd. Laid-back restored Victorian pub, rich in atmosphere and with some beautiful tiled pictures of yesteryear Cardiff. Camp entertainment a speciality, as is the cheap food.

King's Cross ("KX") Hayes Bridge Rd/Caroline St. Large and long-established gay male pub, with few frills but a sociable atmosphere.

The Loft Hayes Bridge Rd/Caroline St. Directly opposite KX, this candlelit place has a mixed gay and het crowd, and good cocktails and bottled beers.

Nightlife and entertainment

There's plenty of choice when it comes to **nightlife** in Cardiff, whether your tastes run to sweaty rock gigs (in English or Welsh), pumping clubs or genteel classical affairs. **Theatre** in Cardiff encompasses everything from the radical and alternative at The Point (see opposite) and Chapter (see opposite) to big, blowzy productions at the New Theatre, on the north side of the city centre east of the castle, or West End spectaculars at the Wales Millennium Centre, home of Welsh National Opera (WMC; @ www.wno.org.uk). The WMC and St David's Hall are the main venues for **classical music**. Cardiff is usually on major acts' world tours, thanks to the Millennium Stadium. There's no shortage of multiplex **cinemas** for the latest blockbusters, though Chapter is best for arthouse movies. If you want to catch **sporting events** on the big screen, the biggest of them all is at the Aussie-themed *Walkabout* pub, at 65–74 St Mary St, which even has individual screens in the men's room so guys won't miss a minute of the action.

Clubs

Buffalo Windsor Place ☏ 029/2031 0312, @ www .myspace.com/wearebuffalobar. Retro restaurant/ bar/club with fabulously quirky decor and a cool vibe from lunchtime until the wee hours.

Clwb Ifor Bach 11 Womanby St ☏ 029/20232199, @ www.clwb.net. Sweaty and massively fun live music and dance club on three floors with nightly gigs, sessions or DJs, including 70s and funk nights. Widely known as the "Welsh club", due to the prevalence of Welsh-language acts and punters, particularly on Sat.

HMS69 Departs/returns Millennium Stadium Taff Meads Embankment Dock ☏ 0777/191 0172, @ www.hms69.com. Three-hour party cruises depart daily at 7.30pm (£30 Mon–Thurs, from £32 Fri–Sun including unlimited beer and wine) for a spin along the Taff and around Cardiff Bay accompanied by an on-board DJ.

Metros (Club Metropolitan) Bakers Row ☏ 029/2037 1549. Grungy venue hosting some of the best metal/ indie/alternative dance nights in town.

Swell Windsor Place ☏ 029/2037 1130, @ www.swellbar.com. Intimate and atmospheric venue – the best place in the capital to catch live jazz and blues.

Tafod 53–59 Despenser St, Riverside ☏ 029/2037 8866, @ www.myspace.com/clwbtafod. Small but hip "underground sound lounge" in the basement of *Nos Da* (see p.114) with top DJs on the decks and live bands.

The Union 3 Churchill Way ☏ 029/2064 1010. Big-name live bands and assorted dance nights in the university's club complex, open to non-students.

Classical and rock music venues

Barfly Kingsway ☏ 029/2039 6589, @ www .barflyclub.com. Dark and cosy club across from the castle that hosts at least a couple of live bands every evening, including many on the verge of making it.

Cardiff Castle Castle St ☏ 029/2087 8100. Increasingly used for big gigs, from Proms-style flag-wavers to visiting rock gods.

Cardiff International Arena Mary Ann St ☏ 029/2023 4500 (enquiries), ☏ 029/2022 4488 (bookings). Large and imposing venue rising high over the city centre's southern streets and playing host to classical concerts, opera and major rock and pop gigs.

Coal Exchange Mount Stuart Square, Cardiff Bay ☏ 029/2049 4917. A lovely Victorian building that has been well converted for all manner of musical events.

Dempseys 15 Castle St ☏ 029/2023 9253 Honest-to-goodness Irish pub with a loyal following and top-notch live music, particularly jazz.

Millennium Stadium Westgate St ☏ 029/2082 2228. Hosts mega-gigs, as well as major sporting fixtures.

Norwegian Church Harbour Drive, Cardiff Bay ☎029/2045 4899. Lovely venue for all kinds of musical and performance evenings.

Royal Oak 200 Broadway, Newport Rd, Roath ☎029/2047 3984. Renowned music pub with acoustic jam sessions on Mon, electric jam sessions on Wed and bands on Fri, all starting from 9pm, and all free.

St David's Hall The Hayes ☎029/2087 8444, ⓦwww.stdavidshallcardiff.co.uk. Part of the massive St David's shopping centre, this large venue is home to visiting orchestras and musicians from jazz to opera, and is frequently used by the excellent BBC National Orchestra of Wales.

University Concert Hall Corbett Rd, Cathays Park ☎029/2087 4816. Hosts public concerts by university and local orchestras, jazz groups and easy-listening ensembles.

Wales Millennium Centre Roald Dahls Plass, Cardiff Bay ☎08700/402000, ⓦwww.wmc.org.uk. Home to Welsh National Opera, along with various other music and dance companies. Also used for touring mega-productions.

Theatre and comedy

Chapter Arts Centre Market Rd, Canton ☎029/2030 4400, ⓦwww.chapter.org. Multifunctional arts complex that's home to fine British and touring theatre and dance companies.

Glee Club Mermaid Quay, Cardiff Bay ☎0870/241 5093, ⓦwww.glee.co.uk. Cardiff's best comedy club, with appearances by some of the biggest names on the British stand-up circuit.

Jongleurs Comedy Club Millennium Plaza, Wood St ☎0870/787 0707, ⓦwww.jongleurs.com. More corporate than the *Glee*, but dependable for decent comedy.

New Theatre Park Place ☎029/2087 8889, ⓦwww.newtheatrecardiff.co.uk. Splendid Edwardian city-centre theatre that plays host to big shows, musicals and pantos.

The Point West Bute St, Cardiff Bay ☎029/2046 0873, ⓦwww.thepointcardiffbay.com. This converted old church is good for experimental theatre, music and dance, as well as more mainstream events.

Sherman Theatre Senghennydd Rd, Cathays ☎029/2064 6900, ⓦwww.shermantheatre.co.uk. An excellent two-auditorium repertory theatre hosting a mixed bag of new and translated classic Welsh-language pieces, stand-up comedy, children's entertainment, drama, music and dance. Many plays on Welsh themes in both English and Welsh.

Cinema

Chapter Arts Centre Market Rd, Canton. Cardiff's main arthouse and alternative film centre.

Cineworld Mary Ann St ☎0871/200 2000. Nicest multi-screen complex in the city centre.

Odeon Red Dragon Centre, Cardiff Bay ☎0871/224 4007. Twelve-screen megaplex in swish new building.

Vue Cinema Millennium Plaza, Wood St ☎0871/224 0240. Flashy multi-screen complex opposite Central station.

Listings

Airport Cardiff International, Rhoose, near Barry ☎01446/711111, ⓦwww.cwlfly.com.

Banks and exchange All major banks have branches along High St or Queen St. In addition there's American Express at 3 Queen St (Mon–Fri 9am–5.30pm, Sat 9am–5pm; ☎029/2064 9301), and Thomas Cook at 16 Queen St (Mon–Fri 9.30am–5pm, Sat 10am–1pm; ☎029/2042 2500); both cash currency and traveller's cheques.

Bike rental Taff Trail Cycle Hire, Cardiff Caravan Park (see p.114), Pontcanna Fields ☎029/2039 8362.

Books Lear's, 37 St Mary St; TSO Bookshop, 18 High St; Waterstone's, 2a The Hayes and in the Cardiff Students' Union in Senghennydd Rd, Cathays.

Bus enquiries Cardiff Bus ☎0871/2002233; National Express ☎0870/580 8080.

Car rental Avis, 14–22 Tudor St ☎029/2034 2111; Enterprise, 45 Penarth Rd ☎029/2038 9222; Hertz, 9 Central Square ☎029/2022 4548.

Cricket Glamorgan County Cricket Ground, Sophia Gardens, Pontcanna Fields ☎0871/282 3401, ⓦwww.glamorgancricket.com.

Dentist For emergency dental work, phone Cardiff NHS Community Dental Service on ☎029/2039 4347.

Football Cardiff City FC, Ninian Park, Sloper Rd ☎029/2022 1001, ⓦwww.cardiffcityfc.co.uk.

Hospital In the first instance, phone NHS Wales Direct on ☎0845/4647.

Internet access Free at Cardiff Central Library (Mon–Wed & Fri 9am–6pm, Thurs 9am–7pm, Sat 9am–5.30pm), though there may be a queue. Otherwise, Internet Exchange, 8 Church St (Mon–Thurs 9am–9pm, Fri & Sat 9am–8pm, Sun 11am–7pm; £1 per 15 min, £7 day).

Laundries Drift Inn, 104 Salisbury Rd, Cathays Park; Launderama, 60 Lower Cathedral Rd.

Newspapers and magazines The Cardiff-based daily *South Wales Echo* is good for listings, especially for films in the city. For a wider overview of arts and events, the free monthly *Buzz* is available from the tourist office, as well as cafés and bars around town.

Pharmacy Boots, 5 Wood St (Mon–Sat 8am–8pm, Sun 6–7pm; ☎029/2023 4043).

Police Cardiff Central Police Station, King Edward VII Ave, Cathays Park ☎029/2022 2111.

Post office The Hayes (Mon–Fri 9am–5.30pm, Sat 9am–12.30pm).

Rugby International matches are held at the Millennium Stadium (☎029/2082 2228), and club matches next door on the smaller Arms Park pitch (☎029/2030 2000).

Swimming pools and spas Welsh Institute of Sport, Sophia Gardens ☎029/2033 8398.

Travel agencies John Cory Travel, Park Place ☎029/2037 1878; Regal Travel, 240 Whitchurch Rd, Cathays Park ☎029/2062 1479; STA Travel, 11 Duke St ☎029/2038 2350.

Around Cardiff

The fairy-tale thirteenth-century fortress of **Castell Coch** stands on a hillside in woodlands at the edge of the city's northern suburbs, while to the west, the **National History Museum** at St Fagans relates the country's history through buildings moved here from all corners of Wales.

Castell Coch

Above the village of **TONGWYNLAIS**, four miles north of Llandaff, the coned turrets of **Castell Coch** (April–Oct daily 9am–5pm; Nov–March Mon–Sat 9.30am–4pm, Sun 11am–4pm; £3.70, audioguide £1; CADW) rise mysteriously out of a steep wooded hillside. A ruined thirteenth-century fortress, Castell Coch was rebuilt into a fantasy castle in the late 1870s by William Burges for the third Marquess of Bute, complete with a working portcullis and drawbridge. Numerous similarities with Cardiff Castle include the lavish decor, culled from religious and moral fables, that dazzles in each room. Lady Bute's bedroom, at the top of one of the three towers, incorporates a fabulously painted double dome, around which are 28 panels depicting frolicking monkeys, some of which were considered lascivious for their day. However, the castle was hardly ever lived in and sees more life today, especially in the tearoom situated in the valet's room. Bus #26A from Central station drops at the castle gates, or the #132 drops in Tongwynlais, from where it's a ten-minute climb.

St Fagans National History Museum and Castle

Separated from Cardiff by a sliver of greenery, the village of **ST FAGANS** (Sain Ffagan), four miles west of the city centre, has a rural ambience only partly marred by the busloads of tourists that regularly roll in to visit the unmissable **St Fagans National History Museum** (daily 10am–5pm; free). A branch of the National Museum and Gallery, it's constructed around **St Fagans Castle**, a country house built in 1580 on the site of a ruined Norman castle and furnished in early nineteenth-century style, complete with heavy oak furniture and solemn portraits. The mansion's formal gardens and eighteenth-century fishponds have also been restored to something akin to their original design.

A collection of period buildings from all corners of Wales has been carefully dismantled and faithfully rebuilt on this site since the museum's inception in 1946. The most impressive element is the fifty-acre **outdoor collection**, particularly the diminutive whitewashed 1777 **Pen-Rhiw Chapel** from Dyfed, the pristine and evocative Victorian **St Mary's Board School** from Lampeter

▲ Castell Coch

and the ordered mini-fortress of a 1772 **Tollhouse** that once guarded the southern approach to Aberystwyth. Many of the domestic structures are farmhouses of different ages and styles – compare, for example, the grandeur of the seventeenth-century red-painted **Kennixton Farmhouse** from Gower or the homely Edwardian comforts of **Llwyn-yr-Eos Farm** with the threadbare simplicity of the Gwynedd farmworkers' **Llainfadyn Cottage**.

The best demonstration of how life changed over the years for a section of the Welsh population comes in the superlative **Rhyd-y-car** ironworkers' cottages from Merthyr Tydfil. Built originally around 1800, each of the six houses, with their accompanying strip of garden, has been furnished in the style of a different era – stretching from 1805 to 1985. Even the frontages and roofs are true to their age, offering a wade through working-class Welsh life over the past two centuries. Next door are the Victorian **Gwalia Stores** from the mining community of Ogmore Vale, whose smell of polished mahogany is as evocative as the starchy-aproned assistants and the jars of boiled sweets that they sell. A large and interesting variety of workplaces, including a stinking **tannery**, a **pottery**, three **mills**, a **bakehouse** and a **smithy**, most of which house people demonstrating the original methods, make up a large number of the remaining buildings.

In St Fagan's village, you'll also find the sublime **restaurant** with rooms ⚘ *The Old Post Office*, on Greenwood Lane (☎029/2056 5400, Ⓦwww .theoldpostofficerestaurant.co.uk; ❺–❻) with beautiful, minimalist rooms and a conservatory restaurant (open lunch Tues–Sun, evenings Tues–Sat) serving classy, suitably expensive, modern European cuisine.

There's an hourly **bus** #320 from Cardiff Central station to the village.

The Vale of Glamorgan

South of the capital the **Vale of Glamorgan**'s rich pastoral landscapes and cliff-fringed coastline, broken by long, sandy beaches, are often overlooked by visitors, though they are worth at least a couple of days' exploration. Lively seaside resorts at **Porthcawl** in the west and **Barry** in the east contrast with the more refined atmosphere of **Penarth**, clinging to the coat-tails of Cardiff. In between lie yawning wide bays and tumbledown castles, linked by bracing coastal walks. At the western tip of the Vale coast is **Kenfig**, a vast, grass-spotted desert of coastal dunes and nature reserves. Inland, the lower parts of the Vale's urban features – such as Wales' international **airport** at Rhoose and occasional looming factories – are set against rolling green pastureland sprinkled with charming, low-key market towns like **Cowbridge**, **Llantrisant** and **Llantwit Major**.

The Vale's proximity to Cardiff makes it easy to explore using **public transport**. The main-line train route through the Vale has a stop at Bridgend, a handy interchange for bus services to the coast and some of the larger inland settlements, while the Vale of Glamorgan line, an alternative route from Cardiff to Bridgend, has stops at Rhoose and Llantwit Major. Barry and Penarth, almost suburbs of Cardiff, are easily reached by bus and train.

Penarth and around

An easy and enjoyable day out from Cardiff, the increasingly upmarket Victorian seaside town of **PENARTH** lies just across the Barrage from Cardiff Bay, accessible by road, train or by the Bay waterbus (see p.111).

The Town

Penarth is linked to Cardiff by half-hourly shuttle trains which ply their way from here, through the capital, and out into the Valleys. From the train station, a path on the right leads up to Stanwell Road, which continues into the clean-cut Edwardian shopping streets of the town centre.

Opposite the station, the red-brick **Turner House Art Gallery** (Tues–Sun 10am–5pm; ☏029/2070 8870; free) on the Plymouth Road hosts top-notch exhibitions, particularly of photography. Running down the left-hand side of Turner House, the Dingle path leads into showy **Alexandra Park**, emblemizing the spirit of Penarth with its flowerbeds and bandstand. Continuing down the hill brings you onto the charmingly fusty **Esplanade**, with a spearmint-green hall on the pier.

You can spend the day **cruising** the local coastline aboard the *Waverley*, a seagoing paddle steamer which makes regular visits to Penarth Pier throughout the summer (though it's sometimes replaced by the more conventionally propelled but no less gracious *Balmoral*). Day-trips range from cruises around Flat Holm to longer journeys up the Severn estuary or across the Bristol Channel to ports on the north Devon coast (£17.95–37; ☏0845/130 4647, ⒲www.waverleyexcursions.co.uk).

Flat Holm and Lavernock Point

Jutting out into the Bristol Channel two miles due south of Penarth, **Lavernock Point** provides a forlorn setting for assorted campsites and pubs, but is notable as the place in which conversation was first heard by means of radio waves. This – as a plaque on the wall of the Victorian church notes – took place on May 11, 1897, when Guglielmo Marconi sent the immortal words "Are you ready?" over to his assistant George Kemp on the island of **Flat Holm** (Ynys Echni), three miles out in the channel, officially Wales' most southerly point.

Over the years, Flat Holm has been used as a Viking anchorage, a cholera hospital and a lookout point. Today it's an interesting and beautifully remote **nature reserve**, the nesting place of thousands of gulls and shelducks. **Boats** operated by the Flat Holm Project, Cardiff Bay (℡01446/747661, Ⓦwww .cardiff.gov.uk/flatholm; £14.75) sail most days between mid-March and late October; book well in advance. Most are day-trips giving three hours on the island (including a history, flora and fauna tour), though it's occasionally possible to stay overnight in a farmhouse **hostel** (£10.50 per person excluding boat transport) on the island if it's not booked out by groups.

Lavernock Point is a fifteen-minute walk from the bus stop on the B4267. Half-hourly bus #94 operates from Cardiff and Penarth, stopping just near the site of archeological digs, **Cosmeston Medieval Village** (daily: May–Sept 11am–5pm; Oct–April 11am–4pm; £3.50), which sometimes hosts events such as jousting.

Practicalities

Penarth's **tourist office** (Easter–Sept daily 10am–5.30pm; ℡029/2070 8849, Ⓔpenarthtic@valeofglamorgan.gov.uk) is at the head of the pier on the Esplanade. **Accommodation** in town is surprisingly sparse; try the soothingly decorated *Hickman Lodge*, 17 Hickman Rd (℡029/2070 1044, Ⓦwww.hickmanlodge.co.uk; ❸), or, on the Esplanade, the smart new *Pebbles Bistro with Rooms* (℡029/2070 0333, Ⓦwww.pebblesbistro.co.uk; ❹–❺), which does great lunchtime and evening meals with a Provençale twist. Other reasonable **restaurants** along Penarth Esplanade include the appealing *Rabaiotti* café; alternatively, head for the *Olive Tree*, 21 Glebe St (℡029/2070 7077; open dinner Tues–Sat and lunch Sun), which does a wonderful three-course table d'hôte for £27.75. There's also good beer and food to be had at several **pubs**: the *Clive Arms* on John Street, up towards the Barrage; the *Windsor*, going down the hill from the town centre on Windsor Road; or, three miles southwest of Penarth on Beach Road, Swanbridge, *The Captain's Wife* (℡029/2053 0066), a wonderful old-fashioned pub overlooking Sully Island at the end of a long winding country lane by the sea wall.

Barry and around

Six miles southwest of Penarth, **Barry** (Barri) is the quintessential Welsh resort of old. A recent clampdown on outdoor drinking, together with a Blue Flag rating for its **beach**, means that although there are a couple of fun pubs here, the town has returned to its traditional roots as a family resort. If you're seeking a bit more solitude, head east around the headland to peaceful Jacksons Bay.

Until the 1880s, when it was developed as a rival port to the Bute family's Cardiff, the main centre for activity, **Barry Island** (Ynys y Barri), was indeed an island due to its position on the tidal estuary, but the docks' construction saw the river diverted. Today, the "island" is pinned out along a cheerful prom. Bang opposite is the **Pleasure Park** (erratic but generally daily: July & Aug 1–10pm; Easter–June & Sept 6–10pm), a collection of rides and fairground attractions.

Barry is best known nowadays as one of the main settings for the BAFTA- award-winning TV sitcom *Gavin & Stacey*, which is mostly filmed here – the tourist office has details of shooting locations.

Dyffryn Gardens and Llanerch Vineyard

The A4226 heads north from Barry, past the child-oriented **Welsh Hawking Centre** (daily except Tues 10.30am–5pm or dusk; £5), where a resident population of over 250 birds of prey can be seen and held. Off to the right, lanes descend to the hamlet of **DYFFRYN** and the magnificent **Dyffryn Gardens** (daily: March–Oct 10am–6pm; £6; Nov–Feb 10am–4pm; £3), set around the Victorian home of a local merchant. Seldom busy, the gardens offer everything from formal lilyponds and billiard-table-smooth lawns to joyous bursts of floral colour and the russets, golds and greens of an arboretum. By the lane junction just south of the gardens, you'll find the **St Lythan Long Cairn**, over four thousand years old. It's nowhere near as impressive, however, as its near neighbour, the **Tinkinswood Long Cairn**, a huge, capstoned burial chamber, around 4500 years old. Legend has it that anyone who sleeps beneath the fifty-ton monolith for a night will either die, go raving mad or become a poet – a threat commonly ascribed to other megalithic sites in Wales, such as Cadair Idris. You'll find it on the other side of the Dyffryn Gardens entrance, just beside the wooded lane between Dyffryn and **St Nicholas**, a village on the A48 just two miles from Cardiff's Culverhouse Cross roundabout.

Among rolling hills four miles northwest of St Nicholas and one mile south of junction 34 of the M4 you'll find **Llanerch Vineyard** (March–Dec daily 10am–5pm; £6). This is Wales' most successful winery, producing around 20,000 bottles of white and rosé Cariad wine each year, most of it sold within Wales. The entry fee includes a self-guided tour among the vines and a patch of ancient woodland and, of course, a taste of the finished product. They also run cookery classes, and offer food and accommodation (see below).

Practicalities

Frequent trains from Cardiff rattle through Barry Docks and Barry stations before terminating at Barry Island, just steps from the **tourist office** (April–Sept daily 10am–6pm; ℡01446/747171). **Accommodation** in Barry town is plentiful enough, though most places are cheap guesthouses away from the waterfront. The cheapest in the area is *Acorns Guesthouse*, at 17 Romilly Rd (℡01446/711666; ❶), with cosy rooms (though no en suites). If your budget's somewhat larger, you might want to consider the exquisite Victoriana of the *Egerton Grey Hotel* (℡01446/711666, ⓦwww.egertongrey.co.uk; ❼–❽), in the hamlet of Porthkerry, a mile west of town. Between Barry and Cardiff Airport, *New Farm* (℡01446/735536, ⓦwww.newfarmbarry.co.uk; ❷), on Port Road West, is a welcoming early seventeenth-century farmhouse B&B that's still a working farm. For smart, contemporary accommodation, your best bet is *Llanerch Vineyard* (see above; ℡01443/225877, ⓦwww.llanerch-vineyard.co.uk; B&B ❸; self-contained studios ❺–❻), which also has a fabulous restaurant.

The Vale coast

West of Barry, the **Vale of Glamorgan** coast alternates between craggy cliffs and wide, white-sand beaches. Considering its location between Wales' two great cities, it's surprisingly quiet, as most of the old-fashioned little towns and seashore villages seem to have escaped the effects of the surrounding industrialization.

Llantwit Major

At first glance, **LLANTWIT MAJOR** (Llanilltud Fawr) appears to be all modern housing estates and rows of shops, but at its heart is a tiny kernel of winding streets. This is where, in around 500 AD, the scholarly St Illtud educated a succession of young men at his monastery, giving the town the chance to claim the title of Britain's earliest centre of learning. Amongst Illtud's pupils were St David as well as St Patrick, who was abducted from the monastery by Irish pirates to become the patron saint of Ireland.

Buses drop passengers behind the modern shopping precinct, from where it's a short walk down East Street into the town centre. The new **train station** on the Vale line is yards away. A miniature **town hall** sits just before the main town square, built in the fifteenth century to replace one destroyed by Owain Glyndŵr; it now serves as an informal **visitor centre** (generally 9am–5pm Mon–Fri; ℡01446/796086). From here, Burial Lane winds its way past the village square and down to the front of the magnificent **parish church**, sheltering in a hollow next to the trickle of the Col Huw River.

The first thing that strikes you about the church is its size: it is, in fact, two churches joined at the tower. The older west church, nearer the stream, dates from around 1100; aisles were added in the twelfth and thirteenth centuries to transform it into the nave of a new church. The west church is notable for the collection of decorative Celtic crosses and stones arranged haphazardly inside. Prize amongst these is the exquisitely carved eighth-century boulder at the back of the church, on which the letters ILT and half of a U (remains of ILLTUD) can still be made out.

At the junction at the top of Burial Lane, Colhugh Street descends for a little over a mile along the scrubby valley of the Col Huw River to the rocky **beach**, popular for surfing and a great starting point for some wonderful walks along the caves and inlets of the stratified cliffs and back into the rolling countryside. The best route to take is the path that runs west along the clifftops for two miles to **St Donat's Bay**, dominated by a mock-Gothic castle, dating back to the fourteenth century, that was bought and restored by US tycoon William Randolph Hearst in the 1930s, and is now the international Atlantic College and multipurpose **arts centre** (information ℡01446/799100, ⓦ www.stdonats .com), at the forefront of Welsh efforts to internationalize local culture. As well as theatre, film, dance, exhibitions and community outreach, the centre hosts the excellent **Beyond the Border Storytelling Festival** (July) and the **Vale of Glamorgan Festival** (Sept).

Accommodation includes the decent *White House* (℡01446/794250, ⓦ www.waleswhitehouse.co.uk; ❸) on Flanders Road, off the road down to the beach; and the friendly *Curriers*, just off the main square on Wine Street (℡01446/793506, ⓦ thecurriers.co.uk; ❷). Rosedew Farm on Ham Lane South incorporates the *Acorn* **campsite** (℡01446/794024; £9.60–10.75 per pitch), with some forty tent pitches and sites for fifty vans.

For **food**, there are cheap takeaways along East Street and its continuation, Boverton Road, or, in the old town centre on Church Street, *Illtyd 216* (℡01446/793800), a gastropub that's winning rave reviews for its local specialities. There's a stack of **pubs** in Llantwit: the *Old Swan Inn* on the Square is the best for food. Four miles east of town, the gorgeous thatched *Blue Anchor* in East Aberthaw is well worth the trip, either for a cosy fireside pint or a brilliant meal.

Southerndown and Ogmore

West of Llantwit Major, the coast ducks and dives past remote cliffs and sandy beaches. **SOUTHERNDOWN** is a diffuse holiday village of touristy pubs and one excellent restaurant – the French-inspired *Frolics* on Beach Road (℡01656/880127; booking advisable). However, the real reason to come here is **Dunraven Bay**, a beautiful, wide beach backed by jagged cliffs of perfectly defined layers of limestone and shale. In the busy car park by Dunraven Beach is the **Heritage Coast Centre** (April–Sept daily 10am–5pm; Oct–March Sat & Sun 10am–5pm; ℡01656/880157), a small information point about walks and drives along this splendid section of the south Wales coastline. Dunraven is at the western end of a magnificent fifteen-mile **coastal walk**, dipping down into tiny, wooded valleys and up across wide stretches of cliff and sand.

The village of **OGMORE** (Ogwr), usually referred to as Ogmore-by-Sea to differentiate it from the hinterland, is a straggling, windswept sort of place, but lies close to the remains of **Ogmore Castle**, situated about a mile north along the coast from Southerndown in a flattened valley. The castle dates from the Norman Conquest in around 1100, but its solid central stone keep, in which a few original windows are still intact, was added later in the twelfth century. Below the castle, you can follow the **stepping stones** across the river.

Ewenny Priory

The village of **EWENNY**, two miles further up the B4524, is interesting mainly for the towering remains of Benedictine **Ewenny Priory** (private), tucked away down leafy lanes three-quarters of a mile to the east. Founded in 1141, the priory's formidable, fortress-like walls were strengthened continuously throughout the thirteenth century, and are still very much intact today, broken only by the two huge gateways in which the portcullis holes can still be seen.

The best views of the priory are from the adjoining priory **church**, divided into two sections by a plain early-medieval rood screen. On the western side (nearest to the rest of the priory) is the nave, whose damp, cold interior includes some splendid Norman windows. This nave served as the parish church, as opposed to the eastern chancel, which housed the monastic chapel.

Merthyr Mawr

On the banks of the Ogmore River two miles west of Ewenny, a narrow lane steers into the small village of **MERTHYR MAWR**, with its neat thatched and whitewashed cottages. The village continues along a wooded glen to its end on the edge of the great dune desert of Merthyr Mawr, stretching over to the distant sea. By the car park is the gaunt ruin of **Candleston**, a fifteenth-century fortified manor house that was abandoned in the nineteenth century as the shifting sands came too close.

Porthcawl

One of Wales' most enduring family resorts, **PORTHCAWL** is poised for a major twenty-first-century overhaul. Plans have been drawn up to transform the waterfront, bestowing the town with amenities including new promenades, leisure facilities and shops. Work should be underway by the time you're reading this. In the meantime, its quaint village centre, invigorating walks, sandy beach and fantastic **surf** make it a great sojourn along the coast.

Half-hourly **buses** connecting Bridgend with Porthcawl stop at the top of the pedestrianized John Street in the town centre. A two-minute walk straight down John Street leads to the Old Police Station, housing both the **tourist office** (Easter–Sept Mon–Sat 9am–5pm, July–Sept also Sun 9am–4pm; Oct–Easter Fri 10am–5pm, Sat 10am–4pm plus either Tues or Thurs 10am–5pm, alternating each week; ☏01656/786639) as well as a local history **museum** (same hours; 50p).

John Street continues down to the Esplanade, Porthcawl's extensive seafront promenade which stretches the full length of the town and changes its name throughout. The section known as the Esplanade comprises a typical array of Victorian and Edwardian hotels along the rocky beach, where you'll find the domed **Grand Pavilion** (box office ☏01656/815995), home to assorted seaside entertainment shows and pantomimes. Eastwards, the Esplanade runs to a lifeboat station at the harbour before veering north alongside the coast under the name of Eastern Promenade, the home of Porthcawl's solid seaside attractions: the **Coney Beach amusement park**, behind whelk stalls and candy floss shops looking out over Sandy Bay and neighbouring Trecco Bay.

On the northwest side of town, a twenty-minute walk from the centre, is the far quieter and more beautiful **Rest Bay**, locally famed as a swimming and **surfing beach**. The Simon Tucker Surfing Academy (℡07815/289761, Ⓦ www.surfingexperience.com), run by champion surfer Tucker, operates from the old car park attendant's hut above the beach and offers tuition, board and wetsuit rental, plus loads of information on the local scene. During the summer, **pleasure steamers** (Ⓦ www.waverleyexcursions.co.uk; around £25) offer occasional day-trips from Porthcawl out into the Bristol Channel.

Accommodation in Porthcawl is plentiful, good value and concentrated around Esplanade Avenue, Mary Street, and along the promenade in its various guises. The fanciest option in town is the shoreline *Fairways Hotel* on West Drive (℡01656/782085, Ⓦ www.thefairwayshotel.co.uk; ❻). The Art Deco elegance of the *Seabank Hotel* on the promenade (℡01656/782261, Ⓦ www.seabankhotel .co.uk; ❺) might appeal too, though there's a minimum two-night stay. Cheaper options include the beautifully decorated *Foam Edge* guesthouse at 9 West Drive (℡01656/782866, Ⓦ www.foam-edge.co.uk; ❸–❹), with brimming cooked Welsh breakfasts, and, cheaper again, *Edmon House*, right in the centre at 33 Esplanade (℡01656/788102, Ⓦ www.edmonguesthouse.co.uk; ❷). **Campers** can stay about fifteen minutes' walk north of town at *Brodawel* (April–Sept; ℡01656/783231; £12 per pitch), a simple field site on Moor Lane; or just outside of Porthcawl on the A4229 at South Cornelly at the well-equipped *Danygraig Holiday Park* (℡01656/740510; £13–18 per pitch).

There are dozens of places to **eat** in the town centre, the best being 🍴 *Coast*, at 2–4 Dock St (℡01656/782025), with its minimalist decor and elegant twists on sturdy Welsh classics. Alternatively, try the *Beach Café* at Rest Bay, a buzzing surfers' hangout. Of the many **pubs**, the *Royal Oak*, at 128 John St, has decent beer and generous food, while in the adjacent village of Newton, *Ye Jolly Sailor Inn* on Church St does great food and sometimes has live music.

Kenfig

The cliffs and beaches north of Porthcawl end at the one-time fishing port and medieval borough of **KENFIG** (Cynffig), two miles up the coast. The village was founded in the Bronze Age, but was subsequently overwhelmed by water and shifting sand dunes, before being rediscovered by fishermen in 1857 when their lines snagged on the submerged ruins. It's now a **nature reserve** (open access; visitor centre Mon–Fri 2–4.30pm, Sat, Sun and school holidays daily 10am–4.30pm), by the tidal **Kenfig Pool**. At low tide, you can see the roofs of the **drowned village** sticking up from the water. The reserve's backdrop takes in the smoking stacks of the Port Talbot steelworks and the great, hazy curve of Swansea Bay stretching for dozens of miles to Gower.

Just up the road, the historic *Prince of Wales* was originally built in 1605 as the replacement town hall for its predecessor, which had been swallowed by the sands. The earlier town hall may have gone, but its ghosts may remain, as there are documented accounts of paranormal activity occurring here. Haunted or not, the beer and food are superb.

The inland Vale

The Vale of Glamorgan's hinterland is speckled with some intriguing towns, villages and ruined castles, connected by narrow, winding, high-hedged lanes.

Llantrisant

LLANTRISANT perches dramatically between two peaks which rise sharply from the rivers Ely and Clun, ten miles west of Cardiff. It was once encircled by fortifications to exploit its natural position as a watching post over the Vale of Glamorgan, and retains its stump of a castle, next to the church.

The town centre is focused on the **Bull Ring**, where there's a suitably wild-eyed statue of **Dr William Price** (1800–93), dressed in his favoured druid's outfit of moons, stars and a fox fur on his head. Dr Price subscribed to radical beliefs for his time – vegetarianism, nudity, republicanism, the unhealthiness of socks, anti-smoking and free love – as well as pointing out the potential environmental disasters of mass industrialization. He is best remembered for burning the body of his dead infant son, Iesu Grist (Welsh for "Jesus Christ"), in an oil drum on Llantrisant Common in January 1884. He was arrested and, in a sensational trial at Cardiff, acquitted, after which cremation was made legal in the UK.

You can learn more about Dr Price in an exhibition in the **Model House Craft and Design Centre** (Tues–Sun 10am–5pm; free), overlooking the Bull Ring, where you'll also find plenty of craft outlets, the excellent *Workhouse* café (housed in the former town workhouse) and a permanent display on the work of the **Royal Mint**.

Cowbridge

High-class boutiques and restaurants line the long and handsome main street of **COWBRIDGE** (Y Bont Faen), Wales' wealthiest town. On the south side of the High Street, Church Street leads under the narrow gatehouse that is the sole survivor of the four that once punctuated the town's fourteenth-century walls.

A little more than a mile south of town, down St Athan Road, a quiet lane fringed with high hedges, there's a tiny lay-by opposite the Regency finery of Howe Mill. A path opposite leads along the bank of the River Thaw for quarter of a mile to the gauntly impressive ruins of **Beaupre Castle**, largely an Elizabethan manor house. Built by the local noble family, the Bassetts, Beaupre is a huge shell of ruined Italianate doorways and vast mullioned windows in the middle of a quiet Glamorgan field.

If you've got some spare cash, Cowbridge will quickly absorb it. There's comfortable **accommodation** at the stylish *Bear Hotel* (☎01446/774814, ⓦ www.bearhotel.com; ❺), a restored twelfth-century coaching inn on the High Street; or, a mile west of town, in the grand old manor house of *Crossways* (☎01446/773171, ⓦ www.crosswayshouse.co.uk; ❸–❹). Cowbridge is chock-full of good **food** possibilities, especially the very reasonable *Farthings Wine Bar*, 54 High St (☎01446/772990) and the posher *Huddart's* restaurant at no. 69 (☎01446/774645; closed Mon). Of the many pubs along the High Street, the *Vale of Glamorgan* ("The Vale") is the cosiest, while the atmospheric thatch-roofed *Bush Inn* in St Hilary serves delicious food.

Neath

The town of **NEATH** (Castell-Nedd), in the Vale of Neath, boasts assorted antiquities. Just west of town off the A465 are the remains of **Neath Abbey** (free access; CADW). The ghostly, dark silhouette of the abbey, founded in the early twelfth century, is wedged in amongst an industrial estate and oily canal. In the sixteenth century, a chunk of the building was converted into a mansion, which later metamorphosed into a copper-smelting works.

A couple of miles north of town, the River Neath passes **Aberdulais**, with its **waterfalls** (March & Nov–Christmas Fri–Sun 11am–4pm; April–Oct Mon–Fri

10am–5pm, Sat & Sun 11am–6pm; £4; NT), still harnessed to generate hydro-electric power. An impressive one hundred and sixty million litres of deep-green water course over the rocks every day.

Three miles away, on the A4109, is the **Cefn Coed Colliery Museum** (April–Oct daily 10.30am–5pm; free), once the world's deepest anthracite mine. There are also some glorious signposted walks from the museum up into the surrounding wooded hills.

The valleys to the east of the Vale of Neath are covered in the Valleys section (pp.92–109).

Swansea

Over half a century ago, Dylan Thomas dubbed his native **SWANSEA** (Abertawe) an "ugly, lovely town" – a scathing but affectionate epithet which was once well deserved, although the famous poet probably wouldn't recognize the place these days. The city was devastated by bombing in World War II and hastily rebuilt, but since the turn of the millennium has been undergoing something of a renaissance, with bright, bold new developments springing up across the city. Even local lass Catherine Zeta-Jones and husband Michael Douglas have acquired a (heavily gated) property just outside town – a source of great pride amongst the city's residents.

Swansea's wide seafront overlooks the huge sweep of **Swansea Bay**, the focal point of much of the redevelopment, particularly around the old docks, and the city now boasts some of the best-funded **museums** in Wales. The seafront arcs around to the Gower peninsula, with the elegant but relaxed seaside resort of **Mumbles**, as well as some of Britain's best **surfing**, on its doorstep.

Some history

The city's Welsh name, Abertawe, refers to the settlement at the mouth of the River Tawe, now being coaxed back to life as part of Swansea's redeveloped waterfront after centuries of use as a repository for Swansea's metal trades. The English name derives from Viking sources, suggesting that a pre-Norman settlement existed in the area. The first reliable records of Swansea date back to 1099, when a Norman castle was built here as an outpost of William the Conqueror's empire. A small settlement subsequently grew near the coalfields and the sea, developing into a mining and shipbuilding centre that, by 1700, was the largest coal port in Wales.

Copper-smelting became the area's dominant industry in the eighteenth century, soon attracting other metal trades to pack out the lower Tawe Valley. Drawn by the town's flourishing metal trades, a swiftly growing port and the arrival of the Swansea Canal, thousands of emigrants moved to the city from all over Ireland and Britain; by the nineteenth century, the town was one of the world's most prolific metal-bashing centres.

Smelting was already on the wane by the beginning of the twentieth century, although Swansea's port continued to thrive. Britain's first oil refinery was opened on the edge of the city in 1918, with dock developments growing up in its wake. Civic zeal, best exemplified by the graceful 1930s Guildhall, was reawakened after the establishment of an important branch of the University of Wales here in 1920. Swansea was devastated during World War II, however, when thirty thousand bombs rained down on the city in just three nights in

140

SWANSEA

▲ Cardiff & M4

River Tawe

SA1

Ferry Port

GRENFELL PARK ROAD

PENTRE GUINEA ROAD

FABIAN WAY

LANGDON ROAD

KINGS ROAD

QUAY PARADE

NEW CUT ROAD

◀ Carmarthen & M4

Train Station

Plantasia

Dylan Thomas Centre 8

Pier of Environment Centre 10

CAMBRIAN PLACE

SOMERSET PL.

Dylan Thomas Theatre 27

Dylan Thomas Theatre 22

S T R A N D

Castle 7

WIND STREET

Action Bikes

St David's Square

Swansea Museum 14 16 17 19

National Waterfront Museum

Castle Street

High Street

Orchard St

DYFATTY ST

Princess Way

St Mary St

Glynn Vivian Art Gallery

Police Station 8

Grove Place

Craddock St

Quadrant Shopping Centre

Market

Bus Station ⓘ

Grand Theatre 9

LC Leisure Complex

Swansea Central Library ⓐ

MARITIME QUARTER

Mount Pleasant

Cromwell Street

Mansell St

The Kingsway

St Helen's Street

Single ton Street

West Way

Page St

OXFORD STREET

3

ST HELEN'S ROAD

20

WESTERN STREET

BEACH ST

ARDWYN ST

OYSTERMOUTH ROAD

23

Guildhall

Dylan Thomas's Birthplace

Terrace Road

BRYN-Y-MOR ROAD

KING EDWARDS ROAD

ST HELEN'S AVENUE

BRUNSWICK STREET

Victoria Park

Patti Pavilion

Dylan's Bookstore

EATON CRESCENT

UPLANDS CRESCENT

E

BRYN ROAD

AVENUE

DYFED

PANT-Y-CELYN ROAD

CRESCENT

DILLWYN

DONKIN DR

Cwmdonkin Park

12

UPLANDS

BERNARD STREET

6

GLANBRYDAN AVENUE

Singleton Park

Swansea University

GLANMOR ROAD

SKETTY ROAD

GLANMOR PARK ROAD

PARC WERN ROAD

BRYN MILL LANE

M U M B L E S

TOWNHILL ROAD

COCKETT RD

VIVIAN ROAD

GOWER ROAD

DE LA BECHE ROAD

TY-COCH ROAD

◀ Gower

Mumbles ▶

N

0   500 yds

© Crown copyright

ACCOMMODATION

Crescent	F
Dragon	B
Hurst Dene	C
Morgans	D
White House Hotel	E
Windsor Lodge Hotel	A

RESTAURANTS, CAFÉS & PUBS

Bella Napoli	14	Govinda's	2	Oceana	9
Café Mambo	6	Ice Bar	15	The Office	4
Cross Keys Inn	13	La Brasseria	10	Pitcher & Piano	17
Didier and Stephanie	20	La Parrilla	8	Pump House	22
Dylan Thomas Centre	18	Miah's	24	Queen's Hotel	21
Eli Jenkins Ale House	16	Monkey Café	1	The Retreat	3
Escape Club	5	Morgans	D	Sketty Hall	23
Exchange	7	No Sign Bar	19	Street Pebble Café Bar	11
				Uplands Tavern	12

1941. Initial rebuilding left the city disjointed, although now, with a population of around 200,000, Swansea boasts resurgent music, club and surf scenes, new attractions and some spirited rebuilding and redevelopment.

Arrival, information and getting around

Swansea is the main interchange station for services out to the west of Wales and for the slow but scenic line across the middle of the country to Shrewsbury in Shropshire. The **train station** is at the top end of the High Street, a ten-minute walk from the **bus station**, which is sandwiched between the Quadrant shopping centre and the Grand Theatre. The municipal **tourist office** (all year Mon–Sat 9.30am–5.30pm; May–Sept also Sun 10am–4pm; ☎01792/468321, ⓔtourism@swansea.gov.uk), where you can pick up the comprehensive bimonthly magazine *What's On*, is on the northwestern side of the bus station.

As most of the sights are within walking distance of each other, **getting around** Swansea is easy. Leafy suburbs near the University, such as Uplands and Sketty, are a bracing half-hour walk from the centre, although buses cover the suburbs thoroughly, and run out to Mumbles and Gower.

Accommodation

Transport is good between Swansea and the surrounding areas, and **accommodation** in the city is less expensive than the Gower. Inexpensive hotels and B&Bs line the seafront Oystermouth Road, with slightly pricier options in the leafy Uplands district. There are no hostels in Swansea, and if you want to camp, you'll have to head out to Gower. In addition to the places listed below, Swansea also has an increasing number of well-situated chain hotels including an Ibis, Marriott, Premier Inn, Village Hotel and Travelodge.

Crescent 132 Eaton Crescent, Uplands ☎01792/466814, ⓦwww.crescentguesthouse .co.uk. Large, sky-blue Edwardian guesthouse with pretty, pastel-shaded en-suite rooms, half of which have superb views over the city and the bay. ②–③
Dragon Kingsway Circle ☎01792/657100, ⓦwww.dragon-hotel.co.uk. Elegant, modernized and very central four-star hotel with luxury amenities including a gym, indoor pool and beauty salon, plus a quality brasserie, lounge bar, piano bar and restaurant. ④–⑦
Hurst Dene 10 Sketty Rd, Uplands ☎01792/280920, ⓦwww.hurstdene.co.uk. Cosy and well-priced B&B in a tall Uplands terrace house, with some self-catering studios and apartments also available (call for prices and minimum stay requirements). ②
Morgans Somerset Place ☎01792/484848, ⓦwww.morganshotel.co.uk. Swansea's showpiece boutique hotel, with 20 elegant rooms in the sumptuously converted old Port Authority HQ. A worthwhile five-star splurge, and not at all stuffy. ⑦–⑨
White House Hotel 4 Nyanza Terrace, Uplands ☎01792/473856, ⓦwww .thewhitehouse-hotel.com. Well-kept guesthouse with excellent rates for well-appointed rooms, all with satellite TV. Extensive breakfasts are included in the rates, and excellent, inexpensive evening meals are available, including vegie options. ④
Windsor Lodge Hotel Mount Pleasant ☎01792/642158, ⓦwww.windsor-lodge.co.uk. Like a country hotel in the city, this 200-year-old house has nicely decorated en-suite rooms, elegant but comfortable lounges, and an evening-only restaurant serving British and French cuisine. ③–④

The City

Swansea's train station faces out onto the **High Street**, which heads south into Castle Street and past the remains of the **castle**. The most obvious landmark of the ruins are the semicircular arcades, built into the wall between 1330 and 1332 by Bishop Gower to replace a Norman predecessor. The castle enjoys a new, improved

▲ Swansea Harbour

setting against the recently overhauled **Castle Square**, a pleasant amphitheatre of steps surrounding a fountain. Running south from the square, Wind Street (so named because it's winding – or at least gently curving) is nocturnal Swansea's main drag, chock-full of bars, pubs and restaurants, with a few more unusual independent establishments in between the theme bars and chains.

A block east of the High Street, the retail park on the Strand, Park Tawe, includes the great pyramidal glasshouse of **Plantasia** (daily 10am–5pm; £3.70), a tropical world of plants, tamarin monkeys, butterflies, parakeets and numerous insects, an aquarium and a thirteen-foot Burmese python.

Alexandra Road forks right off the High Street immediately south of the station, leading down to the **Glynn Vivian Art Gallery** (Tues–Sun 10.30am–5.30pm; free), on the corner of Clifton Hill, a road so steep that the pavement gives way to steps every few yards. This delightful Edwardian gallery houses an inspiring collection of Welsh art including works by Gwen John, her brother Augustus (whose mesmerizing portrait of Caitlin Thomas, Dylan's wife, is a real highlight), and Kyffin Williams; the grimy mining portraits of Josef Herman; and a whole room of huge, frantic canvases by Ceri Richards, Wales' most respected twentieth-century painter. In the early nineteenth century, Swansea was a noted centre of fine porcelain production, of which the gallery houses a large collection, together with pieces of contemporary works from Nantgarw, near Cardiff. Look out too for the frequently changing temporary exhibitions, which are of a consistently high standard.

Swansea's main shopping area is bounded by Kingsway, Princess Way and the Quadrant Centre. The glass-roofed **market** – Wales' largest – is a lively bustle of colourful stalls, fresh flowers and freshly baked food, including local delicacies like laver bread (made from laver, aka seaweed), as well as cockles trawled from the nearby Loughor estuary, typical Welsh cakes, fish and cheeses.

The Maritime Quarter

The spit of land between Oystermouth Road, the sea and the Tawe estuary has been christened the **Maritime Quarter**, with its vast centrepiece marina surrounded by contemporary apartments, cafés, shops, museums and a new leisure centre. Entering the quarter from the east, the main road bridge over the Tawe is guarded by a World War II ack-ack gun which stands as a memorial to the Luftwaffe decimation suffered by Swansea. On Victoria Road, surrounded by a small grid of nineteenth-century and Georgian streets, the **Swansea Museum** (Tues–Sun 10am–5pm; free), or, more properly, the Royal Institution of South Wales, was founded in 1835, making it Wales' oldest public museum. Much of it is still appealingly old-fashioned, with a wizened Egyptian mummy, lots of archeological finds, local porcelain and pottery in ancient glass cases, and a marble bust of Gower son, Edward Evans, who perished with Scott in Antarctica in 1912.

Nearby, in Somerset Place, is the **Dylan Thomas Centre** (daily 10am–4.30pm; free; ☎01792/463980), Wales' National Literature Centre. Housed in a nineteenth-century building and its modern extension, the centre is home to a theatre space, two galleries, a restaurant, bookshops and craft shops, along with unique displays including a mock-up of the shed in which Thomas wrote at Laugharne, where a fascinating video on his life and work plays continuously.

A hundred yards or so west, behind the *Evening Post* building, the city's **Environment Centre** (daily 10am–4pm; free) is housed in the old telephone exchange on Pier Street. As well as a resource centre for all things green, there are regularly changing exhibitions inside.

From here, Burrows Place leads down to the marina and what is arguably the country's finest museum, the **National Waterfront Museum** (daily 10am–5pm; free), which opened in 2005. Carved out of the shell of the old Industrial and Maritime Museum, the original building has been stunningly extended to accommodate wide-ranging exhibitions on Wales' history of innovation and industry. The museum is divided into fifteen zones, each with an interactive take on topics such as energy, landscape, coal, genealogy, networks and money. The whizz-bang technology means you can, for instance, fly over Swansea, explore the people and places of the 1851 census, and go virtual shopping through history. The metals section includes three paternoster lifts whirring around to exhibit some of Wales' many contributions to the world. There are shops, a café and a panoramic waterfront balcony within the complex.

Just north of the museum, on Oystermouth Road, is the latest addition to the area, the state-of-the-art **LC leisure complex** (☎01792/466500, ⓦwww .thelcswansea.com), with a gym, climbing wall, kids' play area, and a waterpark with rides, slides and the "Board Rider", the UK's only standing wave machine; surfing lessons are available for all levels.

To the south, the National Waterfront Museum overlooks a flotilla of yachts bobbing in the marina. Behind John Doubleday's statue of Dylan Thomas (dubbed "A Portrait of the Artist as Someone Else", since it looks nothing like the poet), on Gloucester Place, is the mural-splattered warehouse that has now become the **Dylan Thomas Theatre**, which intersperses productions of his works with offerings by local and visiting companies.

Heading across the River Tawe brings you to the gleaming new **SA1 development**, incorporating apartments, offices and a growing number of restaurants and bars in converted docks warehouses.

West Swansea

West of the city centre, St Helen's Road dips down to the seafront near the tall white tower of the **Guildhall** – a soaring piece of 1930s civic architecture. Within the Guildhall, **Brangwyn Hall** (☎01792/635489 for access) takes its name from Sir Frank Brangwyn, who painted the eighteen enormous British Empire panels lining the hall.

Immediately behind the Guildhall, down by the coast road, the most prominent feature of **Victoria Park** is the **Patti Pavilion**, a graceful green-roofed, glass-paned hall that was a gift from opera singer Adelina Patti, brought here from her home at Craig-y-nos in the Brecon Beacons (see p.223). At the time of writing, restoration work was underway to incorporate a restaurant overlooking the bay – check with the tourist office for updates.

A couple of streets to the north of the Guildhall is King Edward's Road, where, at no. 23, **Dylan's Bookstore** is the city's most comprehensive outlet dedicated to its favourite son.

Three-quarters of a mile further along the coast road, the **Swansea University** campus affords a commanding view over the bay stretching to Mumbles Head. On site is an imaginative performance space, the **Taliesin Arts Centre**, which also incorporates the **Ceri Richards Gallery** (Mon–Fri 10am–5pm, Sat 10am–4pm; free), specializing in touring exhibitions by contemporary Welsh and Celtic artists, as well as the **Egypt Centre** (Tues–Sat 10am–4pm; free), Wales' pre-eminent Egyptology display. The collection is split in two: The House of Death, with its funerary paraphernalia; and The House of Life, covering day-to-day existence, although most of the artefacts come from tombs.

At Blackpill, a mile or so further west and midway between Swansea city and Mumbles, are the **Clyne Gardens** (unrestricted access), the fifty-acre grounds of the Vivian family's old estate, which has lovely walks through rhododendron glades, bog gardens, woods, meadows and past a few follies.

Hourly buses leave the Quadrant bus station towards **Uplands**, which is otherwise a half-hour walk from the city centre. North of the main road, shaded avenues rise up the slopes past the sharp terraces of **Cwmdonkin Park**, where there is a memorial to Dylan Thomas inscribed with lines from *Fern Hill*, one of his best-loved poems. On the eastern side of Cwmdonkin Park is Cwmdonkin Drive (reached from the main road via The Grove), a sharply rising set of solid Victorian semis, where a blue plaque marks no. 5 as **Dylan Thomas' birthplace**.

Eating, drinking and nightlife

Swansea is a city that knows how to have a good time, and works damn hard at it. Most of the **restaurant**, **bar** and **club** action centres on Wind Street and around Kingsway. The city's theatrical and high **cultural** life is also robust and varied.

Restaurants and cafés

Bella Napoli 66 Wind St ☎01792/644611. Superior mid-range Italian eatery, cooking up consistently good pasta, pizza, a daily-changing array of fresh fish, and plenty for vegetarians such as *crespelle formaggio*, an oven-baked pancake stuffed with spinach and ricotta and smothered in béchamel sauce.

Didier and Stephanie 56 St Helen's Rd, Uplands ☎01792/655603. Small, lovely, French restaurant of just ten tables in a beautiful Victorian house, specializing in some fairly obscure regional Gallic surprises.

Dylan Thomas Centre Somerset Place ☎01792/463980. Refined but relaxed snacking or dining in the National Literature Centre, with a good range of reasonably priced Welsh specialities.

Govinda's 8 Craddock St ☎01792/468469. Vegetarian restaurant in the Hare Krishna tradition, selling ultra-cheap wholesome meals and freshly pressed juices.

La Brasseria 28 Wind St ☎01792/469683. Earthy Mediterranean restaurant offering a pared-down menu of meat- and fish-based classics. Closed Sun.

La Parrilla Unit 5 J Shed, Kings Rd ☎01792/464530. Sleek restaurant in a converted warehouse in the SA1 precinct. Excellent seafood.

Miah's St Paul's Church, St Helen's Rd, ☎01792/464084. Sumptuous Indian restaurant, with food to match.

Morgans Somerset Place ☎01792/484848, ⓦwww.morganshotel.co.uk. The huge old boardroom of the Port Authority building now houses this exceptional restaurant, with confident contemporary cooking and dishes such as wild sea bass in vanilla bean sauce.

The Retreat 2 Humphrey St, off Walter Rd ☎01792/457880. Cosy veggie café open for breakfast, lunch and dinner. BYO booze and book ahead for evenings. Open Tues–Sun 10am–9pm.

Sketty Hall Singleton Park ☎01792/284011. Catering academy in beautiful surroundings where you can sample the excellent student cuisine for reasonable prices. Booking essential.

Street Pebble Café Bar 11 Wind St. A wicker, stone and a candlelit interior provide Wind St's most chilled ambience, great for morning smoothies, daytime paninis or Mediterranean food in the evenings.

Bars, pubs and clubs

Café Mambo 46 Kingsway. Popular Latin American bar with tequilas and cocktails, music and a great daytime to early-evening menu.

Cross Keys Inn 12 St Mary St. Swansea's oldest pub, dating from the 1700s, with good food, a beer garden and BBQs in summer.

Eli Jenkins Ale House 24 Oxford St. Yet more Dylan Thomas memorabilia, this time in a pleasant, modern city-centre pub with good beer and decent daytime fare.

Escape Club Northampton Lane, off Kingsway ☎01792/470000, ⓦwww.escapegroup.com. Enormous, purpose-built dance venue that pulls big name DJs for a dizzying array of club nights.

Exchange 10 Strand. Laid-back gay pub that's a good starting point for tapping into the Swansea scene.

Ice Bar 64 Wind St. The Wind St establishment of choice for a younger crowd; loud and lively at all times.

Monkey Café 13 Castle St ⓦwww.monkeycafe.co.uk. Groovy, inexpensive, mosaic-floored café with a relaxed atmosphere and nightly DJs or live music. On a good night, the best in town.

No Sign Bar 56 Wind St. A narrow frontage leads into a long, warm pub interior, one of the oldest in town and easily the best on Wind St.

The meaning of the name is explained in depth in the window.

Oceana 72 Kingsway, ☎0845/2932872, ⓦwww.oceanaclubs.com/swansea. Multi-club spread over three floors with internationally themed bars and dancefloors for serious shakin'.

The Office 2 Castle Gardens, ☎01792/645063. The best place in Swansea to catch live rock.

Pitcher & Piano 58 Wind St. Stripped pine and chrome bar exuding style, individuality and some fine DJs spinning their stuff.

Pump House Pump House Quay. Good on a warm day for a pint overlooking the marina.

Queen's Hotel Gloucester Place, near the marina. Large old hotel and pub firmly in the Swansea seafaring tradition, with good snack lunches and Sunday roasts, plus bags of gritty atmosphere.

Uplands Tavern 42 Uplands Crescent, Uplands. ☎01792/458242, ⓦwww.uplandstavern.co.uk. Former haunt of Dylan Thomas and today a bastion of live music, especially rock, blues, funk and jazz.

Theatre, cinema and classical music

Brangwyn Hall The Guildhall, Guildhall Rd South ☎01792/635432. Vastly impressive music hall in the Art Deco civic centre which hosts regular concerts by the BBC National Orchestra of Wales and others.

Dylan Thomas Theatre Dylan Thomas Square, Maritime Quarter ☎01792/473238, ⓦwww.dylanthomastheatre.org.uk. Reruns of Thomas's classics, intertwined with other modern works in the Little Theatre.

Grand Theatre Singleton St ☎01792/475715, ⓦwww.swanseagrand.co.uk. One of Britain's best provincial theatres, with a wide-ranging diet of visiting high culture, comedy, farce and music.

Odeon Cinema Parc Tawe ☎08712/244007. Ten-screen multiplex.

Patti Pavilion Victoria Park ☎01792/477710. Restored former opera hut of chanteuse Adelina Patti, now hosting numerous gigs and theatrical performances.

Taliesin Arts Centre Swansea University ☎01792/602060, ⓦwww.taliesinartscentre.co.uk. Welsh, English and international visiting theatre, music and film, including offbeat and alternative fare.

Listings

Bike rental Action Bikes, St David's Square, ☎01792/464640.

Books Dylan's Bookstore, Salubrious House, 23 King Edward Rd; Uplands Bookshop, 27 Uplands Crescent; Waterstone's, Oxford St.

Bus enquiries Quadrant Centre bus station, Plymouth St (Mon–Fri 8.30am–4pm, Sat 8.30am–5pm; ☎0871/2002233).

Car rental Enterprise ☎01792/480484 has the best-value rentals, will deliver and pick up, and often have excellent-value weekend specials.

Festivals The annual Swansea Bay Summer Festival takes place from May–Sept, the highbrow Swansea Festival through Oct and the city's Dylan Thomas Festival in early Nov; details from the tourist office.

Football Swansea City FC play at the new Liberty Stadium, Landore (ⓦwww.swanseacity.net).

Hospital Singleton Hospital, Sketty Park Lane, Singleton, West Swansea ☎01792/205666.

Internet access Swansea Central Library, Civic Centre, Oystermouth Rd (Tues–Fri 8.30am–8pm, Sat & Sun 10am–4pm; ☎01792/636464).

Laundries Hafod Laundrette, 16 Neath Rd; Uplands Laundrette, 73 Uplands Crescent.

Pharmacies Kingsway Pharmacy, 39 Kingsway (Mon–Sat 10am–6pm).

Police The main station is on Alexandra Rd (☎01792/456999).

Post office Inside WH Smith, The Quadrant ☎0845/7223344.

Rugby Ospreys Rugby Club, one of Wales' premier sides, play at the new Liberty Stadium, Landore (ⓦwww.ospreysrugby.com).

Surfing Information and equipment (including secondhand boards) from Big Drop Surf Shop, 1 St David's Square, St David's Centre. (☎01792/480481, ⓦwww.big-drop.com).

Swimming The sparkling new Wales National Pool (☎01792/513513, ⓦwww .walesnationalpoolswansea.co.uk) on Sketty Lane near the University is Wales' only 50m facility. There's also swimming at the LC leisure complex (see p.143).

Gower

Thrusting into the Bristol Channel west of Swansea, the nineteen-mile **GOWER** (Gŵyr) peninsula is fringed by sweeping yellow bays and precipitous cliffs, caves and blowholes to the south, and wide, flat marshes and cockle beds to the north. Brackened heaths with prehistoric remains and tiny villages lie between, interspersed with castle ruins, curious churches and the scent of wild garlic.

Gower starts in Swansea's western suburbs, along the coast of Swansea Bay which curves round to a point in the charmingly old-fashioned and increasingly swish resort of **Mumbles** and Mumbles Head, marking the boundary between the sandy sweep of Swansea Bay and the rocky inlets along the southern Gower's serrated coastline. This southern coast is punctuated by sites exploited for their defensive capacities, best seen in the eerie isolation of the sandbound **Pennard Castle**, high above **Three Cliffs Bay**. West, the wide sands of **Oxwich Bay** sit next to inland reedy marshes, beyond which is the picturesque village of **Port Eynon**. West again, the coast becomes a wild, frilly series of inlets and cliffs, capped by a five-mile path that stretches all the way to the peninsula's glorious westernmost point, **Worms Head**.

Rhossili Bay, a breathtaking four-mile span of sand backed by the village of Rhossili, occupies the entire western end of Gower from Worms Head to the islet of **Burry Holms**, and, when conditions are right, provides some of the best **surfing** in Wales. The northern coast merges into the tidal flats of the estuary, running past the salted marsh of **Llanrhidian**, overlooked by the gaunt ruins of **Weobley Castle**, and on to the famous cockle beds at **Penclawdd**.

Gower practicalities

There are no train services on Gower, but with its proximity to urban Swansea, **bus** transport is reasonably comprehensive. Gower Explorer buses run every hour from Swansea's Quadrant bus station to Rhossili and Port Eynon (every two hours to Oxwich and Horton) in South Gower; and through North Gower as far as Llanrhidian (every two hours to Llangennith and Llanmadoc). First

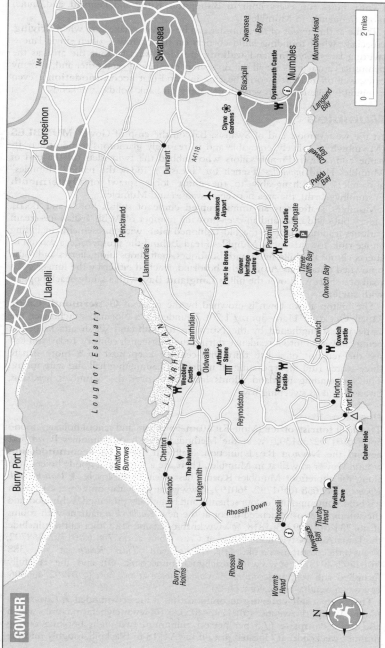

GOWER

Swansea

Swansea
Bay

M4

Gorseinon

Blackpill   Oystermouth Castle Mumbles ⓘ

Mumbles Head

Clyne
Gardens

Langland
Bay

Llanelli

Dunvant

A4118

Caswell
Bay

Pwll Du
Bay

Penclawdd

Swansea
Airport

Pennard Castle

Parkmill Southgate P

Llanmorlais

Parc le Breos

Gower
Heritage
Centre

Three
Cliffs Bay

L
o
u
g
h
o
r
    E
s
t
u
a
r
y

L
L
A
N
R
H
I
D
I
A
N

Llanrhidian

Oldwalls

Arthur's
Stone

Oxwich

Oxwich Bay

Oxwich Castle

Weobley
Castle

Burry Port

Penrice
Castle

Horton

Reynoldston

Port Eynon

Whitford
Burrows

Cheriton

The Bulwark

Culver Hole

Llanmadoc

Langennith

Rhossili Down

Pavliand
Cave

Mewslade Bay Thurba Head

Rhossili ⓘ

Burry
Holms

Rhossili
Bay

Worm's
Head

N

SOUTHEAST WALES

0   2 miles

147

© Crown copyright

Cymru buses run every hour to Bishopston, Kittle and Pennard, and, much more frequently, to Mumbles.

Traffic at the height of the summer can be heavy, so take care when **driving**, especially when rounding blind corners on the narrow – often single-lane – twisting lanes. **Cycling** and **walking** are ideal ways to tour the area, as the peninsula's attractions are all within a short distance of each other and, in many cases, well off-road. It's worth bearing in mind that **accommodation** – even camping – is generally in very short supply on bank holiday weekends.

Mumbles

At the westernmost end of Swansea Bay on the cusp of Gower, **MUMBLES** (Mwmbwls) is a lively, enjoyable and increasingly glamorous seaside town. Its name comes from French sailors who dubbed the twin islets off the end of Mumbles Head *mamelles* (French for "breasts"). Today, the name "Mumbles" also refers interchangeably to the entire loose sprawl of **Oystermouth** (Ystumllwynarth), the area between Swansea and Mumbles.

Mumbles' seafront is an uninterrupted curve of stylish hotels and B&Bs, breezy pubs and cafés and an ever-growing number of Welsh/Italian ice-cream parlours leading down to the old-fashioned **pier**, with amusements including an ice rink, towards rocky Mumbles Head. Behind the promenade, a warren of streets climbs the hills, lined with boutiques, craft shops and galleries and some renowned restaurants. Around the headland, reached either by the longer coast road or a short walk over the hill, is **Langland Bay**, with a sandy beach popular with **surfers**.

The hilltop above town is crowned by the ruins of **Oystermouth Castle** (April–Oct daily 11am–5pm; £1.20). Founded as a Norman watchtower, the castle was strengthened by the Normans to withstand Welsh attacks before being converted into a residence during the fourteenth century. Today you can see the remains of a late thirteenth-century keep next to a more ornate three-storey ruin incorporating an impressive banqueting hall and state rooms. The surrounding parkland affords lush views over the Mumbles headland, Swansea and its sweeping bay.

Practicalities

The small **tourist office** (Mon–Sat 10am–5pm, Sun and school holidays noon–5pm; ☎01792/361302) is in the Methodist church on Mumbles Road, just beyond the Newton Road junction. Staff can advise on **accommodation** around Gower as well as in Mumbles. There are a number of good choices here along the shorefront Mumbles Road. These include the lovely ☂ *Patrick's with Rooms* at no. 638 (☎01792/360199, ⓦ www.patrickswithrooms.com; ➏), which has bold, contemporary colour schemes and beautifully presented Welsh food; and the stunning retro-influenced decor at the new *Knabrock* restaurant-with-rooms at no. 734 (☎01792/361818, ⓦ www.knabrock.com; ➏). Other options include the Laura Ashley-style floral rooms at *Coast House* at no. 708 (☎01792/368702, ⓦ www.thecoasthouse.co.uk; ➌); the elegant *Tides Reach* at no. 388 (☎01792/404877, ⓦ www.tidesreachguesthouse.co.uk; ➌); and the tastefully furnished and very welcoming *Alexandra House* at no. 366 (☎01792/406406, ⓦ www.alexandra-house.com; ➋–➌).

There's great **self-catering** accommodation at the eco-minded ☂ *Clyne Farm Centre*, Westport Avenue (☎01792/403333, ⓦ www.clynefarm.com), which also has a **campsite** (£5 per person, minimum two-night booking during summer weekends). It's located just off the A4118 in Blackpill, roughly midway between Mumbles and Swansea, and you can arrange for someone to come and pick you up if you arrive by public transport.

Mumbles is one of Wales' culinary havens, with some really superb **food**. Daytime highlights include the inexpensive *Coffee Denn*, 34 Newton Rd, particularly good for sweet treats; *Joe's Ice Cream*, 524 Mumbles Rd, which has been making ice cream here for nearly a century and now has several other outlets in south Wales; and *Verdi's*, overlooking the sea near the pier – a Mumbles institution for its lively Welsh–Italian atmosphere and superb pizzas and ice-cream concoctions. For really special lunches or dinners, try the moderately priced *P.A.'s Wine Bar*, 95 Newton Rd (℡01792/367723), for fine fish dishes; the pricier *Knight's* at 614–16 Mumbles Rd (℡01792/363184) for fantastic fusion cuisine; and the incomparable *犬 698* at 698 Mumbles Rd (℡01792/361616), where starters like white bean soup drizzled in truffle oil are followed by beautifully prepared local beef, lamb and seafood. Dylan Thomas' old waterhole, *The Mermaid*, at 686 Mumbles Rd (℡01792/367744), is now a smart restaurant specializing in Gower salt-marsh lamb.

Although the once-legendary "Mumbles Mile" – where stags and hens once ritualistically staggered between the **pubs** along the mile-long stretch of seafront – no longer exists as such, there are still plenty of pubs for relaxed drinking. Places worth a lingering pint include the *Antelope*, the *Oystercatcher* and the *White Rose*.

The south and west Gower coasts

From Mumbles Head, the limestone crags of the **southern Gower coast** twist and delve the fifteen miles or so to Worms Head, at the bottom of Rhossili Bay. Many of the sandy bays between the cliffs are easily accessible by car, so they tend to be crowded in peak season.

From Mumbles Head to Three Cliffs Bay

The first few miles of the southern Gower coast are highly developed, including the popular **surf beach** of **Langland Bay**, between two headlands. The narrow, golden-sanded **Caswell Bay** comes next, from where you can follow the stunning cliff path to the tiny and remote former smugglers' haunt of **Brandy Cove**, or pebbly **Pwlldu Bay**, which is owned by the National Trust and backed by a wooded ravine which offers many stunning walks. Brandy Cove and Pwlldu Bay are inaccessible by car; park in Bishopston village and walk the last mile or so.

Three miles along, huge **Three Cliffs Bay** is one of Gower's finest beaches, at the end of a silent valley fringed by dunes and the eerie ruins of **Pennard Castle**, whose relative inaccessibility ensures that it's never too packed. The best approach is from the car park at **Southgate**, from where you hike a mile or so west along clifftops to Three Cliffs Bay, where you turn inland and follow the boundary of the golf course to the castle. Otherwise, you can try one of the paths that fan out along the tufty valley of the Pennard Pill from **PARKMILL**, a tourist honeypot on the main A4118. Here, the **Gower Heritage Centre** (daily: April–Oct 10am–5.30pm; Nov–March 10am–4.30pm; £4.60) has a working water mill and woollen exhibits.

A mile north of Parkmill (reachable via the lane that heads past the Heritage Centre) is the Neolithic burial chamber (3000–1900 BC) known, in honour of the thirteenth-century lords of Oystermouth Castle, as **Parc le Breos**. Although over-restored, the roofless chamber is impressive for its age and sheer size – seventy feet long and divided into four separate chambers. In 1869, the skeletons of two dozen people were found inside. Just beyond the chamber and to the right, a deep fissure in a limestone outcrop marks the position of the dank and musty **Cathole Rock Cave**, in which flint tools, dating back over 12,000 years have been found.

The best local **B&B** is almost a mile up a lane beside the Heritage Centre: one of the original Gower manor houses, the grand and welcoming *Parc-le-Breos House* (℡01792/371636, ⓦwww.parc-le-breos.co.uk; ❸) does delicious, moderately priced three-course evening meals, rents out bikes, and offers **horseback** sightseeing trips from £28 per half day. **Campers** should make for the *Three Cliffs Caravan Park* at North Hills Farm (℡01792/371218; £13 per pitch; closed Nov–March), overlooking Three Cliffs Bay between Parkmill and Penmaen.

Oxwich

One of the most curious landscapes in Gower is the reedy **nature reserve** around **Oxwich Burrows**, a flatland of salt and freshwater marshes reached via the lane that forks left off the A4118 at the ruined gatehouse of the privately owned Penrice Castle. Close by on the coast, the scattered village of **OXWICH** is grouped next to the gaping sands of Oxwich Bay. The sands and sea around here regularly receive awards, including the coveted blue flag. One way to sample the waters is with Euphoria Sailing (℡01792/234502, ⓦwww .euphoriasailing.com), which offers tuition and rental for sailing, water-skiing and wakeboarding.

The squat **church** of St Illtud sits alone, away from the village, at the top of the beach. A quieter beach can be found just over a mile away at **Slade Sands**, reached along the lane that climbs from the Oxwich crossroads past the ruins of a Tudor manor known as **Oxwich Castle** (April–Sept daily 10am–5pm; £2.70; CADW), a fine example of early sixteenth-century house gentrification by Sir Rice Mansel, member of a powerful Welsh dynasty. His son Edward added the many-windowed eastern range, a pile of rooms with a highly fashionable long gallery that fell into ruin shortly afterwards.

Oxwich's popularity is evident in its plentiful **accommodation**. The *Oxwich Camping Park* on the Penrice road over a mile back from the beach (℡01792/390777; £8–12 per pitch; closed Oct–March) has a swimming pool and laundry on site. On the main street, B&Bs include *Little Haven* (℡01792/390940, ⓦwww.littlehavenoxwich.co.uk; ❷; minimum 2-night stay May–Sept), with a heated outdoor pool; *Surfsound Guesthouse* (℡01792/390822, ⓦwww.surfsoundgower.co.uk; ❸; closed Nov–Feb); and *Woodside* (℡01792/390791; ❷; closed Nov–Feb). Nearby, the plain *Oxwich Bay Hotel* (℡01792/390329, ⓦwww.oxwichbayhotel.co.uk; ❸–❽) is set in splendid isolation by the sands near the church. It's a good place to **eat**, too, with well-prepared seafood and steaks, and some creative vegetarian dishes like a leek, mushroom and potato gratin in white wine.

Horton and Port Eynon

The rocky cliffs from Oxwich Point fade into wide stony bays towards the quiet village of **HORTON**, with a decent beach, and the more touristy **PORT EYNON**, with a clutch of fish and chip shops and the laid-back *Ship Inn*.

The villages' sands and dunes are sheltered by a prominent headland, easily reached by a series of paths that wind their way along the shore from the car park above the bleak ruins of the old shoreline salt house and oyster pools. Owned by the National Trust, the lichen-spattered limestone headland is a wild and windy spot, where tufted grass gives way to sharp limestone crags. A natural cave at the tip can be seen from above, a great dome-shaped chasm that plunges into the hillside. Around the headland to the west is the quite remarkable, but fairly hard to find, **Culver Hole**, built into the cliffs. A man-made cave, it may originally have been a stronghold for the long-gone Port Eynon castle, and has served its time subsequently as a smugglers' retreat, dovecote and armoury.

The headland casts good views over the curve of Port Eynon Bay and the cliffs round to Rhossili, five miles west. The **coastal path** here is the most spectacular walk on Gower, veering along crags above thundering waves for five miles. The only real beach along this stretch is the secluded **Mewslade Bay**, just short of Rhossili and accessible by the path from Pitton. Along the coast walk, about midway between the two villages, is **Paviland Cave**, the site of an astonishing find in 1823, when the skeleton of a Stone Age hunter, at least 19,000 years old, was unearthed. At **Thurba Head**, on the eastern side of Mewslade Bay, there are a few scant remains of an Iron Age hillfort sited magnificently a few hundred feet above the waves.

Port Eynon hogs the accommodation limelight. Its YHA **hostel** (℡0870/770 5998; dorm beds from £15.95), in a beachside Victorian-era lifeboat station, is particularly good. Otherwise, there's the *Culver House Hotel* (℡01792/390755 Ⓦwww.culverhousehotel.co.uk; ❸–❺), or **camping** above the YHA hostel at *Carreglwyd Park* (℡01792/390795; £14 per pitch) or at the family-oriented *Bank Farm* (℡01792/390228; £14.50 per pitch), off the A4118 towards Horton.

Rhossili, Worms Head and Llangennith

Heading west, Gower saves the best for last. The sublimely sited village of **RHOSSILI** (Rhosili) has wraparound views up into the hills and out to sea. It's a great place for coastal walking, particularly out to **Worms Head**, an isolated string of rocks with the spectacular appearance of a basking Welsh dragon, accessible for only five hours around low tide. Take care in this area: the **tidal currents** are extremely dangerous and people have lost their lives here. If you do get cut off, don't attempt to wade back – wait on the promontory until the tide recedes.

At the head of the road, near the village, is a well-stocked, helpful **National Trust visitor centre** (Jan–March Thurs–Sun 11am–4pm; Easter–Oct Mon–Fri 10.30am–5pm, Sat & Sun 10.30am–6pm; Nov–Dec Wed–Sun 11am–4pm; ℡01792/390707), which has continuously updated details of local companies

▲ Kayaksurfing, Rhossili Beach

renting **surfing** and **hang-gliding** equipment. **Tide times** are posted outside for those heading for Worms Head.

Below the village, a great curve of white sand stretches away into the distance, a dazzling coastline vast enough to absorb the crowds, especially if you are prepared to head a little way north towards **Burry Holms**, an islet three miles distant that is cut off at high tide. The northern end of the beach can also be reached along the small lane from Reynoldston, in the middle of the peninsula, to **Llangennith**, on the other side of the towering sandstone **Rhossili Down**, rising up to 633ft. In the village, PJ's Surfshop (℡01792/386669, ⓦwww .pjsurfshop.co.uk) has a wide range of **rental surfboards** (£10 per day), wetsuits (£10 per day) and boogie boards (£5 per day). A mile away at the *Hillend* campsite (see below), the Welsh Surfing Federation's Surf School (℡01792/386426, ⓦwww.wsfsurfschool.co.uk) runs half-day **surfing courses** costing £25 for the first lesson and £20 for subsequent lessons. Also based in Llangennith, Fly West Wales Summer School (ⓦwww.flyspain.co.uk/fly-west-wales) offers **paragliding** trips and tuition, including day-taster courses and tandem flights (both £120), along with longer four- to six-day courses (from £480), and fly from a number of locations, with memorable flights over the coastal dunes.

Accommodation is pretty scarce, but Rhossili village is home to the decent *Worms Head Hotel* (℡01792/390512, ⓦwww.thewormshead.co.uk; ❹–❺; closed late Dec to late Jan), which has what is surely the best aspect of any pub garden in Wales. Nearby Llangennith has two lovely B&Bs: *College House* (℡01792/386214; ❸) in the middle of the village, and the very chilled *Western House* (℡01792/386620, ⓦwww.llangennith.freeserve.co.uk; ❶) on the lane towards the beach. The lane peters out half a mile further at *Hillend* (℡01792/386204; £11–14 per pitch), a fabulous **campsite** behind the dunes and with direct access to the glorious beach. Back in Llangennith village, the *King's Head* is a fine pub for food and drink.

Mid- and north Gower

The great sweep of land that rises to the north of the main Gower road does not attract anything like the number of visitors that the south and west do, due to the lack of comparable coastline.

The Gower's northern fringe comprises a flattened series of marshes and mud flats merging indistinguishably with the sands of the Loughor estuary. Wading birds, gulls and bedded cockles, as well as herds of cattle and wild horses, are all found amongst the flats, dunes and inlets burrowing into the land from the estuary.

Gower's central plateau is a pleasant patchwork of pastoral farmland. Its backbone, the five-hundred-foot-high sandstone ridge Cefn Bryn, stretches across the centre of the peninsula, with wiry peat and grass dotted with hardy sheep, ancient stone cairns and holy wells. The best views over the peninsula are from the road brushing over its roof.

Reynoldston and Arthur's Stone

The **Cefn Bryn** ridge has some great walks, and is most easily explored from the quiet village of **REYNOLDSTON**, grouped around a sheep-filled village green. The village's pub, the ⚔ *King Arthur Hotel* (℡01792/390775, ⓦwww .kingarthurhotel.co.uk; ❸–❺), has comfortable en-suite rooms and dishes up superb meals, as does the luxurious *Fairyhill* (℡01792/390139, ⓦwww.fairyhill .net; ❽–❾), a grand, ivy-clad country-house hotel where a dinner, bed and breakfast package is compulsory on Friday and Saturday nights (£245–355 per double); dinner is optional the rest of the week. The restaurant, serving exceptional

Arthur's Stone

Gower is littered with more dolmens, standing stones and other prehistoric remains than any other landscape in Wales. The most celebrated of all is **Arthur's Stone** (sometimes referred to as King Arthur's Stone), a massive and isolated burial chamber topped by a quartz capstone weighing over 25 tons. The dolmen is thought to be anything up to 6000 years old, while the thrusting, ruptured capstone (which, before it split sometime around 1693, rested on six supporting stones) is mentioned, often as *Maen Ceti*, in documents dating back a thousand years.

Legends abound, including a popular belief that, while walking in Llanelli, King Arthur found a stone in his shoe, removed it and flung it far away, whereupon it landed on Cefn Bryn and swelled in size with pride at having been touched by the king. A more likely explanation for its placement is as a glacial deposit, after which tombs were dug out beneath. Claims also suggest that it's a thirsty stone, occasionally making a nocturnal flit to Port Eynon for a drink in the sea, a reputation that probably arises from its possible position over an underground stream – certainly there are many surfacing around it. And still others believe that it's part of an astronomical alignment along with Lady's Well, a spring deemed holy and now enclosed in a hut, across the road; and Penmaen's ruined chapel and Neolithic burial chamber, some three miles southeast. This alignment is allegedly charged with a special energy that has, in fact, shown up in some curious photographs with streaks and dots in otherwise clear skies. Whatever the case, the views from up here are extraordinary.

cuisine using local Gower and Welsh produce, is also open to non-residents.

From Reynoldston, a dramatic road rises up the slope of Cefn Bryn before skating across its summit in a perfect, straight line. Several tracks lead off from the road affording clear views to both Gower coasts, but you might be best off stopping at the small car park about a mile east of Reynoldston; from here, a path leads about half a mile across the boggy moor to **Arthur's Stone** (see box above).

From Llanrhidian to Llanmadoc

The small village of **LLANRHIDIAN** sits above the largely inaccessible marsh of the same name, which is virtually indistinguishable from the sands of the Loughor estuary. Views from the former village pub, now the exquisite ✴ *Welcome to Town* bistro (closed Mon and dinner Sun; ☎01792/390015), are superb, as is the locally sourced cuisine like scrambled duck egg and smoked salmon followed by roast Gower lamb. Half a mile west, in the hamlet of **Oldwalls**, the *Greyhound Inn* is a cheaper food option, but very good nonetheless. A further mile west is **Weobley Castle** (daily: April–Oct 9.30am–6pm; Nov–March 9.30am–5pm; £2.70; CADW). Gaunt against the backdrop of the marsh and the estuary, the castle was built as a fortified manor in the latter part of the thirteenth century.

The lane continues two miles west to the village of **Cheriton**, with its charming thirteenth-century church, and then on to **LLANMADOC**, where you can park and venture onto the land spit of **Whitford Burrows**, a soft patch of dunes now open as a nature reserve, with the only sea-washed cast-iron lighthouse in the UK. Steep paths lead from Llanmadoc village up **Llanmadoc Hill** to the south. **The Bulwark**, a lonely and windy hillfort, can be seen at the eastern end of Llanmadoc Hill's summit ridge.

Accommodation options along Llanmadoc's main road include the en-suite rooms at *Tallizmand Guesthouse* (☎01792/386373, ⊛www.tallizmand.co.uk; ❷), which has a cosy communal lounge room warmed by an open fire and proper ground coffee at breakfast. You'll find good **meals** and wonderful real ales nearby at the red-trimmed, seventeenth-century *Britannia Inn*.

Travel details

Unless otherwise stated, frequencies for trains and buses are for Monday to Saturday services, Sunday averages 1 to 3 services, though the main routes are more frequent and some routes have no Sunday service at all. See p.38 for more information including websites with route-finder services.

Trains

Cardiff to: Abergavenny (hourly; 40min); Barry Island (every 20–30min; 30min); Bridgend (every 30min; 20min); Bristol (every 30min; 50min); Caerphilly (every 30min; 20min); Carmarthen (6 daily; 1hr 45min); Chepstow (hourly; 40min); Crewe (mostly hourly; 2hr 40min); Haverfordwest (10 daily; 2hr 40min); Holyhead (8 daily; 5hr 10min); Llanelli (17 daily; 1hr 10min); Llantwit Major (hourly; 45min); Llwynypia (every 30min; 50min); London (hourly; 2hr); Maesteg (hourly; 50min); Manchester (mostly hourly; 3hr 10min); Merthyr Tydfil (hourly; 1hr); Neath (hourly; 40min); Newport (every 15–30min; 10min); Penarth (every 20min; 10min); Pontypool (hourly; 30min); Pontypridd (every 15min; 30min); Swansea (every 30min; 50min); Tenby (7 daily; 2hr 30min); Trehafod (every 30min; 30min); Ystrad Rhondda (every 30min; 50min).

Newport to: Abergavenny (hourly; 30min); Bristol (every 30min; 40min); Caldicot (hourly; 10min); Cardiff (every 15–30min; 10min); Chepstow (hourly; 20min); Hereford (hourly; 50min); London (hourly; 1hr 50min); Pontypool (at least hourly; 1hr 15min); Swansea (hourly; 1hr 20min).

Swansea to: Cardiff (at least hourly; 50min); Carmarthen (hourly; 50min); Ferryside (10 daily; 40min); Haverfordwest (7 daily; 1hr 30min); Kidwelly (10 daily; 30min); Knighton (4 daily; 2hr 50min); Llandeilo (4 daily; 1hr); Llandovery (4 daily; 1hr 20min); Llandrindod Wells (4 daily; 2hr 20min); Llanelli (hourly; 20min); Llanwrtyd Wells (5 daily; 1hr 50min); London (2 daily; 3hr); Milford Haven (7 daily; 2hr); Narberth (7 daily; 1hr 20min); Newport (hourly; 1hr 20min); Pembroke (6 daily; 2hr); Tenby (7 daily; 1hr 40min); Whitland (hourly; 1hr 10min).

Buses

Bridgend to: Blaengarw (every 20min; 35min); Cardiff (hourly; 50min); Cowbridge (every 30min; 20min); Cymer (every 15min; 1hr); Kenfig (hourly; 45min); Llantrisant (3 daily; 1hr 20min); Llantwit Major (hourly; 40min); Margam Park (every 30min; 30min); Swansea (hourly; 50min).

Cardiff to: Abergavenny (hourly; 1hr 20min); Aberystwyth (2 daily; 4hr); Bangor (1 daily; 8hr); Barry Island (hourly; 50min); Birmingham (5 daily; 2hr 30min); Blaenafon (hourly, 1 change; 1hr 40min); Brecon (5 daily; 1hr 25min); Bristol (10 daily; 1hr 10min); Caernarfon (1 daily; 7hr 40min); Caerphilly (every 30min; 40min); Cardiff–Wales Airport (every 30min; 30min); Chepstow (hourly; 1hr 20min); Cowbridge (every 30min; 40min); Heathrow Airport (8 daily; 2hr 50min); Lampeter (2 daily; 3hr); Llantwit Major (hourly; 1hr); London (6 daily; 3hr 10min); Machynlleth (1 daily; 5hr 30min); Merthyr Tydfil (every 30min; 45min); Nelson (hourly; 35min); Newport (every 30min; 30min); Penarth (every 30min; 30min); Pontypridd (every 15min; 30min); Senghenydd (hourly; 50min); Swansea (every 30min; 1hr).

Chepstow to: Bristol (at least one daily; 1hr); Caerwent (hourly; 15min); Cardiff (hourly; 1hr 20min); Monmouth (at least hourly; 50min); Newport (hourly; 50min); Penhow (hourly; 40min); Tintern (8 daily; 20min); Trellech (7 daily; 30min); Usk (6 daily; 45min).

Merthyr Tydfil to: Abergavenny (every 30min; 1hr 30min); Brecon (9 daily; 40min); Cardiff (every 30min; 45min); Swansea (hourly; 1hr).

Monmouth to: Abergavenny (6 daily; 40min); Chepstow (at least hourly; 50min); Newport (8 daily; 1hr); Raglan (hourly; 15min); Ross-on-Wye (6 daily; 40min); Tintern (7 daily; 30min); Trellech (8 daily; 20min); Usk (6 daily; 30min).

Neath to: Aberdulais (hourly; 15min); Cymer (hourly; 35min); Pontrhydyfen (hourly; 25min).

Newport to: Abergavenny (hourly; 1hr); Abertillery (every 30min; 1hr); Birmingham (5 daily; 2hr); Blaenafon (every 15min; 1hr); Brecon (every 2hr; 2hr 20min); Bristol (10 daily; 50min); Caerphilly (every 30min; 40min); Caerwent (hourly; 30min); Cardiff (every 30min; 40min); Chepstow (hourly; 50min); London (5 daily; 2hr 50min); Monmouth (8 daily; 1hr); Pontypool (every 15min; 25min); Raglan (8 daily; 45min); Usk (8 daily; 30min).

Swansea to: Aberdulais (hourly; 45min); Aberystwyth (2 daily; 3hr); Brecon (3 daily; 1hr 30min); Bristol (10 daily; 2hr 30min); Cardiff (every 30min; 1hr); Dan-yr-ogof (4 daily; 1hr); Llangennith (3 daily; 1hr 20min); Merthyr Tydfil (hourly; 1hr); Mumbles (every 10min; 15min); Neath (every 30min; 30min); Oxwich (8 daily; 1hr); Pennard (hourly; 30min); Port Eynon (8 daily; 50min); Rhossili (Mon–Sat 10 daily; 1hr).

Southwest Wales

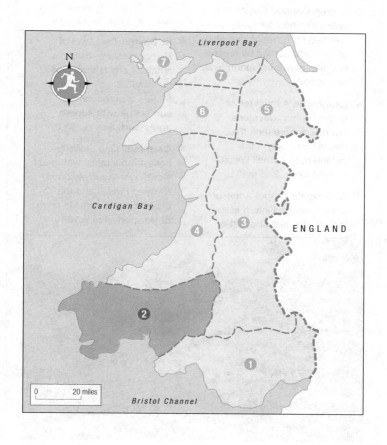

CHAPTER 2 # Highlights

* **The Tywi Valley** Castles, follies and the fledgling National Botanic Garden set amongst one of Wales' lushest and most atmospheric valleys. See p.164

* **Carreg Cennen Castle** The country's finest fortress, perched on a vertiginous plug of rock and framed by green hills and glowering mountains. See p.167

* **Laugharne** A must for all Dylan Thomas devotees, but much more than that, this quirky place is the quintessential small Welsh coastal town. See p.171

* **St Govan's chapel** A tiny grey chapel wedged into a fissure in the cliffs, just above the churning sea: a phenomenal statement of faith and an awesome sight. See p.185

* **Skomer, Skokholm and Grassholm** Rough and rugged islands, where squawking colonies of birds rule the roost. See p.195

* **St Davids** The jewel of Pembrokeshire, Britain's smallest city is surrounded by fabulous scenery and fosters a burgeoning surf scene with superb après-surf. See p.197

* **Carn Ingli** One of Wales' holiest mountains, with great views over the mysterious Mynydd Preseli and the charming little seaside town of Newport. See p.209

▲ St Govan's Chapel

Southwest Wales

The most westerly outpost of Wales, the counties of Carmarthenshire and, in particular, Pembrokeshire attract thousands of visitors each year. The principal draw is the fabulous scenery: bucolic and magical inland, where Carmarthenshire follows the Tywi Valley into the heart of the country; rocky, indented and spectacular around the Pembrokeshire Coast National Park and its 186-mile path. The last remnants of industrial south Wales peter out at **Llanelli**, before the undistinguished county town of **Carmarthen**. Of all the routes that converge on the town, the most glorious is the winding road along the Tywi Valley, past ruined hilltop forts and the **National Botanic Garden of Wales** on the way to **Llandeilo** and Wales' most impressively positioned castle, at **Carreg Cennen**, high up on a dizzy plug of Black Mountain rock. Burrowing further inland, the sparsely populated countryside of remote hills and tiny valleys is broken only by endearing small market towns such as **Llandovery**, the gloomy ruins of **Talley Abbey** and the Roman gold mines at **Dolaucothi**.

The wide sands of southern Carmarthenshire, just beyond Dylan Thomas' adopted hometown of **Laugharne**, merge into the popular south Pembrokeshire bucket-and-spade seaside resorts of **Tenby** and **Saundersfoot**. Tenby sits at the entrance to the south Pembrokeshire peninsula, divided from the rest of the county by the Milford Haven and Daugleddau estuary, which brings its tidal waters deep into the heart of the pastoral county. The peninsula's turbulent, rocky coast is ruptured by some remote historical sites, including the Norman baronial castle at **Manorbier** and **St Govan's chapel**, a minute place of worship wedged into the rocks of a sea cliff near Bosherston. At the top of the peninsula is the old county town of **Pembroke**, dominated by its fearsome castle, across the Milford Haven estuary from small seaside villages and tiny islands along the rugged curve of **St Bride's Bay**, inland of which is the market town and transport interchange of **Haverfordwest**, dull but seemingly difficult to avoid. St Bride's Bay's rutted coastline is one of the most glorious parts of the coastal walk, leading north to brush past the impeccable city of **St Davids**, where the exquisite cathedral shelters from the town in its own protective hollow. St Davids, founded by Wales' patron saint in the sixth century, is a magnet for visitors; aside from its own charms, there are opportunities locally for spectacular coast and hill walks, hair-raising dinghy crossings to local islands, surf galore and numerous other outdoor activities.

The coast turns towards the north at St Davids, becoming the southern stretch of Cardigan Bay. Sixteen miles away by road, and well over thirty by rugged nips and tucks of the coastal walk, is the pretty port of **Fishguard**, terminus for ferries to Rosslare in Ireland. The northernmost section of the Coast Path, from Fishguard to the outskirts of Cardigan and past the delightful little town of **Newport**, is the

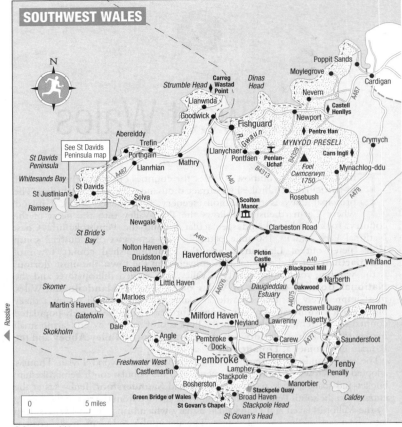

© Crown copyright

most dramatic and remote. To the south and southeast are the eerie **Mynydd Preseli**, relic-spattered mountains overlooking windswept plateaux of heathland and isolated villages – none more remote than along the leafy **Cwm Gwaun**, a lovely and much-bypassed valley cutting through the hills.

Getting around

Despite the remoteness of much of southwestern Wales, public transport is surprisingly efficient and comprehensive, though you'll have to plan carefully. Direct **train** services connect Cardiff and Swansea with Llanelli, Carmarthen, Tenby, Haverfordwest, Milford Haven and Fishguard, while the Heart of Wales line shuffles out of Swansea and Llanelli to Llandeilo and Llandovery before delving into Powys.

Bus services out to the smaller towns and villages are regular and dependable, especially in peak tourist season, when most coastal villages have a fairly regular operation. Carmarthen and Haverfordwest are the principal bus terminuses, with some services radiating out from Tenby, Pembroke and Fishguard. The Pembrokeshire coast is particularly well catered for, with various winsomely

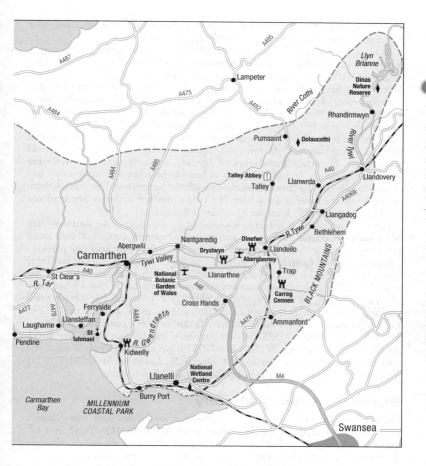

titled services – the Coastal Cruiser, the Puffin Shuttle, the Poppit Rocket and more – operating under the banner of Pembrokeshire Coastal Bus Services. Only in the deserted lanes of northern and eastern Pembrokeshire does bus travel become difficult, although it's excellent walking and cycling country, and there are ample places to rent **bikes** throughout the area. Off the mainland, most of the islands are connected by regular (seasonal) **boat** services, although few of these allow for overnight stops.

Bus and train **timetables** are widely available locally, and online at ⓦwww .pembrokeshiregreenways.co.uk.

From Llanelli to Carmarthen

LLANELLI marks the informal border between anglicized southeast Wales and the *bro*, Welsh Wales, where the native language is part of everyday conversation. The town is famed as the home of the **Scarletts rugby club** (formerly the

Llanelli Scarlets; ☎01554/783900, ⓦwww.scarlets.co.uk), one of Wales' four regional teams, and winners of the Celtic league title in 2004.

To learn something of the metalworking days when the town was known as Tinopolis, visit the **Parc Howard Museum** (April–Sept Mon–Fri 11am–1pm & 2–6pm, Sat & Sun 2–6pm; March–Oct Mon–Fri 11am–1pm & 2–4pm, Sat & Sun 2–4pm; free), half a mile north of the centre, off the A476 Felinfoel road.

There's more of interest two miles east of town, where the **National Wetlands Centre** (daily 9.30am–5pm; £6.95; ⓦwww.wwt.org.uk) overlooks an extensive area of salt marsh dotted with bird hides and landscaped walkways. Uneconomic farmland has been adapted to the needs of wildfowl, with "natural" ponds created around existing mature hedgerows, and even owl nesting sites fashioned from old sewer pipes. Important populations of lapwing, redshank, and over-wintering pintail, widgeon and teal draw legions of birdwatchers, but the centre caters just as well to kids and the curious, mainly through the imaginative Discovery Centre – it's easy to lose most of a day here. The wilder western section is best explored on **free bikes** available from the Discovery Centre.

The wetlands centre is linked to Llanelli but by a section of the fourteen-mile **Millennium Coastal Park** (free access), a traffic-free park-cum-cycle path along the Loughor estuary which forms part of the 300-mile Celtic Trail (see p.54).

Llanelli's **visitor centre** (daily: mid-May to Sept 10am–8pm; Oct to mid-May 10am–5pm; ☎01554/777744) is half a mile south of the town centre beside the coastal path. The pick of the town's **accommodation** is *Llwyn Hall*, Llwynhendy (☎01554/777754, ⓦwww.llwynhall.co.uk; ❺), a comfortable, antique-filled country house with a fine restaurant almost two miles east on the B4297. Otherwise, there are a few fairly ordinary B&Bs, such as *Coastal Park*, 86 Queen Victoria Rd (☎01554/755357, ⓔoffice@awel-y-mor.fsnet.co.uk; ❷). For **food**, *Sheesh Mahal*, 53 Stepney St (☎01554/773773) has some of south Wales' finest curries, while around the corner at 1 Murray St, *Lanostinos* (☎01554/773711) serves up classy brasserie meals and grills for £10–15.

Burry Port and Kidwelly

Both the coastal cycle path and train line run four miles west from Llanelli along the sands of the Loughor estuary to **BURRY PORT** (Porth Tywyn), which is where Amelia Earhart landed after June 1928 after a journey of nearly 21 hours, becoming the first woman to fly across the Atlantic. There's a memorial stone by the pretty little harbour.

A further ten miles along the train line from Llanelli is **KIDWELLY** (Cydweli; request stop only), a sleepy little town dominated by an imposing **castle** (April–Oct daily 9am–5pm; Nov–March Mon–Sat 9.30am–4pm, Sun 11am–4pm; £3.10; CADW), strategically sited overlooking the River Gwendraeth and a vast tract of coast. The castle was established around 1106 by the Bishop of Salisbury as a satellite of Sherborne Abbey in Dorset. On entering through the massive fourteenth-century gatehouse, you can still see portcullis slats and murder holes, through which noxious substances could be tipped onto intruders. The **gatehouse** forms the centrepiece of the impressively intact semicircular outer ward walls, which date from around 1275. Views from the musty solar and hall, packed into the easternmost wall of the inner ward, show the castle's defensive position at its best, with the river directly below. Although the whole castle is long since roofless, the remains are some of the most intact of any medieval Welsh castle that has not been extensively restored. A fourteenth-century town **gate** shields the castle approach from Castle Street, which is the main road through Kidwelly.

A 164-foot brick chimney just over a mile north of town (up Priory Street) marks the modest but informative **Kidwelly Industrial Museum** (May–Sept Mon–Fri 10am–5pm, Sat & Sun noon–5pm; free), housed in a former tinplate works. Many of the works' old features have been preserved, including the rolling mills, where long lines of tin were rolled and spun into wafer-thin slices.

In Kidwelly, there's superb farmhouse **accommodation** at *Penlan Isaf* (①01554/890084, ⓦ www.penlanisaf.co.uk; ②), a dairy farm overlooking town. Daytime **meals** are available at *Time For Tea*, 7 Bridge St. The cosy *Boot and Shoe*, 2 Castle St, is the place for a beer.

St Ishmael and Ferryside

As the train leaves Kidwelly and hugs the side of the River Tywi's estuary, the views out across the water are magnificent. You'll pass by a tiny chapel at **ST ISHMAEL**, built to serve a medieval village that was completely destroyed in a storm three hundred years ago, and is now buried deep beneath the flats, although a huge storm in 2000 briefly revealed some remains.

A mile further on, **FERRYSIDE** (Glanyfferi) is a tiny village that grew as a day-trip destination for Valleys miners. Although the train station still remains (request stop only), Ferryside is tranquil today, its narrow streets facing Llansteffan Castle across the calm waters and circling sea birds. The *White Lion Hotel* on the main square is the best place for **food** and **drink**, though the chips-with-everything, daytime-only *Ferry Cabin*, just across the road, does fresh sea trout – known around these parts as *sewin*.

Carmarthen and around

The ancient capital of its region and county town of Carmarthenshire, **CARMARTHEN** (Caerfyrddin), is a lively market town with 15,000 inhabitants, but does not entirely live up to the promise of its status. There's an undeniably cheerless atmosphere which doesn't encourage you to stay for long – fortunately, with so many beautiful and interesting places nearby, there's little need to. It's the first major town in west Wales, where the native language is heard at all times, and was once – in the early eighteenth century – the largest town in all of Wales on the strength of its position at the tidal limit of the River Tywi.

Founded as a Roman fort, Carmarthen's most popular moment of mythological history dates from the Dark Ages and the supposed birth of the wizard **Merlin** just outside the town (see box, p.162) – Myrddin, in Welsh, gives Carmarthen its name. In 1313, Carmarthen was granted its first charter by Edward I, helping the town to flourish as an important wool centre. It was later taken by Owain Glyndŵr in the early years of the fifteenth century. An eisteddfod was inaugurated in the mid-fifteenth century, and is still used as the basis for today's National Eisteddfod. The importance of the town grew, attracting trade and new commerce, industrial works and a key port.

A mile out of town, **Abergwili** is primarily of interest for the Carmarthen County Museum, and its role as Merlin's resting place.

The Town

Approaching from the train station, the stern facade of the early twentieth-century **Shire Hall** shields the rambling streets of the town centre, and largely swallows up the uninspiring remains of the **castle**, Edward I's reworking of an earlier Norman fortress. The most picturesque eighteenth- and nineteenth-century part of town lies spread out at the base of the castle, around King Street and **Nott Square**, the town's main shopping hub.

From Nott Square, the broad, sloping Darkgate leads down to Lammas Street, a wide Georgian thoroughfare flanked by coaching inns. To the north is the indoor **market**, a great centre for local produce, secondhand books, antiques and endearingly useless tat, with several cheap cafés. On the main market days – Wednesday and Saturday – stalls spill outside. Off Darkgate is Blue Street and the excellent **Origin Dyfed Gallery** (Mon–Sat 10am–5pm; free), the public face of a local art and craft co-operative.

From the other side of Nott Square, King Street heads northeast towards the sturdy tower of **St Peter's church** (often closed). Opposite is the Victorian School of Art that has now metamorphosed into the excellent **Oriel Myrddin** (Mon–Sat 10am–5pm; free), a craft centre and art gallery displaying the work of local artists.

Abergwili

The severe grey Bishop's Palace at **ABERGWILI**, a mile east of Carmarthen, was the seat of the Bishop of St Davids between 1542 and 1974, and now houses the **Carmarthen County Museum** (Mon–Sat 10am–4.30pm; free), a spirited amble through the history of the area. The surprisingly interesting

Merlin

Merlin (Myrddin) is a difficult character to pin down. A mythic figure throughout Europe's Celtic fringe, he is variously described as a wizard and prophet, though over the centuries he has also been called a half-demon and Antichrist, as well as being credited with the creation of Stonehenge. His most common association, of course, is with King Arthur (see box, p.90) to whom he was tutor, wizard and advisor. It was Merlin who arranged Arthur's ascendancy to the throne through the sword-in-the-stone contest, Merlin who founded the Round Table, and Merlin who accompanied Arthur to the Isle of Avalon at the end of his life.

This interpretation dates back to the twelfth-century writings of Geoffrey of Monmouth who, in his *Historia Regum Britanniae* of 1134, drew on all sorts of tales and folklore (plus a fair bit of fabrication) to create the Merlin we know today. He is even credited with inventing the Latinized "Merlin" form to avoid his character being associated with "merde", the French for excrement.

According to Monmouth, Merlin was born in Carmarthen, a conjecture supported half a century later by Giraldus Cambrensis (see box, p.399) who reported the same on his travels around Wales. Monmouth built on earlier stories of very different Merlins under different names – Myrddin Wyllt (Merlin the wild), Merlin Caledonensis (Scottish Merlin), and the most Welsh, Myrddin Emrys (Merlin Ambrosius). These may have been separate people whose stories have blended, or the same person whose stories have diverged in the centuries of telling.

Local legend has it that Merlin lives on under Merlin's Hill, where he will remain until King Arthur and his men rise up when the country is in great danger. Another story tells of Merlin predicting that "when Merlin's tree shall tumble down, then shall fall Carmarthen town". The oak, which once stood in the centre of Carmarthen, died a few years back, but Carmarthen remains. A piece of the tree can be seen in the Carmarthen County Museum.

Today Carmarthen celebrates its legendary connection with the **Gŵyl Myrddyn** (Merlin Festival; ☏01267/232075, ⓦwww.carmarthenshire.gov.uk), which takes place around Carmarthen in mid-June with a funfair, coracle racing, medieval village, fortune tellers and, of course, magicians.

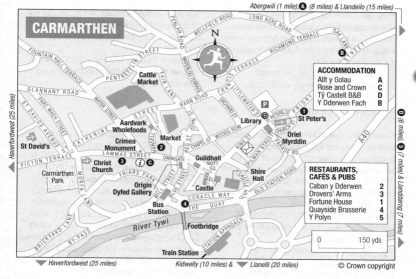

exhibition covers the history of Welsh translations of the New Testament and Book of Common Prayer – both translated for the first time here in 1567. Local pottery, archeological finds, wooden dressers and a lively history of local castles are presented in well-annotated displays, along with material on crime and policing, geology, education, the local coracle industry and the origins of Wales' first eisteddfod in Carmarthen in 1450.

A mile east of Abergwili, the main A40 road passes the sharp slopes of **Merlin's Hill** (Bryn Myrddin), reputedly the sleeping place of the great wizard. Alltyfyrddin Farm, on whose land this lies, has cashed in with the cheesy **Merlin's Hill Centre** (daily: April–Oct 10am–7pm; Nov–March 10am–5pm; £3), full of sub-Harry Potter exhibits aimed mainly at kids, but which at least gives access to the hill.

Practicalities

Trains between Swansea and Pembrokeshire stop at the **train station**, on the south side of the River Tywi. All **buses** terminate at the bus station on Blue Street, north of the river, and many connect with the arrival and departure of trains. The **tourist office** is at 113 Lammas St, near the Crimea Monument (July & Aug daily 10am–5pm; April–June, Sept & Oct Mon–Sat 10am–5pm; Nov–March Mon–Sat 10am–4pm; ☎01267/231557, ⊛www.carmarthenshire.gov.uk), while information on the alternative scene can be found at Aardvark Wholefoods in Mansel Street. For free **internet access** visit the library (Mon–Wed & Fri 9.30am–7pm, Thurs & Sat 9.30am–5pm) on King Street opposite St Peter's church.

The range of **accommodation** and eating in Carmarthen is limited, and few places are truly notable, so the following listings include a selection of places in the adjoining Tywi Valley.

Accommodation

Allt y Golau Feliongwm Uchaf, 8 miles northeast of Carmarthen ☎01267/290455, ⊛www .alltygolau.com. Superb sustainability-minded B&B in a converted 1812 farmhouse with three tastefully decorated rooms and sumptuous breakfasts. Close to the Botanic Garden. ❸

Rose and Crown Lammas St ☎ 01267/232050, ⓦ www.roseandcrowncarmarthen.co.uk. Ancient coaching inn recently refurbished with chic rooms, free wi-fi, DVD players, and full Welsh breakfasts in the bar downstairs. ❹

Tŷ Castell B&B Station Rd, Nantgaredig ☎ 01267/290034, ⓦ www.ty-castell.co.uk.

Wonderful outdoors-oriented farmhouse B&B on the banks of the Towy, 6 miles east of Carmarthen along the A40, with a licensed restaurant on site. ❸

Y Dderwen Fach 98 Priory St ☎ 01267/234193. The best of the central budget B&Bs. Some rooms have bathtubs. ❶

Eating and drinking

Caban y Dderwen 10 Mansel St. The best spot in town for snacks and light lunches, including pan-fried laverbread with cockles (£5.60). Named after the famous oak tree (see p.162) that once stood outside.

Drovers' Arms 106 Lammas St. Unpretentious spot that's more sedate than some of the town's other pubs, with superb beers.

Fortune House 2 Priory St ☎ 01267/243838. Low-cost Cantonese seafood place offering some of the best dining in town.

Quayside Brasserie Coracle Way ☎ 01267/223000. Superb restaurant with a cosy interior and some outside seating. It's

great for fresh local meat, fish and seafood (mains £11–17), and especially popular at lunchtime.

Y Polyn Capel Dewi, Nantgaredig ☎ 01267/290000, ⓦ www .ypolynrestaurant.co.uk. Half-timbered country pub a mile or so north of the National Botanic Garden offering some of the best food in in the area. The modern British cuisine makes superb use of local ingredients and everything is served with relaxed panache. Set dinner cost £22 for two courses, £28 for three. Open for lunch Tues–Fri & Sun, dinner Tues–Sat.

The Tywi Valley

The **River Tywi** curves and darts its way east from Carmarthen through some of the most spellbinding scenery in south Wales. It's not hard to see why the Merlin legend has taken such a hold in these parts – the landscape does seem infused with a kind of eerie magic. The thirty-mile trip from Carmarthen to **Llandovery** is punctuated by gentle, impossibly green hills topped with ruined castles, notably the wonderful **Carreg Cennen** near the appealing town of Llandeilo. Along the way, two budding gardens have sprung up in the last few years: one completely new in the form of the **National Botanic Garden of Wales**; the other a faithful restoration of the original walled gardens around the long-abandoned house of **Aberglasney**.

The tourist office in Carmarthen (see p.163) and a smaller one at Llandeilo (see p.167) have lots of **information** about the Tywi Valley and surrounding area, including the ever-improving array of quality accommodation: we've listed the best of these under the Carmarthen and Llandovery accounts on p.163 and p.169. Regular **buses** run along the A40 between Carmarthen and Llandeilo giving access to Aberglasney and Dinefwr: the #166 runs twice daily from Carmarthen train station to the National Botanic Garden.

The National Botanic Garden of Wales

Though only opened in 2000, the great glass "eye" of the **National Botanic Garden of Wales** (daily: April–Oct 10am–6pm; Nov–March 10am–4.30pm; £8, Nov–Feb £5, small discounts for those arriving by bike or public transport; ⓦ www.gardenofwales.org.uk) has quickly become the centrepiece of the Tywi Valley. Located one mile north of the A48 and seven miles east of Carmarthen, it was conceived as a way of transforming the 500-acre remains of the once immense estate owned by William Paxton, an early nineteenth-century

▲ National Botanic Garden of Wales

London banker. The garden has gradually come to warrant its considerable hype, and enough of the elements are in place to see its huge potential.

A central walkway leads past lakes, sculpture and geological outcrops from all over Wales, with walks down towards slate bed plantings and different wood and wetland habitats. Paxton's double-walled garden has been teased back to life (providing vegetables for the rather disappointing café/restaurant), and enhanced by the addition of a small but exquisite Japanese garden, and a bee garden that's home to a million bees.

At the top of the hill is the garden's most audacious feature: the vast oval **glasshouse** designed by Norman Foster, a stunning piece of architecture that justifies a visit on its own. Inside are plants from regions with a Mediterranean climate: the Cape region of South Africa, southwestern Australia, Chile, California and the Mediterranean itself. Not far away are the remains of **Middleton Hall**, which burnt down in 1931, whose old estate forms the centrepiece of the gardens. A nearby group of buildings house a restaurant, an excellent exhibition about the Welsh herbalists known as the Physicians of Myddfai, and the new Theatre Botanica, all arranged around **Millennium Square**, the venue for open-air concerts and performances. The entire garden has been designed around environmentally sustainable principles: rainwater is caught and used for irrigation; the glasshouses are heated by burning wood coppiced on the grounds; and human waste is transformed into essentially pure water by means of a series of reed beds. A large tract of the surrounding land is being turned over to organic farming using Welsh breeds of cattle and sheep, and the estate's outer edges have been used for re-creations of moorland, spring wood, prairie and native Welsh habitats.

Aberglasney

A natural twin to the Botanic Garden can be found five miles northeast at **Aberglasney** (daily: April–Sept 10am–6pm; Oct–March 10.30am–4pm; £7; Ⓦ www.aberglasney.org), half a mile south of the A40 near Broad Oak. While a partly ruined manor house dating back to the fifteenth century is the estate's centrepiece, it is the stunning **gardens** that have caused all the excitement. Locals had always known about the decaying and abandoned house – which even had listed building status – but it was only in 1994, when the grand eight-columned portico came up for sale at Christie's for £13,000, that the authorities took notice. The portico was withdrawn from sale and reattached to the house as part of the major restoration undertaken by the Aberglasney Trust, although the stabilized shell of the building seems destined to play second fiddle to its remarkable set of gardens. Once massively overgrown, these mostly sixteenth- to eighteenth-century walled gardens have regained much of their original formal splendour, while archeological work has uncovered their history. Especially noteworthy is the replanted kitchen garden and what is thought to be the only secular cloister garden in Britain. A walkway leads around the top of the cloister giving access to a set of six Victorian aviaries, and great views over the Jacobean Pool Garden and the mature woodlands beyond. The highlight, though, is the yew tunnel, a line of five yews planted three centuries ago, and trained over to root on the far side.

In 2005, the central courtyard of the manor house was glassed in to form an atrium populated with subtropical plants – tree ferns, cycads, orchids and more. Dubbed a Ninfarium (after gardens at Ninfa, forty miles outside Rome) it already makes a beautiful counterpoint to the outdoor gardens, and should develop nicely over the next few years. Leave time for tea and cakes outside the lovely **café** built into the wall of the Pool Garden.

Dinefwr Castle and Newton house

The strategic importance of the Tywi Valley is underlined by the tumbledown ruins of **Dinefwr Castle** (unrestricted access; CADW), a mile west of Llandeilo and reached through the extensive Dinefwr Park. Sited on an isolated wooded bluff over the river, the castle was built in the twelfth century by Lord Rhys, who united the warring Welsh princes against the Normans.

By 1523 the castle had become ill-suited to the needs of Lord Rhys's descendants, who aspired to something more luxurious, and eventually, in 1660, built a new residence a few hundred yards away. Now named **Newton House** (mid-March to Oct daily 11am–5pm; Nov to mid-March Fri–Sun 11am–5pm; £6.30; NT), it was much transformed over the centuries, being given a new "Venetian Gothic" facade in the 1860s and then falling into disrepair before being saved in the 1990s. It isn't the most distinguished of stately homes, but the basement and ground floor have been imaginatively set up as though it were a Sunday in 1912. Below stairs you can try your hand at brushing a top hat or correctly folding a shirt before progressing upstairs, where a formal lunch is laid out and a gramophone plays in the drawing room. Up the splendid staircase there are interesting displays on the Rhys family genealogy, the estate's heritage and the local landscape, which can be seen from a conservatory. The lovely **park**, mostly landscaped in the 1770s by George Rhys, now contains rare white cattle and fallow deer.

Llandeilo and around

Beautifully situated on the edge of the magnificent uplands of the Black Mountain, the small, rustic town of **LLANDEILO** is a place in transition. It remains a quiet market town, but now fashions itself as an upscale rural retreat for the aspirational of Swansea, Cardiff and beyond, with a couple of boutique hotels, some fancy shops and galleries, and a handful of delis, cafés and restaurants.

As such, Llandeilo makes the best base for exploring the region, particularly Dinefwr and Carreg Cennan. In town, spend a few minutes in the parish

church of St Teilo on Rhosmaen Street, home to a pair of eighth-century Celtic crosses. The base of the tower houses an interactive display (Tues–Sat 11am–4pm; free) on the **Llandeilo Fawr Gospels**, an eighth-century parchment manuscript which contains the earliest known example of written Welsh. The book itself is in Lichfield Cathedral in England, but computers allow you to browse the pages and learn something of both these gospels and the closely related (and more famous) Lindisfarne Gospels.

Practicalities

There's a small local **tourist office** (Mon–Fri 10.30am–4.30pm, Sat 10.30am–4pm) in the Artwerks craft gallery beside the Crescent Road car park, or you can pick up information on alternative local happenings at the excellent Friends of the Earth-run Green House shop, opposite Barclays bank on Rhosmaen Street.

   Accommodation in town is limited and fairly pricey, but there are several appealing but more modest options in the surrounding countryside. Llandeilo also offers the best **eating** options for miles around.

Accommodation

Abermarlais Caravan Park On the main A40, 6 miles east of Llandeilo ☎01550/777868, ⊛www .abermarlaiscaravanpark.co.uk. Spacious riverside campsite that's perfect for families. £9 per pitch. Closed mid-Nov to mid-March.

   The Cawdor 70 Rhosmaen St ☎01558/823500, ⊛www.thecawdor.com. Llandeilo's focal point, this former coaching inn has been given a major postmodern makeover and boasts delightful, simply decorated rooms (all different) and stunning attic suites. Rooms ❸–❺, suites ❾

Cynyll Farm on the A4069 two miles southeast of Llangadog ☎01550/777316, ⊛www.cynyllfarm .co.uk. Great value, long-standing farmhouse B&B seven miles northeast of Llandeilo. ❶

   Fronlas 7 Thomas St ☎01558/824733, ⊛www.fronlas.com. This large terraced house has been creatively transformed into a modern three-room B&B, all bare boards, flatscreen TVs, wild wallpapers and chic design – right down to the bespoke coffee mugs. There's a strong emphasis on sustainability, and breakfasts are largely organic and made with local ingredients. The lounge has an honesty bar and a good DVD collection. ❹–❺

Penhill Trap, 4 miles southeast of Llandeilo ☎01558/823060, ⊛www.penhill.org.uk. Tranquil and very pleasant one-room B&B a stone's throw from Carreg Cennan castle and well suited for cyclists and walkers. ❸

Eating and drinking

   The Angel 62 Rhosmaen St ☎01558/822765. Convivial pub serving superb bar meals. At £10 for three courses on week nights you can't go wrong, and the menu changes daily. The back room operates as a slightly more formal restaurant, with equally delicious à la carte dining (mains £12–15).

The Angel Inn Salem, 3 miles north of Llandeilo ☎01558/823394. Former village hostelry which has been transformed into a classy gastropub with seriously classy meals all beautifully prepared and presented. Lunch mains £9–15, dinner £15–20. Closed Sun & Mon plus Tues lunch.

Caffi Salvador 3 King St ☎01558/822908. Brand-new tapas bar. Line up the likes of sherry-marinated beef kebab, cannellini bean mash and Basque chicken and chorizo (all £3–4), and help them down with a glass or two. They also run the terribly named but well-stocked Salvador Deli, around the back on Market St.

The Cawdor 70 Rhosmaen St ☎01558/823500. Excellent semi-formal restaurant serving three-course lunches (£13) and sumptuous dinners, which might include grilled duck breast with sautéed celeriac and a red wine sauce (£16). Good wine, guest ales and deep leather sofas attract a broad clientele just for a drink.

Heavenly 64 Rhosmaen St. Great organic ice cream and handmade chocolates that are, well, heavenly.

Carreg Cennen Castle

Isolated in the rural hinterland four miles southeast of Llandeilo is the most magnificently sited castle in Wales. **Carreg Cennen Castle** (daily: April–Oct 9.30am–6.30pm; Nov–March 9.30am–4pm; £3.70; CADW) was constructed on its fearsome outcrop in 1248 (though Sir Urien, one of King Arthur's knights, is said to have built a fortress here earlier), and remained a Welsh stronghold until it fell to the English in 1277, during Edward I's first invasion. It remained in use until 1462, when it was partly destroyed by the Earl of Pembroke, for being a rebel base.

The castle's most striking aspect is its vertiginous location, three hundred feet above a sheer drop into the green valley of the Cennen River. The car park and **farm**, with rare breeds of cows and sheep, are at the bottom of a long path that climbs sharply upwards, with astounding **views** towards the severe purple lines of the Black Mountain, in utter contrast to the velvet greenery of the Tywi and Cennen valleys. The castle seems impenetrable, its crumbling walls merging with the limestone on which it defiantly sits. The highlights of a visit are the views down into the valley and the long descent into a watery, pitch-black cave that is said to have served as a well. Torches (which can be rented for £1.50 from the tearoom near the car park) are essential; it's worth continuing as far as possible and then turning them off to experience absolute darkness. The tearoom has a superb selection of home-cooked Welsh dishes.

Llandovery and around

Twelve miles northeast of Llandeilo, the former cattle drovers' town of **LLANDOVERY** (Llanymddyfri) makes a natural base for exploring the Tywi Valley, with the breathtaking countryside around the Dolaucothi Gold Mine to the west and tranquil Llyn Brianne to the north. The town's architecture and layout have changed little for centuries, the main Broad Street is lined with solid early nineteenth-century town houses and older inns, much as it was when itinerant writer George Borrow visited in 1854 during his grand tour of Wales, remembering it as the "pleasantest little town in which I have halted in the course of my wanderings".

On a grassy mound on the south side of Broad Street, the scant ruins of a **castle** afford fine views over Llandovery's huddled grey buildings and the Bran River, but the real draw is a stunning stainless-steel sculpture of local lord Llywelyn ap Gruffydd Fychan, the "Welsh Braveheart", who was executed in front of the English king Henry IV, for supporting the rebel prince Owain Glyndŵr in 1401.

Above the tourist office (see below), the community-run **Llandovery Heritage Centre** (Easter–Sept daily 9.30am–5pm; Oct–Easter Mon–Sat 10am–4pm, Sun 11am–1pm; donation appreciated) contains a fine section on the legend of the Lady of the Lake from Llyn y Fan Fach, the outlaw Twm Sion Cati, the "Welsh Robin Hood", and seventeenth-century vicar Rhys Prichard, author of *Canwyll y Cymry* ("The Welshmen's Candle"). There's also material on the cattle drovers and their Black Ox bank, which became a part of the present-day LloydsTSB.

Practicalities

The **train station** is on the main A40 just before it becomes Broad Street; **buses** leave from the station and the car park by the Heritage Centre. On Kings Road, the continuation of Broad Street, the joint **tourist office** and Brecon Beacons National Park visitor centre (Easter–Sept daily 9.30am–5pm; Oct–Easter Mon–Sat 10am–4pm, Sun 11am–1pm; ☎01550/720693) is well stocked with leaflets on local walks and natural history, and has an interpretive centre on the Black Mountain.

Cwmgwyn Farm Llangadog Rd, two miles southwest of Llandovery on the A4069 ℡01550/720410, ⓦwww.cwmgwyn-holidays .co.uk. Charming farmhouse B&B with spacious rooms, tasty breakfasts and a wood-beamed lounge complete with inglenook fireplace. ❷
The Drovers 9 Market Square ℡01550/721115, ⓦwww.droversllandovery.co.uk. Cosy accommodation in an eighteenth-century town house with a guests' bar worth checking out. ❶–❸
Erwlon 1 mile east of Llandovery off the A40 ℡01550/720332, ⓦwww.ukparks.co.uk/erwlon. The nearest campsite to town, with caravan sites and camping (£4 per person).

Henllys Estate 2 miles northwest of Llandovery ℡01550/721332, ⓦwww.henllysestate.co.uk. The best-value of the rural B&Bs hereabouts, with lovely oak-floored en-suite bedrooms, digital TV and good breakfasts. ❸
New White Lion 43 Stone St ℡01550/720685, ⓦwww.newwhitelion.co.uk. An understated exterior hides Llandovery's finest accommodation, a lovely combination of modern style and selected antiques. You won't want to leave, and there's little need to with a comfy lounge, honesty bar and meals in their little dining room. Breakfast served until 10.30am. ❺

Eating and drinking

Karahi 34 High St ℡01550/720022. Great new curry restaurant with a standard selection of north Indian curries plus unusual specialities such as fresh salmon *kufta* (£7) and a creamy lamb *pasanda* (£6).
King's Head Inn 1 Market Square. Come to this former drover's coaching inn for their flaky Drovers' beef pie (£8.50), lamb shanks (£9.50) or the best espresso in town.

Red Lion 2 Market Square. An eccentric and bizarrely old-fashioned pub (with beer served in jugs from the barrel) in a red, colonnaded house nestled in an easy-to-miss corner. The landlord, a law unto himself, often chooses to close early.
Royal Oak Inn Rhandirmwyn, 7 miles north (see p.170). Country pub that's well worth the trip for its imaginative menu of nicely cooked classics.

The Dolaucothi Gold Mine and Talley Abbey

West of Llandovery the countryside is blissfully quiet, with a handful of main roads and lanes that rarely carry much traffic. The principal route off the A40 between Llandeilo and Llandovery is the A482, which heads six miles to the **Dolaucothi Gold Mine** (mid-March to Oct daily 10am–5pm; site £3.40, Roman & Victorian underground tours £3.80 each, level-access Long Adit tour £2.50; NT).

This is the only place in Britain where it's certain that the Romans mined gold, laying astoundingly advanced systems to extract the precious metal from the rock; the remains of their workings – a few water channels and an opencast mine – can still be seen around the site. After the Romans left in 140 AD, the mine lay abandoned until 1888, when new shafts were sunk and sporadically exploited until 1938. The site appears much as it would have in the late 1930s, and there are good displays in the exhibit room, but you'll get a much better appreciation by joining one of the hard-hat underground tours deep into the workings, and try your hand at gold panning.

Near the entrance to the mine is a stone marked with indentations supposedly left by five sleeping saints who rested here one night. The event gives its name to the straggling village of **PUMSAINT** (Five Saints). The *Brunant Arms*, a mile east of the gold mine at **CAIO**, offers bags of character, good food and real ales.

Five miles south of Pumsaint, the crumbling twelfth-century tower of Wales' only Premonstratensian **abbey** dominates the village of **TALLEY**, also home to the serene **church of St Michael**, intact from its foundation in 1773 and still including its original box pews. Talley's more recent claim to fame is as the home of Wales' famous **Tipi Valley**, a hippy encampment that was set up in the 1970s near Cwmdu, just south of the village. Controversy has dogged the place ever since, but these days there seems to be a fairly stoic truce between the locals and the tepee dwellers.

Towards Llyn Brianne

The land to the north of Llandovery is equally remote and even more spectacular, with walks following the River Tywi valley and over the hills. As a base, there's the old lead-mining hamlet of **RHANDIRMWYN**, above the winding river, which has some of the best views hereabouts and is accessible by a daily postbus from Llandovery. Here, the popular *Royal Oak Inn* (℡01550/760201, ⓦwww .rhandirmwyn.com; ❷) offers great food, drink and B&B **accommodation**. Two miles north, the basic tap-in-a-field *Gellifechan* **campsite** (℡01550/760397; £6 per pitch) occupies a lovely site by the river.

Four miles beyond Rhandirmwyn, there's a car park (£1) at the Ystradffin chapel for the RSPB's **Dinas Nature Reserve**, deep within which is the reputed hideout cave of Twm Sion Cati (see p.168). You're discouraged from seeking out the bandit's lair lest you disturb the red kites, woodpeckers, nuthatches, redstarts and pipits, but even so, this is a delightful spot with wooden walkways traversing the ancient woodland.

A mile beyond lies **Llyn Brianne**, a reservoir built in the 1970s (to supply Swansea), that has folded well into the contours of the land and offers peaceful shoreline walks.

Southern Carmarthenshire

Frequently overlooked in the stampede towards the resorts of Pembrokeshire, southern Carmarthenshire is a quiet part of the world, its coastline broken by the triple estuary of the Tywi, Taf and Gwendreath rivers. **Llansteffan** huddles below its ruined castle alongside the Tywi, while the Taf estuary is home to **Laugharne**, the region's sole big tourist attraction and a place of pilgrimage for Dylan Thomas lovers.

Beyond Laugharne, the seemingly endless sweep of sand at **Pendine** was once used for land speed record attempts. Inland, dull **Whitland** is historically significant as the site of the first parliament in Wales.

Regular trains connect Carmarthen with Whitland and the west, and buses fill in the gaps, with a service from Carmarthen and St Clears to Laugharne and Pendine. Another service leaves Carmarthen for Llansteffan.

Llansteffan

The pretty village of **LLANSTEFFAN**, on the Tywi estuary ten miles southeast of Carmarthen, is overshadowed by a dramatic ruined **castle** (unrestricted access). This prime example of Norman fortifications was built between the eleventh and thirteenth centuries by the Anglo-Norman de Camille family. The entrance used today is not the original gatehouse, which was converted into living quarters in the fourteenth century: its bricked-up entrance is obvious from outside. In both gatehouses, however, the portcullis and murder holes can still be seen. From atop the towers, it's easy to appreciate the site's defensive position, with far-reaching views in all directions; long before the present castle, there was an Iron Age promontory fort, known to have been occupied from 600 BC.

Returning from the castle to where the path doubles back to the right near a house, continue straight ahead past the house for half a mile then left down the lane towards the beach. The door in the wall on the right conceals **St Anthony's**

Well (Bwthyn Sant Antwn), with its supposed powers of healing for lovesickness. At anything but high tide you can return via the beach.

Llansteffan is attractive enough to justify an overnight stay, perhaps at *Mike & Myra's*, a decent B&B on The Green (℡01267/241262, ⓦwww.llansteffan .net/accommodation; ➋). Two miles back towards Carmarthen, the *Pantyrathro Country Inn* (℡01267/241014, ⓦwww.backpackershostelwales.co.uk; £13 per bunk) offers slightly pokey hostel-style accommodation plus one double room (➊), and also has its own bar and Mexican restaurant.

For **snacks** and Welsh teas try *The Beach Shop*, by the beachside car park, or try *The Village Stores*, on the main street (℡01267/241888), an off-beat little café in the back of a general store. They also open for dinner on Wednesday and Saturday nights, plus Sun lunch.

Laugharne

When quiet, the village of **LAUGHARNE** (Talacharn) is a delightful spot, with a ragged castle looming over the reeds and tidal flats and narrow lanes snuggling in behind. But Laugharne has increasingly been taken over by the legend of Dylan Thomas, the nearest thing Wales has to a national poet.

At the end of an excruciatingly narrow lane (unsuitable for cars) beside the estuary, you'll stumble across the **Dylan Thomas Boathouse** (daily: May–Oct & Easter 10am–5.30pm; Nov–April 10.30am–3.30pm; £3.50; ⓦwww .dylanthomasboathouse.com), the simple home of Thomas, his wife Caitlin and their three children from 1949 until he died from "a massive insult to the brain" (spurred by numerous whiskies) on a lecture tour in New York four years later.

It's an enchanting museum with a feeling of inspirational peace above the ever-changing water and light of the estuary and its "heron-priested shore". Upstairs is given over to a video on Thomas's life and a selection of local artists' views of the estuary and the village – none so rewarding as the one from the windows. Downstairs, the family's living room has been preserved intact, with the rich tones of the man himself reading his work via a period wireless set. Numerous artefacts are encased or on display, and contemporary newspaper reports of his demise show that he was, while alive, a fairly minor literary figure: the *Daily Mirror* manages a small obituary on page five, while even the *Carmarthen Journal* relegates the story to second place behind the tale of a missing local farmer. A

RESTAURANTS, CAFÉS & PUBS

The Cors	C
The Green Room	2
Hurst House on the Marsh	E
New Three Mariners	1

ACCOMMODATION

Ants Hill Caravan Park	B
Boat House Inn	D
Coedllys Country House	A
The Cors	C
Hurst House on the Marsh	E
Swan Cottage	F

LAUGHARNE

0 — 200 yds

small tearoom and outdoor terrace afford views over the water and welcome refreshments. Back along the lane, you can peer into the green garage where Thomas wrote: a gas stove, curling photographs of literary heroes, pen collection and numerous scrunched-up balls of paper on the cheap desk suggest quite effectively that he is about to return at any minute. Thomas and Caitlin, who died in 1994, are buried together in the graveyard of the parish church in the village centre, marked by a simple white cross.

Laugharne is probably the closest to the fictional Llareggub, Thomas' town of darkly rich characters in *Under Milk Wood* – an honour, it is believed, shared with New Quay in Cardiganshire.

The boathouse aside, Laugharne makes little of its literary connections. There's no Thomas Trail, and even Dylan's old boozing hole, **Brown's Hotel** on the

Dylan Thomas

Dylan Thomas (1914–53) was the quintessential Celt – fiery, verbose, richly talented and habitually drunk. Born into a snugly middle-class family in Swansea's Uplands district, Dylan's first glimmers of literary greatness came when he was posted, as a young reporter, on the *South Wales Evening Post* in Swansea; some of the most popular tales in his *Portrait of the Artist as a Young Dog* were inspired by his experiences of working on the newspaper. Thomas' wordy enthusiasm is well demonstrated in a passage describing his gulping down a pint of beer, waiting for the senior reporter to join him for a pub crawl: "I liked the taste of beer, its live, white lather, its brass-bright depths, the sudden world through the wet brown walls of the glass, the tilted rush to the lips and the slow swallowing down to the lapping belly, the salt on the tongue, the foam at the corners."

Rejecting the coarse provincialism of Swansea and Welsh life, Thomas arrived in London as a broke 20-year-old in 1934, weeks before the appearance of his first volume of poetry. Another volume followed shortly afterwards, cementing the engaging young Welshman's reputation in the British literary establishment. He married in 1937 and the newlyweds returned to Wales, settling in the backwater of Laugharne, before moving to New Quay for part of World War II. Short stories – crackling with rich and melancholy humour – tumbled out as swiftly as poems, further widening his base of admirers, although they remained numerically small until well after his death. Like so many writers, he only gained star status posthumously. Despite his evident streak of hedonism and his long days boozing in *Brown's Hotel*, Thomas was a self-disciplined writer, honing his work into some of the most instantly recognizable poetry of the twentieth century, mastering both lyrical ballads of astounding simplicity and rhythmic metre, as well as more turgid, densely layered poetry. Perhaps better than anyone, he writes in an identifiably Celtic, rhythmic wallow. Although Thomas knew little Welsh – he was educated in the time when the native language was stridently discouraged – his English usage is definitively Welsh in its cadence and bold use of words.

Thomas, especially in public, liked to adopt the persona of an archetypal stage Welshman: sonorously loquacious, romantic and fond of a stiff tipple. This role was particularly popular in the United States, where he made lucrative lecture tours; it was on one in 1953 that he died of a massive whisky overdose. One month earlier, he had put the finishing touches to what many regard as his masterpiece: *Under Milk Wood*, the "play for voices". Describing the dreams, thoughts and lives of a straggling Welsh seaside community over 24 hours, the play has never dipped out of fashion and has lured Wales' greatest stars, including Richard Burton and Anthony Hopkins, into the role of chief narrator. The small town of Llareggub (misspelt Llaregyb by the prudish BBC, who wouldn't sanction the usage of the expression "bugger all" backwards) is loosely based on Laugharne, New Quay in Cardiganshire, and a vast dose of Thomas' own imagination.

main street, is temporarily closed. The nicotine-crusted front bar remained largely intact until 2007, but is unlikely to survive current renovations intact.

The main street courses down to the ornate ruins of **Laugharne Castle** (April–Sept daily 10am–5pm; £3.10; CADW). Built in the twelfth and thirteenth centuries, most of the original buildings were obliterated in Tudor times when Sir John Perrot transformed it into a splendid gentleman's mansion. The mix of medieval might and Tudor finery is an intriguing one, especially in the impressive Inner Ward, dominated by two original towers, one of which you can climb for some good interpretive displays and, from the domed roof, sublime views over the huddled town. The "castle brown as owls" (Dylan Thomas) contains an explanatory panel on another famous Welsh writer, Richard Hughes, best known for his novel *A High Wind in Jamaica*, who lodged in the adjoining Castle House between 1934 and 1942.

Opposite the castle entrance is the tiny toytown **town hall**, topped by a whitewashed Italianate bell tower, which once served as a single-cell prison.

Practicalities

Laugharne has no tourist office but is small enough that you'll quickly get your bearings. Book in summer for the limited range of good-quality **accommodation**.

Accommodation

Ants Hill Caravan Park 1 mile north of Laugharne, off the St Clears road ☎01994/427293, Ⓦwww.antshill.co.uk. The closest camping and caravan park to town. £16 per pitch.

Boat House Inn 1 Gosport St ☎01994/427263, Ⓦwww.theboathousebnb.co.uk. Stylish, comfortable four-room B&B right in the centre. Great breakfasts might include vanilla waffles, or smoked salmon.❹

Coedllys Country House Llangynin, 7 miles north of Laugharne ☎01994/231455, Ⓦwww.coedllyscountryhouse.co.uk. Wonderful farmhouse accommodation comprising three lovely rooms, each with antique furniture, classy bedding, quality lotions and a comfy sofa. The hosts are welcoming and have thought of everything including binoculars for guests' use. Tour their farm animal sanctuary or visit the fitness centre (£20 extra), which has an exercise pool, spa and sauna. ❺

The Cors Newbridge Rd ☎01994/427219 Ⓦwww.the-cors.co.uk. A small, gracious country house amid lovely gardens. There are just two, elegantly simple but comfortable rooms and a classy restaurant (see below). ❺

Hurst House on the Marsh Signposted 3 miles south of Laugharne ☎01994/427417, Ⓦwww.hurst-house.co.uk. Chic modern, retro and antique design elements come together at this luxurious boutique hotel, fashioned from farm buildings on the coastal flats, with Bang & Olufsen TVs and stereos, and top-class toiletries. The spa, indoor pool, small cinema and a fine restaurant (see below) complete the setup. Rates from £265. ❾

Swan Cottage 20 Gosport St ☎01994/427409. Appealing one-room B&B with good rates for singles and extended stays. ❷

Eating and drinking

The Cors Newbridge Rd ☎01994/427219 Ⓦwww.the-cors.co.uk. Open Thurs–Sat evenings for excellent modern Welsh cuisine served casually by candlelight. The menu might include smoked haddock crème brûlée or grilled sewin (local trout), with mains for around £15. Bookings essential.

The Green Room Grist Square. Modern coffee shop doing espressos and melts during the day and handmade pizzas at night (except Tues).

Hurst House on the Marsh Signposted 3 miles south of Laugharne ☎01994/427417,

Ⓦwww.hurst-house.co.uk. Stylish bar and an excellent conservatory restaurant with delicious food and immaculate service. Dishes are prepared from largely local ingredients, many from the walled kitchen garden: expect the likes of trout roulade (£7) followed by salt-marsh lamb with cockles and cardamom (£20).

New Three Mariners High St. Cheery pub that offers the best drinking in town and decent bar meals.

Pendine and Whitland

The tatty seaside resort of **PENDINE** (Pentywyn), five miles southwest of Laugharne, is home to a mass of caravan parks and cheap cafés. The resort's crowning glory is its six-mile-long stretch of sand sweeping away to the east, which, for a frenetic few years in the mid-1920s, was the scene of a series of attempts at the world land speed record. In 1927, Malcolm Campbell reached 174.88 miles per hour, a mark that former record holder and Welsh rival J.G. Parry-Thomas thought he could better. A month later, his 27-litre, aircraft-engined and chain-driven *Babs* hurtled along the beach only to explode: its chain decapitated Parry-Thomas. *Babs* was recovered but then buried in the sand for a respectful 42 years, until it was dug up in 1969 and restored. Each July and August *Babs* appears at the seafront **Museum of Speed** (Easter–Sept daily 10am–5pm; free), which otherwise has mildly interesting panels on those heady times and a few motorcycles also used in record attempts. The headquarters for the speed attempts was the *Beach Hotel*, which still displays photographs and mementos of the glory days.

Historically significant **WHITLAND** (Y Hendy Gwyn), five miles north of Pendine, is today a small farming and light industrial town. It was here – in 930 AD – that Hywel Dda ("Hywel the Good"), king of Deheubarth, summoned representatives from all the other Welsh kingdoms to the first all-Wales assembly in order to codify disparate local traditions into common laws for the whole of Wales. They drew up an elaborate code that was strikingly egalitarian, giving bastard children the rights of legitimate siblings, ensuring marriage by common consent, the equal division of land between spouses upon separation and amongst all children after their parents' deaths. Many of these customs survived until the Tudors conquered Wales, and Welsh people today are still proud of the fairness and lack of oppression in that halcyon era, in stark contrast to the laws imposed after Wales' conquest by Edward I. The tales of Hywel Dda are told at a **commemorative centre** (Easter–Sept Tues–Sat 10am–1.30pm & 2–5pm; free), where his laws are inscribed on stone tablets around the walls. It's located 100m from the train station on St Mary Street.

Narberth and the Landsker Borderlands

As you edge west into Pembrokeshire, the first town of any significance is **Narberth**, a cheerful little place with a real community spirit and a burgeoning reputation for its upscale shopping. It's also the "capital" of the **Landsker Borderlands**, a quiet, charming part of mid-Pembrokeshire, dotted with some beautiful villages that are still well off the beaten tourist track. *Landsker* is an Anglo-Saxon word meaning "frontier", referring to the division between Cymric north Pembrokeshire and the anglicized south. The division goes back to the Norman colonization of the south of the county, though the name has only been used since the 1930s. The area is also home to Europe's largest wooden roller-coasters at the **Oakwood** theme park, as well as the wonderful Celtic cross and tidal mill at **Carew**.

Narberth

According to The Mabinogion, a collection of ancient Celtic folk tales and legends, **NARBERTH** (Arberth) was the court of Pwyll, and its ruined **castle** was probably the old home of the Welsh princes. Today, though, its main draw is a growing reputation as Pembrokeshire's prime boutique **shopping** destination

Little England Beyond Wales

Ever since the Normans stormed their way through Wales, securing their hold on Wales with castles, Pembrokeshire has been effectively divided. But its colonization began even earlier, when seaborne Viking raiders seized the best land – the sandy southern coast and the fertile pasture of the Daugleddau estuary – and the Normans only continued an established practice by intermingling with the Vikings (to produce a very English racial mix) and restricting the Celtic Britons (the Welsh) to the northern part of the country.

Today, the racial divide of the past is still evident, delineated by what has become known as the **Landsker Line**, a vestigial boundary through the heart of Pembrokeshire. Along the line are some sixteen castles or castle mounds (such as Roche, Haverfordwest, Llawhaden and Narberth), while on either side of it, the village names are either demonstrably Welsh or anglicized. This historical partition explains why the area south of the line, dubbed **"Little England Beyond Wales"**, has developed mass appeal to English migrants and tourists, while the north tends to attract Celts and other Europeans. Whereas the Tenby and Pembroke area has inclined towards the most Unionist of UK parties, the Conservatives (who hold very little sway in the rest of Wales), the north dallies between the old Liberal tradition and modern Welsh nationalism in the shape of Plaid Cymru.

with a dozen or so clothing, food and homeware shops along High Street. Plan to call in for a couple of hours, eat a good lunch then press on, since there really isn't a great deal else to do. You'll certainly notice the curious, spiky **town hall**, midway down High Street, built in the 1830s to mask the municipal water tank underneath, and now housing a print shop. Further up, **The Queen's Hall**, 44 High St (℡01834/861212, ⓦwww.thequeenshall.org.uk) is one of the best emerging venues in Pembrokeshire, hosting world music concerts, theatre, art exhibitions and more.

Practicalities

The **train station** is at the far eastern end of the town half a mile from the High Street; there's no visitor centre. As well as the following selection of **places to stay and eat**, there are also good accommodation and food options at nearby Lawrenny (see p.176).

Accommodation

Highland Grange Farm Robeston Wathen, 2 miles west of Narberth on the A40 ℡01834/860952, ⓦwww.highlandgrange.co.uk. Reliable guesthouse on a working farm with Shetland ponies. ❷

Jabajak Banc y Llain, Llanboidy Rd, 8 miles northeast of Narberth or 7 miles northwest of Laugharne ℡01994/448786, ⓦwww.jabajak.co.uk.

Relaxed small hotel beside a budding vineyard. The emphasis is mainly on the food (see below), but the rooms, some with four-poster beds, are comfy. ❺–❽

Plas Hyfryd Country Hotel Moorfield Rd, at the north end of town ℡01834/869006, ⓦwww .plashyfrydhotel.com. Comfortable 14-room hotel with restaurant and bar. ❹

Eating and drinking

The Angel At the top of the High St, close to The Queen's Hall. The best spot in town for pub food such as steak and kidney pudding or veggie lasagne (both £7), and there's also a beer garden.
Jabajak Banc y Llain, Llanboidy Rd, 3 miles north of

Whitland ℡01994/448786, ⓦwww.jabajak.co.uk. Bare-boards and rock-walled restaurant where you might order half a dozen pan-fried local scallops (£9) followed by roast Welsh beef with a citrus and cranberry sauce (£20). The wine list is very good.

Kirkland Arms St James St. Memorabilia-filled pub that's great for a beer.

Q Café 44 High St. Modern restaurant and café in The Queen's Hall serving tasty daytime snacks to full evening meals (£10–12) and a daily specials board.

 **Ultracomida** 7 High St ☎ 01834/861491. Perfect for lunch, this little slice of Spain

tucked in behind a fabulous deli has hams hanging from the ceiling and a blackboard menu featuring delicious authentic Spanish morsels, delicious sandwiches, or Serrano ham, goat's cheese salad, or tortilla Española (all £6–8), all washed down with Iberian wines. Lunch served noon–2.30pm, but great coffee and cakes can be had from 10am–4pm.

Blackpool Mill and Oakwood

Narberth lies to the east of the most impressive scenery around the Daugleddau estuary. The tidal reach of the Eastern Cleddau River goes as far as the elegant four-storey **Blackpool Mill** (daily: April–June 11am–5pm; July & Aug 10am–6pm; Sept 11am–4pm; £2), four miles west of Narberth, which was built in 1813 to grind wheat using waterpower.

The A4075 heads south from Blackpool Mill, past a couple of theme parks. The best is **Oakwood** (April–July & Sept–Oct daily 10am–5pm; Aug daily 10am–10pm; £15; Ⓦ www.oakwoodthemepark.co.uk), Wales' largest theme park, and an exciting day out. Its forte is roller coasters, including the *Megaphobia*, the largest wooden roller coaster in Europe, and the stomach-churning *Vertigo* (additional £11). There's also tobogganing, boating, go-karting, a Wild West town and numerous smaller rides.

The Eastern Cleddau

West of Blackpool Mill, quiet lanes wind down towards the muddy banks of the Cleddau estuary amidst a charming landscape of small, inconsequential settlements and some great, if sometimes slightly overgrown, walking following the waymarked **Landsker Borderlands Trail**.

Pretty **LAWRENNY** village, five miles south of Blackpool Mill, is dominated by the four-storey tower of the magnificent twelfth-century **St Caradoc's church**. Half a mile away, the Cresswell and Carew rivers meet at **Lawrenny Quay**, where there's good eating at 🍴 *Quayside*, a licensed café (daily 11am–5pm; closed Oct–Easter) where the staff really care about their food. Super-fresh baguettes compete with daily specials such as goat's cheese tart (£7), served either in the airy pine interior or outside, where you can look out to yachts moored midstream. At the café you can also pick up a laminated sheet for a lovely **loop walk** (3 miles; 1–2hr; 200ft ascent) which weaves through the ancient oaks of Lawrenny Wood and follows the water with views of the privately owned **Benton Castle** on the other bank.

An infrequent postbus runs to Lawrenny from Narberth, giving access to the independent *Millennium Youth Hostel* (☎ 01646/651270, Ⓔ lawrenny.hostel @xifos.co.uk; dorm beds £14), housed in a refurbished Victorian school. There's also accommodation a mile north of Lawrenny Village at *Knowles Farm* (☎ 01834/891221, Ⓦ www.lawrenny.org.uk; ❸), a great organic farmhouse B&B close to the start of some wonderful walks.

Three miles further east, tiny **CRESSWELL QUAY** is home to the ancient, waterfront *Cresselly Arms*, where beer comes in frothing jugs but food is conspicuously absent. On a fine evening when the tide is in, there can be few finer spots for a beer in west Wales.

Carew

The pretty, riverside village of **CAREW** (Caeriw), two miles south of Cresswell Quay and four miles east of Pembroke, is famed for its thirteen-foot **Celtic**

cross, just south of the river crossing, by the main road. Erected as a memorial to Maredydd, ruler of Deheubarth, who died in 1035, the gracefully tapering shaft is covered in fine tracery of ancient Welsh designs.

Beyond the cross, an Elizabethan walled garden houses the ticket office for **Carew Castle and Tidal Mill** (daily: Easter–Oct 10am–5pm; Nov–Easter 11am–3pm; £3.50; ⓦ www.carewcastle.com). Here you can pick up an explanatory leaflet and audioguide (free) for the castle, a hybrid of Elizabethan whimsy and earlier defensive necessity. The building as a whole offers an excellent example of the organic nature by which castles grew, from the Norman tower (believed to be the original gatehouse) and thirteenth-century front battlements to the Tudor gatehouse and Elizabethan mansion grafted onto them all.

A few hundred yards west of the castle is the **Carew French Mill**, last used in 1937 and the only extant tidal mill in Wales. The impressive eighteenth-century exterior belies the pedestrian exhibitions and moderately interesting self-guided audiovisual displays of the milling process inside.

Tenby and around

Situated on a natural promontory of great strategic importance, the beguilingly old-fashioned **TENBY** (Dinbych-y-Pysgod) is everything a seaside resort should be, wedged between two sweeping beaches fronting an island-studded seascape. Narrow streets duck and wind downhill from the medieval centre to the harbour, past miniature gardens fashioned to catch the afternoon sun. Steps down the steeper slopes provide magical views of the dockside arches, while rows of brightly painted houses and hotels are strung along the clifftops. Simply walking around the streets and along the beaches at low tide is a delight, but Tenby is best visited during quiet times such as May or late September – in busy months, you'll be fighting for space with hordes of fellow holiday-makers.

Tenby's pedigree is long. First mentioned in a ninth-century bardic poem, the town grew under the twelfth-century Normans, who erected a castle on the headland in their attempt to colonize south Pembrokeshire and create a "Little England Beyond Wales" (see box, p.175). The town was sacked by the Welsh three times in the twelfth and thirteenth centuries; the last time, in 1260, by Prince Llywelyn himself. In response, the castle was refortified and the stout town walls were built. Tenby prospered as a major port for diverse foodstuffs and fine goods between the fourteenth and sixteenth centuries, but decline followed. Relief came with the arrival of the train line in the mid-nineteenth century, and the town soon became a fashionable resort. Now firmly middle-market, it caters both to a large influx of retirees and more rumbustious fun-seekers – although the town is currently trying to quell its popularity as a destination for hen and stag parties.

Tenby is also one of the major stopping-off points along the **Pembrokeshire Coast Path**, providing walkers with a welcome interlude of glitter and excitement amidst mile upon mile of undulating cliff scenery. The **national park** boundary skirts around the edge of the town, and further along the coast are the two picturesque sandy stop-offs of **Amroth** and **Saundersfoot**. A few miles offshore from Tenby, the monastic **Caldey Island** makes for a pleasant day-trip.

Arrival, information and accommodation

The **train station** is at the western end of the town centre, at the bottom of Warren Street. Some **buses** stop right in the middle of town at South Parade

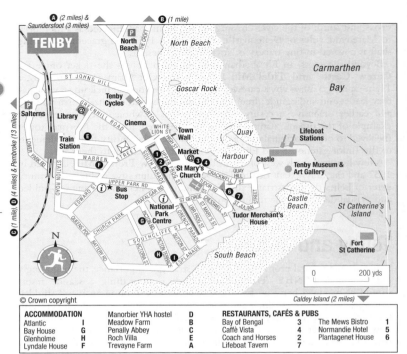

A (2 miles) & Saundersfoot (3 miles)   **B** (1 mile)

G (1 mile) & **D** (4 miles) & Pembroke (13 miles)

Caldey Island (2 miles)

© Crown copyright

ACCOMMODATION				RESTAURANTS, CAFÉS & PUBS			
Atlantic	**I**	Manorbier YHA hostel	**D**	Bay of Bengal	**3**	The Mews Bistro	**1**
Bay House	**G**	Meadow Farm	**B**	Caffè Vista	**4**	Normandie Hotel	**5**
Glenholme	**H**	Penally Abbey	**C**	Coach and Horses	**2**	Plantagenet House	**6**
Lyndale House	**F**	Roch Villa	**E**	Lifeboat Tavern	**7**		
		Trevayne Farm	**A**				

at the top of Trafalgar Road, although most (including National Express coaches) call at the bus shelter on Upper Park Road, just along from the **tourist office** (Easter–Oct Mon–Sat 9.30am–5pm, Sun 10am–4pm; Nov–Easter Mon–Sat 10am–4pm; ☎01834/842402, ✉tenby.tic@pembrokeshire .gov.uk). The **National Park Centre** on South Parade (April–Sept daily 9.30am–5pm; Oct–March Mon–Sat 10am–4.30pm; ☎01834/845040) has interesting displays on the Pembrokeshire coast and around.

A nice way to explore the place is to join Marion Davies for her **Ghost Walk of Tenby** (mid-June to early Sept Mon–Sat at 8pm; £4; reservations recommended on ☎01834/845841, ⓦwww.guidedtourswales.co.uk), which leaves from the *Lifeboat Tavern* in Tudor Square at 8pm and spends an hour and a half exploring the town's past and the people who inhabited it. She also leads other themed walks and offers out-of-season specials – see the notices at the tourist office or contact her directly. For more esoteric information, plus news about forthcoming gigs and festivals, check out Equinox on St Julian Street.

A word of warning to **motorists**: cars are banned in central Tenby throughout July and August (daily 11am–5pm). Free shuttle buses run from the Salterns and North Beach car parks (both pay-and-display), at the west and north side of the town centre, respectively.

Accommodation

As a major resort, Tenby has dozens of hotels and guesthouses, all pressed from much the same mould. Prices are a little higher than elsewhere in west Wales, and in high summer (mid-July to early Sept) the place is full to bursting point; at other times it's not hard to find reasonable **accommodation**. If you don't find anything suitable, consider staying nearby in Saundersfoot, Manorbier or St Florence. There are caravan sites all around Tenby: most take **tents**, especially those around the village of New Hedges, around 1.5 miles north on the A478. In the peak summer season you'll also find tap-in-a-field sites which spring up for a couple of months.

Hotels and guesthouses

Atlantic Esplanade ☎01834/842881, ⓦwww
.atlantic-hotel.uk.com. The best hotel along the
South Beach, with a high standard of rooms (some
with sea views), a couple of good restaurants and a
small indoor pool. Rates include breakfast. ❻–❼

Bay House 5 Picton Rd ☎01834/849015,
ⓦwww.bayhousetenby.co.uk. Considerable
thought has gone into every aspect of this excellent
three-room B&B, from the comfortable, restrained
decor to the delicious breakfasts – especially the
Glamorgan sausages. ❹

Glenholme Picton Terrace ☎01834/843909,
ⓦwww.glenholmetenby.co.uk. Agreeable eight-room
B&B near the town centre, with en-suite rooms. ❷

Lyndale House Warren St ☎01834/842836.
Small, well-maintained B&B near the train station.
Good single rates. ❸

Penally Abbey Penally, 1 mile west of Tenby
☎01834/843033, ⓦwww.penally-abbey.com.
Luxurious country-house hotel on the site of a
sixth-century abbey, with great sea views.
Standards are very high, but the atmosphere is
relaxed and the food unpretentious. ❽

Roch Villa Harding St ☎01834/843096,
ⓔmandy10b@sky.com. Budget B&B with three
shared bathrooms, each with video or DVD player.
Rates are just £15 for bed only, £20 for B&B. ❶

Hostel and campsites

Manorbier YHA hostel Skrinkle Haven, near
Manorbier ☎01834/871803 and 0870/770 5954,
ⓔmanorbier@yha.org.uk. Modern hostel fashioned
from an old MOD building overlooking the cliffs five
miles west of Tenby, near the Manorbier bus route
from town. Meals available. Closed Nov–Feb. Dorm
beds £16–18, rooms ❶

Meadow Farm Northcliff ☎01834/844829. Less
than a mile north of town, this campsite in a grassy
field has only limited facilities but long views over the
town towards Caldey Island – a great alternative to
the family fun-park-style places. Closed Nov–March.
£7 per person.

Trevayne Farm 2 miles north off the A478
☎01834/813402. Family-oriented caravan and
campsite with superb views over Saundersfoot and
the great arc of sand that sweeps round to Amroth
and Pendine. Closed Nov–March. £9–15 per pitch.

The Town

Tenby's old centre is triangular, with two sides meeting at the castle and the third by the remaining **town walls**. South Parade runs alongside the massive twenty-foot-high wall, first built in the late thirteenth century and massively strengthened in 1457 by Jasper Tudor, Earl of Pembroke and uncle of the future king, Henry VII. It was further fortified in the 1580s, when Tenby was regarded as a likely target for the Spanish Armada. The only town gate still standing is **Five Arches** (roughly halfway along the town side of the wall), a semicircular barbican used as an everyday entrance by citizens and peacetime visitors, with hidden lookouts and acute angles to surprise invaders. The wall continues south to the Esplanade, with a long line of snooty hotels facing out over South Beach.

The centre's focal point is the 152-foot spire of the largely fifteenth-century **St Mary's church**, between Tudor Square and St George's Street. Its light interior shows the elaborate ceiling bosses in the chancel to good effect, while fifteenth-century tombs attest to Tenby's mercantile tradition. On the western side of St Mary's runs Upper Frog Street, replete with craft shops and an arcaded indoor **market**, containing craft stalls and gift shops.

Otherwise, it's a pleasure to explore the alleyways and steps in the old town, especially the medieval lanes in the immediate vicinity of the church. Due east, **Quay Hill** runs down towards the harbour past some of Tenby's oldest dwellings, including a **Tudor Merchant's House** (April–Oct daily except Sat 11am–5pm; £2.70; NT), built in the late fifteenth century, when Tenby was second only to

▲ Tenby Harbour

Bristol as a west coast port. The compact house with its Flemish-style chimneypieces is on three floors, packed with furniture, either seventeenth- and eighteenth-century originals or Tudor repro made traditionally without glue or nails: notice especially the superb inlaid 1753 marriage chest.

Crackwell and Bridge streets run down to the **harbour**, which can look idyllic if it's not too crowded. Sheltered by the curving headland and fringed by pastel-hued Georgian and Victorian houses, it's a great place to stroll on a warm evening. By day, it's the departure point for numerous excursion boats, especially the short trip to Caldey Island (see below). Above the harbour is the headland and **Castle Hill**, its grassy slopes rife with Victoriana in the form of huge flowerbeds (including an indigenous small daffodil in springtime), ornate benches, a bandstand and a pompous memorial to Prince Albert – upstaging the ruins of the Norman **castle**, notable for its gatehouse and the all-round view from its windswept tower.

The nearby **Tenby Museum & Art Gallery** (Easter–Oct daily 10am–5pm; Nov–Easter Mon–Fri 10am–5pm; £4), presents an interesting trawl through topics of local interest, notably a broad history of the town and harbour since the tenth century with a scale model showing the town in 1586, before it burst the town walls. The geology section includes ancient axes and a woman's skull dated from around 1300 BC, and there are books from the 1550s written by locally born mathematician, Robert Recorde, who was the first to use the equals symbol. The real attraction, though, is the Wilfred Harrison Gallery, featuring work by Augustus and Gwen John, and locally born Nina Hamnet. Caldey Island also gets a look-in, with material on its Ogham Stone.

From atop Castle Hill, there are great views over the quieter **South Beach**, where the sea recedes so far at low tide that the tiny St Catherine's Island (no access) becomes fully beached. The island is topped by the remains of the 1869 St Catherine's Fort, one of Palmerston's Follies (see box, p.191).

Caldey Island

Caldey Island (Ynys Pyr), three miles off Tenby's Esplanade, was first settled by Celtic monks in the sixth century, perhaps as an offshoot of St Illtud's monastery at Llantwit Major. The community was still thriving in the ninth century when a Latin inscription was added to the island's sixth-century Ogham Stone, but nothing more is known until 1113, when English king Henry I bestowed it on a Norman noble, Robert Fitzmartin. In 1136, it was given to the Benedictine monks of St Dogmael's at Cardigan, who founded their priory here. Upon the dissolution of the monasteries in 1536, the Benedictines left and the island was bought and sold willy-nilly until 1906, when it was again sold to a Benedictine monastic order, and subsequently to Reformed Cistercians. The island has been a monastic home almost constantly ever since, with around twenty monks currently in residence.

Boats leave Tenby Harbour (or Castle Beach when the tide is out) every twenty minutes in season (Easter–Oct Mon–Sat 10.30am–4pm, sometimes until 5pm; £10 return; ☏01834/844453, ⓦwww.caldey-island.co.uk) for the twenty-minute journey to the island. Tickets (not for any specific sailing) are sold at the kiosk in Castle Square, directly above the harbour. A short woodland walk from the island's jetty leads to the island's main settlement: a tiny post office, a popular tearoom and a **perfume shop** selling the herbal fragrances distilled by the monks from Caldey's abundant flora. The narrow road to the left leads down to the heavily restored **chapel of St David**, whose most impressive feature is the round-arched Norman door.

A lane leads south from the village to the old **priory**, abandoned in 1536 and restored at the beginning of the twentieth century. Its centrepiece is the twelfth-century **St Illtud's church**, distinguished by its curiously blunt (and leaning) steeple, and its ownership of one of the most significant pre-Norman finds in Wales. The sandstone **Ogham Stone**, with an inscription from the sixth century (added to, in Latin, during the ninth), was discovered under the stained-glass window on the south side of the nave. The church's rough flooring is largely comprised of pebbles from the island's beaches. The lane continues south from the site, climbing up to the gleaming white island **lighthouse**, built in 1828. Views from here are memorable.

Eating and drinking

There are dozens of **cafés** and **restaurants** around the town, and in high season the beachfronts (especially North Beach) are packed with cheap places that shut up shop in the winter.

Bay of Bengal 1 Crockwell St ☏01834/843331. Reliable BYO curry restaurant. Ask for a seat downstairs, from where there are great bay views.

Caffè Vista 3 Crockwell St. Great little Greek-Australian-run café with excellent panini, espresso and cakes, plus a small selection of dishes such as beef or butterbean stew. Great harbour views from the small terrace, free wi-fi and it's licensed.

Coach and Horses Upper Frog St. Animated, wooden-beamed pub (said to be the oldest in Tenby) with good beer, well-prepared bar meals and some tasty Thai dishes.

Lifeboat Tavern Tudor Square. Popular and enjoyable pub, with a youthful clientele.

The Mews Bistro Upper Frog St ☏01834/844068. Tenby's best fresh fish restaurant, tucked away in a quiet alley and serving the

likes of Tenby sea bass (£17) and Bantry Bay mussels (starter £7, main £14) served with Thai, jalfrezi or Pernod and cream sauces. Mon–Sat for dinner plus summer lunches.

Normandie Hotel Upper Frog St. Old-fashioned pub that's been modernized with bare boards and leather sofas. Head through to the back where *The Stables* wine bar nestles into the ancient town walls.

Plantagenet House Quay Hill ☏01834/842350. This cosy and thoroughly enjoyable restaurant offers some of the best dining in the area, making optimum use of local produce. It's also situated in one of the oldest houses in Tenby – note the massive tenth-century Flemish chimney en route to the loo. Dinner mains go for £18–23 (£15 for vegetarian), but lunch is cheaper (£8 dishes), or just have a drink in the intimate bar.

Listings

Amroth and Saundersfoot

AMROTH, six miles northwest of Tenby, marks the eastern end of the 186-mile **Pembrokeshire Coast Path**, which winds around every cove and cliff in the county, all the way to St Dogmael's, just outside Cardigan. It's a pleasant enough village, with a good beach and **Colby Woodland Gardens** (mid–March to Oct daily 10am–5pm; £4.20; NT), wedged deep into a wooded valley a mile inland. Until the nineteenth century the land now covered by the gardens was mined extensively for anthracite and iron ore, but it's now far more attractive, if hardly spectacular. Highlights include the sloping walled garden (11am–5pm) and, in May and June, the explosion of colour in the numerous rhododendron bushes.

Amroth's **accommodation** is fairly modest, but extends to the simple but comfortable *Ashdale* (℡01834/813853; ❶), a hundred yards south of the beach towards Wiseman's Bridge; and, next door, the very comfortable *Mellieha Guest House* ℡01834/811581, ⓦwww.mellieha.co.uk; ❹). The *New Inn*, next to the beach, is an enjoyable place to eat and drink, if generally packed in summer.

The coast between Amroth and Tenby is one long line of caravan parks, broken only by the picturesque harbour of **SAUNDERSFOOT**, built originally for the export of local coal and anthracite. The industry has long since folded and the predictable clutch of cafés, tacky shops and boisterous fun pubs make the town a popular, good-natured place to hang out beside the wide yawn of sand.

Saundersfoot's **train station** is located over a mile northwest up The Ridgeway from the harbourside **tourist office** (Easter–Oct daily 10am–5pm, plus Sat & Sun Nov–Easter 10am–4pm; ℡01834/813672). If you want to **stay** in the village, try the lovely *Cliff House*, Wogan Terrace (℡01834/813931, ⓦwww.smoothhound.co.uk/hotels/cliffhse; ❸), which has great sea views. High on the hill overlooking the beach, the chic *St Brides Hotel*, St Brides Hill (℡01834/812304, ⓦwww.stbridesspahotel.com; rooms ❼, sea view ❽), is one of Pembrokeshire's finer hotels, remodelled along modern lines, with Welsh art in the public spaces and an elegant restaurant. There's handy **camping** a mile south at *Trevayne Farm* (see p.179)

Saundersfoot has plenty of straightforward **places to eat**, including the *Royal Oak Inn* on Wogan Terrace. Just south of town, the restaurant at the *Swallow Tree Gardens* caravan park (℡01834/812398) is a glorious surprise, offering quality British-pub-style cuisine with stylish twists. A mile and a half north of Saundersfoot towards Amroth, the thoroughly enjoyable *Wiseman's Bridge Inn* is a beachside pub that's good for a drink and a meal.

South Pembrokeshire coast

The southern zigzag of coast that darts west from Tenby is a strange mix of caravan parks and Ministry of Defence shooting ranges above some spectacularly beautiful bays and gull-covered cliffs. For walkers, the coast is constantly

The Pembrokeshire National Park and Coast Path

Of the fourteen national parks in England and Wales, the **Pembrokeshire Coast National Park** is the only one that is predominantly sea-based, hugging the rippled coast around the entire southwestern section of Wales. Established in 1952, the park is not one easily identifiable mass, but rather a series of occasionally unconnected patches of coast and inland scenery. Starting at its southeastern corner, the first segment clings to the coast from Amroth through to the Milford Haven waterway, an area of sweeping limestone cliffs and some fabulous beaches. The second (and by far the quietest) part courses around the inland pastoral landscape of the Daugleddau estuary, which plunges deep into the rural heart of Pembrokeshire southeast of Haverfordwest. Superb for scenic cliff walking, the third section is around the beaches and resorts of St Bride's Bay, where the sea scoops a great chunk out of Wales' westernmost land. In the north of the county, the boundary of the park runs far inland to encompass the Mynydd Preseli, a barren but invigoratingly beautiful range of hills dotted with ancient relics.

Crawling around almost every wriggle of the coast, the **Pembrokeshire Coast Path** winds 186 miles from Amroth in the south, to its northernmost point at St Dogmael's near Cardigan. For the vast majority of the time, the path clings precariously to clifftop routes, overlooking rocks frequented by sunbathing seals, craggy offshore islands, unexpected gashes of sand and shrieking clouds of sea birds. Only on the southwestern end of the Castlemartin peninsula, where the coast is given over to army training camps and rifle ranges, does the path veer inland for any major length; it also ducks briefly inland along the Milford Haven estuary, where the proximity of belching great oil refineries and the huge expanse of hill-backed water provide one of the route's many surprises.

The most popular and ruggedly inspiring segments of the Coast Path are around St Davids Head and the Marloes peninsula, either side of St Bride's Bay; the stretch from the castle at Manorbier to the tiny cliff chapel at Bosherston along the southern coast; and the undulating contours, massive cliffs, bays and old ports along the northern coast, either side of Fishguard. These offer miles of windswept walking amongst great flashes of gorse, heather and seasonal plants, as well as the opportunity to study thousands of sea birds at close quarter. Basking seals are frequent visitors to some of the more inaccessible beaches, particularly around the time when pups are born in the autumn. This is reckoned to be a major cause of the occasional accidents along the route, as people try to gain better views of the creatures and consequently fall over the edge.

Of all the **seasons**, spring is perhaps the finest for walking: the crowds have yet to arrive and the clifftop flora is at its most vivid. The national park publishes the excellent free **newspaper**, *Coast to Coast*, detailing special walks, boat trips and other events, and which you can pick up from visitor centres throughout this chapter. The best **websites** are the general park site ⓦ www.pembrokeshirecoast.org.uk, and ⓦ nt.pcnpa .org.uk, which concentrates on trail-specific info with plenty of trip planning advice.

There are numerous publications about the Coast Path, of which the best is Brian John's *National Trail Guide* (£13), which includes 1:25,000 section maps of the route. Readers with walking difficulties should pick up the *Easy Access Routes* booklet (£3), detailing flatter sections, many of which have been remodelled with gates rather than stiles.

beguiling, as it nips and tucks past some excellent, comparatively quiet beaches, many of which are also accessible by car.

West of Tenby, worthwhile destinations include **MANORBIER**, with its ghostly castle above a small bay, and quintessentially pretty **ST FLORENCE**. You can stroll along the beautiful sandy **Barafundle Bay** and past the **BOSHERSTON** lily ponds at the National Trust's Stackpole Estate, then cross MOD land to the ancient **St Govan's chapel**, squeezed into a rock cleft above the crashing waves. The limestone sea arch known as the **Green Bridge of Wales** is the highlight of the dramatic clifftop scenery hereabouts, which gradually softens towards the village of **ANGLE**, which faces out to the petrochemical installations across the Milford Haven.

Manorbier and St Florence

Three miles southwest of Tenby the Coast Path reaches the glorious, privately owned beach at the 54-acre headland of **Lydstep Haven**; it's a beautiful spot, with limestone caverns to explore in the craggy Lydstep Point, and worth the small parking fee. Although some of the caverns here are only accessible at low tide, the **Smuggler's Cave** is safe at all times. A mile or so further west is the excellent *Manorbier* **YHA hostel** (see p.179).

Manorbier

The next part of the Coast Path veers inland to avoid the artillery range on Old Castle Head, then leads into the quaint village of **MANORBIER** (Maenorbŷr), pronounced "manner-beer", birthplace in 1146 of Giraldus Cambrensis, Gerald of Wales (see p.399), who described the castle here as "excellently well defended by turrets and bulwarks, and ... situated on the summit of a hill extending on the western side towards the sea".

Founded in the early twelfth century as a baronial residence, the **castle** (April–Sept daily 10am–6pm; £3.50; ⓦ www.manorbiercastle.co.uk) sits above the village and its beach on a hill of wild gorse. The Norman walls are very well preserved, surrounding a grass courtyard in which the extensive remains of the castle's chapel and staterooms jostle for position with the nineteenth-century domestic residence. Views from the ramparts are wonderful, taking in the corrugated coastline, bushy dunes, deep-green fields and smoking chimneys of the tinted village houses. In the walls and buildings are a warren of dark passageways to explore, occasionally opening out into little cells populated by lacklustre wax figures, including Gerald himself.

The lane below the castle leads past the curious, elongated tower of **St James' Church**, a Norman structure whose rough stonework has recently been rendered with a "buttermilk limewash" to mimic how the whole church would apparently once have looked. It's a striking sight but not universally popular.

Below the church, a sandy break in the red sandstone cliffs reveals Manorbier's shell-shaped **cove**. For a more secluded bathe, follow the path on the left of the beach (as you face the sea) over the headland called the Priest's Nose, past a Neolithic cromlech (burial chamber) known as the **King's Quoit**, and round for just over half a mile to the steep steps down to often-deserted **Precipe Beach**. At high tide, the beach is entirely flooded, so check times.

St Florence

Three miles north of Manorbier is the delightful little village of **ST FLORENCE**, whose whitewashed stone cottages, many with their original medieval Flemish chimneystacks, huddle around tiny lanes. St Florence was

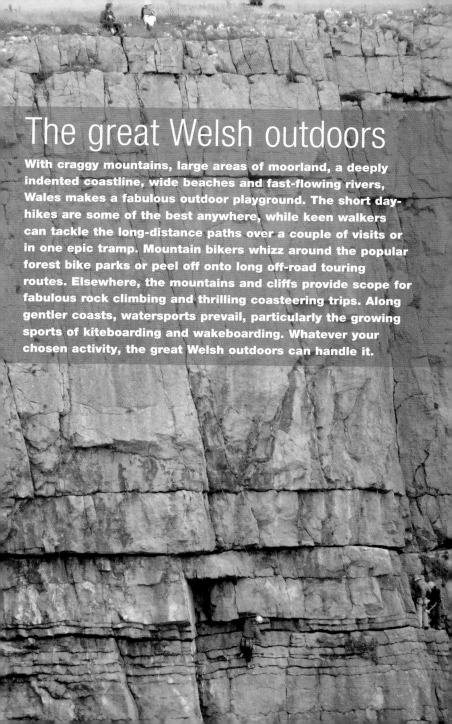

The great Welsh outdoors

With craggy mountains, large areas of moorland, a deeply indented coastline, wide beaches and fast-flowing rivers, Wales makes a fabulous outdoor playground. The short day-hikes are some of the best anywhere, while keen walkers can tackle the long-distance paths over a couple of visits or in one epic tramp. Mountain bikers whizz around the popular forest bike parks or peel off onto long off-road touring routes. Elsewhere, the mountains and cliffs provide scope for fabulous rock climbing and thrilling coasteering trips. Along gentler coasts, watersports prevail, particularly the growing sports of kiteboarding and wakeboarding. Whatever your chosen activity, the great Welsh outdoors can handle it.

Riding the Ymynydd Mojo trail, Cwmcarn ▲

Pembrokeshire coastal path ▼

Rock climbing, Mowingword, Pembrokeshire ▼

Mountain rides

Since the 1990s, the forests of Wales have gained an enviable reputation for top-class **mountain biking**. Every weekend mud-bespattered bikers weave along miles of single-track at key **bike parks** dotted along the mountainous spine of the country – from the Gŵydyr Forest just outside Betws-y-Coed to Cwm Carn in the Valleys northwest of Newport. There's something to suit everyone, from beginners to hardened speed freaks. Elsewhere, off-road cycling is allowed along designated bridleways, including the Snowdon Ranger, Rhyd Ddu and Llanberis paths up Snowdon (detailed on p.378): slog up in the pre-dawn cool for that summit sunrise, or head up for sunset and a nerve-wracking dusk descent.

If you really fancy a challenge, make for **Sarn Helen**, an epic route across the country through Snowdonia and the Brecon Beacons loosely following an old Roman route. At 270 miles long – running from Conwy to Gower – it's reckoned to be the most ambitious off-road ride in Britain and likely to take over a week.

Going cragging

The term "cragging" comes from *craig*, Welsh for cliff, and Wales has some of the finest **rock climbing** in Britain. The scale may not be huge (the highest route only takes you up 800ft) but the quality is excellent, and there's an astonishing variety of routes in a small area. Llanberis, at the foot of Snowdon, is the home of Welsh climbing, with routes ranging from easy hands-on scrambles up mountain ridges to impossibly difficult climbs only achievable by a few dozen people in the world.

In the south of the country, the pick of the crags are the limestone sea cliffs along the **Pembrokeshire Coast**. The bulk of the action happens near Bosherston. The military ordnance testing areas of Range East and Range West here mean that parts of the coast are off limits (permits for some places require climbers to attend a bomb recognition course), but there are plenty of areas with much freer access. Further east, the **Gower peninsula** is also ringed by tempting sea cliffs.

Offshore watersports

Whether you call it **kiteboarding** or kitesurfing, it is hot in Wales. The water may not be that warm, but great sweeping beaches lashed by strong steady winds off the Atlantic make for some excellent spots. Key centres are Rhosneigr on Anglesey, Aberdyfi along the Cambrian Coast, Whitesands Bay in Pembrokeshire, and Rhossili on the Gower peninsula near Swansea. All these places have shops selling gear and offering lessons. It isn't exactly an easy sport to learn, but a class can get you body-dragging (more fun than it sounds) inside a day, and actually riding a board in a couple of days.

Coasteering

Wales may not be at the cutting edge of adventure sports, but it led the way with **coasteering**, an exhilarating combination of hiking, coastal scrambling, swimming and cliff jumping. Clad in a wetsuit, helmet and buoyancy aid, the aim is to make your way as a group along the rugged, wave-lashed coastline. It was pioneered by St Davids-based TYF Adventure (see p.198), who run a range of trips, from the relatively tame to full-on blasts along the coast and even eco-trips suited to families.

▲ Kitesurfing, Rhossili beach, Gower peninsula

▼ Coastal footpath

▼ Coasteering, St Non's Bay

Pembrokeshire coastal path signpost ▲

View of the Black Mountains from the summit of
Sugar Loaf, Abergavenny ▼

Heroic hikes and lengthy rambles

Wales is traced by a spider's web of over a dozen wonderful long-distance paths (LDPs). Three of these – the Pembrokeshire Coast Path, Offa's Dyke Path and Glyndŵr's Way – are additionally designated National Trails, waymarked at frequent intervals by an acorn symbol.

The following is a brief rundown of the most popular LDPs, all of which are also detailed in the Guide.

Cambrian Way (274 miles). The longest, wildest and most arduous of the Welsh LDPs, cutting north-south over the remote Cambrian Mountains. See p.438.

Glyndŵr's Way (123 miles). A lengthy meander amongst the remote mountains and lakes of mid-Wales, visiting sites associated with the great fifteenth-century Welsh hero. See p.260.

Landsker Borderlands Trail (60 miles). Gentle waterways, quiet villages and easy trails characterize this slightly contrived circular walk around the Landsker region in Pembrokeshire. See p.176.

Offa's Dyke Path (177 miles). The classic Welsh LDP, running from Prestatyn in the north to Chepstow in south Wales, largely tracing the line of the eighth-century earthwork along the English border. Mostly wooded lowland walking, with demanding territory through the Black Mountains. See p.257.

Pembrokeshire Coast Path (186 miles). This quintessential Welsh coastal trail dips into quiet coves and climbs over headlands, with sweeping ocean views and plenty of birdlife on the cliffs and offshore islands. See p.183.

Wye Valley Walk (136 miles). A lovely, sylvan, sea-to-source trek following the River Wye from Chepstow to Plynlimon, past rolling countryside and dramatic limestone gorges. See p.78.

For more details on all the outdoor activities mentioned here, see pp.52–57.

once an important port, though its inlet has long since receded, leaving a lovely walk beside the usually dry bed of Ritec stream.

The best place to **stay** is the Georgian *Elmgrove Country House* (☎01834/871255, ⓦwww.elmgrovecountryhouse.co.uk; ⑤), with elegant rooms, a tennis court and a croquet lawn and meals. *Bramley's Tearoom*, at the back of the village garden centre, does cracking Sunday **lunches**, and home-cooked daytime meals the rest of the week. The *Sun Inn* is the pick of the two pubs, serving well-prepared meals.

Stackpole Quay to Angle

One of the best starting points for walks along the breathtaking clifftops is the National Trust's **Stackpole Estate**, which encompasses a couple of miles of coast and some beautiful woods and waterways inland. Road access is at two main points, the westernmost being the rocky harbour of **Stackpole Quay** (parking £2.50). It's one of the smallest harbours you'll find anywhere, with barely enough room for two boats between its slabs of stratified limestone – a gorgeous spot with the added bonus of the *Boathouse Tearoom*, where delicious lunches are served in a sheltered, sunny courtyard. A half-mile walk brings you to **Barafundle Bay**, inaccessible by car and one of the finest beaches in Pembrokeshire, with clear water and a soft, sandy beach fringed by wooded cliffs.

South of the beach, a spectacular stretch of the Coast Path leads to **Stackpole Head**, a tufted plateau on craggy arches jutting into the sea. The *Stackpole Inn* (☎01646/672324, ⓦwww.stackpoleinn.co.uk) nearby serves real ales and does superb pub meals with straightforward lunches (mains £8–9) and more elaborate dinners (mains £12–20) such as pan-fried sea bass or Moroccan lamb cutlets. They also have spacious and pleasant nautically themed rooms (④).

Bosherston and St Govan's Chapel

The path continues around the coast, through the dunes of **Stackpole Warren**, to **BROAD HAVEN** – the next spot on the coast accessible by car – where a nice small beach overlooks several rocky islets managed by the National Trust. Basing yourself here gives good access inland to the nearby **Bosherston Lily Ponds** (free), three reed-fringed fingers of water created in the late eighteenth century for coarse fishing, and now beautifully landscaped, though the lilies don't carpet its surface the way they once did. The westernmost lake remains the prettiest, especially in late spring and early summer, when the flowers are in full bloom. You can still fish here, with a permit (£6 a day; closed mid-March to mid-June) from *Ye Olde Worlde Café*, a hundred yards away in the village of **BOSHERSTON**.

From Bosherston it's a mile to the coast, across the MOD training grounds peppered with warning signs and road barriers that are almost always open at weekends but frequently closed Monday to Friday. Firing orders are posted outside *Ye Olde Worlde Café* or call ☎01646/662367 after 4.30pm for the next day's programme. Continue down the lane through a series of gates and you'll reach a spot overlooking the cliffs where **St Govan's chapel** is wedged. This tiny grey structure is at least eight hundred (and possibly as much as fourteen hundred) years old. Legend has it that St Govan chose this spot to be buried after hoodlums attacked him on the clifftop and the cliffs opened up and folded gently around him, saving him from certain death. Steps descend into the sandy-floored chapel, with its simple stone altar, and thence to a small cell hewn from the rock, containing the fissure that reputedly sheltered Govan. You can follow the steps all the way down to the spume-flecked sea for a magnificent close-up view of the precarious crags, caves and arches.

Accommodation is available at the recently refurbished *St Govan's Country Inn* in Bosherston (℡01646/661311; ●), an enjoyable place which caters mostly to walkers and rock climbers, and serves mountains of inexpensive food (mostly £6–9, including good curries), plus a range of real ales. For excellent, simple **camping** continue through the village towards Broadhaven Beach to *Trefalen Farm* (℡01646/661643; £4 per person), where an open field looks out over the bay.

Range West

All the land beyond the chapel is the MOD's **Range West** and is entirely out of bounds except for the narrow clifftop strip on which the Coast Path runs. This four-mile section runs past a striking cleft known as **Huntsman's Leap** and two isolated beaches at **Bullslaughter** and **Flimston Bay**, to **Stack Rocks**. The only vehicle access to the coast is at the hamlet of **MERRION**, on the B4319, from where a lane (generally open weekends and some weekdays; for 24hr recorded information call ℡01646/662367) runs down to Stack Rocks past the mournful little chapel at **FLIMSTON**, a hamlet forcibly abandoned to the army.

Stack Rocks jut out of the sea here like a series of tall, lichen-spattered stepping stones. A hundred yards further west (as far as you're allowed to go), a graceful limestone arch rises from a wave-flattened rock platform, known as the **Green Bridge of Wales**. On a quiet day, the only company you will have are the shrieking gulls, guillemots and kittiwakes swooping to their perches on the limestone ledges.

Castlemartin, Freshwater West and Angle

Forced to turn inland, the Coast Path continues back up the lane to Merrion and follows the B4319 through the village of **CASTLEMARTIN** – whose church boasts an organ once owned by Mendelssohn. You can **stay** here at the characterful *Old Smithy* (℡01646/661310, ✉paulineforsyth@bigfoot.com; ●), peacefully set in over an acre of land, and with dinner available by arrangement. The Coast Path follows the B4319 a couple of miles to **Freshwater West**, a beach resort that's great for **surfing**, though the currents can be too strong for swimming. Behind the beach, desolate wind-battered dunes make for interesting walking.

The B4319 meets the B4320 from Pembroke near the **Devil's Quoit**, a Neolithic burial chamber topped by an impressive capstone. It continues down the final finger of the peninsula, to the remote village of **ANGLE** at the western end of a wide curve of mud known as **Angle Bay**. Angle consists of one long street, bounded by old, coloured cottages. **West Angle Bay**, a secluded spot a mile to the west of the main village, is better for swimming, and overlooks another of the Lord Palmerston protective forts (see p.191) on **Thorn Island**.

There's no accommodation with a roof in Angle, but you can **camp** at *Castle Farm* (℡01646/641220; £3.50 per person; closed Oct–Easter) just behind the church. For **eating** and **drinking**, try the convivial *Hibernia Inn*, right in the centre; or walk ten minutes east along the shore to the delightful, rustic *Old Point House* inn (closed Tues in winter), whose fire is said to have burned continuously for over three hundred years until the mid-1990s, since when it has only been lit in winter. Quality meals come in large portions: go for the specials board, which usually includes several examples of the day's catch.

Mid-Pembrokeshire

The central slab of Pembrokeshire is generally either ignored or actively avoided by visitors intent on reaching the more obvious coastal pleasures to the south and west. None of the towns here are especially interesting, but they're the largest places hereabouts.

Historically, the most significant is **Pembroke**, the old county town, which sits on the southern side of the Pembroke River, a continuation of the massive **Milford Haven** waterway, described by Nelson as the greatest natural harbour in the world. Yet despite its location and its formidable **castle** (and the nearby ruins of the Bishop's Palace at **Lamphey**), Pembroke is rather dull.

The river links Pembroke to **Pembroke Dock**, on the southern banks of the magnificent Daugleddau River estuary, from where ferries leave for Ireland. Across the water, Quakers founded the town of **Milford Haven**, which has a dramatic setting and a good museum but probably won't detain you long.

Seven miles to the north, the chief town of the region, **Haverfordwest**, is an important market and transport centre. Despite some handsome architecture, it remains rather soulless, though it's made more palatable by its proximity to **Scolton Manor**, which houses the county museum, and **Picton Castle**.

A branch **train line** leaves the main Swansea–Fishguard route at Whitland, calling at Narberth and Tenby en route to Pembroke and Pembroke Dock. A second spur peels off the main line at Clarbeston Road bound for Haverfordwest and Milford Haven. There's a reasonable **bus** service throughout the area, with most routes starting at either Pembroke or Haverfordwest.

Pembroke and around

The old county town of **PEMBROKE** (Penfro) grew up solely to serve its castle, the mightiest link in the chain of Norman strongholds built across southern Wales. Drawn out along a hilltop ridge, the walled town flourished as a port for Pembrokeshire goods to be exported from the main quay, situated alongside the waters below the walls of the castle, to all parts of Britain, as well as Ireland, France and Spain. Though it managed to choose the winning side during the Wars of the Roses, Pembroke was less fortunate in the Civil War, when Cromwell besieged the town.

Though it subsequently became a centre of leather-making, weaving, dyeing and tailoring, Pembroke never regained its former importance, and by the twentieth century the small town was in grave decline, its port long since overtaken by neighbouring sites. One fortunate result of this is that Pembroke is mercifully free of postwar development in the centre, although the fringes around the main street are largely modern and bland.

The town's sole thoroughfare, **Main Street** stretches from the **train station** (as Station Rd) in the east to the mighty walls of the castle. Partway along, Blackhorse Walk runs north beside **St Michael's church**, down to the lovely **Mill Pond** and the most impressive remnants of the thirteenth-century town **walls**, running between the demolished East Gate and **Barnard's Tower**, a medieval towered house attached to the walls. The mill pond is now a nature reserve (unrestricted access) and home to swans and otters.

History buffs shouldn't pass up a trip out to the ruined Bishop's Palace in **Lamphey**, though unless you're off to Ireland you might skip **Pembroke Dock**.

The castle

Pembroke Castle (daily: April–Sept 9.30am–6pm; March & Oct 10am–5pm; Nov–Feb 10am–4pm; £3.50; ⓦ www.pembrokecastle.co.uk) was founded as the strongest link in the chain of fortresses built by the Normans across south Wales. In the early years following the Norman invasion, the people of Deheubarth (west Wales) avoided conquest thanks to a tacit agreement between Rhys ap Tewdwr and the Normans, but after Rhys' death in 1093, Lord Roger de Montgomery immediately invaded the area and built a castle. The castle's powerful bulk, protected by a hill on its southern side and water on the other three, proved impregnable to a Welsh siege for the next four centuries enforcing the rule of "Little England Beyond Wales" (see p.175). In 1452, Henry VI granted the castle to Jasper Tudor, whose nephew Harri was born here, later becoming the Lancastrian heir to the throne, and, in 1485, King Henry VII. During the Civil War, Pembroke was a Parliamentarian stronghold until the town's military governor suddenly switched allegiance to the King in 1648. Cromwell's 48-day siege of the town only succeeded after he cut off its water supply.

Despite Cromwell's battering and centuries of subsequent neglect, the sheer, bloody-minded bulk of Pembroke still inspires awe, even if it's largely due to extensive restoration over the last century. You enter through the soaring gatehouse, home to some excellent displays on the history of the castle and the Tudor empire. You then emerge into the large, grassy courtyard, enclosed by battlements and punctuated by hulking towers where the town walls formerly joined the fortress.

In the inner ward, the 75ft-high Norman **keep** has walls 18ft thick and a crowning dome. Alongside, the Dungeon Tower comes complete with grille to peer through into a gloomy cell below, and there's a Norman Hall whose period arch has been sadly over-restored. Steps at the side of this lead far down into **Wogan Cavern**, a huge natural cavern, dank and slimy, where light beams in through a barred hole in the wall facing out over the waterside path.

The intact towers and battlements contain many heavily restored communal rooms, now empty of furniture (and to a large extent, atmosphere too), although the walkways and dark-roofed passages that connect them give ample chance to chase around spiral stairways into great oak-beamed halls.

Practicalities

Pembroke's **tourist office** (Easter–Oct Mon–Sat 9.30am–5pm, Sun 10am–4pm; ☎01646/622388), on Commons Road parallel to Main Street, can provide a useful free town guide and information on the Pembrokeshire National Park and Coast Path. The library, in same building, offers free **internet access**.

If you decide to **stay**, don't miss *Beech House B&B*, 78 Main St (☎01646/683740; ❶). Rooms (just £18 per person) only have shared bathrooms, but for comfort and hospitality it easily outdoes places charging twice as much. If it's full, try one of the four en-suite rooms at *Tregenna*, 7 Upper Lamphey Rd (☎01646/621525, ⓦ www.tregennapembroke.co.uk; ❷), close to the train station. Pricier places in town aren't great shakes, and you might be better off staying in Lamphey (see opposite), a couple of miles to the southeast, or at *Poyerston Farm* (☎01646/651347, ⓦ www.poyerstonfarm.co.uk; ❹) a top-quality farmhouse B&B two miles northeast of Pembroke.

For good espresso and light **meals** head for *The Cornstore* (closed Sun), down by the river on Northgate Street, or for something more substantial try the nicely cooked restaurant dishes and bar meals at the *Old King's Arms* at 13 Main St. The best of the dozens of **pubs** is the *Old Cross Saws* at 109 Main St, although it's hard to beat a summer evening at the *Waterman's Arms*, over the bridge on Northgate Street, where you can while away the hours on a veranda overlooking the Mill Pond.

Pembroke Dock

Workaday **PEMBROKE DOCK** (Doc Penfro), three miles north of Pembroke, is principally of interest for its ferries to Rosslare in Ireland and its harbourside **Gun Tower**, Front Street (April–Oct daily 10am–4pm; £2), one of Palmerston's Follies (see box, p.191), which houses a few moderately diverting exhibits on the history of the town and the naval nineteenth-century dockyard that was based here.

Pembroke Dock's **train station** is in the centre of town, half a mile east of the **ferry terminal**, from where twice-daily Irish Ferries (℡08705/329543, Ⓦwww.irishferries.com) sail to Rosslare; boats currently depart at 2.45am and 2.30pm, and the journey takes four hours.

One of the few **accommodation** places that accepts late ferry arrivals is *The Blickerage*, 3 Martello Rd (℡01646/689972, Ⓦwww.theblickerage.co.uk; ❷) on St Patrick's Hill, less than half a mile southwest of the ferry terminal. The *Shipwright* pub by the Gun Tower does decent **meals**.

Lamphey

The pleasant village of **LAMPHEY** (Llandyfai), two miles southeast of Pembroke, is best known for the ruined **Bishop's Palace** (daily 10am–5pm; £3.10; CADW) which stands off a quiet lane to the north of the settlement. Dating from at least the thirteenth century and abandoned at the Reformation in the mid-sixteenth century, the palace was built as a country retreat for

The Pembrokeshire energy industries

On both sides of the magnificent Milford Haven waterway, the most prominent features on the landscape belong to the **refineries** that fringe the waters. Storage tankers, observation towers and security fences litter the Coast Path here, the most blighted stretch being the five miles between the west side of the Pembroke River estuary and Angle Bay.

As well as occasional disasters such as the grounding of the *Sea Empress* oil tanker in 1996, the presence of so much polluting and potentially hazardous industry seems totally out of place in this rural corner of Wales. The situation has improved over the years, with one refinery closing down and the two remaining plants cleaning up their acts considerably. But controversy continues as Milford Haven gears up to become the UK's major importer of liquefied natural gas (LNG). As the nation's North Sea reserves run out, Britain is looking to the Middle East to supply its gargantuan needs. Around £4 billion worth of the stuff is supposed to arrive in massive super-tankers over the next fifteen years, mainly from Qatar. A couple of huge new storage and gasification installations are nearing completion, and a new gas-fired power station is being built. To connect these to the gas supply network, a new, buried pipeline threads across south Wales, occasionally veering into northern sections of the Brecon Beacons National Park.

Though the project is enthusiastically backed by the Welsh Assembly and the Pembrokeshire County Council, many locals are less keen. Fears over the safety of tankers and general discontent over the disruption during construction have seen numerous protests but the project rolls inexorably on. Regular gas arrivals are expected by late 2008.

the bishops of St Davids, though it was in use as Crown apartments for a few decades afterwards. Stout walls surround the scattered ruins, with many of the palace buildings having long been lost under the grassy banks. Most impressive are the remains of the Great Hall that form the eastern end of the complex, topped by the fourteenth-century Bishop Gower's hallmark arcaded parapets, similar to those that he built in the Bishop's Palace of St Davids. Lit only by narrow slits, the gloomy hall beneath the Great Hall has the feeling of a crypt.

Lamphey is an agreeable enough place in which to linger, with grand **accommodation** at the slightly over-the-top, *Lamphey Court Hotel & Spa* (℡01646/672273, Ⓦwww.lampheycourt.co.uk; ❼), opposite the Bishop's Palace ruins. Alternatively, sleep comfortably at the characterful three-room Georgian farmhouse *Lower Lamphey Park* (℡01646/672906, Ⓦwww .lowerlampheypark.co.uk; ❸), where some of the outbuildings have been converted into self-catering cottages. It's a few hundred yards north of the *Dial Inn*, on The Ridgeway (℡01646/672426, ❸), which also has rooms and offers a reliable menu and good beer.

Milford Haven

One of the most impressive sights in this part of Wales is the view from the 1970s **Cleddau Bridge** (car toll 75p) between Pembroke Dock and **NEYLAND** on the opposite bank; pedestrians can also cross it. The views over the jutting headlands are magical, especially at sunset, with the masts of boats far below and the full skies reflected in the clear water. Even the refineries look attractive from this far up. If you need to while away an hour or two before (or after) sunset, drop into the *Old Ferry Inn*, immediately below the bridge on the south side, for high-standard but relatively inexpensive meals and real ales. The *Jolly Sailor*, on the north shore, is similar.

The waterway below – the Milford Haven – has long been an important harbour, and was even recognized by William Shakespeare:

...how far it is
To this same blessed Milford; and, by the way,
Tell me how Wales was made so happy as
To inherit such a haven.

(Imogen in *Cymbeline*, Act III, scene 2)

Taking its name from the waterway, the town of **MILFORD HAVEN** (Aberdaugleddau), four miles west of Neyland, was founded in the late eighteenth century by a group of early American Quaker settlers from Nantucket, who were brought to the area to work as whalers. The grid pattern they imposed – principally three streets rising sharply parallel to the waterway – survives today amid new civic and religious buildings. Despite a magnificent site and interesting heritage, Milford Haven hasn't got much going for it. The town has seen hard times of late, with the dead-beat town centre receiving little of the development money pumped into the horribly sterile marina development, where the docks used to be.

The waterside is impressive, though, with tugs and steamers ploughing up the glittering waters of the Haven that stretch out below the pleasant public gardens. Hamilton Terrace skirts around the waterside to the revamped docks, where you'll find the **Waterfront Gallery** and the interesting **Milford Haven Museum** (Easter–Oct Mon–Sat 11am–5pm, Sun during school holidays & bank holiday weekends noon–5pm; £1.50), housed in an eighteenth-century

Palmerston's Follies

The coast of southern Britain, and particularly that of south Pembrokeshire, is littered with what are known as **Palmerston's Follies**, nineteenth-century naval defences that never saw action. During his second term as British Prime Minister in 1860, Lord Palmerston felt that Britain was ill-prepared to withstand any attack made by Napoleon III, who was newly equipped with iron-clad battleships. Britain's navy had been barely upgraded since Nelson's victory at Trafalgar half a century earlier, so a Royal Commission recommended building a series of forts to protect naval dockyards while the navy modernized.

Palmerston got wholeheartedly behind the recommendation and had forts built right along the south coast of England and around Milford Haven and Pembroke. By the time the defences were complete in the 1880s, Anglo-French relations had improved, and the forts were never attacked. Arguably, the forts had been an effective deterrent, but in the public eye they became known as Palmerston's Follies. Most remain inaccessible to the public, though you can visit the Gun Tower at Pembroke Dock.

The best examples around Pembrokeshire are at Tenby, West Angle Bay, West Blockhouse Point and Milford Haven.

---

warehouse originally designed to store whale oil. Exhibits include photographs and mementos from the fishing trade, an explanation of the modern oil industry, details of the Quaker origins of the town and some fascinating archive material showing Milford Haven in wartime.

On the western side of the docks and estuary, **Fort Hubberston** is a Palmerston defence fort (see above), built between 1860 and 1865, which housed some 250 men in the late nineteenth century. It has recently become so rickety and vandalized that access is prohibited. Nearby is the ruined octagonal dome of the **Hakin Observatory**, the sole remaining relic of town founder Charles Francis Greville's dream to build a "mathematical college".

Practicalities

Milford Haven **train station** is located under the Hakin road bridge, next to the docks. The only reasons to stray from the docks area and into the town proper are to visit the **tourist office** at 94 Charles St (April–Sept Mon–Sat 10am–5pm; ☎01646/690866), or west Wales' only professional **theatre**, the recently revamped Torch (☎01646/695267), on St Peter's Road, at the end of Charles Street, which also has a cinema and a good café.

Accommodation is hard to come by, especially during the week. A couple of cheapies worth trying are *Cleddau Villa B&B*, 21 St Anne's Rd (☎01646/690313; ❶), a few yards from the docks towards Hakin; and *Mrs Williams*, 1 Pier Rd (☎01646/694531; ❶), in one of the oldest houses in town, where all rooms have sea views. There's a **campsite** at *Sandy Haven*, near Herbrandston, right by the water two miles west of town (☎01646/698844; £11 per pitch; closed Oct–Easter). Back in town *Martha's Vineyard* (☎01646/697083) on the Marina is a good **eating** option, particularly for fish lovers, or try *Hamiltons*, 26 Hamilton Terrace, a tearoom up by the tourist office, which opens some evenings.

Haverfordwest and around

Ancient but dull **HAVERFORDWEST** (Hwlffordd), seven miles northwest of Milford Haven, grew up around the Gilbert de Clare castle that dominates the skyline to this day. The town prospered as a port and trading centre in the seventeenth and eighteenth centuries, and even deposed Pembroke as the county town of Pembrokeshire, but despite a slew of rich architecture from its glory days, Haverfordwest is scarcely a place to linger.

The diminutive Castle Square forms the heart of the town. From here, a small alleyway to the right of Woolworths ascends to the **castle**, which fails to live up to the expectations created by views of it from below, since there's nothing to see except the dingy shell of the thirteenth-century inner ward. Next to the castle, in the imposing governor's house, is the **town museum** (Easter–Oct Mon–Sat 10am–4pm; £1), a motley collection of minor art pieces and some fairly interesting local history exhibits. Back down below, the Riverside Shopping Centre follows the river from Castle Square up to the Old Bridge, next to the bus terminus and tourist office. The more architecturally appealing parts of Haverfordwest lie up the handsome High Street, rising from the River Cleddau towards the thirteenth-century St Mary's Church.

Practicalities

The **train** station is ten minutes' walk east of the centre, while **buses** come and go from the depot at the end of the Old Bridge, right outside the **tourist office** (May–Sept Mon–Sat 9.30am–5pm; Oct–April Mon–Sat 10am–4pm; ℡01437/763110 ℮haverfordwes.tic@pembrokeshire.gov.uk). The region's best **bike rental** is from Mike's Bikes, 17 Prendergast, (℡01437/760068, ℗www.mikes-bikes.co.uk; closed Sun), a quarter of a mile northeast of the visitor centre, which rents mountain bikes (£12 a day) and hybrid tourers (also £12 a day) with panniers, lock and helmet, and tag-a-longs for kids..

For B&B **accommodation**, try *College Guest House*, 93 Hill St (℡01437/763710; ℗www.collegeguesthouse.com; ❹). If you've got your own transport, however, it's better to drive five miles northeast to *Lower Haythog Farm*, Spittal (℡01437 731279; ℗www.lowerhaythogfarm.co.uk; ❹), with welcoming hosts and evening meals for £23. There's also a **campsite** at the *Rising Sun Inn* in Pelcomb Bridge (℡01437/765171; £8 per pitch), two miles northwest on the A487.

For daytime **food**, grab a freshly filled baguette from *Dylan's*, 23 High St, or an espresso and panini at *Coco* on Castle Square. A great option for lunch or evening meals is *The George's*, 24 Market St (closed Sun), which takes a wholefood approach to delicious peasant dishes. You can eat in a lovely walled garden if the weather allows, or the cellar bistro if not. Four miles northwest of town on the A487, the sublime *Keeston Kitchen* (℡01437/710440; closed Sun evenings and Mon), just before the village of Simpson Cross is superb for seasonal speciality dishes.

Picton Castle and Scolton Manor

The main A40 heads east out of Haverfordwest past the train station. After three miles, signs point two miles south towards **Picton Castle** (April–Sept daily except Mon 10.30am–5pm; £6 including grounds; ℗www.pictoncastle.co.uk), a somewhat graceless hybrid of architectural styles from the fourteenth to the eighteenth centuries, sited in glorious **grounds** with views over the Eastern Cleddau and its valleys.

Four miles northeast of Haverfordwest, along the B4329, **Scolton Manor** (April–Oct daily 10.30am–5.30pm; £2) is a modest stately home, dating from 1840, which forms the nucleus of the Pembrokeshire County Museum. It's a good place to appreciate the lifestyle of a rich Victorian family: the gilt, brocade and fine furnishings upstairs in total contrast with the perfunctory cellar, larder and laundry below. Besides a fine collection of prints and maps detailing some of the lost picturesque estates of Wales, there's a Carriage House filled with traps and a wealth of local artefacts. Having refreshed yourself in the agreeable **café**, check out the surrounding **country park** (daily: April–Oct 9am–6pm; Nov–March 9am–4.30pm; parking £1), whose visitor centre emphasizes environmental awareness.

St Bride's Bay

The most westerly point of Wales, **St Bride's Bay** is one of the country's most enchanting areas, with rocky outcrops, islands and broad, sweeping beaches curving around between two headlands that sit like giant crab pincers facing out into the warm Gulf Stream amidst the crashing Atlantic. The southernmost of these, St Ann's Head, offers calm, east-facing sands at **Dale**, sunny expanses of south-facing beach at **Marloes** and wilder west-facing sands at **Musselwick**. From **Martin's Haven**, boats depart for the offshore islands of **Skomer**, **Skokholm** and **Grassholm**.

The golden sands of the main scoop of St Bride's Bay are backed by teeming, popular holiday villages such as **Little Haven**, **Broad Haven** and **Newgale**. From here, the lacerated coast veers west as **St Davids peninsula**, the stunning cliffs interrupted only by occasional gashes of sand. Just north of **St Non's Bay**, the tiny cathedral city of **St Davids**, founded in the sixth century by Wales' patron saint, is a justified highlight. Rooks and crows circle above the impressive ruins of the huge **Bishop's Palace**, sitting beneath the delicate bulk of the **cathedral**, the most impressive in Wales. The St Davids peninsula, more windswept and elemental than any other part of Pembrokeshire, tapers out just west of the city at the popular **Whitesands Bay** and the hamlet of **St Justinian's**, staring out over the crags of **Ramsey Island**.

Summer transport around the region is excellent, courtesy of the Pembrokeshire **Coastal Bus Service**, which offers assorted shuttle buses with routes centred on Milford Haven and St Davids. Timetables are published online (ⓦ www.pembrokeshiregreenways.co.uk) and in the national park's free newspaper *Coast to Coast*. Note that at busy times **parking** can be hard to come by and is almost always pay-and-display.

Dale, Marloes and the offshore islands

The tiny village of **DALE**, fourteen miles west of Haverfordwest, huddles behind a shingle beach at the head of a huge bite out of the coast. Blighted by views of oil refineries, Dale is not an especially attractive village, but its sheltered, east-facing shore makes it a popular yachting and **water-sports** centre. Activities are focused on the beachside shack of West Wales Wind, Surf and Sailing (ⓣ 01646/636642, ⓦ www.surfdale.co.uk), which offers lessons (April–Oct; £35–65 per half day) at various standards in windsurfing, sailing and kayaking. With adequate proficiency you can rent equipment: a basic windsurfer costs £35 a half day; a superior ensemble £45; and a kayak £20.

There's B&B **accommodation** on the Dale waterfront at the comfortable *Richmond House* (ⓣ 07974/925009, ⓦ www.richmond-house.com; ❸), which also has a family room for £90. Alternatives include *Point Farm B&B* (ⓣ 01646/636541, ⓦ www.pointfarm.info; closed Dec & Jan; ❹) ten minutes' walk along the shore south of Dale, with lovely rooms, sea views and excellent food and hospitality; and the luxurious *Allenbrook* (☎01646/636254, ⓦwww .allenbrook-dale.co.uk; ❺), a charming, richly furnished country house close to the beach. **Eating and drinking** is limited: try the *Boathouse Café*, a good-value, summer-only greasy spoon, or the *Griffin Inn* for real ales and decent bar meals.

The calm waters of Dale are deceptive, and as you head south towards **St Ann's Head** the wind speed whips up, with waves and tides to match. This was the site of the 1996 *Sea Empress* wreck, though thankfully all visible reminders of the oil slick have now vanished.

The coastline here offers invigorating walking. The Coast Path sticks tight to the undulating coastline, passing tiny bays en route to the St Ann's lighthouse. Tucked in the eastern lee of St Ann's Head is **Mill Bay**, where Henry VII landed in 1485, marching the breadth of his native Wales and gathering a loyal army to face Richard III at Bosworth Field.

The coast turns and heads north from St Ann's Head, reaching the sandstone-backed **West Dale Bay**, less than a mile from Dale on the opposite side of the peninsula. Warnings are usually given about the unpredictability of the currents and hidden rocks in the sea here.

Marloes and around

A mile north of Dale, the village of **MARLOES** backs the great sandy curve of **Marloes Sands**, best known for its stunning cliffs of grey, gold and purple folds of rock, alternate layers of grey shale and old red sandstone. At **Three Chimneys**, two-thirds of the way along the beach, three vertical lines of hard Silurian sandstone and mudstone were formed horizontally and forced up by ancient earth movements. There was a fourth "chimney" which crumbled in a severe storm in 1954.

The beach is crowned at its western end by **Gateholm Island**, accessible at mid-tide and below (most easily reached from the YHA hostel – see below, a hundred yards before which is a large National Trust car park). Over 130 Iron Age hut circles, pottery and pieces of jewellery have been found here, on what is thought to have been an ancient monastic community. Today, Gateholm is powerfully atmospheric, though getting topside involves a tricky scramble: head around the left side as you look at the island.

Next up is **MARTIN'S HAVEN**, a cluster of houses and a car park on a slim neck of the peninsula that faces out to Skomer Island. Inexplicably bypassed by the Coast Path is the sublime headland of **Deer Park** the very western tip of this peninsula, reached by a small gateway in the wall just beyond the car park. The park has no deer, but paths radiate out all over the headland, all with stunning views over the offshore islands and St Bride's Bay: if you can catch a decent sunset here, you'll see none better. There's a small Wildlife Trust of South and West Wales information point at Martin's Haven, the principal departure point for **boats** to the offshore islands of Skomer, Skokholm and Grassholm (see below). North of Deer Park, the Coast Path continues less than half a mile from the village of Marloes round to **Musselwick Sands**, a beautiful and unspoilt beach, though it can be dangerous at high tide. Further north along the peninsula is the narrow **St Bride's Haven**, a tiny, sheltered inlet with a small beach at the end of the lane that peters out by the tiny chapel of St Bride. There are some good rock pools around the beach.

There's not much to the village of Marloes, but you can **stay** centrally at *The Clock House* (☎01646 636527, ⓦwww.chmarloes.co.uk; ❹), which has six white and airy rooms with wi-fi. Breakfast is served in their quality

Clockhouse Café. There are several **campsites**, among them the basic *East Hook Farm* (☎01646/636291; £4 per person; closed Oct–Easter) a couple of miles east of Martin's Haven and right beside the Coast Path. The *Marloes Sands* YHA **hostel** (☎0870/770 5958; open May to mid-Sept) consists of a series of converted farm buildings overlooking the northern end of Marloes Sands, with £14 bunks.

Skomer, Skokholm and Grassholm

One of the highlights of this stretch of coast is a boat trip out around the offshore islands, though the only one day-trippers can land on is **Skomer**, a 722-acre flat-topped island that dominates the near horizon. It has one of the finest **sea bird** colonies in northern Europe, the remains of hundreds of ancient hut circles, a stone circle, collapsed defensive ramparts and settlement systems and a Bronze Age standing stone known as Harold's Stone, near the narrow neck where boats land. The stars of Skomer are the 200,000-plus Manx shearwaters, which only leave their burrows at night, though there's a live video of one in a burrow for day visitors to see. There are also puffins (best May to early July), gulls, guillemots, storm petrels, cormorants, shags and kittiwakes. Land birds include buzzards, skylarks, jackdaws, chough, owls and peregrines. If you head to the north of Skomer, facing out over the Garland Stone, there's a good chance of seeing basking grey seals, especially in the autumn. In spring and early summer, wild flowers carpet the island.

Two miles south of Skomer is the 240-acre island of **Skokholm**, whose warm red sandstone cliffs are a sharp contrast to Skomer's grey severity. Britain's first bird observatory was founded here in the 1930s, and the island is still rich in birdlife.

Six miles west of Skomer, the tiny islet of **Grassholm** resembles a small icing-covered cake: the "icing" is, in fact, a swarming mass of 70,000 gannets, one of the largest colonies in the northern hemisphere, that covers well over half the island.

▲ Puffins, Skomer

Boat trips to Skomer are run by Dale Sailing (℡01646/603110, ⓦwww .dale-sailing.co.uk), who operate landing trips on the *Dale Princess* from Martin's Haven (April–Oct Tues–Sun & bank holidays 10am, 11am & noon; £15), giving you several hours to explore the island. They also have one-hour, round-the-island cruises (daily 1pm; £9), and a two-hour evening trip that's great for sea birds (May–July Tues, Weds & Fri at 7pm; £12).

Dale Sailing's trips around Grassholm are either on the *Dale Princess* from Martin's Haven (early April to mid-Aug Mon at 2pm; 3hr; £30), or from Dale on its fast, rigid-inflatable Sea Safari trip (daily 12.30pm; 2hr 30min; £30). Dale is also the departure point for Sea Safari trips around Skomer and Skokholm (Easter–Sept daily 3.30pm & 6.30pm; 2hr 30min; £30).

Birders and those in search of a bit of solitude might fancy full-board **accommodation** on Skokholm. Residential stays have been suspended during renovations but should recommence in 2010. For details contact the Wildlife Trust of South and West Wales (℡01656/724100, ⓦwww.welshwildlife.org).

Little Haven to Solva

Steep streets descend to the sheltered stony beach of **LITTLE HAVEN**, five miles north of Marloes, a picturesque old fishing village and former coal port that's extremely popular with divers and swimmers in summer. At low tide, walks along the shore towards Broad Haven are superb: you can explore caves and rock pools or just enjoy the full westerly skies. **Accommodation** is best just above the village at the welcoming *Bower Farm* (℡01437/781554; ❸). The most noteworthy place **to eat** is *The Swan* (℡01437/781880, ⓦwww .theswanlittlehaven.co.uk), a beachside gastropub serving quality bar meals at lunch (around £9) and offering more refined evening dining with dishes like rib-eye in béarnaise sauce, and asparagus and pea risotto (£15–18), followed by rosewater crème brûlée (£6). For snacks, visit the tearooms inside the post office, where Elvis posters line the walls and The King is usually on the stereo.

Broad Haven and Druidston Haven

The Coast Path cuts inland from Little Haven for a mile to reach brash, popular **BROAD HAVEN** is a dramatic contrast to its unassuming neighbour, especially in summer, with cars cruising its waterfront and holiday-makers spilling out of its pubs. Still, it has a wide beach fringed by fissured and shattered cliffs, and you can rent a sit-on-top kayak or bodyboard from Haven Sports (℡01437/781354, ⓦwww.havensports.co.uk) on Marine Road just behind the *Galleon Inn*.

The modern, spacious *Broad Haven* YHA **hostel** (℡01437/781688 or 0870/770 5728, ℮broadhaven@yha.org.uk; closed Nov–Feb; bunks £14–20, en-suite rooms ❶–❷) is almost on the seafront at the northern end of the village and comes with bunks and a good-value restaurant. There's **B&B** accommodation a mile inland at *Belmont Barn* (℡01437/781372, ⓦwww .belmontbarn.co.uk; ❸), with sea views and use of a kitchenette.

A couple of miles north, the quiet sandy beach at **DRUIDSTON HAVEN** is hemmed in by steep cliffs and reached along small paths at the bottom of the sharply sloping lane from Broad Haven. The best access is from the unique *Druidstone Hotel* (℡01437/781221, ⓦwww.druidstone.co.uk; ❸–❻), a rambling and easy-going place on the cliff with a quirky array of B&B rooms, some with superb sea views, self-catering cottages, including an old circular croquet pavilion, and a cellar bar that spills out onto the clifftops. Rooms are frequently booked months in advance, especially at weekends, though you should still drop by for the varied meals: expect anything from Jamaican jerk chicken (£9) to sea bass in vermouth (£18).

Just before the hotel, Bumpy Lane heads inland for a few hundred yards to the tiny hamlet of **DRUIDSTON**, where you can **camp** at *Shortlands* (℡01437/781234, ⓦwww.bumpylane.co.uk) a small and friendly campsite (£3.50 per person; mid-July to Aug only) on a rare-breeds organic farm with showers and great views of St Bride's Bay. It also has a static caravan and a low-allergen self-catering unit generally let by the week or for short breaks.

Nolton Haven and Newgale

A mile along the coast, **NOLTON HAVEN** is little more than a pub and a picturesque cluster of houses and caravans around a sheltered shingle cove. The next bay north is the vast, west-facing **Newgale Sands**, virtually untouched at its southern end, but popular with families and surfers around the uninspiring village of **NEWGALE**. Here the Newsurf surf shop (℡01437/721398, ⓦwww.newsurf.co.uk) rents gear and offers surfing lessons for £35 a half day. Just behind, Big Blue (℡07816/169359, ⓦwww.bigbluekitesurfing.com) offers kitesurfing, starting with land-based kiting (£40 for 2hr). The *Newgale Camping Site* (℡01437 710253, ⓦwww.newgalecampingsite.co.uk; £5 per person; closed Oct–East) is just across the road from the beach, while the daytime *Sands Café* offers great baguettes, panini, espresso and the likes of green pea and pesto soup (£4) and smoked mackerel pâté (£6).

Immediately north, Brandy Brook disgorges onto the beach, marking the boundary of "Little England Beyond Wales" (see box, p.175) and the furthest extent of Norman colonization of Pembrokeshire.

Solva

Beyond Newgale the coast turns west, rising abruptly to craggy cliffs that make this a wilder, more Celtic landscape than that of southern Pembrokeshire. The Coast Path from Newgale to **SOLVA**, three miles west, is marvellous, with easy clifftop walking, magnificent views over the rippled coast and, in the lee of the Dinas Fach headland, a secluded sandy beach at **Porthmynawyd**. Solva itself is a touristy, picture-postcard village at the top of an inlet running down to **Gwadn beach**. Above this, the **Gribin Headland** between the valleys of the Solva and Gribin rivers affords fantastic views and has an imposing Iron Age earthwork on its summit.

Accommodation in Solva is limited, but you can **stay** in the pretty Lower Village beside the river at *Gamlyn*, 17 Y Gribin (℡01437/721542; ②). The range of food is better, with *The Old Pharmacy*, 5 Main St (℡01437/720005, ⓦwww.theoldpharmacy.co.uk), serving by far the best evening **meals**: expect the likes of lamb kebab with cumin and coriander (£7) followed by garlic sausage and pork belly casserole (£16). There's reliable Indian food at *The Spice Gallery*, 15 Main St.

St Davids

ST DAVIDS (Tyddewi) is one of the most enchanting and evocative spots in Britain. Perched at the very western point of Wales on a windswept, treeless peninsula, this miniature city – really just a large village – clusters around its cathedral, Wales' spiritual and ecclesiastical centre and totally independent of Canterbury.

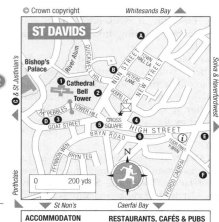

ACCOMMODATON		RESTAURANTS, CAFÉS & PUBS	
Alandale	B	The Bench	4
Pen Albro	D	Cwtch	6
Ramsey House	C	Farmers Arms	3
TYF Eco Hotel	F	The Refectory	1
The Waterings	E	The Sampler	2
Y Gorlan	A	Square Café	5

Traditionally founded by the Welsh patron saint himself in 550, the see of St Davids has drawn pilgrims for a millennium and a half – William the Conqueror included – and by 1120, Pope Calixtus II decreed that two journeys to St Davids amounted to the spiritual equivalent of one pilgrimage to Rome. The settlement grew up around the cathedral, and St Davids today still relies on the imported wealth of newcomers to the area, attracted by its savage beauty.

Arrival, information and activities

Entering St Davids, the main road from Haverfordwest (here called the High Street) passes the National Park **tourist office** (Easter–Oct daily 9.30am–5.30pm; Nov–Easter Mon–Sat 10am–4pm; ☎01437/720392, Ⓦwww.stdavids.co.uk), and carries on for two hundred yards to the **bus stop** in New Street. From May to September, an hourly Celtic Coaster shuttle bus connects the centre of St Davids with White-sands Bay, St Justinian's and Porth Clais. There's no **bike rental** in town itself, but re-Cycles Bike Hire (☎01437/711123) rent out bikes (£10 a day) and will deliver to St Davids. For **internet access** and wi-fi, visit *The Bench* (see p.201).

Several local companies run boat trips to the outlying islands (see p.195), as scheduled at their offices. There are a number of other **outdoor activities** available, most run through TYF, 1 High St (☎01437/721611, Ⓦwww.tyf .com), which pioneered **coasteering**, an exhilarating multi-sport combination which involves scrambling over rocks, jumping off cliffs and swimming across the narrow bays of St Davids peninsula. Coasteering is geared up for just about anyone (there are even itineraries for non-swimmers) and operates throughout the year, with 2.5-hour sessions priced at £50 (£60 in July & Aug). TYF also offer surfing, kayaking and rock climbing (£50/60 half day, £95/100 full day) and can organize multi-day sessions and longer courses.

Accommodation

There are numerous places to **stay** on and around the St Davids peninsula, with prices fairly high in season at the larger hotels, but falling dramatically for the rest of the year. Campsites abound in and around the city.

Hotels and guesthouses

Alandale 43 Nun St ☎01437/720404. Small, friendly, central guesthouse with five en-suite rooms, some with long views. A healthy breakfast is included. ❹

🏃 **Crug Glas** (See map, p.202) Abereiddi, 4 miles northeast of St Davids ☎01348/831302, Ⓦwww.crug-glas.co.uk. Luxurious country house on a working farm. The five large rooms are elaborately decorated with gold fittings, tasselled cushions and either half-tester or four-poster beds, plus there's a wonderfully spacious attic suite. Breakfasts are excellent (great bacon) and delicious four-course evening meals are available for around £25. Rooms ❺, suite ❼

Pen Albro 18 Goat St ☎01437/721865. The cheapest B&B in town; no en suites but a good breakfast, right beside the *Farmers Arms*. ❷

Ramsey House (See map, p.202) Lower Moor ☎ 01437/720321, ⓦ www.ramseyhouse.co.uk. Quality six-room B&B on the road to Porth Clais, with excellent breakfasts: expect the likes of home-made apple and sage sausages and fresh bread. The also do three-course evening meals £20 and have a bar. ❺

TYF Eco Hotel Caerfai Rd ☎ 01437/721678, ⓦ www.tyf.com. Simple 12-room hotel built around a converted windmill and certified both organic and carbon neutral. Rooms (£35) and en-suites (£45) are clean and comfortable, with few frills (apart from wind-up radios). There's a relaxed atmosphere, and you can hang out in the lounge with its honesty bar, or head up to the windmill tower lounge, with great views. Breakfasts are, of course, organic, and the hotel acts as a base for TYF's adventure activities (see p.198). You get a free drink If you turn up without a car. ❶

The Waterings Anchor Drive ☎ 01437/720876, ⓦ www.waterings.co.uk. Very comfortable en-suite rooms and suites in a former marine research establishment, which retains a maritime theme. There are lovely grounds and you can play croquet on the lawn. ❹

Y Gorlan 77 Nun St ☎ 01437/720837. Central guesthouse with en-suite rooms, in a converted Victorian residence. ❹

Hostel and campsites

All the following are marked on the map on p.202.

Caerfai Farm Caerfai Bay, a mile south of St Davids ☎ 01437/720548. The best campsite around, on an organic dairy farm and with great coastal views. No caravans. £6 per person; £4 if you arrive on foot or bike. Closed Oct–April.

Glan-y-môr Caerfai Rd, 0.5 miles south of town ☎ 01437/721788, ⓦ www.glan-y-mor.co.uk. The nearest campsite to town, with a pub and restaurant on site. You can't book – just turn up on spec. £7 per person. Closed Nov–March.

Lleithyr Farm Just off the B4583, 1 mile northwest of St Davids, 0.5 miles short of Whitesands Bay ☎ 01437/720245, ⓦ www.whitesands-stdavids .co.uk. High-standard campsite and caravan park with heated shower rooms in winter. £4 per person; £6 from mid-July to Aug. Closed Jan & Feb.

Rhoson St Justinian's. Basic field campsite with no showers but handy for the boats to Ramsey Island. £3 per person. Closed Nov–Easter.

St Davids YHA Hostel Llaethdy, 2 miles northwest of St Davids near Whitesands Bay ☎ 0870/770 6042, ⓔ stdavids@yha.org.uk. Large, renovated hostel in a former farmhouse and outbuildings. Daytime lockout and 11pm curfew. Closed Nov–March. Bunks £14, rooms ❶

The Town

St Davids High Street courses down to the triangular Cross Square, with its centrepiece **Celtic cross**, and continues under the thirteenth-century **Tower Gate**, which forms the entrance to the serene **Cathedral Close**. The cathedral lies down to the right, hidden in a hollow by the River Alun. This apparent modesty is explained by reasons of defence: a towering cathedral, visible from the sea on all sides, would have been far too vulnerable. On the other side of the babbling Alun lie the ruins of the Bishop's Palace.

There are numerous small commercial **art galleries** and craft outlets throughout St Davids: a few are dreadful, but most reflect the quality of the many artists attracted to this spirited corner of Wales, all of whom claim the area's unique light quality as their inspiration.

The cathedral

The gold-and-purple 125-foot stone tower of the **cathedral** (donation requested; ⓦ www.stdavidscathedral.org.uk) is approached down the Thirty-Nine Articles – steps named after Thomas Cranmer's key tenets of Anglicanism. They descend from beyond the doughty **Gatehouse Tower** (daily 10am–5pm; £1), the last of four medieval originals, which now houses an exhibition about the history of St Davids.

The cathedral tower has clocks on only three sides (the people of the northern part of the parish couldn't raise enough money for one to be installed facing them), and is topped by pert gold pinnacles that seem to glow a different colour from the rest of the building. You enter via a porch in the south side of the low twelfth-century nave, the most striking feature of which is its intricate latticed oak **roof**, built to hide sixteenth-century emergency restoration work undertaken when the nave was in danger of collapse. The nave floor still has a discernible slope and the support buttresses inserted in the northern aisle of the nave look incongruously new and temporary.

At the crossing, an elaborate **rood screen** was constructed under the orders of fourteenth-century Bishop Gower, who envisaged it as his own tomb. Behind the rood screen and the organ, the choir sits directly under the magnificently bold and bright lantern ceiling of the tower, another addition by Gower. The round-headed arch over the organ was built in Norman times, contrasting with the other three underpinning the tower, which are pointed and date from the rebuilding work that took place in the 1220s. At the back of the right-hand choir stalls is a unique **monarch's stall**, complete with royal crest, for, unlike any other British cathedral, the queen is an automatic member of the St Davids cathedral Chapter. The misericords under the choir seats display earthy medieval humour; there's one of a chaotic wild boar hunt and another of someone being seasick. Behind the left-hand choir stalls, the **north transept** contains the tomb of St Caradoc, with two pierced quatrefoils, in which it is believed people would insert diseased limbs in the hope of a cure. Off the north transept, steps from St Thomas' chapel lead up to the **Cathedral Library** (July & Aug Mon–Fri 11am–1pm & 2–4pm; Sept–June Mon only 2–4pm; £1), which includes the Royal Charter of 1995 that granted St Davids city status.

Separating the choir and the presbytery is a finely traced, rare **parclose screen**. The back wall of the **presbytery** was once the eastern extremity of the cathedral, as can be seen from the two lines of windows. The upper row has been left intact, while the lower three were blocked up and filled with delicate gold mosaics in the nineteenth century, surrounded by over-fussy stonework. The colourful fifteenth-century roof, with its deceptively simple medieval pattern, was restored by Gilbert Scott in the mid-nineteenth century. Around the altar, the **sanctuary** has a few fragmented fifteenth-century tiles still in place. On the south side is a beautifully carved sedilla, a seat for the priest and deacon celebrating Mass. To its right are thirteenth-century tombs of bishops Iorwerth (1215–31) and Anselm de la Grace (1231–47), and on the other side of the sanctuary is the disappointingly plain thirteenth-century tomb of St David, largely destroyed in the Reformation.

Behind the filled-in lancets at the back of the presbytery altar is the Perpen-dicular **Bishop Vaughan's chapel**, with an exquisite fan tracery roof built between 1508 and 1522. Bishop Vaughan's statue occupies the niche to the left of the altar. To the right is an effigy of Giraldus Cambrensis, Gerald of Wales, his mitre placed not on his head, but at his feet – a reminder that he never attained the status of bishop to which he evidently aspired. Opposite, facing west, a peephole looks into the presbytery. Around the opening, the four crosses may well predate the Norman church. The bottom cross is largely obscured by a casket, reputedly containing some of the intermingled bones of St David and his friend, St Justinian. Behind the chapel is the ambulatory and the simple **Lady Chapel** with its sentimental Edwardian stained glass. On either side are tombs in wall niches: the one on the left was originally believed to have been for Bishop Beck (1280–96), the builder of St Davids' Bishop's Palace, but now houses Bishop Owen (1897–1926), whose devoted service to the Church in Wales and the Welsh nation is symbolized by the roaring dragon above him.

Guided tours of the cathedral (generally Aug Mon at 11am & Fri at 2.30pm, other times ☎01437/720199, ✉toursofstdavidscathedral@yahoo .co.uk; £4) are arranged at the bookshop in the nave. Also worth noting is the cathedral's **evensong** (every Sun 6pm) when the girls' and men's choirs sing; and the superb annual **music festival**, which takes place in late May/early June. Leave time for a visit to *The Refectory* **café** (see below), connected to the back of the cathedral by a modern **cloister** built on the ruins of the fourteenth-century original.

The Bishop's Palace

From the cathedral, a path leads over the River Alun to the splendid **Bishop's Palace** (April–Oct daily 9am–5pm; Nov–March Mon–Sat 9.30am–4pm, Sun 11am–4pm; £3.10; CADW), built by bishops Beck and Gower in the early fourteenth century. Its huge central quadrangle is enclosed by an array of ruined buildings in extraordinarily rich colours: the green, red, purple and grey tints of volcanic rock, sandstone and many other types of stone. The **arched parapets** along the top of the walls were a favourite motif of Gower, who did more than any of his predecessors or successors to transform the palace into an architectural and political powerhouse. Off the quadrangle, the ruinous yet still impressive **Bishop's Hall** and the enormous **Great Hall**, with its glorious rose window overlay a myriad of rooms adorned by eerily eroded corbels. Beneath the Great Hall are dank vaults containing an interesting exhibition about the palace and the indulgent lifestyles of its occupants. The destruction of the palace is largely due to Bishop Barlow (1536–48), who supposedly stripped the buildings of their lead roofs to provide dowries for his five daughters' marriages to bishops.

Eating, drinking and entertainment

With only one pub to its name, St Davids might appear to be a quiet little backwater. Not so; the city is a real magnet for surfers, outdoor types and musicians. In the summer, and over Christmas/New Year, parties are likely to break out just about anywhere. It's also a good place to eat, and there's something for all tastes and budgets.

The Bench 11 High St ☎01437/721778, ⓦwww .bench-bar.co.uk. Versatile restaurant, café and wine bar that does reasonable pizza and fresh pasta dishes (£7–9), plus good panini and espresso, all served in a sunny conservatory. There's also internet access, and great Italian ice cream to go.

Cwtch 22 High St. Some of the finest dining in Pembrokeshire can be found at *Cwtch* (pronounced "cutsh"), an intimate and easy-going bar and restaurant that's all slate and wood and blackboard menus. Top-quality local ingredients are sourced for unfussy dishes (£27 for three courses) such as roasted red pepper and tomato soup, and hake with lime and anchovy butter. Open for dinner Mon–Sat and Sun lunch. Closed Mon & Tues in winter.

Farmers Arms Goat St. The city's only real pub. Young, lively and very friendly, with a terrace overlooking the cathedral – especially enjoyable on a summer's evening. Good pub food also available.

The Refectory St Davids Cathedral. The modernized interior of the beautiful St Mary's Hall is a great spot for tea and cakes, and also serves delicious meals at moderate prices. Open daytimes, and until 9pm from June–Sept. Free wi-fi.

The Sampler 17 Nun St. Daytime coffee shop serving delicious clotted-cream teas. The walls are covered with an impressive collection of needlework samplers.

Square Café Cross Square. Restful café and mini-gallery with stone-flagged floor and old wooden tables. Perfect for a coffee, home-made cakes and organic sandwiches.

St Davids peninsula

Surrounded on three sides by inlets, coves and rocky stacks, St Davids is an easy base for some excellent walking around the headland of the same name. A mile south, the popular **Caerfai Bay** is a sandy gash in the purple-sandstone cliffs, from which masonry for the cathedral was quarried. Half a mile to the west is the craggy indentation of **St Non's Bay**, where, according to legend, St Non gave birth to St David during a tumultuous storm around 500 AD. A spring opened up between Non's feet, and despite the crashing thunder all around, an eerily calm light filtered down onto the scene.

St Non's received pilgrims for centuries, resulting in the foundation of a tiny chapel in the pre-Norman age, whose successor's thirteenth-century ruins now lie in a field to the right of the car park, beyond the sadly dingy well and coy shrine where the nation's patron saint is said to have been born.

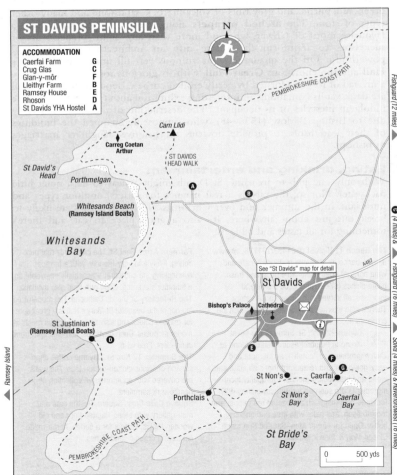

ST DAVIDS PENINSULA

ACCOMMODATION
Caerfai Farm	G
Crug Glas	C
Glan-y-môr	F
Lleithyr Farm	B
Ramsey House	E
Rhoson	D
St Davids YHA Hostel	A

© Crown copyright

The 1934 **chapel**, built in front of the austere 1929 **Retreat House**, was constructed in simple Pembrokeshire style from the rocks of ruined houses, which, in turn, had been built from the stone of ancient, abandoned churches.

Further west, **PORTH CLAIS** is supposedly the place where St David was baptized by the bishop of Munster, who went by the unlikely name of St Elvis. Porth Clais was the city's main harbour, the spruced-up remains of which can still be seen at the bottom of the turquoise river creek. Today, commercial traffic has long gone, replaced by fishing boats and dinghies.

Running due west out of St Davids, Goat Street ducks past the ruins of the Bishop's Palace and over the rocky plateau for two miles to the harbour at **ST JUSTINIAN'S**, little more than a ruined chapel, lifeboat station and ticket hut for the frequent **boats** over to **Ramsey Island** (see below).

Whitesands Bay (Porth Mawr), two miles to the north and reached from St Davids via the B4583 off the Fishguard road, faces west and **surfing** is good. The spectacularly beautiful **Porthmelgan**, a narrow slip of cove reached by a fifteen-minute walk northwest along the Coast Path from Whitesands car park, is far less crowded, largely on account of the dangerous swimming. The thin spit of rock and cliff that juts out into the ocean less than a mile to the west comprises **St Davids Head**, site of an Iron Age coastal fortress, its outline most visible in spring. Rising behind Whitesands and Porthmelgan, the gnarled crag of **Carn Llidi** tops a pastoral patchwork of fields.

Ramsey Island and cruises

The dual-humped plateau of **Ramsey Island**, three miles west of St Davids and half a mile offshore, has been under the able care of the RSPB since 1992 and is quite enchanting. Birds of prey circle the skies above it, but the island is better known for the tens of thousands of sea birds that noisily crowd the sheer cliffs on the western side. On the beaches, seals laze sloppily below the paths worn by a herd of red deer. There's something to see all year round, but spring is great for nesting birds (especially puffins and shearwaters), and autumn for seals with their pups.

Several operators run trips to Ramsey either from St Justinian's or Whitesands Beach, but the only one allowed to **land** you on the island is Thousand Islands

---

Walks around St Davids

OS 1:25,000 Outdoor Leisure map 35 ("North Pembrokeshire") is advised for this walk.

There's some fabulous **coastal walking** around St Davids, much of it along the Pembrokeshire Coast Path, while the useful Celtic Coaster bus service means that you won't need to retrace your steps. The visitor centre stocks a number of leaflets (50p), each detailing a walk along a short section of coast. One good and relatively leisurely **day walk** is the stretch from Caerfai Bay, past Porthclais and round the point to the lifeboat station at St Justinian's. At half tide the waters between here and Ramsey Island churn up into an impressive maelstrom. Another good day walk leaves Whitesands Beach and makes a loop around St Davids Head, one of the most mysterious and magical places in Wales. Evidence of ancient civilization is everywhere, and numerous mystics and seers have pinpointed the area as a focus of the earth's natural energies. Highlights include the rocky summit of **Carn Llidi** (595ft), approached on the south side past two cromlechs (capped burial stones), and **Carreg Coetan Arthur** (Arthur's Quoit), a 6000-year-old burial chamber.

Expeditions, based on Cross Square in St Davids (Easter–Oct daily; ☎01437/721721, ⓦwww.thousandislands.co.uk; £15). Boats depart from St Justinian's at 10am and noon and return at noon and 4pm; you can come back on either boat, allowing you up to six hours' exploration if you leave at 10am and come back at 4pm. Perhaps the best deal is their combined Landing & Around trip (Easter–Oct several daily; £34), which gives you a good look at the wildlife all around.

North Pembrokeshire coast

The stretch of coast immediately north of St Davids forms the very southern sweep of Cardigan Bay and is noticeably less commercialized than the touristy littoral of south and mid-Pembrokeshire. From the crags and cairns above St Davids Head, the Coast Path perches precariously on the cliffs, where only the thousands of sea birds have access.

Although the major income from this part of west Pembrokeshire is now tourism, the remains of old mines, quarries and ports at **Abereiddi** and **Porthgain** bear witness to the slate and granite industries that once employed hundreds of people. Industry dies down towards **Trefin** and up to the more remote beaches and inlets that punctuate the coast as it climbs up to the splendid knuckle of **Strumble Head**. To the east is **Carregwastad Point**, the site of the last invasion of Britain in 1797. The event is also remembered in the port town of **Fishguard**, where local soldiers tricked the invading French into unconditional surrender at the *Royal Oak Inn*.

Abereiddi to Abercastell

Five miles north of St Davids, a small lane tumbles down into the bleak hamlet of **ABEREIDDI**, where you can find tiny fossilized animals in the shale of the black-sand beach. At the back of the beach are remains of workers' huts and a tramway that once climbed over the hill to Porthgain, all part of the village slate quarry that closed in 1904. The quarry itself was dynamited for safety reasons, producing an inland lagoon where the seawater, combined with the minerals, has turned a violent shade of blue.

The lane parallel to the coast passes the hamlet of Cwmwdig Water and leads to tiny **LLANRHIAN**, where a left turn takes you a mile down to the rambling village green of **PORTHGAIN**. This fascinating old port grew up around its slate works, the stumpy remains of which, together with an old brickworks, lime kiln and eerie ruins of workers' cottages, are huddled around the tiny quay. It also has a couple of small art galleries and the eighteenth-century *Sloop Inn*, with numerous photographs of the port in its sepia heyday and a terrace which makes an excellent place to while away a couple of hours before sunset with their real ales and good pub meals. There's also *The Shed* (☎01348/831518; closed Mon), a daytime tearoom and classy evening seafood bistro where £30 will get you three courses, with much of the produce caught locally.

Within walking distance of Porthgain is a brilliant **independent hostel**, ⚐ *Caerhafod Lodge* (☎01348/837859, ⓦwww.caerhafod.co.uk), on the north side of Llanrhian, with a tranquil atmosphere, good views and helpful hosts. They offer self-catering facilities and mostly four-bedded rooms (sheets supplied) for £14 per person. There are also £12 bunks a mile or so east in **Trefin** (Trevine) at *The Old School Hostel,* Ffordd-yr-afon (☎01348/831800, ⓦwww.theoldschoolhostel.co.uk), a former YHA that has been revamped and

▲ Porthgain Harbour

rejuvenated. They also have ultra-cheap doubles (●) for just £28, plus family rooms, do light breakfasts and packed lunches, and operate eco-incentives such as a small discount for those arriving without a car; they also plant a tree for every booking and run on green electricity.

The coastal lane continues east to **ABERCASTELL**, past the 4500-year-old **Carreg Samson** cromlech (burial chamber) at Longhouse, precariously topped by a sixteen-foot capstone. If you're walking, continue past the cromlech and down to the Coast Path to the attractive and popular harbour of Abercastell, once used for the export of limestone and coal. From Abercastell, one of the most scenic parts of the Coast Path zigzags east along the wild, vertiginous cliffs to the point at **Trwyn Llwynog**, about two miles away.

Strumble Head and Carregwastad Point

The headland – known as **Pen Caer** – that rises to the north of Aberscastell, peaking at **STRUMBLE HEAD**, is delightful: tiny hedge-backed lanes bump around between rocky cairns, with fields of wild flowers and sudden glimpses of the shimmering sea. From this remote and spectacular section of the Coast Path there's access to the sandy stretch of **Aber Mawr**, smaller **Aber Bach**, and the west-facing gash of **Pwllcochran**. Nearly two miles further north, there's the simple but fabulously positioned *Pwll Deri* YHA **hostel** (see p.207). Looming large on the inland side of the hostel are the three crags of **Garn Fawr** (699ft): by following a path from the car park at their eastern edge, on the lane up to Strumble Head, you can explore the vestiges of ditches, ramparts and hut circles from its days as an early Iron Age fort.

Strumble Head, just over a mile due north of Garn Fawr, is reached either by the rugged coast path – with astounding views over the two-mile-long "wall" of cliffs to the south – or along a floral country lane. At the headland, the 1908 **lighthouse** is perched atop **Ynys Meicel**, connected to the mainland by a metal footbridge that's closed to the public. It's a peaceful, invigorating spot that's great for sea bird spotting.

Almost three miles on, the hamlet of **LLANWNDA** merits a historical footnote as the site of the **last invasion of Britain** (see box below). The **church of St Gwyndaf** is also well worth a visit for its charming setting, an ancient history which winds back beyond the eighth century, and the collection of pre-Norman carved stones embedded in its walls.

The 1.5-mile **walk** from Llanwnda to **Carregwastad Point** is fabulous, coasting gently down fields and across the top of a craggy cwm. Start off by going over the stile and along the path on the other side of the track from the church entrance. At the coast turn left to reach Carregwasted Point and the memorial plaque commemorating the invasion (see box below), or right to **Aber Felin**, a bay usually littered with grey seals.

Fishguard and Goodwick

Fishguard (Abergwaun), immediately north of Strumble Head, occupies a lofty headland, with the pretty Lower Town on one side and the adjoining port town of **GOODWICK** (Wdig) on the other. Though often seen only as somewhere from which to catch a ferry to Ireland, it's an enjoyable place in its own right, with fine sea views from the easy coastal walks around town.

In the centre of town, the **Royal Oak Inn** was the scene of the surrender of the "last invasion of Britain" in 1797 (see box below). The episode's heroine, Jemima Nicholas, is buried beside the Victorian **parish church** behind the pub.

Opposite, inside the Town Hall, the **Last Invasion Gallery** (Mon–Sat 9.30pm–5pm, Thurs until 6.30pm; free) contains the hundred-foot-long **Fishguard Tapestry**, inspired by the famous Bayeux model and made to mark the event's bicentenary in 1997. The tapestry offers a wonderful pictorial record of the event, depicting the whole story including debauched French soldiers, with one

The last invasion of Britain

In 1797, while Napoleon was absent fighting in central Europe, a newly formed Franco-Irish revolutionary command was trying to make its mark in Paris. Believing that the oppressed countryfolk of Britain would sympathize with their revolutionary views and join their cause, a motley band of "liberators" – some just out of prison and still shackled – hatched a madcap plan to invade Britain. Winds blew their ships from their planned landing place at Bristol and they ended up at **Carregwastad Point**, just south of Fishguard, where the event is marked by a memorial stone. The disorganized army of 1400 made its base at Trehowel Farm, midway between Strumble Head and Llanwnda, which was stocked up with food and drink for an imminent family wedding. Indeed most local farms were full of contraband liquor plundered from a recent Portuguese shipwreck. The would-be conquerors set to the victuals with gusto, swiftly becoming too drunk to do anything except loot the silver plate in Llanwnda's church.

After two days the invasion had collapsed and the invaders surrendered to a local militia at the *Royal Oak* in Fishguard, claiming they had seen "troops of the line to the number of several thousand". No such army was in the vicinity and some say the bleary-eyed French mistook several hundred local women clad in stovepipe hats and red flannel shawls for British Redcoats. While that may not be true, it's a fact that fourteen soldiers were rounded up with a pitchfork by a 47-year-old cobbler's wife, Jemima Nicholas – dubbed ever since the "Welsh Heroine".

unfortunate thief shown with his throat cut on the lower border. A video tells the story of the local artists and embroiderers who made it all happen.

Main Street winds northeast before plummeting down around the coast towards **Lower Town** (Cwm), a cluster of old-fashioned houses and holiday cottages around a muddy, thriving, fishing and pleasure-boat port. Views from Lower Fishguard over the town headland and out to the Goodwick breakwater are superb. Lower Fishguard's moment of glory came in 1971, when it served as the set of Llareggub (see p.172) in the Richard Burton and Elizabeth Taylor movie of Dylan Thomas' *Under Milk Wood*, a film well worth catching if you get the chance.

Practicalities

Buses stop by the town hall in the central Market Square, right outside Fishguard's **tourist office** (Easter–Oct Mon–Sat 9.30am–5pm; Nov–Easter Mon–Sat 10am–4pm; ℡01347/776636, ✉fishguard.tic@pembrokeshire .gov.uk). They also have free **internet access** (15min maximum), or for longer sessions visit the library upstairs (Mon–Sat 9.30pm–5pm, Thurs until 6.30pm). Just steps away, Seaways bookshop on West Street is the best source of books on Wales plus information on Ireland in town.

Quay Road in **Goodwick** is the terminus for **ferries** and catamarans to Ireland (services are detailed on p.214), and is also where you'll find the **train station**. Buses stop right outside the terminal, usually meeting ferries but seldom catamarans. There's also a second **tourist office** (daily: Easter–Oct 9.30am–5pm, Nov–Easter 10am–4pm; free) on the Goodwick foreshore. A **taxi** (℡01348/873075) from here into Fishguard costs about £3.

Accommodation is plentiful; most places are used to visitors coming and going at odd times for the ferries. There's also a fair variety of places to **eat** and **drink**. Over the bank holiday weekend at the end of May, Fishguard hosts the increasingly popular **Fishguard Folk Festival** (ⓦwww .pembrokeshire-folk-music.co.uk), while in late July there's the annual **Fishguard International Music Festival** (℡01348/875538) combining classical, choral, jazz and blues.

Accommodation

Cefn-y-Dre 1 mile out of Fishguard along Hamilton St ℡01348/875663, ⓦwww .cefnydre.co.uk. There's a relaxed and understated elegance to this lovely country house with parts dating back to early sixteenth-century. Just three rooms, attractive breakfasts, tasty breakfasts, and superb home-cooked meals (£25; reserve in advance) prepared by wonderful hosts. ❺

Gwaun Vale Caravan Park 1.4 miles southeast of town on the B4313 ℡01348/874698, ⓦwww .gwaunvale.co.uk. Well-appointed site on the fringes of Cwm Gwaun that is relatively wind-free even when the Coast Path is getting battered. £12 per pitch.

Hamilton Backpackers Lodge 21–23 Hamilton St ℡01348/874797. Cosy, very central and well set-up hostel with dorms, doubles and twins, and a free light breakfast. Bedding is provided. Dorm beds £16, rooms ❶

Plain Dealings Tower Hill ℡01348/873655. Peaceful and attractive top-quality B&B half a mile from the centre, with views of the Lower Town. Closed Nov–Feb. ❸

Pwll Deri YHA hostel 4 miles south of Fishguard ℡0870/770 6004, ✉pwllderi@yha.org.uk. Recently revamped, this is a superbly sited clifftop hostel above the strands of Pwll Deri, with dorms (around £16) and a couple of private double rooms (❶).

Eating and drinking

Bar Five 5 Main St ℡01348/875050, Chic, modern restaurant and bar with great harbour views, sunny terrace and good meals (mains around £13) such as salmon with sorrel sauce or shepherd's lentil pie. Fish caught by the owner determines what's on the daily specials board. Closed Sun & Mon.

Café Celf 16 West St ⓦ www.westwalesartscentre .com. Arty café that's great for a restful cake and espresso or one of their lunch platters (£5–9), including smoked salmon, salami and roast vegetables.

Royal Oak Main Square. Historic pub with real ales and good pub meals (baguettes £4, mains £9)

served in a separate dining area. There are also good-value Sunday lunches, and folk nights on Tues – participants very welcome.

Ship Inn Lower Town. Eccentric, unmissable pub with lots of interesting clutter all over the walls and ceiling, including black-and-white photos of Burton and Taylor shooting *Under Milk Wood* .

Mynydd Preseli

In a county celebrated for some of the most magnificent coastal scenery in Britain, Pembrokeshire's interior is frequently overlooked. The **Mynydd Preseli** (Preseli Mountains) occupy a triangle of land in the north of the county, flecked with prehistoric remains and roughly bounded by the coast in the north, the B4313 to the west and the A478 to the east.

The main A487 coast road is the only major **bus** route hereabouts, cruising from Fishguard to Cardigan through delightful **Newport**, handy for the historic peak of **Carn Ingli**, the bucolic church at **Nevern** with its "bleeding" yew, and the reconstructed Iron Age settlement at **Castell Henllys**. This is also the final (or initial) stretch of the Pembrokeshire Coast Path and the cognoscenti's favourite, with awesome solitude, abundant natural life and stunning cliff formations.

Inland from Fishguard, the **Gwaun River** wriggles southeast through its green cwm, with tiny villages and remote churches seemingly untouched by the modern age. Formed around 200,000 years ago, this is Europe oldest glacial meltwater valley and the subject of many a geology field trip. The brooding mountains hereabouts shelter innumerable standing stones, stone circles, hillforts, cairns and earthworks, several linked by a hike along the **Golden Road**.

The 1:25,000 scale "North Pembrokeshire" Explorer Map (OL35) is extremely useful for **route finding** in the area (even when driving), and local visitor centres stock leaflets detailing walks, including the Golden Road.

Newport, Nevern and the coast

The A487 winds through **NEWPORT** (Trefdraeth), an ancient, proud and wealthy little town that is without doubt the best base in north Pembrokeshire. Set on a gentle slope that courses down to the estuary of the Afon Nyfer, it is a quietly enjoyable place, with superb accommodation, food and drink, welcoming inhabitants and a selection of fine coastal and hill walks on its doorstep. Newport still elects a mayor annually, a legacy of its days as the capital of the Norman Marcher Lordship of Cemmaes. One visible manifestation of this heritage is the annual custom, in August, of "Beating of the Bounds", when the mayor marks out the town's boundaries on horseback.

The town and Carn Ingli

From the main thoroughfare, **Bridge Street**, Long Street and Lower St Mary Street head down to the tidal banks of the Afon Nyfer. A path hugs the southern shore of the estuary, over which squawking sea birds circle and skim the water's edge. Turn east (or take the Parrog Road if you're driving) for a gentle stroll along to the **Parrog**, Newport's nearest beach, mostly shingle but with sandy stretches at low tide. A better beach is the vast dune-backed **Traethmawr**, on the other side of the estuary, reached over the town bridge down Feidr Pen-y-Bont. Just short of the bridge, on the town side, **Carreg Coetan Arthur**, a well-preserved capped burial chamber, can be seen behind holiday bungalows. The footpath that runs along the river either side of the bridge is marked as the Pilgrims' Way; follow it eastwards for a delightful riverbank stroll to Nevern (see p.210), a couple of miles away. Back on Lower St Mary Street, the old town school now contains the **West Wales Eco Centre** (Mon–Fri 9.30am–4.45pm, often longer in summer; free), a venue for exhibitions, advice and resources on various aspects of sustainable living.

South of Bridge Street, a number of pretty thoroughfares rise up to the town's intriguing **castle** (private), a modern residence fashioned out of the medieval ruins. The other obvious landmark is **St Mary's church**, with its original Norman font. Follow Church Street, from the front of St Mary's, for the relatively easy two-hour ascent of **Carn Ingli** (Hill of Angels), once the core of an active volcano and, to many people, one of Wales' holiest mountains. It gets its name from St Brynach, who supposedly lived here in quiet contemplation, with angels as his companions. More certainly, stone embankments of the Iron Age hillfort and the nearby Bronze Age hut circles prove that the hill once had a sizeable community.

Practicalities

The cheerful national park **tourist office** (April–Oct Mon–Sat 10am–5.30pm, plus mid-July to Aug Sun 10am–1.15pm; ℡01239/820912) is on Long Street, as is the **post office**, outside which are boards full of local information. Wholefoods of Newport, on East Street, has news of less mainstream events and rents bikes (£15 per day; ℡01239/820773, ⓦwww.newportbikehire.com) and tag-a-longs for kids (£10).

Though Newport is a small place, the quality of **accommodation** is high. The town is similarly well supplied with places to **eat** and **drink**.

Accommodation

Cnapan Country House East St ℡01239/820575, ⓦwww.cnapan.co.uk. Five comfortable rooms and an old-fashioned friendly welcome are the hallmarks of this long-standing Newport favourite above a great restaurant. Closed Jan & Feb. ❺

The Globe B&B Upper St Mary St ℡01239/820296. About the cheapest place around, with shared bathroom and continental breakfast included in the room rate. ❷

Llys Meddyg East St ℡01239/820008, ⓦwww.llysmeddyg.com. Stylish restaurant-with-rooms fashioned from a Georgian residence. All rooms (and the more spacious suites) have great bedding, classy toiletries and individual decor. Free wi-fi, Rooms ❻, suites ❼

Morawelon Parrog Rd ℡01239/820565. Seaside campsite about 300 yards from town, nicely set in

pleasant gardens and with its own café overlooking the beach and coin-op showers. Closed Nov–Feb. £6–7.50 per person.

Newport YHA hostel Lower St Mary St ℡01239/820080 or 0870/770 6072, ⓔreservations@yha.org.uk. Tucked in behind the Eco Centre, this classy conversion of an old school has bunks and a couple of private rooms. Bunks £16, rooms ❶

Y Bryn Fishguard Rd, 200 yards west of town ℡01239/820288, ⓦwww.brynbedandbreakfast .co.uk. Great value B&B with four unfussy rooms, all with private bathroom (three also have sea views); the spacious attic room is particularly appealing. A full breakfast is served and there's off-street parking. ❸

Eating

The Canteen Market St. Casual restaurant with slate floors and modern wooden tables: a great setting for a good espresso or a meal from the short but well-chosen menu, including

early-evening specials (two courses for £11) and interesting wines by the bottle or the glass.

Cnapan Country House East St ℡01239/820575, ⓦwww.cnapan.co.uk.

Fresh local produce informs the menu at this classic dinner-only restaurant, where spicy mussel chowder might be followed by guinea fowl with gooseberry and elderflower sauce. £22 for two courses, £28 for three. Closed Tues, and for the whole of Jan & Feb. Bookings essential.

Golden Lion East St. Bare stone and timber-beamed pub with real ales, a pool table and a superb menu of carefully prepared pub meals (£9) and fancier restaurant-style dishes (around £15),

both served either in the bar or more formally out the back.

Llys Meddyg East St ☎01239/820008, ⊛www .llysmeddyg.com. A Georgian dining room or the partly walled kitchen garden provide the setting for exquisitely prepared dishes which might include local baby crab cakes with papaya mustard (£9) then wild bass with a sweet and sour mushroom broth (£20). Lunches (around £9) are no less appealing. Closed Mon.

The coast

Either side of Newport, the Coast Path runs through some sublime scenery. To the **west**, the trail edges around the nodule of Dinas Head, en route to Fishguard. Two miles west of New Quay's Parrog beach, there's the popular strand at **Cwm-yr-Eglwys**, where the scant seafront ruins of the twelfth-century **St Brynach's church** are all that survived a huge storm on the night of October 25, 1859, when the rest of the church and some 114 ships at sea were wrecked.

The walk around Dinas Head offers splendid views over the huge cliffs, inhabited by thousands of nesting sea birds between May and mid-July. On the western side of the headland and accessible by car off the A487, is the grey-sand beach of **Pwllgwaelod**. Sadly, the *Sailors' Safety Inn*, where a light was kept burning to help the ships' navigation, closed after 401 years in 1994. Next door, the *Old Sailors* is open throughout the summer season for cream teas, a decent pint or full meals concentrating on seafood.

The segment of Coast Path to the **east of Newport**, running to the fringes of Cardigan at St Dogmael's, is perhaps the wildest and toughest stretch of the whole path: it plummets and climbs passing rocky outcrops, blowholes, caves, natural arches, ancient defensive sites and thousands of sea birds. The only part accessible by car is at the spectacularly folded cliffs of **Ceibwr Bay**, eight miles from Newport near the pretty pastel village of **MOYLEGROVE** (Trewyddel).

Nevern, Pentre Ifan and Castell Henllys

Just over a mile by road to the east of Newport, but about double that along the pleasant riverside walk, the straggling village of **NEVERN** (Nanhyfer) is darkly atmospheric, with a couple of intriguing sights. The ruined and overgrown **castle**, a thirteenth-century replacement of a Norman construction on the site of an earlier Welsh fortress, sits high above the village on a bluff. Below, the brooding bulk of the **church of St Brynach**, founded in the sixth century and with an intact Norman tower, has many features of interest. The churchyard's ancient yews give it a dank, dark presence. Note the second tree on the right, the famous "**bleeding yew**", so called for the brown-red sap that oozes mysteriously from its bark. Legend has it that it will continue to bleed until a Welsh lord of the manor is reinstated in the village castle – unlikely in the foreseeable future, given its tumbledown state. Also outside the church, just by the main doorway, is the stunning **Great Cross**, an inscribed tenth-century Celtic masterpiece standing some 13ft high. St Brynach's interior is no less interesting. If you stand at the back, you can easily divine how the chancel has been built slightly out of alignment with the nave, supposedly to represent Christ's inclined head on the cross. Built into the windowsills of the south transept are two ancient inscribed stones: the **Maglocunus Stone**, with Latin and Ogham inscriptions from about the fifth century AD, and the **Cross Stone**, marked with a very early Celtic cross.

Lanes to the south of Nevern lead to the well-signposted cromlech at **Pentre Ifan**. This vast burial stone – the largest in Wales – with its sixteen-foot arrowhead top-stone precariously balanced on large stone legs, dates back over four thousand years. The views from here are superb, situated as it is on the cusp of the stark, eerie Mynydd Preseli with the pastoral rolls of the countryside to the east.

A couple of miles east of Nevern, signposted off the A487, the Iron Age hillfort of **Castell Henllys** (April–Oct daily 10am–5pm; Nov–March 11am–3pm; ℡01239/891319, ⓦwww.castellhenllys.com; £3.50) is undergoing archeological excavation that is turning up more and more of its past. Some re-created houses, complete with thatch, have been built on their 2000-year-old foundations, and throughout the summer there are ample opportunities to watch ancient skills and learn something of what Iron Age life must have been like here. Children's activities (during the school holidays; £1.50 for 90min; book ahead) give kids a chance to try wool dyeing and basket making. A sculpture trail through the woods and river valley brings to life the tales of The Mabinogion, and further trails lead into the ancient oak woodlands of the adjacent Pengelli Forest. Free one-hour guided tours (11.30am & 2.30pm) come with a strong environmental message, looking at land usage, wood management and conservation.

Cwm Gwaun and the inland hills

Cwm Gwaun, the valley of the burbling River Gwaun is one of the great surprises of Pembrokeshire – a bucolic vale of impossibly narrow lanes, surrounded by the bleak shoulders of bare mountains. It is a timeless place whose residents retain an attachment to the pre-1752 Julian calendar, celebrating New Year on January 13.

Llanychaer and Pontfaen

The B4313 leaves the skirts of Fishguard, heading two miles southeast to tiny **LLANYCHAER** where, opposite the *Bridge End Inn*, a lane runs almost half a mile steeply uphill to the **church** and "cursing" **well** of the lost settlement of **Llanllawer**. The well had a pre-Christian reputation for cementing curses and ill omens if you left a bent pin, although most pilgrims sought miraculous cures, particularly for eye conditions. The lane running east opposite the well and church leads to seven large standing stones – the longest megalithic alignment in Wales – in **Parc y Merw** (the Field of the Dead), just short of Trellwyn Farm.

Back on the B4313, nearly a mile beyond Llanychaer, a lane branches left and drops down into Cwm Gwaun, soon crossing the river near a picnic site from where there are some good walks up into the old oak forests that line the valley.

Three miles off the B4313 you reach the scattered settlement of **PONTFAEN**, complete with its time-warped pub, the rustic and remote 🍴 *Dyffryn Arms,* known as *Bessie's* after its ageing proprietor, where you can enjoy good company in an old-fashioned living room. By doubling back on yourself at the pub and following the lane that crosses the river and rises a quarter of a mile up a sharp hill, you'll reach Pontfaen's exquisitely restored **church**, dedicated, as are so many round here, to St Brynach. The circular graveyard indicates that this was a pre-Christian site of worship before the church was founded, according to traditional belief, by the wandering Breton saint in 540 AD. In the graveyard are two impressive stone crosses, dating from between the sixth and ninth centuries. The intricate interior is notable for a delicious early twentieth-century copy of a Fra Angelico painting of the Madonna, and the church's strange internal angles, known as a squint, that enabled all the congregation, including those in the "cheap" seats, to see what was going on.

Back on the lane that follows the Afon Gwaun, a further two miles brings you to the delightful **Gerddi Penlan-Uchaf** (March–Nov daily 9am–dusk; £2.50), a set of hillside gardens cut through by a stream with wonderful views over the valley. The gardens contain thousands of miniature flowering and alpine plants, and acres of herbs and wild flowers together with some impressive dwarf conifers.

Accommodation in the area is limited, but one place worth seeking out is the very welcoming *Erw-Lon Farm* (☎01348/881297; ❸) on the B4313 overlooking Pontfaen.

Rosebush and the Golden Road

It is further east that the brooding nature of the Mynydd Preseli makes itself most apparent. This is bleak, invigorating countryside, the wild, open hills scattered with the relics of ancient civilizations and, more often than not, the remains of dead sheep that have succumbed to the harsh weather. The characteristic **Preseli blue stone**, which was used to construct Stonehenge, some 140 miles away, between 2000 and 1500 BC, came from these slopes.

Slate is also found hereabouts, and was quarried into the twentieth century near the weird little village of **ROSEBUSH**, just off the B4313 around ten miles southeast of Fishguard. The nineteenth-century Klondike atmosphere of the place is partially explained by the fact that it was built quickly as a would-be resort by the Victorians following the arrival of the railway. The largest of several corrugated iron shacks contains the sawdust-floored *Tafarn Sinc*, or "*Zinc Tavern*" (☎01437/532214; closed Mon in winter), a good spot for a pint and a meal (£8–11) in the garden on a fine day. There's also good **food** at the licensed *Old Post Office* (☎01437/532205; closed Mon), which though noted for its vegetarian and vegan specialities, also does steaks and fish. **Campers** are well served up the road at the well-maintained, lakeside *Rosebush Caravan & Camping Park* (☎01437/532206; ⓦwww.ukparks.co.uk/rosebush; £10 per pitch; closed Nov to mid-March).

A good hike leads from Rosebush along the eastern edge of the coniferous Pantmaenog Forest to the 1760ft summit of **Foel Cwmcerwyn** (4 miles return; 2hr; 800ft ascent), the highest point in Pembrokeshire. This was the site of a legendary battle between King Arthur and his followers and the giant boar, Twrch Trwyth, as detailed in The Mabinogion. Topped by a Bronze Age cairn, the rounded hill sits above **Craig y Cwm**, the last glacial valley (c.8000 BC) in the area.

The main range of the Preselis lies just northeast of the village, crossed by an ancient track, in use for at least 3500 years, known as the **Golden Road**. A hike (8 miles one way; 4–5hr; 1000ft ascent) taking in the best section runs due north out of Rosebush past the old slate quarries through Pantmaenog Forest and up onto the Golden Road.

Turn right to reach many of the Preselis' cairns and ancient sites, such as **Beddarthur**, an eerie stone circle that is supposed to be the great king's burial place, **Carn Menyn**, probably the quarry from which the majority of the Stonehenge boulders were mined, and **Foeldrygarn** ("the Hill of Three

Cairns"), with its hugely impressive Iron Age ramparts and hut circles. Public transport is of little use so plan for a full day out and hike both ways: the perspective is quite different on the way back.

Travel details

Unless otherwise stated, frequencies for trains and buses are for Monday to Saturday services; Sunday averages 1–3 services, though the main routes are more frequent and some routes have no Sunday service at all.

Trains

Carmarthen to: Cardiff (16 daily; 1hr 30min–2hr); Ferryside (14 daily; 10min); Fishguard Harbour (1 daily; 1hr); Haverfordwest (11 daily; 45min); Kidwelly (14 daily; 20min); Llanelli (hourly; 30min); Milford Haven (11 daily; 1hr); Narberth (9 daily; 30min); Pembroke (9 daily; 1hr 20min); Swansea (hourly; 45min); Tenby (9 daily; 50min); Whitland (21 daily; 15min).
Fishguard to: Cardiff (1 daily; 2hr 30min); Swansea (1 daily; 1hr 40min).
Haverfordwest to: Cardiff (8 daily; 2hr 20min); Carmarthen (11 daily; 45min); Milford Haven (11 daily; 20min); Swansea (9 daily; 1hr 30min).
Llanelli to: Cardiff (20 daily; 1hr 30min); Carmarthen (hourly; 30min); Llandeilo (4 daily; 40min); Llandovery (4 daily; 1hr); Llandrindod Wells (4 daily; 1hr 50min); Llanwrtyd Wells (4 daily; 1hr 30min); Pembrey & Burry Port (hourly; 5min); Shrewsbury (4 daily; 3hr 20min); Swansea (hourly; 20min).
Milford Haven to: Carmarthen (11 daily; 1hr); Haverfordwest (11 daily; 20min); Swansea (7 daily; 2hr).
Pembroke to: Lamphey (9 daily; 3min); Manorbier (9 daily; 10min); Pembroke Dock (9 daily; 10min); Swansea (4 daily; 2hr); Tenby (9 daily; 20min); Whitland (9 daily; 50min).
Tenby to: Carmarthen (9 daily; 50min); Lamphey (9 daily; 20min); Narberth (9 daily; 20min); Pembroke (9 daily; 20min); Pembroke Dock (9 daily; 30min); Penally (9 daily; 3min); Saundersfoot (9 daily; 10min); Swansea (4 daily; 1hr 40min); Whitland (9 daily; 30min).
Whitland to: Carmarthen (21 daily; 15min); Haverfordwest (10 daily; 20min); Milford Haven (10 daily; 40min); Narberth (9 daily; 10min); Pembroke (9 daily; 50min); Swansea (7 daily; 1hr); Tenby (9 daily; 30min).

Buses

Carmarthen to: Aberaeron (hourly; 1hr 50min); Aberystwyth (hourly; 2hr 20min); Cardigan (6 daily; 1hr 30min); Cenarth (6 daily; 1hr 15min); Drefach Felindre (6 daily; 45min); Haverfordwest (3 daily; 1hr); Kidwelly (every 30min; 25min); Lampeter (hourly; 1hr); Laugharne (8 daily; 30min); Llandeilo (7 daily; 30min); Llandovery (7 daily; 1hr 20min); Llanelli (every 30min; 1hr); Llansteffan (8 daily; 20min); Narberth (3 daily; 40min); Pendine (8 daily; 40min); Swansea (every 30min; 1hr 20min); Tenby (2 daily; 1hr).
Fishguard to: Cardigan (hourly; 50min); Haverfordwest (hourly; 45min); Newport, Pembrokeshire (hourly; 20min); Rosebush (2 on Tues only; 25min); St Davids (5–8 daily; 50min); Trefin (7 daily; 30min).
Haverfordwest to: Broad Haven (5–7 daily; 20min); Cardigan (hourly; 1hr 20min); Carmarthen (3 daily; 1hr); Dale (3 daily; 55min); Fishguard (hourly; 45min); Manorbier (hourly; 1hr 10min); Milford Haven (every 30min; 25min); Narberth (hourly; 20min); Newgale (hourly; 25min); Newport, Pembrokeshire (hourly; 1hr); Pembroke (hourly; 45min); Rosebush (2 on Tues only; 45min); St Davids (hourly; 45min); Solva (hourly; 40min); Tenby (hourly; 1hr).
Llandeilo to: Carmarthen (7 daily; 30min); Llandovery (9 daily; 40min).
Llandovery to: Brecon (5 daily; 45min); Carmarthen (7 daily; 1hr 20min); Llandeilo (9 daily; 40min).
Llanelli to: Carmarthen (every 30min; 1hr); Kidwelly (every 30min; 30min); Swansea (every 30min; 30–40min).
Milford Haven to: Broad Haven (2 daily; 1hr 20min); Dale (3 daily; 30min); Haverfordwest (every 30min; 25min); Marloes (3 daily; 40min); Pembroke (hourly; 40min); St Davids (2 daily; 2hr 30min).
Narberth to: Carmarthen (3 daily; 40min); Haverfordwest (hourly; 20min); Tenby (hourly; 50min).
Newport (Pembrokeshire) to: Cardigan (hourly; 25min); Fishguard (hourly; 20min); Haverfordwest (hourly; 1hr).
Pembroke to: Bosherston (3 daily; 1hr); Castlemartin (3 daily; 45min); Haverfordwest (hourly; 45min); Manorbier (hourly; 20min);

Milford Haven (hourly; 40min); Pembroke Dock (every 20min; 10min); Stackpole (3–4 daily; 30min); Tenby (hourly; 40min).

Pembroke Dock to: Carew (4 daily; 15min); Pembroke (every 20min; 10min).

St Davids to: Broad Haven (3 daily; 50min); Fishguard (5–8 daily; 50min); Haverfordwest (hourly; 45min); Milford Haven (2 daily; 2hr); Solva (hourly; 10min); Whitesands Bay (April–Sept every 30min; 15min).

Tenby to: Amroth (7–10 daily; 40min); Carmarthen (2 daily; 1hr); Haverfordwest (hourly; 1hr); Manorbier (every 30min; 20min); Narberth (hourly; 50min); Pembroke (hourly; 40min); Pendine (6 daily; 1hr); Saundersfoot (every 30min; 15min).

Ferries

Fishguard to: Rosslare, Ireland (4 daily; 2hr–3hr 30min).

Pembroke Dock to: Rosslare (2 daily; 4hr).

The Brecon Beacons and Powys

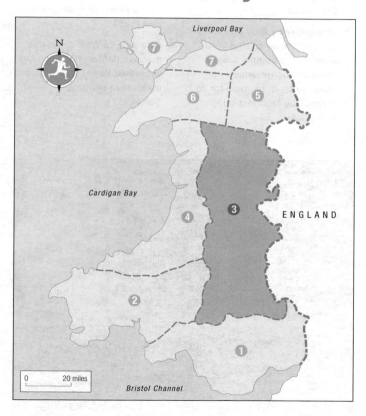

CHAPTER 3 # Highlights

* **Ystradfellte waterfalls**
  Explore the trio of great
  waterfalls in the limestone
  country around Ystradfellte.
  See p.224

* **Glasbury** Canoe downstream
  along the tranquil River Wye.
  See p.233

* **Abergavenny** Dine on locally
  sourced Welsh cuisine from
  some of the country's finest
  chefs at Abergavenny's
  restaurants, or hit town for its
  prestigious food festival.
  See p.235

* **Hay-on-Wye** Browse millions
  of secondhand books at
  over thirty bookshops in this
  bibliophile's paradise.
  See p.242

* **Presteigne** Step back in time
  at the 1868 Judge's Lodging,
  now an evocative museum.
  See p.254

* **Offa's Dyke** Walk along this
  massive earthwork, which has
  separated Wales and England
  for thirteen centuries.
  See p.257

▲ Llanidloes Market

The Brecon Beacons and Powys

The vast inland county of **Powys** takes up a full quarter of Wales. Often traversed quickly en route to the coast, it's well worth exploring in its own right. The most popular area is the **Brecon Beacons National Park** at the county's southern end, an area of moody heights, wild, rambling moors and thundering waterfalls. The main centres within the Beacons are Wales' culinary capital, **Abergavenny**, in the far southeast, and **Brecon**, a traditional market town, army garrison and lively tourist centre.

The bleaker part of the Beacons lies to the west, around the raw peaks of the **Black Mountain** (Mynydd Ddu) and **Fforest Fawr** geopark. A few roads cut through the glowering countryside, connecting key sights such as the immense **Dan-yr-ogof caves** and the mighty caves and waterfalls around the walking centre of **Ystradfellte**. Architecturally charming towns such as **Crickhowell** and **Talgarth**, set in quiet river valleys, also make good bases for walkers to head off into the mountains.

At the northern corner of the national park, the border town of **Hay-on-Wye** is famous for its dozens of secondhand bookshops and attracts thousands of visitors each year for its literary festival. West of Hay, the peaks of the **Mynydd Eppynt** now form a vast training ground for the British army, on the other side of which lie the old spa towns of Radnorshire. Crossed by spectacular mountain roads such as the **Abergwesyn Pass** from Llanwrtyd, the countryside to the north is supremely beautiful, dotted with ancient churches and villages, from the lively border communities of **Presteigne** and **Knighton** to inland centres like **Rhayader**, the nearest centre of population for the grandiose reservoirs of the **Elan Valley**.

The northern portion of Powys, **Montgomeryshire**, is as sparsely populated and remote as its two southern siblings. In common with most of mid-Wales, country towns here such as **Llanidloes** have a sizeable stock of New Age health-food shops, healing groups and arts activity. To the west, the inhospitable mountain of **Plynlimon** is flecked with boggy heathland and gloomy reservoirs, beyond which the hearty town of Machynlleth (covered in Chapter 4) sits out on a limb of Powys. The eastern side of Montgomeryshire is home to the anglicized old county town, **Montgomery**, between the

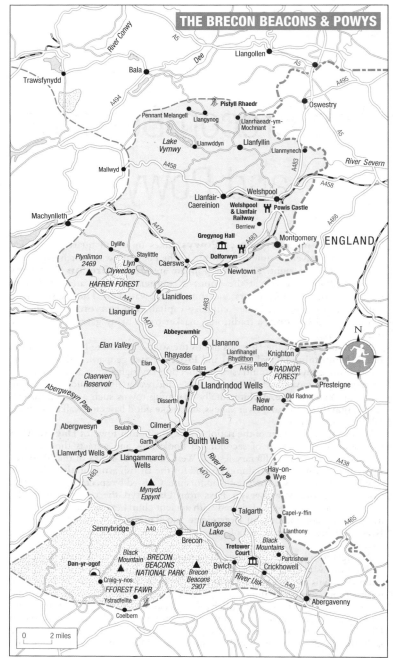

THE BRECON BEACONS & POWYS

River Conwy
Dee
Llangollen
A5
A5
A495
Bala
Trawsfynydd
A494
Oswestry
A5
Pistyll Rhaedr
Pennant Melangell
Llangynog
Llanrhaeadr-ym-Mochnant
Lake Vyrnwy
Llanwddyn
Llanfyllin
Llanmynech
A483
River Severn
A458
Mallwyd
A458
A458
Llanfair-Caereinion
Welshpool
A483
Powis Castle
Machynlleth
A470
Welshpool & Llanfair Railway
Berriew
Gregynog Hall
ENGLAND
Dylife
Staylittle
Caersws
Dolforwyn
Montgomery
A488
Plynlimon 2469
Llyn Clywedog
Newtown
HAFREN FOREST
A44
Llanidloes
A483
Llangurig
A470
Abbeycwmhir
Llananno
Knighton
Elan Valley
Llanfihangel Rhydithon
Pilleth
RADNOR FOREST
Rhayader
Cross Gates
A488
Presteigne
Claerwen Reservoir
Elan
Llandrindod Wells
Old Radnor
Abergwesyn Pass
Disserth
New Radnor
Abergwesyn
Beulah
Cilmeri
Builth Wells
Llanwrtyd Wells
Garth
Llangammarch Wells
River Wye
Hay-on-Wye
A438
Mynydd Eppynt
A470
Talgarth
Capel-y-ffin
A465
Sennybridge
A40
Llangorse Lake
Llanthony
Black Mountain
Brecon
Black Mountains
Dan-yr-ogof
BRECON BEACONS NATIONAL PARK
Tretower Court
Partrishow
Craig-y-nos
Brecon Beacons 2907
Bwlch
Crickhowell
FFOREST FAWR
River Usk
A40
Ystradfellte
Abergavenny
Coelbern

0   2 miles

N

© Crown copyright

robust towns of **Welshpool** and **Newtown**. The northern segment of the county is even quieter, with the only crowds being found along the banks of **Lake Vyrnwy**, a flooded-valley reservoir.

Getting around

Train services are restricted to the Heart of Wales line from Shropshire to Swansea via Knighton, Llandrindod Wells, Llanwrtyd Wells and smaller stops in between, and the Shrewsbury–Machynlleth route through Welshpool and Newtown. Many larger centres such as Brecon, Llanidloes, Rhayader, Builth Wells and Hay-on-Wye rely on sporadic **bus** services, although most places can be reached. One particularly useful service is the three-times-daily #47, which runs up the spine of southern Powys from Brecon through Builth to Llandrindod Wells, where it meets connections for Newtown, Welshpool and the north. Nearby towns such as Wrexham, Abergavenny, Machynlleth and, over the border, Oswestry, all provide useful connection points with local services. Available from libraries, tourist offices and main post offices, the most useful overview of all these services is the free *Wales Bus, Rail and Tourist Map & Guide*, which details operators and their services. On Sundays and bank holidays during summer, the Beacons Bus (see p.221) is ideal for walkers.

Brecon Beacons National Park

With the lowest profile of Wales' three national parks, the **Brecon Beacons** are refreshingly uncrowded, primarily attracting local urban walkers. Spongy hills of grass and rock tumble and climb around river valleys that lie between sandstone and limestone uplands peppered with glass-like lakes and villages that seem to have been hewn from one rock. Known for their vivid quality of light, the hills of the Beacons disappear and re-emerge from hazy blankets of cloud, with shafts of sun sharpening the lush green patchwork of fields.

Covering 520 square miles, the national park straddles southern Powys and northern Monmouthshire from west to east. The most remote parts are around the Black Mountain peaks to the west, with miles of tufted moorland and bleak, often dangerous summits, plummeting to the porous limestone country in the southwestern section, a rocky terrain of rivers, deep caves and spluttering waterfalls. To the northwest, the lonely Black Mountains (not to be confused with the entirely separate Black Mountain to the west) are separated from the Beacons themselves by the Monmouthshire and Brecon Canal, which forges a passage along the Usk Valley. Built around the beginning of the nineteenth century to support coal mining, iron ore and limestone quarrying, the canal is an impressive feat of engineering, successfully steering a 25-mile lock-free stretch (Britain's longest) through some of the most mountainous terrain in Wales. Spreading back from the canal's banks are the region's main residential

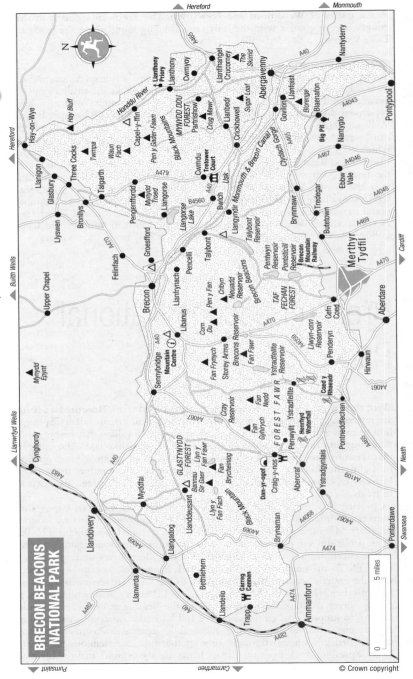

BRECON BEACONS NATIONAL PARK

0 ____ 5 miles

© Crown copyright

areas as well as the majority of its hotels and guesthouses, so it's quite likely that this is where you'll end up staying.

Getting around and accommodation

Getting around the largely rural territory of the Brecon Beacons National Park can be difficult without your own wheels. Abergavenny is the only town with a **train** station, though Merthyr Tydfil, on the southern flank of the park, is well connected by rail to Cardiff. **Buses** are a much better bet, with relatively frequent services (often 4–6 daily) along the major routes; a smattering of services only run on certain days. The main routes are from Abergavenny to Brecon and on to Libanus, Storey Arms, Merthyr and Cardiff (#X43); Brecon to Talgarth, Hay-on-Wye and Hereford (#39/40); and Brecon to Swansea via Craig-y-nos the Dan-yr-ogof Showcaves (#63). Detailed listings of services in the area are contained in the free *Discover the Brecon Beacons* leaflet, available from tourist offices and bus companies. From the May bank holiday weekend until the end of September, the **Beacons Bus** (all day £7) loops around various routes within the park on Sundays and bank holidays – timetables can be downloaded from Ⓦwww.breconbeacons.org. The Cardiff service tows a bike trailer, enabling you to bus it here and cycle back down the Taff Trail (p.228).

The relatively compact nature of the region, the profusion of narrow lanes and the many opportunities to get off-road make this a great place to **travel by bike**: rental locations include Brecon, Abergavenny and Hay-on-Wye. **Horseriding** is also extremely popular and well organized; see the listings throughout this chapter, or visit Ⓦwww.horseridingbreconbeacons.com.

We've listed the Brecon Beacons' best **accommodation** options, though there are plenty more low-budget options, most listed in booklets available from local tourist offices. *Camping on Farms* (downloadable at Ⓦwww.breconbeacons.org /content/visit-us/where-to-stay/camping-on-farms-1) lists around thirty low-cost and free sites scattered throughout the park, while *Bunkhouse Accommodation in the Brecon Beacons* covers two dozen bunkhouses – most charge £10–15 a night. If you're interested in self-catering accommodation, the best locally are *Brecon Beacons Holiday Cottages* (Ⓣ01874/676446, Ⓦwww.breconcottages.com) and the *Abergavenny Farm Holidays Group* (Ⓦwww.afhg.co.uk).

The western Beacons

The western half of the Brecon Beacons National Park comprises the bleak uplands of Black Mountain and Fforest Fawr, and the sparsely populated valleys in between. That this is limestone country is evident everywhere: caves, sink-holes and waterfalls dot the map. From the valleys, invigorating walks or bike rides thread up to the lonely moors for sweeping views across the Beacons.

Black Mountain

The most westerly expanse of upland in the national park is known as the **Black Mountain** (Mynydd Ddu). Despite being named in the singular (as distinct from the Black Mountains further east), the "mountain" actually covers an unpopulated range of barren, smooth-humped peaks that break suddenly at rocky escarpments towering over quiet streams and glacial lakes.

The area provides the most challenging and exhilarating walking in south Wales. Paths cross the wet, wild landscape from Dan-yr-ogof in the east, and from the soaring ruins of Carreg Cennen Castle, just short of Llandeilo in the

A walk around Llanddeusant

The OS Outdoor Leisure 1:25,000 map #12 (Brecon Beacons – Western & Central Area) is recommended for this walk.

Passing both Llyn y Fan Fach and Llyn y Fan Fawr, this bleak and lonely ten-mile circular walk from Llanddeusant weaves through classic glacial scenery: valleys slashed with tumbling streams cut between purple hills, while occasional mounds and moraines of rock debris indicate the force of the ice pushing through the valleys. Such heaps sometimes grew to a size large enough to form a natural dam, building up lakes, such as Llyn y Fan Fach, in their wake.

The walk (10 miles; 4–5hr; 1400ft ascent) starts in Llanddeusant and climbs steeply to Llyn y Fan Fach, from where a precarious path leads around the top of the escarpment, following the ridge to **Fan Brycheiniog** (2630ft), above the glassy black waters of Llyn y Fan Fawr. A remote path heads from here to the cross-moor road, two miles away.

west. Other good starting points for forays into the open Black Mountain uplands are Tyhwnt, near Ystradgynlais, in the south and, in the north, the hamlet of **LLANDDEUSANT**, seven miles south of Llandovery, also home to a cosy **YHA hostel** and **campsite** (T0870/770 5930; closed Nov–Jan; dorm beds from £11.95) in the former village pub. Two miles west of Llanddeusant, you can camp at the pleasant *Pont Aber Inn* (T01550/740202; advance booking required) on the main A4069. The best walk (see box above) from Llanddeusant runs along wooded gulches and moorland bluffs to the twin glacial lakes of **Llyn y Fan Fach** and **Llyn y Fan Fawr**. Llyn y Fan Fach features in one of Wales' most oft-told myths of a beautiful maiden, together with her herd of magic cattle, who rose from the lake to marry a local farmer. The maiden's father had sanctioned the union only on the condition that if the farmer struck his daughter three times, she would return to the lake. Such occasions occurred inadvertently, the final blow being either when he slammed a gate and hit her or when he shook her at a funeral for laughing, depending on which version you hear. The maiden silently left the man and, with her cattle, disappeared beneath the lake's icy waters once more.

The Fforest Fawr geopark

Covering a vast expanse of hilly landscape between the Black Mountain and the central Beacons southwest of Brecon, **Fforest Fawr** (Great Forest) seems something of a misnomer for an area of largely unforested sandstone hills dropping down to a porous limestone belt in the south. The "forest" tag refers more to the old definition of a forest as land used as a hunting ground. In 2005, Fforest Fawr was recognized – and is now subsequently administered – by UNESCO as a geopark, becoming part of the Europe-wide network of other geoparks.

The hills rise up to the south of the A40 west of Brecon, with the dramatic A4067 Sennybridge–Ystradgynlais road scoring the western side of the range and the A470 Brecon–Merthyr road defining the Fforest's eastern limit.

Dan-yr-ogof Showcaves and Craig-y-nos

Travelling south on the A4067, the road soon drops into the upper reaches of the valley of the Afon Tawe, Swansea's river. This is the beginning of the limestone belt, as seen in the hamlet of **Glyntawe** at the **Dan-yr-ogof Showcaves** (April–Oct daily 10am–3pm; Nov–March limited opening hours – call for details; ☎01639/730284, ⓦ www.showcaves.co.uk; £11). Only discovered in 1912, and opened to the public in 1939, it's claimed the caves form the largest system of subterranean caverns in northern Europe. New attractions and a massive marketing campaign have turned the complex into something of a theme park (you enter between a giant fibreglass dinosaur's legs), but the extent and size of the caverns are truly awe-inspiring.

In a self-guided tour, with commentary resonating from loudspeakers, the path first leads you into the **Dan-yr-ogof** cave, the longest showcave in Britain, and a warren of caverns framed by stalactites and frothy limestone deposits. Although the whole cave is known to be around ten miles long, you'll be steered around a circular route of about a mile and a half. Back outside, you pass a recreated Iron Age "village" and walk past yet more fibreglass dinosaurs to reach **Cathedral Cave**, a succession of spookily lit caverns leading into the "cathedral" itself, a hugely impressive 150-foot-long, 70-foot-high cave. Reachable via a precarious path behind the dinosaur park is **Bone Cave**, the third and final cavern, known to have been inhabited by Bronze Age tribes, with some 42 human (and many animal) skeletons found here.

If you want to get an early start on the caves, or use them as a walking base, you can **stay** at on site self-catering units (from £100/150 per three days/week for a double) and **camping** (£5 per person). For £2.50, there's a newly spruced up camping option half a mile north at *Maes-yr-eglwys Farm* (☎01639/730849), up the track behind the church (book through ⓦ www.hoseasons.co.uk). Between there and the showcaves, the *Gwyn Arms* serves decent meals.

A quarter of a mile south of the cave complex is the nineteenth-century **Craig-y-nos Castle** (☎01639/730205, evenings 731167, ⓦ www .craigynoscastle.com; ❸, dorm beds £30), a grand folly built in 1842 and fancifully extended from 1878, when it was bought by Adelina Patti, the celebrated Italian-American opera singer. In her forty years of residence, she turned the place into a diva-esque castle, even adding a scaled-down version of the Drury Lane opera house for performances. After Ms Patti's reign, Craig-y-nos suffered decades of chronic neglect, until it was bought in the mid-1990s, renovated and turned into an oddball (and rather overpriced) **hostel/hotel** and entertainment venue. There are occasional concerts in the opera house, jazz and blues in the bar, history and ghost tours, and a Sunday carvery is available at the **restaurant** (open lunch and dinner by reservation, although frequently closed for private functions). Non-guests can take a free self-guided tour of the ground floor; historian-led tours (£10) are also available on request. Some 44 acres of the castle's grounds form part of the Brecon Beacons National Park and operate as **Craig-y-nos Country Park** (unrestricted access). Its visitor centre (opening hours vary) and car park form the starting point for signposted and leafleted walks around a landscaped site along the banks of the young River Tawe.

Such was Adelina Patti's fame and influence, she even demanded her own private waiting room up at the little railway station, now semi-derelict, at **PENWYLLT**, a mile above the main road to the east. The hamlet is surrounded by a moonscape of quarries and limestone outcrops that makes for superb walking or biking. It is also the HQ of the **South Wales Caving Club** (ⓦ www.swcc.org.uk), first port of call to enquire about exploring the many local cave systems.

Abercraf and Coelbren

The main A4067 continues southwards, alongside the Afon Tawe, to the village of **ABERCRAF** (sometimes Abercrave) on the cusp of the coal-mining Valleys. To the north of the village, the Cribarth mountain resembles a reclining figure and is locally dubbed the Sleeping Giant.

On the back lane to the village of Coelbren is the scruffy but endearing **Cefn-yr-Erw Primate Rescue Sanctuary** (daily 10.30am–dusk; £5). Over sixty primates, rescued from all over the world, including chimpanzees, baboons and gibbons, live alongside Shetland ponies, goats, porcupines and even wolves. Snacks and B&B (☎01639/730276, ⓦwww.cefn-yr-erw.co.uk; ❷) are also available.

With its pebbledash and chapels, **COELBREN** marks the very outpost of the Valleys coalfield. On the north side of the village, a path from a National Trust car park leads down into a gorgeous, wooded ravine and to the ninety-foot exuberance of the **Henrhyd waterfall**, the highest in south Wales, with a rocky ledge behind the fall that can be easily accessed.

Ystradfellte, Penderyn and Pontneddfechan

Continuing east, a wonderful, twisting mountain road crosses the Fforest Fawr and drops down into the valley of the Afon Llia and the limestone crags around the hamlet of **YSTRADFELLTE**. Little more than a handful of houses, a church and a pub, this is, nonetheless, a phenomenally popular centre for walking, as a result of the dazzling countryside on its doorstep. Lush, deep ravines – a total contrast to the barren mountains immediately to the north – carve through the limestone ridge south of the village, with great pavements of bone-white rock littering fields next to cradling potholes, disappearing rivers and thundering waterfalls.

A mile south of Ystradfellte, the River Mellte tumbles into the dark and icy mouth of the **Porth-yr-ogof** cave, emerging into daylight a few hundred yards further south. A signposted path heads south from the Porth-yr-ogof car park and into the green gorge of the River Mellte. Continue for little more than a mile to the first of its three great waterfalls, **Sgwd Clun-Gwyn** (White Meadow Fall), where the river crashes 50ft over two huge, angular steps of rock before hurtling down course for a few hundred yards to the other two falls, the graceful **Sgwd Isaf Clun-Gwyn** (Lower White Meadow Fall), and, a little further on, the mighty **Sgwd y Pannwr** (Fall of the Fuller).

▲ Brecon Beacons

The path continues through the foliage to the confluence of the rivers Mellte and Hepste, half a mile further on. A quarter of a mile along the Hepste is arguably the most impressive of the area's falls, the **Sgwd yr Eira** (Fall of Snow), where the rock below the main tumble has eroded back six feet, allowing people to walk directly behind a dramatic twenty-foot curtain of water – particularly dazzling in afternoon or evening light. There's a shorter signposted path to Sgwd yr Eira from just above Sgwd Isaf Clun-Gwyn, and an even shorter direct two-mile walk from the village of **PENDERYN**, off the A4059 three miles north of Hirwaun, reached by buses from Aberdare. You might want to stop off on the main road through Penderyn at the **Welsh Whisky Distillery** (℡01685/813300, Ⓦwww.welsh-whisky.co.uk), where a new visitor centre should be operational by the time you're reading this – call or check the website for updates.

A less well-known, but equally spectacular, set of waterfall walks heads due north from the village of **PONTNEDDFECHAN**, four miles west of Penderyn, and along the forested valley of the River Nedd (or Neath). A new visitor centre (officially Easter–Oct Mon–Fri 10am–1pm & 1.45–5.30pm, Sat & Sun 9.30am–5.30pm, although hours can vary; ℡01639/721795) here can provide information. There are numerous falls here, the most famous being **Sgwd Gwladus**, an easyish mile's walk along the river from Pontneddfechan, which, like Sgwd yr Eira, overhangs enough to allow you to walk behind. A few hundred yards further, though accessible only via stepping stones and a bit of a scramble that can be tricky after heavy rain, is perhaps the best of all, the sublime **Sgwd Einion Gam**.

In the middle of Ystradfellte, the *New Inn* serves basic meals.

The central Beacons

The **central Brecon Beacons** – after which the whole national park is named – are well set up for walking and pony trekking. The area, to the immediate south of Brecon town, centres on the two highest peaks in south Wales, **Pen y Fan** (2907ft) and **Corn Du** (2863ft), half a mile to the west. Although neither reaches 3000ft, the terrain is unmistakably and dramatically mountainous: classic old red sandstone country with sweeping peaks rising out of glacially carved land.

The combined ascent of **Pen y Fan** and **Corn Du** is the most popular walk in the park. The most direct route up is the well-trampled red-mud path that starts from Pont ar Daf, half a mile south of Storey Arms on the A470 midway between Brecon and Merthyr Tydfil. The ascent is a comparatively easy five-mile round trip, gradually climbing up the southern flank of the two peaks. A longer and generally quieter route (see box, p.226) leads up to the two peaks from the "Gap" route – the pre-nineteenth-century (and possibly Roman) main road winding north from the Neuadd reservoirs through the only natural break in the central Beacons' sandstone ridge to the bottom of the lane. The route eventually joins the main street in the Brecon suburb of Llanfaes as Bailihelig Road. Although the old road is no longer accessible for cars, car parks at either end open out onto the track for an eight-mile round-trip ascent up Pen y Fan and Corn Du from the east.

Brecon

The handsome Georgian buildings of **BRECON** (Aberhonddu) stand at the northern edge of the Beacons, bearing testimony to the town's past importance.

A circular walk around Corn Du and Pen y Fan

The OS Outdoor Leisure 1:25,000 map #12 (Brecon Beacons West & Central) is recommended for this walk.

Few walkers visiting the Brecon Beacons for the first time can resist making an ascent of the two highest peaks: Corn Du and Pen y Fan. Most take one of the shorter routes from the A470 south of Brecon, but connoisseurs prefer this longer and infinitely more rewarding **circular "Gap" route** (8 miles; 4–5hr; 1400ft ascent) that describes a circuit around a ridge-top horseshoe of the Beacons.

The hike starts at the car park by the late-Victorian Neuadd reservoirs. Go through the gate and head down left through a gully and up onto the top of the grassy dam of the lower, smaller reservoir. Go to the end, through the muddy gap and up the hill in front, keeping the partly cleared plantation forest on your left-hand side. Keep to the fairly well-defined track and, when the forest ends, continue up the sharp gradient ahead, keeping the little stream gully on your left. This is the toughest, steepest and often boggiest part of the walk, but before too long you're up on the top of a windy ridge, commanding wide views over the reservoirs, the Beacons and way beyond. Head right along a well-defined path along the ridge top. The slope to the right becomes gradually sharper and more cliff-like as you continue over tiny streams that course down to the valley below. When the ridge on which you're walking narrows to a thin spit, views to the left down the completely uninhabited Cwm Crew are delightful. Corn Du and Pen y Fan are now looming in the foreground – follow the obvious path that strikes up the sandstone ridge to the first summit. Note how eroded the main path from the A470 is when you meet it just short of the peak.

Follow the obvious route from the summit of Corn Du down to a shallow saddle and up again to the peak of Pen y Fan, the highest point in south Wales. From both, the views over the mountains and valleys to Brecon are awesome. You can continue beyond Pen y Fan up to the next summit, Cribyn, and then descend to the Gap, where the wall of hills is breached by a track that is thought to have been a Roman through-route. Alternatively, without missing too much, you can take a right by the stream in the valley between Pen y Fan and Cribyn, following the rough track around the base of Cribyn to meet the Gap track. Turn right and continue along above the Neuadd reservoirs, turning right at the stream gulch to return to the car park.

Today, it's a lively base for walkers and less active visitors alike, with good accommodation, and plenty of places to eat and drink.

A Roman fort was built near here, but the town only started to grow with the building of a Norman castle and Benedictine monastery, founded in 1093 on the banks of the Honddu River, which gives the town its Welsh name. To the dual strands of military and ecclesiastical importance was added the status of regional market centre and cloth-weaving town. In the seventeenth-century Civil War, the townsfolk demonstrated their neutrality between the forces of Parliament and the Crown by demolishing most of the castle and large sections of the town walls, dissipating the appeal for either side of seizing their town.

Information

Brecon's **tourist office** (Easter–Oct Mon–Fri 9.30am–5.30pm, Sat 9.30am–5pm, Sun 9.30am–4pm; Nov–Easter Mon–Fri 9.30am–5pm, Sat & Sun 9.30am–4pm; ☎01874/622485, ✉brectic@powys.gov.uk) is in the Lion Yard car park off Lion Street, next to the Morrisons supermarket and has details of local bus services, which leave from the central Bulwark for Swansea, Cardiff, Abergavenny and Hay-on-Wye. Directly across the car park from the tourist office, the **post office** is inside the Cooperative Foods supermarket.

For details of the town's annual **jazz festival**, held on the second weekend of August, call ☎01874/611622 or visit ⓦwww.breconjazz.co.uk. Noticeboards in the Market Hall foyer on High Street Superior give the lowdown on gigs and other local events. There's free **internet access** at the town library on Ship Street (Mon & Wed–Fri 9.30am–5pm, Tues 9.30am–7pm, Sat 9.30am–1pm).

Accommodation

Ample **accommodation** to suit all pockets exists in Brecon's compact town centre. The suburb of Llanfaes, across the river from the main town, has plenty of smaller hotels and B&Bs on its main street. Book anything up to several months ahead if you're heading here during the jazz festival. See p.232 for options in nearby Bwlch.

Hotels and guesthouses

Beacons Guesthouse 16 Bridge St, Llanfaes ☎01874/623339. Rambling converted town house in an excellent position. Good evening meals also available. ②–③

Cantre Selyf 5 Lion St ☎01874/622904, ⓦwww.cantreselyf.co.uk. Large and imposing seventeenth-century town house, all creaking floors and moulded plaster ceilings, but sensitively modernized with private bathrooms and firm cast-iron beds. Delicious breakfasts, and evening meals by request. ③–④

Castle of Brecon Castle Square ☎01874/624611, ⓦwww.breconcastle.co.uk. Large and sumptuous

hotel built into the castle ruins, overlooking the Usk. All rooms are en suite and have satellite TV; there are also some larger and more expensive rooms with views. ⑤–⑦

The Coach House 12/13 Orchard St ☎0844/3571301, ⓦwww.coachhousebrecon.com. Gay-friendly B&B with well-equipped rooms and a range of holistic therapy treatments available. Great Welsh breakfasts including vegetarian options and a smart new bar/bistro. Can also organize transport for walkers. ②

Lansdowne Hotel 39 The Watton ☎01874/623321, ⓦwww.lansdownehotel.co.uk.

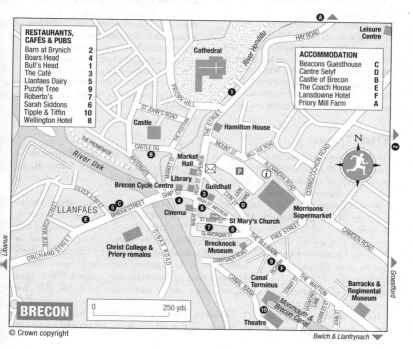

RESTAURANTS, CAFÉS & PUBS
Barn at Brynich 2
Boars Head 4
Bull's Head 1
The Café 3
Llanfaes Dairy 5
Puzzle Tree 9
Roberto's 7
Sarah Siddons 6
Tipple & Tiffin 10
Wellington Hotel 8

ACCOMMODATION
Beacons Guesthouse C
Cantre Selyf D
Castle of Brecon B
The Coach House F
Lansdowne Hotel E
Priory Mill Farm A

BRECON
0   250 yds
© Crown copyright

Bwlch & Llanfrynach ▼

The Taff Trail

Running from Brecon to Cardiff Bay, the 55-mile **Taff Trail** (ⓦ www.tafftrail.org) passes through a spectacular cross-section of south Wales scenery: the Usk Valley, the Brecon Beacons uplands, the former coal-mining Taff Valley and urban parkland. Most of the route – which is open to hikers and bikers – is on forest trails, designated pathways and country lanes and is seldom steep. Pubs and restaurants along the way are marked on the free *Taff Trail* map, available from tourist offices and park information centres, which also shows the location of train stations and the occasional trail-side campsite.

Perhaps the best way to tackle the whole trail is to start in Brecon (where there's bike rental), ride to Cardiff – downhill almost all the way – then catch a train back to Merthyr Tydfil and ride the fifteen miles back over the hills to Brecon. Keen riders could do this in a day, though you might prefer to break the journey in Pontypridd or Cardiff. Also see p.221 for details of the Beacons Bus Cardiff bike service.

Classy town-centre hotel in a handsome Georgian corner house with a restaurant. Rooms are smallish but good value. ❷, family rooms ❹–❺

🏃 **Peterstone Court** Llanhamlach, 3.3 miles east of Brecon ☎01874/665387, ⓦwww .peterstone-court.com. Historic country manor set in lush countryside blending antique and contemporary furnishings. There are also spa facilities, a swimming pool and a good restaurant. ❻–❽

Hostels, bunkhouses and campsites

Llwyn-y-Celyn YHA hostel Libanus, 7 miles southwest of Brecon ☎0870/770 5936, ⓔ llwynycelyn@yha.org.uk. Traditional farmhouse hostel, just off the A470 and main bus route to Merthyr. Closed Dec to mid-Feb. Telephone 48 hours ahead to check availability. Dorms from £11.95.

Priory Mill Farm Hay Rd ☎01874/611609, ⓦwww.priorymillfarm.co.uk. Lovely, low-key

riverside campsite, with bins for log fires. It's on the northern edge of town, reached by a 5min walk along the riverbank. £6 per pitch.

Ty'n-y-Caeau YHA hostel Groesfford, just over 2 miles east of Brecon ☎0870/770 5718, ⓔtynycaeau@yha.org.uk. The nearest YHA hostel to Brecon, reached via the path (Slwch Lane) from Cerrigcochion Rd in town or a mile from bus stops at either Cefn Brynich lock (Brecon–Abergavenny buses) or Troedyrharn Farm (Brecon–Hereford buses). Dorms £13.95 plus some private rooms (❶). Closed Dec–Feb.

Upper Cantref Farm Bunkhouses Cantref Pony Trekking Centre, near Llanfrynach ☎01874/665223, ⓦ www.cantref.com. Overlooking the Cynrig River, three miles southeast of Brecon. Dormitory-style accommodation (£12.50; minimum two-night stay on weekends) with kitchen and showers. Campers can pitch tents in the grounds (£3.50).

The Town

Brecon's imposing central square, at the western end of **The Bulwark** is flanked by the solid-red sixteenth-century tower of **St Mary's Church**, an assortment of old-fashioned shop frontages, and the elegant Georgian portico of the **Wellington Hotel**.

At the junction of The Bulwark and Glamorgan Street is the neo-Grecian frontage of the **Brecknock Museum** (Mon–Fri 10am–5pm, Sat 10am–1pm & 2–5pm, April–Sept also Sun noon–5pm; £1), where there's an interesting walk-through history of Wales and a nineteenth-century assize court, last used in 1971 and preserved in all its ponderous splendour, overseen by the high judge's throne. Elsewhere, there's a finely carved four-poster, inscribed stones dating back to the fifth century and a selection of painstakingly carved Welsh love spoons – some over four hundred years old – that were betrothal gifts for courting Welsh lovers.

Running east, The Bulwark becomes The Watton, where you'll find the foreboding frontage of the South Wales Borderers' **barracks** and its

Regimental Museum (Easter–Sept Mon–Fri 10am–5pm, Sat 10am–4pm, plus certain Sun; Oct–March Mon–Fri 10am–5pm; £3), packed with mementos from the regiment's three-hundred-year existence. Most absorbing are the tales of the 1879 Zulu War when 140 Welsh soldiers faced an attack by 4000 Zulu warriors. From The Watton, a series of small streets runs down to the town's theatre and the northern terminus of the **Monmouth and Brecon Canal**, where afternoon cruises aboard the *Dragonfly* (Easter–Oct; ☎07831/685222, ⓦwww.dragonfly-cruises.co.uk; £6.50) ease their way out of town for enjoyably relaxed two-hour trips. Longer and self-driven trips are available at nearby Talybont-on-Usk (see p.231).

The grid of streets north and west of The Bulwark are packed with Georgian and Victorian buildings and contain some interesting and high-quality independent shops. Northwest, at the crossroads of High Street Inferior, Ship Street descends down to the **River Usk**, the bridge crossing the Usk next to the point where the smaller Honddu River flows in from the north.

From the town centre crossroads, High Street Superior goes north, past the long **Market Hall**, home of a twice-weekly produce market (Tues & Fri) and, on the second Saturday of each month, an excellent **farmers' market**. The road then becomes The Struet, passing the resplendent former timber merchant's home, Hamilton House, at no. 13 (closed to the public).

Over the rushing waters of the Honddu, Priory Hill climbs up to the stark grey buildings of the monastery settlement, centred on the **cathedral**, or Priory Church of St John the Baptist. Its surprisingly lofty interior is graced with a few Norman features intact from the eleventh-century priory that was built here on the site of a probable earlier Celtic church. The hulking Norman font sits at the western end of the nave, near the entrance, from where the south aisle runs down to the most interesting of the many family memorials, the **Games monument** (1555), made up from three oak beds and depicting an unknown woman whose hands remain intact in prayer, but whose arms and nose have been unceremoniously hacked off. There's a relatively interesting **heritage centre** (March–Dec Mon–Sat 10.30am–4.30pm, May–Sept also Sun noon–4pm; free) in a converted sixteenth-century tithe barn in the cathedral close. Among the gilded vestments lies the unusual Cresset Stone, a large boulder indented with thirty scoops in which to place torches. The attached tearooms serve up tasty food.

Between the cathedral and the River Usk, the few remains of the town's **castle** are moulded into the walls of the *Castle Hotel*. The end result is a powerful, if bizarre, amalgam that looks its best from along **The Promenade** by the River Usk, reached from the town-centre side of the river bridge. In high summer, motor and rowing boats can sometimes be rented along the riverbank.

Eating and drinking

There's no shortage of decent places **to eat** in Brecon, although many of the best **restaurants** lie outside town. **Drinking** options are similarly good, although some of the pubs in the near vicinity of the barracks are worth avoiding. While here, be sure to try real ales from the local **Breconshire Brewery** (on tap in many local pubs). Informal brewery tours are planned – check with Brecon's tourist office.

Restaurants and cafés

Barn at Brynich Brynich Caravan Park, off the A470 east of town ☎01874/623480. Cavernous, family-oriented truck stop, but worth investigating for hearty, home-cooked specialities.

The Café 39 High St. Great daytime café, with a warm, relaxed atmosphere and a good range of free trade coffees and hearty soups and sandwiches. It keeps odd hours (usually at least Wed and Sat), but is well worth a visit if open.

Felin Fach Griffin Felinfach, 3 miles northwest of town ☎01874/620111. Superb modern Welsh cuisine in a smart gastropub just off the A470.

Llanfaes Dairy 19 Bridge St. Just across the river, serving scrumptious home-made ice cream.

🏃 Puzzle Tree Corner of the Watton and Rich Way. Brecon's newest pub/nightclub also has outstanding food, from Welsh sausages on mash with onion gravy through to thick steaks and Mexican fare, thanks to its well-travelled local chefs. The only place in town serving nonstop food, from noon until late. Nightclub open Tues–Sat 7pm–2am.

🏃 Roberto's St Mary's St ☎01874/711880. On the outside, this former post office is fronted by typically British red telephone boxes and round, red postboxes. Inside it's a little slice of Italy, with vines adorning the beams, wine bottles lining the walls and Italian classics like creamy salmon risotto.

Tipple & Tiffin Theatr Brycheiniog, Canal Basin. Tapas-style dishes to share, together with a few more substantial options, in this airy waterside bistro. Good for pre-theatre dinner whenever there's a show on.

White Swan Llanfrynach, 3 miles southeast of Brecon ☎01874/665276. Stylish village pub with a tremendous reputation for its local specialities and good wines.

Pubs

Boars Head Ship St. Two very different bars: the front is basic and the best place to meet locals, whereas the back bar is younger and louder.

Bull's Head 86 The Struet. Small and cheery locals' pub, with views over the Honddu River and towards the cathedral. Good-value food (with vegetarian and vegan choices) and occasional live music.

Sarah Siddons High St Inferior. Named after the famous actress, born here in 1755 when the pub was then known as the *Shoulder of Mutton*. A busy place, popular with off-duty soldiers.

Wellington Hotel The Bulwark. Frequent venue for live music, especially jazz.

Activities and entertainment

Signposted 1.5 miles off the A470 (turn off at Libanus), some six miles southwest of the town is the National Park Visitor Centre, also known as the **Brecon Beacons Mountain Centre** (daily: March–June & Sept–Oct 9.30am–5pm; July & Aug 9.30am–6pm; Nov–Feb 9.30am–4.30pm; ☎01874/623366). As well as an excellent café serving hot meals, there are interesting displays on the flora, fauna, geology and history of the area, together with a well-stocked shop of maps, books and guides, which are necessary for the walks that fan out from the centre across the surrounding gorse heathland. Staff here can give experienced hikers details of walks tackling the more challenging peaks of Corn Du and Pen y Fan (see p.225). Buses leave Brecon for Merthyr and stop at Libanus, from where it's a one-mile uphill walk along the lane next to the church up to the centre.

Brecon is well served for sports and recreational facilities: the old-fashioned Coliseum **cinema** is on Wheat Street near the central crossroads (☎01874/622501), while the **Theatr Brycheiniog** at the canal basin (☎01874/611622, ⒲www .brycheiniog.co.uk) offers a good music and theatrical programme. There's an indoor **swimming pool** in the leisure centre a mile northeast of town on the Cerrigcochion road (☎01874/623677). **Bike rental** outlets include the Brecon Cycle Centre, 9 Ship St (☎01874/622651) and Bikes & Hikes (deliveries by arrangement – call ☎01874/610071), both of which offer quality machines for around £25 a day. Hay-on-Wye-based Drover Holidays (☎01497/821134, ⒲www.droverholidays.co.uk) can also deliver bikes to Brecon.

The Usk Valley

Home to the majority of the national park's residents, and hence the greatest concentration of facilities for visitors, the wide, fertile Usk Valley leads southeast from Brecon, running parallel to the Monmouth and Brecon Canal and effectively dividing the Brecon Beacons proper from the Black Mountains

A circular walk around the Eastern Beacons

The OS Outdoor Leisure 1:25,000 map #13 (Brecon Beacons Eastern Area) is recommended for this walk.

Starting at the Blaen-y-glyn car park (SO 064169), on the lane between Talybont and Pontsticill/Merthyr, cross the road and take the track opposite that threads down to the right and passes rapids and falls along the River Caerfanell. Continue for about 600 yards, over a concrete bridge, and take the left path at the fork. This heads uphill, with the plantation forest to your left (and a good comparison with the natural woodland across the valley to the right). Continue into the forest and take the left fork where the path splits into three. After about 300 yards, you come to a clearing, where you take a sharp left over the stream and continue past the picnic tables, fording another stream and taking a sharp right uphill to a fence and stile. Turn right along the forest track, then left at the Torpantau car park entrance, and head up the steep bank for about a third of a mile – the views over the valley of Glyn Collwn are superb here. At the corner of the forest, bear slightly right, away from the stream. It's a hard climb up to the ridge of Craig y Fan Ddu, straight ahead, but well worth it for some stunning vistas. The path swings left, shortly approaching the lip of the slopes to the right. Keep the ridge immediately to your right, cross the stream, and continue across the boggy moorland, still climbing gently. After about a mile, there's a short descent to Bwlch y Ddwyallt, where five paths converge.

Take the first right path, and, after 100 yards or so, strike left, crossing below a peat bog. Cross a stream and head towards the bottom of the rocky edge ahead. A monument, lying between two heaps of twisted metal, marks the spot of a wartime RAF plane crash. Climb up the slope to the top of the ridge, and then walk along its rim in a southeasterly direction, keeping the quarried cliffs to your right. After half a mile, you'll reach a spur of land with steep slopes on either side. Head straight on, down the steep grassy slope in front, across a patch of moor and then right, following a fence, down into the valley. Cross the stile and turn left along the river path, past some little waterfalls. At the footbridge, you can either cross the river and return by the original path, or continue on this bank, past numerous falls and pools. Either way, the road and car park are reached in about 700 yards.

to the northeast. The A40 connects Brecon and Bwlch with Tretower, Crickhowell and Abergavenny, providing a backbone for dozens of minor lanes which twist south over the Brecon Beacons or north into the bucolic head waters of some of the Usk's tributaries.

Talybont and around

Six miles southeast of Brecon, **TALYBONT-ON-USK** is idyllically situated for walks, bike rides or canal trips. The lane heading south of the village over the canal heads towards a number of **reservoirs**, starting with the 323-acre **Talybont reservoir**. It then wiggles up onto the rocky hillsides, past the waterfalls on the Nant Bwrefwr and beyond to the isolated and hauntingly beautiful Neuadd (or Beacons) reservoirs to the north, a good starting point for walks to the summits of Pen y Fan and Corn Du along the old "Gap" route (see box, p.226); or, to the south, the more popular (and hence busier) **Pentwyn** and **Pontsticill** (aka Taf Fechan) **reservoirs**. Two eastbound paths at either end of the Pontsticill reservoir enable escape from fellow walkers in favour of a fairly steep climb up the rocky slopes for wonderful views over the lakes.

Below Pontsticill, the tiny **Brecon Mountain Railway** (Easter–Oct, usually 5–6 trains daily; £9.50 return trip) shuttles passengers along a two-mile section of track on the eastern bank of the reservoir.

Three miles northwest of Talybont, you'll find Cambrian Cruisers (℡01874/665315, Ⓦwww.cambriancruisers.co.uk) at Pencelli wharf, where you can rent narrowboats for short breaks (three nights over the weekend or four nights midweek, both starting from £509), or on a weekly basis (from £702).

Regular Brecon–Crickhowell **buses** stop at Talybont. Amongst the village **pubs**, the *Star Inn* (℡01874/676635; ❸) stands out for its real ale, food, music nights and good **B&B**. Alternatively, *Travellers Rest* (℡01874/676233, Ⓦwww.travellersrestinn.com; ❹) is a homely spot with a roaring fire and a good restaurant and bar that's famed for its tender roast lamb. More upmarket is the *Usk Inn* (℡01874/676251, Ⓦwww.uskinn.co.uk; ❺–❼), a village pub transformed into a country restaurant with eleven comfortable rooms named after birds you'll spot along the River Usk. At Aber, a little over a mile south of Talybont, you can **camp** at the north end of Talybont Reservoir at the basic *Aber Campsite* (£2.60 per person). Over the river is the *Danywenallt* **YHA hostel** (℡0870/770 6136, Ⓔdanywenallt@yha.org.uk; dorm beds from £17.50, rooms ❶), set in a converted farmhouse with a warming woodstove and meals by request (though no self-catering facilities).

Bwlch and around

A few miles northeast of Talybont, the little village of **BWLCH**, served by Regular Brecon–Crickhowell **buses**, is strung out along the A40 with spectacular valley views. The village makes a good, central base for **walks** in the surrounding mountains and for day-trips further afield, and also has a couple of outstanding budget **accommodation** options. *The Star Bunkhouse* (℡01874/730080, Ⓦwww.starbunkhouse.com; dorm beds from £14) primarily caters for groups, but welcomes individual travellers. Directly opposite on the A40, *Beacons Backpackers* (℡01874/730215, Ⓦwww.beaconsbackpackers.co.uk; dorm beds from £17) has sparkling en-suite dorms overlooking the valley and is attached to Bwlch's only **pub**, the 🍴 *New Inn*, an ancient former coaching house and quintessential Welsh village pub with great food (including award-winning chilli), real ales and local events such as quiz nights. If your budget stretches a bit further, *Gliffaes Country House Hotel* (℡01874/730371, Ⓦwww.gliffaeshotel.com; ❺–❾), an Italianate manor set back from the A40 midway between Bwlch and Crickhowell (two miles from both), has grand rooms and serves sumptuous high teas.

Two miles south of Bwlch, across a perilously narrow stone bridge, the beautifully sited village of **LLANGYNDIR** has a handful of atmospheric pubs serving food. From Llangyndir, you can follow a breathtakingly scenic back road over the high moors and down to the eastern Valleys, though you'll need to keep a sharp eye out for errant sheep wandering onto the road.

Llangorse and around

North of Talybont and Bwlch, the B4560 threads its way four miles through rolling countryside to **LLANGORSE** (Llangors), sheltered in the western lee of the Black Mountains. The village is a mile northeast of the reed-shored **Llangorse Lake** (Llyn Syfaddan), which was notorious in medieval times for its supernatural properties (blood-red water, eerie sounds and mythical lost city). A *crannog* (artificial lake island), the only one of its kind in Wales, is thought to have been a ninth-century seat of the royal house of Brycheiniog.

Today, a reconstructed *crannog* at the water's edge has information panels interpreting the lake's history and legends. The *Lakeside* **campsite** (℡01874/658226,

W www.llangorselake.co.uk; £5.50–6.50 per adult, electricity £3.25; closed Nov–Easter) also has boats and bikes for rental. A mile the other side of the village is the **Llangorse Riding & Ropes Centre** (daily 10am–10pm; T 01874/658272, W www.activityuk.com) at Gilfach Farm. Experienced climbers can rent gear cheaply, and there are activity sessions (£13 for 1hr; £16 for 2hr) introducing you to climbing and abseiling. The centre also offers off-road horseriding for beginners and intermediates (£14.50 for 1hr, £28 for 2hr) and hacking for the experienced (£34.50 for 2hr).

The rope centre has an inexpensive **bunkhouse**; preference is generally given to groups using the centre, but it's worth asking, particularly during the school holidays. A mile up the road in Llangorse itself, there's top-quality **B&B** at *Pen-y-Bryn House* (T 01874/658606; ❷). The best food in these parts is at the *Castle Inn*, in the village.

Five miles north of Llangorse, **TALGARTH** is a spirited and friendly village built around its unusual town hall and the hulking **St Gwendoline's church** tower, constructed in the fourteenth century but harking back to Talgarth's position as a defence centre against the Norman invasion. The *Tower Hotel* on The Square (T 01874/711253, W www.towerhoteltalgarth.co.uk; ❷) is the town's main centre for drinking, cooks up wholesome fare like steaks with all the trimmings, and offers **B&B**. There's independent **tourist information** and cheap internet access at the Tower Shop (Easter–Sept Mon, Tues & Thurs–Sat 10am–4pm, Wed & Sun noon–4pm; Oct–Easter Mon, Tues & Thurs–Sat 10.30am–3.30pm, Wed noon–4pm; T 01874/712226), opposite the *Tower Hotel*; it's staffed by volunteers so hours can vary. The local airstrip is the base for the **Black Mountains Gliding Club** (T 01874/711463; flights from £60).

Between Talgarth and the neighbouring village of **BRONLLYS** is **Bronllys Castle**, of which only a large twelfth-century cylindrical tower remains – climb to the top for stunning views up the Llynfi River valley and beyond to the light-washed peaks of the Black Mountains. There are some great places to **eat** and **sleep** around here: just north of Bronllys on the main road, the *Honey Café*, open daily until 10pm, has been around since 1935 and remains popular, especially for its spicy evening menu. Heading up the A470 brings you to Llyswen and the ivy-covered, fifteenth-century *Griffin Inn* (T 01874/754241, W www.griffininn-llyswen.co.uk; ❸), serving delicious local dishes. Directly opposite is the breezy *Wye Knot Stop* daytime café (closed Wed), which serves the best coffee for miles around and has spacious, uncluttered B&B rooms upstairs (T 01874/754247; ❸). Continuing north on the A470 brings you to the luxurious ⚘ *Llangoed Hall* (T 01874/754525, W www.llangoedhall.com; ❾), an ancient castle re-modelled in the early twentieth century by Portmeirion's Clough Williams-Ellis. It's now owned by Sir Bernard Ashley, widower of the late Laura, and its exquisite rooms (from £210) are adorned with fabrics produced by Elanbach, Sir Bernard's on-site textile printing company.

Four miles northeast of Bronllys, just off the A438 on the B4350, the riverside village of **GLASBURY** is home to Wye Valley Canoes (April–Oct; T 01497/847213, W www.wyevalleycanoes.co.uk), where you can rent a boat to paddle the gentle currents of the River Wye. Rental for a five-mile trip downstream to Hay-on-Wye (around two to three hours) costs £15 including minibus pick-up at the other end; longer trips, including multi-day rentals, are also possible. The adjacent *River Café* (Wed–Sat 9am–11.30pm, Sun 9am–5.30pm) occupies the village's former post office and serves heart-starting coffee and home-baked treats; upstairs are four bright en-suite B&B rooms (T 01497/847007; ❸).

Tretower and Pengenffordd

Rising from the valley floor twelve miles south of Talgarth, the solid round tower of the **castle and court** (daily: Easter–Sept 10am–5pm; Oct–Easter 10am–4pm; £3.50; CADW) at **TRETOWER** (Tre-twr) was built to guard the valley pass, and still dominates the skyline from both the A40 and A479. This thirteenth-century tower replaced an earlier Norman fortification, while a grand manor house was built next to it in the late fourteenth century. An open-air gallery and wall walk enable you to view the site on the upper level, while an enjoyable, self-guided audio tour takes you around the site.

Six miles north of Tretower, the hamlet of **PENGENFFORDD** is a good base for walks in the Black Mountains, including up to the vast nearby Iron Age hillfort of **Castell Dinas**, whose 2500-year-old ditches and grass ramparts sit 1500ft up under an outlying crop of the mountain range, commanding views far down the valley of the Rhiangoll River. The friendly *Castle Inn*, at the base of Castell Dinas on the main road in Pengenffordd (☎01874/711353, ⓦwww .thecastleinn.co.uk; ❶), is a favourite base for walkers, offering B&B, camping (£3 per person), bunkhouse accommodation for groups and hearty food and drink (the bar's lively atmosphere makes the rooms noisy on occasion). *Upper Trewalkin Farm* (☎01874/711349; ❸), up in the lanes between Pengenffordd and Talgarth, is a stunningly situated farmhouse B&B with en-suite rooms and staggering views over Castell Dinas and the Black Mountains.

Crickhowell

One of the gems of the Brecon Beacons, **CRICKHOWELL** (Crucywel; locally referred to as "Crick") lies on the northern shore of the wide and shallow Usk. Many a local myth has been spawned by its grand seventeenth-century **bridge** with thirteen arches visible from the eastern end but only twelve from the west. Bridge Street rises from the river and up to the uninspiring mound of the ruined **castle** and the wide **High Street**. Both Bridge and High streets are lined with intriguing shops including old-fashioned butchers and a beautiful small-scale department store, High Street's WM Nicholls & Co, with its original 1920s fittings intact. New Road runs parallel to Bridge Street from the river, passing the steeple of the town's fourteenth-century **church of St Edmund**.

Crickhowell's spectacular northern backdrop is **Table Mountain** (1481ft), whose brown cone presides over the rolling green fields below. The most scenic route up it is along the path that goes off by the electricity substation past The Wern off Llanbedr Road. At the summit are remains of the 2500-year-old hillfort (*crug*) of Hywel, from which Crickhowell takes its name. An alternative, and far shorter, route to Table Mountain starts from the village of **LLANBEDR**, some two miles north of Crickhowell, and heads up alongside the stream behind the *Perth-y-pia* bunkhouse. The views are amongst the best in the area. Many walkers follow the route to the north from Table Mountain, climbing two miles up to the plateau-topped limestone hump of **Pen Cerrig-calch** (2302ft).

Every March, Crickhowell hosts a popular nine-day **Walking Festival** (ⓦwww.crickhowellfestival.com) with guided walks ranging from tough all-day treks to easy strolls, all costing £3 per walk, per person. The other big local event is the **Green Man Festival** (ⓦwww.thegreenmanfestival.co.uk), a three-day folk festival held in mid-August with headline acts like the Super Furry Animals and lots of drum workshops, literary events, a cinema tent, kids' activities, performance art and a "healing field".

Practicalities

The gleaming new **tourist office** (daily: April–Oct 10am–5pm; Nov–March daily 10.30am–4pm; ℡01837/811970) is on Beaufort Street and incorporates an internet café, while upstairs a gallery sells quality local art. **Accommodation** is abundant, with a grand old coaching inn, the *Bear Hotel*, on Beaufort Street (℡01873/810408, Ⓦwww.bearhotel.co.uk; ❺–❼); and the cheerfully relaxed *Dragon* on the High Street (℡01873/810362, Ⓦwww.dragonhotel.co.uk; ❸–❹). For B&B, the en-suite rooms at *Tŷ Gwyn* (℡01873/811625, Ⓦwww.tygwyn .com; ❷), an impressive eighteenth-century stone gatehouse on Brecon Road, just beyond Porth Mawr, are excellent value. The only place to **camp** in town is the manicured *Riverside Caravan Park* on New Road (℡01873/810397, Ⓦwww .riversidecaravanscrickhowell.co.uk; from £3 per tent).

There's no shortage of places to **eat** and **drink** in and around Crickhowell. The smart, contemporary *Number 18*, at 18 High St, is good for daytime snacks, while there's heftier fare, including good curries, at the *Corn Exchange* bar opposite. Evening food is almost universally available in the town's pubs: the *Bear Hotel* (see above) wins legions of awards for its heavenly, if somewhat pricey, bar and restaurant food. Down by the town bridge, the *Bridge End* pub, part of which is an old tollhouse, is an excellent bet for food, including some impressive vegetarian choices. A mile along the A40 towards Brecon is the renowned *Nantyffin Cider Mill* (℡01873/810775), with innovative starters such as beer-battered wild mushrooms, followed by the likes of Welsh black beef with hand-cut chips and a steaming sticky toffee date pudding with butterscotch sauce, all at moderate prices.

The Crickhowell Adventure Gear shop, opposite the market cross at 1 High Street, sells caving and walking paraphernalia, while Mountain and Water (℡01873/831825, Ⓦwww.mountainandwater.co.uk) offers boating, caving, climbing, orienteering and other mountain activities.

Abergavenny

Six miles southeast of Crickhowell, Wales' culinary mecca, **ABERGAVENNY** (Y Fenni) is a vibrant, confident town, though its history is somewhat more chequered. The first main settlement was around the Norman castle, which was built by the English king Henry I's local appointee, Hameline de Ballon, with the express aim of securing enough power to evict local Welsh tribes from the area, an important through route into Wales. Hostility to the Welsh reached its peak at Christmas 1175, when William de Braose, then lord of the town, invited Gwent chieftains to the castle, only to murder them all. The town was shaken badly by the Black Death (1341–51) and a routing by Owain Glyndŵr in 1404, but continued to grow, thanks largely to the weaving and tanning trades that developed from the sixteenth century. The industries prospered alongside Abergavenny's flourishing **market**, still the focal point for a wide area every Tuesday. In World War II, Hitler's deputy, Rudolf Hess, was imprisoned in the town's mental asylum after his plane crash-landed in Scotland in 1941. Today, Abergavenny's combination of urban amenities and countrified setting make it an ideal jumping-off point for forays into the central and eastern sections of the Brecon Beacons.

Arrival and information

Abergavenny is well connected to the national rail network, with fast and frequent trains from Cardiff, Newport and Hereford stopping at its

train station, half a mile southeast of the centre. Buses depart in all directions from Swan Meadows **bus station**, right in the heart of things on Cross Street. The adjacent **tourist office** (daily: April–Oct 10am–5.30pm; Nov–March 10am–4pm; ☎01873/857588, ✆abergavennytic@breconbeacons.org) shares space with the Brecon Beacons National Park office.

Bike rental is available at The Bike Base, 17 Mill St (☎01873/858519, ⓦwww .bikebasewales.com), run by a team of cycling enthusiasts who can deliver bikes throughout the area. To explore the Monmouthshire and Brecon Canal, you can rent **narrowboats** (and day-rental motorboats as well as canoes) from Beacon Park Boats at Llanfoist (☎01873/858277, ⓦwww.beaconparkboats.com), a mile south of town. **Concerts** and **theatre** take place in the Borough Theatre on Cross Street (☎01873/850805).

Accommodation

Accommodation around Abergavenny is abundant and very good value.

Hotels and guesthouses

Angel Hotel 15 Cross St ☎01873/857121, ⓦwww.angelhotelabergavenny.com. Abergavenny's premier hotel, occupying an old coaching inn, now restored to its former glory and providing stylish and very comfortable, rooms in a central location. ⑤–⑥

The Guest House 2 Oxford St ☎01873/854823, ⓦwww.theguesthouseabergavenny.co.uk. Fun seven-room guesthouse (of which two rooms are en suite), with a mini-zoo in the backyard. No credit cards. ②

King's Head Cross St ☎01873/853575, ⓦwww.kingshead.20fr.com. Smartly refurbished town-centre pub next to the market hall; all 14 rooms are en suite. ③

Park Guest House 36 Hereford Rd ☎01873/853715, ✆parkguesthouse @hotmail.com. The cheapest B&B in town, housed in a beautiful Georgian town house near the station and town centre. Exceptionally good value. ②

Pentre House Brecon Rd ☎01873/853435, ⓦwww.pentrehousebandb.com. Roomy, friendly Georgian country house at the turning for Sugar Loaf mountain. Lovely gardens, wonderful breakfasts and a very welcoming atmosphere. Shared bathrooms. ②

Hostels, bunkhouses and campsites

Black Sheep Backpackers 24 Station Rd ☎01873/859125, ⓦwww.blacksheepbackpackers .com. Welcoming hostel right by the station, with accommodation in twin, quad and dorm rooms, and mountain bike rental. Continental breakfast included. Dorm beds £13.50, twin rooms ①

Pyscodlyn Farm 2 miles west of town off the A40 ☎01873/853271, ⓦwww.pyscodlyncaravanpark .com. The nearest place to pitch a tent – all Brecon or Crickhowel-buses pass by. Also organizes fishing licences. £6–13 per pitch.

Smithy's Bunkhouse Lower House Farm, Panty-gelli ☎01873/853432, ⓦwww.smithysbunkhouse .com. Self-catering dormitory accommodation under the slopes of the Sugar Loaf a couple of miles north of town. It's a 5min walk to a real ale pub which also serves food, but otherwise you'll need to bring your own supplies. Dorm beds from £10.

The Town

From the train station, Monmouth Road rises gently into the town centre, becoming Cross Street and, finally, High Street. Off to the right are Monk Street and, next to the blue-turreted Victorian Gothic town hall, the wonderful covered **market** (Tues, Fri & Sat for produce, Wed flea market, regular weekend antiques fairs and Farmers' Market on fourth Thurs of every month).

Any street heading south off Cross or High streets leads to Castle Street, where the dark, fragmented remains of Abergavenny's medieval **castle** languish. The castle's keep was remodelled in the nineteenth century, and sits in the middle of the forsaken ruins like an incongruous Lego model. Serenely situated near the River Usk, at the bottom of the bowl of surrounding hills, it's worth a visit for

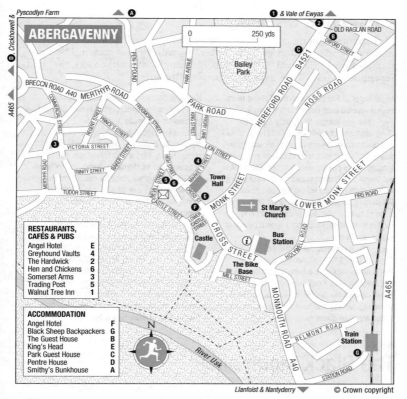

RESTAURANTS, CAFÉS & PUBS

Angel Hotel	E
Greyhound Vaults	4
The Hardwick	2
Hen and Chickens	6
Somerset Arms	3
Trading Post	5
Walnut Tree Inn	1

ACCOMMODATION

Angel Hotel	F
Black Sheep Backpackers	G
The Guest House	B
King's Head	E
Park Guest House	C
Pentre House	D
Smithy's Bunkhouse	A

its quirky **town museum** (Easter–Sept Mon–Sat 11am–5pm, Sun 2–5pm though closed 1–2pm outside school summer holidays; Oct–Easter Mon–Sat 11am–1pm & 2–4pm; free). Displays cover the town's history, using photographs and billboards, and re-created interiors including a saddlery, a sanitized Border farmhouse kitchen of 1890 and Basil Jones' grocery shop, once on Main Street. After the death of Jones' son in 1989, the contents of the shop were transported to the museum lock, stock and biscuit barrel. Some of it was recent, but much of it dated from the 1930s and 1940s – World War II vegetable tins and decorations marked for the coronation of Edward VIII that never happened – and some dating back to the nineteenth century.

Abergavenny's parish **church of St Mary**, on Monk Street, contains effigies and tombs spanning the entire medieval period. Originally built as the chapel of a small twelfth-century Benedictine priory, the existing building goes back only as far as the fourteenth century, although some of the monuments within predate the building itself. There are effigies of members of the de Braose family, along with the tomb and figure of Sir William ap Thomas, founder of Raglan Castle, and Dr David Lewis (died 1584), the first Principal of Jesus College, Oxford. Look too for the **Jesse Tree**, a recumbent, twice-life-size statue of King David's father, which would once have formed part of an altarpiece tracing the family lineage from Jesse to Jesus. The Jesse Window at Llanrhaeadr in the Vale of Clywd (see p.346) tells the same tale.

Eating and drinking

Abergavenny is home to numerous fine eateries, as well as a clutch of cheap takeaways at the bottom of Cross Street, towards the bus station. The town's annual **Food Festival** (ⓦ www.abergavennyfoodfestival.co.uk), in mid-September, is one of the most prestigious in Britain.

Angel Hotel (p.236.) Gracious hotel dining room serving vaunted local cuisine and lavish high teas.

🏃 **The Fox Hunter** Nantyderry, 6.6 miles southeast of town ☏ 01873/881101, ⓦ www .thefoxhunter.com. Award-winning modern British cuisine by TV chef Matt Tebbutt, served in a lovingly restored former stationmaster's house. Closed Mon and dinner Sun. Also organizes "wild food foraging" hunting, gathering and fishing trips on request.

Greyhound Vaults Market St. Great for a wide range of tasty, moderately priced Welsh and English specialities, including a superb choice of vegetarian dishes.

🏃 **The Hardwick** Old Raglan Rd ☏ 01873/854220. Another jewel in Abergavenny's culinary crown, headed up by TV chef Stephen Terry. Creative modern twists on British classics like bubble 'n' squeak topped with a fried organic egg and house-made salad cream. Closed Mon and dinner Sun.

Hen and Chickens Flannel St, off High St. Timeless traditional pub, with the best beer in town and regular live music and events.

Somerset Arms Victoria St, by the junction of Merthyr Rd. Bright and cheerful locals' pub with cheap, hearty food and excellent real ale.

Trading Post 14 Neville St. Trendy coffee house and bistro – a great place for reading the paper over a cappuccino or tucking into inexpensive mains ranging from tortillas to tortelleni. Open until 10pm Thurs–Sat.

🏃 **Walnut Tree Inn** On the B4521 at Llanddewi Sgyrrid, 2 miles north of town ☏ 01873/852797. Legendary foodies' paradise now under the helm of Shaun Hill, drawing diners from afar for its Mediterranean-accented British cuisine like twice-baked goat's cheese soufflé with beetroot or potato and herb gnocchi, and seasonal desserts like elderflower cream with poached gooseberries. Closed Sun & Mon.

The Black Mountains

Appearing only partly tamed by human habitation, the northeastern-most section of the Brecon Beacons National Park, known as the **Black Mountains** (plural, as distinct from the Black Mountain forty miles west) is made up of tiny villages, isolated churches and hedged lanes that fold into the undulating green landscape. The wide valley of the River Usk divides the Beacons heartland from the Black Mountains, whose sandstone range rises to more clearly defined individual peaks than those in the western end of the park.

The most rewarding areas to **walk** are along the lane past Llanthony Priory and along the southern band of peaks, notably Pen Cerrig-calch, Table Mountain and the Sugar Loaf. The mass of rippling hills in the centre and to the north are less easy to reach, although a couple of good paths follow the contours around them.

Blorenge, Sugar Loaf and The Skirrid

From the grounds of Abergavenny Castle, the skyline is dominated by three southern outposts of the Black Mountains that climb out of the river plain. To the southwest is **Blorenge** (1834ft), a corruption of "Blue Ridge", accessible from the road that strikes off the B4246 a mile short of Blaenafon. The open road climbs the shale- and sheep-covered slopes to the car parks near the radio masts. An easy walk from here leads across boggy heathland to a long cairn at the summit, from which there are some glorious views south over the old mining region and north over the Usk Valley, Abergavenny and the Black Mountains. There is a steeper ascent of the Blorenge from **Llanfoist**, a mile southwest of Abergavenny, which cuts past the church and under the canal before zigzagging up the mountain.

The broad and smooth cone of **Sugar Loaf** (1955ft) commands the Black Mountains foothills to the northwest of Abergavenny. Falling away from its summit are paths that scour the windswept slopes before descending to tiny villages in the valleys of the Usk, the Grwyne Fawr and the Grwyne Fechan. The easiest ascent is from the south, taking the right fork of Pentre Lane off the A40, half a mile west of Abergavenny, and following the road that climbs Mynydd Llanwenarth.

At 1595ft, **The Skirrid** (Ysgyryd Fawr) is the most eye-catching mountain in the area. Shooting up from the Gavenny Valley, three miles northeast of Abergavenny, gentle green fields climb about halfway up its flanks, giving way suddenly to purple scrub and bracken. The best path, although it's still a steep ascent, leads from the lay-by on the B4521 just short of the *Walnut Tree Inn* (see p.238). The Skirrid has long been held to be a holy mountain; the almighty chasm that splits the peak is said to have been caused by the force of God's will on the death of Christ, a theory that drew St Michael and legions of other pilgrims to this bleak but breathtaking spot. Another theory claims that Noah's Ark clipped it as it passed by. At the summit, a few leaning boulders are all that remains of a clandestine chapel built by persecuted Catholics.

The Vale of Ewyas

The northern finger of Monmouthshire and the extreme eastern boundary of the Brecon Beacons National Park, stretching along the English border, is one of the most enchanting and reclusive regions in Wales. The main A465 Hereford road leads north out of Abergavenny, passing The Skirrid on the right-hand side. It's worth a quick detour from here (two miles northeast of Abergavenny) to the **Court Cupboard Gallery** (daily 10.30am–4pm, March–Oct open until 5pm; ℡01873/852011, ⊛www.courtcupboardgallery.com), an artists' enclave of workshops within a 500-year-old farm, selling leather crafts (including beautiful handmade bags), jewellery, sculptures, handmade soaps and more. You can often chat with the artists as they work, and the gallery also mounts regular exhibitions as well as art and craft courses.

Back on the A465 six miles north of Abergavenny, a steep, single-track lane diverges west from the village of **Llanfihangel Crucorney** to weave through the Vale of Ewyas along the bank of the Honddu River, past the remote village of **Cwmyoy** with its crooked little church, and on to the crumbling old religious institutions of **Llanthony Priory** and **Capel-y-ffin**. Parallel to the Honddu, a couple of miles and some impressive mountains to the west, is the **Grwyne Fawr**, a sparkling river that flows through the heart of some of Wales' most peaceful and gentle countryside. Folded amongst the contours is one of the country's most perfect small churches at **Partrishow**. Aside from the summer Sunday and bank holiday Monday service from Hay-on-Wye, there are no bus services in this area.

Llanfihangel Crucorney, Partrishow and Cwmyoy

On the main village street of **LLANFIHANGEL CRUCORNEY** (Llanfihangel Crucornau, the "Sacred Enclosure of Michael at the Corner of the Rock") are the odd fifteenth-century **church** and the reputedly haunted **Skirrid Inn**, first mentioned in 1110 and thus thought to be the oldest pub in Wales. During the seventeenth century, some 180 people are believed to have been hanged here – you can still see the beam inside the inn, which bears the scorch marks of the rope. It's an atmospheric spot for a drink; if you're game to experience a ghostly evening complete with a candlelit dinner, historians, spiritual mediums and perhaps other enigmatic "guests", call ☎01543/278075.

From the village, the main road through the valley heads north into the beautiful Vale of Ewyas, along the banks of the River Honddu. After a mile, a lane heads west towards the enchanting valley of the **Grwyne Fawr**, lost deep in the middle of quiet hills. The road is well worth following to the hamlet of **PARTRISHOW**, where a bubbling tributary of the Grwyne Fawr trickles past the delightful **church** and **well** of St Issui (confirm opening times with the Abergavenny tourist office, p.236). First founded in the eleventh century, the tiny church features a lacy fifteenth-century rood screen, carved out of solid Irish oak and adorned with crude symbols of good and evil, most notably in the corner, where an evil dragon consumes a vine, a symbol of hope and well-being – the rest of the whitewashed church breathes simplicity by comparison. Of special note are the wall texts painted over the apocalyptic picture of a skeleton and scythe. Before the Reformation, such images were widely used with the intent of teaching an illiterate population about the scriptures; however, King James I ordered it to be whitewashed over and repainted with scripture texts. Here, the ghostly grim reaper is once again seeping through the whitewash. Encased in glass by the pulpit is a rare example of a 1620 Bible in Welsh.

Back on the main road, the A465 continues to wind its way up the valley's western side, past the fork at the *Queen's Head* pub (☎01873/890241), a great place to **camp** (£3 per person). If you're prepared for some adventurous driving, take the little lane that peels off the main road here, as it dips down over the river and into the village of **CWMYOY** and its wonky **parish church of St Martin**, which has subsided substantially due to geological twists in the underlying rock. Nothing squares up: the tower leans at a severe angle from the bulging body of the church and the view inside from the back of the nave towards the sloping altar, askew roof and straining windows is unforgettable. A few yards below the church, the **Downey Barn Gallery** (☎01873/890993,

▲ Cwmyoy Church

@www.galleriesintheblackmountains.co.uk) occupies a timber barn adjacent to the home of artist and children's author Caroline Downey – you may also get to meet her ginger cat which features in her books. It's open by appointment; you can picnic here for free.

Llanthony

Four miles further into the Vale of Ewyas is the secluded hamlet of **LLANTHONY**, where a handful of houses, an inn and a few farms cluster around the remains of **Llanthony Priory**, whose ruins retain a real sense of spirituality and peace, set against an inspiring backdrop of river and mountain. It's believed the priory was founded on the site of a ruined chapel around 1100 by Norman knight William de Lacy, who was allegedly so captivated by the site that he renounced worldly life and founded a hermitage, attracting like-minded recluses and forming Wales' first Augustine priory. The church and outbuildings still standing today were constructed in the latter half of the twelfth century. Roving episcopal envoy Giraldus Cambrensis visited the emerging priory church in 1188, noting that "here the monks, sitting in their cloisters, enjoying the fresh air, when they happen to look up at the horizon behold the tops of mountains, as it were touching the heavens". A track behind the ruins winds up to the Offa's Dyke Path's atop a lofty, windy ridge.

Fashioned out of part of the tumbledown priory, the *Llanthony Priory Hotel* (☎01873/890487, @www.llanthonyprioryhotel.co.uk; ❸) was built in the eighteenth century as a hunting lodge and has a cellar bar with arches constructed in the twelfth century. Even the most easily accessed of the four antique-laden rooms (with shared bathrooms) involves scaling a narrow spiral staircase, and the tower rooms are several steep flights up; there's also an equally atmospheric restaurant (July & Aug open for lunch daily, dinner Mon–Sat; April–June & Sept–Oct lunch Tues–Sun, dinner Tues–Sat; Nov–March dinner Fri & Sat, lunch Sat & Sun). At the other end of the ruins, *Court Farm* (☎01873/890359, @www.llanthony.co.uk) offers great self-catering units in the farmhouse (April–Sept weekly bookings only, from £305 per week; Oct–March, weekly bookings, or three-night stays for £235), together with a lovely bunkhouse (£10) in an old stone barn called *The Wain House* (usually taken by groups, so minimum charges may apply). Pre-booking is essential for both. There's also basic camping (£3 per person) here, as well as **pony trekking** (half/full day from £25/42). A hundred yards north along the road from the priory the *Half Moon Inn* (☎01873/890611, @www.halfmoon-llanthony .co.uk; ❷) offers solid pub food (including lots of vegetarian options), a toasty open fire and comfy beds.

Capel-y-ffin and the Gospel Pass

From Llanthony, the road climbs alongside the narrowing Honddu River before coasting by ruined farmhouses for four miles to the isolated hamlet of **CAPEL–Y–FFIN**. Locked in the middle of sheer hills, it has a devotional feel, due to the fact that the village is made up of little more than two tiny chapels (one accommodating a congregation of just 20 people) and a curious ruined monastery. A lane forks off by the phone box, leading up to the ruins of the privately owned (and confusingly named) **Llanthony Monastery**, founded in 1870 by the Reverend Joseph Lyne. The religious order failed to survive his death in 1908, but the place later became a self-sufficient outpost of the art world when, in 1924, it was bought by English sculptor, typeface designer and eccentric Eric Gill, whose commune, a motley collection of artists and their families, drew much of their creative inspiration from the area.

From Llanthony Monastery, the hedge-lined road narrows further still as it weaves a tortuous route up into the **Gospel Pass** and out onto the glorious roof of the Black Mountains. A howling, windy moor by **Hay Bluff**, five miles up from Capel-y-ffin, affords panoramic views and terrific walking over springy hills. The road drops just as suddenly as it climbed, descending five miles into Hay-on-Wye.

Facilities around here are essentially limited to *The Grange* (☎01873/890215, ⓦ www.grangetrekking.co.uk; closed Nov–Easter; ❷), a comfortable B&B with extensive gardens in which you can pitch a tent (£5). You can also get well-priced evening meals here, and staff can organize **pony trekking** (from £14 per hour).

Hay-on-Wye and around

The quaint border town of **HAY-ON-WYE** (Y Gelli), at the northern tip of the Brecon Beacons, is synonymous with secondhand books. Since the first bookshop opened here in the 1960s, just about every spare inch of space has been given over to the trade, including the old cinema, houses, shops and even the crumbling stone castle. There are now well over thirty bookshops in town, alongside an increasing number of antique shops, galleries and fine-food haunts.

Always busy, Hay positively bursts at the seams in the last week of May, when fashionable London and international literati decamp here for the

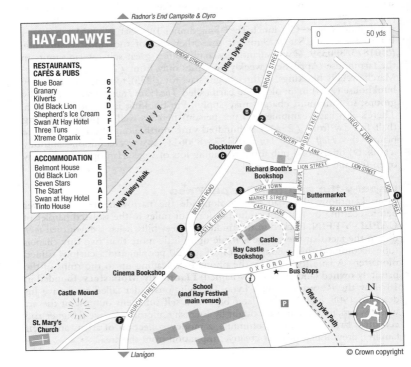

▲ Radnor's End Campsite & Clyro

HAY-ON-WYE

0   50 yds

RESTAURANTS, CAFÉS & PUBS
Blue Boar   6
Granary   2
Kilverts   4
Old Black Lion   D
Shepherd's Ice Cream 3
Swan At Hay Hotel F
Three Tuns   1
Xtreme Organix   5

ACCOMMODATION
Belmont House   E
Old Black Lion   D
Seven Stars   B
The Start   A
Swan at Hay Hotel F
Tinto House   C

Clocktower

Richard Booth's Bookshop

Buttermarket

Castle
Hay Castle Bookshop

Cinema Bookshop

Castle Mound

St. Mary's Church

School (and Hay Festival main venue)

Bus Stops

▼ Llanigon

© Crown copyright

Guardian Hay Festival (℡0870/787 2848, @www.hayfestival.com), a leading literary festival dubbed the "Woodstock of the mind" by former festival attendee, Bill Clinton. The town also fills during the increasingly high-profile single-day **Hay Food Festival** in late June, featuring around fifty artisan producers from across Wales. Any time of year, there's wonderful walking to be had in the surrounding countryside.

Arrival and information

Buses from Brecon and Hereford stop by the Oxford Road car park, next to the **tourist office** (daily: Easter–Oct 10am–5pm, closed 1–2pm Tues, Thurs & Sun; Nov–Easter 11am–1pm & 2–4pm; ℡01497/820144, @www.hay-on-wye .co.uk), which is housed in a modern craft centre and publishes an invaluable **free booklet** detailing the town's bookshops, galleries, restaurants and bars. Staff can also advise on and make reservations for local accommodation, which can sometimes get booked up years in advance during the festival. *Drover Holidays* (℡01497/821 134, @www.droverholidays.co.uk) will deliver **bikes**.

Accommodation

As a major tourist venue, Hay is well served for accommodation, although prices are a little higher here than in other places nearby, and to date there are no hostels. The tourist office has details of dozens of additional romantic options in the surrounding countryside.

Hotels and guesthouses

Belmont House Belmont Rd ℡01497/820718, @www.hay-on-wye.co.uk/belmont. Classy yet affordable Georgian guesthouse, with spacious rooms (some en suite) and friendly family management. ❷–❸

Old Black Lion Lion St ℡01497/820841, @www.oldblacklion.co.uk. The best-known place in town, with excellent accommodation in a candlelit thirteenth-century inn. ❺–❻

Old Post Office Llanigon, 2 miles south of Hay ℡01497/820008, @www.oldpost-office.co.uk. A wonderful seventeenth-century vegetarian B&B which is well placed for local walks, including the Offa's Dyke Path. ❸–❹

Seven Stars Broad St ℡01497/820886. Former town pub near the clock tower, with a good range of simple bedrooms, plus an indoor swimming pool and sauna. ❹

The Start Hay Bridge ℡01497/821391, @www .the-start.net. Lovely renovation of a Georgian riverside house on the far side of the town bridge. ❸

Swan at Hay Hotel Church St ℡01497/ 821188, @www.swanathay.co.uk. The town's most formal hotel, with spotless and attractively furnished rooms, plus elegant dining. ❻–❼

Tinto House Broad St ℡01497/820590, @www .tintohouse.co.uk. Charming old house with a huge, peaceful garden available to guests. ❸

Campsite

Radnors End Five minutes' walk from town across the Wyde-bridge on the road to Clyro ℡01497/820780, @www.hay-on-wye.co.uk /radnorsend. Beautiful setting overlooking Hay with on-site showers and laundry facilities. £5 per pitch.

The Town

The written word is the chief concern of this small market town, and the best place to start sampling the wares is up the track towards the castle that starts opposite the tourist office, where you'll find **Hay Castle Bookshop**, with racks of overspill books stacked in canopied shelves outside, with honesty boxes for payment. The shop specializes in an unlikely mix of photography, transport, humour and Native American history, along with decorative lengths of binding sold by the shelf-foot (popular with interior designers and theme pub developers). Here – or from the tourist office – you can pick up the annually revised

Richard Booth and the Hay book business

Richard Booth, whose family originates in the area, opened the first of his Hay-on-Wye **second-hand bookshops** in 1961. Since then, he has built an astonishing empire and attracted other booksellers to the town, turning it into the greatest market of used books in the world.

Whereas so many mid-Welsh and border towns have seen populations ebb away over the past half-century, Hay is booming on the strength of its bibliophilic connections. Booth views this transformation of a hitherto ordinary little market town as a prototype for reviving rural economies, based on local initiatives and unusual specialisms. This, coupled with Hay's geographical location slap-bang on the Wales–England border and Booth's own self-promotional skills, led him to declare Hay independent of the UK in 1977, with himself, naturally, as king. He appoints his own ministers and offers "official" government scrolls, passports and car stickers to visitors. Although such a proclamation carries no weight officially, most of the people of Hay seem to have rallied behind King Richard and are delighted with the publicity – and visitors – that the town's continuing high profile attracts.

Booth's avant-garde ideas and the events surrounding the 1977 delaration are laid out in his entertaining autobiography, *My Kingdom of Books* (Y Lolfa); he also has a website at ⊛ www.richardbooth.demon.co.uk.

Hay-on-Wye Booksellers, Printsellers & Bookbinders leaflet (free), detailing all the town's booksellers and literary happenings. The **castle** itself, a fire-damaged Jacobean mansion built into the walls of a thirteenth-century fortress, is owned by Hay's ruling "monarch", Richard Booth (see box above).

Most of the town's bookshops cluster on and around Castle Street, such as the **Hay Cinema Bookshop**, housed in the old town cinema and great for new remaindered editions at low prices. Just off the top of Castle Street, **Richard Booth's Bookshop**, at 44 Lion St, is the largest in Hay – a huge, draughty warehouse offering almost unlimited browsing potential among its half a million tomes. These days it's no longer owned by Booth, but still trades under his name. As well as general-category bookshops such as these, there are many highly specialized bookshops, including ones dedicated solely to travel, poetry, children, and even "murder and mayhem".

Around Hay

From Broad Street, Bridge Street passes over the River Wye and climbs the hill towards **CLYRO**, little more than a mile away, home to a couple of small commercial art galleries trading on Clyro's connections with nineteenth-century wandering parson Francis Kilvert. Although Kilvert was vicar of Clyro for only seven years (1865–72), the village, its glorious surroundings and its precisely recorded inhabitants featured prominently in his published diaries, drawing a steady trickle of pilgrims ever since.

The A438 heads south, through the one-horse hamlet of **LLOWES**, whose church of St Meilig houses a hefty three-ton, seventh-century Celtic cross. A mile further, a lane to the right climbs to **MAESYRONNEN**, where the low-roofed barn chapel, built in 1696, is the oldest surviving Nonconformist worship house in Wales. If it's locked, and you want to see the whitewashed interior with its old benches and stacked wooden pulpit, get the key from the Old Post Office in Ffynnon Gynydd, a mile up the lane.

Eating, drinking and entertainment

The *Old Black Lion* and *Swan at Hay Hotel* (p.243 for both) both have tasty bar snacks and pricier restaurants, and are recommended for drinking and dining.

Blue Boar Castle St. Tasteful, wood-panelled real ale pub on the corner with Oxford Rd.

Granary Broad St. Unpretentious, moderately priced café and bistro with a wide range of excellent vegetarian and meat-based meals, many made from local produce. Save space for the wonderful desserts and good espresso. Free wi-fi.

Kilverts Bull Ring at the corner of Market St and Bell Bank ☎ 01497/821042. Warm and friendly locals' pub, with an imaginative, moderate to expensive menu which might extend to crab and prawn terrine or chargrilled sirloin with brandy and mushroom sauce. In summer it's the venue for Hay's only regular live music.

Shepherd's Ice Cream 9 High Town. Daytime Georgian-style ice cream parlour selling local ice cream made from sheep's milk, often in offbeat flavours like blackcurrant cheesecake, rose, or chocolate and chilli.

Three Tuns Broad St. Set in Hay's second-oldest building (after the castle), the ancient stonework, outdoor terrace and crackling open fires make for an atmospheric dining spot. Food includes creations such as honey-glazed Welsh lamb shank with spring onion mash, or smoked haddock, salmon and dill fishcakes, all at moderate prices. Closed Mon and Tues.

XtremeOrganiX 10b Castle St ☎ 01497/847258. The bio-friendly "XOX" has a small day/night café for curries, pizzas, kebabs and burgers, plus a deli and take-away service, where everything, even the soft drinks, is local.

Radnorshire and Montgomeryshire

Even quieter than the quiet Brecon Beacons, the northern tranche of Powys – comprising the old counties of Radnorshire and Montgomeryshire – is a hugely rewarding area to explore. This is farming country, where urban life comes no bigger than a few small market towns. Between the towns, the contours of the impossibly green, sheep-flecked farmland are shaped by the glassy lakes and lively rivers that run down from the open moorland of the Cambrian Mountains, which form Wales' spine. Despite the area's remoteness, the quality and pace of life here has proved irresistible to "alternative" lifestylers over the years, resulting in wholefood cafés and quirky festivals.

In the south of **Radnorshire**, four distinctly different communities jointly form the **Wells towns** (spa towns), each of which grew up around a reputedly health-giving spring. There's more water in the **Elan Valley**, to the west, centred around four interlocking reservoirs and graced by an abundance of red kites. To the east, close to the English border, **Presteigne** is a charming village with a great museum, while for walkers, **Knighton** is ideally situated at the start of **Glyndŵr's Way**, as well as midway along the eighth-century **Offa's Dyke**.

The northernmost section of Powys is mellow **Montgomeryshire**. Good bases include the cheerily offbeat little town of **Llanidloes**, the laid-back northern outpost of **Llanfyllin,** the stately old county town of **Montgomery** and its much larger and more bustling replacement, **Welshpool**.

The Wells towns

Straddling the old border of Brecknockshire and Radnorshire, around fifteen miles north of Brecon, mid-Wales' four former spa towns are strung out along the Heart of Wales rail line and the main A483. All were obscure villages up until the eighteenth century, until royalty and nobility spearheaded the fashion for taking a cure. Once the railway arrived, the four Welsh spas became much more egalitarian, each developing its own distinct clientele and atmosphere.

There westernmost spa of **Llanwrtyd Wells**, hunkered down beneath stunning mountain scenery, is best known for its weird array of offbeat festivals and unusual events. Blink and you'd miss tiny **Llangammarch Wells**, though thriving **Builth Wells** is definitely worth a stop. **Llandrindod Wells** retains some exceptional Victorian-era, architecture but the place is struggling these days.

Llanwrtyd Wells and around

Around twenty miles northwest of Brecon, **LLANWRTYD WELLS** was the spa to which the Welsh − farmers of Dyfed alongside the Nonconformist middle classes from Glamorgan − came to great eisteddfodau in the valley of the Irfon. Nowadays, it's the Welsh capital of **wacky festivals and events** − ranging from the world bog-snorkelling championships to a man-versus-horse race, as well as numerous biking/walking/beer-drinking combination weekends. Call the tourist office for more information or visit ⓦ www.green-events.co.uk.

Main Street runs through the centre of town, crossing the Irfon River just below the main square, Y Sgwar, dominated by a stunning sculpture of a red kite by Sandy O'Connor. Although the sulphurous aroma had been apparent in the area for centuries, it was "discovered" in 1732 by the local priest, Theophilus

▲ Red Kite

Evans, who drank from a vile-smelling spring after seeing a healthy frog pop out of it. The spring, named **Ffynnon Drewllyd** (Stinking Well), bubbles up amongst the dilapidated spa buildings on Dolecoed Road.

Practicalities

Llanwrtyd's hot-pink-painted, independently run **tourist office**, just off the main square (daily except Tues 10am–5pm; ☎01591/610666, ⓦwww.llanwrtyd.com), has cheap internet access and sells homemade baked goods as well as local art and crafts. **Bike rental** is available at Cycles Irfon, a third of a mile northeast of town at *24 Erw Haf, Ffos Road* (☎01591/610668, ⓦwww.cyclesirfon.co.uk). Nearby, also on Ffos Road, you can saddle up for **pony trekking** at *Ffos Farm* (☎01591/610459, ⓦwww.ffosfarm.co.uk).

Accommodation, eating and drinking

Accommodation should be booked well in advance during festivals.

Ardwyn House Station Rd
☎01591/610768, ⓦwww.ardwynhouse .co.uk. Stunning turn-of-the-twentieth-century period piece with rich detailing including roll-top baths in some rooms (all are en suite) and a book-lined billiards room. ❸–❹

Carlton Riverside Llandovery Rd
☎01591/610248, ⓦwww.carltonrestaurant.co.uk. Lovely restaurant, dishing up superb French-inspired Welsh cuisine, plus cosy contemporary rooms. ❸–❺

Drover's Rest Riverside Restaurant By the river bridge ☎01591/610264, ⓦwww .food-food-food.co.uk. Classy and cosy B&B accommodation, both above its restaurant (serving up wholesome traditional Welsh dishes), and in the nearby High View House. Also runs cookery and art classes. ❸

Neuadd Arms In the main square
☎01591/610236, ⓦwww.neuaddarmshotel.co.uk. This lively place is home to the Heart of Wales Brewery, which produces five fabulous ales that you can soak up with good bar food, including some great curries. Also has some fairly basic but generally spacious rooms. ❸

Stonecroft Inn Dolecoed Rd
☎01591/610332, ⓦwww.stonecroft .co.uk. Superb pub with great food, locally brewed real ales, and regular live music as well as beds (from £14) in its self-catering hostel. Check with the tourist office for updates on camping in the area.

Mynydd Eppynt and Llangammarch Wells

To the south of Llanwrtyd Wells, the remote **Crychan Forest** and the rippling mountains of the **Mynydd Eppynt** make up the northern outcrops of the Brecon Beacons, best seen from the roads that snake across the moors from the towns of Garth and Builth. The bulk of the Eppynt, however, has been appropriated by the British Army, as evidenced by the many red flags flying stiffly, warning you not to stop or touch anything.

The B4519 descends dramatically from the Eppynt above a beautifully isolated valley, the **Cwm Graig Ddu**. At the bottom of the hill, a lane forks left to join the River Irfon as it winds to **LLANGAMMARCH WELLS**, four miles east of Llanwrtyd. A mile before the village is the exquisite half-timbered *Lake Country House* (☎01591/620202, ⓦwww.lakecountryhouse.co.uk; ❽–❾), the home of a now defunct barium well that attracted Lloyd George and foreign heads of state seeking cures. It now offers a decadent pool, outdoor hot tub and beauty treatments, as well as fishing on the grounds. The village also has excellent fishing and walking at hand, but there's little to do otherwise.

Abergwesyn and the Abergwesyn Pass

Five miles north of Llanwrtyd, the lane from Llanwrtyd meets up with another road from Beulah at the riverside hamlet of **ABERGWESYN**, home to the

Coed Trallwm Mountain Bike Centre (☎01591/610546, ⓦwww
.coedtrallwm.co.uk), from where three graded trails fan out. You'll need to
bring your own bike, however, as there's no rental here. The centre's visitor
centre occupies a log cabin with an organic café (daily noon–4pm in winter,
longer hours in summer).

From the centre, a magnificent winding road twists up to the **Abergwesyn
Pass**, threading its way up through dense conifer forests to wide, gorse- and
heather-strewn valleys bereft of any sign of human habitation, framed by craggy
peaks and waterfalls. At the little bridge over the tiny Tywi River, a track heads
south past the wonderfully isolated, gaslit *Elenydd Wilderness Hostel* (bookings
☎0870/7708868 or 01443/790720, ⓦwww.elenydd-hostels.co.uk; dorm beds
£10) at **Dolgoch**.

On the other side of the river, a new road channels past the thick forest on to
Llyn Brianne (see p.170), a couple of miles further on. This is as remote a
walking holiday as can be had in Wales – paths lead from Dolgoch, through the
forests and hillsides to the exquisitely isolated chapel at **Soar-y-Mynydd** and
beyond, over the mountains to the next *Elenydd Wilderness Hostel*, Ty'n Cornel,
(also spelt Tyncornel; same contact details and prices as *Elenydd Wilderness Hostel*,
Dolgoch), five strenuous miles from Dolgoch. Advance bookings for both
wilderness hostels are essential during winter.

From Dolgoch, the road continues over expansive terrain before dropping
down along the rounded valley of the Berwyn River and into Tregaron.
Although the entire Llanwrtyd–Tregaron route is less than twenty miles in
length, it takes a good hour for drivers to negotiate the twisting, narrow road
safely. The old drovers, driving their cattle to Shrewsbury or Hereford, would
have taken at least a day or two over the same stretch.

Builth Wells and around

Once the spa of the Welsh working classes, **BUILTH WELLS** (Llanfair ym
Muallt) still has a vibrant, welcoming feel, as well as good amenities and
transport links. The town stretches along the Wye below its architecturally
jumbled High Street, home to some great local shops such as Foreman's
Emporium, at nos. 25–27, a superb stationery and bookshop with many old
and new works on Wales. High Street becomes Broad Street as it descends to
the town bridge, where you'll find an eye-catching mural of Prince Llywelyn
and the multipurpose **Wyeside Arts Centre** (☎01982/552555,
ⓦwww.wyeside.co.uk), converted out of the town's Victorian Assembly
Rooms. On the other side of the river is Builth's major modern source of
prosperity, the **Royal Welsh Showground** (☎01982/553683, ⓦwww.rwas
.co.uk), which hosts numerous agricultural events, together with monthly
flea markets and occasional specialized collectors' fairs. The highlight on its
calendar is the **animated Royal Welsh Show**, Europe's largest agricultural
fair, which takes place over four days in mid- to late July, attracting over
100,000 visitors.

Practicalities

Builth Road **train station** is nearly three miles north of the town and
inaccessible by public transport – a taxi (☎01982/551159 or 553210) costs
about £5. **Buses** depart from the car park by the river bridge, where you'll
find the **tourist office** (Easter–Sept Mon–Sat 9.30am–5pm, Sun 10am–4pm;
Oct–Easter Mon–Sat 9.30am–4pm, Sun 10am–4pm; ☎01982/553307,
ⓔbuiltic@powys.gov.uk), whose staff can provide advice about all the

surrounding area. **Bike rental** is available from John Lloyd at Builth Wells Cycles (℡01982/552923); there's no shop – call for delivery.

Accommodation is cheap: try the *Bron Wye* B&B at 5 Church St (℡01982/553587, Ⓦwww.bronwye.co.uk; ❷), in a nineteenth-century mansion surrounded by gardens and with free in-room wi-fi; the cheerful *Greyhound Hotel* (℡01982/553255, Ⓦwww.thegreyhoundhotel.co.uk; ❹), a few minutes west of the town centre; or, if your budget permits, the impeccably restored *Lion Hotel* (℡01982/553311, Ⓦwww.lionhotelbuilthwells.com; ❻), at the end of the bridge on Broad Street, with contemporary, autumnal-hued rooms. If you prefer something more bucolic, consider one of eight remote **self-catering** cottages around town (℡01591/610229, Ⓦwww.forestcottages.co.uk; two-night minimum stay, from £159).

Builth has numerous cheap daytime cafés, and evening **dining** options are improving all the time: in addition to **pubs** like those at the *Greyhound* and the *Lion* hotels (see above), good bets include the *Calon Wen* bistro on Groe Street and the new riverside *Llanfair Hotel* on The Strand, with a large garden and kids' play area. For plain old **drinking**, head to the *White Horse* or the *Fountain*, both on Broad Street/High Street.

Cilmeri

CILMERI, an unassuming village that straggles along the main A483 road and rail line between Builth and Llanwrtyd, is a place of pilgrimage for many Welsh people, as it was here that the last native Prince of Wales, Llywelyn ap Gruffydd, was slain by the English army in December 1282. On realizing whom they had killed, it's said the English soldiers hacked off Llywelyn's head, whereupon it was dispatched to London and paraded victoriously through the city's streets. A large, pointed granite boulder on a small hillock to the side of the main road marks the spot. The English tablet by the monument calls Llywelyn "our prince". Its Welsh equivalent, tellingly, describes him as *ein llyw olaf* – "our last leader". Semantics aside, you are unlikely ever to see the monument without someone's fresh flowers adorning it.

Llandrindod Wells and around

Following the 1864 arrival of the railway, **LLANDRINDOD WELLS** (Llandrindod; locally referred to as "Llandod" or simply "Dod"), was once Wales' most elegant spa resort. Its Victorian heyday is long since over, however, and although many of the fine buildings from the era still stand, today the town is notoriously plagued by economic and social problems. Still, it's worth a brief stop to admire the faded glamour of its ornate architecture. And, perhaps signalling better times ahead, work is underway to restore the once-lavish **spa pump room** in **Rock Park**, the site of the mineral-rich springs, from where a walking path leads to "**Lovers' Leap**", a Victorian fake cliff overlooking the river.

Buses arrive outside the **train station**, in the heart of town between the High Street and Station Crescent. On the station platform is an old London North Western Railway **signal box** (June–Aug Fri & Sat 11am–3pm; free), which houses an interesting little display about the railway and its spirited survival in the face of repeated plans for closure over the last fifty years. The largest annual event is the **Victorian Festival**, held in the last week of August, which culminates in a firework extravaganza over the town lake. The longer-established annual town **eisteddfod** takes place in early October. **Market day** is Friday.

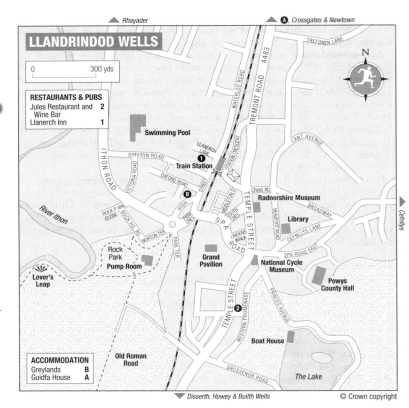

LLANDRINDOD WELLS

N

0   300 yds

RESTAURANTS & PUBS

Jules Restaurant and Wine Bar	**2**
Llanerch Inn	**1**

TREFONEN LANE

WATERLOO ROAD

A483

TREMONT ROAD

LANT AVENUE

Swimming Pool

LLANERCH LANE

DYFFRYN ROAD

ITHON ROAD

STATION CRESCENT

Train Station **1**

VICTORIA ROAD

OXFORD ROAD

HIGH STREET

MIDDLETON ST

B

CRAIG RD.

Radnorshire Museum

BROADWAY

River Ithon

ROCK PARK CLOSE

ROCK HO. RD

NORTON TER.

SOUTH CRES.

SPA ROAD

TEMPLE STREET

BEAUFORT ROAD

Library

CEFNLLYS LANE

Cefnllys

PARK TER.

PARK CRES.

LINDENS WALK

Rock Park Pump Room

Lover's Leap

Grand Pavilion

SPA ROAD EAST

National Cycle Museum

Powys County Hall

TEMPLE STREET

WESTERN PROMENADE

PRINCES AVENUE

2

Boat House

ACCOMMODATION

Greylands	**B**
Guidfa House	**A**

Old Roman Road

GROSVENOR ROAD

The Lake

Disserth, Howey & Builth Wells   © Crown copyright

On Temple Street, the small **Radnorshire museum** (April–Sept Tues–Fri 10am–4pm, Sat 10am–5pm, Sun 1–5pm; Oct–March Tues–Fri 10am–4pm, Sat 10am–1pm; £1) evokes the area's history with exhibits ranging from archeological finds to items from Victorian spa days. The adjacent rockery **grotto**, a nineteenth-century whimsy, was built by a local doctor.

A nostalgic collection of over 250 bikes – including ordinaries (aka penny-farthings), an eight-foot-high "Eiffel Tower" advertising bike from 1899, and trikes – is displayed at Britain's **National Cycle Exhibition** at the corner of Temple Street and Spa Road (March–Oct daily 10am–4pm; call ☎01597/825531 for winter hours; £2.50). Local **walks** from Llandrindod include routes to Cefnllys, taking in the witch's-hat spire of the thirteenth-century **St Michael's Church** and **Bailey Einon Wood** nature reserve; and to Disserth on up into the **Carneddau Hills** – Builth Wells' tourist office (see p.248) has maps and advice.

Should you need to **stay** overnight in town, your best bet is *Greylands* on High Street (☎01597/822253; **②**), a tall Victorian red-brick house in the town centre, near the station. Otherwise head three miles north on the A43 to *Guidfa House*, Crossgates (☎01597/851241, **ⓦ**www.guidfa-house.co.uk; **④**), a relaxing Georgian guesthouse with mostly en-suite rooms, free wi-fi and great meals made from local produce. For **eating** and **drinking**, the sixteenth-century *Llanerch Inn*, on Llanerch Lane, is central Llandrindod's only pub, and predates most of the surrounding town; serving up good-value, well-cooked classics. Alternatively, enjoy a glass of wine and a tasty midday or evening meal at *Jules Restaurant and Wine Bar* on Temple Street.

North and East Radnorshire

Before the reorganization of British counties in 1974, Radnorshire was the most sparsely populated county in either Wales or England, and it's still a remote area, especially to the north and east. In the northwest, **Rhayader** is the only settlement of any real size. Most people base themselves here to explore the wild, spartan countryside to the west of the town, a hilly patchwork of waterfalls, bogland, bare peaks and the four interlocking reservoirs of the **Elan Valley**, built at the beginning of the twentieth century and displaying a grandiose Edwardian solidity.

The countryside to the northeast of Rhayader is slightly tamer, with lanes and bridlepaths delving in and around the woods and farms, occasionally brushing through minute settlements like the village of **Abbeycwmhir**, named for the deserted Cistercian abbey that sits below in the dank, eerie valley of the Clywedog Brook. From here, the hills roll eastwards towards the English border and some of the most intact parts of **Offa's Dyke**, the eighth-century King of Mercia's border with the Welsh princes. The handsome border town of **Knighton** is well geared-up for walkers and cyclists. Seven miles south and inches from England, the dignified town of **Presteigne** contains some intriguing reminders of its former role as the county capital. The River Lugg flows through Presteigne from the Radnorshire hills, passing the isolated church at **Pilleth**, where Owain Glyndŵr captured Sir Edmund Mortimer, agent of the English king, in 1402.

Rhayader and around

RHAYADER (Rhaeder Gwy, literally "waterfall on the Wye"), ten miles west of Llandrindod Wells, lays claim to having the most pubs per capita in the entire UK: twelve, which works out at one for every 173 of the town's population of 2075. Although the waterfall invoked by the town's name virtually disappeared when the town bridge was built in 1780, the Wye still frames the town centre, running in a loop around the western and southern sides. Rhayader was a centre of the mid-nineteenth-century "**Rebecca Riots**", when local farmers disguised themselves in women's clothing in order to tear down tollgates that were prohibitively expensive for travellers and local workers.

Rhayader's four main streets – named North, South, East and West – meet at a small clock tower in the centre of town. Three miles north of town, just off the A470, is the peaceful **Gilfach Farm Nature Reserve** (unrestricted access; free), the showpiece of the Radnorshire Wildlife Trust. Within the 418 acres are meadows, oak forest, moorland, an old railway tunnel that's home to some bats, and river habitats supporting a huge variety of wildlife and flora. The restored longhouse barn has now been kitted out as a **visitor and exhibition centre** (April–Sept Mon & Fri–Sun 10am–5pm), showing live video footage from ten birds' nests around the reserve. To watch **red kites feeding**, head to **Gigrin Farm** (£3), off South Road (the A470 from Builth) on the outskirts of town, where they are lured daily at 3pm (2pm in winter).

Practicalities

Buses stop in the main Dark Lane car park behind the leisure centre. Eighteenth-century coaching inns line the main streets, while more modern **accommodation** includes the cheerful *Brynteg* B&B on East Street (℡01597/810052; ❶), and the *Elan Hotel* on West Street (℡01597/810109, Ⓦwww.elanhotel.co.uk; ❷). The cheapest place in town is *Greenfields* on South Street (℡01597/811101; ❶), which offers B&B and hostel beds (£13–15). Almost two miles northeast of town, off the Abbeycwmhir road, is *Beili Neuadd* (℡01597/810211, Ⓦwww.midwalesfarmstay.co.uk; dorm beds £14, ❷), a laid-back farmhouse B&B which also has a sixteenth-century stone barn **bunkhouse**. There's a **campsite** at *Wyeside* (℡01597/810183; £2 per pitch plus £5.50 per adult), a few hundred yards north of town off the A44, or a quieter and less flashy option a fifteen-minute walk south of town at *Gigrin Farm* (℡01597/810243, Ⓦwww.gigrin.co.uk; £4.50 per tent, £10 per van), the red kite feeding station. **Bikes** can be rented, and all-inclusive cycling packages booked, through the redoubtable Clive Powell Mountain Bikes (℡01597/811343, Ⓦwww.clivepowell-mtb.co.uk) on West Street, which serves yummy baked goods, and sometimes organic evening meals, at its **café** (call ahead as hours vary).

At the junction of West and South streets, *Carole's Old Swan* daytime tearooms is the place to go for steaming jacket potatoes and fabulous cakes. Evening **meals** are good at the moderate *Brynafon* restaurant (℡01597/810735), half a mile south on the road to Builth Wells, or at Rhayader's record number of pubs. Try the lively *Crown Inn* on North Street, or, over Bridge Street in the small hamlet of **LLANSANTFFRAED CWMDEUDDWR**, usually shortened to Cwmdeuddwr, the ancient *Triangle Inn*, where darts players must stand in a special floor hole for fear of spearing the roof.

Elan Valley

Until the last decade of the nineteenth century, the untamed countryside west of Rhayader received few visitors, although the poet Shelley did holiday here: his honeymoon retreat at Nantgwyllt was amongst the couple of dozen buildings submerged by the waters of the **Elan Valley** reservoirs, a nine-mile-long string of four lakes created between 1892 and 1903 to supply water to the rapidly growing industrial city of Birmingham, 75 miles away; in the 1950s, a supplementary reservoir at Claerwen, to the immediate west, was opened (see opposite). Although the lakes enhance an already beautiful and idyllic part of the world, the colonialist way in which Welsh valleys, villages and farmsteads were seized and flooded to provide water for England is something the tourist boards prefer to gloss over. The natural resentment against this has perhaps been best expressed by poet R.S. Thomas in his soulful elegy, *Reservoirs*:

There are places in Wales I don't go:
Reservoirs that are the subconscious
Of a people, troubled far down
With gravestones, chapels, villages even;
The serenity of their expression
Revolts me, it is a pose
For strangers, a watercolour's appeal
To the mass, instead of the poem's
Harsher conditions. There are the hills,
Too; gardens gone under the scum
Of the forests; and the smashed faces
Of the farms with the stone trickle
Of their tears down the hills' side.

The "watercolour's appeal" of the Elan Valley is, nonetheless, extremely strong, not only for the landscape but the profusion of rare plants and birds in the area. **Red kites** are especially cherished – in the 1930s, when numbers were down to just a couple of breeding pairs, the Elan Valley looked set to enter the history books as their last outpost in Britain. Loss of habitat, along with nest robbing by collectors and poisoning at the hands of farmers, were largely to blame, but conservation work undertaken by a few dedicated individuals saved the day. Since then, these birds of prey have staged an impressive recovery, becoming so common they've started repopulating surrounding areas.

From Rhayader, the B4518 heads southwest four miles to **ELAN** village, a curious collection of stone houses built in 1909 to replace the reservoir constructors' village that had grown up on the site. Just below the dam of the first reservoir, **Caban Coch**, the **Elan Valley visitor centre** (mid-March to Oct daily 10am–5.30pm; ℡01597/810898, 🌐www.elanvalley.org.uk), incorporates a permanent exhibition about the history and ecology of the area. Frequent guided **walks** and **Land Rover safaris** head off from the centre. The best place to **stay** here is the *Elan Valley Hotel* (℡01597/810448, 🌐www .elanvalleyhotel.co.uk; ❹–❺), an imposing neocolonial pile on the Rhayader side of Elan village, which offers great food, comfy rooms and a lively bar.

From the visitor centre, a road tucks in along the bank of Caban Coch to the **Garreg Ddu** viaduct, from where you can follow the bank for four spectacular miles to the vast, rather chilling 1952 dam on **Claerwen Reservoir**. More remote and less popular than the Elan lakes, Claerwen is a good base for the more determined walker with paths for eight to ten miles across the harsh terrain to the abbey of Strata Florida or the lonely **Teifi Pools**.

Back at the Garreg Ddu viaduct, a more popular road continues north along the long, glassy finger of **Garreg Ddu** reservoir, before doubling back on itself just below the awesome **Pen-y-garreg** dam and reservoir; if the dam is overflowing, the vast wall of foaming water is mesmerizing. At the top of Pen-y-garreg lake, it's possible to drive over the dam at **Craig Goch** for a close-up view of its gracious curve, elegant Edwardian arches and green cupola. The lake beyond it is fed by the Elan River, which the road crosses just short of a junction. A bleak, invigorating moorland pass heads west from here before dropping into the eerie moonscape of Cwmystwyth (see p.296), while the eastbound road funnels into a beautiful valley back to Rhayader. On the way back, fork off the Elan Valley Road in Rhayader onto the smaller Aberystwyth Road.

The only **bus** route hereabouts is the postbus from Llandrindod and Rhayader (Mon–Fri 2 daily), which continues on to the Elan Valley visitor centre from April to October. Catching the first bus and returning on the second allows you to spend around three hours in and around the visitor centre.

Abbeycwmhir

ABBEYCWMHIR (Abaty Cwm Hir) seven miles northeast of Rhayader, takes its name from the abbey whose sombre ruins (open access; free) lie beneath the village. Cistercian monks founded the abbey in 1146, planning one of the largest churches in Britain, whose 242-foot nave has only ever been exceeded in length by the cathedrals of Durham, York and Winchester. Destruction by Henry III's troops in 1231 scuppered plans to continue the building, however. The sparse ruins of what they did build – a rocky outline of the floorplan – lie in a conifer-carpeted valley alongside a gloomy green lake, lending weight, if only by atmosphere, to the site's melancholic associations. Llywelyn ap Gruffydd's body, after his head had been carted off to London, was rumoured to have been brought here from Cilmeri in 1282, and a new granite slab, carved with a Celtic sword, lies on the altar to commemorate this last native prince of Wales. It should look incongruous, but somehow it only adds to the eerie presence of the ruins and the village. Presiding over the ruins is the resplendent privately owned manor house **The Hall at Abbey-Cwm-Hir** (tours daily – advance booking essential – at 10am, 2pm & 7pm; ☎01597/851727, ⓦwww.abbeycwmhir.com/cms; daytime/evening tours £13/20, gardens only £5), set in twelve acres of flower-filled gardens and woodlands. Family members conduct tours through its 52 sumptuously restored rooms.

Presteigne and around

Twenty miles east of Llandrindod Wells, the charming town of **PRESTEIGNE** (Llanandras) has attracted refugees from the rat race ever since the 1960s, which accounts for the proliferation of craft, antique and bookshops and laid-back cafés occupying the town's gracious and old-fashioned buildings. The town tucks in between the B4362 town bypass and the River Lugg, the border with England, which flows under the seventeenth-century bridge at the bottom of Broad Street. Just before the bridge, the solid parish **church of St Andrew** contains Saxon and Norman fragments, as well as a sixteenth-century Flemish tapestry.

The town's standout attraction is the **Judge's Lodging** (March–Oct daily 10am–6pm; Nov to Christmas Wed–Sun 10am–4pm; £5.25), a fabulously interpreted trawl through the rooms where circuit judges stayed while presiding over the local assizes. Many of its original furnishings had been stashed in the attic, rediscovered only during its recent restoration to its 1868 grandeur. You now follow an audio tour, being "introduced" to characters along the way. Nothing is roped off or hidden behind screens, and it feels more like visiting a private home than a museum, while the oil lamps that light the upper floors and the gas-flame lighting in the servants' quarters provide a whiff of authenticity. Finally you emerge in the courtroom, where an alleged thief that you've "met" in the cells is being tried.

From the Judge's Lodging, Broad Street heads up to the main crossroads, with the High Street forking west and Hereford Street to the east. On the corner of Hereford and Broad streets, the nineteenth-century Italianate Assembly Rooms also house the town's library. High Street is the site of the town's most impressive and intriguing building, the Jacobean **Radnorshire Arms**, built as a private home for Sir Christopher Hatton, Lord Chancellor of England and, allegedly, lover of Queen Elizabeth I, who owned neighbouring property. Later, it became the home of local John Bradshaw who went on to become an English judge and a signatory to the death warrant of Charles I. Bradshaw died in 1659 and was buried in Westminster Abbey, but when Charles II reclaimed the throne in 1660, Bradshaw's body was exhumed and posthumously hanged and beheaded, along with the body of Oliver Cromwell. The building was subsequently owned by wealthy landowner Sir Henry Vaughan, known as a precursor to the Marquis de Sade for his "unnatural and repugnant acts", which eventually resulted in Vaughan being bludgeoned to death by the townsfolk. It was converted into an inn in 1792.

Practicalities

Buses from Knighton, Kington and Leominster stop outside the *Radnorshire Arms* or at the coach park on the bypass. The Judge's Lodging also contains the **tourist office** (March–Oct daily 10am–6pm; Nov to Christmas Wed–Sun 10am–4pm; ☎01544/260650, ⓦwww.presteigne.org.uk). Local **accommodation** options include the Jacobean luxury of the classy *Radnorshire Arms* (see above,

T01544/267406, @www.radnorshirearmshotel.com; ⑤). In the surrounding villages, options range from the sumptuous Victoriana of the award-winning, antique-furnished ⚇ *Old Vicarage* (T01544/260038, @www.oldvicarage -nortonrads.co.uk; ⑤) in Norton, two miles north on the road to Knighton, through to the homelier charms of *Gumma Farm* (T01547/560243; ❶–❷), nearly two miles west on the road to Discoed, where you can also **camp** (from £2 per person). Half a mile nearer town, there's more camping space at the riverside *Rockbridge Park* (T01547/560300, from £5 per person).

Good food options include the family-friendly *Radnorshire Arms* (see opposite); *Emily's Tea Rooms & Restaurant* (closed Mon lunch), on the High Street; and the *Hat Shop Restaurant* (closed Sun), also on the High Street and serving top-notch British cuisine.

Presteigne has become a centre for folk and traditional **music**. Excellent **festivals** in July and over the August bank holiday (details from the tourist office), include one organized by the free music paper *Broad Sheep* (@www .broadsheep.com), available from venues around town.

Old and New Radnor

Just off the A44 six miles southwest of Presteigne, **OLD RADNOR** was once the home of King Harold, killed at the Battle of Hastings by William the Conqueror's troops. The site of his castle is down the lane running southeast from the large, very English-looking **church**, overlooking a wooded vale. Inside the church, a massive eighth-century font on four stone feet is the most remarkable legacy. Opposite, in a rambling, fifteenth-century former farm building, the ⚇ *Harp Inn* (bar & restaurant Tues–Fri 6–11pm, Sat & Sun noon–3pm and 6–11pm; T01544/350655, @www.harpinnradnor.co.uk; ❸) serves delicious Welsh meals like bacon-wrapped wild rabbit in mustard and cream, plus a few Mediterranean excursions and hard-to-find real ales. They also have atmospheric rooms, some with four-poster or wrought-iron beds.

NEW RADNOR, just over two miles to the west, was originally built as a small Norman settlement. In the thirteenth century it was planned to expand it into a major city and capital of Radnorshire, though the project faltered, confirming Wales' antipathy towards large settlements in favour of scattered farmsteads. A Victorian steeple erected to honour local dignitary Sir George Cornewall Lewis (as you enter the village from the A44 to the southeast), is the only feature of the village that seems to suggest any kind of metropolitan status. Its couple of streets are pin-drop quiet, leaving it to the *Radnor Arms* and the *Eagle Hotel*, both on Broad Street, to liven things up. The latter sometimes has live music on Fridays.

The Radnor Forest

North of New Radnor, the deep ravines and wooded hillsides of **Radnor Forest** offer some of the region's best walking and birdwatching. The most popular route is along the driveable track that forks north off the A44 just over a mile west of New Radnor, leading into a thick forest and to the rushing cascade of the **Water-break-its-neck waterfall**, at its icicle-adorned best in winter. The trackway continues on past the heads of numerous steep valleys plunging down to the lowland, giving perhaps the best impression of the area's strange geology, before coming out at the village of **Llanfihangel Rhydithon** some five miles beyond Water-break-its-neck. Paths head off the track to the east, up and over the rounded peaks of the forest and down towards the hamlet of **Casgob**, deep in the northeastern corner. The tiny church here, complete with half-timbered tower, contains a remarkable sixteenth-century amulet, with numerous spiritual symbols, astrological motifs and the word "abracadabra" written as a triangular pattern said by various Gnostics and mystics to have been devised from secret knowledge more powerful than Christianity.

Three miles east of Casgob along tiny lanes, the small village church at **Discoed** is fronted by a yew tree dated to around 5000 years old, making it one of the oldest living organisms in Britain. It's an amazing sight: the centuries have split and cracked the bark, twisting the vast tree in all directions and creating a central chasm big enough to sit in, but fresh green shoots continue to sprout all the same.

The B4536 from Presteigne follows the River Lugg as it skirts the upper edge of the Radnor Forest and passes a delightful example of an unadorned Welsh country church at **PILLETH**. A quiet enough place these days, Pilleth had its moment in the spotlight on Midsummer Day in 1402 when it witnessed the bloodiest and most famous battle of Owain Glyndŵr's war of independence. The English forces, led by Edmund Mortimer, were routed by Glyndŵr's numerically fewer, but far sharper, troops. Mortimer was captured, and 1100 – about half – of the English troops were killed. The mass grave, a mound marked by four pine trees above the church, can still be seen today.

Knighton

Lively, attractive **KNIGHTON** (Tref-y-clawdd, "the town on the dyke"), six miles north of Presteigne, straddles King Offa's eighth-century border and the modern Wales–England divide, and has come into its own as a base for those walking the **Offa's Dyke Path** (see box opposite) and the **Glyndŵr's Way** footpath (see p.260).

So close is Knighton to the border that the town's **train station** is actually in England. From here, Station Road crosses the River Teme into Wales and climbs a couple of hundred yards into the town, joining the pretty Broad Street at Brookside Square. Further up the hill is the town's Victorian clock tower, where Broad Street becomes West Street and the steep High Street soars off up to the left, past rickety Tudor buildings and up to the mound of the old **castle**. In West Street, the excellent **Offa's Dyke Centre** (Easter–Oct Tues–Fri noon–5pm, Sat–Mon 10am–5pm; Nov–Easter call for hours; ☎01547/528753, ⊛www .offasdyke.demon.co.uk) also houses the **tourist office**.

Looming high above Knighton, a mile off the A4113, the **Spaceguard Centre** is housed in the former Powys County Observatory (open year-round, Wed–Sun & bank holiday tours at 2pm & 4pm, plus May–Oct at 10.30am; ☎01547/520247, ⊛www.spaceguarduk.com; £5) and has a planetarium, camera obscura and solar telescope. Call ahead if you're visiting in winter, as it tends to shut for a few days.

Accommodation in Knighton is plentiful and generally good value. Options include the revamped *Knighton Hotel*, right in the town centre on Broad Street (☎01547/520530, ⊛www.knightonhotel.co.uk; ❷); *Fleece House* B&B, at the top of the High Street (☎01547/520168, ⊛www.fleecehouse.co.uk; ❸), with en-suite twin rooms; and the independent hostel *Ffrydd House* (☎01547/520374, ⊛www.border-holidays.co.uk; ❶), 13 Bridge St, in a lovingly restored two-centuries-old house, which has bargain-priced private rooms (no dorms) with shared bathrooms and a large self-catering kitchen. There's cheap **camping** in a field at *Panpwnton Farm* (☎01547/528597; £3.50–4.50 per person), over the river and half a mile up the lane that forks left at the station.

For **eating and drinking**, it's hard to beat the landmark ⚘ *Horse and Jockey* at the town end of Station Road, embracing a sunny courtyard, which has a vast lunch and early-evening menu, and serves huge, tasty pizzas until 11pm and

George Borrow, in his classic book *Wild Wales*, noted that it was once "customary for the English to cut off the ears of every Welshman who was found to the east of the dyke, and for the Welsh to hang every Englishman whom they found to the west of it". Certainly, **Offa's Dyke** has provided a potent symbol of Welsh–English antipathy ever since it was created in the eighth century as a demarcation line by King Offa of Mercia, ruler of the whole of central England. It appears that the dyke was an attempt to thwart Welsh expansionism.

Up to twenty feet high and sixty feet wide, the earthwork made use of natural boundaries such as rivers in its run north to south, and is best seen in the sections near Knighton in Radnorshire and Montgomery. Today's England–Wales border crosses the dyke many times, although the basic boundary has changed little since Offa's day. The glorious **long-distance footpath** (ⓦ www.nationaltrail.co.uk), opened in 1971, runs from Prestatyn on the north Clwyd coast for 177 miles to Sedbury Cliffs, just outside Chepstow, and is one of the most rewarding walks in Britain – neither too popular to be unpleasantly crowded, nor too monotonous in its landscapes. The path is maintained by the Offa's Dyke Association, whose headquarters are in the Offa's Dyke Centre in Knighton (see opposite).

packs in live music and discos as well. For a cheap breakfast or lunch, try *JD's* café on the corner of Broad Street and Station Road.

The local **bike rental** firm, Wheely Wonderful (☏ 01568/770755, ⓦ www .wheelywonderfulcycling.co.uk), is over the border in Shropshire at Petchfield Farm, Elton, near Ludlow, but will deliver to Knighton if you're without a car.

Montgomeryshire

The northern part of Powys is made up of the old county of **Montgomeryshire**, an area of enormously varying landscapes and few inhabitants. The best base for the spartan and mountainous southwest of the county is the spirited little town of **Llanidloes** ten miles north of Rhayader on the River Severn (Afon Hafren), which arrives in the town after rising nearby in the dense **Hafren Forest** on the bleak slopes of **Plynlimon**.

From Llanidloes, one of Wales' most dramatic roads rises past the chilly shores of the **Llyn Clywedog** reservoir, squeezed into sharp hillsides, and up through the remote hamlets of **Staylittle** and **Dylife**. This stark, uplifting scenery contrasts with the gentler, greener contours that characterize the east of the county, where the muted old county town of **Montgomery**, with its fine Georgian architecture, perches above the border and Offa's Dyke. The Severn runs a few miles to the west, near the impeccable village of **Berriew**, home of the offbeat **Andrew Logan Museum of Sculpture** and below the dank hilltop remains of **Dolforwyn Castle**. Further south, the Severn runs through **Newtown**, good as a transport interchange and for followers of **Robert Owen** (see box, p.262).

In the north of the county, **Welshpool** is the only major settlement, packed in above the wide flood plain of the Severn and linked by an impossibly cute toy rail line to **Llanfair Caereinion**. On the southern side of Welshpool is Montgomeryshire's one unmissable sight, the sumptuous **Powis Castle** and its exquisite terraced gardens. The very north of the county is pastoral, deserted and beautiful, particularly around **Lake Vyrnwy**.

Llanidloes and around

Transforming itself from rural village to weaving town and, more recently, into a centre for artists and craftspeople, **LLANIDLOES** (pronounced Thlann-idd-loiss) has managed to avoid the decline of so many other small market towns. The town's four main streets meet at the black-and-white **market hall**, built on timber stilts in 1600, allowing the market – now long since moved – to take place on the cobbles underneath. During the summer months a **museum and exhibition centre** opens upstairs (usually late May–Sept Tues–Sun 11am–4pm; free).

North and south of the market hall are China Street and Long Bridge Street – the latter is good for interesting little shops. Off Long Bridge Street to the east is Church Street, which opens out into a yard surrounding the parish **church of St Idloes** (usually daily 10.30am–3.30pm; call ☎01686/412370 to confirm opening hours), whose impressive fifteenth-century hammerbeam roof is said to have been poached from Abbey Cwmhir.

West of the market hall is Short Bridge Street, a line of fine buildings running down to the River Severn, past two imposing nineteenth-century chapels – one Zionist, one Baptist – staring across the road at each other. Heading the other way from the market hall is Great Oak Street, the town's main thoroughfare. At the western end of the street is the **town hall**, originally built as a temperance hotel to challenge the boozy **Trewythen Arms** opposite.

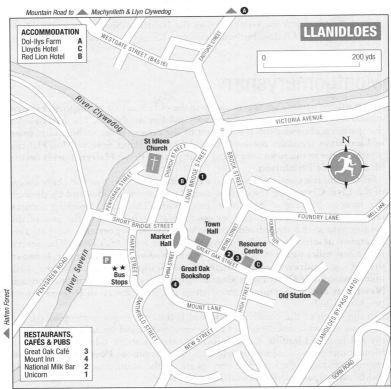

Mountain Road to ▲ Machynlleth & Llyn Clywedog   ▲ **A**

LLANIDLOES

ACCOMMODATION	
Dol-llys Farm	**A**
Lloyds Hotel	**C**
Red Lion Hotel	**B**

0 — 200 yds

WESTGATE STREET (B4518)   EASTGATE STREET

VICTORIA AVENUE

River Clywedog

St Idloes Church

CHURCH STREET   LONG BRIDGE STREET   BROOK STREET

N

PENYGRAIG STREET

SHORT BRIDGE STREET

FOUNDRY LANE   WELL LANE

Town Hall

Market Hall   BETHEL STREET   Resource Centre

CHAPEL STREET   CHINA STREET   GREAT OAK STREET   FOUNDRY   **C**

River Severn

PENYGREEN ROAD

P

★★ Bus Stops

Great Oak Bookshop

HIGH STREET

Old Station

SMITHFIELD STREET   MOUNT LANE

NEW STREET

LLANIDLOES BY-PASS (A470)

GORN ROAD

Hafren Forest ◀

RESTAURANTS, CAFÉS & PUBS	
Great Oak Café	**3**
Mount Inn	**4**
National Milk Bar	**2**
Unicorn	**1**

© Crown copyright

A plaque on the closed hotel commemorates Llanidloes as an unlikely seeming place of industrial and political unrest, when, in April 1839, Chartists stormed the hotel, dragging out and beating up special constables who had been dispatched to the town in a futile attempt to suppress the political fervour of the local flannel weavers.

The town's eclectic **museum** (Easter–Sept daily except Wed 11am–1pm & 2–5pm; Oct–Easter Mon, Tues, Thurs & Fri 11am–1pm & 2–5pm, Sat 10am–1pm; admission by donation) forms part of the town hall complex. The diverting collection ranges from old local prints and mementos, including pictures of boomtown Dylife (see p.260) to a stuffed two-headed lamb, born locally in 1914. Also born locally, as it happens, was **Laura Ashley**'s floral-themed interior decorating empire – the company started just up the road in **Carno** (Ashley herself was born in Merthyr Tydfil).

Practicalities

China Street curves down to the car park from where all **bus** services operate. For news of alternative events – like the **Fancy Dress Night**, on the first Friday of July, when the pubs open late, the streets are cordoned off and virtually the whole town gets kitted out – visit the excellent Resource Centre on Great Oak Street. At the western end of the road is the area's best **bookshop**, Great Oak, with loads of Celtic and Welsh-interest stuff and a barn full of good new and secondhand fiction.

Accommodation includes the delightful *Red Lion Hotel* (☎01686/412270, ⓦwww.llanidloes.com/red_lion_hotel; ❷) on Long Bridge Street, and the cosy *Lloyds Hotel* (☎01686/412284, ⓦwww.lloydshotel.co.uk; ❸), on Cambrian Place, which is also home to a superb **restaurant** serving good-value five-course set menus of an evening – advance booking is essential for both the hotel and the restaurant. There's **camping** around fifteen-minutes' walk north of town at *Dol-llys Farm* (☎01686/412694; £4 per person), which allows campfires down by the River Severn, too.

Other **food** options include wholesome veggie fare in the laid-back *Great Oak Café* on Great Oak Street, or, a few doors down, the *National Milk Bar*. Most of the **pubs** in town also serve food – the inexpensive *Unicorn* on Long Bridge Street and the olde-worlde *Mount Inn* on China Street are the best options.

Llyn Clywedog, Plynlimon, Dylife and Staylittle

Four miles northwest of Llanidloes, the beautiful **Llyn Clywedog reservoir** was built as recently as the 1960s and has settled well into the folds of the Clywedog Valley. At its southern end, the modern concrete dam is Britain's tallest (237ft), towering menacingly over the remnants of the **Bryntail lead mine**, through which a signposted path runs. The roads along the southern shores of Clywedog wind around into the dense plantation of **Hafren Forest**, the only real sign of life and vegetation on the bleak, sodden slopes of **Plynlimon** (Pumlumon Fawr, 2469ft). There's a car park at **RHYD-Y-BENWCH**, in the heart of the forest, from where **walking paths** fan out, the most popular being a six-mile round trip following the River Severn up through the trees, past a waterfall and out to its source, a saturated peat bog in some of the harshest terrain in Wales.

Plynlimon is bleak and difficult walking if you venture beyond the fairly well-trodden path to the Severn's source. Water seeps everywhere in this misty wilderness, with four other rivers – the source of the Wye included – rising on its tufted slopes. The rivers Hengwm, Llechwedd-mawr and Rheidol have been dammed on Plynlimon's western side to form the desolate, black-watered reservoir of **Nant-y-Moch**, reached by road via Ponterwyd (see p.295). There is little sympathetic landscaping here, the lake looking nothing more than the flooded valley that it is.

The hamlet of **STAYLITTLE** (Penfforddlas) – whose English name comes from a village blacksmith who was so quick at shoeing horses his smithy became known as Stay-a-little – is above the Clywedog River at the northern end of Llyn Clywedog. Just north of the village, the mountain road to Machynlleth forks left, running past the plunging ravine of the Twymyn River to the north.

Old mine workings herald the approach to **DYLIFE** (pronounced Duh-levah), a lead-mining community of almost two thousand people in the mid-nineteenth century, with a reputation as a lawless and licentious gambling pit. The mine closed in 1896, and the population has since dwindled to around just twenty (it features on the excellent historical website, Abandoned Communities, at Ⓦ www .abandonedcommunities.co.uk). Fortunately, the village pub – the unpretentious *Star Inn* (Nov–March closed Mon–Fri lunch; Ⓣ 01650/521345; ❷) – valiantly hangs on, and makes a good spot for a meal or bed for the night. There are plenty of wild places to pitch a tent for the night nearby too.

Good walks from Dylife include that up to Pen-y-crocbren, the mine-pocked slope that rises to the south of the village, and west to **Glaslyn**, or "blue lake", and the reedy shores of **Bugeilyn**. The scenically varied **Glyndŵr's Way** footpath (see box below) crosses this patch on its way to Machynlleth. A popular viewpoint on the road two miles west of Dylife has been furnished with a cheery memorial to broadcaster and author **Wynford Vaughan-Thomas** (1908–87), whose outstretched slate hand points out to the dozens of rippling peaks and verdant valleys.

Newtown and around

Despite its name, **NEWTOWN** (Y Drenewydd), thirteen miles northeast of Llanidloes, was founded in the thirteenth century, growing steadily until experiencing a massive population explosion in the nineteenth century as a centre for weaving and textiles – the town once boasted 50 pubs and six breweries. Today, its activity is much reduced, but its compact town centre, straddling the River Severn, has a certain appeal.

Newtown's High Street is home to the original base of the **W.H. Smith** chain of newsagents, now housing a small and reasonably interesting **museum** (Mon–Sat 9am–5.30pm; free) about the company and its growth since it was established in 1792. A block west, the car park is home to the bus depot, tourist office and the **Oriel Davies Gallery** (Mon–Sat 10am–5pm; free), a great gallery of imaginative temporary exhibitions, with a decent café too. On Severn Street, opposite the nineteenth-century red terracotta **clock tower**, is the house in which early socialist **Robert Owen** was born in 1771, now open as

---

Glyndŵr's Way

One of the UK's newer long-distance footpaths, **Glyndŵr's Way** (Ⓦ www.nationaltrail .co.uk/glyndwrsway) weaves for 123 miles through the solitary rural landscapes of Montgomeryshire and northern Radnorshire, from Knighton to Welshpool. Well signposted all the way, though depending rather a lot on lane and road walking, Glyndŵr's Way is far quieter than Offa's Dyke path, both in the number of settlements en route and the number of hikers on the trail. Varied scenery includes barren bog, exhilarating uplands, reservoirs, undulating farmland and sections of river-valley walking. You can pick up an official route guide for £12.99 from tourist offices in the region, or order it online at Ⓦ www.powystrails.org.uk.

a **Memorial Museum** (Mon–Fri 9.30am–noon & 2–3.30pm, Sat 9.30–11.30am; free) that explains this remarkable man's life (see box, p.260). The museum's visitors' book indicates just how much of a shrine the place has become, with a roll call of socialist politicians and trade unionists scrawling their thanks for Owen's work in its pages.

Over the river at 5–7 Commercial St, the **Textile Museum** (opening hours vary – check with Welshpool's tourist office; free) sits above six cramped old weavers' cottages. Exhibits show the dramatic ebb and flow of the town's staple trade, from the flannel and handloom factories of the 1790s, through the social unrest and industrial decline of the 1830s and 1840s (Wales' first Chartist demonstration took place here in 1838), the revival of trade thanks to local entrepreneur Pryce Jones' world-first mail-order service, and its subsequent dwindling to nothing by 1935.

Five miles north of Newtown, the mock-Tudor **Gregynog Hall** was the home from 1920 of Gwendoline and Margaret Davies, aesthete sisters who inherited a vast fortune from their port-building father and spent much of it on a world-class art collection, most of which now resides in Cardiff's National Museum of Wales. Gregynog became the headquarters for their artistic revival, including the establishment of a world-famous small press, which is up and running once more. It's now an extramural outpost of the University of Wales, offering public courses in Welsh language and culture and hosting an annual **music festival** in late June (Ⓦ www.wales.ac.uk/gregynog): the hall is not generally open to the public but you can wander through the grounds at any time.

Practicalities

Newtown's **train station** (complete with a new internet café) is on the southern edge of the town centre. A path heads past the Victorian parish church of St David and up Back Lane to the **bus station**. The Welshpool tourist office (see p.264) can advise on **accommodation**. The best bets are the *Plas Canol* guesthouse, between the station and the town centre at 32 New Rd (Ⓣ01686/625598; ❷), and *Yesterdays* (Ⓣ01686/622644, Ⓦ www.yesterdayshotel.com; ❸), behind the clock tower in Severn Square, with free wi-fi, spacious rooms, and locally sourced Welsh breakfasts.

Eating revolves around the town's numerous cheap daytime cafés and its **pubs** – the *Black Boy* on Broad Street does a fantastic Sunday roast. The *Lion Inn*, by the clock tower, is also good for live music, late drinking and dancing, while Commercial Street's *Bell Hotel* hosts regular live folk, R&B and (especially) blues. *The Angel*, on High Street, is the place to go for a glass of wine.

Dolforwyn Castle

The A483 continues northeast from Newtown, affording occasional glimpses of the River Severn and in almost constant proximity to the reed-filled **Montgomery Canal**. Three miles from Montgomery, a small left turn leads up to the Gothic country house, *Dolforwyn Hall* (Ⓣ01686/630221, Ⓦ www.dolforwyn.co.uk; ❷), and the gaunt remains of **Dolforwyn Castle** (free access). Described by Jan Morris as "the saddest of all the Welsh castles", this was the last fortress to be built by a native Welsh prince on his own soil – Llywelyn ap Gruffydd in 1273 – as a direct snub to the English king, Edward I, who had forbidden the project. Llywelyn built his fortress and started to construct a small adjoining town as a Welsh fiefdom to rival the heavily anglicized Welshpool, just up the valley. Dolforwyn only survived for four years in Welsh hands before being overwhelmed after a nine-day siege by the English, and the castle was left slowly to rot. In the past twenty years, the remains have been excavated, and

Robert Owen, pioneer socialist

Born in Montgomeryshire in the late eighteenth century, **Robert Owen** (1771–1858) left Wales to enter the Manchester cotton trade at the age of 18 and swiftly rose to the position of mill manager. His business acumen was matched by a strong streak of philanthropy towards his subordinates. Fundamentally, he believed in social equality between the classes and was firmly against the concept of competition between individuals. Poverty, he believed, could be eradicated by co-operative methods. Owen recognized the potential of building a model workers' community around the New Lanark mills in Scotland and joined the operation in 1798, swiftly setting up the world's first infant school, an Institution for the Formation of Character and a model welfare state for its people.

Owen's ideas on co-operative living prompted him to build up the model community of New Harmony in Indiana, USA, which he had established between 1824 and 1828, before handing the still-struggling project over to his sons. Before long, and without the wisdom of its founder, the idealistic tenets of New Harmony collapsed under the weight of greed, ambition and too many vested interests. Undeterred, Owen, by now back in Britain, was encouraging the formation of the early trade unions and co-operative societies, as well as leading action against the 1834 deportation of the **Tolpuddle Martyrs**, a group of Dorset farm labourers who withdrew their labour in their call for a wage increase. Owen's later years were dogged by controversy, as he lost the support of the few sympathetic sections of the British establishment in his persistent criticism of organized religion. He gained many followers, however, whose generic name gradually changed from Owenites to "socialists" – the first usage of the term. Owen returned to Newtown in his later years, and died there in 1858.

significant portions of the fragile old castle have emerged on the wind-blown hilltop, with astounding views over the Severn Valley, four hundred feet below.

Montgomery and around

Eight miles northeast of Newtown, the tiny, anglicized town of **MONTGOMERY** (Trefaldwyn) lies at the base of a dilapidated **castle** on the Welsh side of Offa's Dyke and the present-day border. Construction of the castle began in 1233 under the English king, Henry III, and today's remains are not on their own worth the steep climb up the lane at the back of the town hall, although the view over the lofty church tower, handsome Georgian streets and the gargantuan green bowl of hills around the town is stunning. The symmetrical main thoroughfare, Broad Street, swoops up to the red-brick **town hall**, crowned by a trim clock tower. Facing the town hall, turn right on Arthur Street to reach the **Old Bell Museum** (April–July & Sept Wed–Fri & Sun 1.30–5pm, Sat 10.30am–5pm; Aug Mon–Fri & Sun 1.30–5pm, Sat 10.30am–5pm; £1), an unusually enjoyable local history collection featuring artefacts from excavations, scale models of local castles, an old workhouse exhibition and mementos from Montgomery civic life.

At the other end of Broad Street, the rebuilt tower of Montgomery's parish **church of St Nicholas** dominates the diminutive buildings around it. Largely thirteenth-century, the highlights of its spacious interior include the 1600 canopied tomb of local landowner, Sir Richard Herbert, his wife, Magdalen, and their eight children (including Elizabethan poet George Herbert). The two medieval effigies on the floor at the end of the tomb are of uncertain origin, although the farther one is thought to be of Sir Edmund Mortimer ("revolted Mortimer", as Shakespeare had him), son-in-law of Owain Glyndŵr, brother-in-law of Hotspur and once Constable of Montgomery Castle. Equally impressive are the elaborately carved fifteenth-century double screen and accompanying loft, believed to have been built from sections removed from a priory over the border in Cherbury.

Montgomery is near one of the best-preserved sections of **Offa's Dyke**, which the long-distance footpath shadows either side of the B4386 a mile east of the town. Ditches almost twenty feet high give one of the best indications of the dyke's original look, twelve hundred years after it was built. If you want to **stay** here, the rambling black-and-white *Dragon Hotel* (☎01686/668359, Ⓦwww.dragonhotel.com; ❸–❺), by the town hall, has an indoor pool and grand four-poster beds in some rooms. Alternatively, try *Brynwylfa* (☎01686/668555; ❷), with high-quality rooms in a beautiful town house at 4 Bishops Castle St; or the vine-clad *Little Brompton Farm* (☎01686/668371, Ⓦwww.littlebromptonfarm.co.uk; ❷), two miles south of town and handy for the Offa's Dyke path. The Knighton tourist office (see p.256) can also help with accommodation. For **food** and **drink**, head for the lively young *Checkers* pub, on Broad Street.

Berriew

Three miles northwest of Montgomery, the black-and-white Tudor houses in the village of **BERRIEW** (Aberrhiw) are grouped prettily around a small church, the shallow waters of the Rhiw River, and the posh half-timbered *Lion Hotel* (☎01686/640452, Ⓦwww.thelionhotelberriew.com; ❹), which serves excellent home-cooked **meals** (expect the likes of braised Welsh lamb served on creamy mash or an adventurous beetroot, apple and warm goat's cheese risotto).

Just over the river bridge, the flamboyant **Andrew Logan Museum of Sculpture** (Easter weekend noon–6pm; May–Oct Wed–Sun noon–6pm; Nov–Christmas Sat & Sun noon–4pm; Ⓦwww.andrewlogan.com; £3) seems an improbably high-camp addition to the tidy Berriew landscape. In the 1970s, British sculptor Logan inaugurated the Alternative Miss World Contest, a drag-and-grunge ball. Dazzling contestant outfits share space with Logan's oversized sculptures, a gaudy Shiva-figure "goddess of the void" and a twelve-foot-high encrusted glass "cosmic egg".

▲ Zandra Rhodes, Andrew Logan Museum

A mile further down the lane from the museum, where it meets the main A493, you'll find **Glansevern Hall Gardens** (May–Sept Thurs–Sat & bank holidays noon–5pm; £4), spreading around a stately Georgian mansion.

Welshpool

Three miles from the English border and five miles north of Berriew, eastern Montgomeryshire's chief town, **WELSHPOOL** (Y Trallwng), was formerly known merely as Pool, acquiring its prefix in 1835 to distinguish it from the English seaside town of Poole in Dorset. The town's well-proportioned roads are lined with some Tudor and many good Georgian and Victorian buildings, but it's sumptuous **Powis Castle**, one of the greatest Welsh fortresses, that puts Welshpool on most people's agenda.

Arrival, information and accommodation

The neo-Gothic turrets of the old Victorian **train station** (its modern replacement is directly behind) crown Severn Street, which leads down into the town centre crossroads, formed by the intersection of Severn, Berriew, Broad and Church streets. The highly efficient **tourist office** (Easter–Oct Mon–Sat 9.30am–5pm, Sun 9.30am–4pm; Nov–Easter Mon–Fri 9.30am–5pm, Sat & Sun 9.30am–4pm; ☏01938/552043, ✉weltic@powys.gov.uk), is fifty yards up Church Street in the Vicarage Gardens car park opposite the Spar supermarket.

There's plenty of **accommodation** in the area. Bang in the centre at the main crossroads, the traditional Georgian *Royal Oak* coaching inn (☏01938/552217, ⓦwww.royaloakhotel.info; ⑤) has comfortable en-suite rooms. Dozens of **B&Bs** line Salop Road, as well as Berriew Road, where *Traethllawn B&B* (☏01938/555696, ⓦwww.traethllawn.co.uk; ②) has fresh, contemporary rooms. Out of town, try the *Trefnant Hall Farm* (☏01686/640262, ⓦwww.trefnanthall.com; ①–②), with its splendid Georgian architecture, four miles southwest of Welshpool, beyond Powis Castle. **Camping** is good at the *Green Dragon Inn*, a mile along the Shrewsbury road at Buttington (☏01938/553076; from £4 per person).

The Town

Two hundred yards along Severn Street from Welshpool's modern **train station**, a humpback bridge over the much-restored **Montgomery Canal** hides the **canal wharf** and a wharfside warehouse that has been carefully restored as the **Powysland Museum** (Mon, Tues, Thurs & Fri 11am–1pm & 2–5pm; May–Sept also Sat & Sun 10am–1pm & 2–5pm; Oct–April also Sat 11am–2pm; free), an impressively wide collection covering the history of the local area. The entrance is heralded by Andrew Logan's spangly blue outsized handbag, beyond which displays include archeological finds from a local neolithic timber circle and Roman remains through to exhibits showing the changing patterns of domestic and civic life, as well as surprises like an intricate model of a guillotine carved from mutton bones, left behind by prisoners of the Napoleonic Wars.

Broad Street is the most architecturally interesting of the streets leading off from the town's central crossroads, with the ponderous Victorian town hall and its dominating clock tower overlooking Tudor and Jacobean town-houses. On New Street, behind the NatWest bank, you can wander around an early eighteenth-century circular **cockpit**, where cockfights were once held (confirm your visit with bank staff; free). Broad Street changes name five times as it rises up the hill towards the tiny Raven Square terminus station of the **Welshpool & Llanfair Railway**, half a mile beyond the town hall. The eight-mile narrow-gauge line

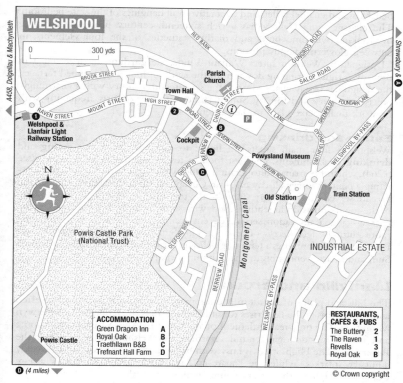

WELSHPOOL

0 — 300 yds

A458, Dolgellau & Machynlleth

Shrewsbury & A

RED BANK

GUNGROG ROAD

SALOP ROAD

BROOK STREET

Parish
Church

Town Hall

MOUNT STREET

HIGH STREET

RAVEN STREET

❶

**Welshpool &
Llanfair Light
Railway Station**

BROAD STREET

CHURCH STREET

MILL LANE

FOUNDARY LANE

GREENFIELDS

SMITHFIELD

WELSHPOOL BY-PASS

❷

ⓘ

P

Ⓑ

Cockpit

BERRIEW ST

SEVERN STREET

❸

OLD A1010

LANE

Ⓒ

Powysland Museum

SEVERN ROAD

N

OLDFORD RISE

Montgomery Canal

Old Station

Train Station

**Powis Castle Park
(National Trust)**

BERRIEW ROAD

WELSHPOOL BY-PASS

INDUSTRIAL ESTATE

ACCOMMODATION	
Green Dragon Inn	A
Royal Oak	B
Traethllawn B&B	C
Trefnant Hall Farm	D

Powis Castle

| RESTAURANTS,
CAFÉS & PUBS	
The Buttery	2
The Raven	1
Revells	3
Royal Oak	B

Ⓓ (4 miles) ▼

© Crown copyright

(generally 2–5 trains a week Easter–Oct, increasing to daily services late July to Aug; £11.20 return; ☎01938/810441, ⓦwww.wllr.org.uk) originally operated for less than thirty years, closing in 1931 – these days, scaled-down engines once more chuff along the equally small-scale valleys of the Sylfaen Brook and Banwy River to the quiet village of **LLANFAIR CAEREINION**, where the *Goat Hotel* does good pub food. Leaflets describing circular **walks** here can be picked up from Welshpool's tourist office.

Powis Castle

In a land of ruined castles, the sheer scale and beauty of **Powis Castle** (April–Oct Mon & Thurs–Sun castle 1–5pm, gardens 11am–6pm; July–Aug Tues–Sun, same times; castle and gardens £10.50, gardens only £7.50; NT) stands out. Located a mile from Welshpool up Park Lane on the site of an earlier Norman fort, work on the castle was started in the reign of Edward I by the Gwenwynwyn family; to qualify for the site and the barony of De la Pole, they had to renounce all claims to Welsh princedom. In 1587, Sir Edward Herbert bought the castle and began to transform it into the Elizabethan palace you see today.

Inside, the **Clive Museum** – named after the son of Clive of India, who married into the family in 1784 – provides a lively account of the British in India, through diaries, notes, letters, paintings, tapestries, weapons and jewels, although it's the sumptuous period rooms that impress most, from the vast and kitsch frescoes by Lanscroon above the balustraded staircase to the mahogany bed, brass and enamel toilets and decorative wall hangings of the state bedroom. The elegant Long Gallery has a rich sixteenth-century plasterwork ceiling overlooking winsome busts and marble statuettes of the four elements, in between glowering family portraits.

Designed by Welsh architect William Winde, the **gardens** are spectacular in their own right. Dropping down from the castle in four huge stepped terraces, the design has barely changed since the seventeenth century, with a charmingly precise orangery and topiary. Summertime outdoor concerts, frequently with firework finales, take place in the gardens.

Eating and drinking

Welshpool's four main streets are home to most of the town's **eating** and **drinking** establishments. The best food in town is at the *Royal Oak* pub (see p.264), which has managed to retain its olde-worlde grandiosity while incorporating a contemporary all-day café-bar. Cheap and filling breakfasts, lunches and teas are served in *The Buttery*, opposite the town hall on the High Street. Many of the town's **pubs** do lunchtime food, with some, notably *The Raven*, up by the narrow-gauge train station, serving decent evening meals as well. For something more cutting-edge, *Revells* (Thurs–Sat, plus Sun lunch; ☎01938/559000), on Berriew Street, combines a tempting delicatessen with a daytime café-bar (closed Sun) and smart evening bistro fare, within a striking Art Deco building.

Llanfyllin and around

The hills and plains of northern Montgomeryshire conceal a maze of deserted lanes and farms as the land rises towards the foothills of Denbighshire's Berwyn Mountains. The only real settlement of any size is **LLANFYLLIN**, a handsome and friendly hillside town, ten miles northwest of Welshpool in the valley of the River Cain. The High Street is busy with bright pubs, cafés, shops and a weekly Thursday market, while the square-cut, red-brick parish church is a rare example of eighteenth-century church building in Wales.

The best place to stay in the area is the tranquil, ivy-draped seventeenth-century 🏡 *Cyfie Farm* (☎01691/648451, ⓦ www.cyfiefarm.co.uk; ❻), in a beautiful garden setting just south of the tiny village of Llanfihangel-yng-Ngwynfa, which also serves up four-course evening meals around its big communal table. In Llanfyllin itself, on the High Street, there's the fine *Seeds* **restaurant** (☎01691/648604), with good vegetarian options.

The Tanat and Rhaeadr valleys

Parallel to the valley of the River Cain, north of Llanfyllin, are the lush valleys of the Afon Tanat and its tributary, the Rhaeadr – a beguiling and sparsely populated backwater, set against the looming Berwyn Mountains.

The small, low-roofed village of **LLANRHAEADR-YM-MOCHNANT**, six miles north of Llanfyllin, is best remembered as the parish of Bishop William Morgan, who translated the Bible into Welsh in 1588 (see p.424), a pivotal act which ensured the survival of the old tongue. The village has three great **pubs** – the *Three Tuns*, *Hand Inn* and *Wynnstay Arms* – and excellent-value **B&Bs** such as the beautifully decorated Victorian *Bron Heulog* on Waterfall Street (☎01691/780521, ⓦ www.bronheulog.co.uk; ❷–❸).

Llanrhaeadr lies at the foot of the wild walking country of the southern Berwyn Mountains. From the middle of the village, Waterfall Street becomes a lane that courses northwest for four miles to a dead end at the enchanting **Pistyll Rhaeadr**, Wales' highest waterfall at 240ft. The river tumbles down the crags in two stages, flowing under a natural stone arch known as the Fairy

Bridge. It's well worth walking to the top of the fall for the dizzying views down the valley, as well the chance to follow further paths leading up into the moody Berwyns. Pistyll Rhaeadr is rich in legend, which you can absorb at the riverside *Tan-y-Pistyll* licensed **café**. The café's owners also offer **B&B** (℡01691/780392; ❸) and a lovely **campsite** (from £5 per person) in the back field, and operate various spiritual retreats.

East from Llanrhaeadr, the B4396 runs, along the Tanat Valley and through the village of **LLANGEDWYN**. A mile or so after the village, few visitors make it up one of the left turns leading to **SYCARTH**, only a mile from the English border, but one of the most Welsh of all shrines: a grass mound marks the site of Owain Glyndŵr's ancestral court, reputedly a palace of nine grand halls. Bard Iolo Goch immortalized this Welsh Shangri-la as a place of "no want, no hunger, no shame/No-one is ever thirsty at Sycarth".

Just east of Sycarth, the English–Welsh border tightly encircles the 740-foot limestone crag of **Llanymynech Rocks** (now a nature reserve), before cutting down to run right through the middle of the village of **LLANYMYNECH**.

Heading **northwest from Llanrhaeadr**, the B4391 hugs the river as far as the sleepy former mining village of **LLANGYNOG**, where it heads north into the Berwyn Mountains and Denbighshire. A lane by the bridge leads to a stunning four-mile hike over the top of Y Clogydd and down to the elfin charms of Pistyll Rhaeadr (see p.266). Less strenuously, you can walk (or, less strenuously still, drive) two miles further up the Tanat Valley to the hamlet of **PENNANT MELANGELL**, sitting low in a quiet, sheer-sided valley of sparkling brooks, and the site of one of Wales' most enduring sites of pilgrimage. Legend has it that the eighth-century saint Melangell was praying in the valley when a hare being chased by a hunt pack led by Prince Brochwel took refuge in her skirts. The hounds drew to a sudden stop before her and fled howling. The prince drew his horn to his lips to call them, only to find himself unable to remove it. The prince was so moved by Melangell's gentle humanity that he granted her the valley, in which she built a religious community. The little **church** (opening hours vary; contact the Welshpool tourist office) here dates from the eighth century; inside, a twelfth-century shrine and supposed effigy of St Melangell lie beneath an exquisite barrel roof. Melangell's grave is in the semicircular *cell y bedd* at the back of the church. Intact Norman features include a window in the main church, the south door porch and the font.

Lake Vyrnwy

A few miles south of **Pennant Melangell**, the magnificent **Lake Vyrnwy** (Llyn Efyrnwy) combines its functional role as a water supply for Liverpool with Victorian self-aggrandizement in the shape of the huge nineteenth-century dam and Disneyesque turreted straining tower. Constructed during the 1880s, Vyrnwy was the first of the massive reservoirs of mid-Wales. The village of **Llanwddyn** was flattened and rebuilt at the eastern end, its people receiving only meagre compensation for the loss of their homes. The story is told, somewhat apologetically, in the **Vyrnwy Visitor Centre** (April–Oct daily 10.30am–5.30pm; Nov–March Sat & Sun 10.30am–4.30pm; free), which is located on the western side of the dam and coexists with an **RSPB Visitor Centre** (same hours). RSPB staff here are in charge of a small hide across the road, where you can sit and watch forest birds (and cheeky squirrels) attacking the feeders outside the windows. A few yards down the road, the *Artisans Coffee Shop* (℡01691/870377), **rents out bikes**.

Quality **accommodation** in the immediate surroundings includes the *Lake Vyrnwy Hotel* (℡01691/870692, ⓦwww.lakevyrnwy.com; ❻–❾), a lavish spa retreat overlooking the waters above the southeastern shore. Its restaurant serves fresh-as-it-gets Welsh cuisine (the hotel's kitchen even has its own flock of sheep), but a lakeside afternoon high tea is perfect if you just want to have a look around. There's a great **B&B** just beyond the visitor centre at *The Oaks* (☎01691/870250, ⓦ www.vyrnwyaccommodation.co.uk; ❸), and daytime snacks and full evening **meals** are available at *Lake View* (☎01691/870286), on the lakeside road beyond the *Lake Vyrnwy Hotel*. If you're **camping**, there are a handful of pitches at *Fronheulog* (☎01691/870662, ⓦ www.fronheulog-caravan-park.co.uk; £2.50 per person), at the top of the hairpin bends on the road to Llanfyllin.

Note that Lake Vyrnwy isn't accessible by public transport (not even taxis), so you'll need your own vehicle to get there.

Travel details

Unless otherwise stated, frequencies for trains and buses are for Monday to Saturday services, Sunday averages 1 to 3 services, though the main routes are more frequent, while some routes have no Sunday service at all. See p.38 and p.219 for more information including websites with route-finder services.

Trains

Abergavenny to: Cardiff (hourly; 40min); Hereford (hourly; 20min); Newport (hourly; 30min); Pontypool (hourly; 10min).

Knighton to: Llandrindod Wells (4 daily; 40min); Llanwrtyd Wells (4 daily; 1hr 10min); Shrewsbury (4 daily; 1hr); Swansea (4 daily; 3hr 10min).

Llandrindod Wells to: Knighton (4 daily; 40min); Llanwrtyd Wells (4 daily; 30min); Shrewsbury (4 daily; 1hr 40min); Swansea (4 daily; 2hr 20min).

Welshpool to: Aberystwyth (6 daily; 1hr 30min); Birmingham (6 daily; 1hr 30min); Machynlleth (6 daily; 1hr); Newtown (6 daily; 20min); Pwllheli (4 daily; 3hr); Shrewsbury (6 daily; 20min).

Buses

Abergavenny to: Brecon (7 daily Mon–Sat; 1hr); Cardiff (hourly; 1hr 20min); Clydach (hourly; 30min); Crickhowell (7 daily Mon–Sat; 20min); Llanfihangel Crucorney (6 daily; 15min); Merthyr Tydfil (hourly; 1hr 30min); Monmouth (6 daily; 40min); Newport (hourly; 1hr 10min); Pontypool (hourly; 25min); Raglan (6 daily; 20min).

Brecon to: Aberdulais (2–3 daily; 1hr 30min); Abergavenny (every 2hr Mon–Sat; 1hr); Builth Wells (1–3 daily Mon–Sat; 40min); Cardiff (1 daily; 1hr 25min, otherwise change at Merthyr); Craig-y-nos/Dan-yr-ogof (2–3 daily; 30min); Crickhowell (7 daily Mon–Sat; 25min); Hay-on-Wye (7 daily; 45min); Hereford (7 daily; 1hr 45min); Libanus (9 daily; 10min); Llandrindod Wells (3 daily Mon–Sat; 1hr); Merthyr Tydfil (10 daily; 40min); Newport (5 daily; 1hr 50min); Pontypool (6 daily; 1hr 20min);

Sennybridge (2–3 daily; 20min); Swansea (2–3 daily; 1hr 30min); Talgarth (6 daily; 30min); Talybont (7 daily Mon–Sat; 20min).

Builth Wells to: Llandrindod Wells (hourly Mon–Sat; 20min); Rhayader (2 daily Mon–Sat; 20min).

Hay-on-Wye to: Brecon (7 daily; 50min); Hereford (6 daily; 1hr); Llandrindod Wells (1 daily Wed & Sat; 1hr).

Knighton to: Ludlow (3 daily; 1hr 10min); Presteigne (7 daily; 30min).

Llandrindod Wells to: Aberystwyth (1 daily; 2hr); Brecon (3 daily Mon–Sat; 1hr); Builth Wells (hourly; 20min); Disserth (2 daily; 15min); Elan Village (1 postbus daily Mon–Fri; 40min); Hay-on-Wye (1 daily Wed & Sat; 1hr); New Radnor (2 daily Mon–Sat; 30min); Newtown (3 daily; 1hr 10min); Rhayader (3 daily; 30min).

Llanfyllin to: Oswestry (3 daily Mon–Sat; 45min); Welshpool (1 daily Mon–Sat; 40min).

Llanidloes to: Aberystwyth (5 daily; 1hr); Newtown (9 daily; 30min); Ponterwyd (1 daily; 40min); Shrewsbury (4 daily; 2hr); Welshpool (5 daily; 1hr 10min).

Llanwrtyd Wells to: Builth Wells (3 daily; 45min).

Oswestry (Shropshire) to: Chirk (hourly; 30min); Llanfyllin (3–4 daily; 50min); Welshpool (5 daily; 1hr); Wrexham (hourly; 1hr).

Shrewsbury (Shropshire) to: Llanidloes (4 daily; 2hr); Welshpool (7 daily; 50min).

Welshpool to: Berriew (6 daily Mon–Sat; 20min); Llanidloes (5 daily; 1hr 10min); Llanfyllin (1 daily Mon–Sat; 40min); Llanymynech (5 daily; 30min); Montgomery (4 daily Mon–Sat; 25min); Newtown (7 daily; 40min); Oswestry (5 daily; 1hr); Shrewsbury (7 daily; 50min).

The Cambrian coast

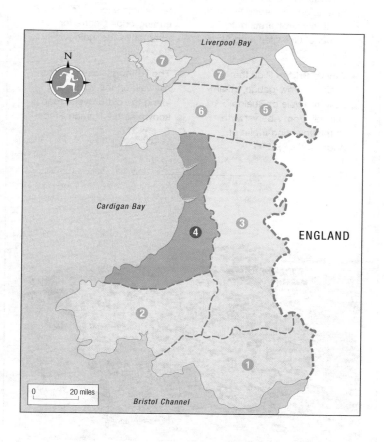

CHAPTER 4 # Highlights

✳ **New Quay** Follow Dylan Thomas's footsteps through the salty seaside town that inspired *Under Milk Wood*. See p.277

✳ **Aberaeron** Hit town for Aberaeron's Seafood Festival, or simply stroll around its colourful Georgian harbour. See p.279

✳ **Devil's Bridge** Ride the scenic narrow-gauge, steam-powered Vale of Rheidol Railway from Aberystwyth to this towering triplet of bridges. See p.295

✳ **Cadair Idris** Hike up southern Snowdonia's highest peak for swooping views and the chance to become a poet … or go mad. See p.298

✳ **Machynlleth** Learn about renewable energies at the cutting-edge Centre for Alternative Technology. See p.299

✳ **The Rhinogs** Take a Welsh hill walk on the wild side along the old drovers' road known as the Roman Steps. See p.317

▲ Ceredigion coast

The Cambrian coast

ardigan Bay (Bae Ceredigion) takes a huge bite out of Wales' west coast, stretching from the Pembrokeshire peninsula in the south to the Llŷn in the north. Between these two points lies the Cambrian coast, stretching up from Cardigan to Harlech and the shores of Tremadog Bay.

Before the nineteenth-century construction of the railway and improved roads, the Cambrian Mountains, split by tumbling rivers, served to isolate this stretch of coast from the rest of Wales, with only narrow passes and cattle-droving routes pushing through the rugged terrain to the markets in England. Today development is still low-key, with large sand-fringed sections sprinkled with enchanting coastal resorts.

The Cambrian coast starts where the rugged seashore of Pembrokeshire ends, continuing in much the same vein of great cliffs, isolated beaches and swirling sea birds, punctuated with *sarnau*, stony offshore reefs largely exposed at low tide. North of the charismatic town of **Cardigan**, the coast breaks at some popular seaside resorts – the best being **Llangrannog** and **New Quay** – before the tiny Georgian harbour town of **Aberaeron**, now the headquarters of the county of Ceredigion.

A bucolic **inland** alternative to the coastal resorts follows the **River Teifi**, which meets the sea at Cardigan and meanders eastwards through lush meadows past a clutch of small towns, prominent among them the stalwart market centre of **Newcastle Emlyn**, the ancient university town of **Lampeter** and the charmingly old-fashioned community of **Tregaron**.

The coastal and inland routes connect at the cosmopolitan "capital" of mid-Wales, **Aberystwyth**, built on the estuary of the **Rheidol**, a fast-falling river with dramatic ravines that make for great walking country. A narrow-gauge railway, an attraction in itself, climbs out of Aberystwyth to **Devil's Bridge**, where three bridges, one on top of the other, span a plunging chasm of cascading waterfalls.

Although situated in the far west of Powys, this chapter includes **Machynlleth**, at the head of the Dyfi estuary, the seat of Owain Glyndŵr's putative fifteenth-century Welsh parliament and still a thriving market centre. Just outside the town is the **Centre for Alternative Technology**, Britain's renowned and very topical showpiece for sustainable living and renewable energy resources.

The main road continues due north from Machynlleth into the old county of **Meirionydd**, now part of Gwynedd. The train line and small coastal road skirt west around **Cadair Idris**, the monumental mountain that dominates the southern third of **Snowdonia National Park**. Each of the mountain's crag-fringed faces invites exploration, but it is best approached from the south, where the narrow-gauge Talyllyn rail line reaches the tiny settlement of **Abergynolwyn**, a great base for the unhurried delights of the **Dysynni Valley**. Cadair

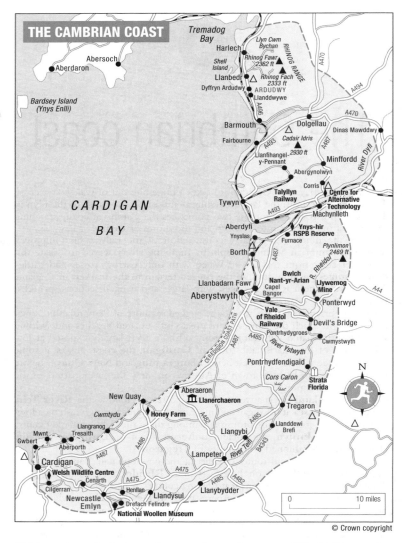

THE CAMBRIAN COAST

Tremadog Bay

Abersoch
Aberdaron

Bardsey Island
(Ynys Enlli)

CARDIGAN
BAY

Harlech
Llyn Cwm Bychan
Shell Island
Rhinog Fawr 2362 ft
RHINOG RANGE
Llanbedr
Rhinog Fach 2333 ft
Dyffryn Ardudwy
ARDUDWY
Llanddwywe

Barmouth
Dolgellau
Dinas Mawddwy
Fairbourne
Cadair Idris 2930 ft
Llanfihangel-y-Pennant
Minffordd
Abergynolwyn
Corris
Centre for Alternative Technology
Talyllyn Railway
Machynlleth
Tywyn

Aberdyfi
Ynys-hir RSPB Reserve
Ynyslas
Furnace
Plynlimon 2469 ft
Borth
Bwlch Nant-yr-Arian
Llywernog Mine
Llanbadarn Fawr
Capel Bangor
Aberystwyth
Ponterwyd
Vale of Rheidol Railway
Devil's Bridge
Pontrhydygroes
Cwmystwyth
River Ystwyth
Pontrhydfendigaid
Cors Caron
Strata Florida

New Quay
Aberaeron
Llanerchaeron
Tregaron
Cwmtydu
Honey Farm
Llangranog
Tresaith
Llangybi
Llanddewi Brefi
Mwnt
Aberporth
Gwbert
Lampeter
River Teifi
Cardigan
Welsh Wildlife Centre
Cenarth
Cilgerran
Henllan
Llandysul
Llanybydder
Newcastle Emlyn
Drefach Felindre
National Woollen Museum

River Dyfi
River Rheidol

0   10 miles

N

© Crown copyright

Idris's northern flank slopes down to the market town of **Dolgellau**, at the head of the scenic Mawddach estuary and linked by waterside path to the likeable resort of **Barmouth**. The coastal strip then broadens out with complex dune systems protecting the approaches to **Harlech** and its virtually intact castle, the southernmost link in Edward I's chain of thirteenth-century fortresses, perched high on its rocky promontory.

Getting around

The most relaxing way to get fairly swiftly to, and along, the Cambrian coast is on the mid-Wales **train** line from Shrewsbury in England through to Machynlleth. At

Machynlleth, the line splits: one branch runs south to Aberystwyth, from where you can pick up the Vale of Rheidol line to Devil's Bridge; the other swings north, calling at 25 stations in under sixty miles before terminating at Pwllheli on the Llŷn. The Day Ranger and Evening Ranger (see Basics, p.37) tickets offer flexible and relatively cheap travel.

Buses offer similar services to the trains, also extending south to Cardigan and inland to all towns of any size, although many villages aren't served by public transport at all. There's also the express TrawsCambria service from Cardiff and Swansea to Bangor and through Aberystwyth, Machynlleth, Dolgellau and Porthmadog. In summer, the Cardi Bach bus runs from approximately the last Saturday in June to the last Sunday in September (but not Wednesday) between Cardigan and New Quay – tourist offices in these two towns have timetables and route maps. This service can be flagged down anywhere along the route (providing it's safe for the driver to stop).

Detailed information on bus and train services as far as Machynlleth appears in the Gwynedd and Ceredigion regional transport guides, available at tourist offices. Alternatively, information is available from Traveline Cymru (℡01871/2002233, ⓦwww.traveline-cymru.org.uk). See also p.320.

Walkers can now set out on the scenic **Ceredigion Coast Path** (ⓦwww .walkcardiganbay.com), opened in 2008, which follows the coast for 63 wind-blown miles from Cardigan to Ynyslas.

From Cardigan to Aberaeron

Wales' highest sea-cliffs, safe, sheltered beaches, great coastal walking, and a resident pod of bottlenose dolphins all characterize the southern section of the Ceredigion coastline. Many of the coast's settlements retain a timeless, salty charm: the one-time smuggler's port of **New Quay** uncoils down the hair-raisingly steep hillside to the craggy coastline, while smaller places like **Llangrannog**, **Penbryn**, **Mwnt** and **Tresaith** juxtapose rolling pastoral countryside and wide, sweeping beaches, and brightly painted cottages huddle around the boat-filled harbour at **Aberaeron**. Just inland, at the mouth of the Teifi, is the pretty and cheerful old county town of **Cardigan** with an excellent range of pubs, shops and accommodation.

The main A487 road runs parallel to the coast, meeting the sea at Aberaeron. The regular #550 bus service links the larger seaside villages and towns along this stretch. The summer-only Cardi Bach bus (#600) connects all the villages and coves between Cardigan and New Quay.

Cardigan and around

Until the River Teifi silted up in the nineteenth century, **CARDIGAN** (Aberteifi) was one of the greatest sea-ports in Britain, although these days there's little evidence of its former status. It is, however, a sprightly little town, with some great diversions and a relaxed ambience. The town's castle, slowly being salvaged from dereliction, was founded by the Norman lord Roger de Montgomery in 1093 and was the site of the first Welsh eisteddfod in 1176.

On the south side of the river, away from the town centre, an old granary houses the **Cardigan Heritage Centre** (Canolfan Hanes Aberteifi; March–Oct daily 10am–5pm; free). The first section houses a coffee shop and exhibition about the rise and fall of the port of Cardigan, including shipping history and memories of the emigration boats that set sail for Canada and the

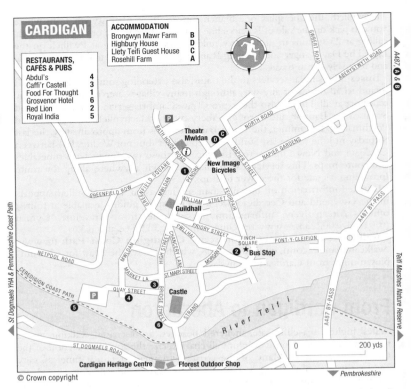

USA. The excellent second section takes a diverting look at Cardigan's long history. There's usually a temporary exhibition or two to finish off the tour. Adjacent to the Heritage Centre, the Fforest Outdoor Shop (☏01239/613961, ⓦcardiganbayactive.co.uk) runs guided **canoeing** trips and more adventurous **kayaking** trips (each £30) bumping over a few rapids.

Across the river towards the town centre, the currently out-of-bounds castle bulges at the town end of the medieval bridge. Sweeping up a hill around the site, Bridge Street becomes the picturesque High Street – leading off from here are narrow thoroughfares crammed with Georgian and Victorian buildings. High Street wends past pubs and shops to the spiky turrets of the **Guildhall**. Through the Guildhall courtyard is the town's bustling **covered market** (daily except Wed & Sun), an eclectic mix of locally produced food and plenty of browsable oddities. A couple of hundred yards up High Street (at this point called Pendre) from the Guildhall, Bath House Road dips down to the **Theatr Mwldan** (☏01239/621200, ⓦwww .mwldan.co.uk), a great place for exhibitions and performances. Priory Street leads down the hill from the Guildhall, past the council offices and on to Finch Square, where buses terminate.

While in the area, it's worth visiting the castle-crowned village of Cilgerran and the Welsh Wildlife Centre (see p.281), four miles by road but just a mile or so by cycling or walking along a riverside path; the tourist office can provide directions.

The **Ceredigion Coast Path** (see p.273) starts (or ends, depending on which way you tackle it) at the Teifi estuary, right in town opposite the Cardigan Heritage Centre.

Practicalities

Cardigan's friendly **tourist office** (July–Aug daily 10am–6pm; Sept–June Mon–Sat 10am–5pm; ☎01239/613230, ⓔcardigantic@ceredigion.gov.uk) is in the foyer of Theatr Mwldan on Bath House Road. There's **bike rental** from New Image Bicycles on Pendre (☎01239/621275).

For **accommodation**, try the basic but decent *Highbury House*, the old county jail, on Pendre (☎01239/613403; ❶–❷), or the neighbouring *Llety Teifi Guest House* (☎0781/3892431; ⓦwww.llety.co.uk; ❹–❺), a raspberry-pink place with ten contemporary broadband-equipped rooms. If you want to base yourself here while exploring the area (and you have your own transport), try the sixteenth-century riverside *Rosehill Farm* self-catering cottage in Llangoedmor, a mile and a half east of town (☎01239/612019, ⓦwww .rosehillfarm.co.uk; closed Nov–March; from £324 per week; ❸). Cardigan is just beyond the northern end of the Pembrokeshire Coast Path, which terminates four miles from town on the other side of the Teifi estuary at Poppit Sands, site of the nearest **YHA hostel** (☎0870/770 5996, ⓔpoppit@yha .org.uk; closed Nov–Feb), a newly renovated place with dorm beds from £9.95. From May to late September the Poppit Rocket bus service (2–3 daily, 3 services per week rest of year) will take you there, and the year-round #407 stops within half a mile. **Camping** is allowed in the hostel grounds. Slightly nearer to Cardigan is the *Brongwyn Mawr Farm* caravan park (☎01239/613644; from £9.50), which also takes tents. It's just north of the village of Penparc, which itself is two miles north of Cardigan on the A487.

Cardigan's colourful streets are lined with great daytime **eating** options: the home-made cawl at the *Caffi'r Castell*, on the corner of Quay and High streets, is wonderfully warming on a chilly day, while the *Food For Thought* café, at 13 Pendre, offers a good range of wholesome snacks and strong coffee. In the evenings, go for a fine curry at *Abdul's* on Quay Street (☎01239/621416) or the trendy floating restaurant *Royal India* (☎01239/621444) at the far end of Quay Street. Alternatively, head to the *Red Lion* **pub** on Pwllhai near Finch Square or the *Grosvenor Hotel*, overlooking the river on Bridge Street, for a meal or just a drink. Alternatively, there are some fabulous pubs in the surrounding villages, most notably the *Crown Inn* at Llwyndafydd (see p.277) and the *Nag's Head* at Aber-Cych (see p.282).

The southern Ceredigion coast

Cardigan's outskirts quickly give way to the rippled cliffs, expansive beaches and hedged lanes of the southern Ceredigion coast. The Gwbert road heads out of the town's neat suburbs before descending to the estuary edge and the straggling seaside village of **GWBERT**, a peaceful spot with good sea views best enjoyed from the **Cardigan Island Coastal Farm Park** (Easter–Oct daily 9.30am–6pm or dusk; £3.50), a great place for kids, offering the chance to spot dolphins and fur seals on a coastal walk.

A mile or so to the east, tiny lanes bump down to the isolated little hamlet of **MWNT**, where the exquisite sandy beach and cliffs are under the custodianship of the National Trust. Set in windswept solitude above the cliffs, the tiny, white-washed church is the oldest in Ceredigion – its foundation dates back to the sixth century, although most of today's thickset building dates from the thirteenth century. Mwnt's finest hour came in 1155, when invading Flemings landed here, only to be routed by the Welsh. The occasion, which became known as *Sul Coch y Mwnt*, the Bloody Sunday of Mwnt, has been periodically remembered through the whole skeletons and other human bones that have been unearthed en masse in the vicinity. There's some good **camping** at Mwnt, though come supplied, as there are no shops nearby. Further along the track from the church is *Tŷ Gwyn*, a fairly basic site. Alternatively, a walk up through the wooded ravine behind the church brings you to the well-equipped *Blaenwaun Farm* site (☏01239/613456; £8–17.70 per pitch), also reached on the back lane from Felinwynt.

Heading northeast past **ABERPORTH**'s twin beaches, which wrap around two adjoining bays, brings you to the scenic hamlet of **TRESAITH**. just around the rocks from its compact beach is a sandy cove with its own natural after-sea shower – a **waterfall** crashing down from the River Saith above. There's often good **surf** (heed the signs if you're swimming here, though, as there's a risk of being cut off by the tide at the northern and southern ends), as well as **dinghy races** on calmer summer Sundays. From Tresaith you can pick up the clifftop coast path and follow it around to the wide, sandy, National Trust beach at **PENBRYN**. While here, don't miss a real ale or fantastic pub fare at the bustling 🍺 *Ship Inn* (☏01239/811816, ⓦwww .shiptresaith.co.uk; ❺), which also has comfy **rooms** with fantastic sea views. Other **accommodation** options include the rich Georgian ambience of *Glandŵr* (☏01239/811442, ⓦwww.glandwrtresaith.co.uk; ❺–❻) at the top of Tresaith village on the road to Aberporth; and, a little further along, a wonderful tent-only clifftop **campsite** at the far end of the *Llety Caravan Park* (☏01239/810354, £13–15 per pitch), from where a pretty footpath descends straight to the beach. For something a little different, you can camp in a tepee for £20 at *TipiWest* on Hendre Farm, just south of Aberporth (☏07813/672336, ⓦwww.tipiwest.co.uk).

Just along the coast, three miles northeast of Tresaith, **LLANGRANNOG** is the most attractive village on the Ceredigion coast, wedged in between hills covered with bracken and gorse. The very narrow streets wind their way to the

▲ Mwnt Church

tiny seafront, catering for visitors with a couple of cafés and pubs and assorted sporting activities. The beach can become congested in midsummer – a quieter alternative is to head north over to **Cilborth Beach**, reachable in ten minutes along the coast at low tide or via a cliff path leading along the glorious National Trust headland towards **Ynys Lochtyn** and a couple of other remote strips of sand – a circuit that can be completed in about an hour. In Llangrannog, you can **stay** at the seafront *Pentre Arms* (℡01239/654345, ⓦwww.pentrearms .co.uk; ➋–➎), where it's worth shelling out a bit extra for a sea-view room.

Signs around Llangrannog point to seemingly unlikely local activities: **skiing** and **snowboarding**. There's a decent artificial slope a mile east of the village at the Urdd Centre (℡01239/654473), just off the B4321; lessons, as well as numerous other outdoor activities, are available.

From Llangranog, you can walk along the coast path towards New Quay Head, where seasonal wild flowers swath wind-blasted hillsides and cliffs that drop dramatically into clear seas. The next bay north is the glorious cave-walled beach at **CWMTYDU**, approached along tiny lanes winding steeply down from above. Two miles inland is the village of **LLWYNDAFYDD**, where the excellent ⚒ *Crown Inn* (closed Sun eve in winter) is famed for its food such as leek- and apricot-stuffed trout in almond sauce, and succulent steaks. There's also very good accommodation nearby on the A487 in Pentregat at the lovely Georgian *Grange Country House* (℡01239/654121; ➎), and, on the same estate, at the working *Grange Farm* (℡01239/654252; ➋).

New Quay

NEW QUAY (Cei Newydd) lays claim to being the original Llareggub in **Dylan Thomas's** *Under Milk Wood* (see p.172). Certainly, it has the little tumbling streets, pastel-painted Victorian terraces, cobbled harbour and dreamy isolation that Thomas evoked so successfully in his "play for voices", as well, perhaps, as the darkly eccentric characters he describes. Moreover, the poet's own experience in New Quay (he and his young family lived here during the last half of World War II) showed him the odder side of human nature. Thomas's metropolitan ways and poetic demeanour did not go down too well in such a close-knit little town, particularly so with an ex-commando officer, fresh home from the war, with whom he had a row in the *Black Lion* pub. The soldier, convinced that his wife was in a *ménage à trois* with Thomas and his wife Caitlin, followed the writer home and shot at his rented bungalow, the *Majoda*, with a machine gun, while the family was inside. The officer was charged with attempted murder in June 1945, and acquitted. Dylan Thomas and family left the area soon afterwards. Thomas's eventful time in New Quay was the subject of the 2008 film, *The Edge of Love* (see p.510), and much of the filming took place in the area.

Two free leaflets from the tourist office each highlight places where the poet spent time: *Dylan Thomas' Ceredigion*, which guides you through local villages, and *Dylan Thomas' New Quay* **walking trail**, concentrating on places he lived and his favourite pubs. If nothing else, pop into the *Black Lion* on Glanmor Terrace, with its collection of Thomas memorabilia, and *The Seahorse*, known to Thomas as the *Commercial* and the model for the *Sailor's Arms* in *Under Milk Wood*.

The town and around

New Quay's main road cuts through the upper, residential part of town, past Uplands Square, from where acutely inclined streets plunge down to a pretty

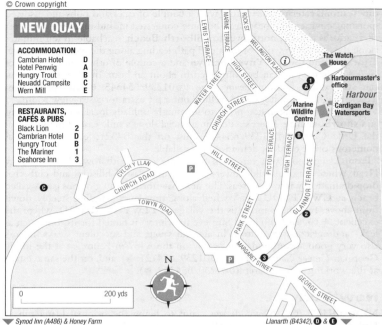

NEW QUAY

ACCOMMODATION
Cambrian Hotel	D
Hotel Penwig	A
Hungry Trout	B
Neuadd Campsite	C
Wern Mill	E

RESTAURANTS, CAFÉS & PUBS
Black Lion	2
Cambrian Hotel	D
Hungry Trout	B
The Mariner	1
Seahorse Inn	3

The Watch House

Harbourmaster's office

Harbour

Marine Wildlife Centre

Cardigan Bay Watersports

0 — 200 yds

N

▼ *Synod Inn (A486) & Honey Farm*

Llanarth (B4342), **D** *&* **E** ▼

harbour, formed by its sturdy stone quay, and with a small, curving **main beach**. Back from the sand, the higgledy-piggledy lines of multicoloured shops and houses comprise the **lower town**, the more traditionally seaside part of New Quay, full of standard-issue cafés, pubs and beach shops. A good stop is the **Marine Wildlife Centre** (April–Oct daily 10am–5pm; donation requested), tucked away down the slipway above the main harbour beach, which contains some interesting exhibits on the dolphins, sea birds and seals that inhabit Cardigan Bay. Staff will also point you to the best spots on land from which to see dolphins.

It's easy to escape the town's bustle (such as it is). The northern stretch of beach soon gives way to a rocky headland, **New Quay Head**, where an invigorating path steers along the top of the sheer drops to **Bird Rock**, aptly named for the profusion of razorbills and guillemots nesting here, and beyond to Cwmtydu. A map is available from the tourist office.

Dolphin-watching and **fishing** boat trips (see box opposite) ply the local waters. Various courses in **kayaking**, **windsurfing** and **sailing** are offered by Cardigan Bay Watersports (℡01545/561257, ⓦwww.cardiganbaywatersports .org.uk), down by the main beach.

Two miles inland at Cross Inn, the well-signposted **New Quay Honey Farm** (May–Oct Mon–Sat plus bank holidays 10am–5.30pm; £3.20) does a great job of illustrating the life and works of bees, together with chances to sample the honey and delicious mead produced here.

Practicalities

Buses stop at the south end of town on Park Street, from where any road heading downhill will bring you to the harbour and the **tourist office** (April–Sept Mon–Sat 10am–5pm; ℡01545/560865, ⓔnewquay@ceredigiontic.gov.uk), on the corner of Church Street and Wellington Place. Ensure when you're making enquiries that you specify New Quay in Wales, as distinct from Newquay in Cornwall, as it's not uncommon for people to inadvertently book themselves into the wrong country.

Accommodation is fairly limited, although in summer locals put up signs outside their houses advertising rooms for rent. For B&B, the *Hungry Trout*, above the harbour on South John Street, (℡01545/560680, Ⓦwww.thehungrytrout.co.uk; ❸–❺) has a couple of delightful rooms, while down the street towards the harbour is the attractively refurbished *Hotel Penwig* (℡01545/560910; ❸). Less than a mile out of town on the B4342, towards the village of **Gilfachreda**, is the landmark, white-painted *Cambrian Hotel* (℡01545/ 560295, Ⓦwww.cambrianhotelnewquay.co.uk; ❸), which has beautiful, understated rooms and original features like stained-glass leadlight windows. Nearby, there's a quiet caravan and tent **campsite** on the B4342 at *Wern Mill* (℡01545/580699; £6–10 per pitch), although the nearest to town is the *Neuadd* campsite (℡01545/560709; £6–10 per pitch), behind the *Penrhiwllan Inn* at the top of the hill on the main road (A486) to Synod Inn.

An ever-changing cluster of **cafés** overlooks New Quay's harbour, the pick being the stalwart, *The Mariner*, with its wide range of classic seaside fare (fish and chips, ice cream, et al). For restaurant food, your best bet in town is the *Hungry Trout* (see above), with locally caught fish and an imaginative vegetarian selection. Meals are also good at New Quay's **pubs**, notably the *Black Lion*, which has a great garden overlooking the bay; the *Cambrian Hotel* (see above); and the *Seahorse Inn*, on Margaret Street, where you'll find good food, a friendly crowd and regular live music.

Fuelled by a huddle of pubs and a transient young population, summer nights can be boisterously good-natured. It's a great base at any time of the year, with coastal walks, beaches and boat trips. **New Year's Eve** here is legendary, when virtually the whole town gets kitted out in fancy dress and spends most of the night locked in the pubs or dancing out in the streets, followed by a three-legged race around the pubs on New Year's Day.

Aberaeron and around

In complete contrast to the precipitous, zigzagging streets of New Quay, **ABERAERON**, seven miles up the coast, faces away from the ocean, its brightly coloured Georgian houses and level streets clustered instead around the town's internal harbour. Aberaeron's harmonious maritime appearance results from its being built in one fell swoop during the early nineteenth century by

Dolphin-spotting

One of only two pods in Britain, the Cambrian coast's **bottlenosed dolphins** are one of New Quay's major attractions, and can often be seen frolicking by the harbour wall, particularly when the tide is full and the weather calm. A mile-wide strip of the coastal waters forms the Ceredigion Marine Heritage Coast, in summer plied by boat trips geared around potential sightings. The pleasure jaunts run by **New Quay Boat Trips**, based at the harbourmaster's office on the harbour wall (April–Oct daily; ℡01545/560800 daytime, 560375 evenings; £8 for 1hr, or £15 for 2hr), are the cheapest, but chances of a sighting are even better on the environmentally oriented **Dolphin Survey Boat Trips** (℡01545/560032; from £18 for 2hr), which go further offshore and up along the heritage coast on data-gathering exercises, accompanied by an on-board ranger; book at the Marine Wildlife Centre (see opposite).

the Reverend Alban Gwynne. After the 1807 Harbour Act paved the way for port development, Gywnne spent his wife's inheritance dredging the Aeron estuary as a new port for mid-Wales and constructing a formally planned town around it – reputedly from a design by John Nash.

Georgian planning is most evident around the central **Alban Square**, with graceful, small-scale terraces of quoin-edged buildings and the odd pedimented porch. From the square, a grid of narrow streets stretches away to the sea at **Quay Parade**, a neatly ordered line of colourful houses on the seafront.

The southern end of Aberaeron's stony **beach** is marginally better than its northern extent, but the most agreeable activity is simply ambling around the waterfront and grazing in the cafés and pubs. The tourist office rents "town trail" audio guides (£5 refundable deposit) for a two-hour stroll around the sights. Off the main road at the southern end of town, a cluster of ageing stone buildings house **Clôs Pengarreg** (summer daily 10am–6pm; rest of year Mon–Fri 10am–4pm), a better-than-average collection of craft shops. Steep but stunning walks extend along the **coast path** south to Cei Bach and New Quay – pick up a route plan from the tourist office.

The town is positively hopping during its fun-filled **festivals** (contact the tourist office for details). Its finest hour is the annual **Seafood Festival**, held on a Sunday in early July, with live entertainment and loads of free food and drink. Other festivities include the **Cob Fair** (mid-Aug), with horses – as well as local art and crafts – taking over the streets; and the **Aberaeron Carnival** (late Aug), when the town swings to live jazz.

Practicalities

Buses stop on the A487, here known as Bridge Street, from where it's a five-minute walk along Market Street to the **tourist office** on Quay Parade (July–Sept daily 10am–5pm; Easter–June & Oct–Easter Mon–Sat 10am–5pm; ☎01545/570602, ✉aberaeron@ceredigion.gov.uk). There's a good supply of decently priced **accommodation** in and around Aberaeron. Overlooking the harbour on Cadwgan Place are the *Coedmor*, at no. 2 (☎01545/571615, Ⓦwww.coedmorbandb.co.uk; ❹), and the traditional *Arosfa*, at no. 8 (☎01545/570120; ❹). The best place in town is the central, cobalt-blue ⚥ *Harbourmaster Hotel* (☎01545/570755, Ⓦwww.harbour-master.com; ❻), with ultramodern rooms, great breakfasts and a relaxed, informal atmosphere. Next door, the new, boutique ⚥ *Pen Cei Guest House* (☎01545/571147, Ⓦwww.pen-cei-guest-house.co.uk; ❻) is an oasis of crisp cotton sheets, fresh flowers and mod cons including wi-fi.

The closest **campsite** is the *Aeron Coast Caravan Park* (☎01545/570349, £14–23 per pitch), just north of town on the A487, next to the petrol station. Alternatively try the laid-back shoreline site next door at *Drefnewydd Farm* (☎07971/402201; from £10 per pitch).

Far and away the best place to **eat** in Aberaeron is the laid-back bistro at the *Harbourmaster Hotel* (see above; closed Sun eve), with delicious lunches, imaginative evening dishes and an abundance of Antipodean wines (bookings essential). Alternatives include the buzzing ⚥ *Hive on the Quay*, Cadwgan Place (☎01545/570445; closed mid-Sept to April), which serves fine local seafood in its airy conservatory and scrumptious **honey ice cream** to eat in or take away. Of the many cafés in town, *Ji-binc*, on Market Street within the gallery of the same name, is a good choice. *La Cucina*, on Alban Square, bakes its own bread, pastries and other treats.

The *Harbourmaster* (see above) doubles as a convivial bar, specializing in Welsh real ales, which has become the focal gathering point for the town. Other

drinking options include the *Monachty Arms* at 7 Market St, with a harbourside beer garden, and the *Black Lion*, Alban Square.

Llanerchaeron

Three miles east along the A482 from Aberaeron is **Llanerchaeron** (house and gardens late March to Oct Wed–Sun 11am–5pm; £6.70; parkland all year dawn–dusk; free; NT), the substantially restored remains of a late eighteenth-century Welsh country estate. Bequeathed to the National Trust in 1989, Llanerchaeron is a remarkable example of a type of holding once common in these parts. Over the last decade or so, a century of decline has been arrested and partially reversed, leaving the Nash-designed main house in pristine shape. The original, mostly Edwardian furnishing and fittings are in place, along with an extensive and eclectic collection of small antiques – glassware, spectacles, fans, etc – amassed by London dealer Pamela Ward.

The set-piece rooms only hint at the fact that this was someone's home little more than two decades ago, something which is much more apparent in the servants' quarters and the serviced courtyard which acted as laundry, dairy, salting room and home brewery. The estate is a working organic farm, with a considerable vegetable- and fruit-growing enterprise in the **walled garden**, a time capsule of horticultural history, featuring early greenhouses and hotbeds with underground heating styled on Roman hypocausts.

The #X40 bus from Aberaeron to Lampeter passes within half a mile of the site, though you might find it just as easy to ride (or walk) the two miles along the **cycle path** connecting Aberaeron with Llanerchaeron. Apart from a small hill in town, the route is flat, as it follows the old railway line: access is off South Road in Aberaeron.

The Teifi Valley

The meandering Teifi is one of Wales' most eulogized rivers for its spawning fish, otter population and the coracles that were a regular feature from pre-Roman times. The river flows through undulating, vivid-green countryside to the river's estuary at Cardigan, dotted with a string of pleasant little market towns with a strong Welsh ambience.

The river is tidal almost as far up as the massive ramparts of **Cilgerran Castle**, and the nearby **Welsh Wildlife Centre**, though it narrows appreciably by the time it reaches the rapids at **Cenarth**, four miles beyond. Further upstream, it swirls around three sides of another fortress at **Newcastle Emlyn**, and also takes in the ancient university town of **Lampeter**. Beyond here, the river passes through harsher landscapes for eleven miles to **Tregaron**, a good base for nearby **Llanddewi Brefi**, with some spectacular walks up into the Abergwesyn Pass (see p.248) and the reedy bogland of **Cors Caron**. The river's infancy can be seen in the solid village of **Pontrhydfendigaid**, famed for its annual eisteddfod, and the nearby ruins of **Strata Florida Abbey**, beyond which the river emerges from the dark and remote **Teifi Pools**.

Cilgerran and the Welsh Wildlife Centre

Just a couple of miles up the Teifi from Cardigan (four miles by road) is the commandingly situated village of **CILGERRAN**. Behind the wide main street, the massive ramparts of the **castle** (daily: April–Sept 9.30am–6pm; Oct 9.30am–5pm; Nov–March 9.30am–4pm; £3.10; CADW) rise on a high wooded bluff above the river, which was still navigable for seagoing ships during the castle's construction in 1100. A few years later, in 1109, Nest (the "Welsh Helen of Troy") was abducted here by a lovestruck Prince Owain of Powys. Nest's husband, Gerald of Pembroke, escaped by slithering down a toilet waste chute through the castle walls.

The massive dual entry towers still dominate the castle, and the outer walls are some four feet thicker than those facing the inner courtyard. Walkways high on the battlements – not for vertigo sufferers – connect the other towers. The outer ward is a good example of the evolution of the keepless castle throughout the thirteenth century. Any potential attackers would be waylaid instead by the still-evident ditch and the outer walls and gatehouse, of which only fragmentary remains can be seen. Another ditch and drawbridge pit protect the inner ward underneath the two entry towers.

A **footpath** runs from the castle to the river's edge, flanked by display boards telling the story of the emigrants who departed from Cardigan to America, and the history of the Teifi Valley industries, particularly quarrying, brick-making and coracle fishing. If you want to see coracles in action, the best bet is Cilgerran's fun annual **coracle races**, which take place in August – the Cardigan tourist office (see p.275) has details.

A mile or so north of Cilgerran, a long driveway leads to the extensive **Teifi Marshes Nature Reserve** (unrestricted access), encompassing several important habitats – reed beds, meadows, marshes and untouched oak woodland – for otters, badgers, butterflies and birds, including Wales' largest resident group of Cetti's Warblers. A herd of **buffalo**, brought in to control invasive bulrushes, wander incongruously amongst the native inhabitants and can be seen from the various trails which access viewing hides. The modern timber-and-glass **Welsh Wildlife Centre** (Easter–Oct daily 10.30am–5pm; free) here has some informative displays and a good, spacious café with expansive views over the reserve. There's an adventure playground to keep kids entertained, and three-hour **kayak** or **canoe trips** (£30; book on ☏01239/613961) through a wooded valley upstream as far as Cilgerran Castle.

Although four miles from Cardigan by road, the reserve is only a little over a mile upstream, and can be easily reached on foot or bike along a riverside path.

Cenarth

A lure for tourists since the nineteenth century, **CENARTH**, seven miles upstream from Cardigan, is still chock-full of tearooms and gift shops thanks to its **rapids**, situated close to the main road. The low cataracts are a result of the Teifi being split by rocks as it tumbles and churns its way over the craggy limestone. The path to the rapids runs from opposite the *White Hart* pub and past the **National Coracle Centre** (Easter–Oct daily except Sat 10.30am–5.30pm; £3; other times by appointment on ☏01239/710980), a small museum with intriguing displays of original coracles from all over the world, half of them from Wales. You may still see fishermen fishing for salmon from these traditional boats, which the fishermen strap to their backs to haul upstream. Adjacent to the Coracle Centre, the *Three Horseshoes* pub (☏01239/710119) serves good bar meals (bookings advised), while two miles southwest along the B4332 at Aber-Cych, the *Nag's Head* is worth seeking out for its full-flavoured beers brewed on the premises. The website ⓦwww.visitcenarth.co.uk is a handy resource if you want to spend some time in the area, otherwise Cardigan's tourist office (see p.275) can book accommodation.

Newcastle Emlyn and around

An ancient farming and droving centre, **NEWCASTLE EMLYN** (Castell Newydd Emlyn) still retains an earthy agricultural feel, particularly on Thursdays, the busy and bellowing market day. The swooping meander of the Teifi River made the site a natural defensive position, first built on by the Normans. The "new" **castle** – of which only a few stone stacks and an archway survive – replaced this original fortress in the mid-thirteenth century. Although the ruins aren't impressive, the river setting, surrounded by grazing sheep and rugby fields, is quintessentially Welsh. The castle is tucked away at the bottom of dead-end Castle Terrace, which peels off the main street by a squat little stone **market hall**. Unsurprisingly, Bridge Street (Heol yr Bont), heads down from here to the stone bridge over the Teifi. That's about it for sights, but there are some great pubs and decent enough places to eat, along with a strong sense of community, an eclectic range of shops and unhurried charm.

Practicalities

Posters around town will give you the lowdown on local events, while the town's website (Ⓦwww.newcastle-emlyn.com) has some good stuff on it. There's free internet access at the library on Church Lane, which spurs off Bridge Street opposite the market hall.

In town, the *Emlyn Arms* **hotel** on Bridge Street (Ⓣ01239/710317, Ⓦwww .emlynarmshotel.com; ❸) is an appealing old coaching inn with comfortable modern rooms. Further out, the *Maes-y Derw* guesthouse (Ⓣ01239/710860; ❷–❸), half a mile towards Cardigan on the A484, has spacious Edwardian rooms, a good restaurant and private fishing.

The best place to **eat and drink** is the *Bunch of Grapes*, a stylish bar on Bridge Street, with guest real ales and live folk music most Thursdays in summer. Next door, the cosy *Royal Spice* does good curries. Straightforward boozing is best at the *Ivy Bush*, a gnarled old local on Emlyn Square.

Museum of the Welsh Woollen Industry

The lower Teifi's prolific past as a weaving centre is best seen in the village of **DREFACH FELINDRE**, five miles southeast of Newcastle Emlyn. At the beginning of the twentieth century, this was at the heart of the Welsh wool trade, with 43 working mills in and around the village. One of these, the Cambrian Mills, has been turned into the National Museum's **Museum of the Welsh Woollen Industry** (daily: April–Sept 10am–5pm; Oct–March Tues–Sat 10am–5pm; free). The museum's excellent exhibits span the entire process – from the different wools produced by Wales' eleven million sheep, through demonstrations of working presses and looms to stunning examples of the finished flannels, shawls and blankets. Throughout, video footage and informative wall displays put the industry into its social and cultural contexts. There's also an authentic working mill, the **Melin Teifi** (generally Mon–Fri 10am–4pm), on site, which sells its own produce. Twenty miles of paths, along which workers walked to the mills, radiate from the museum. Regular buses (#460/#461) between Cardigan and Carmarthen, via Newcastle Emlyn, pass nearby.

Llandysul and Llanybydder

The region's pace slows down even further as the lanes reach **LLANDYSUL**, sitting pretty above the Teifi some eight miles east of Newcastle Emlyn. Two main streets run parallel through the village, the lower one brushing past the massive Early English-style **church of St Tysul**. Two centuries ago, the church porch served as a goalpost in the annual match of *cnapan*, an anarchic and extremely rough, day-long football-like game which ran the length of the village. Inside the church, there's an inscribed altar stone, thought to date from the sixth century, in the Lady Chapel.

Most of Llandysul's shops and pubs are on the upper main street. The biggest reminder of the area's strong agricultural pedigree is the monthly **horse market** in the otherwise sleepy village of **LLANYBYDDER** (sometimes anglicized to Llanbyther on old road signs), some ten miles east of Llandysul along the Teifi. Held on the last Thursday of every month, the market is one of Britain's largest, bringing buyers, sellers and neighing horses together from all over the country, and evoking a bygone era.

Lampeter

Five miles further along the Teifi from Llanybydder, the old-fashioned town of **LAMPETER** (Llanbedr Pont Steffan; often known as Llambed) is best known as a remote outpost of the British university system, St Davids University College, Wales' first, founded in 1822 by the Bishop of St Davids to aid Welsh theological students unable to travel to England for their education; it only became part of the University of Wales in the 1970s. Though the town has less than three thousand residents, it's a lively place, with frequent gigs and theatre performances and an eclectic population of current students, graduates who forgot to leave, hippies and farmers.

The town's few low-key sights can be explored on a decent heritage trail, with plaques marking out historical places of interest, and is accompanied by a leaflet that you can pick up at the library. The town's three main streets – High, Bridge and College – meet at **Harford Square**, named after the local landowning family responsible for the construction of the early nineteenth-century **Falcondale Hall**, now an opulent hotel (see below), on the northern approach to Lampeter.

The main buildings of the **University College** lie off College Street, and include C.B. Cockerell's original stuccoed quadrangle of buildings, dating from 1827 and modelled along the lines of an Oxbridge college. Tucked right underneath the main buildings, the motte of Lampeter's long-vanished **castle** forms an incongruous mound amidst such order.

On the other side of Harford Square, the **High Street** is the most architecturally distinguished part of town, its eighteenth-century coaching inn, the *Black Lion*, dominating the streetscape; you can see its old stables and coach house through an archway.

Practicalities

There's no tourist office, but the town's website, Ⓦ www.lampeter.org, has contact details for accommodation, while noticeboards in the Mulberry Bush wholefood shop at 2 Bridge St carry information about local B&Bs and longer lets. Aberaeron's tourist office (see p.280) can also help. For central **accommodation** try the *Haulfan Guest House*, 6 Station Terrace (Ⓣ 01570/422718, Ⓦ www .haulfanguesthouse.co.uk; ❶–❷), a good B&B behind University College; the recently refurbished *Black Lion* on the High Street (Ⓣ 01570/422490; ❸); or the Italianate *Falcondale Mansion Hotel* (Ⓣ 01570/422910, Ⓦ www.falcondalehotel .com; ❻), within Falcondale Hall (see above), a Victorian pile surrounded by fourteen acres of parkland, located a third of a mile west along High Street then twice that along its stately drive. It's now part of the Best Western chain, and kitted out with mod cons.

If you're interested in self-catering **holiday cottage** accommodation in these parts, check the collection of beautifully restored properties run by *Under the*

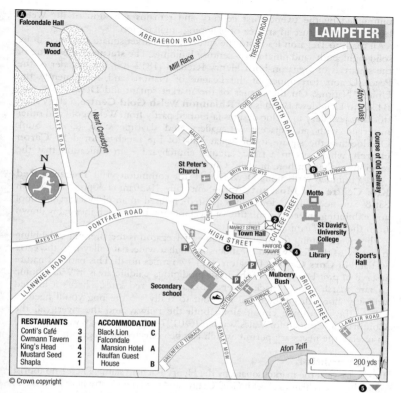

© Crown copyright

Thatch (☎01239/851410, ⓦwww.underthethatch.co.uk). As the name suggests, a few are traditional Ceredigion thatched cottages, but there are also Romany caravans and an outrageous 1970s woodland "love shack". Rates fluctuate wildly depending on seasonal demand (see the website for prices and availability; the best deals are available last minute); lets are generally weekly or half-weekly.

Lampeter's restaurant scene is fairly limited, though there's decent daytime **eating** at the *Mustard Seed* on College Road. Make sure you at least stick your head into *Conti's Café* on Harford Square, plastered with ageing accolades for its rich home-made ice cream. In the evenings, it's either pub food (notably the *King's Head* on Bridge Street) or the *Shapla* on College Street, which does the best curries for miles around. **Drinking** is better, with the friendly and fairly studenty *King's Head* (see above) serving very well-kept beer, and the *Cwmann Tavern*, half a mile down the road running south out of town, which is the best local bet for beery **live music** gigs and sessions.

The area's **festivals** include August's Women in Tune music camp (ⓦwww .womenintune.org.uk), which was hanging on at the time of writing despite a lack of funding; and late July's Food Festival (details from ☎01570/24271).

Tregaron and around

On the cusp of the verdant Teifi Valley and the desolate moors rising above it, the small town of **TREGARON**, ten miles northeast of Lampeter, feels almost untouched by the twenty-first century and remains a bastion of the Welsh language and culture in an area of galloping anglicization.

All roads to Tregaron lead into the spruced-up market square, hemmed in by solid eighteenth- and nineteenth-century buildings. The **statue** in the centre of the square is of Tregaron-born Henry Richard (1812–88), the founder of the Peace Union, forerunner of the League of Nations and, subsequently, the United Nations. On the corner of the market square and Dewi Road (the B4343 to Llanddewi Brefi) is the **Rhiannon Welsh Gold Centre**, a classy shop stocking jewellery in Celtic designs fashioned partly from Welsh gold and other materials, with an adjacent art gallery and daytime **café** (closed Sun). Overlooking the square is the squat bulk of the much-restored **St Caron church**, which sits in a large, circular churchyard – an indication that the religious settlement here predates Christianity.

Just a hundred yards along Dewi Road is the community-run **Tregaron Red Kite Centre and Museum** (April–Sept daily 10.30am–4.30pm; Oct–March Sat & Sun noon–4pm; donation requested), housed in an old Victorian school and exhibiting an eclectic mixture of local memorabilia, much inevitably drawn from the area's farming tradition.

The river running through the middle of Tregaron is the Brennig, a babbling tributary of the Teifi which meanders through a wide, flat valley into the eerie wetland of **Cors Caron** (Tregaron Bog), two miles north. This national nature reserve of peat bog is one of the most prodigious wildlife areas in Wales, home to rare marsh grasses, black adders, buzzards and red kites. There's a limited walkway along the disused rail line, but to really see the bog you'll need to follow the three-mile circuit along both the railway and the river; call the Countryside Council for Wales warden (℡01974/298480, ⊛www.ccw.gov.uk) to reserve the necessary permit, which can be collected in Tregaron.

Practicalities

Buses arrive at the market square, by the Henry Richard statue. There's no tourist office, but the Rhiannon Welsh Gold Centre and the Kite Centre have leaflets and can provide some assistance. Local **accommodation** is severely limited, although the oak-beamed, thirteenth-century *Talbot Hotel*, a classically symmetrical old drovers' inn on the square (℡01974/298208; ⊛www.talbothotel-tregaron .com; ❸), is a cosy spot to stay or to **eat**, and also excels with live roots **music** (folk, blues and so on), often featuring surprisingly big names (details at ⊛www .cambriaarts.org.uk). For plain **drinking**, hit *Y Llew Coch* (The Red Lion) by the river bridge, a youthful pub with a pool table and bar games.

Llanddewi Brefi

Heol Dewi, the road from Tregaron runs three miles south past a cottage hospital and along the Teifi to the little village of **LLANDDEWI BREFI**. If the road sign's been stolen (again), it's because of Llanddewi's fame as the fictitious home of Dafydd, the "only gay in the village" from the BBC comedy *Little Britain*. Souvenir T-shirts nodding to this unlikely notoriety are available in the village shop.

Llanddewi Brefi's previous claim to fame was the legend of 118 Welsh churchmen who met here in 519 AD and summoned Dewi Sant (St David). On appearing, Dewi began to speak to the men, but had trouble being heard, until the ground beneath him shuddered ominously and suddenly rose, giving him a natural platform to continue speaking – the massive **parish church** of St David sits on the mound to this day. Part of the church wall consists of two discernible stones inscribed with fragments of Latin script. These were originally part of a single memorial that dated from within a century of David's death – the first recorded mention of the Welsh patron saint – but they were broken up, reportedly, by an illiterate eighteenth- or nineteenth-century mason.

Pontrhydfendigaid, Strata Florida and the Teifi Pools

Six miles northeast of Tregaron, the last village on the Teifi is austere **PONTRHYDFENDIGAID** ("Bridge near the ford of the Blessed Virgin"), a grey-stoned cluster remarkable for its annual May eisteddfod in the enormous village pavilion, recently rebuilt and accommodating up to 3000 spectators. The infant Teifi flows in from the east, followed by a road that, after a mile, reaches the atmospheric ruins of the mighty **Strata Florida Abbey** (May–Sept daily 10am–5pm; £3.10; Oct–April unrestricted entry), originally located in Ystrad Fflur, "the valley of the flowers", two miles away, but relocated in its early years to this equally fertile spot. This Cistercian abbey was founded in 1164, swiftly growing into a centre for milling, farming and weaving, and becoming an important political centre for Wales. In 1238, a dying Llywelyn the Great, fearful that his work of unifying Wales under one ruler would disintegrate, summoned the lesser Welsh princes here to command them to pay homage to his son, Dafydd.

Although very little survived Henry VIII's dissolution of the monasteries, the huge, Norman west doorway gives some idea of the church's vast dimensions. Fragments of one-time side chapels include beautifully tiled medieval floors, and there's also a serene cemetery, but it's really the abbey's position that impresses most, in glorious rural solitude against wide open skies and sheep-flecked hills. A yew tree in the neighbouring graveyard shades the spot where Dafydd ap Gwilym (see p.292), fourteenth-century bard and contemporary of Chaucer, is said to be buried.

The narrow lane running due east from Strata Florida leads to Tyncwm, a farm with bridleways to the drenched grass and craggy outcrops around the **Teifi Pools**, a series of sombre lakes where the Teifi River rises. This is demanding but rewarding walking country where you may be tempted to strike out over the rocky, squelchy moorland down to the Claerwen Reservoir (see p.253). More direct access to the pools can be had from the lane that forks off the B4343 in the village of **Ffair-Rhos**, a mile north of Pontrhydfendigaid.

The best bet for **accommodation**, **eating** and **drinking** in the area is Pontrhydfendigaid's ⚞ *Llew Du* (Black Lion) pub (☏01974/831624, Ⓦblacklionhotel.co.uk; ❸), which is particularly welcoming to cyclists and walkers, and has a roaring fire when the temperature drops.

Aberystwyth

Midway along the Cambrian coast, spirited **ABERYSTWYTH** (or "Aber", as it's known locally) is a blast of fresh sea air. The presence of Aberystwyth University, one of the UK's most prestigious educational institutions (the Prince of Wales himself, Prince Charles, studied here), and Wales' National Library, makes the city home – it's claimed – to more books per capita than anywhere else in the world. There are plenty of other cultural and other diversions in town too, as well as an array of Victorian and Edwardian seaside trappings including a charming pier.

Aberystwyth's anti-establishment past and anarchic soul manifest in diverse ways. Pubs – and there are loads – stay open late, the political scene is green-tinged, and the town overall is emphatically Welsh – making it an easy-going and enjoyable place to gain an insight into the national psyche.

The precursor of Aberystwyth is the inland village of **Llanbadarn Fawr**, the seat of Wales' oldest bishopric between the sixth and eighth centuries, whose massive parish church still reeks of past power. Aberystwyth and Llanbadarn grew together around the church and the seafront thirteenth-century castle, minting its own coins and headquartering Owain Glyndŵr's revolutionaries in the Middle Ages. The *Cymdeithas yr Iaith* (Welsh Language Society) was founded in Aberystwyth in 1963 and is still located in the town, while the National Library was established here in 1907.

Two long bays skirted by pebbly beaches curve between twin rocky heads: Constitution Hill to the north, and Pen Dinas to the south above the town harbour's marina, where both the Rheidol and Ystwyth rivers empty into the sea. The town rises up towards the east from the flat plains in between the two, peaking in the district of **Penglais**, where the graceful Portland stone buildings of the National Library and the modernist blocks of the university gaze over the town's rooftops.

Arrival and information

Aberystwyth's twin **train stations** (one for main-line trains and one for the Vale of Rheidol line) adjoin each other on Alexandra Road, a ten-minute walk from the seafront on the southeastern side of the town centre. **Local buses** stop outside the main-line station, with **long–distance** ones thirty yards to the north along Alexandra Road.

The **tourist office** (July & Aug daily 10am–6pm; Sept–June Mon–Sat 10am–5pm; ☎01970/612125) is located a ten-minute stroll from Alexandra Road down Terrace Road towards the seafront. Tourist office staff can also help with accommodation and sell tickets for local events. At the time of writing there was nowhere to rent bikes in town; check with the tourist office. There's free **internet** access at the public library on Corporation Street (Mon–Fri 9.30am–8pm, Sat 9.30am–5pm).

Siop y Pethe, on North Parade, has a huge array of Welsh-interest **books**, plus magazines and music in both Welsh and English. Galloway, on Pier Street, also has a wide range, while Ystwyth Books, near the Market Hall on Princess Street, buys and sells secondhand titles.

Accommodation

With plenty of **places to stay**, accommodation is generally quite reasonably priced and easy to find, though everywhere fills up to the gills during graduation week (usually the second or third week of July), when prices invariably jump. Guesthouses and B&Bs predominate; anywhere on the seafront is likely to charge a premium.

Hotels and guesthouses

Bodalwyn Queens Ave ☎01970/612578, ⓦwww.bodalwyn.co.uk. Spacious, stylishly decorated guesthouse blending contemporary and older furnishings. All rooms have well-appointed en-suite bathrooms, and breakfast is served in a sunny conservatory. ❷–❸

Conrah Country House Rhydgaled, Chancery ☎01970/617941, ⓦwww.conrah.co.uk. Elegant Georgian country-house hotel four miles south of town along the A487, with luxurious rooms,

comfortable lounges, sauna, heated indoor pool and a superb restaurant, all set amid 22 acres of beautifully landscaped grounds. ❻–❼

Harry's 40–46 North Parade ☎01970/612647, ⓦwww.harrysaberystwyth.com. Excellent mid-range conversion of four terraced houses in the heart of town, with a fabulous restaurant and bar downstairs (p.293). All rooms are en suite. ❹–❺

Helmsman 43 Marine Terrace ☎01970/624132, ⓔhelman_guesthouse@hotmail.com. Tall seafront

ABERYSTWYTH

ACCOMMODATION

Bodalwyn	A
Conrah Country House	I
Glan-y-mor Leisure Park	H
Harry's	F
Helmsman	C
Maes-y-Môr	D
Plas Dolau	J
Richmond	B
Savannah	E
Yr Hafod	G

RESTAURANTS, CAFÉS & PUBS

Castle Hotel	9
Gannets Bistro	4
Harry's	F
Little Italy	3
MG's Café	6
Orangery	2
Rummers	11
Shilam Tandoori	10
Ship and Castle	5
Treehouse	1
Y Cŵps	8
Yr Hen Llew Du	7

H (3 miles), Borth (5 miles) & Machynlleth (20 miles)

Llanbadarn Fawr (0.5 miles) & (2.5 miles)

Midfield (1.5 miles), (3 miles) & Cardigan (40 miles)

Constitution Hill

Cliff Railway

On Your Bike

North Road

Town Hall

Cinema

Queen's Road

Terrace Road

North Parade

Portland Road

Portland St

Bath St

Marine Terrace

Penglais Road

Northgate St

Poplar Row

Bronglais Hospital

Llanbadarn Road

Aberystwyth University

Students Union

Aberystwyth Arts Centre

National Library of Wales

Ceredigion Museum

Library

Pier

Pavilion

North Beach

University College of Wales

War Memorial

St Michael's

Castle

New Promenade

New St

New Street

Vine Street

Pier St

Eastgate

Market Street

Dark Gate Street

Market

Queens St

Grays Inn Rd

Bridge St

Mill St

High St

Vulcan St

Sea View Pl

South Rd

Pier Pl

South Marine Ter

Tabernacle Chapel

Trefechan Rd

Pen-Yr-Angor

Penparcau Road

Marina

River Rheidol

South Beach

CARDIGAN BAY

Pen Dinas

Train Station

Bus Stops

Vale of Rheidol Railway

Park Avenue

Alexandra Road

Plascrug Avenue

Stanley Road

School of Art

Boulevard St Brieuc

Sports Ground and Plascrug Leisure Centre

Cefnllan

200 yds

N

THE CAMBRIAN COAST

4

289

© Crown copyright

guesthouse in the middle of the curving Promenade. Book early for a sea view. ❷–❸

Richmond 44–45 Marine Terrace ☎01970/612201, ⓦwww.richmondhotel.uk.com. Comfortable, family-run seafront hotel, with a full complement of en-suite rooms (most with sea views), plus a restaurant, bar and small garden. ❺

Savannah 27 Queens Rd ☎01970/615131, ⓦwww.savannahguesthouse.co.uk. Well-priced family-run guesthouse close to the town centre, with some en-suite rooms. ❸

Yr Hafod 1 South Marine Terrace ☎01970/617579, ⓦwww.yrhafod.co.uk. The best seafront accommodation, with spacious, well-maintained and tastefully decorated rooms (some en suite), appealingly situated south of the castle. ❷–❸

Hostels, campsites and self-catering

Aberystwyth University Penglais ☎01970/621960, ⓦwww.aber.ac.uk/visitors. During the university's summer recess (mid-June to mid-Sept) the university offers some single-bed

accommodation in self-contained flats including bed linen, full cooking facilities and access to the university facilities, including two sports halls and a heated pool. ❶

Glan-y-mor Leisure Park Clarach Bay ☎01970/828900, ⓦwww.sunbourne.co.uk. Situated on the other side of Constitution Hill, to the north of Aberystwyth, with a variety of options including on-site caravans and tent pitches, plus a superb range of leisure facilities including (for an extra fee) a heated indoor pool and gym. From £13 per pitch.

Maes-y-Môr 25 Bath St ☎01970/639270, ⓦwww.maesymor.co.uk. Brightly painted and very central hostel with cheap single and twin rooms and a good guests' kitchen. ❶

Plas Dolau Lovesgrove, three miles east of town. Well-run hostel, catering primarily to groups, in a characterful Victorian mansion. The bunks (from £15) come equipped with linen and there are extensive cooking facilities. Buses #525 and #526 will drop passengers at the end of the hostel drive. ❷

The Town

The 430-foot **Constitution Hill** (Y Graig Glais) rises sharply from the rocky beach at the long Promenade's northern end. It's accessible on foot, but if you don't fancy the invigorating but stiff walk up, you can take the clanking 1896 **cliff railway** (daily mid-March to early Nov 10am–5pm; early Nov to mid-March Wed–Sun 10am–5pm; £2.95 return; ⓦwww.aberystwythcliffrailway .co.uk), which creeps up the crooked tracks at scarcely more than walking pace from the grand terminus building at the top of Queen's Road, behind the Promenade.

At the summit you'll find a café, picnic area, telescopes and an octagonal **camera obscura** (hours as for railway; free), a device popular in the pre-TV era using a mirror and hefty lens to project close-up and long-shot views over the town, the surrounding mountains and bays, plus a vista of the hordes of caravans to the north, resembling legions of tanks poised for battle. The existing structure was built in the 1980s on the ground plan of the original, but with its scale expanded to make it the largest of its type in the world.

From the bottom of Constitution Hill, the **Promenade** – officially Marine Terrace – arcs away to the south, past ornate benches decorated with snakes, a continuous wall of hotels and guesthouses, a prim bandstand and a shingle beach. Terrace Road peels off to the left after a couple of hundred yards, almost immediately reaching the tourist office and the **Amgueddfa Ceredigion** (Ceredigion Museum; Mon–Sat 10am–5pm; free), atmospherically housed in the ornate Edwardian Coliseum music hall. Mementos of the building as a theatre and cinema give a sense of place to an otherwise disparate collection, including cosy reconstructed cottages, dairies complete with separating and churning equipment, a nineteenth-century pharmacy, exhibits on the local geology and a surprisingly interesting look at the history of weights and measures.

Marine Terrace continues to the spindly **pier**, beyond which a John Nash-designed turreted **villa** dominates the seafront. Dating from 1790, the villa was massively extended in the 1860s, as a hotel designed to soak up the anticipated masses arriving on the new rail line. The venture failed, though, and in 1872, it was sold to the fledgling university, whose property it remains. The Promenade cuts around the front of the building to a rocky headland, where the **castle** ruins (unrestricted access) stare blankly out to sea. Built by Edward I as part of his conquest of Wales, the thirteenth-century fortress is more notable for its breezy position than for the buildings themselves, of which the two outer gates are the most impressive remains. South of the castle is the quieter, sandy beach along South Marine Terrace, which peters out by the wide **harbour**, the mouth of the Rheidol and Ystwyth rivers. The quietest beach is further south still, across the other side of the rivers' mouth, at **Tanybwlch**. High above the shingle strand is the Iron Age hillfort of **Pen Dinas** (413ft), crowned with what looks like a chimney – actually an 1853 memorial to the Duke of Wellington. Paths lead to the top from the car park at Tanybwlch.

The rest of town

A couple of blocks inland from the Promenade, you'll find the terminus of the **Vale of Rheidol Railway** (see p.294), next to the main-line train station on Alexandra Road. A hundred yards north of the station, Stanley Road forks off to the right, leading down to the splendid **School of Art** (Mon–Fri 10am–5pm; free) at Buarth Mawr. Originally bequeathed to the university by the Davies sisters of Gregynog Hall (see p.261), this impressive Edwardian building, topped with a distinctive cupola, has been the home of the art department since 1995. The public galleries on the ground floor mount both touring exhibitions and rotating exhibitions from the university's extensive permanent collection, with an emphasis on Welsh art.

▲ Art Nouveau tearoom, Aberystwyth

North Parade meets up with Queen's Road at the bottom of Northgate Street; the latter winds east, becoming Penglais Road as it climbs the hill towards the university's main campus and the fascinating **National Library of Wales** (Mon–Sat 9.30am–5pm; free; Ⓦ www.llgc.org.uk). Housed in a massive white stone Edwardian building overlooking the town, the library's fine manuscripts include the oldest extant Welsh text, the twelfth-century *Black Book of Carmarthen*, and the earliest manuscript of The Mabinogion. Temporary exhibitions are held in the corridors near the entrance, the upstairs Gregynog Gallery and the downstairs Peniarth Gallery, and are invariably excellent. Displays from the library's permanent collection of books, manuscripts and papers include the **World of the Book**, which looks at the history of the written word and publishing in Wales. Free tickets need to be obtained in advance for entry into the **Reading Rooms**, which boast an enormous range of texts, maps, photos and documents, including, as one of the UK's copyright libraries, copies of every new book published in Britain. You'll need two forms of ID, including one that shows your current address. Hour-long **guided tours**, also free, take place on Mondays at 11am (reservations essential; call ☏ 01970/632800). The National Library is also home to the impressive exhibition and performance space, the **Drwm**.

While in the Penglais area, you might want to check out the excellent **Aberystwyth Arts Centre**, a quarter of a mile further up the hill from the National Library in the middle of the university's main campus. A curious mix of 1960s brutalism and postmodern elegance, the Arts Centre is a great place to while away an hour or two, taking in the various temporary art and ceramics exhibitions, browsing the designer crafts and bookshops, catching a movie or enjoying a drink in the café, which affords sublime views over the town and bay.

Elsewhere, visitors are welcome to attend rehearsals of the Côr Meibion Aberystwyth **male voice choir**, if it's not on tour; the tourist office has details of venues and times. To unwind, the Plascrug Leisure Centre (☏ 01970/624579), off the Llanbadarn Road, has two indoor pools, a sauna and solarium, squash and tennis courts, and a multi-gym.

Llanbadarn Fawr

A mile inland from the main resort is **LLANBADARN FAWR**, the original settlement from which Aberystwyth grew. Now all but intertwined with Aberystwyth proper, its knot of busy roads would warrant little attention except for the stunning sight of the massive **St Padarn parish church**. The present structure was completely rebuilt in the thirteenth century, but religious association with the spot goes back to the Breton St Padarn establishing a monastic settlement here in the second half of the sixth century, decades before even St Augustine's mission to the English of 597 AD.

Inside the church, opposite the main door, hangs an enlargement of a page from *Rhygyfarch's Psalter* of 1079, one example of the beautifully decorated texts for which the monks of Llanbadarn became renowned. In the south transept, there's a fascinating exhibition on St Padarn's monastic foundation and the area's history that includes two beautiful tenth-century crosses, moved inside from the churchyard in 1916. The taller one, about eight feet high, is woven with exquisite Celtic tracery. Perhaps the most entertaining part of the exhibition deals with poet **Dafydd ap Gwilym** (c.1320–70) and his upbringing in Llanbadarn parish. His poem *Merched Llanbadarn*, ("Women of Llanbadarn") tells of his frustration at sitting in the church watching the beautiful parish girls, as demonstrated in its opening extract:

Plygu rhag llid yr ydwyf,
Pla ar holl ferched y plwyf!
Am na chefais, drais drawsgoed,
Onaddun'yr un erioed,
Na morwyn fwyn ofynaig,
Na merch fach, na gwrach, na gwraig.

Passion doubles me over,
Plague take all the parish girls!
Because, frustrated trysting,
I've had not a single one.
No lovely, longed-for virgin,
Not a wench nor witch nor wife.

Eating, drinking and entertainment

Aberystwyth's cultural and gastronomic life is a cosmopolitan, year-round affair, thriving on students in term time and visitors in the summer. As well as a varied range of **pubs** and **restaurants**, the town is a good place to hear Welsh **music** and a lively centre for theatre and cinema. For a slice of Edwardian gentility, take afternoon tea in one of the seafront hotels along the Promenade. Daytime **café** culture is booming in the town centre, and the Arts Centre (see opposite) is home to no less than two fabulous cafés and two bars.

Restaurants and cafés

Gannets Bistro 7 St James Square ☎01970/617164. Small, long-established restaurant reliably producing delicious and imaginative dishes using local farm produce and seafood. Open Wed–Sat.

Harry's 40–46 North Parade ☎01970/ 612647, ⓦwww.harrysaberystwyth.com. One of the best restaurants in town, yet fun and informal, serving the likes of salmon and prawn rillette and roasted half duck, with a daily specials board. Book ahead.

Little Italy 51 North Parade ☎01970/625707. Cosy and atmospheric local favourite serving generous pizzas and pastas at very reasonable prices. Good seafood antipasti and a wide range of vegetarian options, too.

MG's Café 26 Chalybeate St. Comfy sofas, newspapers and Aberystwyth's best espresso, along with a range of savoury dishes and tasty cakes.

Orangery Market St ☎01970/617606. Sophisti- cated wine and tapas bar which also does well- priced meals.

Shilam Tandoori Station Building, Alexandra Rd ☎01970/615015. Superb modern Indian restau- rant with unusual specialities and good vegetarian choices.

Treehouse 14 Baker St ☎01970/615791. Upbeat, mostly vegetarian organic food shop and restaurant, good for veg rissoles, pizza slices, fruit smoothies, good coffee and a range of daily specials. Closed Sun.

Pubs

Castle Hotel 37 South Rd. Built in the style of an ornate Victorian gin palace, this pub hosts live local bands at weekends and has a good bar menu with vegetarian specialities.

Rummers Bridge St. Late-opening, popular pub and wine bar with sawdust on the floor, outside seating by the river and live music Thurs–Sun.

Ship and Castle Corner of Vulcan and High sts. Nautical-style bar, with a good range of beer, cider and food. Hosts regular Welsh and Irish folk music, best on Wed.

Y Cwps (*Coopers Arms*), Llanbadarn Rd. Fun and friendly Welsh local, with regular folk and jazz nights and jam sessions.

Yr Hen Lew Du (*The Old Black Lion*), Bridge St. Boisterous, very Welsh and hugely enjoyable pub. Easily the best place in Aberystwyth to catch an international match on the big screen.

Entertainment

Aberystwyth Arts Centre The University, Penglais ☎01970/623232, ⓦwww.aberystwythartscentre .co.uk. The town's main venue for arthouse cinema, touring theatre, classes, events and wide-ranging temporary exhibitions. From late July through Aug there's always some kind of music on – anything from classical music to popular shows.

Commodore Cinema Bath St ☎01970/612421. Screens mainstream current releases.

Drwm National Library, Penglais ☎01970/632548, ⓦwww.drwm.llgc.org.uk. Hip new centre for film, lectures and concerts.

Around Aberystwyth

Immediately inland of Aberystwyth is the **Vale of Rheidol**, a region of forested glades and remote villages, easily accessed by road or, more enjoyably, rail, by the narrow-gauge steam train that serves the area, terminating at the spectacular **Devil's Bridge**.

The coast north of Aberystwyth draws sunseekers to the beach at **Borth** and the dunes close to the mouth of the Dyfi estuary. Birdwatchers will prefer to head further northeast to the RSPB's **Ynys-Hir Nature Reserve**, with its complex series of habitats.

The Vale of Rheidol

From Aberystwyth, the River Rheidol winds its way up to a secluded, wooded valley, where occasional old industrial workings have moulded themselves into the contours, past waterfalls and minute villages. These glorious landscapes are best seen from aboard one of the trains of the **Vale of Rheidol Railway** (July & Aug at least two services daily; Easter–June, Sept & Oct two services five or six days per week; £13.50 return; ☎01970/625819, ⓦwww.rheidolrailway .co.uk), a narrow-gauge steam train which huffs and puffs along twelve miles of sheer rock faces, climbing six hundred feet in the process. It was built in 1902, ostensibly for the valley's lead mines but with a canny eye on its tourist potential. For many years it operated as part of British Rail's network, running steam trains into the late 1980s (some twenty years after steam locos had ceased operating elsewhere), until being sold to the private group which now operates it using authentic Rheidol rolling stock. The trip takes one hour each way, and is most enjoyable from the comfortable first-class observation carriage (£2 extra each way) or the open-sided "summer car".

If you'd rather drive, the easiest way is to take the A4120 along the south side of the valley direct to Devil's Bridge (see opposite) or the A44 along the north side; the two meet at Ponterwyd. You can also explore the valley by bike using the **Rheidol Cycle Trail**, a combination of designated cycle paths and quiet country lanes which runs eighteen miles from Aberystwyth to Devil's Bridge: the tourist office in Aberystwyth has a free leaflet outlining the route.

The tiny hamlet of **CAPEL BANGOR**, five miles east of Aberystwyth along the A44, is home to the **Rheidol Riding Centre** (☎01970/880863, ⓦwww.rheidol-riding-centre.co.uk), offering a variety of lessons and leisure rides for all standards. The 300-year-old *Tynllidiart Arms* merits a stop for its homebrew beer and summertime draught cider. Nearby, the **Cwm Rheidol Reservoir** is reached by a narrow riverside route off the main road. This is the final element in a small, showpiece hydroelectric scheme that starts high in the headwaters of the Rheidol River at the Nant-y-moch Reservoir. An **information centre** (Easter & May–Sept 11am–3.30pm; free) explains the scheme's significance, and a visit is essential to appreciate the free 45-minute tour of the **power station**, where impressive sluices and channels funnel the water according to need. The reservoir dam and weir are floodlit nightly, from dusk until 11pm in the summer, 10pm in the winter. Behind the visitor centre, the **Magic of Life Butterfly House** (Easter–Sept daily 10am–5pm; Oct 10am–4pm; £5.50) houses dozens of beautiful butterflies and moths in a wild garden and tropically heated polytunnel.

Some remains of old lead workings are evident on the banks of the reservoir, although the valley's mining legacy is better seen further along, as the road begins to narrow before finally disappearing into a wood as a mud track. From here, paths rise either side of the river to overlook the burned orange spoil, vividly coloured water and bright plants, fitted snugly into their green landscape. A sharp path on the south side of the river climbs up to Rhiwfron halt on the Rheidol Railway (see opposite).

Llywernog Mine Museum and Ponterwyd

Heading east, the A44 winds up into **galena** country, tucked between the bleak moorland of Plynlimon (see p.259) and the rugged mountains to the south. The silver-rich lead ore was found throughout the region and scores of mines sprang up, each plugging away at the lode until waterlogging made the mines uneconomic. In the boom years, the latter half of the 1800s, the whole of northern Ceredigion lured speculators and opportunists by the trainful. The remains – waste tips scarring hillsides and shafts pockmarking former sites – are now mostly hidden amongst the exotic evergreens of the Rheidol Forest. Both remains and forest can be visited on wonderful walks and mountain bike rides from the **Bwlch Nant-yr-Arian visitor centre** (daily: Easter–Sept 10am–5pm; Oct–Easter generally 10am to dusk; entry free; ℡01970/890694, ⓦwww.nantyrarian.com), seven miles east of Capel Bangor. A free leaflet details a half-hour all-access walkway around a small lake, plus a couple of longer hikes (1hr & 2.5hr). The visitor centre's café terrace is perfect for viewing the **red kite feeding** that takes place at 3pm during daylight saving (or 2pm during non-daylight saving). If you've brought a bike along (there are no rentals available here), the woods also offer top-class **mountain biking**, notably on the 16km Summit Trail, which is classed as difficult and will take at least an hour and a half.

The forest's lush foliage makes it difficult to imagine how stark the valley once looked. A truer picture unfolds a mile further east with the impressively barren scenery around the **Llywernog Mine Museum & Caverns** (Easter– May daily 10am–5pm; June–Aug 10am–6pm; Sept–Nov daily 11am–5pm; £6.95; ⓦwww.silverminetours.co.uk), which opened in the 1740s and closed in the early twentieth century, then reopened in the early 1970s. The site has since expanded in an appropriately rustic manner. A low-key mock-up of a working mine, housing an interesting museum, leads on to a collection of rusted machinery and the dank, dark mine itself, visitable on a rewarding thirty-minute underground tour. Topside, you can pan for "fool's gold" or dowse for veins of galena.

The largest settlement to spring up around the mines was **PONTERWYD**, a mile from Llywernog on the banks of the Rheidol. Walking aside, there's little of interest here; indeed, one of the funniest sections in George Borrow's *Wild Wales* tells of his night in the inn at Ponterwyd – now the *George Borrow Hotel* (℡01970/890230, ⓦwww.thegeorgeborrowhotel.co.uk; ❶–❹) – when the pompous Englishman met his match in a pugnacious landlord, who, even in 1854, was complaining about the numbers of unimaginative tourists ignoring his and other local villages and flocking instead to Devil's Bridge.

Devil's Bridge

Folk legend, incredible scenery and travellers' lore combine at **DEVIL'S BRIDGE** (Pontarfynach), a tiny settlement twelve miles east of Aberystwyth – reached by road (A4120) or the Vale of Rheidol Railway – built largely for the growing visitor trade of the last few hundred years.

The main attraction is the Devil's Bridge itself, where three roads (the A4120, the B4343 and the B4574) converge and cross the churning River Mynach yards above its confluence with the Rheidol to form three bridges, one on top of the other. The road bridge in front of the alpine *Hafod Arms* hotel (see below) is the most recently built of the three, dating from 1901. Immediately below it and wedged between the rock faces are the stone bridge from 1753, and, at the bottom, the original bridge, dating from the eleventh century and reputedly built by the monks of Strata Florida Abbey.

To see the bridges – and it is well worth it – you have to enter the **turnstiles** on either side of the modern road bridge. With your back to the hotel, the right-hand side (£1) is the shorter route, signposted to the Punch Bowl. Slippery steps lead down to the deep cleft in the rock, where the water pounds and hurtles through the gap crowned by the bridges. The Punch Bowl is the name given to a series of rock bowls scooped by the sheer power of the thundering river, which rushes through past bright-green mossy rocks and saturated lichen.

On the opposite side of the road is a **ticket office** (Easter–Oct daily 9.45am–5pm) – pay £2.50 or pass through turnstiles (£2) when closed – which opens out onto a path leading down into the valley and ultimately to the crashing **Mynach Falls**. The scenery here is magnificent: sharp, wooded slopes rising away from the frothing river, with distant mountain peaks surfacing on the horizon. A platform overlooks the series of falls, from where a steep flight of steps takes you further down to a footbridge dramatically spanning the river at the bottom. Note that Devil's Bridge has been a popular day excursion for centuries; to escape some of the inevitable congestion, consider visiting at the beginning or end of the day, or out of season.

The railway terminates half a mile away at a tinpot shack, just by Devil's Bridge **post office**, which has some worthwhile booklets on local walks. For **accommodation**, there's the rather plush *Hafod Hotel* (℡01970/890232, ⓦ www.thehafodhotel.co.uk; ❹–❺), midway between the station and the bridges, and reasonably priced **camping** at *Woodlands Caravan Park* (℡01970/890233, ⓦ www.woodlandsdevilsbridge.co.uk; £9.50–11 per pitch) by the petrol station, just beyond the bridges. The *Hafod Hotel* serves decent **food** (closed Mon evenings), as do a couple of simple cafés nearby.

The Vale of Ystwyth

The Ystwyth River runs pretty much parallel to the Rheidol, a couple of miles to the south. Four miles south of Devil's Bridge is the quiet village of **PONTRHYDYGROES**, the former centre of local lead-mining activity. The B4574 climbs out of the village and past the delightful country estate of **Hafod**, once the seat of a great house belonging to the wealthy Johnes family. In the late eighteenth century, Thomas Johnes commissioned a mansion here in the Picturesque style; it was added to by John Nash, amongst others, but ravaged by fire in 1807. The sumptuous replacement house was demolished in 1958 as an unsafe ruin, and all that remains is the beautiful estate Johnes landscaped and forested two hundred years ago. The church, off the B4574, is the best place to embark on the waymarked **trails** that lead through the estate, past its trickling streams, monumental relics and planted glades, down to the river. A bridge spans the river, where paths fan out along its banks and up through the tiny valley of the Nant Gau.

Continuing east, a small road grinds uphill into the bizarre moonscape surrounding **CWMYSTWYTH**, a small, semi-derelict village at the bottom of a valley of old lead mines, deserted in the late nineteenth century when the mines were exhausted. The river shimmers past abandoned shafts, tumbledown cottages, twisted tramways and grey heaps of spoil littering spartan hillsides. The isolated road continues to climb the uninhabited slopes, before dropping down into the Elan Valley and its reservoirs.

North from Aberystwyth

The A487 runs north from Aberystwyth towards Machynlleth, slicing between the mountains to the east and the flat lands bordering the vast Dyfi estuary. The seaward plain is one of the most surprising landscapes in Wales, at its heart a raised bog, **Cors Fochno**, visible from the main road but better viewed from the rail line or the coastal B4353. This road sneaks through **Borth**, stretching for nearly two miles along the seafront, to the **nature reserve** at Ynyslas, the best place to explore the sand dunes.

Inland, attractions worth a detour from the A487 include the roadside village of **Furnace**, with its eighteenth-century iron foundry and access to the lovely **Artists' Valley**, and nearby **Ynys-hir**, an RSPB nature reserve with an impressive range of bird habitats.

Borth and Ynyslas can be reached from Aberystwyth on buses #511 and #512. The #28 and #X32 to Machynlleth run through Furnace and Ynys-hir. You can also get to Borth and Machynlleth by train.

Borth and Ynyslas

Hemmed by the sea on one side and a vast peat bog on the other, **BORTH**, five miles north of Aberystwyth, is an old fishing village that gradually adapted to tourism, mainly in the shape of the caravan parks that still fringe the village. The linear village is strung out along one ruler-straight street (High Street) which regularly gets battered by weather fronts from the Atlantic, with ferocious winds in winter. Its shallow **beach**, some three miles in length, is excellent: swimming is fine as long as you don't go too far up towards the mouth of the Dyfi. Kids will enjoy the creatures at the **Animalarium** zoo, half a mile off High Street (daily: Easter–Oct 10am–6pm; Nov–Easter 11am–4pm; £7.50). The section of the Ceredigion **coast path** (p.273) between Borth and Aberystwyth (3hr one way) is a wonderful up-and-down route with some great beach stops. You can also easily return by bus or train.

Accommodation mainly revolves around the caravan parks, but there's a lovely Edwardian **YHA hostel** at the northern end of the High Street (Easter–Oct; ☎0870/770 5708, ✆borth@yha.org.uk; ❶), with dorm beds from £9.95 and some double and family rooms, as well as a licensed bar. For **eating** there are a few cafés and **pubs**, the best of which is the *Railway Hotel*.

To the north, the flat landscape meets the formidable sand dunes that line the southern side of the Dyfi estuary. The road follows the coast a couple of miles to **YNYSLAS**, entrance to the dramatic estuary-side **Ynyslas nature reserve** (unrestricted access), most notable for its birdlife. In winter, wading and sea birds feed amongst the dunes and mud flats, while in summer, butterflies flit amongst vibrant sand plants growing in the grass. The views here stretch inland to the mountains, along the estuary and coast, and over the river to the colourful huddle of Aberdyfi. Staff at the Countryside Council for Wales **visitor centre** (Easter–Sept daily 10am–4pm; ☎01970/872901) – the starting point for guided walks and tours most summer weekends – can point you to a short circular dune walk or half a mile along the beach to a **fossilized forest**. At low tides, the sands near the water's edge are studded with the petrified stumps of a dozen or so 5000-year-old trees, a reminder that the coast was some twelve miles away when these trees were in their prime. A more romantic explanation is the Welsh legend that tells of a drowned land known as Cantre'r Gwaelod which was protected by sea walls and floodgates. Their keeper, Seithenyn, happened to get drunk the night of an almighty storm and the sea burst through, drowning a thousand people and fourteen settlements.

The Borth road rejoins the A487 a couple of miles south of the hamlet of **FURNACE** which, as its name suggests, grew principally as an industrial centre, firstly around silver refining and then iron smelting. Both activities centred around the **Dyfi Furnace** (unrestricted access), a barn-like building constructed to harness the power of the Einion River, with an immense water wheel driving the bellows. Take five minutes to stroll around the back to a picturesque waterfall.

The adjacent narrow lane follows the river through a forest and out into the idyllic **Cwm Einion**, known as "Artists' Valley" because of its popularity with nineteenth-century landscape painters. A parking area about a mile and a half along the lane gives access to footpaths which head up into the deserted foothills of Plynlimon (see p.259), across the spongy moors and through dark conifer forests to the remote glacial lakes of **Llyn Conach** and **Llyn Dwfn**, three miles away.

Half a mile north of Furnace, a short lane runs seaward to *Ynyshir Hall* hotel and restaurant (see p.302) and the RSPB's **Ynys-hir Nature Reserve** (reserve daily 9am–9pm or dusk; visitor centre April–Oct daily 10am–5pm, Nov–March Wed–Sun 10am–4pm; £2). The thousand-plus-acre site comprises five distinct habitats. Redstarts, pied-flycatchers and warblers flit about the ancient hanging oak woodland so typical of mid-Wales; cormorants flock to the estuarine salt marshes; red-breasted mersangers and elusive otters inhabit the freshwater streams and pools; remnant peat bogs are a riot of wild flowers in spring; and winter brings water rails to the reed beds to join the herons. The attractions are obvious to the birders who return time and again to the network of hides, but there's enough along the one- or two-hour designated trails to interest anyone, and most weekends there are special-interest guided walks (call for details on ☎01654/700222 or visit ⓦwww.rspb.org.uk/wales).

Southern Cadair Idris and the Dyfi and Talyllyn valleys

The southern coastal reaches of Snowdonia National Park are almost entirely dominated by **Cadair Idris** (2930ft), a five-peaked massif standing defiant in its isolation. Tennyson claimed never to have seen "anything more awful than the great veil of rain drawn straight over Cader Idris", but catch it on a good day, and the views from the top – occasionally stretching as far as Ireland – are phenomenal. During the last Ice Age, the heads of glaciers scalloped out two huge cwms from Cadair Idris' distinctive dome, leaving thousand-foot cliffs dropping away on all sides to cool, clear lakes. The largest of these amphitheatres is Cwm Gadair, the **Chair of Idris**, which takes its name from a giant warrior poet of Welsh legend, although some prefer the notion that Idris' Chair refers to a seat-like rock formation on the summit ridge, where anyone spending the night (specifically New Year's Eve, some say) will become a poet, go mad or die.

Cadair Idris' southern limits are lapped by the broad expanse of the Dyfi estuary, which in turn bleeds into the grand scenery of the **Dyfi Valley**, often described as one of the greenest corners of Europe. The valley's focal point is the engaging town of **Machynlleth**, which lies just south of the renowned **Centre for Alternative Technology**.

Small-scale coastal resorts are peppered throughout the region including **Tywyn**, from where you can ride the narrow-gauge **Talyllyn Railway** seven

4

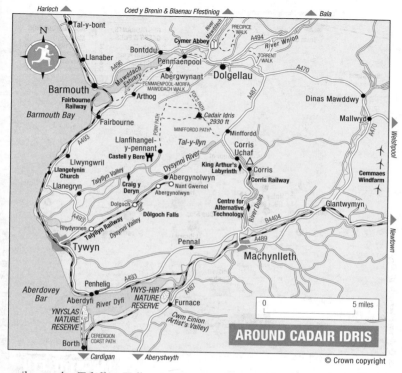

Around the map labels:
Harlech ▲ Coed y Brenin & Blaenau Ffestiniog ▲ ▲ Bala
Tal-y-bont
PRECIPICE WALK
Cymer Abbey
River Wnion
A494
Bontddu
TORRENT WALK
Llanaber
Penmaenpool
Abergwynant
Dolgellau
A470
PENMAENPOOL-MORFA MAWDDACH WALK
Mawddach Estuary
A496
Barmouth
Arthog
Fairbourne Railway
Barmouth Bay
Dinas Mawddwy
Fairbourne
Cadair Idris 2930 ft
Mallwyd
A487
MINFFORDD PATH
Llanfihangel-y-pennant
Tal-y-llyn
Minffordd
A470
Castell y Bere
Corris Uchaf
Welshpool
Llwyngwril
Dysynni River
King Arthur's Labyrinth
Corris
Cemmaes Windfarm
Llangelynin Church
Talyllyn Valley
Abergynolwyn
Corris Railway
Llanegryn
Craig y Deryn
Nant Gwernol
Abergynolwyn
River Dulas
Newtown
Dolgoch
Centre for Alternative Technology
Glantwymyn
Dôlgoch Falls
A493
Rhydyronen
Talyllyn Railway
Dysynni Valley
B4404
Tywyn
Pennal
A489
Machynlleth
Penhelig
A493
Aberdovey Bar
Aberdyfi
River Dyfi
YNYS-HIR NATURE RESERVE
A487
Furnace
0   5 miles
YNYSLAS NATURE RESERVE
CEREDIGION COAST PATH
Cwm Einion (Artist's Valley)
AROUND CADAIR IDRIS
Borth
▼ Cardigan   ▼ Aberystwyth
© Crown copyright

miles up the **Talyllyn Valley** to **Abergynolwyn** at the foot of Cadair Idris, within a short distance of the brooding thirteenth-century **Castell-y-Bere** and the inland cormorant colony at **Craig yr Aderyn**.

A well-coordinated network of bike routes, trains, steam rail lines and buses make **getting around** the area easy.

Machynlleth and around

MACHYNLLETH (pronounced Mah-hun-cthleth, and referred to locally as Mac) is Wales' "alternative" capital in more ways than one. Shortlisted as a possible capital of Wales in the 1950s and site of Owain Glyndŵr's totemic fifteenth-century Welsh parliament, it retains its handsome architecture, while the town's excellent facilities, lively atmosphere and proximity to the coast make it an ideal jumping-off point for exploring the area. It also boasts a long tradition of progressive and environmentally conscious thinking and innovation, long before such concerns became universally fashionable.

It's difficult to imagine a nation's capital consisting of just two intersecting streets, but that's essentially what Machynlleth is. The A489 enters the town from the east becoming the wide main street, **Heol Maengwyn**, busiest on Wednesdays, when a lively **market** swings into action. Heol Maengwyn comes to an end at a T-junction, under the gaze of a fanciful **clock tower**, built in 1873 by local landowner, the Marquess of Londonderry, to commemorate his son and heir's coming of age.

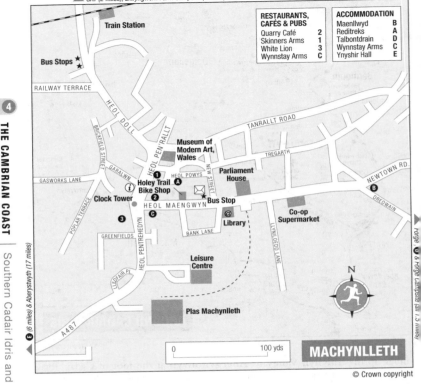

CAT (2 miles), Llwyngwern Farm Campsite (3 miles) & Corris YHA (5 miles)

Train Station

Bus Stops

RAILWAY TERRACE

THE CAMBRIAN COAST | Southern Cadair Idris and the Dyfi and Talyllyn valleys

RESTAURANTS, CAFÉS & PUBS	
Quarry Café	2
Skinners Arms	1
White Lion	3
Wynnstay Arms	C

ACCOMMODATION	
Maenllwyd	B
Reditreks	A
Talbontdrain	D
Wynnstay Arms	C
Ynyshir Hall	E

HEOL DOLL

TANRALLT ROAD

BRICKFIELD STREET

GARALWN

HEOL PEN'RALLT

NEW STREET

TREGARTH

NEWTOWN RD.

GASWORKS LANE

Museum of Modern Art, Wales

HEOL POWYS

Parliament House

DREGWAIN

Holey Trail Bike Shop

Clock Tower

HEOL MAENGWYN

Bus Stop

POPLAR TERRACE

Library

Co-op Supermarket

BANK LANE

LLYN-LLOED LANE

GREENFIELDS

HEOL PENTREHEDYN

Leisure Centre

LLEFAIR PL.

A487

Plas Machynlleth

N

0   100 yds

MACHYNLLETH

© Crown copyright

(6 miles) & Aberystwyth (17 miles)

Forge & Forge Campsite (all 1.5 miles)

The Town

Glyndŵr's partly fifteenth-century **Parliament House** (Easter–Sept Mon–Sat 10am–4pm; other times by arrangement on ☏01654/702827; free) sits halfway along Heol Maengwyn, a modest looking black-and-white-fronted building concealing a large interior. Displays chart the course of Glyndŵr's life, his military campaigns, his downfall, and the 1404 parliament in the town, when he controlled almost all of what is now known as Wales and even negotiated international recognition of the sovereign state. The sorriest tales are from 1405 onwards, when tactical errors and the sheer brute force of the English forced an ignominious end to the great Welsh uprising.

Opposite the Parliament House, a path leads into the landscaped grounds of **Plas Machynlleth**, the elegant seventeenth-century mansion of the Marquess of Londonderry. Its solitude is entirely intentional: in the 1840s the Marquess bought up all the surrounding buildings and had them demolished, and rerouted the main road away from his grounds. There's also a great daytime tearoom here.

Back into town, past the clock tower and up Heol Pen'rallt towards the station, is the **Museum of Modern Art, Wales** (MOMA Cymru: Mon–Sat 10am–4pm; free; ☏01654/703355; ⓦwww.momawales.org.uk). Housed in Y Tabernacl, a beautifully serene old chapel converted into a cultural centre, it hosts an ongoing programme of temporary exhibitions, including some from its own growing collection. It is also the place to go for films, theatre, comedy, concerts and the August Gŵyl Machynlleth festival, which combines classical and some folk music with theatre and debate.

Between late July and late August each year, the **Cambrian steam train** (℡01524/732100, 🌐www.westcoastrailways.co.uk) runs from Machynlleth to Porthmadog from Monday to Friday (£28 return) and, on Wednesday and Friday only, on to Pwllheli (£33 return); you can also join it in Tywyn and Barmouth.

Owain Glyndŵr

No name is so frequently invoked in Wales as that of **Owain Glyndŵr** (c.1349–1416), a potent figurehead of Welsh nationalism ever since he rose up against the occupying English in the first few years of the fifteenth century.

Little is known about the man described in Shakespeare's *Henry IV, Part I* as "not in the roll of common men". There seems little doubt that the charismatic Owain fulfilled many of the mystical medieval prophecies about the rising up of the red dragon. He was of aristocratic stock, and had a conventional upbringing, part of it in England of all places. His blue blood – he was directly descended from the princes of Powys and Cyfeiliog – furthered his claim as Prince of Wales, and as a result of his status, he learned English, studied in London and became a loyal, and distinguished, soldier of the English king, before returning to Wales and marrying a local woman.

Wales in the late fourteenth century was a turbulent place. The brutal savaging a century earlier of Llywelyn the Last and Edward I's stringent policies of subordinating Wales had left a discontented, cowed nation where any signs of rebellion were sure to attract support. Glyndŵr became the focus of the rebellion through a parochial problem: his neighbour in Glyndyfrdwy, the English Lord of Ruthin, seized some of his land and when the courts failed to back him, Glyndŵr took matters into his own hands. With four thousand supporters and a new declaration that he was Prince of Wales, he attacked Ruthin, and then Denbigh, Rhuddlan, Flint, Hawarden and Oswestry, before encountering an English resistance at Welshpool. However, whole swaths of north Wales were his for the taking. The English king, Henry IV, dispatched troops and rapidly drew up a range of severely punitive laws against the Welsh, even outlawing Welsh-language bards and singers. Battles continued to rage, with Glyndŵr capturing Edmund Mortimer, the Earl Marcher, in Pilleth in June 1402. By the end of 1403, he controlled most of Wales.

In 1404, Glyndŵr assembled a parliament of four men from every *commot* (community) in Wales at Machynlleth, drawing up mutual recognition treaties with France and Spain. At Machynlleth, he was also crowned ruler of a free Wales. A second parliament in Harlech took place a year later, with Glyndŵr making plans to carve up England and Wales into three as part of an alliance against the English king: Mortimer would take the south and west of England, Thomas Percy, Earl of Northumberland, would have the Midlands and North, and Glyndŵr himself Wales and the Marches of England. The English army, however, concentrated with increased vigour on destroying the Welsh uprising, and the Tripartite Indenture was never realized. From then on, Glyndŵr lost battles, ground and castles and was forced into hiding; dying, it is thought, in Herefordshire.

Anti-Welsh laws stayed in place until the accession to the English throne of Henry VII, a Welshman, in 1485. Wales became subsumed into English custom and law, and Glyndŵr's uprising became an increasingly powerful symbol of frustrated Welsh independence. In modern times, the shadowy organization that surfaced in the early 1980s to burn the holiday homes of English people and English estate agents dealing in Welsh property took the name Meibion (the sons of) Glyndŵr.

The figure of Glyndŵr, his trademark double-pointed beard to the fore, can often be seen gracing Welsh pub signs of inns called the Prince of Wales – as distinct to those who, by dint of being the first-born son of the reigning British monarch, have occupied the title ever since. See also p.469.

Machynlleth's **train station** is a five-minute walk up Heol Pen'rallt from the town's central clock tower, which is the main **bus stop**, though many also call at the train station. Just by the clock tower, the **tourist office** (Easter–Sept Mon–Sat 9.30am–5pm, Sun 9.30am–4pm; Oct–Easter Mon–Sat 10am–5pm, Sun 10am–4pm; ☎01654/702401, ✉mactic@powys.gov.uk) occupies the oldest shop in Wales, the fifteenth-century Royal House. The library (Mon & Fri 9.30am–1pm & 2–7pm, Tues & Wed 9.30am–1pm & 2–5pm, Sat 9.30am–1pm) on Heol Maengwyn has free **internet access**.

Machynlleth has become something of a **mountain biking** mecca, with a number of excellent purpose-built routes in the vicinity. The best place for information and **cycle rental** is The Holey Trail at 31 Heol Maengwyn (☎01654/700411). Guided biking holidays can be booked through *Reditreks* bunkhouse (see below).

Accommodation is plentiful and of a high standard. At the top end, there's the laidback grandeur of the *Wynnstay Arms* on Heol Maengwyn (☎01654/702941, ⊛www.wynnstay-hotel.com; ❺–❼), with cosy guest lounges where you can curl up with a book. Mid-range B&Bs include the *Maenllwyd* on Newtown Road (☎01654/702928, ⊛www.maenllwyd.co.uk; ❸), the eastward extension of Heol Maengwyn. With your own transport, you'll find the welcoming *Talbontdrain* just four miles south of town, in stunning countryside beyond the village of Forge (☎01654/702192, ⊛www.talbontdrain.co.uk; ❷–❸). If money's no object, the Relais & Chateaux luxury of *Ynyshir Hall*, situated near the Ynys-hir Nature Reserve (see p.294) at Eglwysfach, six miles southwest on the A487 (☎01654/781209, ⊛www.ynyshir-hall.co.uk; from £285; ❾) is sublime. In central Machynlleth, *Reditreks* **bunkhouse**, off Heol Powys, (☎01654/702184, ⊛www.reditreks.com) has beds for £15 and **camp** sites in their grassy yard for £5. Reditreks also organize guided mountain bike rides from £40. Otherwise, the nearest camping is three miles north near the Centre for Alternative Technology (CAT) at *Llwyngwern Farm* (☎01654/702492; £7–10 per pitch).

There are plenty of **cafés**, **restaurants** and **pubs** in the town, including a popular veggie wholefood café, the CAT-run *Quarry Café*, near the clock tower on Heol Maengwyn, with noticeboards listing info about healing workshops and so on. Lunch and dinner are great at the ⚲ *Wynnstay Arms* (see above), which serves inventive Welsh dishes like roast partridge in bayleaf gravy, will cook any fish that you might catch, and also has a superb pizzeria in its courtyard bar. The *Skinners Arms*, round the corner on Heol Pen'rallt, is cheaper but cosy and good for food or beer. Drinking is at its liveliest either at the *Skinners Arms*, or the oak-beamed *White Lion* by the clock tower.

Centre for Alternative Technology and Corris

Three miles north from Machynlleth up the A487 is the **Centre for Alternative Technology** (CAT) or *Canolfan y Dechnoleg Amgen* (daily: Easter–Sept 10am–5.30pm; Oct–Easter 10am–dusk; £8.40 summer, £6.40 winter, 50 percent discount to those arriving by bike or public transport; ☎01654/705950, ⊛www.cat.org.uk). Since its inception during the oil crisis of 1974, seven acres of a once-derelict slate quarry have been turned into an almost entirely sustainable community, generating eighty percent of its own power from wind, sun and water. But this is no back-to-the-land hippie commune. Right from the start, the idea was to embrace technology – much of the on-site equipment was developed and

▲ Centre for Alternative Technology

built here, reflecting the centre's achievements in this field – and, most importantly, to promote its application in urban situations.

CAT's water-balanced (turbine-powered) **cliff railway** (Easter–Oct only) whisks visitors 200ft up from the car park to the beautiful main site, sensitively landscaped using local slate and wood, and you can easily spend half a day sauntering around. There's plenty for kids to do, including a **children's theatre** (mainly mid-July to Aug), while the wholefood **restaurant** turns out delicious food and the excellent **bookshop** stocks a wide range of alternative literature, along with crafts and intriguing toys.

Primarily, though, this is a working community which exists more to educate by example than entertain, partly facilitated by the environmental information centre housed in a rammed-earth building. Residential **volunteer programmes** are offered, the most popular being a guide to building your own energy-efficient home. For £10 per night to cover bed and board, you can get a week-long taster of life and work at the centre between March and September – enquire as far ahead as possible, as placements are limited and in high demand.

Corris

The spirit of CAT extends three miles higher up the valley to **CORRIS**, a small former slate-quarrying settlement in the middle of the Dyfi Forest. In the centre of the village is the **Corris Railway and Museum** (generally Sundays April–Sept and four times a week in school holidays; £4; ☎01654/761303, ⓦwww.corris.co.uk). The line currently shuttles passengers a mere half-mile and back – including a stop with a guided tour and talk, taking about fifty minutes all-up – though there are plans to restore a further two miles. The line is part of the old narrow-gauge railway that linked the slate quarries of the Dulas Valley with the main line at Machynlleth.

Corris station is a short signposted walk from the former village school, now operating as the ecologically minded ⅍ *Canolfan Corris* **hostel**, Old Road (mid-Feb to Oct & weekends Nov–Feb; ☎01654/761686, ⓦwww.corrishostel .co.uk; dorm £15). It's the kind of place where you can easily end up staying longer than intended – in dorms, family rooms and even tents; reasonably priced, healthy meals are available and there are kitchen facilities. There's also fabulous food and drink at the village's lovely old **pub**, the 🥢 *Slaters' Arms*, on the central crossroads. Up on the main road above Corris, there's another **bunkhouse** in the old *Braich Goch* pub (☎01654/761229, ⓦwww .braichgoch.co.uk; £16), which can arrange all manner of sporting and outward-bound activities.

Half a mile further up the valley, the **Corris Craft Centre** occupies a former slate mine, and houses the local **tourist office** (Easter–Oct daily 10am–5.30pm; ☎01654/761244, ⓔcorris.tic@gwynedd.gov.uk), a few run-of-the-mill craft shops, a decent café, a good children's playground, and a couple of modest attractions. **King Arthur's Labyrinth** (late March to Oct daily 10am–5pm, call for winter hours; £6.50, or £8.55 with Bard's Quest; ☎01654/761584, ⓦwww.kingarthurslabyrinth.com) is based deep within the flooded tunnels of a former quarry. Led by a guide dressed as a monk, the boat trip into the heart of the mountain is huge fun, with son et lumière tableaux illustrating various Welsh legends. The **Bard's Quest** (£4.10, or £8.55 with the Labyrinth) outdoor floral maze reveals "mystical stories echoing across the ages" by way of various iconic figures you meet along the way, and is a great way to help ensure these Welsh stories are retained by younger generations.

Aberdyfi

The proud maritime heritage of **ABERDYFI** (sometimes spelt as the anglicized Aberdovey) has largely been replaced by the life of a well-heeled resort. With its south-facing aspect across the Dyfi estuary backed by lush mountains, Aberdyfi has one of the highest proportions of holiday homes anywhere on this coast (and with some of the highest property prices, too). There's sporadic canoe and sailboard rental on the beach, but not much else in the way of activities. Swimming is possible, but tidal currents make it potentially hazardous, so aim to swim close to high tide, or keep in the shallows.

In the mid-nineteenth century, the town, with its seamlessly joined eastern neighbour, **Penhelig**, built shallow-draught coastal traders for the inshore fleet, a past remembered in the small historic and **maritime display** in the tourist office (see below).

Practicalities

Aberdyfi is served by two equally inconvenient **train** stations: the request-only Penhelig, half a mile east (the most convenient for the centre of town); and Aberdyfi, half a mile west of the **tourist office** at Wharf Gardens (Easter–Oct daily 9.30am–5.30pm; ☎01654/767321, ⓔticaberdyfi@hotmail.com), near where the #28 **bus** stops.

None of the **accommodation** here is particularly cheap: the nearest thing to a budget option is the *Cartref Guest House*, Penrhos, near Aberdyfi train station (☎01654/767273, ⓦwww.cartref-abedovey.co.uk; ❶–❸). The swankiest options are the *Llety Bodfor* (☎01654/767475, ⓦwww.lletybodfor.co.uk; ❻–❼) on the seafront, where you can even buy the designer furnishings in your room; and the 🥢 *Penhelig Arms Hotel*, near Penhelig train station (☎01654/767215, ⓦwww.penheligarms.com; ❹–❺), which has attractively streamlined contemporary rooms and also boasts a nautical-style **restaurant** with expertly cooked seafood, turf-based specialties including honey-roasted duck, vegetarian options like beanburgers with curried apple chutney, and an extensive wine list. Lighter **meals** are offered at the good-value *Grapevine*, at 1 Chapel Square

(☎01654/767448), which offers bistro-type fare. In the evening, the landmark *Dovey Inn*, a few doors along, does good bar meals and, along with the *Britannia Inn* at 13 Sea View Terrace, has the liveliest atmosphere.

Tywyn and the Talyllyn Railway

With its four miles of sandy beach, the traditional, down-to-earth seaside resort of **TYWYN** ("The Strand"), four miles north of Aberdyfi, makes a handy base for the Talyllyn and Dysynni valleys. At the east end of the long High Street, the Norman nave of the **Church of St Cadfan** (daily 9am–5pm, later in summer) houses one of the town's few real sights – the five-foot-high **St Cadfan's Stone**, which bears the earliest example of written Welsh, dating back to around 650 AD.

The town's main attraction, however, is the cute **Talyllyn narrow-gauge railway** (April–Oct & late Dec daily, plus some winter weekends; ☎01654/710472, ⓦwww.talyllyn.co.uk; £12 unlimited one-day travel), the inspiration for Thomas the Tank Engine. which tootles seven miles inland through the delightful wooded Talyllyn Valley to Nant Gwernol. From 1866 to 1946, the rail line was used to haul slate from the Bryn Eglwys quarry near Nant Gwernol to Tywyn Wharf station. Four years after the quarry's closure, rail enthusiasts took over the running of services, making this the world's first volunteer-run railway. The round trip (at a maximum 15mph) takes two hours, but you can get on and off as frequently as the schedule allows, taking in some fine broadleaf **forest walks**. The best of these starts at Dolgoch Falls station, where three trails (maximum 1hr; leaflet 30p from tourist office or downloadable free at ⓦeryri-npa.gov.uk) lead off to the lower, mid- and upper cascades. At the end of the line, more woodland walks take you around the site of the old slate quarries. In mid-August each year, the schedule is disrupted by the "Race the Train" event, when runners attempt to beat the train on its fourteen-mile trip to Abergynolwyn and back. Some do.

The **Narrow-Gauge Museum** (open when trains are running; free) at Tywyn Wharf station contains displays about the railway, other narrow-gauge lines in Britain and much about Thomas the Tank Engine. Of the original Talyllyn rolling stock, two steam engines and all five of the oak and mahogany passenger carriages still run up to Nant Gwernol.

From late July to late August, the **Cambrian steam train** (see p.301) calls at Tywyn's main station; travelling to Porthmadog from Monday to Friday (£22 return) and, on Wednesday and Friday only, on to Pwllheli (£27 return).

Practicalities

The three main roads in Tywyn – the High Street, Pier Road and the Aberdyfi road – meet at the **main train station**, which also serves as the principal **bus** stop. The **tourist office** is in front of the Leisure Centre on High Street (Easter–Sept Mon, Tues & Thurs–Sat 9.30am–1pm & 2–5pm; ☎01654/710070, ⓔtywyn.tic@gwynedd.co.uk); Pier Road makes for the beach; and the Aberdyfi road heads south past the Talyllyn **narrow-gauge train station** (Tywyn Wharf) two hundred yards away.

The cheapest **accommodation** is the at basic *Llys Maldwyn* B&B, opposite the tourist office on the High Street (☎01654/711058; ❷) and at the *Sunningdale*, also on the High Street (☎01654/710248; ❷). *Monfa Guest House*, 4 Pier Rd (☎01654/710858, ⓦwww.monfa.co.uk; ❸), between the seafront and the High Street, is a more comfortable alternative, in a classical Victorian town-house. The handiest **campsite** is the *Vaenol Camping Park* (open March–Nov; ☎01654/710232; £10 per pitch), ten-minutes' walk from town on the Aberdyfi road.

Good daytime **food** is served up at the *Town & Gown* on Marine Parade (the prom), where you can eat while browsing thousands of secondhand books. There are plenty of cafés in the town centre, and staple bar **meals** are dished up at the *Tredegar Arms* (known as "The Tred"), a welcoming High Street pub. You'll also find reasonably priced lunches and dinners at the *Whitehall Hotel* ("The White"), on Corbett Square. There are occasional **Wurlitzer concerts** (ⓦwww.organ.co.uk/tywyn) at the Neuadd Pentre on Brook Street.

The Talyllyn and Dysynni valleys

The **Talyllyn Valley** starts at the northeast by Minffordd and follows the River Dysynni as far as Abergynolwyn. Here the valley splits into two, some ancient geological upheaval having forced the river to abruptly switch its course north, forming the **Dysynni Valley** and leaving its original course beside the Talyllyn Railway all but dry. Although a quick tour around the sites won't take more than a half a day, the area is monumentally beautiful, and the superb lowland or mountain **walking** (particularly on Cadair Idris) warrants more time.

Bus #30 serves the Talyllyn Valley, running from Tywyn to Abergynolwyn and continuing to Minffordd (where you can catch #32 or #X32 to Dolgellau or Machynlleth). The Talyllyn narrow-gauge railway runs from Tywyn to Abergynolwyn station, half a mile short of the village, and then continues on to Nant Gwernol, just past the village but off the road.

The Talyllyn Valley

From Tywyn, the B4405 up the **Talyllyn Valley** runs parallel to the Talyllyn Railway (see p.305), meeting it at **Dolgoch Falls**, the site of some delightful wooded walks, and also home to the peaceful *Dolgoch Falls Hotel* (☎01654/782258, ⓦwww.dolgochfallshotel.co.uk; ❹), with a tearoom serving light lunches and a cosy restaurant serving dinner (both generally open daily April–Sept). A few hundred yards further on is the superbly situated farmhouse B&B, *Tan-y-Coed-Isaf*

Cadair Idris: the Minffordd Path

The OS Explorer 1:25,000 map OL23, "Cadair Idris & Llyn Tegid", is recommended for this walk.

The most dramatic ascent of Cadair Idris follows the **Minffordd Path** (6 miles; 5hr; 2900ft ascent), a justifiably popular route which makes a full circuit around the rim of **Cwm Cau**, probably the country's most impressive mountain cirque.

The path starts just west of the *Minffordd Hotel* at the junction of the A487 and the B4405. From the car park, follow the signs along an avenue of horse chestnuts and up through the woods, heading north. You will reach a fork: take the left path that wheels around the end of Craig Lwyd into Cwm Cau, and before you reach the lake, fork left and climb onto the rim of Cwm Cau, following it round to **Penygadair** (2930ft; see also p.311), the highest point on the massif. Here, there's a circular shelter and a tin-roofed hut originally built for dispensing refreshments to thirsty Victorians, and now affording none-too-comfortable protection from wind and rain.

The shortest descent follows the summit plateau northeast, then down to a grassy ridge before ascending gradually to **Mynydd Moel** (2831ft), from which you get a magnificent view down into a cwm containing the waters of Llyn Arran. The descent starts beside the fence which you cross just before the summit – follow the fence south all the way to the fork below Cwm Cau.

(☎01654/782639; ❷; open March–Oct), just two miles short of the twin valleys' only real settlement, **ABERGYNOLWYN**. Here, a few dozen quarry workers' houses crowd around the *Railway Inn*, which serves the best range of real ales for miles, together with some great food.

The Dysynni Valley branches northwest here, but the Talyllyn Valley continues northeast for a couple of miles to the serene **Tal-y-Llyn Lake** (Llyn Mwyngil). The chief interest here is the fifteenth-century **St Mary's church** on the southern shores of the lake, a fine example of a small Welsh parish church, unusual because of its chancel arch painted with an alternating grid of red and River white roses, separated by grotesque bosses.

The lake itself is frequently stocked with brown trout and, occasionally, migratory sea trout and salmon are also found here. Talyllyn Fisheries, beside the lake, issues fishing permits (£15 per day), and rents out boats with outboard engines (£18) plus tackle. Talyllyn Fisheries is part of the angling-oriented *Týnycornel* hotel (☎01654/782282, ⓦwww.tynycornel.co.uk; ❷–❹), which also has a sauna, mountain bikes for guests and an excellent range of bar lunches, plus à la carte evening meals; the half-board deals are the best value here. The nearby sixteenth-century *Pen-y-Bont* (☎01654/782285; ❹), next to the church, is a less expensive option, with a good bar and an affordable restaurant. Better value still is the lovely *Dolffanog Fawr* B&B (☎01654/761247, ⓦwww.dolffanogfawr .co.uk; ❹), set in a converted farmhouse a mile further on near the top of the lake, serving a daily changing menu featuring local produce.

Just before the B4405 meets the A487 at **MINFFORDD** is the access point for the finest ascent of Cadair Idris (see box opposite), together with a great **campsite**: *Dôl Einion* (☎01654/761312; from £6.50 per pitch).

The Dysynni Valley

The **Dysynni Valley** has more to offer in the way of sights, although a lack of public transport makes it difficult to explore. A mile and a half northwest of Abergynolwyn, a side road cuts northeast to the hamlet of **LLANFIHANGEL-Y-PENNANT** and the scant ruins of the native Welsh **Castell-y-Bere** (unrestricted access; CADW), a fortress built by Llywelyn ap Iorwerth (Llywelyn the Great) in 1221 to protect the mountain passes. After being besieged twice in the thirteenth century, this castle – one of the most massive of the Welsh castles – was consigned to seven centuries of obscurity and decay. Like so many of the native fortresses, Castell-y-Bere seems to rise almost imperceptibly out of the rock upon which it was built. With large slabs of the main towers still standing, there's plenty to poke around, but it's primarily a great place just to sit or picnic, with good views to Cadair Idris and Craig y Deryn (see below).

A few hundred yards beyond the castle, you'll come to the centre of Llanfihangel and its stocky little **church of St Michael**, which has a couple of interesting exhibits in its vestry, including a fabulous 3-D map of the valley, some fourteen feet long and built to a scale of one foot to one mile from patchwork and cloth. There are also some exhibits centred on **Mary Jones** – famed for her 1800 Bible-buying walk to Bala (see box, p.389) – including photos from 1921 detailing the unveiling of her monument, which can be found a little further up the lane at the ruined **Tŷn-y-ddôl** (unrestricted access). Tŷn-y-ddôl marks the beginning of a path (10 miles; 7hr; 2900ft ascent) up Cadair Idris, though it's a longer and far less exciting route than the one described in the box opposite.

Three miles seaward from Tŷn-y-ddôl, along the Dysynni Valley road, around thirty breeding pairs of cormorants colonize **Craig y Deryn** (Birds' Rock), a stunning 760-foot-high cliff four miles from the coast. As the sea has gradually withdrawn from the valley, the birds have remained loyal to their home, making this Europe's only inland cormorant nesting site. It's reachable via a path (2 miles; 1hr; 750ft ascent) from two miles west of Abergynolwyn – the well-equipped *Llanllwyda* **campsite** (℡01654/782276; £6/8 per tent/van site) is conveniently placed at the start of the path.

The lane snakes back towards the coast, reaching the village of **LLANEGRYN** three miles on. Half a mile northwest of the village, the little hilltop **church** has an unexpectedly beautiful rood screen, probably carved in the fifteenth century, which is said to have been carried overnight from Cymer Abbey (see p.312) after its dissolution. Check with the tourist office at Tywyn to confirm it's open when you visit.

Just over two miles west of Llanegryn, where the northbound A493 swings dramatically around to hug the coast, is the wonderful *Cae Du* clifftop campsite (℡01654/711234; from £8 per pitch), half a mile short of the hamlet of **LLANGELYNIN**. Here, a track descends seawards off the main road to another ancient **church** (check opening times with the Tywyn tourist office): a mainly eleventh-century building on the foundations of an eighth-century structure, and bare but for a few basic pews and a bier which was carried by horses. Just outside the porch is the grave of Abram Wood, patriarch of Y Teulu Wood, a clan of Romanies who settled in Wales at the beginning of the eighteenth century. Continue along the main road for the cheerful village of **LLWYNGWRIL** and its atmospheric tearoom and **gallery** (ⓦwww.llwyngwril-gallery.co.uk), housed in an old chapel and hosting regular events such as concerts.

Northern Cadair Idris and the Mawddach Estuary

Gouging their way deep into the heart of the mid-Wales mountains, the Mawddach Estuary's broad tidal flats create dramatic backdrops from every angle. With the sun low in the sky and the tide ebbing, the constantly changing course of the river trickles silver through the golden sands. That colour isn't just an illusion: the sands actually do contain gold, albeit in tiny amounts, as the abandoned mines littering the hills around testify. Spasmodic gold fever still occasionally hits the region's main town, **Dolgellau**, but most people come here for excellent walking up Cadair Idris and along the estuary, or to hit the beaches, particularly at **Barmouth**, the area's main resort.

Fairbourne

The blink-and-you'll-miss-it settlement of **FAIRBOURNE**, on the southern side of the Mawddach Estuary, was developed in the late nineteenth century as the country estate of the chairman of the McDougall's flour company. There's a decent beach and sublime views along the coast and across the estuary, but otherwise the only attraction is the steam-hauled **Fairbourne Railway** (Easter & May to late Sept 4–9 trains daily; £7.20 return), with a gauge of just one foot. The railway makes a pleasant alternative route across the estuary to Barmouth, starting across the road from the **train station** and running a mile to a connecting **passenger ferry** (Easter–Sept; £2.50) which takes you the rest of the way.

Midway between Fairbourne and the ferry's departure point, a halt on the railway line boasts a name to outdo even Llanfairpwll on Anglesey, the gimmicky

Gorsafawddacha'idraigodanheddogleddollônpenrhynareurdraethceredigion ("The station on the Mawddach with dragon's teeth on the north Penrhyn Drive on the golden Cardigan sands"). The "dragon's teeth" are, alas, a set of grim concrete defences left over from World War II.

Dolgellau

The old county town of Meirionethshire, **DOLGELLAU** still maintains an air of unhurried importance, never more so than when all the area's farmers roll up for market day. Its dark buildings gleam forebodingly in the frequent downpours, but in fine weather, the lofty crags of Cadair Idris perfectly frame the stone squares and streets.

Dolgellau is a much older town than appearances suggest, lying at the junction of three Roman roads which converged on a now vanished military outpost. It was here that Owain Glyndŵr assembled the last Welsh parliament in 1404, and later signed an alliance with Charles VI of France for providing troops to fight against Henry IV of England. Seventeenth-century Quakers sought freedom from persecution here, and in the 1860s, Dolgellau became the focus of numerous **gold rushes**, drawing waves of prospectors to pan the estuary or blast levels into Clogau shale or mudstone sediment under the Coed y Brenin Forest. The quartz veins yielded some gold, but in quantities too small to make much money.

As the most convenient access point to the southern reaches of the Snowdonia National Park, Dolgellau is a decent and enjoyable base today. As well as offering some wonderful **walks,** notably an easy stroll along the Mawddach Estuary and a strenuous hike up Cadair Idris, Dolgellau offers plenty of evening diversions in the form of good pubs and restaurants and a fair bit of live music, none more so than during the awesome **Sesiwn Fawr** (see p.321).

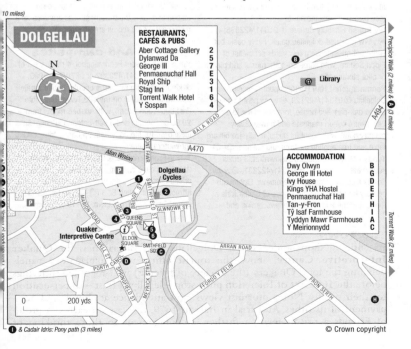

DOLGELLAU

N

RESTAURANTS, CAFÉS & PUBS

Aber Cottage Gallery	2
Dylanwad Da	5
George III	7
Penmaenuchaf Hall	E
Royal Ship	3
Stag Inn	1
Torrent Walk Hotel	6
Y Sospan	4

Library

Afon Wnion

BALA ROAD

BONT FAWR

A470

P

Dolgellau Cycles

SMITHFIELD ST

GLWNDWR ST

MARION ROAD

LION ST

BRIDGE ST

P

QUEENS SQUARE

Quaker Interpretive Centre

ELDON SQUARE

WELL ST

PORTH CANO

SPRINGFIELD ST

SMITHFIELD SQ

MEIRICK STREET

ARRAN ROAD

FFORDD Y FELIN

FRON SERTH

ACCOMMODATION

Dwy Olwyn	B
George III Hotel	G
Ivy House	D
Kings YHA Hostel	E
Penmaenuchaf Hall	F
Tan-y-Fron	H
Tŷ Isaf Farmhouse	I
Tyddyn Mawr Farmhouse	A
Y Meirionnydd	C

0   200 yds

& Cadair Idris: Pony path (3 miles)

© Crown copyright

10 miles)

Precipice Walk (2 miles) & (3 miles)

Torrent Walk (2 miles)

Arrival, information and accommodation

Dolgellau doesn't have a train station, but is well served by **buses** from Bala, Barmouth and Machynlleth, which all pull into Eldon Square, home to the **tourist office** (Easter–Oct daily 9.30am–5.30pm; Nov–Easter Mon & Thurs–Sun 9.30am–4.30pm; ☎01341/422888, ✉tic.dolgellau@eyri-npa .gov.uk), along with theQuaker Interpretive Centre (see below). The tourist office and interpretive centre are volunteer-staffed, so hours can vary, with lunchtime closures outside peak season. There's **internet access** at the library (Mon & Fri 10am–7pm, Tues & Thurs 10am–5pm, Wed 10am–1pm, Sat 10am–noon) on the northeastern edge of town on the Bala Road. **Bike rental** is availableat Dolgellau Cycles on Smithfield Street (☎01341/423332, ⓦwww.dolgellaucycles.co.uk).

While there's commendable **accommodation** in Dolgellau itself (some catering to the legions of mountain bikers frequenting Coed-y-Brenin), there are more appealing options scattered around the district, some so close to Cadair Idris that you can start your hike at the back door.

Hotels and guesthouses

Dwy Olwyn Coed y Fronallt, Llanfachreth Rd ☎01341/422822, ⓦwww.dwyolwyn.co.uk. Homely guesthouse in landscaped gardens with Cadair Idris views. It's a 10min walk from the centre – cross Bont Fawr (Big Bridge) and turn right. ❶

George III Hotel Penmaenpool, 4 miles west of Dolgellau ☎01341/422525, ⓦwww.georgethethird .co.uk. Superb seventeenth-century hotel right by the Mawddach Estuary (bus #28). Some rooms are in former train station buildings, and the restaurant (see p.313) is outstanding. ❻

Ivy House Finsbury Square ☎01341/422535, ⓦwww.ivyhouse-dolgellau.co.uk. Fairly basic but well-kept guesthouse a few yards southeast of Eldon Square, with some en-suite rooms and plenty of bike storage. ❷–❸

Penmaenuchaf Hall Penmaenpool, 4 miles west of Dolgellau ☎01341/422129, ⓦwww.penhall.co.uk. Grand oak-panelled house, formerly home to a Lancashire cotton magnate and now a classy country hotel, with beautiful decor, a full-size billiard table and free angling for trout and salmon. ❹–❻

Tyddyn Mawr Farmhouse Islawrdref, 3 miles southwest of Dolgellau ☎01341/422331, ⓦwww .lokalink.co.uk/dolgellau/tyddynmawr. Eighteenth-century farmhouse on the slopes of Cadair Idris at the foot of the Pony Path. Very welcoming and great value, with open fireplaces and en-suite rooms. Check ahead for winter closures. ❸

Tŷ Isaf Farmhouse Llanfachreth ☎01341/423261, ⓦwww.tyisaf78.freeserve.co.uk. Small, comfortable seventeenth-century guest-house in three acres of grounds close to the Precipice Walk. Great £15 communal dinners and generous breakfasts. No credit cards. ❷

Y Meirionnydd Smithfield Square ☎01341/422554, ⓦwww.clifton-house-hotel .co.uk. Good-value hotel built in an ex-police station and jail – the basement cells are used as a restaurant. Some rooms are en suite. ❷–❻

Hostels and campsites

Kings YHA Hostel Penmaenpool, 4 miles west of Dolgellau ☎01341/422392 or 0870/770 5900, ✉kings@yha.org.uk. Large country house a mile up a wooded valley off the #28 Tywyn bus route (last bus around 7pm), with six-bed rooms from £9.95 per person and a self-catering kitchen. An ideal base for the Pony Path up Cadair Idris. Check for winter closures.

Tan-y-Fron Arran Rd ☎01341/422638, ⓦwww .tanyfron.co.uk. Well-appointed and reasonably priced camping and caravan site next to an attractively furnished B&B (❷–❸) of the same name, 5min walk from town. £9–19 per pitch.

The Town

Its enticing shops aside, central Dolgellau's only diversion is the **Quaker Interpretive Centre**, above the tourist office, with explanatory panels detailing the local Quakers' (the Society of Friends) well-recorded sufferings before the 1689 Act of Toleration put a stop – legally, at least – to persecution for their pacifist Nonconformist views, non-attendance at church and non-payment of its tithes. At a trial in Bala in 1679, this last sin earned a group of Friends a prison term, a further encouragement to those thinking of

The OS Explorer 1:25,000 map OL23, "Cadair Idris & Llyn Tegid", is recommended, particularly for the ascent of Cadair Idris.

Torrent Walk

The attractive lowland **Torrent Walk** (2 miles; 1hr; 100ft ascent), follows the course of the Clywedog River as it carves its way through the bedrock. Stroll downstream past the cascades and through some gnarled old woodland that drips with antiquity. Bus #32/ X32 can take you the 2.5 miles east along the A470, from where it's a couple of hundred yards or so down the B4416 (signposted to Brithdir) to a sign on the left-hand side marking the beginning of the walk.

Precipice Walk and New Precipice Walk

Though the path is narrow in places and there are some steep banks, the **Precipice Walk** (3–4 miles; 2hr; negligible ascent) can hardly be called precipitous. In fact it is very easy-going, simple to follow and has great views to the 1000-foot ramparts of Cadair Idris and along the Mawddach Estuary – best in late afternoon or early morning sun. The path makes a circuit around Foel Cynwch, starting three miles north of Dolgellau from a public car park on the road to Llanfachreth. For those without a vehicle, there's access from a path beside Cymer Abbey (see p.312). Even less precipitous, the **New Precipice Walk** (4 miles; 2hr; 700ft ascent) combines luscious views of the estuary with a ramble along the old tramways of the Foel Ispri gold mine. Access is easiest from the signed path at the very western end of Llanelltyd village, two miles northwest of Dolgellau.

Penmaenpool–Morfa Mawddach Walk

Beside the Mawddach Estuary's broad sands, a disused rail line makes for easy going on the **Penmaenpool–Morfa Mawddach Walk** (8 miles one way; 3hr; flat), starting in Dolgellau at the car park by Bont Fawr (Big Bridge). The first two miles are the least interesting, so it makes sense to catch the #28 bus to the **RSPB Nature Information Centre** (Easter & late May to Sept daily 11am–5pm; Easter to late May Sat & Sun noon–4pm; free) in an old rail signal box at Penmaenpool, just by a wooden toll bridge (daily 8am–7pm; cars 50p, pedestrians 20p) linking the two banks of the estuary. From there the path (also a popular cycle trail) hugs the estuary bank all the way to Morfa Mawddach, from where you can walk across the bridge to Barmouth or catch the bus back to Dolgellau. Another good scheme is to take the bus to Morfa Mawddach and walk back to Penmaenpool, or use the Cambrian coast railway to Morfa Mawddach.

Pony Path

If the weather is good and you are well kitted out, don't miss the classic **Pony Path** (6–7 miles; 4–5hr; 2500ft ascent), a straightforward and enjoyable route up Cadair Idris which starts from the car park at Tŷ Nant, three miles southwest from Dolgellau along the Cadair road. Turn right, then right again at the telephone box, following the path to "Cader Idris". Already, the views to the craggy flanks of the massif are tremendous, but they disappear as you climb steeply to the col, where you turn left on a rocky path to the summit shelter on **Penygadair** (2930ft; see also p.306). The descent is either by the same route or (with some care and considerable efforts to minimize erosion) by taking the first part of the Fox's Path down to Llyn y Gadair. From the summit, go northeast to a grassy plateau then north to a couple of cairns and down to Llyn y Gadair. By the lake, forsake the rest of the Fox's Path in favour of a less obvious route heading off from the northwest corner of the lake, eventually meeting the Pony Path again. Note that there are no buses up the Cadair road.

following the two thousand Welsh Quakers who had already fled to the United States and started the Pennsylvania towns of Bangor, Bryn Mawr and others. The building also houses a **national park exhibition** concentrating on southern Snowdonia.

Around Dolgellau

Gold frenzy first hit Dolgellau when flecks of gold were discovered in the Mawddach silt by the Romans. Later, the thirteenth-century Cistercian monks based at **Cymer Abbey** (open access; free; CADW), two miles north of Dolgellau, were given "the right in digging or carrying away metals and treasures free from all secular exaction". The fine location at the head of the Mawddach Estuary is typical of this austere order, but unfortunately the surrounding caravan site mars the effect of the remaining Gothic slabs. A path beside the abbey makes an alternative approach to the Precipice Walk (see box, p.311).

Precious metal was also the raison d'être for the village of **BONTDDU**, four miles west along the A496 towards Barmouth. This is the source of gold used in royal wedding rings, and if you walk up the wooded valley north of the village, you'll come across mine workings past and present.

Eating, drinking and entertainment

Dolgellau and the surrounding area are blessed with some good **eating** options, particularly by day. Evening life focuses on the numerous pubs, together with odd concerts and performances – see local noticeboards. The public are welcome at weekly rehearsals of the town's male voice choir, Côr Meibion Dolgellau, at Ysgol Gynradd (Wed 8pm). The annual **Sesiwn Fawr** (bookings on ☎08712/301314, ⓦwww.sesiwnfawr.co.uk), literally "Big Session", is just that: a long weekend during mid-July of bands and musical shenanigans taking place in the riverside meadows below the bridge, with plenty more music and mayhem to be found in the town's pubs.

▲ The Coal Porters at Dolgellau's Sesiwn Fawr

Aber Cottage Gallery Smithfield St
ⓣ01341/422460, ⓦwww.abercottagegallery.com.
Cosy place filled with works by the artist-owner,
and one of Dolgellau's nicest daytime cafés for a
warming lunch or a cuppa.

Dylanwad Da 2 Smithfield St
ⓣ01341/422870. Consistently the best
restaurant in town, with creative, affordable
dishes – like Thai seafood soup and cumin-
spiced salmon or Moroccan lamb stew – and
great desserts served in simple surroundings.
Also open for good coffee and cakes 10am–4pm.
Closed Feb.

George III Penmaenpool (see p.310). Superb spot
for an afternoon drink or delicious locally inspired
dishes from the à la carte menu such as the "lamb
turner", pastry-topped minted lamb in a creamy
honey sauce.

Penmaenuchaf Hall Penmaenpool (see p.310).
Superior modern British cuisine in a gazebo-style
setting, complete with fresh flowers, flowing white
tablecloths and candlelight. A three-course set
menu costs £35, and there are some superb
vegetarian options.

Royal Ship Queen's Square. Large and cheerful old
coaching inn, with good beer and decent food too.

Stag Inn Bridge St. Straightforward town-centre
pub with good beer and a garden.

Torrent Walk Hotel Smithfield Square. The
liveliest pub in town, though with some quiet
corners for more peaceful drinking.

Y Sospan Queen's Square ⓣ01341/423174.
Dependable café/bistro behind the tourist office,
serving reasonable coffee, decent daytime meals
and better dinners (booking necessary), all at
modest prices.

Barmouth and around

Cluttered with shops selling takeaway food, buckets and spades, and pleasure-
beach sideshow attractions, lively **BARMOUTH** (Abermaw) tucks in
beneath steep cliffs, lapped by both estuary and sea. The best approach is via
the 2253-foot-long rail bridge, created for the nineteenth-century English
Midlands sea-bathers who popularized the town, which traverses 113 rickety-
looking wooden spans across the Mawddach River estuary south of town.

Barmouth was once a shipbuilding centre, and a maritime air lingers around
the quay at the south end of town, departure point for a **passenger ferry** to
Fairbourne (Easter–Oct; as frequently as custom demands; £2.50 return), as well
as several sea-fishing and sightseeing trips (enquire on the quay). In late June each
year, the highly competitive **Three Peaks Race** (ⓦwww.threepeaksyachtrace
.co.uk) starts here, a two to three day amateur monohull yachting event entailing
navigation to Caernarfon, the English Lake District and Fort William in Scotland,
and a run up the highest peak in each country. The current record, set in 2002,
is two days, fourteen hours and 22 minutes.

The quay is also where you'll find the **RNLI Lifeboat Museum** (Easter–
Sept daily 10.30am–4.30pm; free), with its workaday exhibition of lifesaving
paraphernalia, and the **Tŷ Gwyn Museum** (July–Sept daily 10.30am–5pm;
free), a medieval tower house where Henry VII's uncle, Jasper Tudor, is said to
have plotted Richard III's downfall. First recorded in a poem around the middle
of the fifteenth century, the house was thought to have been destroyed until
renovations in the 1980s revealed its identity. It now contains displays on the
Tudor dynasty, as well as explanatory panels on local shipwrecks.

On the hill behind, the **Tŷ Crwn Roundhouse** (same hours as Tŷ Gwyn
museum) acted as a lockup for drunken sailors in the eighteenth century. The
circular design was reputedly conceived to prevent the Devil lurking in any
corners and further tempting the incarcerated mariners. It now houses some old
photos of Barmouth.

One prominent local shipwreck was that of the 700-ton Genoese galleon the
Bronze Bell, which sank in 1709 five miles northwest of here, complete with its
cargo of Carrara marble virtually identical to the stuff Michelangelo had once
used. Forty or so two-ton blocks of marble still lie on the seabed but one piece
was raised in the 1980s, and fashioned by local sculptor Frank Cocksey into

Walks from Barmouth

The best lowland walk on the Cambrian coast, the **Barmouth–Fairbourne Loop** (5 miles; 2–3hr; 300ft ascent) makes a superb circuit around Barmouth and Fairbourne, with fine mountain, estuarine and coastal views all the way. The route can be done with almost no walking at all using the rail line to Fairbourne, the Fairbourne narrow-gauge railway and the ferry across the mouth of the estuary, but walking allows for seemingly infinite variation. The route first crosses the rail bridge (60p return toll) to Morfa Mawddach station, follows the lane to the main road, crosses it onto a footpath that loops around the back of a small wooded hill to Pant Einion Hall, then follows another lane back to the main road near Fairbourne. Turn north for 400 yards, then left down the main street of Fairbourne to the sea, walk north along the beach and you can catch the ferry back to Barmouth. Any desired extension to the walk is best done from Morfa Mawddach, where the route described meets the Penmaenpool-Morfa Mawddach Walk (see box, p.311). Follow it for a mile to Arthog where a small road and a mesh of paths lead up past waterfalls to the beautiful **Cregennan Lakes** (NT).

The **Panorama Walk** (10min) is more famous, but apart from the fine estuary view, its chief quality is its brevity, the viewpoint being only yards away from the nearest road. By taking in **Dinas Oleu** (Fortress of Light), the cliffs immediately above Barmouth, which became the National Trust's first property in 1895, it can be turned into a decent walk (3 miles; 2hr; 400ft ascent). Essentially the route follows Gloddfa Road opposite Woolworth's on High Street onto the exposed clifftops, where there is a map of the reserve. Go through the metal gate and follow the path past Frenchman's Grave to a road where you turn left to the Panorama Viewpoint. Return by the same route.

"**The Last Haul**", which stands at the junction of The Quay and Church Street. Three centuries of undersea corrosion have left the surface fabulously pockmarked, though the quality of marble comes through in the carved section which depicts three fishing generations working together to haul in a catch.

From late July to late August, the **Cambrian steam train** (see p.301) calls at Barmouth; travelling to Porthmadog from Monday to Friday (£20 return) and, on Wednesday and Friday only, on to Pwllheli (£25 return).

Practicalities

Buses from Harlech and Dolgellau stop on Jubilee Road, near the **train station** and just a few yards from the **tourist office** on Station Road (Easter–Oct daily 10am–5pm, and until to 5.50pm during summer school holidays; Nov–Easter 10am–4.30pm; ☎01341/280787, ⍟www.barmouth-wales.co.uk). Free **internet access** is available at the library on Talbot Square, and there's basic **bike rental** from the Birmingham Garage on Church Street (☎01341/280644).

Barmouth has plenty of **accommodation**, although booking ahead is advised in July and August. Among the usual cheap cafés, there are quite a few decent places to **eat**, the majority clustered at the south end of town where The Quay meets Church Street, which is also the best area for **pubs**.

Accommodation

Hotels and guesthouses

Bae Abermaw Hotel Panorama Hill ☎01341/280550, ⍟www.baeabermaw.com. Very un-Barmouth, this former Victorian hotel is now ultra-contemporary, with minimalist white-on-white rooms, an elegant bare-boards lounge and a pricey but sublime restaurant (see below), almost all with unfurling views over Cardigan Bay. ❻–❽

Endeavour Marine Parade ☎01341/280271, ⍟www.endeavour-guest-house.co.uk. Fresh, neutral-toned B&B with sea views from all rooms, and en suites and wi-fi in most. ❷

Llwyndû Farmhouse Llanaber, 2 miles north of Barmouth ☎ 01341/280144, ⊛ www.llwyndu-farmhouse.co.uk. A gem of a B&B with en-suite rooms in a seventeenth-century farmhouse building (complete with mullioned windows and inglenook fireplace) and adjacent converted barn. Also wonderful table d'hôte meals (see below). ❺
Wavecrest Hotel 8 Marine Parade ☎ 01341/280330, ⊛ www.barmouthbandb.com. One of the best beachfront B&Bs, with antique-furnished en-suite rooms, organic breakfasts and bike storage. ❷–❸

Campsite

Hendre Mynach Llanaber Rd, one mile north of town ☎ 01341/280262, ⊛ www.hendremynach .co.uk. Barmouth has loads of places to camp, the closest – and least afflicted with fixed caravans – being this well-set-up place just off the beach. £8–22 per tent. Closed Jan & Feb.

Eating, drinking and entertainment

Bae Abermaw (see opposite). Comfy chairs, wooden floors, white walls and a wintertime fire all enhance the best of modern British cuisine served here – from grilled black bream with cockles and caper butter to seared venison and ginger-and-date pudding for dessert.
Indian Clipper Church St ☎ 01341/280252. A great South Asian balti house which serves well-prepared and tasty meals including plenty of vegetarian dishes. Unlicensed, but you can bring your own booze.
Isis The Quay. The pick of the quayside places with brimming baguettes, loaded pizzas and straightforward low-cost meals (including vegetarian options) and good espresso. Closed Oct–Feb.

Last Inn Church St ☎ 01341/280530. A cosy bar in a former cobbler's shop where you can also get good pub meals such as Thai red chicken curry and sirloin steak. The outdoor tables catch the afternoon sun.
Llwyndû Farmhouse Llanaber, 2 miles north of Barmouth ☎ 01341/280144, ⊛ www.llwyndu-farmhouse.co.uk. Delicious evening meals served in the romantic lamplit dining room with candles flickering on the tables (meals Mon–Sat; from £24.50; available for guests and non-guests). Arrive early for pre-dinner drinks around the fireplace.
Tal y Don High St. Traditional and friendly pub with well-kept real ales.

Ardudwy

North of Barmouth, the coast opens out to a narrow coastal plain running a dozen miles towards Snowdonia and flanked by the heather-covered slopes of the Rhinog Mountains, five miles inland. This is **Ardudwy**, a fertile land used as a fattening ground for black Welsh cattle on their way to the English markets, and now tamed by caravan sites and golf courses.

No modern road crosses the Rhinos to the east, but until the early nineteenth-century building of coach roads, the existence of two mountain passes (see box, p.317) made this a strategic and populous area, as the number of minor Neolithic burial chambers and small Iron and Bronze Age forts testify. Further up the coast, the town of **Harlech** was built as one link in Edward I's chain of magnificent fortresses. It is the only sizeable town in the region, followed in importance by **Llanbedr**, from where a road runs west to the dune-backed camping resort on Shell Island, and another rises east, splitting into two delightfully remote valleys.

Bus #38 services the coast from Barmouth to Harlech, then inland to Blaenau Ffestiniog. The Cambrian coast train line covers the same route to Harlech, from where it makes for Porthmadog on the Llŷn.

Llanddwywe and Dyffryn Ardudwy

Two of the most accessible and impressive Neolithic sites in Ardudwy are in the contiguous twin villages of **LLANDDWYWE** and **DYFFRYN ARDUDWY**, five miles north of Barmouth. Turn right opposite the church in Llanddwywe and continue for a mile to get to **Cors-y-Gedol Burial Chamber** (unrestricted entry), a large capstone on deeply embedded uprights. Follow the path to the right at the far end of Ffordd Gors; the one straight ahead leads to the old drovers' bridge at **Pont Scethin** and the Roman Steps (see opposite). More substantial than Cors-y-Geddol, the **Dyffryn Ardudwy Burial Chambers** (unrestricted entry; CADW) are signposted just off the main road behind the school. Two supported capstones lie amongst a bed of small boulders, the base stones of a mound thought to have been a hundred feet long. Finds from a dig here in the 1960s – including pottery, finely polished stone plaques and bones – are on display at the National Museum in Cardiff.

If you're travelling by train, get off at Talybont, walk north to visit the two sites and rejoin the line at Dyffryn Ardudwy, a walk of three miles in all. Just beyond Dyffryn Ardudwy station is the southern entrance to the **Morfa Dyffryn National Nature Reserve**, a coastal dune system stretching up to Shell Island (see below) notable for its flora, particularly the marsh helleborine. This is a fragile zone and large areas are fenced off, but there's beach access across a boardwalk. Follow the path from Dyffryn Ardudwy station through the caravan parks and the dunes to the splendid, vast **beach**. A section of shore a few hundred yards to the north serves as Wales' only official **nudist beach** (well, when it's warm enough).

Llanbedr and around

LLANBEDR, three miles north of Dyffryn Ardudwy, is home to more Neolithic sights. There are two imposing **standing stones** at the northern end of the village, in the field to the northwest of the petrol station; sadly, though, they and an oak tree are incarcerated behind a rusty fence. Across the road from the stones is the parish **church of St Peter**, which contains an ancient stone grooved with a spiral pattern, a common design from other pre-Christian sites. The central ⚓ *Victoria Inn* (℡01341/241213, ⓦwww.vic-inn.co.uk; ❹) is a winner for its beer garden and à la carte meals made from produce from its own market garden.

Though Llanbedr itself has only limited interest, there's plenty to do in the area. A lane forks off the main road in the village centre, snaking its way alongside the babbling Afon Artro, past the train station and redundant airfield to **Shell Island**, or Mochras, two miles away (£5 per car). A peninsula at anything other than high tide, the island is reached by a tidal causeway and offers the chance to swim, sail, look for wild flowers or scour the beach for some of the two hundred varieties of shell found here. The *Shell Island* complex houses a **restaurant**, deservedly popular for its Sunday roast lunch, and forms the centrepiece of the three-hundred-acre, tent-only **campsite** (℡01341/241453, ⓦwww.shellisland .co.uk; £6–7 per person), Europe's biggest, which spreads along the beach from the harbour down to the vast dunes of Morfa Dyffryn. Although it can get crowded during the school summer holidays and warm bank holiday weekends, campers must pitch tents a minimum of twenty yards from each other (unless agreed with your neighbours), guaranteeing solitude amongst quite spectacular scenery, with some of the best sunsets in north Wales. At low tide you can see a line of rocks in the sea leading out towards Ireland, known as Sarn Badrig (St Patrick's Causeway) and traditionally thought to be the road to a flooded land known as the Cantre'r Gwaelod ("The Low Hundreds").

East of Llanbedr, a narrow road dives through gorgeous woods as it follows the Afon Artro six miles to the waters of **Llyn Cwm Bychan**, deep in the heather and angular rocks of the Rhinog range. Pay the farmer to park on the

The northern **Rhinogs** offer some surprisingly tough walking. At under 2500ft, they're hardly giants, but the typically large, rough, gritstone rocks hidden in thick heather make anything but the most well-worn paths hard-going and potentially ankle-twisting. The rewards for your efforts are long views across Cardigan Bay, a good chance of stumbling across a herd of feral goats and a strong sense of achievement. The two walks described here start at the head of different valleys (see opposite & below), but share a common summit, that of Rhinog Fawr. Ambitious walkers might try combining the two (10 miles; 7hr; 3700ft ascent), using paths that only approximately follow those marked on the OS Landranger 124 1:50,000 "Porthmadog & Dolgellau" map or the 1:25,000 Explorer OL18 "Harlech, Porthmadog & Bala" map.

Cwm Bychan Walk #1

The **Cwm Bychan walk** (5 miles; 3–4hr; 1900ft ascent) starts at the car park in Cwm Bychan, following signs up through a small wood then out onto the open moor and up to the misnamed **Roman Steps**. These guide you up to a pass, Bwlch Tyddiad, giving views east to Bala and beyond. Continue a couple of hundred yards past a large cairn to a smaller one signalling a much less well-defined path leading south and steeply up. Beyond Llyn Du, the terrain gets steeper still, and you may have to use your hands to finally reach **Rhinog Fawr** (2362ft). The standard route is then to retrace your steps, but in good weather you can descend the same way you came for a few hundred yards and seek out a line running northwest from the shoulder towards Gloyw Llyn. From there, with some effort, you can pick up a path by following the obvious watercourse along a small stream to the head of Llyn Cwm Bychan.

Cwm Bychan Walk #2

The second walk (6–7 miles; 5–6hr; 2900ft ascent) starts by the Maes-y-Garnedd farmhouse at the head of Cwm Nantcol and makes a fairly rugged circuit over Rhinog Fawr and Rhinog Fach. Follow the track north from the car park to the house, into the fields and over the stile, then turn northeast and walk gradually towards the base of the rocky southwest ridge, following the white marker posts. Eventually, the path turns north to a cairn on the skyline, then east following more cairns up the ridge to the summit trig point of **Rhinog Fawr** (2362ft).

To approach Rhinog Fach you first have to make an arduous descent into Bwlch Drws Ardudwy (The Pass of the Door of Ardudwy). From the summit of Rhinog Fawr head southeast towards a couple of cairns, then with Rhinog Fach ahead of you keep left, descending on whatever looks like it has had the most use. Eventually you'll reach the col, where you cross the stone wall and start on a fairly clear line up **Rhinog Fach** (2236ft). Explore the summit ridge to get the best views either way, then descend to Cwm Nantcol by first walking to a rocky ledge overlooking Llyn Hywel to the south. From here you should be able to see a scrappy path running very steeply down to the lake on the right-hand edge of the ledge. You'll have to use your hands at times, and there are sections of scree, but you're soon on a clear path that skirts north around the base of Rhinog Fach towards Bwlch Drws Ardudwy. When you reach the path through the pass, turn left and follow it back to Cwm Nantcol.

property here to take the path up to the **Roman Steps** – most likely a medieval packhorse route, made of flat slabs cutting through the range – onto Rhinog Fawr (see box above). Branching off the Cwm Bychan road a mile out of Llanbedr, another delightful road leads to **Cwm Nantcol**, the next valley south. Two hundred yards up the lane, **Capel Salem** was where Sidney Curnow Vosper's famous 1908 painting of the same name was modelled – a

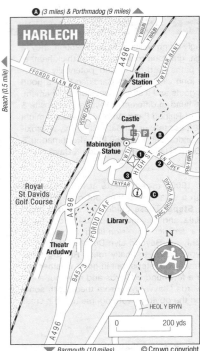

ACCOMMODATION

Byrdir	**C**
Castle Cottage	**B**
Maes-y-Neuadd	**A**

RESTAURANTS, CAFÉS & PUBS

Castle Cottage	**B**	Maes-y-	
Cemlyn	**1**	Neuadd	**A**
Lion Hotel	**2**	Plâs Café	**3**

copy hangs inside. Further up the lane, follow the signs to the Nantcol Waterfalls for a basic but blissfully secluded **campsite** (☎ 01341/241209, ⓦ www .nantcolwaterfalls.co.uk; £6 per person) by the river.

North of Llanbedr the A496 climbs gently for a mile or so to **Chwarel Hên Slate Caverns** (Easter to Sept daily 10am–5pm; Oct daily 11am–4pm; £4.30) at Llanfair, a small slate quarry visited on a self-guided underground tour. A few yards further on, a small road branches down to the hamlet of **Llandanwg**, a great place to get out onto the dunes, with a small church that has to be periodically dug out of the sand by youth scheme workers so that the occasional service can be held. From the top road in Llanfair, a lane to the right ascends into spectacular hill country, a crisscross of dry stone walls, sheep and prehistoric relics.

Harlech

One of the highlights of the Cambrian coast, three miles north of Llanbedr, **HARLECH** makes a dramatic first impression. Its commanding castle clings to a rocky outcrop, while the charming township cloaking the hill behind the fortress takes in one of Wales' finest views: over the Morfa Harlech dunes across Cardigan Bay to the Llŷn, and north to the jagged peaks of Snowdonia. There are plenty of inviting places to eat, drink and stay in the town's narrow streets, plus wonderful walking country and superb beaches on the doorstep.

Practicalities

Harlech's **train** station is on the main A496 under the castle. Most **buses** call both here and at the southern end of High Street, a couple of hundred yards from the welcoming **tourist office** (Easter–Oct daily 9.30am–5.30pm; ☎01766/780658, ⓔticharlech@eryri-npa.gov.uk). The tourist office is volunteer staffed, so hours can vary, including lunchtime closures (usually 12.30–1.30pm) outside peak season. **Theatr Ardudwy** (☎01766/780667, ⓦwww.theatrardudwy.com), on the A496, occasionally puts on decent plays and shows recent releases at the only cinema in the district.

Accommodation

For accommodation, your best bets are the reliable small hotel, *Byrdir*, 200 yards from the tourist office on High Street (☎01766/780316, ⓦwww.byrdir.com; ❸;

closed Nov), with five en-suite rooms and meals available; the contemporary yet cosily informal "restaurant with rooms", *Castle Cottage*, Pen Llech (℡01766/780479, Ⓦwww.castlecottageharlech.co.uk; ❻–❼); and *Maes-y-Neuadd* (℡01766/780200, Ⓦwww.neuadd.com; ❻–❽), three miles north in Talsarnau in a substantially modernized country-house hotel (parts of which date from the fourteenth century) set in beautiful grounds.

Eating and drinking

Castle Cottage and *Maes-y-Neuadd* (see above) are both superior top-end places to **dine**. For something less expensive, try ⚓ *Cemlyn* (℡01766/780637) on the High Street – by day, an upmarket café serving the best loose-leaf teas and espresso coffees around, and by night a quality restaurant for which booking is advised. Alternatively, Harlech's most happening pub, the *Lion Hotel*, Pen Dref, just up from the central crossroads, is great for hand-pumped ales and good home-cooked bar meals, while the unpretentious licensed café and restaurant *Plâs Café* (℡01766/780204; closed Jan) on the High Street serves well-prepared lunches and afternoon teas in a glass-fronted dining room or on a garden terrace with sensational views, as well as inexpensive to moderately priced evening meals.

The Town

Harlech's showpiece is its substantially intact **castle** (daily April–Oct 9am–5pm; Nov–March Mon–Sat 9.30am–4pm, Sun 11am–4pm; £3.70; CADW), rising mightily on its 200-foot bluff. Intended as one of Edward I's Iron Ring of monumental fortresses (see p.435), construction of Harlech castle began in 1283, just six months after the death of Llewelyn the Last. It was built of a hard Cambrian rock, known as Harlech grit, hewn from the moat where sheep now peacefully graze. One side of the fortress was originally protected by the sea – the waters have now receded, though, leaving the castle dominating a stretch of duned coastline.

The castle has seen a lot of action in its time: it withheld a siege in 1295, was taken by Owain Glyndŵr in 1404, and the youthful, future Henry VII – the first Welsh king of England and Wales – withstood a seven-year siege at the hands of the Yorkists from 1461 to 1468, until the castle was again taken. It subsequently fell into ruin, but was put back into service for the king during the Civil War, and in March 1647 it became the last Royalist castle to fall.

The first defensive line comprised the three successive pairs of gates and portcullises built between the two massive half-round towers of the **gatehouse**, where an exhibition now outlines the castle's history. Much of the outermost ring has been destroyed, leaving only the twelve-foot-thick curtain walls rising up 40ft to the exposed battlements, and only the towering gatehouse prevents you walking the full circuit. Outside the castle, a modern equestrian **statue** by Ivor Roberts depicts a scene from The Mabinogion, recalling a semi-mythical era long before Edward's conquest. The heroic giant and king of the British, Bendigeidfran (Brân the Blessed), ruled the court at Harlech, which needed to ally itself with the Irish. Bendigeidfran's sister Branwen (White Crow) married the king of Ireland and bore him a son, Gwern, but war soon broke out and Gwern was killed. The sorrowful uncle and dead nephew are **The Two Kings** of the sculpture's title.

Reachable via Beach Road, which shoots off the main road through Harlech, directly below the castle, the town's **sand dunes** and **beach** are among the finest on the coast. On the way to the sands, you'll brush past the ultra-exclusive **Royal St David's golf course**, venue of many a championship.

Travel details

Unless otherwise stated, frequencies for trains and buses are for Monday to Saturday services; Sunday averages 1–3 services, though the main routes are more frequent and some routes have no Sunday service at all. See p.38 and p.273 for more information including websites with route-finder services.

Trains

Aberdyfi to: Barmouth (10 daily; 30min); Machynlleth (8–10 daily; 20min); Porthmadog (7 daily; 1hr 20min); Pwllheli (7 daily; 1hr 40min); Tywyn (10 daily; 5min).
Aberystwyth to: Borth (9 daily; 12min); Machynlleth (9 daily; 30min).
Barmouth to: Aberdyfi (10 daily; 30min); Harlech (7 daily; 25min); Machynlleth (8–10 daily; 50min); Porthmadog (7 daily; 45min).
Harlech to: Barmouth (7 daily; 30min); Machynlleth (6 daily; 1hr 20min); Porthmadog (7 daily; 20min).
Machynlleth to: Aberdyfi (8–10 daily; 20min); Aberystwyth (9 daily; 30min); Barmouth (10 daily; 50min); Birmingham (7 daily; 2hr 15min); Harlech (7 daily; 1hr 20min); Porthmadog (7 daily; 1hr 45min); Shrewsbury (7 daily; 1hr 20min).
Tywyn to: Aberdyfi (10 daily; 5min); Barmouth (7 daily; 25min); Harlech (7 daily; 1hr); Machynlleth (7 daily; 30min); Porthmadog (7 daily; 1hr 10min).

Buses

Aberaeron to: Aberystwyth (every 30min; 40min); Cardigan (8 daily; 50min); Carmarthen (10 daily; 1hr 40min); Lampeter (10 daily; 40min); New Quay (hourly; 20min).
Aberdyfi to: Machynlleth (8 daily; 20min); Tywyn (8 daily; 10min).
Aberystwyth to: Aberaeron (every 30min; 40min); Borth (hourly; 20min); Caernarfon (4 daily; 3hr); Cardigan (9 daily; 1hr 30min–2hr); Carmarthen (mostly hourly; 2hr 20min); Devil's Bridge (2 daily Mon–Sat; 50min); Lampeter (Mon–Sat hourly; 1hr 15min); Machynlleth (hourly; 45min); New Quay (hourly; 1hr); Ponterwyd (7 daily Mon–Sat; 30min); Pontrhydfendigaid (3 daily Mon–Sat; 45min); Tregaron (7 daily; 45min); Ynyslas (hourly; 30min).

Barmouth to: Bala (mostly hourly; 1hr); Blaenau Ffestiniog (5 daily; 1hr); Dolgellau (hourly; 30min); Harlech (hourly; 30min); Llangollen (mostly hourly; 2hr); Wrexham (mostly hourly; 2hr 30min).
Cardigan to: Aberaeron (8 daily; 50min); Aberporth (hourly; 25min); Aberystwyth (9 daily; 1hr 30min–2hr); Carmarthen (hourly; 1hr 30min); Cenarth (10 daily; 25min); Cilgerran (8 daily; 10min); Drefach Felindre (hourly; 30min); Newcastle Emlyn (10 daily; 25min); New Quay (hourly; 1hr).
Dolgellau to: Bala (10 daily; 35min); Barmouth (hourly; 30min); Llangollen (mostly hourly; 1hr 30min); Machynlleth (mostly hourly; 30min); Porthmadog (6 daily; 40min); Tywyn (8 daily; 55min).
Fairbourne to: Dolgellau (8 daily; 20min); Tywyn (8 daily; 35min).
Harlech to: Barmouth (hourly; 30min); Blaenau Ffestiniog (4 daily; 35min); Dyffryn Ardudwy (mostly hourly; 15min).
Lampeter to: Aberaeron (10 daily; 40min); Aberystwyth (Mon–Sat hourly; 1hr 15min); Carmarthen (mostly hourly; 1hr); Llanddewi Brefi (6 daily Mon–Sat; 25min); Tregaron (Mon–Sat 8 daily; 20–35min).
Machynlleth to: Aberdyfi (8 daily; 20min); Aberystwyth (hourly; 45min); Corris (hourly; 15min); Dolgellau (mostly hourly; 30min); Tywyn (8 daily; 35min).
New Quay to: Aberaeron (hourly; 20min); Aberporth (hourly; 40min); Aberystwyth (hourly; 1hr); Cardigan (hourly; 1hr).
Tregaron to: Aberystwyth (9 daily; 1hr); Lampeter (Mon–Sat 8 daily; 20–35min); Llanddewi Brefi (Mon–Sat 6 daily; 10min).
Tywyn to: Aberdyfi (8 daily; 10min); Abergynolwyn (3 daily; 18min); Corris (3 daily; 30min); Dolgellau (8 daily; 55min); Fairbourne (8 daily; 35min); Machynlleth (8 daily; 35min).

The North Wales borderlands

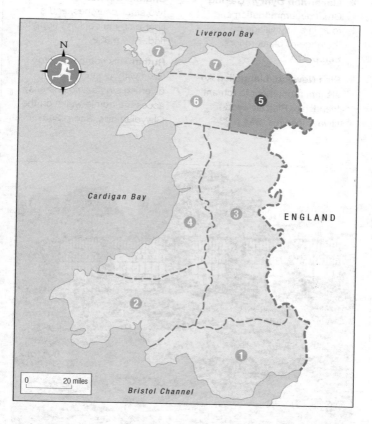

CHAPTER 5

Highlights

✳ **Erddig** The most interesting stately home in Wales, complete with finely preserved servants' quarters, outbuildings and gardens. See p.328

✳ **Llanarmon Dyffryn Ceiriog** Great accommodation and food in a tiny village on the edge of bleak moors. See p.330

✳ **Plas Newydd, Llangollen** An elegant monument to romantic friendship, Plas Newydd always inspires. See p.334

✳ **Castell Dinas Brân, Llangollen** Hike up to this ragged ruin of a Welsh castle for a breath of air and great views. See p.336

✳ **Rug Chapel and Llangar Church, Corwen** One ticket, two small churches, and a finer pair you couldn't hope to find. See p.339

✳ **Ruthin** This compact hilltop town with its cluster of diverting sights also has easy access to gentle walks on the Clwydian hills. See p.343

▲ Plas Newydd, Llangollen

5

The North Wales borderlands

The **North Wales borderlands** is a schizophrenic region encompassing both industrialized flatlands that spill over the border from England and attractive folds of green hill country that are as Welsh as anywhere. There's plenty to see here, but few of the region's sights top most people's list, and visitors often travel through with their minds set firmly on the more obvious destinations further west. The three main routes through the region – the Dee Valley, the Vale of Clwyd, and Deeside – all start in the English border country known as the **Marches**, an area long contested by the Welsh and English. At its heart is the borderlands' largest conurbation, **Wrexham**, where the light industrial hinterland is leavened by the packaged mining and smelting heritage along the **Clywedog Valley**.

The only extant Marcher fortress of note is **Chirk Castle**, south of Wrexham, a potent reminder of the centuries after the Norman conquest of England, when powerful barons fought the Welsh princes for control of these fertile lands. The castle makes a fine introduction to the **Dee Valley**, the umbilical cord which runs between the Welsh borders and the rugged mountains of Snowdonia. The Dee Valley remains more firmly Welsh than the Marches, and three hundred years after the arrival of the Normans, the area was the site of the first big revolt against them. From his base near **Corwen**, Wales' greatest hero, Owain Glyndŵr, attacked the property of a nearby English landowner, sparking a fourteen-year campaign which, at its height, saw Glyndŵr ruling most of Wales. Little remains to commemorate the era, and most people drive through oblivious of its heritage. **Llangollen** is the valley's main draw, with an international eisteddfod folk music festival each July and a broad selection of ruins, rides and rambles to tempt visitors throughout the rest of the year.

The bucolic lands to the north reward a leisurely approach. The historic but dull market town of **Mold** is the gateway to the bald tops of the **Clwydian Range**, easy walking country that overlooks the pastoral **Vale of Clwyd**. Its gentle contours and minor sights take time to appreciate, including the appealing town of **Ruthin** with its fine medieval buildings and jail tour, and **Denbigh**, surmounted by its craggy castle.

The fastest route through the borderlands follows the A55 close to the coast. This initially runs through **Deeside**, a wedge of former mining communities set between the salt marshes of the Dee estuary and the

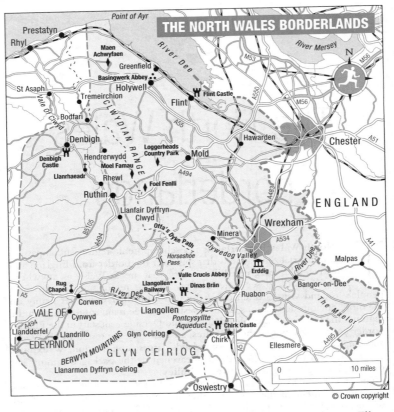

THE NORTH WALES BORDERLANDS

© Crown copyright

Clwydian Range. The area has its share of modest and varied offerings: **Flint**, the first link in Edward I's Iron Ring of castles; and understated **Holywell**, whose quiet attractions include St Winefride's Well, a pilgrimage site of varied fortunes during the last 1300 years.

Getting around

The region is best explored by car, but public transport will get you most places. **Trains** are good for Deeside and Wrexham, but otherwise you'll be reliant on **buses**. The main routes to Snowdonia are from Wrexham to Llangollen, where you can pick up a bus to either Betws-y-Coed or Bala. Further north, the #51 links Ruthin and Denbigh with Rhyl on the north coast, and the #11 visits Flint and Holywell on its run between Chester and Rhyl.

Wrexham and the Clywedog Valley

While not a classically pretty place, **WREXHAM** (Wrecsam), the largest town in North Wales, has a boisterous charm and some fine older buildings amidst the identikit chainstores. Having long looked more to the industrial northwest

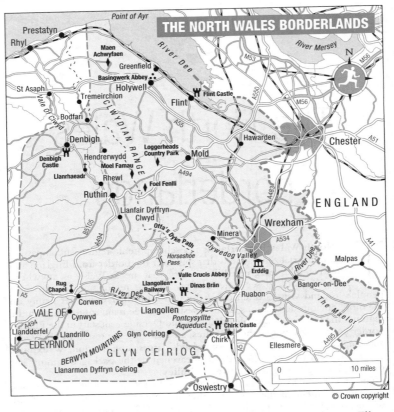

of England than its own Welsh hinterland, Wrexham's Welshness is only loudly and proudly flaunted when the Welsh football team plays international matches at the town's Racecourse Ground (home for the rest of the time to Wrexham Football Club).

Once a medieval marketplace for the fertile lands all around, Wrexham developed as an administrative centre before the discovery of iron ore, coal and lead combined to jettison the town into the industrial age. The legacy of these times is best seen to the south and west of town in the **Clywedog Valley**, which played a key role in the early part of the Industrial Revolution. Its sites have now been smartened up as Wrexham's chief attractions, the finest being the National Trust's splendidly evocative stately home, **Erddig**.

The Town

Though it is pleasant enough wandering around the centre with its Edwardian arcades and two Victorian market halls, the town's real highlight is the imposing **St Giles' Church** (daily 10am–4pm; free), whose Gothic tower (open Thurs & Sat at 12.30pm; £2.50) gracefully rises above the knot of lanes at the end of Hope Street. Topped off with a steeple in the 1520s, the tower's five tiers, rising to four hexagonal pinnacles, are replicated at America's Yale University in homage to the ancestral home of the college's benefactor, Elihu Yale, whose tomb is here at the base. The engraved stone in the tower wall near his grave came from the university, replacing one that now holds up a replica tower there. The spacious interior boasts the scant remains of a late fifteenth-century mural of *The Last Judgement* above the entrance to the chancel, and an abundance of Victorian and contemporary stained glass. The church is approached through wrought-iron gates installed between 1718 and 1724 by famed Welsh ironworkers Robert and John Davies of Bersham, also responsible for the striking gates at Chirk Castle and St Peter's Church in Ruthin.

From St Giles' you can head northeast to the small but engaging **Wrexham County Borough Museum**, Regent Street (Mon–Fri 10am–5pm, Sat 10.30am–3pm; free; set to close for refurbishment from August 2009 until July 2010). In the meantime, its central room exhibits a ramshackle array of artefacts from the town's nineteenth-century boom years, alongside Roman nuggets and the remarkable remains of the Bronze Age Brymbo Man, who was unearthed from a local sandstone burial cist complete with his pottery beaker and flint knife. Two smaller galleries house temporary exhibitions, usually on local themes.

Practicalities

Wrexham has two **train stations**, half a mile apart. Chester, Chirk and Shrewsbury trains call only at Wrexham General on Regent Street, ten minutes' walk northwest of the centre, while services from Liverpool (change at Bidston on the Wirral line) call there on request before Wrexham Central, incorporated into the Island Green shopping centre behind Hill Street, in the middle of town. National Express buses from Birmingham, London and Glasgow and assorted local services arrive at the **bus station** on King Street.

The **tourist office** is on Lambpit Street (April to mid-Oct Mon–Fri 10am–5pm, Sat 9am–4pm; mid-Oct to March Mon–Sat 10am–4pm; ☎01978/292015, Ⓦwww.borderlands.co.uk). There's free **internet** access at the library and pay facilities at @rrow CyberWorld (Mon–Sat 9am–6pm) on Vicarage Hill.

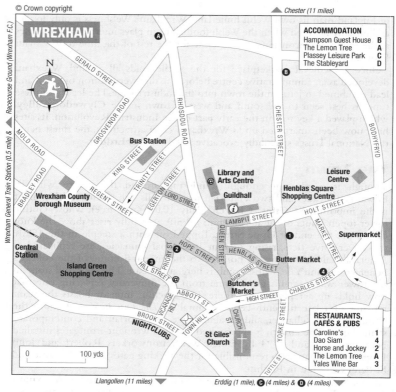

© Crown copyright

▲ Chester (11 miles)

WREXHAM

Ⓐ

ACCOMMODATION
Hampson Guest House   B
The Lemon Tree   A
Plassey Leisure Park   C
The Stableyard   D

GERALD STREET
GROSVENOR ROAD
MOLD ROAD
BRADLEY ROAD
RHOSDDU ROAD
KING STREET
REGENT STREET
TRINITY STREET
EGERTON STREET
LORD STREET
CHESTER STREET
BODHYFRYD
HOLT STREET
MARKET STREET
CHARLES STREET
YORKE STREET
TUTTLE ST
CHURCH ST
TOWN HILL
VICARAGE HILL
BROOK STREET
ABBOTT ST
HILL STREET
PRIORY ST
HOPE STREET
QUEEN STREET
HENBLAS STREET
BANK STREET
HIGH STREET
LAMBPIT STREET

Bus Station

Wrexham County Borough Museum

Central Station

Island Green Shopping Centre

Library and Arts Centre

Guildhall ⓘ

Leisure Centre

Henblas Square Shopping Centre

Supermarket

Butter Market

Butcher's Market

St Giles' Church ✝

NIGHTCLUBS

❸
❷
❶
❹

0 _____ 100 yds

▼ Llangollen (11 miles)   Erddig (1 mile), Ⓒ (4 miles) & Ⓓ (4 miles) ▼

Ⓐ Ⓑ

Ⓝ Racecourse Ground (Wrexham F.C.) & ▲
Wrexham General Train Station (0.5 mile) ◄

RESTAURANTS, CAFÉS & PUBS
Caroline's   1
Dao Siam   4
Horse and Jockey   2
The Lemon Tree   A
Yales Wine Bar   3

Accommodation

There's a reasonable choice of places to stay in Wrexham, but for something more upscale it's worth pushing on to Llangollen or Ruthin.

Hampson Guest House 6 Chester Rd ☏01978/357665, ⓦwww.wrexhamhotels .com. Pleasant, central, renovated B&B with some en-suite rooms, full breakfast, free broadband and nice lawns for a relaxing sundowner. ❷

The Lemon Tree 29 Rhosddu Rd ☏01978/261211, ⓦwww.lemon-tree.net. Modernized hotel converted from an old Gothic school priory, with small and simple yet tasteful en-suite rooms (some with canopy beds and DVD players), and a good restaurant where breakfast is served. ❹

Plassey Leisure Park Four miles south at Eyton ☏01978/780277, ⓦwww.plassey.co.uk. Wrexham's nearest campsite, pricey but with tent and caravan facilities, an indoor swimming pool, nine-hole golf course and microbrewery. £22 per pitch

The Stableyard High St, 4 miles southeast in Bangor-on-Dee ☏01978/780642, ⓦwww .stableyard.co.uk. Attractive rooms and superb meals in a seventeenth-century tavern, set in an appealing, ancient village. Self-catering also available. ❷

Eating, drinking and entertainment

Wrexham has a tolerable range of places to **eat** and **drink**. At weekends, the area around the junction of Brook Street and Vicarage Hill features a handful of reasonable **nightclubs**; and there's more highbrow diversion in the form of several **male voice choir** evening practice sessions in local halls (all year except Aug on Mon, Wed, Thurs & Sun): call the tourist office for details.

Caroline's 45 Chester St. The best of the daytime cafés, with some outside eating and a range of budget sandwiches, panini and snacks.
Dao Siam 13 Charles St ℡01978/351071. Good-quality Thai restaurant, with most mains £8–10. Takeaways available. Closed Sun.
Horse and Jockey Corner of Hope and Priory sts. Thatched, characterful old cottage, long since converted into a convivial low-beamed pub serving good beer and decent food.

The Lemon Tree 29 Rhosddu Rd ℡01978/261211. Bustling, brightly decorated Italian restaurant, café and bar with an extensive menu of ciabattas and pasta dishes for lunch (£6–7) and a wider range of vegetarian and meaty dishes for dinner (2/3 courses for £18/21). Save room for tiramisu or chocolate truffle ice cream.
Yales Wine Bar Hill St. The best bet in town for live bands or special entertainment; look out for posters around town advertising events.

The Clywedog Valley

The **Clywedog Valley** – forming an arc around the western and southern suburbs of Wrexham – was the crucible of industrial achievement in the northern Welsh borders during the eighteenth century. Iron production boomed here, thanks to an abundance of ore deposits and cheap waterpower harnessed from the River Clywedog. As the Industrial Revolution forged ahead, coal became a more important energy source than water and factories moved away, closer to their raw materials, leaving the valley in peace. The long-abandoned industrial ruins here – principally a mine, a mill and an ironworks – have been partly restored and are now waypoints on the seven-mile-long **Clywedog Valley Trail**. The area is all a bit over-packaged, but no less interesting for that, and you can see everything in one long, varied day, making use of the free *Clywedog Valley Trail* leaflet available from tourist offices and any of the sites. Aside from Minera and Nant Mill, all the sites lie within a couple of miles of the centre of Wrexham, and can be visited on foot. To tackle the whole valley in a day (a total of 9 miles walking), catch a #10 or #11 bus to Minera, walk the full length of the **Clywedog Trail** to Erddig, then wander the mile and a half back into Wrexham.

There isn't a lot to see at the **Minera Lead Mines** (Easter to mid-July Sat & Sun 10am–5pm; mid-July to early Sept Mon & Thurs–Sun 10am–5pm; free), four miles west of Wrexham. Many of the surface workings are still incompletely excavated, but the engine house and a pithead derrick have been largely rebuilt, together with some ore-processing machinery by the small museum in the former ore house. For a better impression of the mine's layout, walk up onto the hill behind – a heather-clad moor on the fringe of an area called **World's End** – and look back on the valley. In the eighteenth century this was full of mines extracting galena, a silver-and-zinc-rich lead ore, from shafts over 1200ft deep.

From the lead mines, a path leads for a mile and a half east along the River Clywedog to the child-oriented **Nant Mill** visitor centre (Easter–Sept daily 10.30am–4.30pm; Oct–Easter Sat & Sun 10.30am–4.30pm; free), where you can pick up leaflets for nature trails leading to a very visible section of **Offa's Dyke** in the woods nearby. The Clywedog Valley Trail runs through the wood to **Bersham Ironworks** (Easter & mid-July to early Sept daily except Tues & Wed noon–5pm; free), established in the seventeenth century and expanded by Cumbrian ironmaster John "Iron-Mad" Wilkinson who, in 1775, patented his new method for horizontally boring out cylinders. This produced the first truly circular, smooth bore iron, perfect for highly accurate cannons – hundreds were made here for the American Civil and Napoleonic wars – and the production of fine tolerance steam-engine cylinders. Engineer James Watt was a big customer, producing steam engines that made water-powered sites unprofitable and eventually put Bersham out of business.

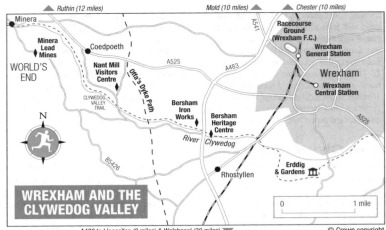

Ruthin (12 miles) ▲   Mold (10 miles) ▲   ▲ Chester (10 miles)

Minera
Minera
Lead
Mines
Coedpoeth
Nant Mill
Visitors
Centre
WORLD'S
END
CLYWEDOG
VALLEY
TRAIL
Offa's Dyke Path
A525
A483
A541
Racecourse
Ground
(Wrexham F.C.)
Wrexham
General Station
Wrexham
Wrexham
Central Station
A525
Bersham
Iron
Works
Bersham
Heritage
Centre
River Clywedog
N
B5426
Rhostyllen
Erddig
& Gardens 🏛

WREXHAM AND THE
CLYWEDOG VALLEY

0   1 mile

A483 to Llangollen (8 miles) & Welshpool (30 miles) ▼   © Crown copyright

After nearly two centuries of neglect, the ironworks' remains are now being unearthed, revealing a broad area of knee-high foundations around the old foundry. This survived largely intact though it saw service as a corn mill and still retains its huge water wheel. The foundations really only serve to help you visualize the layout, which is better explained inside the foundry and put in context ten-minutes' walk away at the **Bersham Heritage Centre** (Easter–Oct Mon–Fri 10am–5pm, Sat & Sun noon–5pm; free), which has a room dedicated to Wilkinson.

From the Bersham Heritage Centre it's only a mile and a half along the trail to Erddig.

Erddig

Despite the closure of the ironworks, coal continued to be mined around Bersham until 1986. After World War II, coal tunnels were pushed under the local stately home, **Erddig**, 1.5 miles south of Wrexham (last two weeks in March and Oct daily except Thurs & Fri noon–4pm; April, May & Sept daily except Thurs & Fri noon–5pm; July & Aug daily except Fri noon–5pm; £9.40, outbuildings & gardens only £6; NT), adding subsidence to the troubles of an already decaying building. Ever since it was built in the late seventeenth century, its owners – all seemingly called Simon or Philip Yorke – had a hands-off attitude; especially the fourth Simon Yorke, who inherited Erddig in 1922. Largely through poverty he failed to install electricity, running water, gas or a phone, and ignored the chronic damp that had the Chinese hand-blocked paper peeling off the walls. The National Trust took charge in the 1970s, since when it has restored the house to its 1922 appearance and returned the jungle of a garden to its formal eighteenth-century plan.

The house itself isn't especially distinguished, but, as nothing was ever thrown away, the collection of fine furniture and portraits – including one by Gainsborough of the first Philip Yorke – is unusually complete. The real interest, however, lies in the servants' quarters, particularly the Servants' Hall, where specially commissioned portraits of eighteenth- and early nineteenth-century staff members are accompanied by personalized dedications in verse written by a Yorke – an extraordinary display of benevolence. You can also see the blacksmith's shop, stables, laundry, the still-used bake house and kitchen.

Reserve an hour for the **walled garden**, saved from the worst excesses of the eighteenth-century landscaping craze despite the attentions of William Emes, a contemporary of Capability Brown, who worked on the surrounding parkland. Manicured box hedges delineate beds planted with pleached lime trees, the walls support some 150 species of ivy, and apple trees produce fruit celebrated during an annual apple festival in early October.

To return to Wrexham from Erddig Hall, head half a mile or so northeast to *Squire Yorke Inn*, from where it's about a mile along the road.

The Dee Valley

The **Dee Valley** has long been the main transport route from the English Marches to Snowdonia, and it remains the most interesting route west. The course of the River Dee is traced by Thomas Telford's A5 road between London and Holyhead which approaches the region past **Chirk**, with its fine Marcher castle. From Chirk, the bucolic Glyn Ceiriog is a peaceful alternative to the more bustling charms of **Llangollen** with its hilltop castle ruins, broken-down abbey and medieval bridge over the river. Upstream, Owain Glyndŵr's stronghold, **Corwen**, deserves a stop to explore a couple of beautiful small churches.

Chirk and Glyn Ceiriog

The peaceful vale of **Glyn Ceiriog**, which runs parallel to the Dee Valley three miles to the south, is a blissfully quiet and starkly beautiful part of the country billed as the "Little Switzerland of Wales" (though that's more than a little optimistic). Other than **Chirk Castle** at the entrance to the valley, there are no compelling sights to draw you here, but the area makes a perfect getaway from the rigours of touring Wales.

Chirk and Chirk Castle

The Normans founded **CHIRK** (Y Waun) almost a thousand years ago, their motte remaining as a small tree-covered mound at the southern end of this pleasant enough village with long views up the valley to the Berwyn hills.

For 400 years until 2004, the Myddleton family occupied the massive drum-towered **Chirk Castle** (July & Aug Tues–Sun 11am–5pm; mid-March to June & Sept Wed–Sun 11pm–5pm; Oct Wed–Sun 11am–4pm; £8.80, garden only £6.20; NT), squatting ominously on a rise half a mile to the west of Chirk. Roger Mortimer began the construction of this Marcher fortress at the behest of Edward I during the thirteenth century, and it eventually fell to the Myddletons.

The approach to the castle is guarded by a magnificent white, Baroque **gatescreen**, the finest work done by the Davies brothers of Bersham, who wrought it between 1712 and 1719. The ebullient floral designs are capped by the Myddleton coat of arms and a red hand, the principal element on the local lairds' coat of arms and the source of all the "Hand" hotels which dot the region. The gates are flanked by a pair of wolves, perhaps a memorial to one of the last wolves in Wales, said to have kept watch over the moat in the 1680s.

From the gates, a mile-and-a-half-long oak-lined avenue leads up to the castle, an austere-looking place softened only by its mullioned windows. The original plan was probably to mimic Beaumaris Castle, started just a couple of

A short walk from Chirk

On the way back from Chirk Castle stop by Chirk train station for a fun short walk (1.5 miles; 30–45min; flat) along the Shropshire Union Canal that takes in a tunnel, an aqueduct and the English border. About 50 yards west of the station a short track leads down to the entrance to the 421-metre Chirk Tunnel. Walk south through the tunnel (torch handy but not absolutely essential) which emerges at the start of Chirk Aqueduct over the River Ceiriog, and a parallel rail viaduct. You can walk to the far end where the canal crosses into England. Return the way you came, or avoid the tunnel using Station Road which runs above it.

months earlier, but Chirk lacks Beaumaris's purity and symmetry. The east and west walls are both incomplete, stopping at the half-round towers midway along the planned length, and the towers have been cut down to wall level, probably after the Civil War when taller towers would have been vulnerable to mortar attack. Internal modifications have been no less extensive, leaving a legacy of sumptuous rooms reflecting sixteenth- to nineteenth-century tastes, many returned to their former states after some Victorian meddling by Pugin in the 1840s. Since the Myddletons' departure, the **east wing** has been opened up, with rooms including one of the last great Welsh family libraries, with volumes dating back to 1535.

After touring the house, spend an hour exploring the beautiful ornamental **gardens** (which open an hour earlier than the castle and close an hour later) or tracing the section of Offa's Dyke that runs across the front of the house, though it was flattened in 1758 for use as a cart track.

Glyn Ceiriog

Chirk Castle guards the entrance to the Glyn Ceiriog Valley, for centuries an important route into the heart of Wales and over the Berwyns into Snowdonia. These days it is the minor B4500 which runs beside the river for five miles through the hamlet of Pontfadog to the slightly larger Glyn Ceiriog, then on a further four miles to **LLANARMON DYFFRYN CEIRIOG** (usually referred to as Llanarmon DC), an appealing small village consisting of nothing but a church, a post office and some excellent **accommodation** in a couple of high-quality country inns, both serving excellent **meals**. Though **trains** on the Shrewsbury to Wrexham line stop at Chirk's station on Station Avenue, and **buses** infrequently penetrate the Glyn Ceiriog Valley as far as Llanarmon DC, you really need your own transport to explore the valley.

Accommodation, eating and drinking

Ddol-Hir On the B4500 a mile west of Glyn Ceiriog ☎01691/718681. Small riverside caravan park and campsite. £14 per pitch.

Fron Frys Glyn Ceiriog ☎01691/718880, ⊚www .fronfrys.co.uk. Lovely B&B in converted farm buildings on a smallholding about a mile out of the village towards Oswestry. ❷

Hand Hotel Llanarmon DC ☎01691/600666, ⊚www.thehandhotel.co.uk. Converted sixteenth-century farmhouse with a convivial wood-beamed bar and relaxed dining room with top-quality food. Try to get one of the older, more atmospheric but

less well-appointed rooms (❻) rather than those in the modern extension. ❺–❻

West Arms Llanarmon DC ☎01691/600665, ⊚www.thewestarms .co.uk. Ancient farmhouse-turned-inn with stone-flagged floor and a gorgeous inglenook fireplace. There are a couple of cheaper, more modest rooms, but you'll really want one of the older rooms, which have bags of character. Stay for the sumptuous dinners (£33 for three courses) and affordable bar meals. ❻/❽

Llangollen and around

Clasped tightly in the narrow Dee Valley between the shoulders of the Berwyn and Eglwyseg mountains, **LLANGOLLEN** is the embodiment of a Welsh town in both setting and character. Along the valley's floor, the waters of the River Dee (Afon Dyfrdwy) cut a wide arc around the base of **Dinas Brân**, a conical tor surmounted by the ruins of a native Welsh castle. At the apex of the bend, the Dee licks the angled buttresses of Llangollen's weighty Gothic bridge, which has spanned the river since the fourteenth century. On its south bank, half a dozen streets, their houses harmoniously straggling up the rugged hillsides, are labelled in both Welsh and English, and form the core of the scattered settlement flung out across the low hills. With its wealth of historical sights, Llangollen is very popular throughout the summer, particularly in early July when the town struggles to cope with the thousands of visitors to Wales' celebration of worldwide folk music, the **International Music Eisteddfod** (see box, p.334).

As the only river crossing point for miles, Llangollen was an important town long before the early Romantics arrived at the end of the eighteenth century, when they were cut off from their European Grand Tours by the Napoleonic Wars. Turner came to paint the swollen river and the Cistercian ruin of **Valle Crucis**, a couple of miles up the valley; John Ruskin found the town "entirely lovely in its gentle wildness"; and writer George Borrow made Llangollen his base for the early part of his 1854 tour detailed in *Wild Wales* (see "Books", p.503). The rich and famous came not only for the scenery, but to visit the celebrated **Ladies of Llangollen**, an eccentric couple who became the toast of society from their house, **Plas Newydd**. But by this stage, some of the town's

Thomas Telford (1767–1834)

The English poet Robert Southey dubbed **Thomas Telford** the "Colossus of Roads" in recognition of his pre-eminence as the greatest road builder of his day, if not the greatest ever. Throughout the early years of the nineteenth century, he managed some of the most ambitious and far-reaching engineering projects yet attempted, and there was seldom a public work on which his opinion wasn't sought.

Born in Scotland, he was apprenticed to a stonemason in London where he taught himself engineering architecture, eventually earning himself a position working for the Ellesmere Canal Company, which was planning a canal to link the Severn, Dee and Mersey rivers. His reputation was forged on the **Pontcysyllte Aqueduct**, part of the **Llangollen Canal** which, though one of his earliest major projects, was recognized as innovative even before he had completed it. Though lured away to build the Caledonian Canal in Scotland and St Katherine's Docks in London, he continued to work in Wales, reaching the apotheosis of his road-building career by pushing the London–Holyhead Turnpike through Snowdonia.

After the 1800 Act of Union between Britain and Ireland, a good road was needed to hasten mail and to transport the new Irish MPs to and from parliament in London. What is now the A5 was wedged into the same valley as Telford's Llangollen Canal, then driven right through Snowdonia with its gradient never exceeding 1:20. The combination of its near-level route and the high quality of its well-drained surface cut hours off the journey time, but the Dublin ferries left from Holyhead on the island of Anglesey, separated from the mainland by the Menai Strait. Telford's solution and his greatest achievement was the 580-foot-long **Menai Suspension Bridge**, strung 100ft above the strait to allow tall ships to pass under. Though the idea wasn't completely novel, the scale and the balance of grace and function won the plaudits of engineers and admiring visitors from around the world.

rural charm had been eaten up by the works of one of the century's finest engineers, Thomas Telford (see box, p.331), who squeezed both his **London–Holyhead trunk road** and the **Llangollen Canal** alongside the river. Canal trips run east to his majestic nineteen-span **Pontcysyllte Aqueduct** over the Dee, while steam-hauled trains now ply the reconstructed track west beyond the head of the canal at the Horseshoe Falls. If none of this is energetic enough, try the panoramic Llangollen History Trail along the limestone escarpment to the north of town (see box, p.337).

Arrival, information and getting around

Buses are the only form of public transport to reach Llangollen, with local services (and the daily Wrexham–London National Express coach: tickets from the visitor centre) stopping on Market Street. The nearest **train station** is five miles away at Ruabon, and passed by frequent buses on the Llangollen–Wrexham run. With your own vehicle, the most spectacular way to approach Llangollen is over the 1350-foot Horseshoe Pass (A542) from Ruthin.

The **tourist office** (Easter–Oct daily 9.30am–5.30pm; Nov–Easter daily 9.30am–5pm; ☏01978/860828, ⓔllangollen@nwtic.com) is in Y Capel on Castle Street, just south of the bridge and less than a hundred yards from the bus stop on Market Street. There's a smart art gallery in the same building, along with the town's library (closed Thurs & Sun), which has free **internet access**.

Buses in the immediate locality are fairly infrequent, so you might as well resign yourself to **getting around** on foot: no great hardship, as even Valle Crucis, the most distant sight, is only a mile and a half along the towpath.

If you fancy something more energetic than the hikes up to Dinas Brân and along the valley (see box, p.337), consider **renting a bike** from ProAdventure,

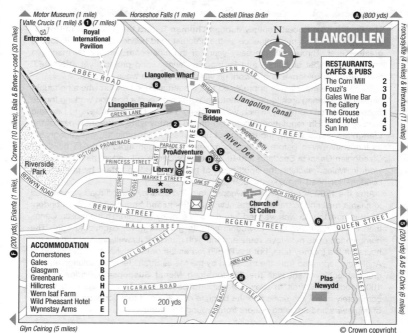

23 Castle St (☎01978/861912, ⓦwww.proadventure.co.uk) who offer hardtails for £18 a day. They also run all sorts of adventure activities and courses including canyoning (£44 for a half day; book in advance). Bookings are also advised for modest **rafting trips** (£40 for 2hr session; £50 on Sat) on the bouncy but less than menacing waters of the Dee run by Whitewater Active (☎1978/860763, ⓦwww.whitewateractive.co.uk) at Mile End Mill, a mile upstream from Llangollen along Berwyn Road. Skilled kayakers can use the slalom course all day for £5.

Accommodation

Llangollen is a fine place to **stay**, with some very pleasant B&Bs and a few luxury options, but no hostel. Finding rooms can be a chore in the middle of summer, especially during the eisteddfod (the week beginning the first or second Tuesday of July), though this is alleviated by people letting out one or two bedrooms in the peak period. The tourist office can book you into these, as well as the ordinary guesthouses that are dotted all over the valley. If you're looking for upscale **country retreats**, consider those a few miles away at Llanarmon DC (see p.330) and in the Vale of Edeyrnion (see p.339).

Cornerstones 15–19 Bridge St ☎01978/861569, ⓦwww.cornerstones-guesthouse.co.uk. The slightly over-the-top exuberance of this luxury B&B can easily be excused when you see the river views from three of the five rooms spread across three adjacent houses, one dating back to the sixteenth century. Amenities include DVD library, free wi-fi, well-appointed guest lounges and an extensive breakfast, plus there are midweek deals. ➍

Gales 18 Bridge St ☎01978/860089, ⓦwww.galesofllangollen.co.uk. Very comfortable and central guesthouse above the restaurant of the same name (or in the house next door), some with brass beds and oak beams. ➍

Glasgwm Abbey Rd ☎01978/861975, ⓔglasgwm@llangollen.co.uk. Very relaxed B&B where the relatively modest facilities are compensated by engaging hosts whose tastes are reflected in the decor of the doubles, twin and single (which has its own deep bath). Plenty of books, and the guest lounge has a piano. ➋

Greenbank Victoria Square ☎01978/861835, ⓦwww.thegreenbankhotel.com. Refurbished and good-value guesthouse with clean, bright, simply furnished rooms, free wi-fi and a good restaurant and bar on site. ➋

Hillcrest Hill St ☎01978/860208, ⓦwww.hillcrest-guesthouse.com. Appealing licensed Victorian guesthouse up towards Plas Newydd with excellent breakfasts. Cheaper deals at quiet times. ➌

Wern Isaf Farm ☎01978/860632, ⓦwww.wernisaf.supanet.com. Simple but lovely farmhouse campsite on the flanks of Dinas Brân just under a mile steeply up Wern Rd (turn right over the canal on Wharf Hill). £7–10 per site and there are some hookups. Open April–Oct.

Wild Pheasant Hotel Berwyn Rd, half a mile west along the A5 ☎01978/860629, ⓦwww.wildpheasanthotel.co.uk. Venerable hotel with an older wing of standard rooms and a luxurious, tastefully decorated new wing, plus spacious suites. Guests have free use of the modern spa pool, steam room and sauna (£10 day pass for non-guests). Frequent three-night deals for the price of two. ➏/➐

Wynnstay Arms Bridge St ☎01978/860710, ⓦwww.wynnstay-arms.co.uk. Ageing hotel with reasonable rooms, but primarily of interest for the three 6–10 bed en-suite bunkhouses, all with bedding and breakfast provided in the hotel. At £22.50 a head it works out okay for singles and can be fun for groups, but couples can sleep better at some of the cheaper B&Bs for just a few pounds more.

The Town

Few visitors can resist admiring the view up the valley from the parapet of the **town bridge** which, though widened and strengthened over the years, has spanned the river since the fourteenth century. Below it, the Dee pours through the fingers of shale which make up the unimaginatively dubbed "Town Falls" rapids. The bridge runs onto Castle Street, which heads due south past the

Llangollen is heaving in summer, but never more so than during the second week of July, when for six days the town explodes into a frenzy of music, dance and poetry. The **International Music Eisteddfod** comes billed as "the world's greatest folk festival" but unlike the National Eisteddfod (see colour insert), which is a purely Welsh affair, the Llangollen event draws amateur performers from fifty countries, all competing for prizes in their chosen disciplines. Throughout the week, dances and choral performances take place at Plas Newydd, Valle Crucis and just about anywhere that a group of people can congregate, though competitive performances are concentrated in the main venue, the **Royal International Pavilion**, on the north bank just west of the town bridge. When the day's competition is over, headlining stars often pack out the pavilion: a few years back, Luciano Pavarotti and his 200-strong entourage fronted up on the fortieth anniversary of his first performance here.

The festival has been held in its present form since 1947, when it was started more or less on a whim by one Harold Tudor to soothe the social wounds of World War II. Forty choirs from fourteen countries performed at the first (entirely choral) event, and it expanded, drawing praise quickly from Dylan Thomas, who declared that "the town sang and danced, as though it were right". Today over 12,000 international musicians, singers, dancers and choristers descend on this town of 3000 people, further swamped by up to 150,000 visitors. While the whole setup can seem oppressive, there is an irresistible *joie de vivre* as brightly costumed dancers walk the streets and fill the restaurants and fish and chip shops.

Unless you are going specifically for the eisteddfod, the week beginning the first or second Tuesday of July is a good time to stay away. Accommodation should be booked (most easily through the tourist office) several months in advance, though **tickets** (☏01978/862001, ⊛www.international-eisteddfod.co.uk) for all but the headlining shows can be obtained much closer the time, often on the day itself. All-day access to the main site, with no guarantee of a seat, costs as little as £8 a day.

Since the late 1990s the eisteddfod has been followed by the less frenetic **Llangollen Fringe** (☏01978/860600, ⊛www.llangollenfringe.co.uk), with a number of more "alternative" acts – music, dance, comedy and so on – performing in the town hall on Castle Street over the last two weeks in July.

---

tourist office. Bibliophiles should cross the road to *Maxine's* café, above which there's a cavernous secondhand **bookshop**.

Llangollen takes its name from the **Church of St Collen** on Church Street, off Castle Street (late May–Sept Tues–Sat 2–6pm; free). Dedicated to a sixth-century saint, the church features a fine fifteenth-century oak hammerbeam roof, said to have come from Valle Crucis (see p.337). The graveyard is of equal interest for the triangular, railed-off monument to Mary Carryll erected by her mistresses, the Ladies of Llangollen (see below), who are also buried with her in the churchyard and commemorated on the other two sides of her pillar.

Plas Newydd

Standing in twelve acres of formal gardens, half a mile up Hill Street from the southern end of Castle Street, the two-storeyed mock-Tudor **Plas Newydd**, Butler Hill (Easter–Oct daily 10am–5pm; £3.50) was, for almost fifty years, home to the celebrated **Ladies of Llangollen**. Lady Eleanor Butler and Sarah Ponsonby were a couple of Anglo-Irish aristocrats, who tried to elope together at the end of the eighteenth century. After two botched attempts dressed in men's clothes, they were grudgingly allowed to leave in 1778 with an annual allowance of £280, enough to settle in Llangollen, where they became the country's most celebrated lesbians – though apparently they were affronted by the suggestion that their relationship was anything other than chaste. Regency society was captivated by their "model friendship" in what Simone de Beauvoir called "a peaceful Eden on the edge of the world". Despite their desire for a "life of sweet and delicious retirement", they didn't seem to mind the constant stream of gentry who called on them. They found the Duke of Wellington a "charming young man, hansom, fashioned tall and elegant" and commemorated his visit in typically self-absorbed manner by engraving "E.B & S.P. 1814" over the mantelpiece in the Oak Room. Walter Scott was also well received, though he found them "a couple of hazy or crazy old sailors" in manner, and like "two respectable superannuated clergymen" in their mode of dress. Thomas de Quincey humoured the ladies, if only to bend their favour towards his friend Wordsworth, who had displeased them by referring to their house as "a low roofed cot" in an inelegant poem he had composed in the grounds.

An excellent, self-guided **audio tour** (free) leads you around the half-dozen rooms of the modest black-and-white timbered house. Most of the walls are covered in a riotous frieze of dark wood panelling: a wonderful, if slightly oppressive, effect set off by a mixed bag of furniture in a style similar to that owned by the ladies. As a counterpoint you can also visit the spartan attic room where their loyal housekeeper, Mary Carryll, lived. Outside, take time to wander through the formal **grounds** (unrestricted access; free), including the **knot garden**, which perfectly complements the front of the house.

The north bank of the Dee

Wherever you are in Llangollen, the hills echo to the shrill cry of steam engines easing along the **Llangollen Railway** (April–Oct 3–8 services most days; call ahead at other times; £9 return; ☎01978/860979; ⓦwww.llangollen-railway .co.uk). Shoehorned into the north side of the valley, it runs west from Llangollen's time-warped station past Glyndyfrdwy, near the Horseshoe Falls, as far as Carrog, eight miles up the valley: eventually (perhaps by 2010) it's planned to go a further two miles to Corwen. Operating along a restored section of the disused Ruabon–Barmouth line, belching steam engines creep along the river bank, hauling ancient carriages which sport the liveries of their erstwhile owners.

Most visitors simply ride to the end of the line and back, but consider getting off partway along and walking back to town along the Dee Valley Way (see box, p.337), perhaps stopping for a pint in the riverside pub at Carrog. If you've got kids in tow, look out for the three nine-day "Day Out With Thomas" sessions (typically in Feb, Aug & Oct), when Thomas the Tank Engine and his friends ply the tracks. Summer also brings evening trips when you can get on-board for a pie and a pint, and there are occasional driver-experience courses, letting you behind the controls of a steam loco (from £150 for 2hr).

Across the road from the station, **Llangollen Wharf** is the starting point for trips along the Llangollen Canal. Until the coming of the railway in 1865, the waterway was the only means to carry slates from the quarries on the Horseshoe Pass. Designed by Thomas Telford as a water supply for the Shropshire Union Canal, the Llangollen canal was one of Britain's finest feats of canal engineering. The canal starts at **Horseshoe Falls**, an artificial, crescent-shaped weir built in 1806 to feed water into the canal. Telford managed to avoid using locks for the first fourteen miles by building the thousand-foot-long **Pontcysyllte Aqueduct** 126ft above the river, at **Froncysyllte**, four miles east, employing long cast-iron troughs supported by stone piers – a bold move for its time.

Narrowboats run from the Horse Drawn Boat Centre on Llangollen Wharf (Easter–Oct daily; ☎01978/860702, ⓦwww.horsedrawnboats.co.uk), offering 45-minute rides in a horse-drawn narrowboat (£5) and a two-hour motorized

▲ Narrow boat crossing Thomas Telford's Pontcysyllte Aqueduct

trip down to and across the Pontcysyllte Aqueduct (£10). Alternatively, you can drive to the *Telford Inn* in Froncysyllte (which has a good garden bar) on the A542 – or walk the towpath – and take a 45-minute narrowboat ride with Aqueduct Cruises (☎01691/690322, ⓦwww.canaltrip.co.uk; hourly from 2pm most days in summer; £4.50) across the aqueduct and back. Another possibility, if you can organize a group of up to ten, is to rent a self-steer narrowboat for the day from Anglo Welsh at Froncysyllte (☎0117/304 1122, ⓦwww.anglowelsh.co.uk; weekdays £99, weekends £120). You can travel west as far as Llangollen and east across the aqueduct to Chirk; there are a couple of good pubs for lunch.

Castell Dinas Brân

It's the view both ways along the valley which justifies a 45-minute slog up to **Castell Dinas Brân** (Crow's Fortress Castle), perched on a hill 800ft above the town, and reached by a signposted path from Llangollen Wharf. The lure certainly isn't the few sad but evocative vaulted stumps that stand in poor testament to what was once the district's largest and most important Welsh fortress. Built by the ruler of northern Powys, Prince Madog ap Gruffydd Maelor, in the 1230s, the castle rose on the site of an earlier Iron Age fort. Edward I soon took it as part of his first campaign against Llywelyn ap Gruffydd (see p.469), and the castle was left to decay. John Leland, Henry VIII's antiquarian, finding it "all in ruin" in 1540.

Although not much to look at, it's a great place to be when the sun is setting, imagining George Borrow sitting up here translating seventeenth-century bard Roger Cyffyn:

Gone, gone are thy gates, Dinas Brân on the height!
Thy warders are blood-crows and ravens, I trow;
Now no-one will wend from the field of the fight
To the fortress on high, save the raven and the crow.

Walking west from the town bridge, you'll soon see the 6000-seat, white plastic **Royal International Pavilion**, which was designed to evoke the shape of the traditional marquee formerly erected on the eisteddfod site each year, but looks more like some giant armoured reptile. Outside the eisteddfod season, the auditorium acts as a concert venue and sports hall, the foyer operates as a **gallery** (Mon–Fri 10am–4pm; free) with reputable changing exhibitions of international fine art and north Welsh crafts, and side rooms host workshops ranging from alternative medicines to Chinese brush painting.

Following the A542 or the canal towpath a mile west, you pass Llangollen's **Motor Museum** (March–Oct daily 10am–5pm; winter by appointment on ☎01978/860324; £3), a shed full of lovingly restored not-so-vintage cars and vans supplemented by a small **canal exhibition**, which admirably explains the construction of the Llangollen Canal in the context of Britain's canal building mania at the end of the eighteenth century.

Half a mile beyond, the gaunt remains of **Valle Crucis Abbey** (April–Sept daily 10am–5pm, £2.70; Oct–Easter unrestricted access; CADW), stand in Glyn y Groes, the "Valley of the Cross". In 1201, Madog ap Gruffydd Maelor of Dinas Brân chose this majestic pastoral setting for one of the last Cistercian foundations in Wales, as well as the first Gothic abbey in Britain. Despite a devastating fire in its first century, and a complement of far from pious monks, it survived until the Dissolution in 1535. The church fell into disrepair, after which the monastic buildings, in particular the monks' dormitory, were employed as farm buildings. Later, Turner painted the abbey, imaginatively shifting Dinas Brân a couple of miles west onto the hill behind.

Though less impressive than Tintern Abbey, Valle Crucis does greet you with its best side, the largely intact west wall of the church pierced by the frame of a rose window. At the opposite end, the equally complete east wall guards a row of six graves, one of which is said to contain Owain Glyndŵr's resident bard, Iolo Goch. There are displays on monastic life upstairs, reached by a detour through the mostly ruined cloister and past the weighty vaulting of the chapter house.

The cross that gives the valley its name is the eight-foot-tall **Eliseg's Pillar** (unrestricted access; CADW), four hundred yards north by the A542. Erected to a Prince of Powys in the ninth century by his great-grandson, it originally stood 25ft high but was smashed during the Civil War in the 1640s. The stump remains, but you can now only see half of the full 31 lines glorifying the lineage of the Princes of Powys, which Celtic scholar Edward Llwyd translated from the remaining pieces in 1696.

Walks from Llangollen

Llangollen is a great place to explore on foot, perhaps using a narrowboat or steam train to shorten a loop. The Explorer map 225, "Llangollen & Berwyn", is useful for the following walks.

Llangollen History Trail (6 mile loop; 3–6 hr; 500ft ascent). The tourist office stocks the free *Llangollen History Trail* leaflet which details this easy-to-follow loop, initially following the canal towpath to Horseshoe Falls, then visiting Valle Crucis Abbey and Eliseg's Pillar before returning to town via Dinas Brân.

Dee Valley Way This well-marked route along the north side of the Dee Valley between Llangollen and Corwen is 15 miles long, but can be broken into smaller sections, or shortened by taking the Llangollen Railway to Glyndyfrdwy or Carrog then walking back. A free booklet from the tourist office explains the route, pinpoints pubs and discusses points of interest along the way.

Eating, drinking and entertainment

Llangollen boasts a fairly good selection of **restaurants,** and there's no shortage of daytime **cafés**. Picnic ingredients are best bought at Bailey's Delicatessen on Castle Street, next to the tourist office. Outside the eisteddfod and its fringe, there's not a great deal of **nightlife**, but local bands (and occasionally bigger acts) do play from time to time, and it's always worth checking if there is anything going on at the eisteddfod site. The **Royal International Pavilion** on Abbey Road (☎01978/860111) serves as a year-round venue for anything from choral and classical concerts to pull-out-the-stops rock gigs. You can listen to the **male voice choir** in full song at 7.30pm on Fridays at the *Hand Hotel*, 26 Bridge St.

The Corn Mill Dee Lane ☎01978/869555. Superb conversion of a town-centre mill, with riverside decking that catches the afternoon sun. Good all day for coffee and well-prepared café-bar food such as beef and horseradish sandwiches (£5.25) and mains (£9–14) like tuna salad with wasabi and free-range chicken with black pudding mash. The real ales are well kept.

Fouzi's Castle St ☎01978/861340. Smart modern daytime café serving panini, stuffed baguettes (£4–5), plus a few mains (£6), daily specials and good espresso.

Gales Wine Bar 18 Bridge St ☎01978/860089. Old church pews, a blackboard menu of delicious, bistro-style food

(mains £9–13) and a good selection of wines from around the world make this long-standing place a Llangollen favourite. Closed Sun.

The Gallery 15 Chapel St ☎01978/860076. Friendly evening-only restaurant serving a good range of medium-priced pizza and pasta dishes. Closed Sun & Mon.

The Grouse Carrog, just off the A5, eight miles west of Llangollen. Smart, modernized country pub with decent meals and outdoor seating overlooking the River Dee. Accessible on the Llangollen Railway.

Sun Inn Regent St. Convivial locals' pub that stays open later than most in town and puts on live bands every Fri & Sat night.

Corwen and around

In the early fifteenth century, Welsh rebel, local landowner and scourge of Henry IV, Owain Glyndŵr, set out from **CORWEN**, ten miles west of Llangollen, to wrest back all Wales from the English barons (see p.469). His likeness atop a modern equestrian statue in the centre of town looks set to terrorize his persecutors once again, and he is further recalled in the ill-cared-for south porch of the thirteenth-century church of St Mael and St Julien, where the shape of a dagger incised into a grey stone lintel is known as **Glyndŵr's Sword**. He is said to have cast the "sword" in anger at the townspeople from atop the hill behind, though it actually predates him by half a millennium.

In Glyndŵr's time cattle-droving routes from Anglesey and from Harlech met at Corwen for the final push to the English markets. Subsequently a major rail junction, Corwen is now a quiet market town with a couple of fine ancient churches nearby. Glyndŵr aficionados will probably be interested in the thirty-foot-high truncated cone of **Owain Glyndŵr's Mount**, on the south bank of the Dee just over three miles east on the road to Llangollen, where he is supposed to have stood on lookout for his enemies. He may well have done so, but the earthworks are more likely to be a Norman motte-and-bailey castle.

Corwen's charms don't justify stopping overnight, although the dowdy but clean *Corwen Court*, London Road (☎01490/412854; ❶ closed Dec–Feb), offers **B&B** with a difference: converted from a police station and courthouse, the cells are now single rooms (£20 each), while the sergeant's family's quarters have been converted into doubles. If that doesn't suit, *Bron-y-Graig* (☎01490/413007, ⓦwww.north-wales-hotel.co.uk; ❷) is only a few yards east along the A5, and offers authentically renovated Victorian rooms in a house built for the Sheriff of Denbigh. They do a room-only deal for £45 for two; meals and self-catering cottages are also available.

Buses on the Llangollen–Bala route stop in the centre of Corwen.

Rug Chapel and Llangar Church

Taking its name from the Welsh word for heather, **Rug Chapel** (Easter–Sept Wed–Sun 10am–5pm; £3.70; CADW), a mile west of Corwen on the A494, is one of Wales' best examples of an unaltered seventeenth-century church. Along with the Gwydyr Uchaf Chapel, near Llanrwst (see p.365), it gives a charming insight into worship three hundred years ago, when Mass was a private clerical devotion, with the congregation kept behind rood screens.

Rug didn't entirely escape, but much here is as it was built in 1637 by the former privateer and collaborator on William Morgan's Welsh Bible (see p.424), William Salusbury. The plain exterior design gives no hint of the richly decorated interior: wooden angels support a roof patterned with stars and amoebic swirls, and a painting of a skeleton said to represent the transient nature of life and the inevitability of death. Informative displays in the ticket office give more details of the building's use.

Your ticket to Rug Chapel also entitles you to an escorted visit from there to another little-changed church, **Llangar** (normally locked, phone Rug Chapel on ☎01490/412025 for tour times, usually Easter–Sept Wed–Sun 1pm, and to arrange a visit), a mile to the south off the B4401, which dates back to the fourteenth century. Parish boundary changes in 1853 made this church redundant, saving its extensive fifteenth-century wall paintings and seventeenth-century figure of death from obliteration. The interior woodwork is wonderful, from the beamed roof and minstrel's gallery down to the eighteenth-century box pews.

The Vale of Edeyrnion

West of Corwen, the A5 provides the quickest route to Betws-y-Coed and the mountains of Snowdonia. An alternative route heads south through the Vale of Edeyrnion to the watersports centre of Bala, through the peaceful villages of Cynwyd, Llandrillo and Llandderfel and past a couple of the best country hotels in the area. Buses on the Llangollen–Bala route go right through the valley. None of the villages is particularly interesting, but all make convenient bases for hikes on the largely undiscovered Berwyn Range to the east (see box, p.340), where you can walk all day without seeing a soul.

The first village, two miles south of Corwen, is **CYNWYD**, home to the budget *Pen-y-Bont Fawr* B&B (☎01490/412663, ✉robert.wivell@btopenworld .com; ❶), in a converted barn behind the *Prince of Wales* pub. The Berwyns are equally accessible from **LLANDRILLO**, where, after a day in the hills, you can rest your head at the excellent *Y Llwyn Guesthouse* (☎01490/440455; ❷), in the centre near the post office. Alternatively, luxuriate in the elegant Georgian surroundings of *Tyddyn Llan Country House*, on the B4401 towards Bala (☎01490/440264, ⓦwww.tyddynllan.co.uk; ❻); its superb restaurant ranks among the best in Wales (3 courses for £45).

For sheer grandeur, and the opportunity to stay in a house once frequented by Queen Victoria, you can't beat the hand-painted and intricately carved nineteenth-century interiors of *Palé Hall*, three miles south of Llandderfel (☎01678/530285, ⓦwww.palehall.co.uk; dinner and B&B for two ❽), located in peacock-inhabited grounds beside a trout stream available for guests' use. Superb meals (£33 for three courses) are also served to

The OS 1:50,000 Landranger 125 map is recommended for this walk.

Henry II's 1165 expeditionary force encamped on the Berwyn Hills, until forced to flee back to England by the Welsh weather and the guerrilla tactics of Owain Gwynedd. Legend has it that the king beat his retreat along the ancient high-moor trackway, thereafter known as Ffordd Saeson (Englishman's Road). Whether he did or not, the path makes for a good route up onto these lonesome rocky heather-clad outcrops. The **walk** (10 miles; 5–6hr; 2500ft ascent) follows part of Ffordd Saeson starting from Cynwyd about a hundred yards north of *Y Llew Glas* (The Blue Lion) pub then up through a forest to the deep heather moorland pass of **Bwlch Cynwyd** (1700ft). From Bwlch Cynwyd, the circular route leads south, but if the skies are clear, the lone summit of **Moel Fferna** (2067ft), a mile or so to the north, makes a rewarding detour. South from Bwlch Cynwyd, follow the path beside the fence for a couple of miles across desolate, somewhat featureless land to the summit of **Pen Bwlch Llandrillo Top** (2037ft), then drop down the other side to an ancient drovers' road. Known locally as the Maid's Path, it was once the harvest-time route for girls heading east from Llandrillo, sometimes as far as Llanarmon Dyffryn Ceiriog, five miles from here (see p.330). If you don't have your own transport, try walking over the Berwyns from the Vale of Edeyrnion into Glyn Ceiriog: it is the closest you'll get to experiencing what the drover's life must have been like.

Near where you meet the drovers' road, a much later traveller is commemorated by a stone to "A Wayfarer 1877–1956, a lover of Wales". In the days before knobbly tyres and gas mono-shock suspension systems, one W.M. Robinson rode up here by bicycle, unwittingly laying the groundwork for scores of mountain bikers now following his lead along the bridleways.

The cairned summit of **Cadair Bronwen** (2575ft), a mile and a half south of the memorial, is the only place in Wales where you can pick cloudberries (sharp-tasting orange blackberries); otherwise head east for Glyn Ceiriog or west for the Vale of Edeyrnion. After half a mile on the westerly path, a sign points to Llandrillo, while an unsigned path forks right to Cynwyd. The track to Llandrillo heads downwards and under the lip of the hill on which **Moel Tŷ Uchaf**, a quite stunning 3500-year-old stone circle, can be found.

non-residents: forest mushroom risotto and fillet of duck might be followed by vanilla pannacotta.

If your budget won't stretch to these kind of prices, continue along the B4401 past **LLANDDERFEL** to *Melin Meloch*, just two miles short of Bala (℡01678/520101, ⓦ www.melochmill.com; ⊙), a B&B partly built from a converted fourteenth-century water mill beside the Dee.

Mold and the Vale of Clwyd

One of the least-travelled paths through northwest Wales leaves the English Marches at the market town of **Mold**, crosses the soft contours of the **Clwydian Range** – along whose tops runs a section of the **Offa's Dyke long-distance path** – and approaches the north coast through the wide and fertile **Vale of Clwyd**, which follows the sandstone course of the barely noticeable River Clwyd (Afon Clywedog). Nineteenth-century poet Gerard Manley Hopkins eulogized the valley where he studied for the priesthood, celebrating its beauty in some of his best-loved works, "*The Windhover*", "*In the Valley of the Elwy*" and "*Pied Beauty*". Linked by quiet roads through a patchwork of small farms, two attractive towns of warm-hued stone sit on hillocks above the valley. The ancient market town of **Ruthin** is the pick of the two, with its thirteenth-century castle, compact core of medieval buildings, intriguing jail and a host of good places to stay. Four miles north is **Denbigh**, best known for its "hollow crown", the high-walled castle ruin that rings the hilltop behind the town.

The frequent #51 **bus** connects Ruthin and Rhyl via Denbigh.

Mold

The slow pace of **MOLD** (Yr Wyddgrug) is only disrupted by its Wednesday and Saturday **markets**, when stalls supplant cars along the High Street. Despite a good deal of interesting history tied to the town, there's no great reason for a visit, except perhaps en route over the Clwydian Hills into the Vale of Clwyd.

Mold was founded during the reign of William Rufus, though only a copse of beeches atop a mound mark the site of the motte-and-bailey fortifications on **Bailey Hill**, at the top of High Street. Built for the local Norman lord, Robert de Montalt, its commanding view over the River Alyn (Afon Alun) shows the strategic value of the site. First taken by Owain Gwynedd in 1157 and again in 1199 by Llywelyn the Great, it alternated between Welsh and Anglo-Norman control until Edward I's clampdown on the region. In 1465, during the War of the Roses, local lord Rheinallt ap Gruffydd captured the Mayor of Chester, took him back to the Tower in Nercwys and presented him with a pie containing the rope that would be his noose. Henry VII's assumption of the throne, after his victory at the Battle of Bosworth, stamped some stability on the area.

In gratitude for Henry's victory, his mother, Margaret Beaufort, commissioned the airy Perpendicular **St Mary's Church** (sometimes open summer Wed & Sat) at the foot of Bailey Hill. While largely restored by Gilbert Scott in the nineteenth century, the north aisle retains its original oak roof carved with Tudor roses, and a quatrefoil and animal frieze beneath the small clerestory windows.

Among the Tudor stained glass, a Victorian window is Mold's meagre memorial to its most famous son (at least to English-speakers) and Wales' greatest painter, the eighteenth-century landscapist **Richard Wilson**, whose grave is by the church's north entrance. Although Wilson co-founded the Royal Academy in 1768 and was later acclaimed by Ruskin, his work was undervalued and he died a pauper.

Mold is no Welsh-language stronghold, so it seems ironic that it is **Daniel Owen**, a local tailor and nineteenth-century novelist, who should be commemorated by a statue, outside the library. "Not for the wise and learned have I written, but for the common people" is inscribed below, and it was his bluntly honest accounts of ordinary life that made him so unpopular with the Methodist leaders of the community. Writing only in Welsh, Owen became his country's most prominent writer of the late nineteenth century. A room full of memorabilia takes up a sizeable portion of the small but effective **museum**, housed in the same building as the town's library and tourist office (Mon, Tues, Thurs & Fri 9.30am–7pm, Wed 9.30am–5.30pm, Sat 9.30am–3pm; free).

Practicalities

Mold has no train station, but regular **bus** services stop behind the cattle market east of High Street, from where it's five minutes' walk down King Street to Earl Road and the **tourist office** (Easter–Oct Mon–Fri 9.30am–5pm, Sat 9.30am–3pm; Nov–Easter Mon–Fri 10am–4pm; ☎01352/759331, ✉mold@nwtic.com), in the same building as the library.

There's nowhere worth recommending to **stay** in town, but you can **eat** well enough at several cheap cafés, or head to the fish-oriented *56 High Street*, 56 High St (℡01352/759225; closed Sun & Mon), with a sparse, modern interior, a range of tasty mains for £10–15 and two-course lunch specials for £9. The best of the **pubs** for both meals and drinking, is *We Three Loggerheads*, opposite Loggerheads Country Park, while **entertainment** revolves around the region's major arts centre, Clwyd Theatr Cymru (℡0845/330 3565, ⓦwww.clwyd-theatr-cymru.co.uk), a mile east on the A494, which stages quality theatre and cinema, aided by revenue from its excellent arts bookshop and café.

Loggerheads Country Park and the Clwydian Range

When Mold's charms begin to fade, head west along the A494 to the wide open spaces of the **Clwydian Range**. You might consider stopping at the family-oriented **Loggerheads Country Park**, three miles west of Mold, which offers forest walks and nature trails with views of the Clwydian Range. You can pick up more information at the **visitor centre** by the entrance (May–Oct daily 10am–5.30pm; Nov–April Sat & Sun 10am–4pm; ⓦwww .loggerheadsarea.co.uk). Bus #1 between Mold and Ruthin comes this way, and from early July to Sept the Clwydian Ranger runs two daily services from Mold to Bwlch Penbarras.

Beyond Loggerheads, the B5429 branches right off the A494 following an old turnpike route between Mold and Ruthin. It climbs up to **Bwlch Penbarras**, a shallow pass where the road meets the **Offa's Dyke long-distance path** (though not the Dyke itself), which runs along these bald tops following the line of a Bronze Age trading route, past the remains of six Iron Age hillforts. The highest point is the 1820-foot **Moel Famau**, topped by a truncated **Jubilee Tower**. The subject of many a disparaging remark when it was built in 1810 to celebrate George III's fifty-year reign, this Egyptian-style structure was never completed. The planned pyramid was to rise to 150ft but was damaged in a storm in 1860 and only partially repaired in 1970. The ruins may not be much, but on a clear day the views over the Vale of Clwyd as far as Snowdon and Cadair Idris make a walk out here worthwhile (see box below). Proximity to Liverpool, Chester and Wrexham, and the relatively gentle terrain, make this a popular spot at weekends: stick to weekdays if possible.

Walks to Foel Fenlli and Moel Famau

The 1:50,000 OS Landranger 116 "Denbigh & Colwyn Bay" map is recommended for these walks.

From the car park (small charge) at Bwlch Penbarras (see above) you can make the steep climb southwards to the most impressive of the Clwydian hillfort sites on 1800-foot **Foel Fenlli** (1 mile return; 40min; 500ft ascent). Excavations here have uncovered 35 hut circles within earthworks three-quarters of a mile across. The height from ditch bottom to bank top reaches 35ft in places, with triple defences on the less easily defended eastern flank. Aerial shots make much more of this than is visible on the ground, but that doesn't detract from the walk.

From the same car park, a broad path leads a mile and a half north to **Moel Famau** (3 miles return; 1–2hr; 650ft ascent) and the Jubilee Tower (see above).

For more information, pick up the *Discover Moel Famau Country Park* leaflet from the Ruthin or Mold tourist office.

Ruthin

With its attractive knot of half-timbered buildings, a handful of sights and some of the finest food and lodgings in the area **RUTHIN** (Rhuthun), ten miles west of Mold, should not be missed. The town is built on a commanding rise in the Vale of Clwyd, close to lands held by Owain Glyndŵr during his quest for dominion over all of Wales in 1400.

St Peter's Square

Before making tracks for Ruthin Gaol it's worth spending a few minutes around **St Peter's Square**, the hub of the town's medieval street plan. **St Peter's Church** (daily 9am–4pm or thereabouts) is approached via a lovely pair of iron gates wrought by the Davies Brothers (who also made the gates of St Giles' church in Wrexham and those at Chirk Castle). The ceiling of its north aisle consists of 408 carved black oak panels with Tudor Rose bosses, reputedly donated by Henry VII from Basingwerk Abbey (see p.350) in gratitude to those who helped him take the English throne. Get someone to turn the lights on for you if you can; alternatively, simply consult the grotesque faces and floral and geometric designs reproduced on a panel opposite the door. One of the busts on the north wall is of Gabriel Goodman, who, in 1574, while Dean of Westminster, re-founded the **grammar school** that had been closed by Henry VIII forty years earlier; the building still stands behind the church, next to the Christ's Hospital Almshouses, which Goodman built in 1590 as a gift to the town.

Goodman was born beside St Peter's Square in Exmewe Hall (now Barclays bank), outside which sits an unimpressive chunk of limestone known as **Maen Huail**. A less-than-convincing story has Arthur and Huail, brother of a Welsh chieftain called Gildas, fighting over the attentions of a woman. Huail pierced

▲ Eyes of Ruthin

Joint tickets for Nantclwyd House and Ruthin Gaol cost £6.50, or £9 including Llangollen's Plas Newydd (p.334).

Arthur's thigh, giving him a permanent limp, but promised never to mention Arthur's loss of face. Inevitably, though, Huail couldn't resist taunting him about it and an incensed Arthur had him beheaded on this stone.

Standing isolated on the other side of the square is one of the many timber-framed buildings around town. Now the NatWest bank, it was built in 1401 as a courthouse and prison and still retains under the eaves the barely visible stump of a **gibbet**, last used in 1679 to hang a Franciscan priest. However, the most photographed building in town is the **Myddleton Arms pub**, built in 1657 in Dutch style and topped by seven dormer windows known as "The Eyes of Ruthin", which overlook the square.

The rest of town and around

Heading off the square towards the castle, you'll find the medieval **Nantclwyd House**, Castle Street (April–Sept Fri–Sun 10am–5pm; £3.60), a restored, timber-framed town house partly dating back to 1435, making it the oldest town house in Wales. Restored from near dereliction using authentic techniques, it's a wonderfully higgledy-piggledy place, with wonky oak floors, interesting nooks and crannies, and a general atmosphere which makes you feel like you're nosing around someone's home. The house has been extended and updated over five centuries, and the major phases of its existence have been recreated in the seven main rooms which include a Jacobean bed chamber, a Stuart study, a Victorian schoolroom and an entrance hall of 1942, which looks much as it did when the last family moved out in 1984. Outside there's a walled garden and a pretty little summerhouse.

Windows in the summerhouse overlook **Ruthin Gaol** (April–Oct daily 10am–5pm; Nov–March Sat & Sun 10am–5pm; Ⓦwww.ruthingaol.co.uk; £3.50), five-minutes' walk down Clwyd Street from St Peter's Square. Though there was a prison on the site from 1654 to 1916, the so-called "Gruelling Experience" focuses on the Victorian era and the four-storey cell block (1866) inspired by London's Pentonville, designed to improve living conditions and penal correction, with one prisoner per cell and the requirement to work while incarcerated. Most upper-floor cells are now used as council offices and county archives, but you can poke around elsewhere, perhaps following the free audio guide which traces the prison life of a mythical "Will the Poacher". Informative panels in the lower cells and prison kitchen explain daily prison life and behind-the-scenes operations along with the real meaning of "screws" and "bobbies" and the source of the expression "money for old rope". One tale tells of John Jones, the "Welsh Houdini", who seemingly spent half his life escaping from prisons. He absconded from Ruthin in 1913 before being shot five days later.

It is also worth spending a little time in the new **Ruthin Craft Centre** (daily 10am–5.30pm; free; ℡01824/704774, Ⓦwww.ruthincraftcentre.org.uk), 300 yards west of St Peter's Square down Market Street. Set up as Wales' Centre for the applied arts, the centre occupies a zinc and stone building housing three galleries, six artists' studios, workshops, a shop and café. Check out the website for forthcoming events.

If Ruthin's huddle of buildings becomes too claustrophobic, you can take one of the nearby **walks** along the Clwydian Range to Moel Famau and Foel Fenlli (see box, p.342), or go **horseriding** at the Ruthin Riding Centre (℡01824/703470, Ⓦwww.ruthinridingcenter.com) in Pentre Coch, four miles north of town.

Festivals

Ranging from the epic to the absurd, Wales' wealth of festivals sees all walks of life partying in muddy fields across the country. Many of the events on the nation's annual calendar are uniquely Welsh, from traditional eisteddfodau through to mellow folk and grittier, grungier rock festivals showcasing established and up-and-coming talent. Not surprisingly, there are also plenty with a distinctly surreal edge – from parading around Llangynwyd village with a horse's skull to welcome in the new year (the Mari Lwyd) to snorkelling through the peat bogs of Powys.

Procession of the Bards, Royal National Eisteddfod, Cardiff ▲

Festival-goers, Royal National Eisteddfod ▼

Royal Welsh Show prizewinners ▼

The eisteddfod

The centrepiece of Welsh culture is the **eisteddfod** (plural eisteddfodau), originally meaning "a meeting of bards". These days it covers anything from a village festival to two cultural extravganzas: the **International Music Eisteddfod** (see p.334), held on a purpose-built fixed site at Llangollen in July and open to international competitors; and the roving **Royal National Eisteddfod** in August. The National is *the* Welsh festival: the vast *maes* (field) hosts art, craft, literature, rock music, Welsh-language lessons, theatre and major music and poetry competitions. The similarly nomadic **Urdd Eisteddfod** ("youth eisteddfod") takes place in May. The National and the Urdd are the largest indigenous cultural festivals of their kind Europe-wide. Although everything is conducted in *Cymraeg*, the Welsh language, simultaneous translation makes it easy for anyone to join in. See p.50 for more details.

Royal Welsh Show

Even if your interest in rural life goes no further than a Sunday afternoon stroll, the **Royal Welsh Show** – aka the *sioe fawr* ("big show"), held in July at the massive showground just outside Builth Wells – is a top day out. You can watch the ultra-serious judging of prize cows, pigs, chickens, horses or sheepdogs, competitive sheep-shearing or wood chopping, displays of falconry and craftsmanship, or simply feast on farm-fresh produce in the food halls. Hundreds of stallholders sell everything from artisan products to agricultural equipment and, if you stay overnight, you'll find the already lively town of Builth positively hopping with high-spirited crowds come the evening. See p.248 for more details.

The Guardian Hay Festival

The Brecon Beacons town of **Hay-on-Wye** ("is that some kind of sandwich?" – Arthur Miller) is a bibliophilic treat year-round, with over thirty second-hand bookshops. But its annual ten-day literary festival is the *pièce de résistance* for any serious print junkie. The marquee-filled meadow where the festival takes place is an idyllic venue to hear the world's leading writers give voice to their words, with the pauses, nuances and inflections that only the author can convey. See p.242 for more details.

▲ Judging time at the Royal Welsh Show

▼ Guardian Hay festival

Sesiwn Fawr

Dolgellau's **Sesiwn Fawr** ("big session") lives up to its name, as one of the biggest and best rock festivals in Wales. To get the full experience, you need a weekend ticket, a tent, gum boots to slosh through the mud, and an iron constitution for partying hard. Bands and DJs from Wales, other Celtic cultures and beyond perform across six stages, with yet more music in the town's cosy pubs. See p.312 for more details.

▼ Cadair Idris looms over Sesiwn Fawr

Faenol festival

Held in the sylvan surrounds of the Faenol Park, near Caernarfon, opera superstar Bryn Terfel's four-day **Faenol** festival sees international orchestras and opera divas mingle with rock gods and native Welsh talent every August. Reserved seating is available right in front of the stage, but the quintessential Faenol experience involves buying a promenade ticket, bringing a blanket to spread out on the lawns, and being prepared for informal competition over who's packed the poshest picnic. See p.51 for more details.

▼ Singing along at Sesiwn Fawr

Wakeboarding ▲

Abergavenny Food Festival ▼

World Bog-snorkelling Championship, Lianwrtyd Wells ▼

Wakestock

Mixing wakeboarding contests and surfing on the beaches of the Llŷn peninsula with BMX-riding, cutting-edge live music and DJs, July's **Wakestock** festival, attracting tens of thousands of bleached-haired punters, is proof of just how far and how quickly Wales' whole watersports scene has come in recent years. See p.51 for more details.

Food glorious food

Foodies are flocking to Wales in ever-increasing numbers for its smorgasbord of fresh food and its burgeoning number of festivals. Chief among them is September's **Abergavenny Food Festival**, showcasing celebrity chefs. Other culinary celebrations include early July's **Aberaeron Seafood Festival**, late July's **Big Cheese** in Caerphilly and October's **Anglesey Oyster Festival**. See pp.50–52 for more details.

Weird and wonderful

When it comes to weird festivals, **Llanwrtyd Wells** is Wales' undisputed capital. This tiny Powys town hosts the annual **Man versus Horse** race (with both equine and human winners in its time), a beer-quaffing/mountain biking **Real Ale Wobble** race, and the **World Bog-snorkelling Championship**, as well as a mind-boggling array of other oddball events.

The Welsh fondness for **dressing up** gets full play at Llanidloes fancy dress night in early July and on New Year's Eve in New Quay. Alternatively, you could ring in the New Year all over again two weeks later on 13 January in Pembrokeshire's **Cwm Gwaun** (see p.211), where they still prefer to use the Julian calendar. See pp.50–52 for more details.

Ruthin Castle

Hidden away in the trees a quarter of a mile south of town lie the restored, red sandstone ruins of **Ruthin Castle**, which now operates as a hotel. The castle was built by Edward I and by the beginning of the thirteenth century was owned by Lord de Grey of Ruthin, a favourite of Henry IV, who used his influence to have local landowner, Owain Glyndŵr, declared a traitor and acquire his land. In response, Glyndŵr crowned himself Prince of Wales and besieged Ruthin, razing the town once he had plundered the goods brought to its fair by the English. The castle went on to resist the Parliamentarians for eleven weeks during the Civil War, eventually falling to General Mytton in 1646, after which it was destroyed. In 1963, it was partially restored as a **hotel**, with Italian and rose gardens landscaped around the ancient moat and crumbling ruins. Strictly speaking, the grounds are open to residents and peacocks only, but you can wander through if attending one of the tacky medieval banquets or drinking in the panelled library bar.

Practicalities

Buses from Denbigh, Rhyl and Mold all stop on Market Street, which runs between St Peter's Square and the Craft Centre, which contains an unstaffed **visitor information** point. There's **internet** access at the library on Record Street. You can **eat** and **sleep** well in Ruthin, though rooms should be reserved ahead at weekends, when accommodation fills up with guests attending weddings at the castle.

Accommodation

Firgrove Country House On the B5105 a mile southeast of Ruthin ☏01824/702677, ⒲www.firgrovecountryhouse.co.uk. A large Georgian house with manicured gardens, offering B&B and one self-catering cottage. Everything is done with an understated elegance, and the five-course dinners with wine (£35) are superb. ❹

Gorphwysfa B&B 8a Castle St ☏01824/702529, ⒺMarg@gorphwysfa .fsnet.co.uk. Comfortable wood-panelled sixteenth-century Tudor town house in the heart of town, with three spacious rooms and a very welcoming atmosphere. ❷, en suite ❸

Manorhaus 10 Well St ☏01824/704830, ⒲www.manorhaus.com. Fluffy duvets, bright colours and bold art works characterize this lovely eight-room boutique hotel in a Georgian house, complete with a small gym, sauna, DVD/CD, book and games library, and excellent restaurant and bar. ❺

Minffordd Campsite ☏01824/707169. Simple, tent-and-campervan-only site two miles north of Ruthin and just east of Rhewl: follow signs for Gellifor then turn right 150 yards after a pair of stone bridges. £6 per pitch.

Rhydonnen Llanychan, a mile north of Ruthin ☏01824/790258, ⒲www.rhydonnen.co.uk. A well-appointed B&B in a fifteenth-century black-and-white farmhouse steeped in history. ❸

Eating and drinking

Crown House Well St. Pleasant daytime café that's good for sandwiches, panini and bagels (£3–4).

Manorhaus 10 Well St. Stylish decor, subdued lighting and understated service make this a superb place for dinner (£23/28 for 2/3 courses), which might include dishes such as pea and mint risotto and pork and black pudding tournedo. Desserts are delectable and the wine list should keep most people very happy.

On the Hill Restaurant 1 Upper Clwyd St ☏01824/707736. This cosy wood-floored restaurant is hard to beat for its bistro-style meals (mains £10–15) and excellent selection of wines.

Ruthin Castle ☏01824/702664, ⒲www .ruthincastle.co.uk. Nip into this grand and extensively refurbished baronial castle for a bar meal or a drink in the lovely panelled library bar. You might even be tempted by the ersatz Welsh medieval banquets (£40).

Ye Olde Cross Keys On the B5105 a mile southeast of Ruthin ☏01824/705281. Welcoming pub serving pub meals well above the normal standard but at modest prices.

Llanrhaeadr

Just off the A525, four miles north of Ruthin (and accessible on bus #51), **St Dyfnog's Church** seems much too large for the tiny hamlet of **LLANRHAEADR**. In the sixth century St Dyfnog established a hermitage here on the site of a healing well, and donations from pilgrims funded the building of the present church in 1533. Typically for the area it has twin naves and, though heavily restored in 1880, drips with original features, including a glorious carved barrel roof with vine-leaf patterns and outstanding stained glass.

The **Jesse Window**, at the east end of the north aisle, depicts the descent of Jesus through the House of Israel from Jesse, the father of King David. Regarded as one of the finest such Jesse windows in Britain, it draws you in to the Virgin and Child, surrounded by 21 of their bearded, ermine-robed ancestors, whose names are recorded in medieval Latin. The window is believed to be contemporary with the church, though it was removed and stored in an oak chest during the Civil War, which is when its companion in the south aisle is thought to have been destroyed. In the nineteenth century, fragments which may have belonged to it were found nearby and pieced together to form the west window.

Denbigh and around

The hilltop castle ruins dominating the Vale of Clwyd eight miles north of Ruthin herald **DENBIGH** (Dinbych), a former bastide town which tumbles down the hill towards its medieval centre. The glove-making industry for which the town was once famed has vanished, leaving it merely hosting a Wednesday market and servicing the sprawling postwar development on its outskirts.

The market takes place just off the broad central section of the High Street, which is surrounded by a pleasing array of colonnaded medieval buildings. Thankfully, they haven't been over-restored and, together with the more modern structures in their midst, help retain a working town atmosphere. Beside *The Old Vaults* pub on the High Street, Broomhill Lane runs up past the crumbling **Burgess Gate**, the former northern entry to the town, to the vast grassy ward of the ruined **Denbigh Castle** (April–Sept daily 10am–5pm, £3.10; Oct–March daily 10am–4pm, free; CADW).

For a long time, the River Clwyd formed the border of England and Wales, guarded here by a now vanished castle built by Dafydd, brother of Llywelyn ap Gruffydd ("the Last"). This probably gave the town its name, meaning "small fort", though it's more imaginatively attributed to John Salusbury, a medieval knight said to have rid the town of a dragon, triumphantly returning with its head to cries of "Dim Dych!" (No More Dragon!). Dafydd's castle put up strong resistance but eventually fell to the English, enabling Edward I to fortify Rhuddlan and Ruthin, and entrust Denbigh to Henry de Lacey, Earl of Lincoln. By 1282 he had barely begun the town walls and ordered each of his 63 burgesses to "find a man armed in Denbigh to guard and defend the town". This wasn't enough to repel a Welsh revolt in 1294, which though rapidly suppressed, goaded de Lacy into work on the castle proper, employing many of the concepts already implemented by Edward's architect, James of St George.

The most imposing remnant is the **gatehouse**, with three octagonal towers enclosing an originally vaulted hall, making it one of the finest defensive structures of the era. You enter beneath a weathered statue of Edward I in a niche, flanked on the right by the Prison Tower (stained by five garderobes discharging into a common cesspit) and the Porter's Lodge Tower on the left. From here, you can walk the only remaining section of the wall, extending as far as the Great Kitchen Tower with its two huge fireplaces. On the far side, the Postern Tower was heavily strengthened after 1294, as were the **town walls** that formed the outer ward branching off at the castle walls. Continue along the short section of wall walk (key from the tourist office) down to the **Goblin Tower** from where, at the end of a six-month-long siege in 1646, Charles I threw the castle keys onto the heads of the all-conquering Roundheads.

In 1563, Elizabeth I sold the castle to her favourite, Robert Dudley, Earl of Leicester, who in 1579 chose a site just below the castle for the church that he hoped would supplant St Asaph cathedral, four miles to the north. It was never completed, but the shell still stands today as **Leicester's Folly**.

Practicalities

All **buses** stop on High Street, just along from the sixteenth-century County Hall, which contains the **library** (Mon & Wed 9.30am–7pm, Tues, Thurs & Fri 9.30am–5pm, Sat 9.30am–12.30pm), which has free **internet access** and a supply of tourist **information** leaflets.

About the only **accommodation** in the centre is *Cayo Guesthouse*, 74 Vale St (℡01745/812686, @stay@cayo.co.uk; ❷), a few hundred yards down the main St Asaph road. With your own transport, go for the relaxed and welcoming *Bach Y Graig* (℡01745/730627, ❻www.bachygraig.co.uk; ❹) a sixteenth-century farmhouse on a working dairy farm in Tremeirchion, four miles northeast along the A543. It has its own woodland trail, and there are self-catering cottages (minimum one-week stay in summer). The handiest **campsite** is the *Station House Caravan Park* (℡01745/710372; £8–10 per pitch) at Bodfari, reached on bus #14.

Eating and drinking in Denbigh are limited: the best bests are on Back Row, parallel to the High Street: try *The Glass Onion* for inexpensive daytime snacks or *The Eagle* for straightforward but well-cooked pub meals. Alternatively, head out to *The White Horse Inn* (℡01824/790218, ❻www.white-horse-inn.co.uk), three miles southeast at Hendrerwydd, a superb country gastropub with top-quality meals (mains £15–19) and a cosy bar with an array of real ales and single malts.

Deeside

The industrial hinterland that spreads over the English border from Chester can best be avoided by heading directly for **Deeside**, a narrow littoral flanking the River Dee estuary. Most visitors shoot past on the A55 expressway, but a short detour onto the A548 is rewarded by a few mildly interesting sights. The crumbling castle remains at **Flint** should only detain you briefly, though you may want longer to pay homage to St Winefride and her healing waters at **Holywell**, especially if you're drawn to the adjacent minor collection of historic industrial buildings of the **Greenfield Valley Heritage Park** or the gorgeous carved Celtic cross of **Maen Achwyfaen**.

The salt-soaked fields alongside the Dee estuary support huge numbers of waders and **wildfowl**, which come to feed on the sands and mud flats left by retreating tides. At the RSPB's **Point of Ayr** site (unrestricted access), around seven miles northwest of Holywell, plovers, oystercatchers and Europe's largest concentration of pintails winter here, pushing the bird population into six figures.

Flint

If you're travelling on the North Coast train line, take one of the regional services which stop at **FLINT** (Y Fflint), seven miles north of Mold, and spend the hour between trains rambling around the buff sandstone ruins of **Flint Castle** (unrestricted access; CADW), two-minutes' walk over the footbridge from the station. Started in 1277, this was the first of Edward I's Iron Ring of fortresses (see p.435), standing sentinel over once-important shipping lanes into Chester. The ten-foot-thick pockmarked walls form a square with drum towers at all except the southeast corner, where a small moat and drawbridge separate the castle from the well-preserved Great Tower, or Donjon. Uniquely in Britain, this was intended as the castle's main accommodation and last place of retreat, and came equipped with its own well. Together with its large grassy outer ward and the adjoining town, the castle formed a unified enclave known as a "bastide". Flint can claim to be the first borough in Wales to receive its charter, in September 1284. Until then, towns didn't really exist in essentially rural Wales.

Flint's greatest hour came in 1399 when Richard II was lured here from the safety of Conwy Castle and captured by Henry Bolingbroke, the Duke of Lancaster and future Henry IV. Shakespeare dramatized the event in *Richard II*, when in response to Bolingbroke's, "My gracious Lord, I come but for mine own", the defeated king replies, "Your own is yours, and I am yours, and all". Even Richard's favourite greyhound is said to have deserted him at this point.

During the Civil War, Flint remained Royalist until taken in 1647 by General Mytton, who so effectively dismantled it that only six years later it was practically buried in its own ruins. It was in this condition when Celia Fiennes found it on the brief – and generally displeasing – Welsh leg of her journeys around Britain between 1698 and 1712. She described Flint as "a very ragged place", and things haven't changed much. **Trains** pass every 30–60 minutes and the #11 Arriva **bus** leaves from outside the train station every half-hour, bound for Chester and Rhyl.

Holywell and around

A place of pilgrimage for thirteen hundred years, **HOLYWELL** (Treffynnon), just off the A55 four miles northwest of Flint, is fancifully billed as "The Lourdes of Wales", though without the tacky souvenir stalls selling Virgin Mary lighters. Instead, Holywell is a quiet little town that modestly plays down its ancient appeal. The source of all the fuss is **St Winefride's Well** (daily: April–Sept 9am–5.30pm; Oct–March 10am–4pm; 60p; ⓦ www.saintwinefrideswell .com), a sacred and ancient spring that was first recorded by the Romans, who used its waters to relieve rheumatism and gout. The Roman connection sheds considerable doubt on the veracity of local legends said to date back to 660 AD or thereabouts. The virtuous Winefride (*Gwenfrewi* in Welsh) was decapitated here after resisting the amorous advances of Prince Caradoc, and the well is said to have sprung up at the spot where her head fell. When St Beuno, her uncle, placed her head beside the body, a combination of prayer and the waters revived her, setting her on track for the rest of her life as an abbess at Gwytherin Convent near Llanrwst.

Richard I and Henry V provided regal patronage, ensuring a steady flow of believers to what became one of the great shrines of Christendom. After the Reformation, pilgrimages – now punishable by death – became more clandestine, and the well became a focal point of resistance to Protestantism. A century and a half later, the Catholic king of England, James II, came here to pray for a

▲ The Healing Pool, St Winefride's Well

son and heir; the eventual answer to his prayers threatened a Catholic succession and contributed to the overthrow of the House of Stuart.

Pilgrims spent the night praying in the Perpendicular **St Winefride's Chapel** (key from the ticket office; CADW), built around 1500 to enclose three sides of the well. Henry VII's mother, Margaret Beaufort, paid for the construction and earned herself a likeness amongst the roof bosses that depict the life of St Winefride in the ornate, Gothic fan-vaulted crypt that surrounds the well. With the gloom only cut by light from votive candles, she's not that easy to see now.

Pilgrimages still take place, mainly on St Winefride's Day, the nearest Sunday to June 22, when over five hundred pilgrims are led through the streets by the Bishop of Wrexham. The procession ends by the open side of the crypt where a few dozen faithful wade through the waters of a calm pool three times in the hope of curing their ailments. Sadly, a pump now fills the pool after mine working disrupted the spring's source in 1917. Immersion isn't limited to the procession: anyone, whatever their beliefs, can take the cure, though most choose to go in the summer "Curing Season".

A small **exhibition** features ancient boards inscribed with major donations, a collection of cast-off crutches, and banners once carried on pilgrimages. The former custodian's house contains a small **museum** (April–Sept Wed, Sat & Sun noon–4pm) with more painted banners and a beautiful silver reliquary designed to display Holywell's relic – part of Winefride's thumb bone – which is the subject of daily **veneration**.

Practicalities

Frequent **buses** along the coast call at the bus station at the southern end of High Street, so you shouldn't need to spend the night here. If you do decide to **stay**, the best choice is the oak-beamed, partly sixteenth-century *Greenhill Farm* (☎01352/713270, ⓦwww.greenhillfarm.co.uk; ❷), reached by heading a few yards northeast from Winefride's Well on the B5121 and then taking the second left opposite the *Royal Oak* pub. There are several perfectly adequate cafés and pubs along High Street. Alternatively, drive two miles south along the B5026 to the *Glan-yr-Afon Inn*, Milwr (☎01752/710052), which has a great reputation for its cooking and real ales.

Greenfield Valley and Basingwerk Abbey

A path heads a mile towards the sea from St Winefride's Well along the trackbed of an old pilgrims' train line to the wooded **Greenfield Valley Heritage Park**. Five ponds and a series of millraces lead to the restored remains of copper works and cotton mills set around the ruinous **Basingwerk Abbey** (unrestricted access; CADW). Most of the extant slabs of stonework are the remains of domestic buildings used by the abbot and twelve monks of the Savignac order. The abbey's history is told in the **visitor centre** (April–Oct daily 10am–4.30pm; free), which also serves as the entrance to the **Greenfield Valley Farm and Museum** (same hours; £3.50), a collection of reconstructed buildings from around North Wales, many saved from demolition. Particularly interesting are the Victorian school and the agricultural buildings, the latter preserved as a working farm where you can feed the animals. Come on Sunday afternoon, when there are workshops, demonstrations and guided countryside walks.

Maen Achwyfaen

If you've got your own transport, it's well worth making an excursion four miles west from Holywell to the impressive **Maen Achwyfaen** or "Stone of Lamentation" (unrestricted access; CADW), Britain's tallest **Celtic cross**. Though the shaft, incised with interwoven latticework, is over 10ft high and crowned with a wheel cross, this thousand-year-old monument is little celebrated and stands alone in a field. To get there, take the A5026 to the northwest of Holywell, turning right onto the A5151, then taking the third exit at the first roundabout and following signs to Treloyan for a little over a mile.

Travel details

Unless otherwise stated, frequencies for trains and buses are for Monday to Saturday services, Sunday averages 1–3 services, though the main routes are more frequent and some routes have no Sunday service at all.

Trains

Flint to: Chester (at least hourly; 15min); Llandudno Junction (at least hourly; 40min); Prestatyn (at least hourly; 15min).
Wrexham to: Chirk (5 daily; 1min); Shotton, for Liverpool (hourly; 1hr).

Buses

Chirk to: Llangollen (7 daily; 20min); Oswestry (hourly; 20min); Wrexham (hourly; 40min).
Corwen to: Bala (8 daily; 40min); Denbigh (hourly; 1hr); Llangollen (8 daily; 20min); Ruthin (hourly; 25min).
Denbigh to: Corwen (hourly; 1hr); Rhyl (every 20min; 45min); Ruthin (hourly; 30min); St Asaph (every 20min; 20min).

Flint to: Mold (hourly; 20min); Prestatyn (every 30min; 50min).
Llangollen to: Bala (8 daily; 1hr); Chirk (7 daily; 20min); Betws-y-Coed (3 daily; 1hr); Corwen (8 daily; 20min); Glyn Ceiriog (6 daily; 30min); Wrexham (at least hourly; 40min).
Mold to: Chester (every 30min; 1hr); Flint (hourly; 20min); Ruthin (8 daily; 40min); Wrexham (at least hourly; 40min–1hr).
Ruthin to: Corwen (hourly; 25min); Denbigh (hourly; 30min); Mold (daily; 40min).
Wrexham to: Chester (every 15min; 40min); Chirk (hourly; 40min); Llangollen (at least hourly; 40min); Mold (at least hourly; 40min–1hr); Oswestry (hourly; 1hr).

Snowdonia and the
Llŷn

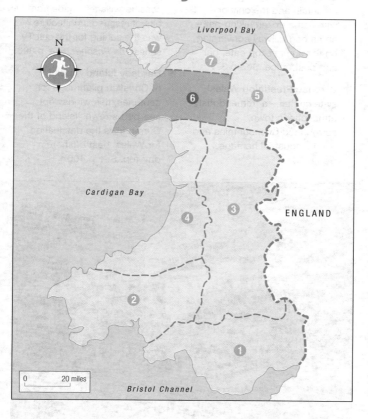

CHAPTER 6

Highlights

* **Welsh Slate Museum** Learn how slate was hewn from the hills around Llanberis and something of the lives of those who worked the quarries. See p.375

* **Snowdon** Wales' highest mountain and the only one with half a dozen hiking paths and a cog railway converging on the summit-top café, bar and post office. See p.377

* **Blaenau Ffestiniog** Wales' slate capital – a tremendously atmospheric town, surrounded by mountains and rich in industrial heritage. See p.384

* **Ffestiniog Railway** The finest of Wales' narrow-gauge railways, running thirteen miles from the coast high into the heart of the mountains. See p.396

* **Portmeirion** This surreal seaside "village", made from bits of rescued architecture, was the setting for the cult TV series *The Prisoner*. See p.396

* **Bardsey Island** A point of Christian pilgrimage for centuries, this windswept sea-bird-strewn "Island of the Currents" is the destination for Wales' best offshore day-trip. See p.406

▲ Portmeirion

Snowdonia and the Llŷn

W hat the coal valleys are to the south of the country, the mountains of Snowdonia (Yr Eryri) are to the north: the defining feature, not just in their physical form but in the way they have shaped the communities within them. Trapped between the brash coastal resorts in the north and the thinly inhabited hill tracts of mid–Wales to the south, this mountainous kernel is north Wales' crowning glory, a tightly packed bundle of soaring cliff faces, jagged peaks and plunging waterfalls. Snowdonia is the heart – and undisputed highlight – of the massive **Snowdonia National Park** (Parc Cenedlaethol Eryri), an 840-square-mile area which extends north and south, beyond the bounds of Snowdonia and this chapter, to encompass the Rhinog range, Cadair Idris and 23 miles of superb Cambrian coastal scenery. It is this concentrated section, little more than ten miles by ten, that most people mean when they refer to Snowdonia: staggeringly beautiful and home to Wales' highest mountain, **Snowdon** (Eryri), where winter snows cling to 3000-foot peaks well into April.

Not surprisingly, the massif is the region's focus, and there are enough mountain paths to keep even the most jaded walking enthusiast happy for weeks. But Snowdonia isn't all walking. Small settlements are dotted in the valleys, making great bases or places to rest. Chief among them are **Betws-y-Coed** and **Llanberis**, the latter linked to Snowdon's summit by mountain rail, while others, like **Beddgelert** and **Blaenau Ffestiniog**, are former mining or quarry towns still brimming with interest. Over the barren hills on the eastern fringes of Snowdonia, **Bala** tempts with watersports: either lake sailing or whitewater rafting down the Tryweryn.

West of here, the mountain landscape bleeds gently into the softer contours of the **Llŷn**, which juts into the Celtic Sea at a near right angle to the Cambrian coast. Linked to Snowdonia by the magnificent, narrow-gauge **Ffestiniog Railway**, its first settlement is the harbour town of **Porthmadog**, best known these days for its proximity to the Italianate dream village of **Portmeirion**. The Welsh castle at Cricieth and the museum devoted to Lloyd George a couple of miles away are amongst the good reasons to pause before Wales ends in a flourish of small coves around **Abersoch** and **Aberdaron**. Finally, roads loop back along the Llŷn to the tip of the north coast where **Caernarfon**, the heart of one of the most nationalist, Welsh-speaking areas in the country, is overshadowed by its mighty castle.

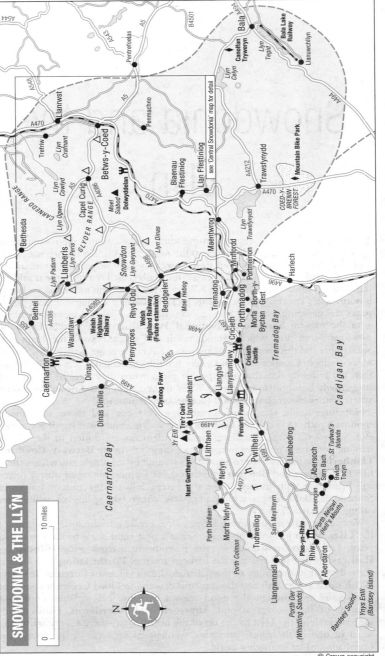

SNOWDONIA & THE LLŶN

10 miles

N

0

354

© Crown copyright

Getting around

Getting to the fringes of Snowdonia from elsewhere in Wales is easy: main-line **trains** run along the coast to nearby Bangor, while the Conwy Valley line branches at Llandudno Junction, penetrating to Betws-y-Coed and on to Blaenau Ffestiniog. Here, you can transfer to the useful and highly scenic Ffestiniog Railway for Porthmadog – the latter is also a stop on the Cambrian Coast line, shuffling daily around the coast to Pwllheli on the Llŷn.

There are frequent **bus** services from Llandudno Junction (close to Llandudno and Conwy) up the Conwy Valley to Llanrwst, where you can change for Betws-y-Coed. From there, the Snowdon Sherpa services (see box, p.360) provide access to Bethesda, Llanberis, Beddgelert and Porthmadog, each with good connections to the coast. Pwllheli is the main transport hub for the Llŷn, with buses to most parts of the peninsula leaving from near the train station. Routes and times are all fully detailed on the free *Gwynedd Public Transport Maps and Timetables*, available from tourist offices and bus stations.

Current **discount fares** include the **Red Rover** (£4.95; buy on the first bus), good for one day's bus travel anywhere in northwest Wales as far south as Aberystwyth, and east to Llandudno and Corwen. If you intend to travel by both bus and train, there's the **North and Mid-Wales Rover**, available from any staffed train station: a one-day pass costs £22; four days in any eight costs £47. It includes access to the Ffestiniog and Welsh Highland (Caernarfon) narrow-gauge railways.

Roads throughout the region are well surfaced but also well travelled, making **cycle touring** less appealing than it might seem. That said, the views are great, parking isn't a problem, and the quieter roads on the Llŷn are perfect for relaxed pedalling. You can also explore the ever-expanding network of **cycle tracks** and get off-road among the pines of Coed-y-Brenin south of Blaenau Ffestiniog and the Gwydir Forest near Betws-y-Coed.

Snowdonia

To Henry VIII's antiquarian, John Leland, **SNOWDONIA** seemed "horrible with the sight of bare stones"; these days, it's widely acclaimed as the most dramatic and alluring region in Wales, a compact, barren land of tortured ridges dividing glacial valleys where the sheer faces belie the fact that the tallest peaks only just top three thousand feet. It was to this mountain fastness that Llywelyn ap Gruffydd, the last true Prince of Wales, retreated in 1277 after his first war with Edward I; it was also here that Owain Glyndŵr held on most tenaciously to his dream of regaining the title for the Welsh. Centuries later, the English came to remove the mountains; slate barons built huge fortunes from Welsh toil and reshaped the patterns of Snowdonian life forever, as men looking for steady work in the quarries fled the hills and became town dwellers.

From the late eighteenth century, Snowdonia became the focus for the first truly structured approach to geological research. Early proponents of this new science pieced together the glacial evidence – scoured valley walls, scalloped mountainsides and hanging valleys – to come up with the first reliable proof of the last Ice Age and its retreat ten thousand years ago. These pioneers produced

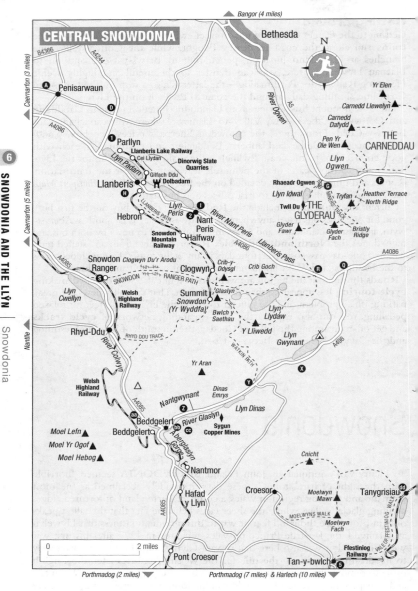

the rock-type classifications familiar to any students of the discipline: Cambrian rock takes its name from the Roman name for Wales, Ordovician and Silurian rocks from the Celtic tribes, the Ordovices and the Silures.

Botanists found rare alpine flora, writers produced libraries full of purple prose, and Richard Wilson, Paul Sandby and J.M.W. Turner all came to paint the landscape. Soon, those with the means began flocking here to marvel at the

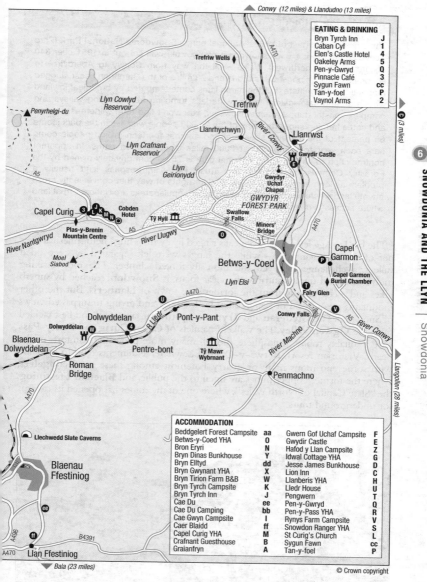

Conwy (12 miles) & Llandudno (13 miles)

EATING & DRINKING

Bryn Tyrch Inn	J
Caban Cyf	1
Elen's Castle Hotel	4
Oakeley Arms	5
Pen-y-Gwryd	Q
Pinnacle Café	3
Sygun Fawn	cc
Tan-y-foel	P
Vaynol Arms	2

A470

Trefriw Wells

Penyrhelgi-du

Llyn Cowlyd Reservoir

Trefriw

River Conwy

Llanrhychwyn

Llanrwst

Gwydir Castle

Llyn Crafnant Reservoir

Llyn Geirionydd

Gwydyr Uchaf Chapel

GWYDYR FOREST PARK

A5

Capel Curig

Cobden Hotel

Tŷ Hyll

Swallow Falls

Miners' Bridge

A470

Plas-y-Brenin Mountain Centre

A5

River Llugwy

Capel Garmon

River Nantgwryd

Moel Siabod

Betws-y-Coed

Capel Garmon Burial Chamber

Llyn Elsi

Fairy Glen

Dolwyddelan

Dolwyddelan

A470

R Lledr

Pont-y-Pant

Conwy Falls

River Machno

River Conwy

A5

Blaenau Dolwyddelan

Pentre-bont

Tŷ Mawr Wybrnant

Roman Bridge

Penmachno

Llechwedd Slate Caverns

Blaenau Ffestiniog

ACCOMMODATION

Beddgelert Forest Campsite	aa	Gwern Gof Uchaf Campsite	F
Betws-y-Coed YHA	O	Gwydir Castle	E
Bron Eryri	N	Hafod y Llan Campsite	Z
Bryn Dinas Bunkhouse	Y	Idwal Cottage YHA	G
Bryn Elltyd	dd	Jesse James Bunkhouse	D
Bryn Gwynant YHA	X	Lion Inn	C
Bryn Tirion Farm B&B	W	Llanberis YHA	H
Bryn Tyrch Campsite	K	Lledr House	U
Bryn Tyrch Inn	J	Pengwern	T
Cae Du	ee	Pen-y-Gwryd	Q
Cae Du Camping	bb	Pen-y-Pass YHA	R
Cae Gwyn Campsite	I	Rynys Farm Campsite	V
Caer Blaidd	ff	Snowdon Ranger YHA	S
Capel Curig YHA	M	St Curig's Church	L
Crafnant Guesthouse	A	Sygun Fawn	cc
Graianfryn		Tan-y-foel	P

ee

ff

A496

B4391

A470

Llan Ffestiniog

Bala (23 miles)

© Crown copyright

plunging waterfalls and walk the ever-widening paths to the mountaintops. Today, thousands of hikers arrive every weekend for some of the country's best walks over steep, exacting and constantly changing terrain. In recognition of the region's scientific importance, as well as its scenic and recreational appeal, Snowdonia became the heartland of Wales' first, and still largest, national park (see box, p.358).

6

SNOWDONIA AND THE LLŶN | Snowdonia

357

Snowdonia National Park

The oldest and largest of Wales' national parks, **Snowdonia National Park** (Parc Cenedlaethol Eryri; ⊛www.snowdonia-npa.gov.uk) was set out in 1951 over 840 square miles of northwest Wales – all the way from Conwy to Aberdyfi – to encompass the Rhinogs, Cadair Idris and 23 miles of the Cambrian coast. Jagged mountains predominate, but the harsh lines come tempered by broadleaf lowland woods around calm glacial lakes, waterfalls tumbling from hanging valleys and complex coastal dune systems. However, you won't find total wilderness: sheep and cattle farming supports many of the 27,000 people who live in the park (some 65 percent of them Welsh speakers) and another fourteen million people come here each year to tramp almost 2000 miles of designated paths. In apparent contradiction to its name, the national park is 75 percent privately owned by the Forestry Commission and National Trust. However, trespass isn't usually a problem as long as you keep to the ancient rights of way that conveniently cross private land where needed. Many of the most popular areas are National Trust land where access is unrestricted.

The last Ice Age left a legacy of peaks ringed by cwms – huge hemispherical bites out of the mountainsides – while the ranges were left separated by steep-sided valleys, a challenge for even the most fly-footed climber. The most striking monument, and understandably the clear focus, is **Snowdon**, reached by superb hikes and a cog railway from the former slate town of **Llanberis**. But the other mountains are as good or better, often far less busy and giving unsurpassed views of Snowdon. The **Glyderau** and **Tryfan** are particular favourites and best tackled from the **Ogwen Valley**. The walkers' hamlets of **Capel Curig** and **Pen–y–Pass** have a suitably robust atmosphere, though many more prefer the comforts of the nearby Victorian resort, **Betws-y-Coed**. Elsewhere, settlements tend to coincide with some enormous mine or quarry. Foremost among these are **Beddgelert**, where the former copper mines are open to the public, and **Blaenau Ffestiniog**, the "Slate Capital of North Wales", where one of the mines has opened its caverns for underground tours.

▲ Snowdonia National Park

If you're serious about doing some **walking** – and some of the walks described here *are* serious, especially in bad weather (Snowdon gets 200 inches of rain a year) – you need a good map, such as the 1:50,000 OS Landranger 115 or the 1:25,000 OS Explorer OL17. Always check mountain weather conditions before setting out: latest reports are usually posted on the doors or noticeboards of outdoor shops and tourist offices, while the Met Office (℡0870/900 0100, ⓦwww.metoffice.co.uk) has dedicated mountain forecasts.

Accommodation inside the Snowdonia National Park is strictly limited, and most is on the fringes. The main exception is Betws-y-Coed, a village packed with guesthouses, all of them filling up early during the busy summer season. Elsewhere in Snowdonia are B&Bs, hostels, bunkhouses and basic campsites, mostly geared towards walkers and climbers. In all, there are six **YHA hostels** within five miles of Snowdon's summit, and a further half-dozen other budget places. Even with a medium-sized backpack, walking from one to another makes a welcome change from the usual circular walks.

Betws-y-Coed and around

Sprawled out across a flat plain around the confluence of the Conwy, Llugwy and Lledr valleys, **BETWS-Y-COED** (pronounced "betoos-er-coyd") should be the perfect base for exploring Snowdonia. Its riverside setting, overlooked by the conifer-clad slopes of the **Gwydyr Forest Park**, is undeniably appealing, and the town boasts the best selection of hotels and guesthouses in the region, but after an hour mooching around the outdoor equipment shops and drinking tea you are left wondering what to do. The town is touted as "the gateway to Snowdonia", but none of the serious mountain walks starts from here, just a couple of easy strolls (see box, p.363) to its two main attractions, the **Conwy Falls** and **Swallow Falls**. In recent years, Betws-y-Coed has become something of a magnet for **bikers**, both those with polished chrome hogs parked outside the town's pubs and cafés, and mud-bespattered mountain bikers returning from the pleasures of the Gwydyr Forest.

The quieter valleys in the vicinity can often be a lot more appealing than the town itself. The rail line from the coast comes up the **Conwy Valley** past **Llanrwst**, five miles north of Betws-y-Coed, a town graced by a fine bridge attributed to Inigo Jones and a couple of beautifully decorated chapels. The train continues south from Betws-y-Coed up the **Lledr Valley**, a wonderfully scenic journey passing the lonely **Dolwyddelan Castle**, on its way to the slate town of Blaenau Ffestiniog. South of Betws-y-Coed, a minor road leads to **Penmachno** and the house of William Morgan, who first translated the Bible into Welsh. Walkers bound for the high hills will be heading west beside the **River Llugwy** to the mountain centre of Capel Curig and beyond to Llanberis and the Ogwen Valley.

Most of the land around Betws-y-Coed and along the Conwy Valley was part of the Gwydyr Estate owned by the Wynn family, descended from the kings of Gwynedd and the most powerful dynasty in the region until the male line died out in 1678; several place names are reminders of the family's might.

Arrival and accommodation

Betws-y-Coed is arranged in a flat triangle bounded by the Conwy and Llugwy rivers and the A5, which forms the town's High Street. Access is easy, either by train or bus from the north coast, or by car along the A5 from

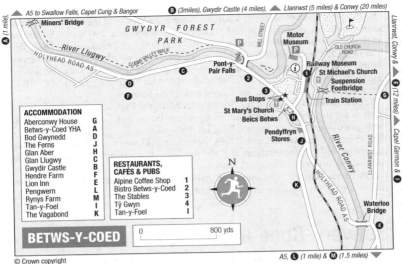

Llangollen. The **tourist office** (daily: Easter to mid-Oct 9.30am–5.30pm; mid-Oct to Easter 9.30am–4.30pm; ☎01690/710426, ✉tic.byc@eryri-npa .gov.uk), in Royal Oak Stables, has displays giving a quick overview of Snowdonia. Across the lawn, the **train station** also acts as the hub for **buses**, which fan out towards the peaks around Snowdon (see box, p.370), and to Penmachno, Llanberis, Conwy and Llandudno. For **internet access**, visit *The Vagabond* (see p.361) or the library in Llanrwst.

Accommodation

Betws-y-Coed has plenty of **accommodation**, but has to cope with an even larger numbers of visitors pushing prices up in the summer. Expect to pay a few pounds more than in other towns in Snowdonia, and don't be surprised to find the places listed below full if you arrive late in the day.

Parking, buses and the Snowdon Sherpa

Parking is regular expense in Wales. In the mountainous core around Snowdon, visitors are encouraged to park in surrounding towns and use the comprehensive bus system to get into the mountains. The **Snowdon Sherpa** is a catch-all name for a handful of interconnecting bus services plying the roads between Betws-y-Coed, Bethesda, Llanberis, Caernarfon and Porthmadog. Most meet at Pen-y-Pass, and a **day ticket** (£4; buy from the driver) will give you one day's unlimited travel within this area throughout the day. On summer weekends and school holidays, some services use open-top double-deckers.

Major routes through northern Snowdonia are:

#S1 Llanberis to Pen-y-Pass via Nant Peris.

#S2 Betws-y-Coed to Pen-y-Pass.

#S4 Caernarfon to Pen-y-Pass via Waunfawr and Beddgelert.

#S6 Bethesda to Pen-y-Pass via Llyn Ogwen, Capel Curig and the *Pen-y-Gwryd Hotel*.

#S97 Betws-y-Coed to Porthmadog via Capel Curig, Pen-y-Pass and Beddgelert.

B&Bs and hotels

Aberconwy House Lôn Muriau, Llanrwst Rd
☎01690/710202, ⊛ www.aberconwy-house.co.uk.
A friendly and well-appointed Victorian guesthouse,
with doubles, twins and family rooms to suit most
needs: four rooms enjoy superb views over Betws-
y-Coed and the Llugwy Valley and one comes with
a four-poster bed. To get there on foot, cross the
suspension bridge behind the train station; by car,
take the A470 towards Llanrwst. ❹

🚶 **Bod Gwynedd** Holyhead Rd, half a mile
towards Capel Curig ☎01690/710717 ,
⊛ www.bodgwynedd.com. New and welcoming
B&B in a Victorian house on the edge of town with
uncluttered rooms, white linen, powerful showers
and one room with a four-poster. ❸

The Ferns Holyhead Rd ☎01690/710587,
⊛ www.ferns-guesthouse.co.uk. Nicely appointed
guesthouse with seven pleasant and good-value
rooms, plus an attractive self-catering cottage out
back. ❷–❸

Glan Aber Holyhead Rd ☎01690/710325, ⊛ www
.glanaberhotel.com. Reasonable town-centre hotel
with bar, plus a kind of hostel with two bunks to a
room (£15 per head) but no self-catering facilities:
optional £5 breakfast. Good bike storage. ❶/❹

Glan Llugwy On the A5 towards Capel Curig, 300
yards beyond Pont-y-Pair ☎01690/710592,
⊛ www.glanllugwysnowdonia.co.uk. One of the
cheapest B&Bs around, with one en suite.
Rooms ❷, en suite ❸

🚶 **Gwydir Castle** 3 miles north on the B5106
☎01492/641687, ⊛ www.gwydir-castle
.co.uk. Gwydir represents one of the best
opportunities in Wales to stay in an authentic castle
that still maintains the air of a family home. Two
splendid bedrooms have been fitted out in baronial
style with four-poster beds, deep baths and
elegantly eclectic decor. There's no TV but you can
relax in the oak-panelled parlour, where a hearty
breakfast is served. ❺

Lion Inn Gwytherin ☎01745/860123, ⊛ www
.thelioninn.net. For peace and relaxation (no TV, no
internet, no mobile coverage) stay at this renovated
pub in a tiny village in a fold of rolling hills nine
miles east of Llanrwst. A couple of the tastefully
upgraded rooms come with bathtub, and there's an
extensive DVD library if a few pints in the pub

doesn't suit. Breakfast and excellent meals (£10
mains) are served in the bar or restaurant. ❹

🚶 **Pengwern** Allt Dinas, a mile east on the
A5 ☎01690/710480, ⊛ www
.snowdoniaaccommodation.com. Beautiful,
welcoming and tastefully decorated country
house set in two acres of woods with just three
rooms plus a separate self-catering cottage let
from around £350 a week in summer. ❺

Tan-y-Foel Capel Garmon ☎01690/710507,
⊛ www.tyfhotel.co.uk. Ultramodern public spaces
and stylish, luxurious rooms in a sixteenth-century
farmhouse make this one of the best small
country hotels in the district, with sweeping views
across eight acres of grounds to the Conwy Valley
and outstanding three-course dinners (£42). Take
the A470 towards Llanrwst then turn right after
two miles. ❽

Hostels and campsites

Betws-y-Coed YHA A5, 2 miles west of Betws-y-
Coed ☎01690/710796, ⊛ www.swallowfallshotel
.co.uk. Pleasant, modern hostel with dorms (from
£15), and rooms (including some doubles), plus
breakfasts and packed lunches available (both £5).
It's next door to the otherwise nondescript *Swallow
Falls Hotel* (which has a bar and restaurant), and a
nice campsite (£5 per person). ❶

Hendre Farm Holyhead Rd, half a mile towards
Capel Curig ☎01690/710133. The closest tent site
to town with fairly basic facilities and tent sites at
£4.50 per person.

Rynys Farm 2 miles southeast of town on the A5
near the Conwy Falls ☎01690/710218, ⊛ www
.rynys-camping.co.uk. Charming farm campsite
and caravan park in peaceful undulating terrain,
and with great valley views and good facilities
(hook-ups £2). £5 per person.

🚶 **The Vagabond** Craiglan Rd
☎01690/710850, ⊛ www.thevagabond
.co.uk. Excellent and central independent hostel
with 36 bunks (with sheets) in 4–8 bunk dorms, and
good facilities including cheap internet and wi-fi,
secure bike lockup and off-street parking. There's a
self-catering kitchen but they also serve good
breakfasts (£4), evening meals (£7) and have an
inexpensive bar with seating on the patio. Bookings
recommended at weekends. £14 per bunk.

The Town

Betws-y-Coed was founded in the fifth or sixth century, when a monastic cell
earned the settlement the moniker of the "oratory in the forest". Apart from
some lead mining, it remained a backwater until 1808, when road improvements brought the Irish Mail this way. As part of the A5 construction, Telford
completed the graceful cast-iron **Waterloo Bridge** in 1815, complete with

spandrels which use the emblems (rose, thistle, shamrock and leek) of the four countries of the then newly formed United Kingdom. The improved access lured landscape painters David Cox and J.M.W. Turner, who in turn alerted the leisured classes to the town's beauty. Anglers keen to exploit the richly stocked pools came too, but it was the arrival of the train line in 1868 that really lifted Betws-y-Coed's status to genteel resort. Sights in town are few, but include the **Pont-y-Pair Falls**, a low cataract where the waters of the River Llugwy thunder over assorted boulders and funnel under the adjacent Pont-y-Pair ("Bridge of the Cauldron"). On sunny days the stone slabs around the falls are always littered with people relaxing after long walks or too much outdoor clothing shopping.

Adjoining the train station, the **Conwy Valley Railway Museum** (daily 10.15am–5pm; £1.50) is a fairly dull collection of memorabilia and shiny engines, slightly enlivened by a model of a Welsh slate quarry and the opportunity for kids to take a short ride on a miniature train (£1.50) or tram (£1). Pick up a key here if you fancy visiting the interior of the fourteenth-century **St Michael's church**, most interesting for the twelfth-century font and a carved effigy of an armoured knight, whose inscription identifies him as Gruffydd ap Dafydd Goch, the grandson of Llywelyn ap Gruffydd's brother, Prince Dafydd.

Activities

There are several easy to moderate **walks** around Betws-y-Coed (see box opposite). For more of a workout, there's also **mountain biking** in the Gwydyr Forest Park, one of the top trail-riding locales in Wales. The classic route is the Marin Trail (25km loop; 2–4hr) with mostly forest track ascents and numerous single-track descents of varying difficulty. The scenery is great, with mountain views along the higher sections. **Rent a bike** either from Lightspeed, Holyhead Road (£20/day, £30 for full suspension) or Beics Betws (℡01690/710766, ⓦwww.bikewales.co.uk), in the street up behind the post office, who offer two grades of hardtail (£14/18 and £18/25 per half/full day).

The nearest **horseriding** is at Gwydyr Riding and Trekking Stables (℡01690/760248, ⓦwww.horse-riding-wales.co.uk; 2hr for £28), seven miles south of Betws-y-Coed in Penmachno. **Anglers** with a rod licence (available from any post office) and their own tackle can try hooking salmon and sea trout on stretches of the Conwy and Llugwy within town (£18 a day; mid-March to mid-Oct), and brown and American brook trout on Llyn Elsi in the hills just south (£13 a day; late March to late Oct only). For details, pick up the free Betws-y-Coed Anglers Club leaflet from the tourist office or Pendyffryn Stores, on Holyhead Road, which also sells gear.

Eating and drinking

For a town so geared to tourism that it's hard to turn around without knocking someone's cream tea onto the floor, there are surprisingly few really good places to **eat**. Many of the more visible ones along the main road are quite mediocre, but better options do exist.

Entertainment doesn't usually stretch much further than a beer in one of the pubs, though a couple of **male-voice choirs** give performances during summer: a different choir performs each week in St Mary's Church (Sun at 8pm; £5), and there's a free performance every second Friday (8.30–10pm) at *The Stables*.

Alpine Coffee Shop In the train station. Bright, wooden-floored daytime café with art on the walls and an appealing range of sandwiches, wraps and vegetarian dishes, as well as speciality teas, espresso and hikers' packed lunches (£7). Loses marks for lack of attention to detail and uninterested staff.

Bistro Betws-y-Coed Holyhead Rd ☎01690/710328. Excellent, casual, wood-floored restaurant where dishes are all named in Welsh, reflecting their insistence on using local produce. Lunches might just be sandwiches (£6–9) or Glamorgan sausage with a basil and tomato sauce (£8.50), but everything is beautifully presented. Dinners might stretch to breasts of local wood pigeon with a chilli-spiced plum jam (£5) followed by Menai Strait sea bass with a garlic, leek and chorizo stir fry (£15).

The Stables *Royal Oak Hotel*, High St. The town's liveliest bar, with good beer, stacks of outdoor seating, jazz on summer Thurs, and a good range of bar food, pizzas and grills at reasonable prices. Their signature haddock, chips and mushy peas is good value at £7.50.

Tŷ Gwyn On the A5 ☎01690/710383, ⊛www.tygwynhotel.co.uk. Convivial wood-beamed hotel with excellent meals served either in the low-roofed bar or the slightly more formal restaurant. The Conwy *moules marinière* (£6) are excellent, and might be followed by roast venison with mushroom risotto (£15) or home-made steak and kidney pie (£10).

Tan-y-Foel (See "accommodation"). Dinner (£43 for three courses) is the highlight of any stay here. The restaurant only seats ten, and everything is carefully cooked to order. Expect the likes of duck breast with spiced pearl barley and pear chutney followed by wild turbot, Conwy crab and squid ink risotto. Guests have priority for reservations and smart dress is required.

Conwy Falls, Fairy Glen and Tŷ Mawr Wybrnant

None of the attractions of Betws–y–Coed can compete with getting out to the gorges and waterfalls in the vicinity, and **walking** is the ideal way to see them (see box below). A few miles upstream of Betws-y-Coed, the River Conwy

Walks around Betws-y-Coed

These two lowland walks explore the valleys and waterfalls on the outskirts of town. Neither is circular, so unless you plan to hitch back, consult bus timetables first to avoid a long wait for the infrequent services.

The **Conwy Gorge walk** (3 miles; 1hr 15min; descent only) links two of the district's best-known natural attractions, Fairy Glen and the Conwy Falls (see p.364), by way of a cool green lane giving glimpses of the river through the woods. Catch the #64 bus (8 daily) to the *Conwy Falls Café*, then after having a look at the falls, walk a hundred yards back along the road towards Betws-y-Coed and follow a path parallel to the river through the trees. After about half an hour, you'll see the gate to Fairy Glen on your left. Returning to the main path, continue to the *Fairy Glen Hotel*, where you can cross the river by Beaver Bridge, turn right and follow a minor road a mile back to town.

The car park on the north side of the Pont-y-Pair bridge marks the beginning of the **Llugwy Valley walk** (6 miles; 2hr 30min; 600ft ascent), a forested path following the twisting and plunging river upstream to Capel Curig. With the A5 running parallel to the river all the way, there are several opportunities to cut short the walk and hitch or wait for the bus back to Betws-y-Coed. Less than a mile from Pont-y-Pair, you first reach a ford where the Roman road Sarn Helen crossed the river, then pass the steeply sloping Miners' Bridge, which linked miners' homes at Pentre Du on the south side of the river to the lead mines in the Gwydyr Forest. With its plunge pools and rocky diving platforms this is a wonderfully refreshing place to take a dip. The path follows the river on your left for another mile to a slightly obscured view of Swallow Falls. Detailed maps available from the tourist office in Betws-y-Coed show numerous routes back through the Gwydyr Forest, or you can continue half a mile to the road bridge by Tŷ Hyll and follow the right bank to Capel Curig, passing the scant remains of the Caer Llugwy, a Roman fort, and a couple more treacherous rapids: The Mincer and Cobden's Falls.

plunges fifty feet over the **Conwy Falls** into a deep pool. After slotting £1 into the turnstile beside the *Conwy Falls Café* (reached by the #64 bus 8 times daily), you can view the falls on the right and a series of rock steps to the left, originally cut as a kind of primitive fish ladder, which is now superseded by a tunnel through the rock on the far side.

A mile or so downstream, after negotiating a continuous series of tortuous rapids, the churning waters of the Conwy negotiate a staircase of drops and enter **Fairy Glen**, a cleft in a small wood which takes its name from the Welsh fairies, the Tylwyth Teg, who are said to be seen hereabouts. Take the A470 towards Blaenau Ffestiniog and turn up the lane beside the *Fairy Glen Hotel*. From the car park here (£1) a short path (20min each way; 50p) leads to the glen.

Just above Conwy Falls is the river's confluence with the River Machno, which drains the hills around the small village of **Penmachno**, a couple of miles upstream. Some two and a half miles beyond Penmachno stands the isolated and little-visited cottage of **Tŷ Mawr Wybrnant** (late March–Sept Thurs–Sun noon–5pm; £3; NT). Here, Bishop William Morgan, the man who first translated the Bible into Welsh (see p.424), was born in 1545 and lived until his teenage years, when he decamped to Gwydyr Castle to pursue his education. The original cottage has been restored to something like its sixteenth-century appearance: all bare stone and beams, with a gaping fireplace supporting a huge, sagging beam dating back to the thirteenth century. Its star attraction is the collection of Bibles and prayer books, including a Morgan original.

The Llugwy Valley: Swallow Falls and the Gwydyr Forest

The **Swallow Falls** (a mistranslation of *Rhaeadr Ewynnol*, or "foaming cataract"; £1) lie two miles west of Betws-y-Coed along the A5 towards Capel Curig. Such easy access makes this one of the region's most-visited sights, but it's really no more than a straightforward, pretty waterfall with the occasional mad kayaker scraping down the precipitous rock. Pay your £1 and you can walk down to a series of viewing platforms.

Less than a mile beyond, the road crosses the river passing **Tŷ Hyll** (Easter–Oct daily 9.30am–5pm; Nov–Easter Mon–Fri variable hours; ☎01690/720287, ⓦwww.snowdonia-society.org.uk; £1), known as the "Ugly House" for its chunky appearance. Decked out with period furniture and surrounded by a cottage garden, wildlife pond, and forest full of easy paths, it is also the headquarters of the Snowdonia Society, an environmental campaigning group which lobbies to preserve the region's ecological and social integrity. From Tŷ Hyll, the A5 follows the River Llugwy upstream past a number of roadside cataracts – most notably opposite *Cobden's Hotel* – and on to Capel Curig.

The Lledr Valley

The train line up the Conwy Valley from Betws-y-Coed follows the twists of the beautiful **Lledr Valley** to Blaenau Ffestiniog, the river flowing through deciduous and pine forests that give way to the smooth, grassy slopes of the Moel Siabod before the route bores through over two miles of slate – the longest rail tunnel in Wales. Take this trip while you can: the section of the line between Betws-y-Coed and Blaenau Ffestiniog seems to be always under threat of closure.

The A470 runs parallel to the river from Betws-y-Coed to Blaenau Ffestiniog. Four miles south of Betws-y-Coed, you come to Pont-y-Pant station, where the Roman road Sarn Helen crosses the river on a clapper bridge and follows its banks to Dolwyddelan. The *Lledr House* **independent hostel** (℡01690/750202, Ⓦwww.ukyh.com; ❶), across the river from the station, is an ideal starting point for a walk up Moel Siabod (see box, p.368), and has beds in double, twin and family rooms with self-catering facilities for £12 a head (bedding included).

A mile further on is **DOLWYDDELAN** village, well placed for the southern approach to Moel Siabod and only a mile east of lonely **Dolwyddelan Castle** (April–Sept Mon–Sat 10am–5pm, Sun 11.30am–4pm; Oct–March Mon–Sat 10am–4pm, Sun 11.30am–4pm; £2.70; CADW), commanding the head of the valley. Llywelyn ap Iorwerth ("the Great"; see p.469) may well have been born here, since his father was reputedly responsible for its construction at the end of the twelfth century. The strategic site, on the important route from Aberconwy to the north and Ardudwy to the south, was soon turned against him when Edward I took the castle, refortified it and used it to further subdue the Welsh. By the end of the fifteenth century, it had become redundant and lay abandoned until the Wynns of Gwydyr treated it to a suitably Victorian reconstruction, complete with fanciful battlements and a new roof. Today, it shelters only a small exhibition on native Welsh castles, but affords a panoramic view of Snowdonia from between its castellations.

If you want to stay around here, the castle custodian runs the neighbouring *Bryn Tirion Farm* B&B (℡01690/750366; ❸), a **campsite** (£3 per person; closed Nov–Feb) and a comfortable, self-catering **bunkhouse** (open all year; £13 per person), with bedding supplied. Back in the centre of Dolwyddelan, *Elen's Castle Hotel* (℡01690/750207, Ⓦwww.elenscastlehotel.co.uk; ❸) has cosy rooms and serves good, inexpensive bar food and pricier meals. The best **pub** is the welcoming *Y Gwydyr*, on the main road in Dolwyddelan, where Sunday lunch is served.

The Conwy Valley: Capel Garmon, Llanrwst and Trefriw

The Conwy River leaves Betws-y-Coed along its broad pastoral corridor to the sea flanked on the left by the bald tops of Snowdonia's northeastern bulwark, the mighty Carneddau range. More manageable hills lie to the east, where Neolithic dwellers left their mark in the **Capel Garmon Burial Chamber** (unrestricted access; CADW), a heavily reconstructed, multi-chambered burial site built between 2500 and 1900 BC. It's an atmospheric spot, comprising some rough stones lining a series of linked pits, with a central chamber covered by an enormous capstone. The site is a five-minute signposted walk across farmland two miles southeast of Betws-y-Coed, half a mile south of the tiny hilltop village of **CAPEL GARMON**.

Llanrwst

Five miles north of Betws-y-Coed, **LLANRWST** was once the largest wool market in north Wales, had a spell as a centre for harp manufacture in the eighteenth century, and is still the most economically important town in the valley, retaining Wednesday and Friday livestock **markets**, and a general one each Tuesday. The latter takes place on the central Ancaster Square, close to the **Llanrwst Almshouse Museum**, at 1 Church St (Tues–Fri 10.30am–3.30pm, Sat & Sun noon–3.30pm; £2), occupying a set of almshouses dating back to 1610, and which only finally closed in 1976. Two rooms are done in period style (1610 and 1850 respectively), while exhibits in others cover the town's history and detail the lives of some of the residents. A few yards further down the street,

St Gwrst Church contains a fine rood screen and, in the south transept (separate entrance: £1 donation requested), the thirteenth-century carved stone coffin (minus its lid) of Llywelyn the Great.

Inigo Jones is said to have spent his early years in Llanrwst, and the great seventeenth-century architect was at least partially responsible for the town's most noted sight, the beautifully proportioned, humpback **Pont Fawr** (Big Bridge). In summer, its single lane struggles to cope with the traffic across it to **Tu Hwnt i'r Bont**, a photogenic, fifteenth-century, ivy-clad former court-house that's now a café (open Easter–Oct) serving traditional afternoon teas.

Buses and trains stop close to Ancaster Square, where the Italian-oriented *La Barrica* bistro does good daytime **meals** and sandwiches. Alternatively pick up picnic supplies from *Blas ar Fwyd* deli, 25 Station Rd, or try *Amser Da* (Good Times) across the road at no. 34 (T01492/641188), which does dishes like smoked duck salad (£6) and local trout with blanched almonds (£11). Since it's so close to Betws-y-Coed, few people choose to **stay** in Llanrwst, though you may come for free **internet access** at the library (Mon, Wed & Fri 10am–5.30pm, Wed 10am–7pm, Sat 10am–1pm) on Station Road just north of town.

Gwydir Castle and Gwydyr Uchaf Chapel

Across the river, half a mile west of Llanrwst, is Richard Wynn's ancestral home, **Gwydir Castle** (March–Oct daily 10am–4pm; £4), actually a low-slung manor house begun around 1490 on the site of a fortified house a century older. Despite additions in the sixteenth and nineteenth centuries, with parts plundered from the post-dissolution Maenan Abbey, the ivy- and wisteria-covered building is a fabulous model of early Tudor architecture.

Its core is a three-storey solar tower, whose windows relieve the gloom of the great halls, each with enormous fireplaces and stone-flagged or heavy timber floors. Most of the original fittings and Tudor furniture were sold in 1921, and much of the rest of the house was ruined in a fire a few months later. The subsequent restoration was kept simple – tapestries cover the solid stone walls, a few tables and chairs are scattered about and there's some fine painted glass. Some of the original furnishings have been tracked down, including the heavily carved oak panels, Baroque door-case and fireplace, and abundant gilded Spanish leather of the magnificent **Dining Room**. This was initially installed by Richard Wynn around 1642, and is again attributed to Inigo Jones. The complete set was bought during the 1921 sell-off by American newspaper magnate William Randolph Hearst and shipped across the Atlantic. New York's Metropolitan Museum acquired it in 1956 and kept it boxed up for forty years until it was sold back to the castle in 1996 and re-installed.

Outside, the main attraction is the **Dutch Garden**, with its fountain, peacocks and Cedars of Lebanon dating back to 1625. There's also excellent accommoda-tion (see p.361).

A few hundred yards from his home, Richard Wynn built his own private **Gwydyr Uchaf Chapel** (key from Gwydir Castle by appointment on T01492/641687; free; CADW) in 1673. The plain exterior is in striking contrast to the unashamedly Baroque interior, with its roof beams cut into angelic figures. The inward-facing pews are unusual, but it's the painted ceiling that's really outstanding, depicting the Creation, the Trinity and the Day of Judgement.

Trefriw and Llyn Crafnant

The small village of **TREFRIW**, two miles north of Llanrwst, is home to the **Trefriw Woollen Mills** (mill Easter–Sept Mon–Fri 10am–5pm, shop daily all year; free), whose demonstrations of late nineteenth-century weaving methods, using power from the stream outside, make for a more compelling visit than other mills around north Wales. In the second century, Romans garrisoned on the banks of the Conwy recognized the restorative properties of the iron-rich waters of **Trefriw Wells** (Easter–Sept Mon–Sat 10am–5pm Sun 11am–5pm; Oct–Easter Mon–Sat 10am–5pm; £3), a mile and a half north of the village. An interesting, if laboured, twenty-minute self-guided tour visits a robust pair of gentlemen's and ladies' bathhouses, complete with slate tubs built around 1700. You can also sample the waters – they taste a little like sucking a rusty nail, but their invigorating, curative powers are extolled by the numerous testimonials kept in the café.

A signposted road back in the village close to the woollen mills leads three miles southwest to **Llyn Crafnant**, a calm reservoir hemmed in by mountains, and one of the more popular local beauty spots. Alternatively, take the steep lane south of the village towards the neighbouring lakes of **Llanrhychwyn** and **Llyn Geirionydd**. There are numerous other small pools in the vicinity, many bordered by forest, and it's a lovely area for a picnic, a gentle walk or a swim.

If you want to **stay** in Trefriw, try the tastefully appointed *Crafnant Guesthouse* (℡01492/640809, ⓦwww.trefriw.co.uk; ❷, two-night minimum stay; closed Nov–Jan), right in the village on the B5106.

Capel Curig and the Ogwen Valley

Tantalizing glimpses of Wales' highest mountains flash through the forested banks of the Llugwy as you climb west from Betws-y-Coed on the A5, but you don't spot Snowdon until the final bend before **Capel Curig**. This tiny walkers' village makes a perfect base for the two valleys that plunge westwards deep into the mountains. The A4086 follows Nant Gwryd southwest to the Snowdon massif, while the A5 prises apart the Carneddau and Glyder ranges to the northwest, forging through the **Ogwen Valley** to tatty **Bethesda**, home to one of Wales' last surviving slate quarries.

As you cross the watershed between the Llugwy and Ogwen rivers, the frequently mist-shrouded Carnedd range to the north glowers across at the Glyder range and its triple-peaked **Tryfan**, arguably Snowdonia's most demanding mountain. This forms a fractured spur out from the main range and blocks your view down the valley, the twin monoliths of Adam and Eve that crown Tryfan's summit picked out on the skyline. The courageous (or foolhardy) make the jump between them as a point of honour at the end of every ascent. West of Tryfan, the road follows a perfect example of a U-shaped valley, carved and smoothed by rocks frozen into the undersides of the glaciers that creaked down **Nant Ffrancon** ten thousand years ago.

Capel Curig

There's scarcely a building in tiny **CAPEL CURIG**, six miles west of Betws-y-Coed, that isn't of some use to hikers. Foremost among them is **Plas y Brenin: The National Mountain Centre** (℡01690/720214, ⓦwww.pyb .co.uk), a quarter of a mile along the A4086 to Llanberis from the town's main road junction. Built around a former coaching inn and hotel, the centre runs internationally renowned residential courses in hiking, mountaineering, kayaking, skiing and rock climbing (see p.65). Daily mountain weather forecasts are available from reception. If you're just passing through and don't have your own equipment, the two-hour indoor climbing, lake canoeing and dry-slope skiing sessions held during August and other school holidays (£15) may be of interest. Kids who want a full-day taster of canoeing, skiing and abseiling can be left on the "3 in a Day" adventure session (£35), where adults are welcome too. There is also a climbing wall (daily 10am–11pm; £4), a dry ski slope (daily 10am–4pm; £5 per hr including ski rental, £20 per hr for instruction; call for availability) and bar (see below). Plas-y-Brenin also rents out all kinds of hiking, camping and mountaineering gear at reasonable prices. For **mountain bike rental** you'll need to visit Beics Betws in Betws-y-Coed (see p.362).

Despite Capel Curig's popularity amongst hikers, the only major **walk** from here is up Moel Siabod (see box below), but the village acts as a base for the Ogwen Valley and Snowdon. The A4086 runs four miles southwest to the *Pen-y-Gwryd Hotel* (see p.381). From here, the A498 continues south to Beddgelert, past the best view of Snowdon's east face, while the A4086 branches west to Llanberis, passing Pen-y-Pass, the start for the best-known Snowdon walks.

Practicalities

Snowdon Sherpa **buses** (see box, p.360) service Capel Curig, but if bus times are unsuitable you can always walk here from Betws-y-Coed along the River Llugwy (see box, p.363) – a pleasant three-hour walk in good weather. There are several **places to stay** (see below), but only a couple of places to **eat** and **drink**. The *Pinnacle Café*, at the intersection of the main road junction in the village, offers cheap but basic hikers' fare, though generally you're far better served at the 🦌 *Bryn Tyrch* (see below), with its warm and lively bar, hearty food, garden seating and a wonderful view of Snowdon. Many dishes are vegetarian, and this is one of the very fewestablishments in the whole of Snowdonia to make any real attempt to please vegans. Expect the likes of *spanakopita*, Hungarian goulash and Cajun chicken (all £11). The *Snowdon Bar* at Plas y Brenin has cheap **internet** access (and free wi-fi), and hosts talks and slide shows of recent international expeditions (usually Mon, Tues & Sat at 8pm; free).

A walk from Capel Curig

The 1:50,000 OS Landranger 115 map ("Snowdon/Yr Wyddfa") or the 1:25,000 OS Explorer OL17 map ("Snowdon & Conwy Valley") are recommended for this walk.

If you approached **Capel Curig** from the west, you won't have looked twice at the rounded grassy back of **Moel Siabod** (2862ft), but its eastern aspect is another matter – a challenging ridge affording a magnificent summit view of the Snowdon Horseshoe.

The mountainous section of the east ridge walk (5 miles; 4hr; 2200ft) is circular and brings you back into the Llugwy Valley. The route starts from opposite the YHA hostel in Capel Curig, crossing the concrete bridge and following the right bank downstream past the falls by *Cobden's Hotel* to the Pont Cyfyng road bridge (30min), an alternative starting point for the walk. Taking the road south, turn right on the second path signposted to Moel Siabod. This quickly rises out of the valley and keeps to the left of the mountain, past a disued slate quarry and across some boggy land, before the long scramble up the east ridge. Once found, the path is fairly clear, but it weaves around outcrops where a moment's inattention could be perilous. The summit is flat and uninteresting, so once you've admired Snowdon, turn northeast and follow the craggy summit ridge, which eventually starts to drop across grass to the moors below, soon rejoining your ascent route for the hike back to Pont Cyfyng.

Accommodation

Bron Eryri A5, 1 mile outside the village towards Betws-y-Coed ☏01690/720240, ⓦwww .eryriguesthouse.fsnet.co.uk. Comfortable and welcoming B&B. ❷

Bryn Tyrch Campsite A5, 0.3 miles towards Betws-y-Coed ☏01690/720414. Basic grassy site with token showers and very simple bunkhouses (bring everything). Bunks £6, camping £4 per person.

Bryn Tyrch Inn A5, 0.3 miles towards Betws-y-Coed ☏01690/720223, ⓦwww.bryntyrchinn .co.uk. Recently renovated ten-room inn offering simple but tasteful rooms with well-appointed bathrooms and TV. Also has four-bunk rooms (£25 per person B&B, minimum 3 in one room). Two-night minimum stay at weekends; midweek and off-season discounts often available. ❹

Capel Curig YHA A5, 0.5 miles towards Betws-y-Coed ☏0870/770 5746, ⓔcapelcurig@yha.org.uk. Busy hostel. Rates include a full breakfast, and packed lunches (£4–5) are available. Generally closed Nov–Feb. Bunks £18–20, rooms ❶

St Curig's Church A5, by the intersection in the heart of the village ☏01690/720469, ⓦwww.stcurigschurch.com. Great B&B fashioned from a former church which comes complete with a domed gilded mosaic of Christ in the pool and TV room. One room has a four-poster, two share the family's bathroom (complete with deep bath) and all are very comfortable. A recess off the lounge has bunks for four (£15 a head plus £5 for optional breakfast), and everyone has access to a hot tub with views of the stars and mountains. Shared bath ❸, en suite ❹

The Ogwen Valley

Five miles west of Capel Curig the gentle **Ogwen Valley** fills with the waters of Llyn Ogwen, a post-glacial lake formed behind time-compacted moraine left by the retreating ice. At its western end stands **IDWAL COTTAGE**, the only settlement in the valley and so small it isn't named on most maps, comprising just a mountain rescue centre, a snack bar and a YHA hostel clustered around a car park. The main reason to come here is to tackle some of Wales' most demanding and rewarding hikes (see box, pp.370–371), or start the easier twenty-minute walk to the magnificent, classically formed cirque, **Cwm Idwal**.

The evidence of glacial scouring is so clear here that you wonder why it took geologists so long to work out the process that created these hollowed faces and scored rocks. In 1842, Darwin wrote of his visit with the geologist Adam Sedgewick eleven years earlier, recalling "Neither of us saw a trace of the wonderful glacial phenomena all around us". The cwm's scalloped floor traps the beautifully limpid **Llyn Idwal**, which reflects the precipitous grey cliffs behind, split by the jointed cleft of **Twll Du**, the Devil's Kitchen. Down this channel, a fine watery haze runs off the flanks of **Glyder Fawr**, soaking the crevices where early botanists found the rare arctic-alpine plants (see Contexts, p.489) that were the main motivation for designating Cwm Idwal as Wales' first **National Nature Reserve** (NT) in 1954. The rowan, bilberry and heather in a small but luxuriant fenced-off control area shows how the area might look in a few decades time if the authorities succeed in keeping sheep out of the cwm, though this is proving problematic.

Geomorphologists pay more attention to the twisted rocks beside Twll Du, one of the few places where you can see the downfolded strata of what is known as the Snowdon syncline, evidence that the existing mountains sat between two much larger ranges some 300 million years ago. To their left, the smooth inclines of the Idwal Slabs act as nursery slopes for budding rock climbers.

The nature reserve is accessed by an easy, well-groomed path which leads up from the car park, beside the *Ogwen Falls* snack bar (daily 8.30am–5pm, later on summer weekends). A five-minute walk down the valley from the car park, the road crosses a bridge over the top of **Rhaeadr Ogwen** (Ogwen Falls), which cascades down this step in the valley floor. Before you put your camera away, look under the road bridge, where you'll see the simple mortarless arch of a bridge, part of the original packhorse route that followed the valley before Telford pushed the Holyhead road through.

Practicalities

Five **buses** a day run along the valley between Bethesda and Capel Curig, with connections to Betws-y-Coed and Bangor. A **footpath** covers the length of the valley from Capel Curig to Idwal Cottage, following a five-mile-long packhorse route which runs parallel to the fast and fairly busy road. **Accommodation** in the valley is limited and primitive. Almost four miles west of Capel Curig

Walks from Ogwen: The Glyderau and the Carneddau

The OS 1:25,000 map OL17 ("Snowdon & Conwy Valley") is highly recommended for all these walks. The 1:50,000 Landranger 115 ("Snowdon/Yr Wyddfa") also covers the whole area. For a general layout see our Snowdonia map, pp.356–357.

Either side of the Ogwen Valley, the mountains divide into two ranges: the spiky **Glyderau** to the south, and the more rounded **Carneddau** to the north.

The Glyderau

"Tourists" climb Snowdon, but mountain connoisseurs almost invariably prefer the sharply angled peaks of the **Glyderau**, with their challenging terrain, an entertaining high-level jump, cantilevered rocks and views back to Snowdon. The sheer number of intersecting paths make it almost impossible to choose one definitive route through the range so we've described individual ascents which you can piece together into a loop that suits your group. All times given are for the ascents: expect to take approximately half the time to get back down.

Tryfan: If you've got the head for it, the North Ridge of Tryfan (1 mile; 1hr–1hr 30min; 2000ft ascent) is one of the most rewarding scrambles in the country. It's not as precarious as Snowdon's Crib Goch, but you get a genuine mountaineering feel as the valley floor drops rapidly away and the views stretch further and further along it. The route starts in the lay-by at the head of Idwal Lake and goes left across rising ground, until you strike a path heading straight up following the crest of the ridge to the 3002-foot summit. Anyone who has seen pictures of people jumping the five-foot gap between Adam and Eve, the two chunks of rhyolitic lava which crown this regal mountain, will wonder what the fuss is about until they get up there and see the mountain dropping away on all sides. In theory the leap is trivial, but the consequences of overshooting would be disastrous.

There are two other main routes up Tryfan. The first follows the so-called Miners' Track (2 miles; 2hr; 1350ft ascent) from Idwal Cottage, taking the path to Cwm Idwal then, as it bears sharply to the right, keeping straight ahead and making for the gap on the horizon. This is Bwlch Tryfan, the col between Tryfan and Glyder Fach, from where the South Ridge of Tryfan (800 yards; 30min; 650ft ascent) climbs past the Far South Peak to the summit. This last section is an easy scramble. The second route, which is more often used in descent, follows Heather Terrace (1.5 miles; 2hr; 2000ft ascent), which keeps to a fault in the rock running diagonally across the east face. The start is the same as for the north ridge, but instead of following the ridge, you cut left, heading south until you arrive between the South and the Far South peaks. A right turn then starts your scramble for the summit.

Glyder Fach: The assault on Glyder Fach (3260ft) begins at Bwlch Tryfan, reached either by the Miners' Track from Idwal Cottage or by the South Ridge from Tryfan's summit. The trickier route follows Bristly Ridge (1000 yards; 40min; 900ft ascent), which isn't marked on OS maps but runs steeply south from the col up past some daunting-looking towers of rock. In good conditions, it isn't so difficult, and saves a long hike southeast along a second section of the Miners' Track (1.5 miles; 1hr 30min; 900ft ascent), then west to the top. The summit is a chaotic jumble of huge grey slabs that many people don't bother climbing up, preferring to be photographed on a massive cantilevered rock a few yards away.

🏕 *Gwern Gôf Uchaf* campsite (☎01690/720294, ⊛www.tryfanwales.co.uk) is superbly sited right at the base of Tryfan, and offers £4 **camping**, a modern shower block, and a good 14–berth bunkhouse (£8 per person) with a fully equipped kitchen and a drying room: bring a sleeping bag and food. A mile further on at the western end of Llyn Ogwen, the self-catering *Idwal Cottage* **YHA hostel** (☎0870/770 5874, ✉idwal@yha.org.uk; Feb–Oct and some

Glyder Fawr: From Glyder Fach, it is an easy enough stroll to the 3280-foot summit of Glyder Fawr (1 mile; 40min; 200ft ascent), reached by skirting round the tortured rock formations of Castell y Gwynt (the Castle of the Winds) then following a cairn-marked path to the dramatic summit of frost-shattered slabs angled like ancient headstones.

Glyder Fawr is normally approached directly from Idwal Cottage, following the Devil's Kitchen Route (2.5 miles; 3hr; 2300ft ascent) past Idwal Cottage, then to the left of the Devil's Kitchen, zigzagging up to a lake-filled plateau. Follow the path to the right of the lake; then, where paths cross, turn left for the summit.

A southern approach to Glyder Fawr (3 miles; 2hr 30min; 2100ft ascent) leaves from beside the YHA hostel at Pen-y-Pass (see p.381), following a "courtesy path" marked at key points by faint red flashes of paint. It rises steeply behind the hostel heading northwest, but turns north for the summit to avoid straying onto the screes on the flanks of the neighbouring mountain, Esgair Felen.

The Carneddau

The appearance of the **Carneddau** could hardly be in greater contrast to the jagged edges of the Glyderau, on the other side of the Ogwen Valley. These peaceful giants, which present the longest stretch of ground over three thousand feet in England and Wales, form a rounded plateau stretching to the cliffs of Penmaenmawr on the north coast. The sound of a raven in the neighbouring mist-filled cwms, and the occasional wild pony, can often be your only company on inclement days, but in fine weather the easy walking and roof-of-the-world views make for a satisfying day out.

Though the tops are fairly flat once you're up there, getting to them can be a hard slog. The start from Idwal Cottage is the most strenuous, requiring a long push up the shaley south ridge from the stile beside the road bridge at the foot of Ogwen Lake. If you can, avoid this in favour of the fine Carneddau loop (9 miles; 5hr; 3500ft ascent), starting from the lay-by at the head of the lake near Tal y Llyn Ogwen farm and taking in the range's four mighty southern peaks. The path keeps to the right of the farm, then follows boggy land by a stream towards its source, Ffynnon Lloer, before turning left up the east ridge of Pen yr Ole Wen (3212ft), with its magnificent view down into Nant Ffrancon and back to Tryfan. In clear weather, you can see the route running north past Carnedd Fach, and what looks to be a huge artificial mound, to Carnedd Dafydd (3425ft). After a short easterly descent, the path skirts the steep Ysgolion Duon cliffs, then climbs over stones to the broad, arched top of Carnedd Llywelyn (3491ft), the highest of the Carneddau and surpassed in Wales only by two of Snowdon's peaks, Yr Wyddfa and Crib-y-ddysgl.

For little extra effort, enthusiasts can summit Yr Elen (3152ft), a short distance to the northeast, but most will be content with the easterly descent to Craig yr Ysfa, a sheer cliff which drops away into the vast amphitheatre of Cwm Eigiau to the north. Continuing with care, skirt around the north of Ffynnon Llugwy reservoir and climb to the grassy top of Penyrhelgi-du (2733ft), from where there's a steady broad-ridged descent to the road near Helyg. The mile-long trek back west to the starting point is best done on the old packhorse route running parallel to the A5, and linked to it occasionally by footpaths.

winter weekends) has bunks for £17–19 and camping for £9, but no meals. The only other amenity in the valley is the *Ogwen Falls* snack bar (see above).

Llanberis and Snowdon

Mention **LLANBERIS**, ten miles west of Capel Curig, to any mountain enthusiast and **Snowdon** immediately springs to mind. The two seem inseparable, not least because of the five-mile-long umbilical cord of the **Snowdon Mountain Railway** (see p.374), Britain's only rack and pinion railway, which bonds the town to the summit, and the popular path running parallel to the tracks (see box, p.378). Llanberis is the nearest you'll get in Wales to an alpine climbing village, its single main street thronged with weather-beaten walkers and climbers decked out in Gore-Tex and fleece, high fashion for what is otherwise a dowdy town. Most are Snowdon-bound, others are just making use of abundant budget accommodation and the best facilities this side of Betws-y-Coed.

At the same time, Llanberis is very much a Welsh rural community, albeit a depleted one now that slate is no longer being torn from the flanks of Elidir Fawr, the mountain separated from the town by the twin lakes of Llyn Padarn

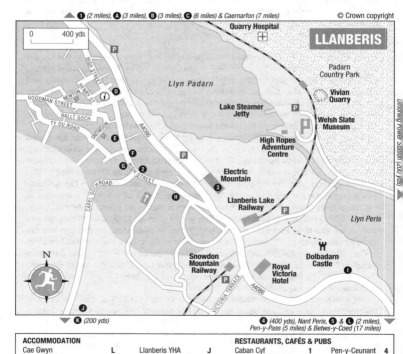

ACCOMMODATION				RESTAURANTS, CAFÉS & PUBS			
Cae Gwyn	L	Llanberis YHA	J	Caban Cyf	1	Pen-y-Ceunant	4
Dolafon Hotel	H	Llwyn Celyn Bach	K	Connections Café	3	Pete's Eats	D
Erw Fair	E	Pete's Sleeps	D	The Heights	F	Ty'n Rhos	C
Graianfryn	B	Plas Coch	G	The Peak Restaurant	2	Vaynol Arms	5
The Heights	F	Snowdon Cottage	I				
Jesse James' Bunkhouse	A	Ty'n Rhos	C				

and Llyn Peris. The **quarries**, which for the best part of two centuries employed up to three thousand men to chisel out the precious slabs, closed in 1969, leaving a vast staircase of sixty-foot-high terraced platforms as a testament to their labours. At much the same time, proposals were tabled for a power station to be built on the former quarry sites. Environmentalists were incensed that this fragile spot on the fringes of the national park could be desecrated. The people of Llanberis, still reeling from the closure of the quarries, had no such qualms, and in the end both parties were pacified: the project went ahead underground.

Arrival, information and accommodation

With no train or National Express services, the easiest way to get here is by **bus**: #85 from Bangor, #88/9a from Caernarfon or the #S1 Snowdon Sherpa service. All stop along High Street outside either of the two outdoor equipment shops, both just a few steps from the town's **tourist office**, 41b High St (Easter–Oct daily 9.30am–4.30pm; Nov–Easter Mon & Fri–Sun 10.30am–3.30pm; ☎01286/870765, ✉llanberis.tic@gwynedd.gov.uk). There's **internet** access at *Pete's Eats* and free wi-fi at *Caban Cyf* (see p.377 for both).

There's a wealth of low-cost **accommodation** and **campsites** in or close to town, as well as up at Pen-y-Pass (see p.381). Luxurious places are harder to find, so if you have your own transport and don't mind being a few miles further from the mountain, you might prefer to stay in places listed under Caernarfon or Bangor.

Hotels and guesthouses

Dolafon Hotel High St ☎01286/870993, ⓦwww.dolafon.com. Appealing, well-priced B&B in its own grounds, with spacious, comfortable rooms. ③

Erw Fair High St ☎01286/872400, ⓦwww.erwfair.com. Large house with tidy B&B rooms, (half of them en suite), a comfy lounge and hearty breakfasts. ②–③

Graianfryn Penisarwaun, 3 miles northwest of Llanberis ☎01286/871007, ⓦwww.fastasleep.me.uk. An exclusively vegetarian and vegan wholefood B&B in a Victorian farmhouse. Home-grown vegetables are used in the three-course evening meals (£18). ②

The Heights 74 High St ☎01286/871179, ⓦwww.heightshotel.co.uk. B&B catering primarily to the walking and climbing set, with comfortable en-suite rooms with TV, dorms (see "Hostels" below) and the liveliest bar in town. ②

🏃 **Plas Coch** High St ☎01286/872122, ⓦwww.plas-coch.co.uk. One of the nicest places in town, tastefully renovated and maintained to a high standard, with en-suite rooms plus a separate bathroom with tub for post-hike soaks. Great breakfasts too, plus free internet and wi-fi. There's one cheaper attic room (②). ③

Snowdon Cottage A4086, 0.5 miles southeast of central Llanberis ☎01286/872015. Three-room B&B (including a single at £27) in a renovated eighteenth-century cottage with a cosy guest lounge and open fire that's perfect after a blustery

day in the hills. Run by a walker who's always keen to help get you on the trail. ②

Ty'n Rhos Llanddeiniolen, 6 miles northwest of Llanberis ☎01248/670489, ⓦwww.tynrhos.co.uk. The plushly furnished rooms (some with mountain views) in this peaceful country house are little havens, but the cosy lounge, and airy conservatory will lure you out, as should the superb house restaurant. ⑤, suites ⑦

Hostels, bunkhouses and campsites

Cae Gwyn Nant Peris, 2 miles southeast of Llanberis ☎01286/870718. Fairly basic campsite and primitive bunkhouse (bring everything) with showers, almost opposite the *Vaynol Arms* pub towards Pen-y-Pass. Budget-minded climbers and mountain bikers make up the bulk of the clientele. Camping £5 per person, bunkhouse £10.

The Heights 74 High St ☎01286/871179, ⓦwww.heightshotel.co.uk. Accommodation in eight-bed dorms in *The Heights* hotel (see above). No self-catering facilities, and you'll need to bring a sleeping bag or duvet; towels can be rented (£2.50). Bed only £12.50, B&B £17.50.

Jesse James' Bunkhouse Buarth y Clytiau, Penisarwaun ☎01286/870521. The original bunkhouse, large, rambling, clean and efficiently run since 1966 by a former mountain guide. Dorm beds £12–15 a night (sleeping bag and towel required) or separate, slightly comfier self-contained rooms (mostly £25 a head). Take the A4086 two miles towards Caernarfon, turn right onto the A4244 and continue for a mile. No credit cards; phone ahead. ❷

Llanberis YHA Llwyn Celyn ☎ 0870/770 5928, ⒺⒺ llanberis@yha.org.uk. Well-appointed but not especially atmospheric YHA hostel with bunks (£16–18) and some twin rooms, a 700-yard uphill slog along Capel Goch Rd. ❶

Llwyn Celyn Bach Capel Coch Rd ☎ 01286/870923. Farmer's field site 200 yards beyond the *Llanberis YHA* hostel, with showers and toilets. £4 per person.

Pete's Sleeps 40 High St ☎ 01286/872135, ⓌⓌ www.petes-eats.co.uk. Fairly basic dorms (£13 per bed) above *Pete's Eats* café (see p.377), plus a couple of twin rooms (for just £32 per room without breakfast) with access to self-catering facilities. ❶

The town and around

At first acquaintance Llanberis isn't a stunning-looking place. Snowdon's summit isn't visible from most of the town and the hillside on the northern side to Llyn Padarn and Llyn Peris has been chewed away by decades of slate mining, leaving tiers of blue–grey rubble covering the mountainside. Yet it's an oddly compelling scene, especially when low cloud shrouds the workings and the hilltop Dolbadarn Castle looms from the murk like a lonely sentinel.

Though such days are great for exploring the Dinorwig Slate Quarries and the Welsh Slate Museum, if the weather is really bad you're better off underground visiting the Dinorwig Power Station. When the sun breaks out there's also a choice of two narrow-gauge railways, the most celebrated being the wonderful Snowdon Mountain Railway to Wales' highest point.

Llanberis also offers myriad activities – from playing around in boats on the lake to scrambling, mountain biking and paragliding.

Snowdon Mountain Railway

The **Snowdon Mountain Railway** (mid-March to Oct 6–25 trains daily; ☎ 0870/720 0033, ⓌⓌ www.snowdonrailway.co.uk; summit return £22) was completed in 1896, and trains (sometimes pushed by seventy-year-old steam locos) still climb to the summit in just under an hour. The most heavily maintained track in Britain, the rails follow the shallowest approach to the top of Snowdon, struggling for five miles and three thousand feet up a mostly one-in-eight gradient.

Times and type of locomotive vary with demand and season, but whether hauled by steam or diesel, the full round trip takes two and a half hours, with half an hour on top. In summer (especially July, Aug and weekends in Sept) trains are often full, so book a day or so in advance. Those who reserve a day in advance by phone (£3.50 booking fee) and travel on the 9am train go for half price. If you walk up by one of the routes detailed in the box on pp.378–379, you can still take the train down.

The railway **starts** at the southeastern end of Llanberis opposite the *Royal Victoria Hotel*, and climbs past the summertime swimming hole at Bishop's Falls to the new *Hafod Eryri* **summit** café (mid-May to Oct). Inside is a bar and a post office where, for a few pence, you can buy a "Railway Stamp" to affix to your letter – along with the Royal Mail one – thereby entitling you to use the highest postbox in the UK and enchant your friends with a "Summit of Snowdon – Copa'r Wyddfa" postmark. In bad weather, trains terminate at **Clogwyn station**, thirty minutes' walk from the summit.

For a full description of Snowdon and walks on the mountain, see pp.377–380.

Dolbadarn Castle and the Dinorwig Power Station

Perched on a rock between the twin lakes of Llyn Padarn and Llyn Peris, where it once guarded the mouth of the Llanberis Pass, a single dramatic tower and some scattered masonry are all that remain of **Dolbadarn Castle** (unrestricted access; CADW). Built in the thirteenth century, its construction is usually attributed to Llywelyn ap Iorwerth ("the Great"), even if its circular keep is more redolent of a Norman Marcher fort than a native Welsh castle. Close up, there's not a lot to look at, but, viewed across Llyn Padarn and framed by the grey crags of the Pass behind, it is easy to see why both Richard Wilson and Turner came to paint it.

Views to the north are dominated by the entrance to the **Dinorwig Pumped Storage Power Station**, hollowed out of the ground in the mid-1970s starting just five years after the quarries closed. Unlike most power stations, this actually consumes more electricity than it produces, but benefits the national grid by being able to instantly produce electricity to cope with the early evening surge in demand. Within ten seconds it can attain its maximum power output (1800 megawatts), by letting the contents of the Marchlyn Mawr reservoir rapidly empty through its turbines into Llyn Peris; then, when the demand lessens, pumping it up again. The hour-long **bus tour** (Easter–Oct daily, plus selected winter days; ☎01286/870636, ⑩ www.electricmountain.co.uk; £7) through its rock-hewn tunnels to the powerhouse below is one of Snowdonia's more popular rainy day activities, so book ahead if the weather turns foul.

Tours leave roughly every half-hour from the **Electric Mountain complex** (June–Aug daily 9.30am–5.30pm; Sept–May daily 10am–4.30pm; free) by the lake on the A4086, which bypasses the town centre. Electric Mountain also contains a good café (see p.377) and an interesting little **boat display** featuring a twelfth-century wooden craft which was discovered near the lake in the 1970s.

Padarn Country Park: the Welsh Slate Museum and the Llanberis Lake Railway

At **Padarn Country Park** (unrestricted access), across Llyn Padarn from Llanberis, lakeside oak woods are gradually recolonizing the discarded workings of the defunct **Dinorwig Slate Quarries**, formerly one of the largest slate quarries in the world. Equipment and engines that once hauled materials up inclined tramways have been partly restored and punctuate the paths which link the levels chiselled out of the hillside. One of the most interesting spots is right near the parking area, where you can walk through a rock arch to the flooded **Vivian Quarry**, a dramatic spot and a popular destination for **scuba divers**. Leaflets outlining the various walking trails are available for a few pence from a small kiosk nearby, or you can just set off meandering around the old slate workings and through the ancient woodlands of Coed Dinorwig, making for the period-furnished **Quarry Hospital** (May–Sept 11am–4.45pm; free), where the resident surgeon patched up gruesome injuries from gunpowder blasts and falling rock.

The fort-like complex of buildings at the base of the main tramway was once the quarry's maintenance workshops, but now houses the **Welsh Slate Museum** (Easter–Oct daily 10am–5pm; Nov–Easter daily except Sat 10am–4pm; ⑩ www.nmgw.ac.uk; free). The fifty-foot-diameter water wheel that once powered cutting machines through a cat's cradle of lineshafts, countershafts and flapping belts still turns, but no longer drives the machinery. Though most of the equipment dates back to the early part of the twentieth century, it was still in use until the quarries closed and is quite familiar to the former quarry workers who demonstrate their skills at turning an inch-thick slab of slate into six, even eight, perfectly smooth slivers. The slate was delivered to the slate-dressing sheds by means of a maze of tramways, cranes and rope lifts, all kept in good order in the

▲ Llanberis Lake Railway

fitting and repair shops. As you pass through, look out for the scales used to calculate the price each rock cutter would be paid for his work, before the typical deductions for the amount of rope and gunpowder he used to extract the diverse types of slate. Some of these are displayed nearby and range from mottled burgundy and bottle green to every shade of grey. Look out, too, for the set of four slate workers' cottages transported to the site from nearby Tanygrisiau and now kitted out in the style of historical periods related to the quarries.

To keep everything in working order, the craftsmen here operate an ageing foundry, producing pieces for the scattered branches of the National Museum of Wales, as well as repairing the rolling stock that plies the adjacent **Llanberis Lake Railway** (July & Aug 4–10 services daily; mid-March to June, Sept & Oct 4–5 services daily; £6.50 return). The original railway, which from 1843 to 1961 transported slate and workers between the Dinorwig quarries and Port Dinorwig on the Menai Strait, was sold for scrap. Enthusiasts subsequently relaid a tame two-mile stretch to Pen Llyn along the shores of Lake Padarn. The smoking tank engine takes about forty minutes for the round trip, and although there's nothing much to do at the other end, you might want to stop off halfway back at Cei Llydan station and spend time at the **Cwm Derwen Visitor Centre** (generally open when trains are running; free), which illustrates the history of the woodland that spreads up the slopes behind the rail tracks.

Throughout summer, a small jetty near the slate museum is home to the *Snowdon Star*, a lake steamer which runs forty-minute narrated **cruises** on Llyn Padarn (May–Oct daily 11am–5pm; £5).

Activities

By far the most popular activity around Llanberis is getting out on foot, particularly on Snowdon, whose vast, steep-sided cwms have become a summer playground for rock athletes picking their way up impossibly sheer faces. If you're not equipped or confident enough to go **climbing** or **scrambling** by yourself, engage the services of one of the many mountain guides based around Llanberis such as High Trek Snowdonia, Tal y Waen, Deiniolen (☏01286/871232,

@ www.climbing-wales.co.uk), which does good packages. When inclement weather forces climbers off the crags, the keen ones make straight for the huge indoor climbing wall at **Beacon Climbing Centre**, four miles west from Llanberis in Ceunant (Mon–Fri 11am–10pm, Sat & Sun 10am–10pm; T01286/650045, @ www.beaconclimbing.com; £6), which offers taster sessions (£50 total for 1–3 people).

As well as being one of the most popular walking routes up Snowdon, the **Llanberis Path** (see box, p.378) is designated a bridleway, making it, the Snowdon Ranger Path and the Pitt's Head Track to Rhyd-Ddu, open for **cyclists**. A voluntary agreement bans bike access to and from the summit tracks between 10am and 5pm from May to September, but otherwise these paths are open to cyclists. Currently, there is no bike rental in Llanberis: Caernarfon is the closest.

Further challenges await at the **High Ropes Adventure Centre**, by the slate museum (T01286/872310, @ www.ropesandladders.co.uk), where for £20 you get a couple of hours with an instructor helping you push your boundaries among the treetops.

Eating, drinking and entertainment

While Llanberis isn't spilling over with good places to **eat**, it does have something to suit all pockets. Pretty much all there is lies on High Street, where you'll find a couple of likeable **pubs**. Alternatively, Bangor and Caernarfon are both only eight miles away.

Caban Cyf Yr Hen Ysgol, Brynrefail, 2.3 miles northwest of Llanberis. Relaxed, licensed daytime café, with big windows overlooking the woods. Predominantly organic, local or fair-trade ingredients go into their breakfasts (£4–6), sandwiches, baguettes and mains such as bean burritos (£5.25) and a range of blackboard specials. A great place to hang out on a wet day. Free wi-fi.

Connections Café Electric Mountain building. Good spacious café with outdoor seating and a range of espresso coffees, jumbo rolls and baguettes, Welsh rarebit, daily specials (£6) and rich ice cream.

The Heights 74 High St. One of the liveliest bars in town, with real ales, sports TV, and a range of fairly basic inexpensive meals such as veg or meat lasagne, curry and gammon steak (£7.50–10).

The Peak Restaurant 86 High St T01286/872777. This unflashy open-kitchen restaurant serves easily the best food in Llanberis. Try the toasted haloumi with roast vegetable couscous and mint salad (£6), perhaps followed by their signature bouillabaisse with fresh prawns, salmon and halibut (£17) and a home-made dessert. Bookings recommended. Open Wed–Sun evenings; booking advised.

Pen-y-Ceunant Snowdon Path @ www.ceunant .co.uk. Snug, slate-floored eighteenth-century cottage, 400 yards steeply uphill along the Llanberis Path, serving hikers and all comers with Welsh teas, coffee and snacks until 9pm daily. Visit if only to see the cottage, decorated with paintings and prints by Kyffin Williams and other Welsh artists.

Pete's Eats 40 High St. Climbers fortify themselves on Pete's large portions of top-value caff food and a few more delicate dishes. Free jukebox, heaps of magazines and maps to browse, and cheap internet access. Daily 8am–8pm or later.

Ty'n Rhos Llanddeiniolen, 6 miles northwest of Llanberis T01248/670489, @ www.tynrhos.co.uk. Even if you're not staying here it's worth a visit for the delicious and immaculately presented three-course dinner (£35). Local Welsh produce is given a French, fine-dining twist in dishes such as fillet of Welsh beef with foie gras. There's a great wine list, too.

Vaynol Arms Nant Peris, 2 miles east of Llanberis. Cosy pub, the only one before Pen-y-Gwryd, with good beer, decent meals and a convivial atmosphere. Full of locals midweek, and climbers and campers at weekends.

Snowdon

The highest British mountain south of the Scottish Grampians, the **Snowdon** massif (3650ft) forms a star of shattered ridges with three major peaks – Crib Goch, Crib-y-ddysgl and Y Lliwedd – and the summit, **Yr Wyddfa**, crowning the lot. If

All the following paths are easy to follow in good weather, but the 1:25,000 OS Explorer OL17 map ("Snowdon & Conwy Valley") is still recommended. There's also a series of leaflets (40p each, available from visitor centres) detailing the individual routes up the mountain.

Llanberis Path

The easiest and longest route up Snowdon, the **Llanberis Path** (5 miles to summit; 3hr; 3200ft ascent), following the rail line, is widely scorned by the sort of serious hiker who wouldn't use the railway or deign to visit the summit café. Victoria Terrace runs off the A4086 opposite the *Royal Victoria Hotel* and becomes a path which soon passes the *Pen-y-Ceunant* tearoom (see p.377). The summit gradually comes into view as you rise towards the midway point and the *Halfway House Café* (June–Sept daily 10am–5pm; Easter–June & Sept–Dec weekends 10am–5pm). From here there are views of Clogwyn Du'r Arddu (The Black Cliff, or "Cloggy" to its friends), an ominous sheet of rock which frames a small lake. Today, climbers virtually sprint up the face, which caused an early exponent to lament, "No breach seems either possible or desirable along the whole extent of the west buttress. Though there is the faintest of faint hopes for a human fly rather on the left side." The path next passes Clogwyn station, from where you get a great view down onto the Llanberis Pass. This soon disappears as the path gets steeper, passing the low remains of stables where mule trains used to rest. Bwlch Glas (Green Pass) is marked by the "Finger Stone" where the Snowdon Ranger Path (see opposite) and three routes coming up from Pen-y-Pass join the Llanberis Path for the final ascent to Yr Wyddfa. Llanberis Path is the route used by the annual Snowdon Race which takes place on the second Saturday in July, with the leading runners recording times of only a little over an hour for the combined ascent and descent.

The Miners' Track

The **Miners' Track** (4 miles to summit; 2hr 30min; 2400ft ascent) is the easiest of the three routes up from Pen-y-Pass. Leaving the car park, a broad track leads south then west to the former copper mines in Cwm Dyli. Dilapidated remains of the crushing mill perch on the shores of Llyn Llydaw, a tarn-turned-reservoir with one of the worst eyesores in the park, an overground pipeline slicing across Snowdon's east face to the power station in Nantgwynant. Skirting around the right of the lake, the path climbs more steeply to the lake-filled Cwm Glaslyn, then again to Upper Glaslyn, from where the measured steps of those ahead warn of the impending switchback ascent to the junction with the Llanberis Path.

Pig Track

The stonier **Pig Track** (3.5 miles to summit; 2hr 30min; 2400ft ascent) is really just a shorter and steeper variation on the Miners' Track, leaving from the western end of the Pen-y-Pass car park and climbing up to Bwlch y Moch (the Pass of the Pigs), which gives the route its name. Ignore the scramble up to Crib Goch (part of the Snowdon Horseshoe) and traverse below the rocky ridge looking down on Llyn Llydaw and those pacing the Miners' Track, content that you're already 500ft up on them. They'll soon catch up, as the two tracks meet just before the zigzag up to the Llanberis Path. The path is also known as the PYG track, supposedly after the nearby *Pen Y Gwryd Hotel*: no one seems able to settle the argument.

Snowdon Horseshoe

Some claim that the **Snowdon Horseshoe** (8 miles round; 5–7hr; 3200ft ascent) is one of the finest ridge walks in Europe. The route makes a full anticlockwise circuit around the three glacier-graven cwms of Upper Glaslyn, Glaslyn and Llydaw. Not to be taken lightly, it includes the knife-edge traverse of Crib Goch. Every summer's day, dozens of people find themselves straddling the lip, empty space on either side, and wishing they weren't there. In winter conditions, an ice axe and crampons are the minimum requirement. The path follows the Pig Track to Bwlch y Moch, then pitches right for the moderate scramble up to Crib Goch. If you baulk at any of this, turn back. If not, wait your turn, then painstakingly pick your way along the sensational ridge to Crib-y-ddysgl (3494ft), from where it's an easy descent to Bwlch Glas and on to Yr Wyddfa. Having ticked off Wales' two highest peaks, turn southwest for a couple of hundred yards to a marker stone where the Watkin Path (see below) drops away to the east. Follow it down to the stretched saddle of Bwlch-y-Saethau (Pass of the Arrows), then onto the cairn at Bwlch Ciliau from where the Watkin Path descends to Nantgwynant. Ignore that route, continuing straight on up the cliff-lined northwest ridge of Y Lliwedd (2930ft), then descend to where you see the scrappy but safe path down to Llyn Llydaw and the Miners' Track.

Snowdon Ranger Path

Many of the earliest Snowdon climbers engaged the services of the Snowdon Ranger, who led them up the comparatively long and dull but easy **Snowdon Ranger Path** (4 miles to summit; 3hr; 3100ft ascent), on the now unfashionable south side of the mountain. The path starts from the *Snowdon Ranger YHA Hostel* (see p.383) on the shores of Llyn Cwellyn, five miles northwest of Beddgelert. To the left of the hostel, a path leads up a track then ascends, steeply flattening out to cross sometimes boggy grass, eventually skirting to the right of the impressive Clogwyn Du'r Arddu cliffs (see Llanberis Path, opposite). This is another steep ascent that eventually meets the Llanberis Path at Bwlch Glas.

Rhyd Ddu Track

The **Rhyd Ddu Track** (4 miles to summit; 3hr; 2900ft ascent) has two branches, one starting from Pitt's Head Rock, two and a half miles northwest of Beddgelert, the other from the national park car park in Rhyd Ddu, a mile beyond that. They join up after less than a mile's walk across stony, walled grazing land, and after crossing a kissing gate continue to the northwest up to the stunning final section along the rim of Cwm Clogwyn and the south ridge of Yr Wyddfa. The Welsh Highland Railway (or the #S4 bus) makes it easy to turn this and the Snowdon Ranger Path into a loop.

Watkin Path

The most spectacular of the southern routes up Snowdon, the **Watkin Path** (4 miles to summit; 3hr; 3350ft ascent), is also the one with the greatest height gain. From Bethania Bridge, three miles northeast of Beddgelert in Nantgwynant, the path starts on a broad track through oaks opening up to long views of a series of cataracts. Ascend beside these to a disused inclined tramway where the track narrows before reaching the natural amphitheatre of Cwm Llan. The ruins of the South Snowdon Slate Works only briefly distract you from Gladstone Rock, at which, in 1892, the 83-year-old Liberal statesman, then in his fourth term as British Prime Minister, officially opened the route. A narrower path wheels left around the base of Craig Ddu, then starts the steep ascent past Carnedd Arthur to Bwlch Ciliau, the saddle between Y Lliwedd (see Snowdon Horseshoe opposite) and the true summit (Yr Wyddfa), then turning right for the final climb to the top. The Watkin Path can be easily turned into a loop by descending the top section of the Pitt's Head Track then continuing down Bwlch Main to the saddle and cutting east into Cwm Llan and down.

height were its only quality, it would be popular, but Snowdon also sports some of the finest walking and scrambling in Wales. Its Welsh name, Eryri, is derived from either *eryr* (land of eagles) or *eira* (land of snow); since the eagles have long gone, the latter is more appropriate, with winter snows lingering well into April.

Some hardened outdoor enthusiasts dismiss Snowdon as overused, and it certainly can be crowded. A thousand visitors a day press into the postbox-red carriages of the Snowdon Mountain Railway (see p.374), while another fifteen hundred pound the well-maintained paths to make this Britain's most-climbed mountain. Opprobrium is chiefly levelled at the train for its mere existence, and at the brand new **Hafod Eryri** ("dwelling place atop Snowdon"), café and bar on the summit for selling the country's highest pint of beer. But at least there's a warm place for walkers to rest, and those unable to walk up have the chance of seeing the **view** over most of north Wales — and even across to Ireland on exceptionally clear days.

There is no longer a tumulus on the top of Snowdon, but the Welsh for the highest point, Yr Wyddfa, means "The Burial Place" — near proof that people have been climbing the mountain for millennia. More recently, early ascents were for botanical or geological reasons — 500-million-year-old fossil shells can be found near the summit from when Snowdon was on the sea bottom — but the Welsh naturalist Thomas Pennant came up here mainly for pleasure, and in 1773, his description of the dawn view from the summit in his *Journey to Snowdon* encouraged many to follow. Some were guided by the Snowdon Ranger, Evan Roberts, from his house on the south side (now a YHA hostel), but the rapidly improving facilities in Llanberis soon shifted the balance in favour of the easier Llanberis Path, a route later followed by the railway. This remains one of the most popular routes, though many prefer the three shorter and steeper ones from the Pen-y-Pass car park at the top of the Llanberis Pass. By far the most dramatic, if also the most dangerous, is the wonderful Snowdon Horseshoe, which calls at all four of the high peaks.

The Llanberis Pass and Pen-y-Pass

The steady Llanberis Path which grinds up Snowdon's gentlest ascent may be the most popular single route up the mountain, but more walkers start from the

---

King Arthur and Snowdon

From the departure of the Romans until the tenth century, Welsh history is pervaded by **legends** of King Arthur (see p.90), Gwrtheryn (Vortigern) and Myrddin (Merlin; see p.162). Arthur's British (as opposed to Anglo-Saxon) blood gives him a firm place in Welsh hearts, and while Caerleon in southeast Wales lays a powerful, though not incontestable, claim to being the site of Arthur's court, Snowdon is often held to be his home.

It was atop Dinas Emrys, the seat of Gwrtheryn's realm near Beddgelert, that the most potent symbol of Welsh independence, the Red Dragon, earned its colours. The Celtic king, Gwrtheryn, was trying to build a fortress to protect himself from the Saxons, but each night the earth swallowed the masonry. Myrddin divined this to be caused by two dragons sleeping underground: one white, the other red. When woken, they fought unendingly, symbolizing the Red Dragon of Wales' perpetual battle with the White Dragon of the Saxons.

Arthur's domain was higher up the mountain. Llyn Llydaw aspires to being the lake into which Bedivere cast Arthur's sword, Excalibur, after Arthur was mortally wounded by an arrow while on the point of vanquishing his nephew Modred at Bwlch-y-Saethau (The Pass of the Arrows), thirteen hundred feet above the lake.

lofty saddle at the top of the **Llanberis Pass**, the deepest, narrowest and craggiest of Snowdonia's passes, running five miles east from Llanberis itself. At its head is the YHA hostel, café and car park that make up **PEN-Y-PASS**, the base for the Miners' Track, the Pig Track and the demanding Snowdon Horseshoe (see box, p.378). These all leave from the car park, while a route up Glyder Fawr (see box, p.371) follows a "courtesy path" to the west of the hostel.

Frequent #S1 Snowdon Sherpa **buses** travel daily to Pen-y-Pass, worth catching even if you have a car, since the Pen-y-Pass car park is almost always full and costs £4 (£2 after noon). If you use the park-and-ride facility at the bottom of the pass close to the *Vaynol Arms*: parking costs £4 all day and entitles you to a free all-day Snowdon Sherpa bus pass.

The only **accommodation** at Pen-y-Pass is the **YHA hostel** (℡0870/770 5990, @penypass@yha.org.uk; £18; open all year), which has full daytime access, limited free parking, a few two-bedded rooms, plus videos on climbing and kayaking and a bar licence. A mile east is the nearest **pub** with accommodation, the 🍴 *Pen-y-Gwryd Hotel* (℡01286/870211, ⊛www.pyg.co.uk; ❺; two-night minimum at weekends; closed Nov & Dec, open weekends only Jan & Feb), a wonderfully rustic place with ageing furniture, magnificent Edwardian bathrooms, an outdoor sauna, and a lot of muddy boots in the bar. Amongst others, the first successful expedition up Mount Everest in 1953 stayed at the hotel while doing final equipment testing, and took time out to sign the ceiling: Edmund Hillary, Chris Bonnington, Doug Scott and Portmeirion designer Clough Williams-Ellis are all there. The Everest team also brought back a piece of the mountain, which now sits in pride of place in the bar. Rooms (some en suite) are priced per person, and are good value for singles. If you stay, expect a congenial though somewhat regimented atmosphere and lots of plain home cooking (£28 for a five-course meal).

Beddgelert and around

At the confluence of the Glaslyn and Colwyn rivers on the south flank of Snowdon sits the picture-postcard village of **BEDDGELERT**. The village comprises little more than a few dozen hard grey houses, but is curiously enchanting, with its front gardens and window boxes bursting with flowers, and lots of spots to mooch, eat and drink. Tourists already throng Beddgelert on sunny summer days and the crowds are likely to become denser from 2009, when it will become the principal halt on the Welsh Highland Railway (see p.412) between Caernarfon and Porthmadog.

If you tire of the village, it's easy enough to embark on one of the longer walks described in the box on p.383. A shorter and more celebrated excursion takes you four hundred yards south, along the right bank of the Glaslyn, to the spot that gives the village its name, **Gelert's Grave** (*bedd* means "burial place"). A railed-off enclosure in a field marks the final resting place of Prince Llywelyn ap Iorwerth's faithful dog, Gelert, who was left in charge of the prince's infant son while he went hunting. On his return, the child was gone and the hound's muzzle was soaked in blood. Jumping to conclusions, the impetuous Llywelyn slew the dog, only to find the child safely asleep beneath its cot and a dead wolf beside him. Llywelyn hurried to his dog, which licked his hand as it died. In fact, the story is an eighteenth-century invention by a local publican, though it's suceeded in luring punters ever since. The real source of the name is probably the grave of Celert, a sixth-century British saint who supposedly lived hereabouts.

Beddgelert makes less of its other legendary animal, **Rupert the Bear**. Arthur Bestall, who wrote and illustrated the *Daily Express* cartoon strip for thirty years from 1935, spent much of his later years in Beddgelert, and "The Followers of Rupert Bear" have contributed to the planting of Cae Gel, a picnic meadow near the banks of the River Glasyln, just over the footbridge in town.

Almost a mile north on the A498, the red-brown stain on the hillside opposite identifies the family-oriented **Sygun Copper Mine** (daily: Easter–Oct 9.30am–5pm; Nov–Easter 10.30am–4pm; ⓦ www.syguncoppermine.co.uk; £8), whose ore drew first the Romans, then nineteenth-century prospectors. The dilapidated remains of what was once the valley's prime source of income have now been restored and made safe for the cool (9°C) 45-minute self-guided **tour** up through the multiple levels of tunnels and galleries. At stations along the way the disembodied voice of a miner describes his working life. Afterwards, you're free to potter around the ore-crushing and separation equipment, or go gold panning (£2).

For something more active, there's good **mountain biking** for all abilities in the Beddgelert Forest a mile out on the Caernarfon road and a mile uphill from the *Beddgelert Forest Campsite* (see below). **Bike rental** is available from Beddgelert Bikes (☎01766/890434, ⓦ www.beddgelertbikes.co.uk; £10/20 for two hours/full day).

Practicalities

Beddgelert is on two **bus** routes: the #S4 Snowdon Sherpa from Caernarfon and the #S97 between Betws-y-Coed, Pen-y-Pass and Porthmadog. All stop on the main street just yards from the **tourist office** (Easter–Oct daily 9.30am–5.30pm; Nov–Easter Fri, Sat & Sun 9.30am–4.30pm; ☎01766/890615, ⓦ www.beddgelerttourism.com). There's a **post office** in the centre of the village, but no banks and only limited grocery shopping.

Accommodation

Accommodation is limited and quite expensive. If you're wanting to make an early start on the Snowdon walks you'll find the hostels better sited.

Hotels and guesthouses

Beddgelert Bistro & Antiques Waterloo House ☎01766/890543. Three attractive en-suite rooms, above a restaurant and tearoom, directly opposite the bridge. ❷

Colwyn A498 ☎01766/890276, ⓦ www .beddgelertguesthouse.co.uk. Central 300-year-old cottage guesthouse with comfortable, renovated rooms, a beamed lounge and an open fire. ❸

🏃 **Sygun Fawr** 0.7 miles northeast off the A498 ☎01766/890258, ⓦ www.sygunfawr.co.uk. This partly seventeenth-century country house in its own grounds is the pick of the local hotels. Some of its comfy rooms have views of Snowdon, and there are two- and three-night deals which include dinner at the superb restaurant (see below). ❺

Hostels and campsites

Beddgelert Forest Campsite A498 ☎01766/890288, ⓦ www.forestholidays.co.uk.

Excellent, reasonably priced campsite a mile out of the village with two-person pitches for £9–14 (depending on time of year) and hiker/biker sites for £5 per person. Closed Nov to mid-Dec.

Bryn Dinas Bunkhouse Nantgwynant, 3 miles northeast on the A498 ☎01766/890234, ⓦ www .bryndinasbunkhouse.co.uk. At the foot of the Watkin Path, with fully self-catering cabins sleeping one to six (£10 per person). Bring a sleeping bag.

Bryn Gwynant YHA Hostel A498, 4 miles northeast of Beddgelert ☎0870/770 5732, ⓔ bryngwynant @yha.org.uk. Beautifully sited in a former mansion in Nantgwynant, near the start of the Watkin Path, with dorm beds and private rooms. Meals are available, the hostel is also licensed. Only open Aug–Oct and limited times in winter. Dorms £14–17, rooms ❶

Cae Du Camping 10min walk towards Capel Curig on the A498 ☎01766/890345, ⓦ www .caeducampsite.co.uk. Spacious and peaceful site with showers. £16 per pitch. Closed Nov–Feb.

Hafod y Llan Nantgwynant, 1 mile north on the A498 ℡01766/510129. Tent-only site on a farm purchased by the National Trust and managed to enhance the landscape and for nature conservation. Campfires are permitted. £3.50 per person. Closed Nov–March.

Snowdon Ranger YHA Hostel Rhyd Ddu, 5 miles northwest of Beddgelert on the A498 ℡0870/770 6038, ℮snowdon@yha.org.uk. A former inn, at the foot of the Snowdon Ranger Path. Bunks are mostly in two- and four-bed rooms, meals are available and the place is licensed. Open April–Aug; call for other times. Dorms £14–18, rooms ❶

Eating and drinking

Beddgelert Bistro & Antiques Waterloo House ℡01766/890543. Scones with clotted cream by day; wild goose breast in triple sec, Anglesey lobster or leek and mushroom pie (£12–20) by

night. There's a cosy cellar bar, too. Book ahead for dinner.

Glaslyn Ices/Cafe Glyndŵr On the south side of the river bridge. Great ice-cream shop with three

Walks from Beddgelert

Two fine hikes up Snowdon start near Beddgelert, and there are a couple of good ones closer to town: all are covered by OS 1:25,000 OL17 ("Snowdon & Conwy Valley") and 1:50,000 115 ("Snowdon/Yr Wyddfa") maps.

The Aberglaslyn Gorge

This fairly easy walk follows the short but very picturesque **Aberglaslyn Gorge** (4 miles; 2hr 30min; 600ft ascent), and returns to the Sygun Copper Mine (see p.382) on a path up Cwm Bychan between Mynydd Sygun and Moel y Dyniewyd. Cross a footbridge over the Glaslyn River in the village and follow the left bank downstream until you meet the Welsh Highland Railway. Continue between the railway and the river as the train line ducks through two tunnels.

The path meets the road at Pont Aberglaslyn – the tidal limit before The Cob was built at Porthmadog – where you can either retrace your steps, or head north up Cwm Bychan on a path near the exit of the disused railway tunnel. It's about a two-mile valley walk to the copper mines, from where a track follows the left bank of the River Glaslyn back to Beddgelert.

Moel Hebog

From Beddgelert, you are unlikely to have missed the lumpish **Moel Hebog** (Bald Hill of the Hawk; 2569ft) to the west of the village. It forms the highest point on a fine panoramic ridge walk (8 miles; 5hr; 2800ft ascent) which also takes in the lesser peaks of Moel Lefn, and Moel yr Ogof (Hill of the Cave), named after a refuge used by Owain Glyndŵr when fleeing the English in 1404, after his failed attempt to take Caernarfon Castle. The final forest section can be a bit disorientating, even in good weather, so be sure you have a compass.

Start half a mile northwest of the centre of Beddgelert on the A4085, where Pont Alyn crosses the river to Cwm Cloch Isaf Farm. Follow the signs to a green lane, which soon leads up onto the broad northeast ridge, all the time keeping left of the Y Diffwys cliffs. The summit cairn is joined by two walls, the one to the northwest leading down a steep grassy slope to Bwlch Meillionen, from where you can ascend over rocky ground to Moel yr Ogof, or descend to the right, and then skirt left in a probably fruitless attempt to find the elusive Glyndŵr's Cave. From the top of Moel yr Ogof, it's a clear route north to Moel Lefn, then down to a cairn from where you can plan your descent. The easiest line is to Bwlch Cwm-trwsgl, near the highest point of the Beddgelert Forest, where a stile over a wire fence leads into the forest. Both the maps cited above show a clear, though not always easy-to-follow, route to Beddgelert Forest Campsite, where you turn right and tramp a mile along the A4085 to reach Beddgelert.

dozen flavours to take away, and a surprisingly good family-style restaurant tucked in behind. **River Garden Restaurant** ☎01766/890551. Centrally located, with a waterside terrace and hearty breakfasts, meals (£10–12) and cream teas.

Sygun Fawr 0.7 miles northeast off the A498 ☎01766/890258, ⓦwww.sygunfawr.co.uk. Open to non-residents, with beautifully prepared four-course evening meals (£23) served in a snug dining room. Bookings recommended. Closed Mon & Thurs.

Blaenau Ffestiniog and around

Snowdonia's most southerly major settlement, **BLAENAU FFESTINIOG** (*Blaenau* means "head of the valley", in this case the lush Vale of Ffestiniog) cowers at the foot of stark thousand-foot mountains strewn with heaps of splintered slate. The town attracts some of Snowdonia's worst weather, and when clouds hunker low in the great cwm and rain lashes the grey roofs, walls and paving slabs it looks terrifically gloomy. Fortunately, on days when every tourist office in north Wales is packed with wet visitors wondering what to do, Blaenau Ffestiniog is at its most dramatic, and besides, its slate mine will keep you dry.

Thousands of tons of slate a year were once hewn from the labyrinth of caverns beneath the town, and exported worldwide. Nowadays, only two mines manage to keep ticking over (one of them aided by earnings from tours) and the loss of a steady income has hit the town hard. Its population has dropped to less than half its 1910 peak of 12,000, and the town's economy now leans on tourism, generated by its mine tour and the fact that it's at the junction of two of the finest train journeys in Wales: the narrow-gauge **Ffestiniog Railway** which winds up from Porthmadog, and the Lledr Valley rail line to Betws-y-Coed.

The town and mine tours

It's hard to get a real feeling of what slate means to Blaenau Ffestiniog without a visit to **Llechwedd Slate Caverns**, on the A470 a mile north of town (daily: March–Sept 10am–6pm; Oct–Feb 10am–5pm; last tour 45min before closing; single tour £9.25, both tours £14.75; ⓦwww.llechwedd-slate-caverns.co.uk), which presents entertaining and informative insights into the rigours of a miner's life. There's no charge to walk around the reconstructed Victorian mining village and to watch slate being split, shaped and engraved, though you'll want to change money into pennies and farthings at the Old Bank to buy something from the old-style sweet shop or buy a drink at the *Miners Arms* pub.

To visit some of the 25 miles of tunnels and sixteen working levels, however, you need to take one of two 45-minute tours. Using a small train, the **Miners Tramway** tour takes you a third of a mile along one of the oldest levels, cut in 1846, disembarking to admire the enormous Cathedral Cave and the open-air Chough's Cavern – both tilted at 30° to follow the slate's bedding plane – as you are plied with facts on slate mining. The scale of the place is awe-inspiring even without the unconvincing tableaux of Victorian miners at work chained high up in the tops of the caverns. On the wilder **Deep Mine** tour you're bundled onto special carriages and lowered to one of the deepest parts of the mine down a 1-in-1.8 incline – Britain's steepest underground inclined railway. After donning waterproofs and headgear, you head off into the tunnels, guided by an irksome taped spiel of someone pretending to be a Victorian miner. That said, the content is good, concentrating on the working and social life of the miners who never saw daylight in winter, taking their breaks in a dank underground shelter known as a *caban*. The long caverns angling back into the gloom

The Welsh slate industry

Slate is as much a symbol of north Wales as coal is of the south: it too peaked around the beginning of the twentieth century and shaped society throughout the period of British mass industrialization, drawing thousands from the impoverished hills to the relative wealth of the new towns which sprang up around the quarries.

Slate derives its name from the Old French word *esclater*, meaning "to split" – a perfect description of its most highly valued quality. Six hundred million years ago, what is now north Wales lay under the sea, gradually accumulating a thousand-foot-thick layer of fine-grained mud which metamorphosed into the purplish Cambrian slates of the Penrhyn and Dinorwig quarries and the hundred-million-year-younger blue-grey Ordovician slates of Ffestiniog.

The Romans recognized the potential of the substance, and used it as **roofing material** for the houses of Segontium (see p.412), while Edward I used it extensively in his Iron Ring of castles around Snowdonia. But it wasn't until around 1780 that Britain's Industrial Revolution took hold, leading to greater urbanization and a demand for roofing slates. As cities grew during the nineteenth and early twentieth centuries, millions of tons of slate were shipped around the globe, primarily for use as a cheap and durable roofing material. Hamburg was re-roofed with Welsh slate after its fire of 1842, and it is the same material that still gives that rainy-day sheen to interminable rows of English mill-town houses.

By 1898, Welsh quarries – run by the English, like the coal and steel industries of the south – were producing half a million tons of dressed slate a year (and ten times as much slate waste), almost all of it from Snowdonia. At Penrhyn and Dinorwig, mountains were hacked away in terraces, sometimes rising 2000ft above sea level, with teams of **workers** negotiating with the foreman for the choicest piece of rock and the selling price for what they produced. They often slept through the week in damp dormitories on the mountain, and tuberculosis was common, exacerbated by slate dust. At Blaenau Ffestiniog, the seams required mining underground rather than quarrying, but conditions were no better; miners even had to buy their own candles, their only light source. Few workers were allowed to join Undeb Chwarelwyr Gogledd Cymru (the North Wales Quarrymen's Union), and in 1900, the workers in Lord Penrhyn's quarry at Bethesda went out on **strike**. For three years they stayed out – one of Britain's longest-ever industrial disputes – but failed to win any concessions. Those who got their jobs back were forced to work for even less money as a recession took hold, and although the two world wars heralded mini-booms as bombed houses were replaced, the industry never recovered its nineteenth-century prosperity, and most quarries and mines closed in the 1950s.

Welsh slate was firmly established as the finest in the world at the 1862 London Exhibition, where one skilled craftsman produced a sheet 10ft long, 1ft wide and a sixteenth of an inch thick – so thin it could be flexed. Slate is now produced worldwide, and although none beats the quality of north Wales' output, this is little compensation as the region struggles to compete with inferior but half-priced Spanish slate. The Snowdonia National Park Board once insisted on local slate for roofing, but pressure from the European Union now forces them to accept slate "equivalent in colour, texture and weathering characteristics". The last criterion is a moot point, as the Spanish industry is still young, but in the meantime, slate is being shipped from Spain while Welsh slate lies in the ground and unemployed quarrymen kick their heels. The remaining quarries produce relatively small quantities, much of it used for floor tiling, road aggregate or an astonishing array of ashtrays and coasters etched with mountainscapes. More memorable are the roadside fences made from lines of broken, wafer-thin slabs, the beautifully carved slate fire surrounds and mantelpieces occasionally found in pubs and houses, as well as Westminster Abbey's memorial to Dylan Thomas, which is made entirely of Penrhyn slate.

The curse of the Rhododendron

It is against the pervasive greyness of Blaenau Ffestiniog that Snowdonia's **rhododendron** (specifically *Rhododendron ponticum*) invasion is most evident. Come in June, and many of Snowdonia's valleys are a riot of lilac and purple blooms. There's no doubting their aesthetic appeal, but these choking mats of foliage block footpaths and are high on ecologists' hate lists. In their native Himalayas they grow into trees, but in Britain, where they've spread from the cultivated gardens of grand houses, they've become a noxious weed. Native flora can't compete with the dense canopy that cuts out so much sunlight that nothing can grow underneath – a major threat to native birds and insects which thrive in more open scrub. Volunteer action groups periodically target particular areas, blitzing a valley by digging out all the plants, but the rhododendron is proving difficult to contain.

become increasingly impressive, culminating in one filled by a softly lit, limpid pool. The site was the setting for the first ever Welsh-language film, *Y Chwarelwr* (The Quarrymen) in 1935.

Slate from the Llechwedd quarry (and dozens of others that once existed) made the first part of its journey to markets around the world on the **Ffestiniog Railway** (see p.396) which took the dressed and packed product down to the ships at Porthmadog, thirteen miles away. Whether you're heading to Porthmadog or just want to ride the train, it's worth considering doing part of the journey on foot (see box, opposite).

Practicalities

By **car**, Blaenau Ffestiniog is most dramatically approached from the north via the Lledr Valley, climbing over the Crimea Pass between the Manod and Moelwyn mountains and plunging down into the town's shattered landscape. The **train station**, where High Street becomes Church Street, serves both the Ffestiniog narrow-gauge line from Porthmadog and main-line train services from Betws-y-Coed and Conwy. **Buses** stop outside the train station or along High Street. Opposite the station is the **tourist office** (Easter–Oct daily 9.30am–12.30pm & 1.30–5.30pm; ☎01766/830360), while a few doors away the *Bridge Café* has low-cost **internet access**.

The best **place to eat** is *Bistro Moelwyn*, 10 High St (☎01766/832358, ⊛www.bistromoelwyn.co.uk), which is open daily for coffees and snacks and Thursday, Friday and Saturday evenings for the likes of free-range chicken (£13) or borlotti bean and mushroom stew (£12). There's good pub food at *The Commercial* on Commercial Square half a mile north. The chippy across from the *Commercial* is the best in town.

To listen to a **male voice choir** practice (usually Tues, Thurs & Fri at 7.30pm) get directions from the tourist office.

Accommodation

Many of Blaenau Ffestiniog's visitors ride the train up from Porthmadog, visit a slate mine and leave, so **accommodation** is limited, but excellent value. The nearest campsite is the low-priced *Bryn Tirion* four miles north in the Lledr Valley (see p.364).

Bryn Elltyd 1 mile from Blaenau in Tanygrysiau ☎01766/831356, ⊛www.accommodation -snowdonia.com. A very popular, environmentally friendly option overlooking Llyn Ystradau, run by a

mountain leader. Excellent evening meals are available from £13. ❸

Cae Du 1.5 miles south on the A470 ☎01766/830847, ⊛www.caedu.co.uk. A comfy, sixteenth-century beamed farmhouse, beautifully situated at the end of a long drive, and with guided walks available. ❷

🏃 **Cae'r Blaidd** 3 miles south on the A470 ☎01766/762765, ⓦwww.caerblaidd.fsnet .co.uk. Wonderfully spacious Victorian country house set in four acres of woodland with just three rooms, two with fabulous views of the Moelwyn mountains.

Sustaining breakfasts and professionally served table d'hôte dinners (£18 for 3 courses) are very good and the hosts run an extensive array of guided hiking, climbing and scrambling trips (see website). ❹

Isallt Guest House Church St ☎01766/832488, ⓦwww.isallt.com. Very reasonably priced B&B with a variety of rooms, all en suite, a DVD library and wi-fi available on request. ❷

Llan Ffestiniog, Trawsfynydd and Coed-y-Brenin

Slate waste surrounds Blaenau Ffestiniog on three sides, but the fourth drops away into the bucolic **Vale of Ffestiniog**, best explored using the Ffestiniog Railway, or on the walk described in the box below. In the woods around Tanybwlch train station, Snowdonia National Park's study centre, **Plas Tan y Bwlch** (☎01766/772600, ⓦwww.plastanybwlch.com), runs numerous courses throughout the year – see the website for details. Many are taught in Welsh or bilingually, and suitable for Welsh-language beginners (see Basics, p.66).

Heading south from Blaenau Ffestiniog, the A470 runs through the village of **LLAN FFESTINIOG** (Ffestiniog on maps, but just Llan locally), three miles away, broadly following the remains of the old Great Western Railway route which ran across the broad open moors of the Migneint to Bala. Rusted rails run four miles further south to the greatest blot on the national park's landscape, the defunct **Trawsfynydd Nuclear Power Station**, which closed in 1995, but which isn't scheduled to be removed for 130 years.

The A470 continues seven miles south towards Dolgellau, past the evergreen **Coed y Brenin** (The King's Forest), Wales' premier **mountain-biking** destination, with miles of dreamy single-track. At the **visitor centre** (in theory April–Oct daily 10am–5pm; Nov–March Fri–Mon 10am–5pm; ☎01341/440666; parking £3 all day) you can rent bikes (from £22 per day), pick up a free trail map, and afterwards, shower (£1) and recover in the good café.

A walk down the Vale of Ffestiniog

The 1:50,000 OS Landranger map 124 ("Porthmadog & Dolgellau") is useful for this walk.

This gentle walk down into the **Vale of Ffestiniog** (4–5 miles; 2–3hr; descent only) follows the railway line from Tanygrisiau station down to Tan-y-Bwlch, from where you catch the train back to Tanygrisiau – check train times at Tanygrisiau station and buy your ticket when you start to ensure a place on the return train. The walk can also be done from Blaenau Ffestiniog, but this involves a fairly dull first mile, easily avoided by catching the Ffestiniog Railway (or driving) to Tanygrisiau station.

Start at Tanygrisiau station. From here, turn right then take the second left – not the road beside the reservoir but the next one following the footpath signs. Cross the train line and pass a car park on your left before turning left down a track and skirting behind the powerhouse. The path then sticks closely to the railway tracks (occasionally crossing them), following the train line to its 360° loop, through sessile oak woods and past several cascades all the way to Tan-y-Bwlch, offering some great views south to the Rhinogs and west to the Glaslyn estuary en route. Even when there are several paths, you can't go far wrong if you keep the train lines in sight. The *Oakeley Arms* pub near Tan-y-Bwlch, is a good place to while away the time until the next train (or the one after that).

Bala

East of Trawsfynydd, the A4212 climbs twenty miles over open moors, past Canolfan Tryweryn (see p.390) to the little town of **BALA** (Y Bala). Located at the northern end of Wales' largest natural lake, **Llyn Tegid** (Bala Lake), Bala is a major watersports centre with a modest sideline in remote walks on little-visited hills. Thankfully, the tourist hype about "Teggy", a legendary beast lurking in the lake's waters, hasn't done to Bala what the Nessie industry has done in Scotland. The four-mile-long body of water is perfect for **windsurfing**, with buffeting winds whipping from the coast up the Talyllyn Valley and between the Aran and Arenig mountains that flank the lake.

Bala's second lake, **Llyn Celyn**, five miles west of town, isn't that much smaller than Llyn Tegid, but is very much an artificial affair created amid huge controversy in the 1960s, to supply Liverpool, in England, with its drinking water. A modern chapel on the shore commemorates the valley-bottom village of Capel Celyn, which was flooded to create the reservoir.

The Town

The narrow town sits slightly back from the lake edge, perhaps to avoid the legendary catastrophe that drowned the old town, which stood where the lake now is. The story tell of the quasi-legendary prince Tegid Foel, who was warned by a voice that because of his cruelty to his people "Vengeance will come". On the birth of his son, he held a banquet at which a hired harpist heard a voice saying "Vengeance has come". A bird led him away onto a hill where he slept, waking to find the town submerged beneath the lake which took the prince's name.

Bala has a role in Welsh history that far outweighs its current, rather modest status. The Romans built a fort at the southern end of the lake (not open to the public), then the Normans erected a motte. This tree-covered **Tomen-y-Bala**, on Heol y Domen off the northern end of the High Street (generally open 9am–dusk; free) gives a panoramic view over the town. But it was **socks** that brought the town its fame. Until the Industrial Revolution killed the trade, most local men and women were involved in knitting, even clothing George III, who wore Bala stockings for his rheumatism. During this period, the people of Bala became noted for their piety and followed the preachings of Nonconformist ministers Thomas Charles and Michael D. Jones (see box opposite). Charles is buried a mile south in the churchyard at Llanycil; his statue stands outside the Presbyterian church on Tegid Street, and a plaque locates his former home at 68 High St, in what is now a Barclays bank. A nearby plaque records Mary Jones' walk (see box opposite).

The only other thing to do around town is ride the **Bala Lake Railway** (late March–Sept 4 trains most days; £7.50 return, £4.50 single; ℡01678/540666, Ⓦwww.bala-lake-railway.co.uk), which starts at Llanuwchllyn, six miles southwest of town, and runs for four miles along the route of the former Ruabon–Barmouth standard-gauge line, which closed in 1963. Despite the use of renovated north Wales slate quarry trains, it's one of Wales' least interesting narrow-gauge runs, though a ride can be combined with a visit to the *Eagles Inn* (see p.390).

Practicalities

The best approach to Bala is the A4212 from south of Blaenau Ffestiniog over the wild uplands between the twin peaks of Arenig Fawr and Arenig Fach. Unfortunately, this can't be done by public transport as Bala's only **bus** is the #X94, which

Thomas Charles and Michael D. Jones

During the seventeenth and eighteenth centuries, the religious needs of the Welsh were being poorly met by the established Church. None of the bishops were Welsh, few were resident, and most regarded their positions as stepping stones to higher appointments. The preachings of the newly emerging Nonconformists – Quakers, Baptists and, later, Calvinist and Wesleyan Methodists – were therefore welcomed by the people. Congregations swelled from the middle of the eighteenth century, but conversion didn't get into full swing until the effects of itinerant religious teachers improved literacy and the strident sermons of native Welsh-speakers fired their enthusiasm. There were already over twice as many chapels as Anglican churches when the chief protagonist of Methodism in Wales, **Thomas Charles**, gave the movement a massive boost through the founding of the British and Foreign Bible Society, a group committed to distributing local-language Bibles worldwide.

Charles had already reprinted Bishop Morgan's 1588 original Welsh translation, but was down to his last copy when 16-year-old **Mary Jones** (see p.307), the daughter of a poor weaver from the other side of Cadair Idris, arrived on his doorstep. She had saved money for six years to buy a Bible from Thomas Charles and, in 1800, walked the 25 miles to Bala, barefoot some of the way, prompting Charles to found the society.

Despite the rise in Nonconformism, many of the more pious converts sought greater religious freedom, something denied them in Wales by the oppression of both the English Church and State. In 1865, reformist preacher **Michael D. Jones** recruited around Bala for the 153 Welsh settlers who subsequently sailed for Argentine Patagonia and established Y Wladfa, "The Colony", the remains of which can still be found in the Chubut Valley. Jones stayed in Wales, setting up the Bala-Bangor Theological College and leading campaigns for Welsh causes, and many now regard him as "the father of modern Welsh nationalism".

runs from Chester and Llangollen through the Vale of Edeyrnion to Dolgellau and Barmouth, stopping on High Street. The **tourist office** on Pensarn Road (April–Oct daily 10am–5pm; Nov–March Mon & Fri–Sun 10am–4pm; ℡01678/521021, ✉bala.tic@gwynedd.gov.uk), is half a mile south along High Street in the same building as the Penllyn Leisure Centre. **Bike rental** is available from R.H. Roberts at 7 High St (℡01678/520252; £13 a day), and there's **internet** access and wi-fi at *Cwpwrdd Cornel* café, 64 High St.

Accommodation

Bala and its immediate vicinity have plenty of places to **stay**, but you can also make the most of the surrounding countryside by staying in the Vale of Edeyrnion, northeast of the town (see p.339).

Abercelyn 1 mile south of Bala on the A494 ℡01678/521109, ⊛www.abercelyn.co.uk. The pick of the local mid-range places, this fine country house occupies an eighteenth-century former rectory. Rooms (two with bathtub) are stylishly understated, and there are also three self-catering cottages. One night-stays attract a £10–14 supplement. ❸

Bala Backpackers 32 Tegid St ℡01678/521700, ⊛www.bala-backpackers.co.uk. Extensively renovated hostel in a central Bala house offering beds (£12–13) in both small dorms and larger ones partitioned into smaller areas. There are also a private twins (some en suite), most in an adjacent house. Cook for yourself or order breakfast in advance (£3.50). Open May–Sept and winter weekends. Rooms ❶, en suite ❷

Bala Bunk House Tomen-y-Castell on the A494, 1.5 miles north of Bala ℡01678/520738, ⊛www .balabunkhouse.co.uk. Self-catering bunkhouse with small dorms (£15), one self-contained unit sleeping six, and communal lounge and cooking areas. Duvets can be rented (£2) if you haven't brought a sleeping bag.

Bryn Tegid Country House Llanycil, 1.5 miles south on the A494 ☏ 01678 521645, ⓦ www .bryntegid.co.uk. Attractive country house surrounded by lovely grounds and woodland with two of the three spacious rooms overlooking Llyn Tegid. ⑤
Monfa 95 Tegid St ☏ 01678/520059. The cheapest B&B rooms (with shared bathrooms) in town. ②

Pen-y-Bont ☏ 01678/520549, ⓦ www .penybont-bala.co.uk. The nearest campsite to town, by the outlet of the lake on the B4319 Llangynog Rd. £14 per tent. Closed Nov to mid-March.
Tyn Cornel 4 miles west along the A4212 ☏ 01678/520759, ⓦ www.tyncornel.co.uk. Camping and caravan park next to the National Watersports Centre; usually packed with paddlers at weekends. £7 per person. Closed Nov–Feb.

Eating and drinking

Bala is small, but still has its fair share of decent **restaurants** and **pubs**.

Caffi'r Cyfnod High St. A legend in Bala, this café was founded in 1885 and is still going strong for breakfasts, sandwiches and cheap lunches.
Eagles Inn 5 miles southwest at Llanuwchllyn. Cosy local half a mile from the Lake Railway station, which serves excellent bar meals (mostly £7–10) with several vegetarian options and a kids' menu. Also handy for the male voice choir rehearsals which take place in the village hall at 7.30pm on Thurs.

Plas-yn-Dre 29 High St ☏ 01678/521256. Spacious and airy bistro popular with locals for dishes such as chicken penne with mushrooms and asparagus (£11.50) or pan-fried rib-eye (£15). There's decent espresso at its café next door.
Rainbow's End 102 High St. Quality espresso and cakes in a former chapel above a craft shop, with some outdoor seating.
The Ship 30 High St. The best of the town's straightforward drinking pubs.

Watersports

The only real **whitewater-rafting** trips in Wales take place at **Canolfan Tryweryn** (☏ 01678/521083, ⓦ www.ukrafting.co.uk), the National White Water Centre, four miles west up the A4212. When water is released – typically around 200 days a year – it crashes down a mile and a half through the slalom site where frequent competitions take place on summer weekends. Go for two

▲ Whitewater rafting at Canolfan Tryweryn

runs down (40–60min; £31), a two-hour session (typically 4 runs; 4–7 people for £235 midweek, £310 at weekends), or, stepping up a notch, try the Orca, a two-person inflatable in which you tackle the rapids unguided (half day £72 per person). Wetsuit rental is extra. Proficient **kayakers** can also take to the water (£7 per day for Canoeing Association members, £14 others).

Down on the shores of Llyn Tegid by the tourist office, Bala Adventure and Watersports Centre (℡01678/521059, ⓦwww.balawatersports.com) runs courses in windsurfing, open-water kayaking and sailing. These are mostly aimed at groups but you can get individual instruction for around £35 a half day. The centre also rent kayaks (£16 for 2hr), canoes (£30), windsurfers (£24) and more.

The Llŷn

An undulating spur from Snowdonia's mountainous heartland, the **Llŷn** takes its name from an Irish word for "peninsula", an apt description for this most westerly part of north Wales, which, until the fifth century, had a significant Irish population and which still maintains an atmosphere reminiscent of parts of western Ireland. The Llŷn's cliff-and-cove-lined finger of land juts out south and west, separating Cardigan and Caernarfon bays, its hills tapering away along the ancient route to **Aberdaron**, from where pilgrims sailed for **Ynys Enlli (Bardsey Island)**. Ancestors of those last Irish inhabitants may have been responsible for the numerous hillforts and cromlechs found on the Llŷn, particularly the hut circles of the **Tre'r Ceiri** hillfort. But these days, it's the beaches that lure people to the south-coast family resorts of **Criccieth**, **Pwllheli** and **Abersoch**. Unless you want to rent windsurfers or canoes, it's preferable to make for the far quieter coves punctuating the north coast, or press on along the narrow roads that dawdle down towards Aberdaron.

The Llŷn is approached through one of two gateway towns linked by the A487, an effective boundary between Snowdonia proper and the peninsula. **Porthmadog** is primarily of interest for its proximity to the private dream village of **Portmeirion**, reached on Wales' finest narrow-gauge train line, the **Ffestiniog Railway**. The Llŷn's northern coast comes to an abrupt end at the mouth of the Menai Strait, guarded by the awesome fortress that forms the centrepiece of **Caernarfon**, a good base for both the Llŷn and central Snowdonia.

Nowhere in Wales feels more remote than the tip of the Llŷn or is more staunchly Welsh; defiantly so, over eight decades after the meeting in Pwllheli that saw the formation of the Welsh nationalist party, Plaid Cymru (see Contexts, p.482). In most local shops you'll only hear Welsh spoken and Stryd Fawr is used instead of High Street. To some extent it is a reaction (or over-reaction) to the increasing number of English-speakers moving here or buying second homes (see box, p.392).

The Llŷn's bountiful caravan parks can seem unappealing to campers, and often only accept families and couples, but a local ruling allows anyone with a

Holiday homes and incomers

For decades the biggest threat to rural Wales was **depopulation**, as workers and their families fled the declining quarry, pit and farming villages. Now repopulation is the hot issue as self-appointed guardians of both the language and the rural way of life fight a rearguard action against incomers – predominantly wealthy English, buying up coastal cottages as weekend getaways.

During the 1980s, north and west Wales witnessed a spate of **arson attacks** on holiday homes conducted by the shadowy **Meibion Glyndŵr**, or "Sons of Glyndŵr". Though their campaign petered out by the 1990s, newcomers keep arriving and pushing house prices beyond the reach of locals.

Some **incomers** are permanent migrants sympathetic to the Welsh way of life, but others – particularly the second-home owners who might only spend the odd weekend there – make little attempt to integrate. It is the latter contingent that enrages Cymuned (literally "Community"; ⓦ www.cymuned.org), a pressure group formed in 2000 to campaign for the preservation of rural communities and the Welsh language. It advocates a minimum ten-year residency clause for home buyers; planning permission to turn a permanent dwelling into a second home; investment in schemes to help residents buy property locally; and a Welsh-learning requirement for residents. Opponents suggest this would create a divided Wales and effectively a "language ghetto" in the north and west, but such talk is bending ears in Gwynedd County Council.

Plaid Cymru, the Welsh nationalist party, takes a broader view, citing economic deprivation as the main issue. After all, being unable to afford property isn't restricted to rural Wales; people in Cardiff (let alone London) have more trouble buying a house than most in Gwynedd. Some argue that communities might do better embracing incomers, exploiting any economic spin-off and using that to help preserve the culture and language.

field to run a **campsite** for one month a year, and through the summer they spring up everywhere.

Trains and National Express **buses** serve both Cricieth and Pwllheli, leaving an extensive network of infrequent buses to cover the rest. Better still, the peninsula's quiet narrow lanes through rolling pastoral land are ideal for cycling, and you can **rent bikes** in Pwllheli and Porthmadog.

Porthmadog and around

The Vale of Ffestiniog and Beddgelert's Glaslyn River meet the sea at Tremadog Bay, where the Cambrian coast makes a sharp left to become the south side of the Llŷn. The bustling town of **PORTHMADOG** drapes itself around the northern shore of Traeth Bach, the mountain-backed common estuary, sadly making little of its wonderful position. It was once the busiest slate port in north Wales, and is now a pleasant enough town to use as a base for visiting the Italianate folly of **Portmeirion**, two miles east of Porthmadog, and the wonderful **Ffestiniog Railway** that originally carried down slates from Blaenau Ffestiniog.

Arrival, information and accommodation

The main-line **train** station and the Welsh Highland Railway (Caernarfon Branch) station are at the north end of the High Street, near the Tesco supermarket where National Express **buses** from Liverpool, Manchester and London stop. The Ffestiniog Railway's Harbour Station is located down by the harbour, about half a mile to the south. Just north of here, the helpful **tourist office** (Easter–Oct daily 9.30am–5pm; Nov–Easter Mon–Sat 10am–4pm; ℡01766/512981, ⓦwww.porthmadog.co.uk) is at the southern end of the High Street. There's free **internet** at the library on Chapel Street. Note that Dolgellau buses go inland through Coed-y-Brenin: take the train if you want to stick to the coast.

Porthmadog has a fair range of low-cost and moderately priced places to stay, but excels in luxury **accommodation**.

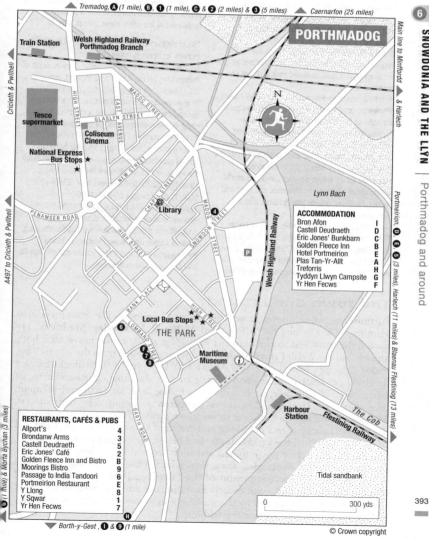

▲ Tremadog, Ⓐ (1 mile), Ⓑ, ❶ (1 mile), Ⓒ & ❷ (2 miles) & ❸ (5 miles)　　▲ Caernarfon (25 miles)

PORTHMADOG

Train Station

Welsh Highland Railway
Porthmadog Branch

◄ Criccieth & Pwllheli

Main line to Minffordd ► & Harlech

HIGH STREET

MADOC STREET

EAST AVENUE

GLASLYN STREET

Tesco
supermarket

Coliseum
Cinema

NEW STREET

National Express
Bus Stops ★
★

CHAPEL STREET

@ Library

PENAMSER ROAD

◄ A497 to Criccieth & Pwllheli

HIGH STREET

SNOWDON STREET

MADOC STREET

❹

P

Lynn Bach

N

Welsh Highland Railway

Portmeirion, Ⓓ Ⓔ ❺ (3 miles); Harlech (11 miles) & Blaenau Ffestiniog (13 miles) ►

ACCOMMODATION
Bron Afon	I
Castell Deudraeth	D
Eric Jones' Bunkbarn	C
Golden Fleece Inn	B
Hotel Portmeirion	E
Plas Tan-Yr-Allt	A
Treforris	H
Tyddyn Llwyn Campsite	G
Yr Hen Fecws	F

BANK PLACE

HIGH STREET

Local Bus Stops ★ ★
★

THE PARK

❻

LOMBARD STREET

Ⓕ
❼
❽

Maritime
Museum ⓘ

GARTH ROAD

◄ Ⓖ (1 mile) & Morfa Bychan (3 miles)

Harbour
Station

Ffestiniog Railway

The Cob

Tidal sandbank

RESTAURANTS, CAFÉS & PUBS
Allport's	4
Brondanw Arms	3
Castell Deudraeth	5
Eric Jones' Café	2
Golden Fleece Inn and Bistro	B
Moorings Bistro	9
Passage to India Tandoori	6
Portmeirion Restaurant	E
Y Llong	8
Y Sqwar	1
Yr Hen Fecws	7

0 　　　　　　　 300 yds

393

▼ Borth-y-Gest, ❶ & ❾ (1 mile)　　　Ⓗ

© Crown copyright

Hotels and guesthouses

Bron Afon Borth-y-Gest, 1 mile southwest of Porthmadog ☎01766/513918. Attractive, en-suite B&B rooms in this pretty village with fabulous views across the bay to the mountains. Also offers separate self-catering facilities accommodation. ❷

Castell Deudraeth Portmeirion ☎01766/770000, ⓦwww .portmeirion-village.com. Chic designer hotel in a remodelled Victorian "castle" decorated in muted tones with the finest fittings, including widescreen TVs with episodes of *The Prisoner* on DVD. Only 10min walk from Portmeirion village, where you're free to roam and use the outdoor heated pool. So classy you'll want to stay a week. ❽

Golden Fleece Inn Tremadog, 1 mile north of Porthmadog ☎01766/512421. The best bet for pub accommodation, with pleasant rooms above an excellent bar. ❷

Hotel Portmeirion Portmeirion ☎01766/770000, ⓦwww.portmeirion-village.com. Elegant suites in the hotel or in serviced cottages throughout Portmeirion village, meeting international hotel standards but with little of the quirkiness you'd hope for (and the choicest ones are booked months in advance at peak times). While the more expensive suites will strain your credit, it's worth asking about low-season, midweek and weekend breaks. Facilities include tennis courts and a heated outdoor pool. ❽

Plas Tan-Yr-Allt 1 mile north of Porth-madog and immediately east of Tremadog on the Beddgelert road ☎01766/514545, ⓦwww .tanyrallt.co.uk. Cool and stylish conversion of a small Georgian mansion (once the home of the poet Shelley), run by a wonderfully flamboyant gay couple who stamp their personality on the place. Rooms are very comfortable, exquisite breakfasts are served overlooking Tremadog Bay, and you should really stay for the delicious evening meals. ❼

Treforris Garth Rd ☎01766/512853. Pleasant shared bathrooms in a large house overlooking the harbour to the west. Take Bank Place off High St then left onto Garth Rd – a 15min walk in all. ❶

Yr Hen Fecws 16 Lombard St ☎01766/514625, ⓦwww.henfecws.com. Relaxed, pleasant B&B with comfy, uncluttered rooms, beside a popular restaurant of the same name (see p.398). ❸

Bunkhouse, self-catering and campsites

Eric Jones' Bunkbarn Tremadog, 2 miles north of Porthmadog on the A498 to Beddgelert, opposite *Eric Jones' Café* (see p.398) ☎01766/512199, ⓦwww.ericjones-tremadog.co.uk. Rock climbers' bunkhouse where you can get a mattress for £5 a night, or basic camping for £4 per person.

Hotel Portmeirion Portmeirion ☎01766/770000, ⓦwww.portmeirion-village.com. This hotel (see above) also lets luxurious self-catering cottages by the week, or half-week in winter. The cottages sleep two (£635–990 a week), four (£750–1200), or up to eight people (£1000–1700).

Tyddyn Llwyn Black Rock Rd ☎01766/512205, ⓦwww.tyddynllwyn.com. A superior family campsite on a grassy hillside, with all facilities and a bar, a 15min walk along the road to Morfa Bychan following Bank Place southwest off High St. £14 per tent. Closed Nov–Feb.

The town and around

Porthmadog would never have existed at all without the entrepreneurial ventures of a Lincolnshire MP named **William Alexander Madocks**. He named the town and its elder brother Tremadog, a mile to the north, after both himself and the Welsh Prince Madog, who some say sailed from the nearby Ynys Fadog (Madog's Island) to North America in 1170. In 1805, Madocks fancied he could get himself some good grazing land by draining a thousand acres of estuarine mud flats here; he bought Ynys Fadog, built an earth embankment, then started on Tremadog. The towns prospered and, buoyed by their success, Madocks embarked on a project to enclose a further 7000 acres by sealing off the Glaslyn estuary with a mile-long embankment known as The Cob, southeast of present-day Porthmadog. Madocks died before the project came to fruition, but the Glaslyn River was rerouted and soon scoured out a deep watercourse close to the north bank, ideal for a slate wharf. This was the first of several which, boosted by the completion of the Ffestiniog Railway in 1836, spread along a waterfront thick with orderly heaps of slate and the masts of merchant ships. The slate traffic ceased by the middle of the twentieth century, and today only a few dozen yachts grace the harbour.

The waterfront is still the most interesting place to wander, with a bunch of old slate buildings overlooking yachts bobbing on the tide. If the weather is fine, and particularly towards sunset, you can't go far wrong with a gentle stroll along The Cob, with the occasional steam-hauled Ffestiniog Railway service adding atmosphere to views up the estuary towards Snowdon. Ffestiniog trains leave from Harbour Station, also the terminus (from mid-2009) for Welsh Highland Railway trains bound for Beddgelert and Caernarfon.

Porthmadog has a third, more child-oriented, narrow-gauge line, also confusingly known as the **Welsh Highland Railway** (mid-March to Oct 5–6 services daily; £5.50; ☏01766/513402, ⓦwww.whr.co.uk), running from close to the train station. Come 2009 it will hook into the main Welsh Highland line from Caernarfon and will probably run trips as far as the RSPB's **Glaslyn Osprey Project** (mid-March to Aug; free) at Pont Croesor, where telescopes and CCTV cameras allow you to watch eggs hatch and young develop. Fans can ride the footplate (£3 extra for diesel, £6 for steam), though you need to be over 18.

A confusion of railways

Apart from the standard gauge Cambrian Coast line, Porthmadog now has three tourist-oriented narrow-gauge railways. The most established is the **Ffestiniog Railway**, which runs from Harbour Station to the slate town of Blaenau Ffestiniog. This is also the terminus for the **Welsh Highland Railway: Caernarfon Branch** which, by Easter 2009 should connect Porthmadog via Beddgelert to Caernarfon. Confusingly, there's also the **Welsh Highland Railway: Porthmadog Branch**, which has a different terminus, on the north side of town, but also connects to the line to Beddgelert and Caernarfon.

It's a tangled story. The original Welsh Highland Railway from Porthmadog to Caernarfon was pulled up decades ago, but the Welsh love affair with restoring railways as steam-driven tourist attractions kicked in and two organizations began running trips on short sections of track, one from Caernarfon and one from Porthmadog. Plans to reconnect the two lines and form Britain's longest narrow-gauge railway (running just over 25 miles) brought years of squabbling for the two Welsh Highland Railways.

Permission for the project finally came from the Department of Transport in 1999, with £4.3 million of Millennium lottery money also forthcoming. Farmers with land along the route (and the ramblers who regularly walked it), however, were not pleased, and with much public support the National Farmers' Union launched an appeal for a judicial review. Though unsuccessful, this didn't stop individual farmers from doing their best to obstruct work on the old track-bed where it ran across their land. The feats of engineering needed to reopen the old line are staggering: over twenty bridges have been rebuilt; walking and cycling paths re-routed; four tunnels down the Aberglaslyn Gorge near Beddgelert (see p.383) needed extensive safety work; and to link up with the Ffestiniog Railway's Harbour Station at Porthmadog, trains have to run across a street. And most of this within a national park.

Emotions in the area are very mixed about the possible benefits of the line. The Department of Transport made great play of its potential for locals, as well as tourists, claiming that it would restore the missing link in a rail loop (main line: Bangor–Betws-y-Coed–Blaenau Ffestiniog; Ffestiniog Railway: Blaenau Ffestiniog–Porthmadog; and Welsh Highland Railway: Porthmadog–Caernarfon) which somehow ignored the fact that the Bangor–Caernarfon rail line, an essential link in the chain, was removed in the 1960s and is now a cycle track. Furthermore, with the steep gradients and twisting route of the WHR, it's unlikely to be a journey fast enough to satisfy the needs of commuters.

The Ffestiniog Railway

The **Ffestiniog Railway** (April–Oct 4–8 services daily; Nov–March services several days a week; return to Blaenau Ffestiniog £17.50; return to Tan-y-Bwlch £10.80; discount on last train of the day; a £34 combo ticket gets one adult and one child to Blaenau Ffestiniog and back, plus a ride on the Welsh Highland Railway; ☎01766/516000, ⓦwww.festrail.co.uk) is Wales' finest narrow-gauge rail line, twisting and looping up 650ft from Porthmadog to the slate mines at Blaenau Ffestiniog, thirteen miles away. The gutsy little engines make light of the steep gradients and chug through stunning scenery, from broad estuarine expanses to the deep greens of the Vale of Ffestiniog, only fading to grey on the final approaches to the slate-bound upper terminus at Blaenau Ffestiniog.

When the line opened in 1836, it carried slates from the mines down to the port with the help of gravity, horses riding with the goods before hauling the empty carriages back up again. Steam had to be introduced to cope with the 100,000 tons of slate that Blaenau Ffestiniog was churning out each year in the late nineteenth century, but after the slate-roofing market collapsed between the wars, passengers were carried instead until the line was finally abandoned in 1946. Most of the tracks and sleepers had disappeared by 1954, when, encouraged by the success of the Talyllyn Railway (see p.305), a bunch of dedicated volunteers began to reconstruct the line, only completing the entire route in 1982.

Leaving Porthmadog, trains cross The Cob then stop at Minffordd, an interchange point for the Cambrian coast main line and the mile-long walk to Portmeirion. Short **nature trails** spur off from Tan-y-Bwlch (the fourth station), as does the longer Vale of Ffestiniog walk (see box, p.387) which passes Dduallt station by the spiral on its way to Tanygrisiau. The full round trip to Blaenau Ffestiniog takes almost three hours, but you can get on and off as frequently as the timetable allows, and the journey is included in the North and Mid-Wales Freedom of Wales Flexi Pass (see Basics, p.37). It costs £2.50 each way for bikes, but call first to confirm that there's room for them. Sit on the right of the carriage going up to get the best view of the scenery; for more legroom or to sit in the observation carriage you'll need to pay £4 each way for a first-class upgrade.

Tremadog, Borth-y-Gest and Morfa Bychan

Even without your own vehicle it's easy to explore a couple of local villages. A mile north of Porthmadog, **Tremadog** was founded by William Madocks around 1805, and though really just the intersection of three streets, offers a good example of early town planning.

Almost equally handy is **BORTH-Y-GEST**, a small former boat-building village enveloping a picturesque harbour a mile south of Porthmadog. There's nothing to do here but enjoy the estuary views, maybe stay at *Bron Afon* (see p.394) and eat at one of the waterfront cafés or, more formally, at the delectable *Moorings Bistro* (see p.398). The #99 bus (hourly) runs here from Porthmadog, but the coastal walk (20min: follow Lôn Cei) makes a particularly nice summer evening stroll.

If all the sand and water around Porthmadog leaves you hankering for a swim, **Black Rock Sands**, three miles west of Porthmadog at **MORFA BYCHAN**, is the best beach: a two-mile swath of golden sands with sublime views down to Harlech and up to the peaks of Snowdonia.

Portmeirion

Porthmadog's other major attraction is the unique Italianate private village of **PORTMEIRION** (daily 9.30am–5.30pm; ⓦwww.portmeirion-village.com;

£7; free afternoon entry if you pre-book a meal at the *Porthmeirion Hotel*, or have lunch at *Castell Deudraeth*), set on a small rocky peninsula in Tremadog Bay, three miles east near Minffordd. You can walk there in an hour from Porthmadog, or catch the #1b bus, main-line or Ffestiniog trains to Minffordd, from where it's a signposted 25-minute walk.

Portmeirion was the brainchild of eccentric architect **Clough Williams-Ellis** and his dream to build an ideal village to enhance rather than blend in with its surroundings, using a "gay, light-opera sort of approach", as Williams-Ellis himself described it. The result is certainly theatrical: a stage set with a lucky dip of unwanted buildings arranged to distort perspectives and reveal tantalizing glimpses of the sea or the expansive sands behind. The village is perhaps best known as "The Village" in the 1960s British cult TV series *The Prisoner*, which is due to be reprised with a belated second series in 2009 (though it will mostly be shot in South Africa rather than Portmeirion).

In the 1920s, Williams-Ellis began scouring Britain for a suitable island – he believed only an island could provide the seclusion for his project – but having found nothing he could afford, was gratified to be offered a piece of wilderness four miles from his home, Plâs Brodanw, at Garreg (see below). A Victorian house already on the site was turned into a hotel, the income from which provided funds for Williams-Ellis's "Home for Fallen Buildings". Endangered buildings from all over Britain and abroad were broken down, transported and rebuilt, every being style being plundered: a neoclassical colonnade from Bristol; Siamese figures on Ionic columns; a Jacobean town hall; a Buddha; and the Italianate touches, a campanile and a pantheon. Williams-Ellis designed his village around a Mediterranean piazza, piecing together a scaled-down nest of loggias, grand porticoes and tiny terracotta-roofed houses, and painting them in pastels: turquoise, ochre and buff yellows. Continually surprising, with hidden entrances and cherubs popping out of crevices, the ensemble is wildly eclectic, yet never quite inappropriate.

More than three thousand visitors a day come to ogle in summer, when it can be a delight; fewer in winter, when it's just plain bizarre. And for one weekend in March, Portmeirion hosts *The Prisoner* convention (check links on Ⓦwww.portmeirion-village.com for details) when fans book the place out to re-enact scenes as best they can – though, as much of the series was shot in the studio, the juxtaposition of Portmeirion's buildings doesn't match that of *The Village*.

Sometimes dismissed as the grandest folly of all and a symbol of Britain's fascination with eccentrics, Portmeirion at least supports Williams-Ellis's guiding principle that natural beauty and profitable development needn't be mutually exclusive. Architectural idealism aside, it was always intended to be self-sustaining, much of the finance coming from the opulent waterside *Hotel Portmeirion* (see p.394). In the evening, when the village is closed to the public, guests see the place at its best: peaceful, even ghostly. The hotel also utilizes many of the cottages in the village, so much of your time will be spent outside, or popping into shops selling *Prisoner* memorabilia or gaudy Portmeirion pottery. Guests and visitors can eat at the expensive hotel-restaurant (see p.396), but most will be content with a couple of cafés – better still, bring a picnic and find a spot on the paths that wind through the exotic forest which backs Portmeirion.

Clough Williams-Ellis's talents are also in evidence four miles northeast of Portmeirion at his ancestral home **Plâs Brodanw** (daily 9.30am–5.30pm; £3), near Garreg, where whimsical topiary creates a formal, yet not quite manicured, setting for a solid Welsh stone house. The house itself is closed to the public, leaving only the gardens and some of the grounds, visited by following the "To the Tower" sign opposite the entrance. A ten-minute woodland walk brings you to the outlook tower, with expansive views of Porthmadog and the Moelwyns.

Eating, drinking and entertainment

Eating is fairly limited in Porthmadog itself, though there are also good options in Tremadog and Portmeirion. As usual, there are plenty of good places to **drink**, some selling brews from the town's Purple Moose brewery.

Allport's Corner of Snowdon and Madog sts. Ordinary-looking fish and chip shop frequently claimed to be the best in the region – or Wales, even.

Brondanw Arms Llanfrothen, 5 miles northwest of Porthmadog. This slate-floored traditional inn, known locally as *Y Ring*, has real ales, a beer garden, kids' play area, decent bar meals and occasional live music.

Castell Deudraeth Portmeirion ☎01766/770400. Conservatory brasserie overlooking a walled garden – much younger and hipper than the nearby *Portmeirion Restaurant*. Modern Welsh grills take precedence (2 courses for £18.50), and they also do an excellent Sunday lunch.

Eric Jones' Café 1 mile east of Tremadog on the A498. Good, solid food, wolfed down by climbers of the Tremadog crags across the road. There's a good noticeboard, a small stock of climbing gear and guidebooks for sale. Usually open to 6pm, later on summer weekends.

Golden Fleece Inn and Bistro Tremadog. An ancient coaching inn on Tremadog's main square, with a cramped "cave bar" serving meals (£8–10) around the fire or in the courtyard. There's a blackboard bistro menu in the restaurant out the back (generally Thurs–Sat) with most mains £9–12. Tues is folk night.

Moorings Bistro 4 Ivy Terrace, Borth-y-Gest, 1 mile south of Porthmadog ☎01766/513500. Great little spot specializing in local seafood, and also

serving a great Sunday roast lunch (£10) and local ales. Closed all day Mon & Tues, and Sun evenings.

Passage to India Tandoori 26a Lombard St ☎01766/512144. Typical curry restaurant menu disguises the fact that this is one of the best such places around. Most dishes are £6–8 and there's a good selection of chef's specials.

Portmeirion Restaurant *Hotel Portmeirion* ☎01766/770480. Delightful, slightly formal hotel restaurant with views across the Traeth Bach sands serving inventive modern cuisine; lamb with garlic-roasted leeks or halibut with chargrilled artichokes; about £21 for lunch, £18–24 for dinner mains. Smart attire (no jeans or trainers) required in the evening. Reservations advised.

Y Llong (The Ship) 14 Lombard St. Cosy pub with a stock of real ales, a lively atmosphere and free wi-fi.

Y Sgwar The Square, Tremadog ☎01766/515451. Well-prepared and presented meals at this simple but stylish restaurant – good for a steak-and-ale pie at lunch (£9), or dinner starting with Chinese duck pancakes (£16 for 2) then lamb shank with leeks (£13).

Yr Hen Fecws 16 Lombard St ☎01766/514625. Bistro-style place that's all stone walls, wooden floors and dim lighting, with an imaginative menu including some tasty vegetarian dishes. Expect the likes of crispy duck with garlic mash (£15) and baked goat's cheese with aubergine (£12).

Cricieth and around

In the 1980s, seeing defaced road signs around north Wales was an everyday occurrence, as nationalists made their point about monoglot English instructions with the help of paint. Nowadays, most signs are bilingual, but **CRICIETH**, five miles west of Porthmadog, is one of the few places you'll still see a bit of daubing. Official signs spell the name with a double C in the middle, which is a sound produced by the English alphabet, not the Welsh, where one C suffices; consequently, the offending extra letter gets ritually removed.

Cricieth, however, has depended on the English for its growth, and it's still smarter and more anglicized than its neighbouring towns. When sea-bathing became the Victorian fashion, English families descended on Cricieth's sweeping sand and shingle beach and built long terraces of guesthouses (many now

Giraldus Cambrensis and his journey through Wales

Through his books *The Journey Through Wales* and *The Description of Wales*, Norman-Welsh **Giraldus Cambrensis** (Gerald of Wales, or Gerallt Cymro) has left us with a vivid picture of life in Wales in the twelfth century. Gerald worked his way up the ecclesiastical hierarchy, but failed to achieve his lifelong goal, the bishopric of St Davids, mainly because of his reformist ideals.

Gerald's influence in Wales made him the first choice when Baldwin, the Archbishop of Canterbury, needed someone to accompany him on his 51-day tour around Wales in 1188, preaching the cross and recruiting for a third Crusade, designed to dislodge the Muslim leader Saladin from Jerusalem. During the tour, Gerald amassed much of the material for his books, where he sensitively portrayed the landscape and its people, judging that "Welsh generosity and hospitality are the greatest of all virtues", but warning "If they come to a house where there is any sign of affluence and they are in a position to take what they want, there is no limit to their demands". But on the whole, he shows sympathy for the Welsh, coming up with a conclusion that has an oddly contemporary ring: "if only Wales could find the place it deserves in the heart of its rulers, or at least if those put in charge locally would stop behaving so vindictively and submitting the Welsh to such shameful ill-treatment".

retirement homes). These days, beach-bound holiday-makers go further west, leaving a quietly amiable resort that makes a convenient touring base for the peninsula and Porthmadog.

The only real sight is the battle-worn **Cricieth Castle** (April–Oct daily 10am–5pm; Nov–March Fri & Sat 9.30am–4pm, Sun 11am–4pm; £3.10; open and free of charge on other days 10am–4pm; CADW), dominating the coastline with what remains of its twin, D-towered gatehouse. The castle was started by Llywelyn ap Iorwerth in 1230, but strengthened and finished by Edward I, who took it in 1283. During his 1404 rebellion, Owain Glyndŵr grabbed it back, only to raze it and leave little remaining besides an outline of broken walls and the gatehouse. Nowadays, it's a great spot to sit and look over Cardigan Bay to Harlech or down the ripples of the Llŷn coast in the late afternoon, but leave time for the workaday exhibition on Welsh castles and a wonderful animated cartoon based on the twelfth-century Cambrian travels of Giraldus Cambrensis (see box above) in the ticket office. If all you want are glorious views, clamber up the neighbouring hill behind Marine Terrace. The view there is as good and is set off by the hulking castle.

Practicalities

Both National Express **buses** from the north Wales coast and frequent local buses from Porthmadog and Pwllheli stop at Y Maes, the open square at the centre of town flanked by The Green, just a couple of hundred yards east of the Cambrian coast **train station**. The nearest tourist offices are at Porthmadog and Pwllheli. For such a small town, good **restaurants** are surprisingly abundant in Cricieth. It also hosts the annual **Cricieth Festival** (ⓦ www.cricciethfestival .co.uk), which takes place over the third week of June in venues all over town, and features jazz and classical music, lectures, art shows and plenty for kids.

Accommodation

Glyn y Coed Porthmadog Rd, 100 yards along the A497 ☎ 01766/522870, ⓦ www.glynycoedhotel .co.uk. Newly refurbished small hotel with ten pretty rooms, some with sea views. ❸

Mynydd Du ☎ 01766/522294. Simple campsite a mile towards Porthmadog on the A497. Closed Nov–Feb. £10 per pitch.

Mynydd Ednyfed Caernarfon Rd, 1 mile north on the B4411 ☎01766/523269, ⓦwww.criccieth.net. Elegant, renovated country house with gym and solarium set in attractive grounds, plus a very good restaurant with an extensive wine list. ⑤

Tyddyn Morthwyl Farm and Caravan Park ☎01766/522115. Not the closest but the nicest campsite, on the Caernarfon Rd, 1.5 miles north of Cricieth. £10 per pitch includes hot showers. There's a spacious bunkhouse in converted farm buildings for £6.50 a night. Book ahead and bring a sleeping bag.

Eating and drinking

Blue China Tearooms Marine Terrace. Down by the sea, this is the pick of the bunch for daytime coffee and cake.
Cadwalader's Castle St. Founding outlet of this regional ice-cream empire, now with a spacious airy café and great sea views. Come for coffee, smoothies, tasty pies, or one of their rich ice creams in dozens of flavours. Closed weekdays Nov–March.
The Moelwyn 27–29 Mona Terrace ☎01766/522500, ⓦwww.themoelwyn.co.uk.

Casual yet stylish restaurant with white linen tablecloths, sea views and a seasonal menu which might include pan-fried chicken livers (£6) followed by oak-smoked haddock with a Welsh rarebit topping (£15). Closed winter weekends.
Mynydd Ednyfed Caernarfon Rd, 1 mile north on the B4411 ☎01766/523269, ⓦwww.criccieth.net. Upscale cuisine served in a candlelit conservatory with mains (£11–17) such as chargrilled salmon fillet with crispy duck in a red wine and hoi sin sauce.

▲ Statue of Lloyd George, Caernarfon

Llanystumdwy

Though born in Manchester, the Welsh nationalist, social reformer and British Prime Minister David Lloyd George (1864–1945) lived in his mother's home village of **LLANYSTUMDWY**, a mile west of Criccieth, until 1880, when he was sixteen. He grew up in Highgate House, the home of his uncle, the village cobbler, which is now part of the **Lloyd George Museum** (Easter & May Mon–Fri 10.30am–5pm; June Mon–Sat 10.30am–5pm; July–Sept daily 10.30am–5pm; Oct Mon–Fri 11am–4pm; £4). It kicks off with an informative thirty-minute film on the life of this witty and powerful orator described by Churchill as "a man of action, resource and creative energy, [who] stood, when at his zenith, without a rival". An extensive collection of gifts, awards and caskets honouring Lloyd George with the freedom of various cities illustrate the great man's popularity, and the displays are full of anecdotes and little-known facts about him. Read between the lines to get a sense of the betrayal felt by many Welsh nationalists as his interest turned from the politics of Wales to those of Westminster.

Rustic late nineteenth-century beds and dressers furnish Lloyd George's wooden-floored two-up, two-down house, in a garden laid out much as it would have been in Lloyd George's day. Before ambling through the garden, walk down the path towards the River Dwyfor, beside which Lloyd George is buried under a memorial – a boulder and two simple plaques designed by Portmeirion's creator Clough Williams-Ellis (see p.397). **Bus** #3 runs from Porthmadog and Criccieth, through the village on its way to Pwllheli.

Penarth Fawr

Five miles west of Criccieth along the A497, signposts point down a tiny lane half a mile inland towards **Penarth Fawr** (Easter–Sept Tues–Fri 10am–5.30pm, Sat & Sun 2–5.30pm; free), a compact fifteenth-century hallhouse built to a common standard for the Welsh gentry. Constructed in 1416, the rare aisle truss hall was originally heated by a huge central hearth, replaced in the seventeenth century by the large fireplace you see today. Alterations at that time included the insertion of an upper floor – a dismantled beam from this work is on display, bearing the date 1656.

Pwllheli and around

The undoubted "capital" of the Llŷn, **PWLLHELI** (pronounced something like "Poothl-heli") is a strange place: not quite a seaside resort, nor a town that exploits its illustrious history. Although the town appears largely Victorian, Pwllheli's market charter dates back to 1355: the Wednesday **market** takes place on Y Maes. It was also here at the *Maesgwyn Temperance Hotel* (now a pet shop marked with a plaque) in August 1925 that six people met to form Plaid Cymru (see Contexts, p.482). Even in the height of summer, you'll hear far more Welsh spoken here than English.

From Y Maes, Ffordd-y-Cob leads south, past the spruce **marina**, packed with yachts, to Pwllheli's **West End**, a Victorian seaside development of pastel-shaded villas that seem ripe for renovation. The marina is lively all summer, with **boat trips** to Bardsey Island (see p.406). The *Shearwater* (Easter–Oct only; ℡01758/613000) runs a morning cruise (2hr; £25) along an impressive section of coast, an afternoon cruise (3hr; £35) that includes a non-landing circuit of Bardsey Island, and an evening cruise (2hr; £30).

Activity peaks in early July for **Wakestock** (⦿ www.wakestock.co.uk), when 20,000 spectators arrive for a celebration of wakeboarding, skateboarding, BMX and music: Groove Armada, The Streets and Duffy headlined in 2008.

Practicalities

The town spreads out from Y Maes, where National Express and local **buses** pull in. The **train station**, the northern terminus of the Cambrian coast line, stands a few yards to the east, opposite the **tourist office** (April–Oct daily 9am–4.30pm; Nov–March Mon–Wed, Fri & Sat 10.30am–4.30pm; ☎01758/613000, pwllheli .tic@gwynedd.gov.uk) on Station Square. **Internet** is available at the library on Penlan Street (free) and at the K2 Synergy computer shop, 67 Stryd Fawr (closed Sun), which also has wi-fi.

The main reason to **stay** is to spend a night at ⚑ *Plas Bodegroes*, Efailnewydd, two miles northwest of Pwllheli on the A497 (☎01758/612363, ⦿ www.bodegroes .co.uk; ⊙; closed Sun & Mon). It's probably the nicest place to stay on the Llŷn, set in a very swish Georgian country house surrounded by wonderful parkland. The rooms are comfortable yet understated, the service attentive but relaxed. The restaurant (closed Sun evening and Mon) offers sumptuous dining in Wales' longest-standing Michelin-starred establishment. Modern interpretations of traditional dishes are presented for lunch and dinner (£42.50 for three courses), the wine list is superb and Sunday lunch costs a modest £18.50. If you can't stretch to *Plas Bodegroes*, try the simple, shared-bathroom B&B accommodation at *Bank Place*, Stryd Fawr (☎01758/612103; ❷), or continue on to Cricieth or Abersoch.

Eating in town is best at *Penlan Fawr*, 3 Penlan St (☎01758/612864), a four-hundred-year-old pub that's always lively, serves cask ales and does decent meals, especially the Sunday lunches. Alternatively, try *The Mariner*, on Station Square below the tourist office, which does bargain sandwiches and light lunches, plus good-value steak and fish staples in the evening.

Llanbedrog

LLANBEDROG, four miles west of Pwllheli, is a delightful village with a wonderful beach and one of Wales' oldest public art galleries, **Plas Glyn-y-Weddw** (mid-July to early Sept daily 10am–5pm; mid-Sept to early July daily except Tues 10am–5pm; ⦿ www.oriel.org.uk; free). Solomon Andrews, the Cardiff entrepreneur who built Pwllheli's West End, bought the Victorian Gothic mansion in 1896 and turned it into a genteel centre for the arts, with pleasure gardens and legendary tea dances. All rooms peel off a spectacular galleried hallway under a huge stained-glass window and a gorgeous hammerbeam oak roof, topped with a lantern. The exhibitions combine pieces from the gallery's permanent collection with touring works, often with a Welsh theme. There's also a lovely conservatory tearoom in which to sit and gaze out at the sea.

It's a short stroll from Glyn-y-Weddw down to **Traeth Llanbedrog**, a charming strand whose restored, pastel-hued beach huts attest to its ownership by the National Trust. From the southern end of the beach, a steep, fairly rough path climbs through a wooded glen onto a towering headland known as Mynydd Tir-y-Cwmwd, where the sweeping views are shared by the **Iron Man**, a contemporary wrought-iron sculpture designed and built locally to replace an eight-foot ship's figurehead erected there in 1919.

The village is also blessed with a couple of excellent **places to eat**. Besides the tearoom at Plas Glyn-y-Weddw, there's the *Gallery*, an appealing bistro down by Traeth Llanbedrog with a cosy interior, beachside seating and a good range of snacks (£5–7) and mains (£10–15). The *Ship Inn* at Bryn-y-Gro, half a mile north, serves good meals and has a very popular summertime beer garden.

Abersoch and around

After the distinctly Welsh feel of Pwllheli, **ABERSOCH**, seven miles southwest along the coast, comes as a surprise. This former fishing village, pitched in the middle of two golden bays, is a largely anglicized resort, catering to affluent boat-owners and holidaying families. At high tide the harbour is attractive and the long beach is a fine spot, even if it's barely visible under beach towels at busy times – although a short walk along the shore shakes off most of the crowds.

Surfers make for **Porth Neigwl** (Hell's Mouth), two miles to the southwest, which is one of the finest **surf** beaches in Wales – though beware of the undertow if you're swimming. Sun-seekers should head a mile north to a fine stretch of beach backed by *The Warren* holiday park.

If baking on the beach isn't active enough, you might fancy trying your hand at **watersports**. The West Coast Surf Shop, Lôn Pen Cei (℡01758/713067, ⓦwww.westcoastsurf.co.uk), rents surfing gear (boards £10, wetsuits £8) and offers lessons (£30 for 2hr). Throughout summer, Offaxis, right in the centre of town (℡01758/713407, ⓦwww.offaxis.co.uk), runs a wakeboarding and surfing academy (£30 per lesson) and rents gear, while Abersoch Sailing School (March–Oct; ℡01758/712963, ⓦwww.abersochsailingschool.com) runs lessons and rents Lasers and other craft on the town's main beach.

For something a bit less outdoorsy, bus #18 can take you two miles to **Llanengan**, a short walk from the beach of Porth Neigwl, where you can also visit the gorgeous twin-aisled fifteenth-century **St Engan's Church** (instructions for obtaining the key are inside the porch). Its twin altars and rood screens are integral parts of decoration, unchanged by the eighteenth- and nineteenth-century reformist zeal that altered most other churches. While there, visit the *Sun Inn*, a cosy pub serving reasonable bar meals, with a pleasant beer garden.

Practicalities

Buses from Pwllheli loop through the middle of Abersoch, stopping near the **tourist office** on Lôn Pen Cei (Easter–Sept daily 10.30am–3pm; Oct–Easter Sat & Sun 10.30am–3pm; ℡01758/712929, ⓦwww.abersochtouristinfo.co.uk). To continue to Aberdaron by bus, you must take a Pwllheli-bound service as far as Llanbedrog, then change onto the #17.

There are lots of places to stay in and around Abersoch, but **accommodation** can be tight over summer and at weekends during spring and autumn. Almost all the **campsites** in villages around Abersoch are family-oriented places, so groups need to look reputable to be admitted. Ask the tourist office for a list of places with a freer regime.

Abersoch is increasingly well supplied with decent **places to eat**. Almost all are along Lôn Pen Cei and most are packed in summertime (but seldom open in winter). The varied **Abersoch Jazz Festival** (ⓦabersoch.co.uk/jazzfestival) is held annually in several local venues over the second weekend in June.

Accommodation

Angorfa Lôn Sarn Bach ℡01758/712967, ⓦwww.angorfa.com. Superior modern budget B&B. Rates include breakfast. ❸

Goslings at the Carisbrooke Lôn Sarn Bach ℡01758/712526, ⓦwww.goslingsabersoch.co.uk. Friendly, central a/c restaurant (see below) with rooms, including en-suite doubles, family rooms with DVD players and a couple of self-catering flats nearby. Delicious breakfasts, too. ❺

Porth Tocyn 2.5 miles south of Abersoch, on the road through Sarn Bach and Bwlchtocyn ℡01758/713303, ⓦwww.porth-tocyn-hotel.co.uk. Luxurious country-house hotel with an outdoor pool, excellent restaurant and great views of Cardigan Bay. Closed early Nov to mid-March. ❼

Rhydolion Llangian, 1 mile northwest of Abersoch ☎ 01758/712342, ⊛ www.rhydolion.co.uk. Small, welcoming tent and caravan site which accepts groups, 15min walk from Porth Neigwl beach. It

also has a couple of very well-appointed, self-contained units. Camping £6 per person.

Sgobor Unnos Tanrallt Farm, Llangian, 2 miles west of Abersoch ☎ 01758/713527, ⊛ www.tanrallt.com. Self-catering bunkhouse/hostel located in Llangian (bus #18 from Pwllheli or Abersoch; 4 daily). Bunks cost £15 with continental breakfast. ❶

Eating and drinking

Abersoch Café Lôn Pen Cei. Good café serving panini, jacket potatoes and daily specials (£6–9), plus espresso.

Brig in the *Harbour Hotel* on Lôn Sarn Bach. About the best spot in town for a few pints.

🏃 **Goslings at the Carisbrooke** Lôn Sarn Bach ☎ 01758/712526, ⊛ www .goslingsabersoch.co.uk. Casual wood-floored bistro (plus some outside seating) with a short menu plus daily specials, all simply cooked from fresh ingredients. Mains range from a succulent Welsh steak burger (£7) to barbecue ribs (£10) and

smoked salmon salad (£13). Generally open weekends only.

Mañana Lôn Pen Cei (no bookings accepted). Casual, fairly inexpensive Mexican restaurant that's always popular with locals.

Porth Tocyn 2.5 miles south of Abersoch, on the road through Sarn Bach and Bwlchtocyn ☎ 01758/713303, ⊛ www.porth-tocyn-hotel.co.uk. It's been one of Abersoch's best restaurants for half a century, and still welcomes non-residents to its panoramic dining room for superb meals (£33 for two courses, £39 for four), and Sunday buffet lunch (£23).

Aberdaron and around

At the lime-washed fishing hamlet of **ABERDARON**, two miles short of the tip of the Llŷn, you really feel you're at the end of Wales. For the best part of a thousand years up to the sixteenth century the inn and church here were the last stops on a pilgrim trail to Ynys Enlli or Bardsey Island, around the headland. Just back from the water, the fourteenth-century stone *Y Gegin Fawr* (The Big Kitchen) served as the pilgrims' final gathering place before the treacherous crossing, and now operates as a café. The twelfth-century **church of St Hywyn** (daily: Easter–Oct 10am–6pm; Nov–Easter 10am–4pm; free) on the cliffs behind the stony beach still serves its original purpose, and was ministered by one of Wales's greatest modern poets, R.S. Thomas (see box opposite), until he retired in 1978. Displays on Thomas have pride of place in the twin-naved interior, beside material on Enlli and its pilgrims, and a pair of Latin-inscribed sixth-century gravestones – among the earliest Christian artefacts in Wales.

In the early years of his retirement, Thomas lived five miles east of Aberdaron in a cottage in the grounds of **Plas yn Rhiw** (mid-March to April & Oct Thurs–Sun noon–5pm; May, June & Sept daily except Tues & Wed noon–5pm; July & Aug daily except Tues noon–5pm; £3.60; NT), a Regency manor house on Tudor foundations at the western end of Porth Neigwl. The house was derelict in 1938 when it was bought by Thomas' moneyed friends, the Keating sisters, who restored it with the help of Portmeirion architect Clough Williams-Ellis, whose offbeat touch is evident in the flattened arches and a Gothic doorway rescued from a demolished castle. Unlike many National Trust mansions, this is a manageable and relaxed place, filled with rustic furniture like a 1920s oil stove used by Honora Keating until her death in 1981, and her accomplished watercolours. The upstairs sitting room is notable for its six-foot-thick wall containing a fireplace, a spiral staircase and a window nook overlooking gorgeous gardens almost overgrown with fuchsias, hydrangeas, roses and wild flowers.

Having made your way out as far as Aberdaron, it's worth using the village as a base for exploring the narrow lanes at the end of the peninsula, leading to the National Trust property around **Mynydd Mawr**, the hill overlooking Bardsey Sound. A minor road weaves west to the headland of **Braich-y-Pwll**, two miles west of Aberdaron, from where a short path heads down the cliffs to the ruins of St Mary's church, the crossing point at the end of the Pilgrim's Way. The road continues from here to the top of Mynydd Mawr, from where the medieval patchwork of ancient fields which make up the tip of the Llŷn are clearly visible.

Alternatively, head two miles north to the clean, safe and secluded bay of **Porth Oer** (NT), known as "Whistling Sands" for the white sands which squeak as you walk on them. Barring a small beach shop in high summer, the only amenities are the clifftop and coastal paths leading away.

Practicalities

Without your own transport, the only way to reach Aberdaron is the fairly infrequent #17 **bus** from Pwllheli. There's no tourist office, but information is available on Ⓦ www.aberdaronlink.co.uk. **Accommodation** is quite limited and hard to get in summer. *Brynmor B&B* (Ⓣ01758/760344; ❷), has some fairly simple rooms with shared bath, and there are a couple of hotels right in the centre with en-suite rooms: *The Ship* (Ⓣ01758/760204; ❸) is comfortable enough; while *Tŷ Newydd* (Ⓣ01758/760207; ❺), has recently been revamped and has some sea-view rooms. The area has lots of good **campsites** including *Mynydd Mawr* (Ⓣ01758/760223, Ⓦ www.aberdaroncaravanandcampingsite.co.uk; £7 per pitch; closed Nov–Feb), a peaceful grassy spot right by the entrance to Mynydd Mawr.

R.S. Thomas

The reclusive poet **R.S. (Ronald Stuart) Thomas** was something of a Welsh anti-hero. Born in Cardiff in 1913, he worked as a minister in rural parishes throughout Wales, most famously in Aberdaron where he spent his last couple of working decades and much of his retirement until his death in 2000. It was Thomas' fourth volume of poetry, published in 1955, that brought him lasting recognition, something consolidated with his best-known collections – *The Bread of Truth* (1963) and *Not that he brought Flowers* (1968).

R.S. Thomas's poetry is dark and spartan, illuminated with shafts of vision and clarity. Common themes include religion (Christianity in particular), rural and pastoral strands and the eternal poetic topic of love in human relationships. However, it's in his Welsh-themed work that Thomas most savagely and thrillingly hits the mark. *Selected Poems*, published by Bloodaxe, is a good starter anthology of his work.

I never wanted the drab rôle
Life assigned me, an actor playing
To the past's audience upon a stage
Of earth and stone; the absurd label
Of birth, of race hanging askew
About my shoulders. I was in prison
Until you came; your voice was a key
Turning in the enormous lock
Of hopelessness. Did the door open
To let me out or yourselves in?

For light **meals**, try the *Hen Blas Café* in the middle of the village. For bar snacks and full dinners, there's the *Tŷ Newydd Hotel* (see above), with a restaurant overlooking the beach.

Ynys Enlli (Bardsey Island)

Bardsey Island or **Ynys Enlli** (The Island of the Currents) rises out of the ocean two miles off the tip of the Llŷn, separated from it by a strait of churning, unpredictable water. This national nature reserve has been an important pilgrimage site since the sixth century, when St Cadfan set up the first monastery here: three visits were proclaimed equivalent to one pilgrimage to Rome. Legend claims Bardsey as "The Isle of Twenty Thousand Saints", most likely remembering not saints, but huge numbers of pilgrims who came to die at this holy spot. By the twelfth century, Giraldus Cambrensis was already claiming that "the bodies of a vast number of holy men are buried there", and that "no one dies there except in extreme old age, for disease is almost unheard of". Numerous other stories tell of the burial place of Myrddin (Merlin) and the former Bishop of Bangor, St Deiniol, but the only hard evidence is the remaining **bell tower** of the thirteenth-century Augustinian Abbey of St Mary and a few Celtic crosses scattered around it. After the dissolution of the monasteries in 1536, piracy became the focus of the island's economy for over a century, gradually giving way to agriculture and fishing.

Interesting though the abbey ruins and later buildings are, most visitors come to watch **birds**. Among the dozen or so species of nesting sea birds are Manx shearwaters, fulmars and guillemots, and an amazing number of vagrants turn up after being blown off course by storms. Few other people bother to make the journey, as **boats** are dependent on sea conditions and a viable load of passengers. The cheapest crossings are with Aberdaron-based Bardsey Boat Trips (£28; ☎07971/769895, ⓦwww.bardseyboattrips.com); while Enlli Charters (☎0845 811 3655, ⓦwww.enllicharter.co.uk) run from Pwllheli (£35), and sometimes Porth Meudwy (£30), a tiny cove half a mile south of Aberdaron. All give around four hours on Bardsey.

For details of the half-dozen **houses** on the island, rented out by the week (April–Oct only), contact the Bardsey Island Trust (☎0845/811 2233, ⓦwww .bardsey.org). There are no facilities on the island and only one resident family.

The north Llŷn coast

Sprinkled with small coves and sweeping beaches between rocky bluffs, the **north Llŷn coast** is a dramatic contrast to the busier south. It has few settlements of any size and lots of quiet little beaches. The most popular (though seldom thronged) is **Porth Dinllaen** with its pub gorgeously sited beside the sand. A rockier coastline is accessible from the Welsh language school at Nant Gwrtheyrn, which is overlooked by the heights of **Tre'r Ceiri** with its prehistoric hillfort remains. The road northeast from Tre'r Ceiri towards Caernarfon now bypasses one of north Wales' finest churches, the austere **Clynnog Fawr**.

Even at the best of times, bus services are infrequent and badly timed, so you're far better off with your own car or bike. Amenities are also thinly scattered hereabouts – a few campsites dotted around, and the odd shop and pub in a village.

Nefyn and Porth Dinllaen

There isn't much to recommend **NEFYN**, the largest of the peninsula's northern communities, but neighbouring **MORFA NEFYN**, a mile to the west, and the adjacent shoreline hamlet of **PORTH DINLLAEN**, both benefit from having lost the 1839 battle to become the terminus for ferries to Ireland. Now owned by the National Trust, Porth Dinllaen is just a pristine sweeping bay backed by a handful of houses and the popular waterside *Tŷ Coch Inn* (closed Sun evening), a beautiful spot for a beer. Easiest access is to walk half a mile along the beach from the National Trust's Porth Dinllaen car park in Morfa Nefyn.

There's comfortable B&B **accommodation** nearby at *Llys Olwen* in Morfa Nefyn (℡01758/720493, ⓦwww.llysolwen.co.uk; ❷), which serves evening meals for £19.

Nant Gwrtheyrn and Tre'r Ceiri

Northeast of Nefyn the mountains of Yr Eifl rise steeply only to plummet into the sea to the north. A fold in the mountains called **Nant Gwrtheyrn** (Vortigern's Valley) is supposed to be the final resting place of the Celtic chieftain Vortigern, who was responsible for inviting the Saxons to Britain after his magician, Myrddin (Merlin), had seen the struggle of the two dragons – the red of the ancient Britons and the white of the Saxons. Vortigern should be pleased to know that his valley is now doing its best to atone for his error, by keeping the ancient British language alive at the impressive **Nant Gwrtheyrn: The Welsh Language and Heritage Centre** (℡01758/750334, ⓦwww .nantgwrtheyrn.org), in rows of converted granite quarry cottages at the foot of the valley. The centre is primarily set up for residential courses entirely in Welsh (see p.66), but is also a beautiful spot to spend a couple of hours exploring the three-mile **nature trail**, strolling through old mine workings and learning all about the place at the Heritage Centre (April–Sept daily 11am–3pm; free). The centre is reached down a narrow, precipitous two-mile track from **Llithfaen**, three miles east of Nefyn: look for signs to "Canolfan Genedlaethol Iaith".

Back on the northern coast road (B4417) it's less than two miles northeast to reach the steep path (4km return; 2hr; 800ft ascent) to the **Tre'r Ceiri** or "Town of the Giants" hillfort (unrestricted access), easily the finest prehistoric remains on the Llŷn. Crowning the entire rounded top of the second-highest of the three Yr Eifl mountains, the hillfort is a massive tumble of rocks, mostly formed into the waist-high walls of about 150 dry-stone hut circles surrounded by a rampart twelve feet high in places. The site is Bronze Age, but the huts are probably only a couple of thousand years old. Locals refer to them as *Cytiau Gwddelod* or "Irishmen's Huts", possibly recalling the Irish immigrant population on the Llŷn in the first few centuries AD, when five hundred people lived on this inhospitable site. Today, the ruins command a stunning **view** over the whole peninsula. The infrequent #14 bus from Tudweiliog passes the foot of the main path up, near a lay-by on the B4417, 0.6 miles west of **Llanaelhaearn**, itself reached by the hourly bus #12 from Pwllheli.

Clynnog Fawr

The last worthwhile stop on the #12 bus route to Caernarfon is **CLYNNOG FAWR**, four miles beyond Llanaelhaearn. Rich in ancient spiritual connections, its large, airy, early sixteenth-century **Church of St Beuno** (generally Easter–Oct 9am–6pm) is built on foundations laid by Saint Beuno in the sixth century. This monastic settlement would have been an important stop for pilgrims bound for Ynys Enlli, ensuring a hefty income that probably financed this impressive church. The interior combines spartan whitewash and limestone flags with wealthier flourishes like the fine hammerbeam roof with ornamental bosses, lovely choir stalls and imposing chancel. St Beuno's stone, a boulder used as a prayer stone or a boundary marker around the eighth century, can be seen in the chapel adjacent to the bell tower, while St Beuno's Well bubbles forth on the other side of the main road, about two hundred yards southwest of the church. Between church and well, a lane to Bach Wen Farm heads seawards – park by the entrance to the farm and follow a grassy lane turning off southwest to the spectacularly situated **Clynnog dolmen**. Lying beneath the peaks of Bwlch Mawr and Gyrn Goch, it's a perfect little cromlech, topped with a superbly hewn capstone featuring 110 mysterious cupped hollows.

The road to Caernarfon passes the gates of Parc Glynllifon (see p.414) and close by the Inigo Jones Slateworks (see p.413).

Caernarfon and around

It was in **CAERNARFON** in 1969 that Charles, the current heir to the throne, was invested as Prince of Wales, a ceremony that reaffirmed English sovereignty over Wales in the midst of one of the most nationalist of Welsh-speaking regions. Since 1282, when the English defeated Llywelyn ap Gruffydd, the last Welsh Prince of Wales, the title has been bestowed on heirs to the English throne, usually in a ceremony held either at Windsor Castle or in Westminster Abbey in London. However, in 1911, the machinations of Lloyd George – MP for Caernarfon, Welsh cabinet minister and future Prime Minister – ensured that the investiture of the future King Edward VIII would take place in the centre of his constituency: a paradoxical move for a nationalist, but one that undoubtedly helped to advance Lloyd George's career.

By the time it was Charles' turn, nationalist activism was on the rise and two of the more militant cadres of the so-called Free Wales Army tried to blow up the Prince's train but succeeded only in killing themselves, an event still mourned by their successors Meibion Glyndŵr, the Sons of Glyndŵr (see p.392 & p.484). Charles' 25-year commemorative return visit in the summer of 1994 was less than triumphant, a low-key affair most significantly characterized by the local constabulary ruling that the local joke shop risked committing a public-order offence by selling "wingnut" ears and Prince Charles masks.

Caernarfon is a town where ardent support for Plaid Cymru guarantees the party a seat in Westminster, and the local dialect is barely intelligible even to other Welsh-speakers. It is also the county town of Gwynedd, a suitable title for what is one of the oldest continuously occupied settlements in Wales, once the site of the Romans' most westerly legion post. Today, Caernarfon is primarily of interest for its awesome castle and town walls: the rest of town is nothing special, and fails to exploit its magnificent setting, where the tidal mouth of the River Seiont meets the Menai Strait.

Arrival, information and accommodation

With no main-line train station, the hub of Caernarfon's public transport system is Penllyn, where both National Express and local **buses** arrive just a few steps from the central Y Maes (Castle Square). The **tourist office** (Easter–Oct daily 9.30am–4.30pm; Nov–Easter Mon–Sat 10am–4pm; ☎01286/672232, ✉ caernarfon.tic@gwynedd.gov.uk) is on Castle Street.

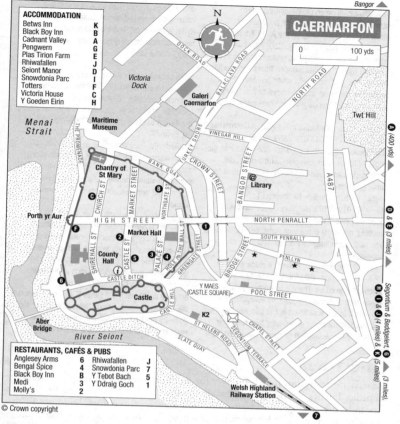

ACCOMMODATION
Betws Inn	K
Black Boy Inn	B
Cadnant Valley	A
Pengwern	G
Plas Tirion Farm	E
Rhiwafallen	J
Seiont Manor	D
Snowdonia Parc	I
Totters	F
Victoria House	C
Y Goeden Eirin	H

RESTAURANTS, CAFÉS & PUBS
Anglesey Arms	6	Rhiwafallen	J
Bengal Spice	4	Snowdonia Parc	7
Black Boy Inn	B	Y Tebot Bach	5
Medi	3	Y Ddraig Goch	1
Molly's	2		

© Crown copyright

There's free **internet** access at the **library** on Bangor Street (Mon, Tues, Thurs & Fri 10am–7pm, Wed 10am–1pm, Sat 9am–1pm), and free **wi-fi** at the *Anglesey Arms* (see p.412).

Central Caernarfon has decent **accommodation** for all pockets, and there are some lovely farmhouse B&Bs in the vicinity, particularly *Tŷ Mawr Farm* in Llanddeiniolen, halfway between Caernarfon and Bangor (see p.440).

Hotels and guesthouses and hostels

Betws Inn Betws Garmon, 5 miles southeast on the A4085 ☏ 01286/650324, ⓦ www .betws-inn.co.uk. A low-beamed former drovers' inn (some parts from 1620) with stylish modern touches. Guests share a cosy lounge with huge inglenook fireplace (lit in winter), and there are excellent three-course dinners (£18–25) by arrangement. ⑤

Black Boy Inn Northgate St ☏ 01286/673604, ⓦ www.welsh-historic-inns.com. Characterful low-beamed rooms in what is said to be the town's oldest building (bar the castle), plus newer en-suite rooms and good-value singles. Rooms ③, en suites ④

Pengwern Saron, 3 miles southwest of Caernarfon ☏ 01286/831500, ⓦ www.pengwern.net. Friendly, top-quality, B&B in a rural setting, with characterful rooms and farm-fresh evening meals (£25). Take the A487 south across the river then turn right towards Saron – *Pengwern* is just over two miles down on the right. Closed Nov–Feb. ④

Plas Tirion Farm Llanrug, 3 miles east of Caernarfon on the A4086 ☏ 01286/673190,

@ www.plas-tirion.co.uk. Welcoming Welsh farmhouse B&B, furnished with antiques. **②**

Rhiwafallen Llandwrog, on the A499 4.5 miles south of Caernarfon ☎ 01286/830172, @ www.rhiwafallen.co.uk. Delightful restaurant with five en-suite rooms, all with wooden floors and modern furnishings, and most with white-painted fireplaces and deep double-ended baths. There's also an elegant lounge and excellent restaurant (see p.413). **⑥**

Seiont Manor Llanrug, 3 miles east of Caernarfon on the A4086 ☎ 0845/072 7550, @ www.handpicked.co.uk. Rustic edifice converted into the region's finest hotel, complete with indoor pool, good restaurant, sauna and even fishing within the hotel grounds. **⑦**

Victoria House 13 Church St ☎ 01286/678263. Very comfortable and good-value B&B within the town walls. Rooms (all doubles, no twins) come with flatscreen TV/DVD, free wi-fi, complimentary drinks and internet access. **⑤**

Y Goeden Eirin Dolydd, 4 miles south of Caernarfon ☎ 01286/830942, @ www.ygoedeneirin.co.uk. There's no doubting the eco credentials of this classy B&B, as everything is turned off at the wall when not in use. But there's nothing austere about effortlessly tasteful decor either in the spacious loft or rooms converted from outbuildings. Dinner (£25 for 4 courses) is a relaxed affair served on oak tables overlooked by Kyffin Williams' art. There's also a self-catering beach cottage sleeping a few miles away (£300–500 a week). **④–⑤**

Hostel and campsites

Cadnant Valley ☎ 01286/673196, @ www.cwmcadnantvalley.co.uk. Pleasant wooded campsite 10min walk east of town near the start of the A4086 to Llanberis. Closed Nov–Feb. £12–15 per tent.

Snowdonia Parc Waunfawr ☎ 01286/650409, @ www.snowdonia-park.co.uk. Attractive year-round campsite four miles southeast on the A4085, right by a station on the Welsh Highland Railway and a good brewpub. £12 per pitch, showers included.

Totters Plas Porth Yr Aur, 2 High St ☎ 01286/672963, @ www.totters.co.uk. Caernarfon's only backpacker hostel is one of the best in Wales. Centrally located, with clean dorms (£15 including continental breakfast) and some lovely communal spaces, including a fourteenth-century cellar kitchen. There's also a great attic en-suite double with sea views (£45) and a separate self-contained house across the road sleeping six (£20–25 per person). Staff can direct you to all manner of local activities and lend you a bike. **①**

The Town

Caernarfon may not match Conwy for the sheer pleasure of simply wandering around, but it's slowly getting its act together, and there's a lot to be said for meandering among the seventeenth- and eighteenth-century buildings in the knot of streets wedged between the **town walls**. These are as complete as those at Conwy, but so boxed-in by modern buildings that they're far less striking, and there's currently no way to get onto them.

Caernarfon Castle

In 1283, Edward I started work on **Caernarfon Castle** (April–Oct daily 9am–5pm; Nov–March Mon–Sat 9.30am–4pm, Sun 11am–4pm; £5.10; CADW), the strongest link in his Iron Ring (see p.435) and the decisive hammerblow to any Welsh aspirations of autonomy. Until Beaumaris Castle was built to guard the other end of the Menai Strait, Caernarfon was the ultimate symbol of Anglo-Norman military might and political wrangling. With the Welsh already smarting from the loss of their Prince of Wales, Edward reputedly rubbed salt in their wounds by justifying his own infant son's claim to the title, having promised them "a prince born in Wales who could speak never a word of English", and subsequently presenting them with the newborn baby that had arrived after his pregnant wife had been forced to take up residence in the castle. The story is almost certainly apocryphal, since Edward's son, though born at Caernarfon, wasn't invested until seven years later.

However, Edward attempted to woo the Welsh with gestures to certain local legends. The Welsh had long associated their town with the eastern capital of

▲ Caernarfon Castle

the Roman Empire: Caernarfon's old Roman name, Caer Cystennin ("Fort of Constantine") alludes to the emperor after whom Constantinople was named, and there are even some dreamers who claim that Constantine himself was born here. Edward's architect, James of St George, exploited this connection in the distinctive limestone and sandstone banding and polygonal towers, both reminiscent of the Theodosian walls still standing in present-day Istanbul.

The other legend to influence the castle was the medieval legend known as the **Dream of Macsen Wledig**, in which the eponymous Welsh hero (the Roman legionnaire Maximus) dreams about "a fair fortress at the mouth of a river, in a land of high mountains, opposite an island, and a tower of many colours at the fort, and golden eagles on the ramparts". When it came to finishing off the turrets in 1317, Edward III perfected the accuracy of this description by adding eagles – also, ironically, the standard of Owain Gwynedd. These are weathered almost beyond recognition now, but the rest of the castle is in an excellent state of repair, thanks largely to Anthony Salvin's nineteenth-century reconstruction, carried out after Richard Wilson and J.M.W. Turner had painted their Romantic images of it.

As a military monument of its time, the castle is supreme, and it still has a brooding, imperious presence. Seized only once, before it was finished, it then withstood two sieges by Owain Glyndŵr with a complement of only 28 men-at-arms. Entering through the **King's Gate**, the castle's strength is immediately apparent. Between the octagonal towers, embrasures and murder-holes cover no fewer than five gates and six portcullises once you've crossed the moat, now bridged by an incongruous modern structure. Inside, the huge lawn gives a misleading impression, since both the wall dividing the two original wards and all the buildings that filled them crumbled away long ago.

The towers are in a much better state, linked by such a honeycomb of wall-walks and tunnels that a tour can be exhausting. The King's Tower at the western end is the loftiest and most striking, its three slender turrets adorned with eagle sculptures affording superb views of the town. Displays and a short film outline the castle's history and importance. To the south, the Queen's Tower is entirely taken up by the numbingly thorough **Museum of the Royal Welch Fusiliers** detailing the victories of Wales' oldest regiment through collections of medals, uniforms and a brass howitzer captured from the Russians at the Battle of the Alma in the Crimea in 1854. Crossing the upper ward from here, you pass the site of the original Norman motte, now faced in Dinorwig slate as part of the dais for the investiture of the Prince of Wales. Displays on the most recent ceremony, and others since the pageant was moved here in 1911, are presented in the **Prince of Wales Exhibition** in the Northeast Tower, just beyond the dais.

Other sights

Leaving the castle, turn left then first right to find the **Chantry of St Mary**, a restored fourteenth-century edifice built into a corner of the town wall on Church Street, that's chiefly notable for the Jesse Window in the south wall. Unfortunately, it's usually closed except for services.

Just outside the walls here is the Victoria Dock, where the **Maritime Museum** (open sporadically; £1) touches the expected bases. The only way to get out on to the Strait these days is on the *Queen of the Sea* (June–Sept daily; ☎01286/672772; £5.50), which embarks on forty-minute **cruises** from the footbridge below the castle.

On the eastern side of town, a ten-minute walk along the A4085 Beddgelert road brings you to the western end of the Roman road from Chester, a location commemorated by the **Segontium Roman Fort and Museum** (daily except Mon 12.30–4.30pm; free; CADW). The Romans occupied this five-acre site for three centuries from around 78 AD, though most of the remains are from the final rebuilding after 364 AD. This was the base of Maximus, the Spanish-born pretender to the imperial throne who was declared Emperor by his British troops in 383 AD, and made a failed march on Rome. The remains of Segontium are about as impressive as his march, seldom more than shin-high and somewhat baffling, making the museum and displays pretty much essential.

Welsh Highland Railway

Trains on the **Welsh Highland Railway** (mid-March to Oct 2–6 trains most days; ☎01766/516000, ⓦwww.welshhighlandrailway.net), run from the small station on St Helen's Road. The full line to Porthmadog via Beddgelert (see box, p.395) should be up and running by Easter 2009. The steam- or diesel-hauled trains currently make a leisurely rural seventy-minute run twelve miles southeast to Rhyd Ddu (unlimited one-day travel £17.50, Caernarfon–Waunfawr return £10). Notable stops along the way include Waunfawr, where there's the *Snowdonia Parc* pub and a pleasant campsite, and the *Snowdon Ranger* YHA hostel. Both the *Snowdon Ranger* and the Rhyd Ddu stations are right by the base of paths up Snowdon, meaning that you can actually hike up the mountain from Caernarfon. A combo ticket (£32) gives a round-trip journey from Caernarfon to Rhyd Ddu, a return trip on the Ffestiniog Railway from Porthmadog to Blaenau Ffestiniog, and a ride on the Porthmadog branch of the Welsh Highland Railway.

Eating, drinking and entertainment

Caernarfon boasts a number of low-key and likeable restaurants which may well be the focus of your evening's entertainment, as there's little else going on. The main exception is **Galeri Caernarfon**, Victoria Dock (☎01286/685222, ⓦwww.galericaernarfon.com), an arts and entertainment complex which puts on a wide range of plays, shows mainstream and more arty movies (mainly Wed evenings) and includes gallery space and a café/bar.

For news of alternative events, check out the noticeboards in the old **Market Hall** on Palace Street, home to a number of interesting shops and stalls.

Anglesey Arms The Promenade. The sea wall outside makes this the best pub for soaking up the afternoon sun, and it also has good real ales and decent bar meals.

Bengal Spice 11 Palace St ☎01286/676797. Reliable curry restaurant and takeaway with fab balti dishes (£6–8).

Black Boy Inn Northgate St ☎01286/673604, ⓦwww.welsh-historic-inns.com. The closest Caernarfon comes to an old-fashioned British pub, with a choice of two low-beamed bars and the best bar meals in town.

Medi Chapel St. Youthful, multi-floored bar that always kicks off at weekends.

Molly's 6 Castle St ☎01286/673238. Relaxed bistro over three floors with an eclectic menu. Tuna sandwiches (£3.50), goats cheese crostini with aubergine relish (£5.50) and butternut and lentil curry (£6) are typical for lunch, while dinner is more formal with mains (£13–15) stretching to pork loin with apple and thyme cream sauce. Closed Tues.

Rhiwafallen Llandwrog, on the A499 4.5 miles south of Caernarfon ☎01286/830172, ⓦwww.rhiwafallen.co.uk. Classy little conservatory restaurant with rural views and a short menu (three courses for £30; Sun lunch £20) on which

local produce features prominently. Expect the likes of pea and mint soup with buffalo mozzarella toasts followed by beef sirloin with shitake mushrooms and a watercress and blue cheese salad. Dinner Tues–Sat plus Sun lunch.

Snowdonia Parc Waunfawr ☎01286/650409. Rural pub four miles southeast of town by Waunfaur station on the Welsh Highland line, with beer brewed on site and decent pub meals. Bus #95 to Beddgelert goes right by.

Y Ddraig Goch 4 Eastgate St ☎01286/678011. Excellent little café and bar that's particularly worth seeking out for its live music. There are always posters in the window showing what's coming up.

Y Tebot Bach 13 Castle St. Modern food with old-fashioned attention to detail in this chip-free tearoom that's good for sandwiches, salads, home-baked cakes and cream teas throughout the day. Closed Sun & Mon.

Around Caernarfon

One of the most enjoyable ways to get out into the area around Caernarfon is to follow either of two walking and **bike paths** along the route of a disused railway: Lôn Las Menai, accessed from Victoria Dock and running north for four miles to Y Felinheri (Port Dinorwig) and thence via lanes to Bangor. In the other direction and leaving town alongside the line of the restored Welsh Highland Railway on St Helen's Road, Lôn Eifion heads twelve miles south to Bryncir, and then via lanes to Cricieth. There's **bike rental** for around £16 for 6hr from Beics Menai, 1 Slate Quay (☎01286/676804). You might also consider catching the Welsh Highland Railway to Dinas then walking the three miles back along Lôn Eifion.

Spectacular **scenic flights** (£39 per person for 20min; ☎08707/541500) over Snowdonia and Anglesey are available from Caernarfon's tiny airport, eight miles south of town at Dinas Dinlle (bus #91; not Sun in winter).

North of Caernarfon

Three miles northeast of Caernarfon, just west of the village of Bethel on the B4366, the **Greenwood Forest Park** (mid–March to Aug daily 11am–5.30pm; Sept & Oct daily 11am–5pm; ☎01248/670076, ⓦwww.greenwoodforestpark.co.uk; £9.80, reduced prices in winter) is primarily a family fun park geared around keeping kids happy with small boats, slides, longbow shooting, adventure playgrounds and the like. Located on the fringe of a copse of managed woodland, it has grown from a desire to celebrate the life of trees, and its roots are still evident. You enter though a large barn built using ancient methods and forty tons of green Welsh and English oak trees, its gargantuan beams held together with pine struts and wooden pegs. Tree and forest ecology is explored through a blend of the scientific, the spiritual (due attention is paid to Celtic tree spirits and the like) and the sensory: you're invited to punch the bark of a redwood to see how "soft" it is, identify aromatic woods from their smell and try out an Ethiopian wood pillow.

South of Caernarfon

The Lôn Eifion bike path runs south from Caernarfon right by the **Inigo Jones Slateworks**, Groeslon (daily 10am–5pm; ⓦwww.inigojones.co.uk; £4.50), on the A487 six miles south of Caernarfon. Slate has been fashioned in roadside sheds here since 1861, when the factory was started by one Inigo Jones, a local man apparently unrelated to the seventeenth-century architect. Many of the inscribed slate plaques adorning public buildings around north Wales were cut here, ample excuse for an interesting calligraphy exhibition that forms part of the 45-minute self-guided audio tour. You can even try your hand at chiselling out a few random chips of slate to appreciate the skill of the carvers here.

A mile west, off the A499 near Llandwrog, **Parc Glynllifon** (daily 10am–5pm; craft workshops and café free, grounds £4) occupies the grounds of the sombre nineteenth-century Glynllifon Hall (not open to the public), once home of Lord Newborough. Easy trails weave through a pleasant woodland garden complete with arboretum, but time is equally well spent at the former workshops, now given over to well-respected craftspeople including one of Wales' top artistic blacksmiths, Ann Catrin Evans.

Travel details

Unless otherwise stated frequencies for trains and buses are for Monday to Saturday services; Sunday averages 1–3 services, though the main routes are more frequent and some routes have no Sunday service at all.

Trains

Betws-y-Coed to: Blaenau Ffestiniog (6 daily; 30min); Llandudno (4 daily; 45min); Llandudno Junction (6 daily; 30min).

Blaenau Ffestiniog to: Betws-y-Coed (6 daily; 30min); Llandudno (4 daily; 1hr 10min); Llandudno Junction (6 daily; 1hr); Porthmadog by Ffestiniog Railway (Easter–Oct 4–8 daily; 1hr).

Criccieth to: Porthmadog (8 daily; 10min); Pwllheli (7 daily; 15min).

Porthmadog to: Barmouth (8 daily; 50min); Blaenau Ffestiniog by Ffestiniog Railway (Easter–Oct 4–8 daily; 1hr); Harlech (8 daily; 20min); Machynlleth (8 daily; 1hr 50min); Pwllheli (7 daily; 25min).

Pwllheli to: Criccieth (7 daily; 15min); Porthmadog (7 daily; 25min).

Buses

Aberdaron to: Pwllheli (9 daily; 40min).
Abersoch to: Pwllheli (11 daily; 15min).
Bala to: Corwen (8 daily; 40min); Dolgellau (8 daily; 35min); Llandrillo (8 daily; 25min); Llangollen (8 daily; 1hr).
Beddgelert to: Caernarfon (8 daily; 30min); Pen-y-Pass (5 daily; 25min); Porthmadog (7 daily; 25min).
Betws-y-Coed to: Bethesda (5 daily; 40–60min); Blaenau Ffestiniog (7 daily; 25min); Capel Curig (every 30min; 10min); Idwal Cottage (5 daily; 20min); Llangollen (3 daily; 1hr); Llanrwst (hourly; 10min); Penmachno (9 daily; 10min); Pen-y-Pass (every 30min; 20min).

Blaenau Ffestiniog to: Betws-y-Coed (7 daily; 25min); Harlech (4 daily; 40min); Llandudno (7 daily; 1hr 10min); Porthmadog (hourly; 30min).
Caernarfon to: Bangor (every 20min; 30min); Beddgelert (8 daily; 30min); Chester (1 daily; 3hr); Criccieth (6 daily; 35min); Llanberis (hourly; 25min); Porthmadog (at least hourly; 50min); Pwllheli (hourly; 45min).
Capel Curig to: Bethesda (5 daily; 20min); Betws-y-Coed (every 30min; 10min); Idwal Cottage (5 daily; 10min); Pen-y-Pass (every 30min; 10min).
Criccieth to: Caernarfon (6 daily; 35min); Llanystumdwy (every 30min; 5min); Porthmadog (every 15–30min; 15min); Pwllheli (every 15–30min; 25min).
Llanberis to: Bangor (hourly; 45min); Caernarfon (hourly; 25min); Nant Peris (every 30min; 10min); Pen-y-Pass (every 30min; 15min).
Llanrwst to: Betws-y-Coed (hourly; 10min); Conwy (every 30min; 40min).
Nefyn to: Pwllheli (roughly hourly; 15min).
Pen-y-Pass to: Beddgelert (5 daily; 25min); Betws-y-Coed (every 30min; 20min); Capel Curig (every 30min; 10min); Llanberis (every 30min; 15min)
Porthmadog to: Beddgelert (7 daily; 25min); Blaenau Ffestiniog (hourly; 30min); Caernarfon (at least hourly; 50min); Criccieth (every 15–30min; 15min); Dolgellau (6 daily; 50min); Pwllheli (every 15–30min; 40min).
Pwllheli to: Aberdaron (9 daily; 40min); Abersoch (11 daily; 15min); Caernarfon (hourly; 45min); Chester (1 daily; 4hr); Criccieth (every 15–30min; 25min); Nefyn (roughly hourly; 15min); Porthmadog (every 15–30min; 40min).

The north coast and Anglesey

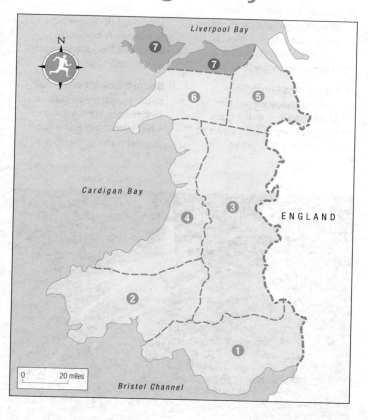

CHAPTER 7

Highlights

* **The Great Orme** Ride the San Francisco-style cable car or aerial gondola to the summit of Llandudno's limestone hummock, before delving into Bronze Age copper mines. See p.428

* **Conwy** The pick of North Wales towns with its imposing castle and intact ring of medieval walls enclosing a fascinating centre. See p.431

* **Menai Strait** Look back from Anglesey across the Menai Strait, with the great bridges framing long views of Snowdonia. See p.444

* **Penmon Priory** Lovely twelfth-century church containing ancient stonework, hidden in an almost forgotten corner of Anglesey. See p.449

* **Newborough Warren** Easy strolls through ecologically important dune systems to the lovely peninsula known as Llanddwyn Island. See p.452

* **South Stack** Wheeling sea birds, stunning sea cliffs, a picturesque lighthouse on a small island and some great coastal walking. See p.456

▲ South Stack Lighthouse

The north coast and Anglesey

Wales' **north coast** and its natural extension, **Anglesey**, encompass both the geographical extremities of the country and the extremes of Welsh life. Walking around most of the brash seaside towns along the eastern section of the coast, only the street signs give any indication that you are in Wales at all: further west, there are places where English is seldom spoken other than to visitors. Scattered along the coast, dramatically situated castles work as a superb antidote to the lowbrow hedonism of the resorts.

Two major forces shaped the region into what it is today. In the thirteenth century, the might of English king Edward I all but crushed the Welsh princes and forced their armies out of the area, whereupon Edward set about building the castles that finally subjugated them.

Though there were earlier castles, the first major success was at **Conwy** where the castle was surrounded by a "bastide" (fortified) town and the garrison and burghers were interdependent. Economically and politically marginalized, the Welsh retreated west to Anglesey, where the English wielded less influence. In response, Edward sited his final castle at **Beaumaris**, a highly advanced concentric design, protecting the entrance to the **Menai Strait**, the treacherous channel that separates the Isle of Anglesey from the mainland.

The second sweeping change came in the late nineteenth and early twentieth centuries, when the benefits of the Industrial Revolution finally loosened the shackles on English mill-town factory workers enough for them to take holidays. Beachfront towns sprang up, catering to the summer visitors who arrived by the trainload. The setup isn't so different today, but cars have all but taken over from the train, caravans are as popular as guesthouses and amusement arcades rule. The stretch of coast from **Prestatyn** to **Colwyn Bay** epitomizes the image of the shabby, tacky British seaside resort – whereas Victorian **Llandudno** was always a posher resort and remains a cut above the rest. With no real beach, Llandudno's neighbour, **Conwy**, is a different proposition, with its tight kernel of ancient buildings overshadowed by a fine castle.

If it's beaches you're after, you'll find that more discerning swimmers and windsurfers shun the mainland coast, heading instead through the university town of **Bangor** to the island of **Anglesey**, a patchwork of rural communities dotted with burial chambers, standing stones and mysterious alignments, as well as being home to Wales' greatest concentration of Neolithic remains. The southwestern resorts of **Rhosneigr**, **Rhoscolyn** and **Trearddur Bay** are the favoured spots, but in scenic terms there's much to be said for the extensive dune system of **Newborough** and the sea cliffs around **South Stack**, both great for birdwatching. Lastly, the ferries from **Holyhead**, at the western end of the island, provide the fastest route to Dublin and Dun Laoghaire in Ireland.

Getting around

The A55 dual carriageway allows you to drive from the Welsh border just south of Liverpool through Anglesey to Holyhead in little over an hour, bypassing all the coastal towns and skirting the northern reaches of Snowdonia. However, unless you take one of the slower alternative routes along the coast, you'll see much more on the **train**, which hugs the coast, linking all the resorts to Bangor, then across to Anglesey for the run to Holyhead.

With the exception of National Express **bus** services from Manchester, Liverpool and other English cities to Bangor and Holyhead, bus travel is much more piecemeal, although services are fairly frequent. We've listed all useful buses in the text, while a series of excellent **timetables** is available free at tourist offices and bus stations. Current **discount fares** include the **Red Rover** (£4.95; buy on the first bus), good for one day's bus travel anywhere in northwest Wales as far south as Aberystwyth, and east to Llandudno and Corwen.

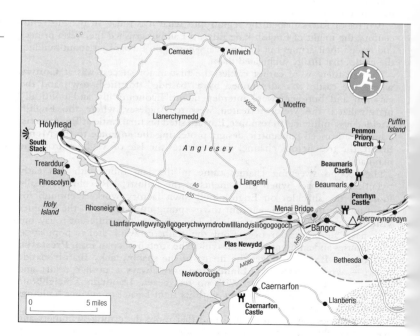

The north coast

Wales' northern seaboard elicits strong reactions. Many return annually to the inexpensive holiday resorts at its eastern end, while others sneer as they pass them by en route to the more highbrow attractions further west. Either way, the initial strip of the **north coast** proper is the ugliest in Wales, an endless array of caravan parks with barely an arm's length between adjacent vehicles – packed each year with fun-seekers from Merseyside and the rest of northern England. The amusements scattered along the promenades and beachfronts seem designed to keep you off the beaches: wise counsel, since the sea here is none too clean. Of the resorts, uninspiring **Prestatyn**, is notable mainly as the starting, or finishing, point of the Offa's Dyke long-distance path, while loud and tacky **Rhyl** offers good budget accommodation and is close to several inland attractions. **Colwyn Bay** is smarter, but pales next to its far superior western neighbours, Conwy and Llandudno.

The great sweep of the north coast is interrupted by the **Great Orme**, a massive limestone hummock that rises above **Llandudno**, queen of the north Wales coast for over a hundred years. Neighbouring **Conwy** is more appealing still, packing more sights than the rest of the coast put together within the girdle of 700-year-old town walls which spur off from the mighty castle. The A55 expressway is held tightly to the coast by the northern fringes of Snowdonia's Carneddau range for the final fifteen miles to **Bangor**, home to north Wales' only university, and consequently its liveliest town.

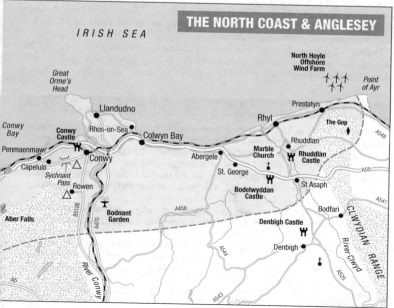

Prestatyn to Colwyn Bay

Almost all the vituperative comments aimed at the north Wales coast are aimed squarely at this heavily populated twenty-mile stretch of amusement arcades, bingo halls, caravan sites and negligible beach. Of the resorts, the best known is **Rhyl** – big, brash and ballsy but with more gentle attractions nearby including the cathedral at tiny **St Asaph**, one of Edward I's castles at **Rhuddlan** and the collection of Victorian portraits and furniture at **Bodelwyddan Castle**. There's little to keep you in **Prestatyn**, although it is the starting point for the Offa's Dyke long-distance path, and close to the Neolithic mound of the **Gop**. The more architecturally coherent, if hardly exciting, **Colwyn Bay** is marginally the nicest of the main resorts.

Prestatyn and around

PRESTATYN is a likeable enough market town, though it's really only of interest as the northern terminus of the 177-mile Offa's Dyke Path, which runs from here to Chepstow (see box, p.257). The more committed traditionally start at least ankle-deep in the water, then cross the beach onto Bastion Road. The path then follows High Street, through the main shopping area, to the *Cross Foxes* pub, from where acorn-marked signs guide you up to the hills behind. You won't come across any of the Offa's Dyke earthworks until the path gets south of the River Dee, since the route planners rightly preferred to send hikers across the Clwydian Range rather than to the scrappy industrial towns of Trevor and Ruabon on the dyke's route. On a good day, though, the view from atop the Clwydian Range is tremendous – east to Liverpool, west to Snowdonia, and north past the offshore windfarm to Blackpool. Beside the beach, the joint **Offa's Dyke Path Centre** and **tourist office** (July–Sept daily 10.30am–4.30pm; Easter–June Sat & Sun 10.30am–4.30pm; ☎01745/889092), contains an interpretive diagram of the route and a stack of leaflets, maps and guides for walkers.

Trains on the north coast line stop in the centre of town, close to the bus station, and a fifteen-minute walk from the central beach and tourist office along Bastion Road. You'll probably want to continue along the coast rather

---

Windfarms in Wales

Britain has hardly been a world leader in renewable energy, but in the 1990s, Welsh hillsides sprouted a dozen or so **windfarms**, comprising some 400 graceful white wind turbines peeking from behind trees or dominating ridgelines. By the turn of the millennium three percent of the UK's energy came from renewable sources. Around the same time, the government set the goal of producing fifteen percent of all its energy sustainably by 2020, a target it is almost certain to miss (probably by a mile).

Complaints about the constant low drone from turbine blades and the visual impact on some of Britain's most beautiful scenery has prompted the development of offshore windfarms, such as the 30-turbine **North Hoyle** windfarm, five miles off the coast of Prestatyn, and the nearby 25-turbine **Rhyl Flats** windfarm, due for completion in 2009. On grey days you can't see them from land, but on clear days they're a striking sight, glistening white on the horizon. Together, these 300-foot-high turbines will soon produce enough power for 80,000 homes. British electricity consumers can support offshore wind power by buying their power from Juice (Ⓦ www.npowerjuice.com).

▲ North Hoyle offshore windfarm

than **stay** here, but there are comfortable en-suite rooms a *Plas Ifan*, 17 Ffordlas (☎01745/887883, Ⓦwww.plasifan.com; ❸) near the *Cross Foxes* pub (see above). The waterfront *Beaches Hotel*, Beach Road East (☎01745/853072, Ⓦwww.thebeacheshotel.com; ❻), has comfy rooms and an indoor pool. The family-oriented *Nant Mill* (☎01745/852360; £13 per pitch; closed mid-Oct to mid-March) is a simple grassy **campsite** a mile east along the A548.

For **eating**, *Suhail Tandoori*, at 12 Bastion Rd on the A548 (☎01745/856829), serves moderately priced Indian food in a converted church near the station.

The Gop

If you've got your own transport, head four miles southeast of Prestatyn to the **Gop**, a neglected piece of ancient history that's Britain's second largest artificial Neolithic mound after Silbury Hill in Wiltshire. Unlike Silbury, which was built on a flat floor, the Gop was constructed on top of an existing hill, crowning an already splendid viewpoint with a mysterious mound – prehistoric remains have been found both in the mound itself and in the caves directly below the hill. The superb **views** over the Clwydian hills from the top are accessed via a path from above the village of **Trelawnyd**, on the A5151. In Trelawnyd, park about 200 yards up High Street and walk along a narrow gravel lane on the left following the discreet yellow discs to the Gop – about fifteen-minutes' walk in all.

Rhyl and around

For raw and raucous seaside shenanigans, **RHYL** (Y Rhyl), three miles west of Prestatyn, is probably your best bet in Wales. The two-mile long Promenade is a powerful assault on the senses, all pulsing lights, whooping arcade games and the ever-present smell of candyfloss and vinegar on chips. While no one would claim that Rhyl is a sophisticated tourist destination, it's as decent a place as any for a cheap, cheerful holiday blowout, especially if you're with kids.

Starting at the tarted-up eastern end of the Promenade, the slides and surfing-wave pool of north Wales' most popular tourist attraction, the **Sun Centre** (mid-March to mid-Sept Tues–Sun 10.30am–5.30pm, plus weekends through

Oct; £7.95; ☎01745/344433, ⓦwww.rhylsuncentre.co.uk), form the main lure. Further west, the **SeaQuarium** (daily: March–Oct 10am–5pm; Nov–Feb 10am–4pm; £6.50; ⓦwww.seaquarium.co.uk) recreates several coastal environments. Its star attraction is the shark tunnel, where dogfish, basking sharks and various eels drift leisurely around you until the day's highlight: feeding time.

Yet further along lies the **Children's Village**, a garish splatter of candy-coloured huts, toddler rides, and a five-screen cinema near the 240-foot **Skytower** (mid-March to mid-Sept Tues–Sun 10.30am–5.30pm, plus weekends through Oct; £2), an observation platform that ascends a huge concrete mast. Across the road, kids squeal at the ghoulish surprises in the **Terror Tombs** (daily 10am–6pm; £2.95).

Practicalities

The **train station** and **bus station** are adjacent, near the intersection of the A548 (Russell/Wellington roads) and the High Street. From the bus station, High Street runs four blocks to the Promenade and the **tourist office** (May–Sept daily 10am–5pm; Oct–April Mon–Fri 9.30am–4.30pm; ☎01745/355068, ⓔrhyl.tic@denbighshire.gov.uk), in the heart of the Children's Village.

Competition has forced **B&B** prices down to some of the lowest in Wales: try *Melbourne*, 8 Beechwood Rd (☎01745/342762, ⓦwww.the-melbourne.co .uk; ❶, en suite ❷), off East Parade near the Sun Centre, or *Kilkee Guesthouse*, 50 River St (☎01745/350070; ❸), off the right-hand side of Wellington Road, walking west from the tourist office. For a bit of luxury, *Barratt's*, Ty'n Rhyl, 167 Vale Rd (☎01745/344138, ⓦwww.barrattsoftynrhyl.co.uk; ❺), has an excellent on-site restaurant (see below) and offers sumptuous and well-appointed rooms. Despite the vast number of caravan parks in the area, the nearest **campsite** is four miles east at *Nant Mill* (see p.421).

Cheap cafés and takeaways abound in Rhyl, but classier **eating** also exists. *Deli-t-full*, 10 Bodfor St, near the train station, is a spruce daytime café which does good sandwiches, wraps and jacket spuds, while *Boswell's* on Bodfor Street (☎01745/355492) offers an eclectic range of inexpensive bistro food and a healthy wine and cocktail list. Pricey *Barratt's* (see above) is the best place in town, offering modern cuisine in Rhyl's oldest house.

Rhuddlan

RHUDDLAN, three miles to the north of Rhyl, and essentially a suburb of it, lies on the banks of a tidal reach of the Clwyd River (Afon Clywedog) and is dominated by the large and impressive hollow ruin of **Rhuddlan Castle** (April–Sept daily 10am–5pm; £3.10; CADW). Constructed between 1277 and 1282 by Edward I during his first phase of castle-building, Rhuddlan was designed as both a garrison and royal residence, commanding a canalized section of the then strategic river that allowed boats to service the castle and provided water for the huge stone-lined moat. **Gillot's Tower**, by the dock gate, provided protection for the supply ships. The massive towers were the work of James of St George, who was responsible for the concentric plan that allowed archers on both outer and inner walls to fire simultaneously. This had become irrelevant by 1648, when Parliament forces took the castle during the Civil War and demolished it. Stairs now give access to the top of the East Gatehouse.

Important though the castle was, Rhuddlan earns its position in Welsh history as the place where Edward I signed the **Statute of Rhuddlan** on March 19, 1284, consigning Wales to centuries of subjugation by the English that many insist still continues. The ceremony took place on the site of **Parliament**

House, on the main street 200 yards to the north. A sign on the building cynically claims that the Statute secured Welsh "judicial rights and independence", despite the fact that Edward laid down the laws by which the Welsh should be governed, including the outlawing of the native language in any official capacity.

Rhuddlan is served by the frequent #51 **bus** from Rhyl.

St Asaph

Six miles south of Rhyl, a single main street forms the heart of Britain's second smallest city, **ST ASAPH** (Llanelwy). While the city of St Davids in Pembrokeshire is slightly less populous, St Asaph boasts the country's smallest **cathedral** (daily 9am–6.30pm) – a squat-towered edifice no bigger than many village churches.

The town's Welsh name (meaning "the church on Elwy River") dates back to around 570 when St Asaph succeeded the cathedral's founder, St Kentigern, as abbot, and became its first bishop. Both are commemorated in the easternmost window in the north aisle of the cathedral. In 1282, Edward I's men ravaged the church, leaving the incumbent bishop Anian II (whose effigy is in the south aisle) with the task of building the present structure, which itself was attacked in 1402 by Owain Glyndŵr, though only the woodwork was lost and soon replaced.

From 1601 until his death in 1604, the bishopric was held by **William Morgan** (see box, p.424), who was responsible for the translation of the first Welsh-language Bible in 1588. An octagonal monument in the churchyard on the north side of the cathedral commemorates the work of Morgan and his fellow translators, including William Salusbury and Gabriel Goodman (see p.343). This is Morgan's only memorial; his grave under the presbytery has been unmarked since Giles Gilbert Scott's substantial restoration in the 1870s. Around a thousand Morgan Bibles were printed – one for every church in the land – of which only nineteen remain, one of them displayed in the south aisle along with Elizabeth I's 1549 copy of *The Book of Common Prayer* that only slightly predated Salusbury's New Testament translation of 1567. In the south transept you'll find a handsome collection of psalter and prayer books, along with an exquisite sixteenth-century ivory Madonna, said to have come from the Spanish Armada.

In a similar vein, the churchyard of St Kentigern and St Asaph's Church, a couple of hundred yards down High Street, contains the tombstone of Richard Robert Jones, the nineteenth-century compiler of a Welsh-Greek-Hebrew dictionary. Usually known as Dic Aberdaron, after the fishing village where he was born in 1780, he lived more or less as a tramp whilst acquiring command of fifteen languages and smatterings of another twenty. His tombstone is engraved with a few lines by Ellis Owen, which translate as:

A linguist eight times above other linguists – truly he was
A dictionary of every province.
Death took away his fifteen languages.
Below he is now without a language at all.

Practicalities

The A55 runs close by St Asaph, but without your own transport you're reliant on local **buses**, which all stop outside the cathedral. There's comfortable **accommodation** at *Plas Elwy* (℡01745/582263, ⓦwww.gtleisure.co.uk /plaselwy; ③), on The Roe – down High Street from the cathedral, across the river bridge then right; and excellent B&B a couple of miles east at *Tan-yr-Onnen*,

Until 1588 only English Bibles had been used in Welsh churches, a fact which rankled Welsh-born preacher **William Morgan**, who insisted: "Religion, if it is not taught in the mother tongue, will lie hidden and unknown". This was the professed reason behind Elizabeth I's demand for a translation, though her subjects' disaffection could be most conveniently controlled through the church. Four clergymen took up the challenge over a period of 25 years, but it is Morgan who is remembered: working away in Llanrhaeadr-ym-Mochnant (see p.266), he so neglected his other duties that he needed an armed guard to get to his services and was said to preach with a pistol at his side.

The eventual translation was so successful that the Privy Council decreed that a copy should be allocated to every Welsh church. Though it was soon replaced by a translation of the Authorized Version, Morgan's Bible differs little in style from the latest edition used in Welsh services today. More than just a basis for sermons, The *Welsh Bible* (*Y Beibl*) served to codify the language and set a standard for Welsh prose. Without it the language would probably have divided into several dialects or even followed its Brythonic cousin, Cornish, into history.

Waen (℗01745/583821, Ⓦwww.northwalesbreaks.co.uk; ❹). For something special, head four miles west to the picturesque hamlet of **St George** and the 🍴 *Kinmel Arms* (℗01745/832207, Ⓦwww.thekinmelarms.co.uk; restaurant and hotel closed Sun & Mon; ❼), a lovely seventeenth-century pub with chic, modern and gorgeously furnished rooms.

You can get snacks, coffee and picnic supplies from the Farm Shop, halfway down High Street. For more substantial **meals**, try the *Plough Inn*, The Roe, home to a lively bar with several real ales on tap and a wide selection of bar meals (£8–10). Alternatively, head out to the 🍴 *Kinmel Arms* (closed Sun & Mon) for a wide selection of fine beer and wine, great espresso, classy brasserie lunch mains (£7–11) and fancier à la carte dishes in the evenings (£13–20).

Marble Church and Bodelwyddan Castle: the National Portrait Gallery

At **BODELWYDDAN**, two miles west of St Asaph along the A55 expressway, the slender 202-foot limestone spire of **Marble Church** stands as a beacon over the flat coastal plain. The spire's finely worked Gothic tracery is its most impressive feature, and is continued inside around the marble arcades that give the church its name.

Half a mile to the south amid landscaped grounds, **Bodelwyddan Castle** (April–July, Sept & Oct daily except Fri 10.30am–5pm; Aug daily 10.30am–5pm; Nov–March Thurs 10.30am–5pm, Sat & Sun 10.30am–4pm; £5 including audio tour; Ⓦwww.bodelwyddan-castle.co.uk) is essentially a nineteenth-century country mansion, its opulent Victorian interiors re-created during its restoration in the 1980s, after sixty years during which it was home to Lowther College girls' school. It now houses one of four provincial outposts of the **National Portrait Gallery**, specializing in works contemporary with the castle.

Most of the hundred paintings are on the ground floor, approached through the "Watts Hall of Fame", a long corridor lined with 26 portraits of eminent Victorians by G.F. Watts, among them Millais, Rossetti, Browning and Walter Crane. In the Dining Room, two portraits highlight the Pre-Raphaelite support for social reform: William Holman Hunt's portrayal of the vociferous opponent of slavery and capital punishment, Stephen Lushington; and Ford Madox

Brown's double portrait of Henry Farell, prime mover in the passing of the 1867 Reform Bill, and suffragette Millicent Garrett. Works by John Singer Sargent and Hubert von Herkamer also adorn the room, which, like the others, is furnished with pieces from the Victoria and Albert Museum in London. The table and chairs originally belonged to one Alfred Waterhouse, who designed the superb walnut and boxwood grand piano.

More worthy Victorians line the Library, which leads on to the Ladies' Drawing Room, where a beautiful Biedermeier sofa outshines the paintings of nineteenth-century society ladies. A grand staircase leads up to further examples of nineteenth-century portraiture and an interesting exhibit on the castle's time as Lowther College.

The #51 **bus** from Rhyl or Rhuddlan, brings you within ten-minutes' walk of both the castle and the church.

Colwyn Bay and Rhos-on-Sea

COLWYN BAY (Bae Colwyn), twelve miles west of Rhyl, has marginally more charm than its eastern neighbours, with its hilly setting, architecturally intact Victorian main street and old-fashioned seafront enhanced by a semi-working pier. Perhaps the nicest way to explore town is by heading along the shore; the Prestatyn to Rhos-on-Sea **cycle path** offers good views – you can rent a bike from West End Cycles (℡01492/530269) at 121 Conwy Rd in Colwyn's West End.

Two miles inland and steeply uphill, the **Welsh Mountain Zoo** (daily: March–Oct 9.30am–6pm; Nov–Feb 9.30am–4pm; £8.75; ⓦwww .welshmountainzoo.org), which boasts Californian sea lions, snow leopards and free-flying raptor displays. A free shuttle bus runs every twenty minutes (Easter to mid-Sept) between the zoo and the town's train station.

Colwyn Bay merges into **RHOS-ON-SEA**, whose ninety-minute **Harlequin Puppet Theatre** (July, Aug and most school holidays daily 3pm & Wed 8pm; £5; ℡01492/548166) is pitched at both adults and kids and is one of the very few remaining marionette acts in the British tradition.

At Rhos Point, half a mile further on, the minuscule **St Trillo's chapel** has seating for just six worshippers, so may have standing room only during the services (generally Sun at 8am, 9am & 11am). The chapel stands over an ancient healing well and was reputedly the launch point of Prince Madoc ap Owain Gwynedd's voyage to America in 1170 – Welshmen and women the world over like to claim that he was the first European to visit the New World, over three hundred years before Christopher Columbus.

Trains stop on the Colwyn Bay seafront. There are plenty of guesthouses and dining options nearby, though you're better off staying and eating in nearby Llandudno or Conwy.

Llandudno

The twin limestone hummocks of the 680-foot **Great Orme** and its southern cousin the Little Orme provide a dramatic frame for the gently curving Victorian frontage of **LLANDUDNO**, Wales' most enduring archetype of the genteel British seaside resort. The core of the town occupies a low isthmus between two beachfronts: Llandudno Bay, where the older set of promenading devotees can be found huddled in the glass frontages of once grand hotels, and the less developed West Shore. Despite the arrival of more rumbustious fun-seekers, Llandudno retains an undeniably dignified air, but steers clear of retirement-home stagnation.

The town's early history revolves around the Great Orme, where St Tudno, who brought Christianity to the region in the sixth century, built the monastic cell that gives Llandudno its name. When the early Victorian copper mines seemed exhausted, local landowner Edward Mostyn began a venture to exploit the growing craze for sea bathing, with a resort for the upper middle classes. As MP for the constituency, with the Bishop of Bangor in his pocket, Mostyn was able to tease through an enclosure act giving him the rights to develop the land.

Within fifty years of its foundation in 1854, Llandudno had become synonymous with the Victorian ideal of a refined resort, drawing music stars such as Adelina Patti and Jules Rivière, the French conductor who sat in a gilded armchair facing the audience as he waved his bejewelled ivory baton. Mostyn Street, with its wrought-iron and glass verandas, was said to have some of the finest shops outside London, patronized by the likes of Bismarck, Napoléon III, Gladstone and Queen Elizabeth of Romania, who stayed here for five weeks in 1890 and reputedly gave the town its motto *Hardd, haran, hedd*, meaning "beautiful haven of peace". Mostyn Street's emporia are less exalted today, but as the coast's largest town Llandudno is a bustling place, its ever-improving selection of chic hotels and quality restaurants setting it above much of the immediate area.

Arrival, information and getting around

Direct trains from Chester and Betws-y-Coed, and indirect ones from Bangor (change at Llandudno Junction near Conwy) terminate at the forlorn **train station**, five minutes' walk from the **tourist office** on Mostyn Street (Easter–Sept Mon–Sat 9am–5.30pm, Sun 9.30am–4.30pm; Oct–Easter Mon–Sat 9am–5pm; ☎01492/876413, ⊛www.visitllandudno.org.uk). Local **buses** from Bangor, Betws-y-Coed, Conwy and Rhyl stop on Mostyn Street, while National Express services (bookings at the tourist office) uses the coach park on Mostyn Broadway.

The tourist office stocks a free map of Great Orme footpaths, though most people drive or use the tram or cable car (see p.430). Alpine (☎01492/876606) run **tours** for those in a hurry. These include trips in a 1950s vintage bus (3 daily year round; £5) along Marine Drive, leaving from North Parade near the pier; and an open-top double-decker bus looping from Llandudno to Conwy and back (late May to mid-Sept every 30min 10am–4pm; £6.50). **Bikes** can be rented from Snowdonia Cycle Hire (☎01492/878771, ⊛www.snowdoniacyclehire.co.uk; £17 a day, £12 half-day), who deliver and collect bikes within six miles of Llandudno at no extra charge.

There's free **internet** access at the library (Mon, Tues & Fri 9am–6pm, Wed 10am–5pm, Thurs 9am–7pm, Sat 9.30am–1pm) and low-cost internet and wi-fi at *Nineteen* (see p.431).

Accommodation

With several hundred **hotels**, finding somewhere to stay in Llandudno isn't usually a problem: competition keeps **prices** low and rates are often cheaper if you stay for two or more nights. In high summer (and especially bank holidays), booking ahead is wise: if everywhere below is full, your best bets for inexpensive accommodation are St David's Road and Deganwy Avenue, each of which has almost a dozen guesthouses. The nearest **camping** is in Conwy.

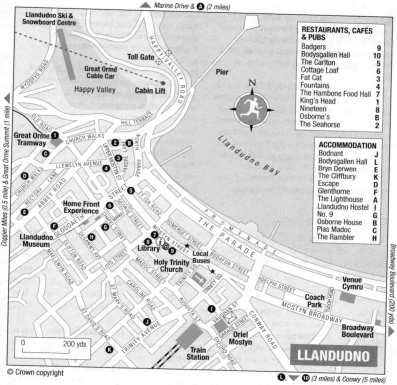

© Crown copyright

Map labels:
Marine Drive & **A** (2 miles)
Llandudno Ski & Snowboard Centre
Toll Gate
Great Orme Cable Car
Happy Valley
Cabin Lift
Pier
Llandudno Bay
N
HAPPY VALLEY ROAD
WYDDFYD ROAD
OLD ROAD
HILL TERRACE
Great Orme Tramway **1**
CHURCH WALKS
LLEWELYN AVENUE
ABBEY ROAD
RECTORY LANE
UPPER MOSTYN STREET
NORTH PARADE
VAUGHAN LANE
Home Front Experience
Llandudno Museum
GLODDAETH
CLIFTON ROAD
MOSTYN STREET
GEORGE STREET
CHAPEL STREET
TUDNO STREET
TY ISA ROAD
SOMERSET STREET
THE PARADE
PROMENADE
BODAFON STREET
Library
Holy Trinity Church
Local Buses
MADOC STREET
LLOYD STREET
LLEWELYN AVENUE
ST MARY'S ROAD
ST DAVID'S ROAD
CAROLINE ROAD
TRINITY AVENUE
TRINITY SQ
GARAGE STREET
AUGUSTA ST
VAUGHAN ST
ADELPHI STREET
CONWAY ROAD
OXFORD ROAD
Oriel Mostyn
Train Station
Venue Cymru
Coach Park
MOSTYN BROADWAY
Broadway Boulevard
LLANDUDNO

Copper Mines (0.5 mile) & Great Orme Summit (1 mile)

Broadway Boulevard (200 yds)

L, ▼ **10** (3 miles) & Conwy (5 miles)

0 200 yds

RESTAURANTS, CAFÉS & PUBS
Badgers — 9
Bodysgallen Hall — 10
The Carlton — 5
Cottage Loaf — 6
Fat Cat — 3
Fountains — 4
The Hambone Food Hall — 7
King's Head — 1
Nineteen — 8
Osborne's — B
The Seahorse — 2

ACCOMMODATION
Bodnant — J
Bodysgallen Hall — L
Bryn Derwen — E
The Cliffbury — K
Escape — D
Glenthorne — F
The Lighthouse — A
Llandudno Hostel — I
No. 9 — G
Osborne House — B
Plas Madoc — C
The Rambler — H

Bodnant 39 St Mary's Rd ☎01492/876936, ⓦwww.bodnantguesthouse.biz. Comfortable six-room guesthouse (including two singles for £35) on a tree-lined street. **3**

Bodysgallen Hall 3 miles south of town on the A470 ☎01492/584466, ⓦwww.bodysgallen.com. One of the top country hotels in Wales, set in a partly seventeenth-century house surrounded by 200 acres of terraced lawns and gardens. There are antique-filled rooms, all beautifully decorated and festooned with flowers, in the house itself and in cottages in the grounds. **8**

Bryn Derwen 34 Abbey Rd ☎01492/876804, ⓦwww.bryn-derwen.co.uk. Sumptuous yet informal small hotel at the foot of the Orme, with huge Victorian common areas, off-street parking and home-cooked meals. Licensed. Closed Dec & Jan. **6**

The Cliffbury 34 St David's Rd ☎01492/877224, ⓦwww.thecliffbury.co.uk. A recent overhaul brings stylish feature wallpapers and sparkling white bathrooms to the seven individually decorated rooms in this hotel on a quiet street. There's wi-fi and home-style three-course evening

meals (£15). Superior rooms are bigger and come with DVD player and robes. Generally two-night minimum. **3–4**

Escape 48 Church Walks ☎01492/877776, ⓦwww.escapebandb.co.uk. Chic, boutique B&B with nine lovely individually designed rooms combining clean-lined modernism with retro or antique touches. Aveda toiletries, wi-fi, classy breakfasts and a guest lounge with honesty bar complete the package. **5**

Glenthorne 2 York Rd ☎01492/879591. Very good guesthouse with seven comfy rooms and a welcoming atmosphere, plus good-value three-course evening meals (£12). **2**

The Lighthouse Marine Drive ☎01492/876819, ⓦwww.lighthouse-llandudno.co.uk. Very comfortable B&B in a former lighthouse fabulously sited on cliffs over 300 feet above the northern end of the Great Orme. All the rooms are completely different (though all have sea views), and include one where the lamp turned until decommissioning in 1985. **8**

Llandudno Hostel 14 Charlton St ☎01492/877430, ⓦwww.llandudnohostel.co.uk. Family-run, forty-bed hostel in the centre of town with dorm beds (£17), doubles, a family room and a friendly atmosphere. Sheets, towels and a continental breakfast are supplied, but there's no self-catering kitchen. Often full with school groups during termtime, so call ahead. ❶

No. 9 9 Chapel St ☏01492/877251, ⌨www .no9llandudno.co.uk. Excellent value and very welcoming B&B with tastefully decorated rooms (all with DVD players), comfy guest lounge, free internet access, wi-fi throughout, and very good breakfasts. There's also an en-suite single (£29), one room with a bathtub and a cosy, attic studio flat with kitchen (£40 without breakfast). No credit cards. ❷

Osborne House 17 North Parade ☏01492 /860330, ⌨www.osbornehouse.co.uk.

Effortless elegance and pampering (antique beds, marble bathrooms, widescreen TV, deep bath and shower) in enormous suites overlooking the Promenade, plus an attached restaurant (see p.431). ❻

Plas Madoc 60 Church Walks ☏01492/876514, ⌨www.plasmadocguesthouse.co.uk. Comfortable guesthouse at the base of the Great Orme with rooms decorated predominantly in white, and with a superior room with bath and good views over the town. Full breakfasts include the option of soy milk, vegan sausages and the like. Free wi-fi. ❸–❹

The Rambler 15 Deganwy Ave ☏01492/875618. One of the cheapest B&Bs around, clean and well run, with a mix of rooms with and without en suite. ❶–❷

The Town

While much daytime activity revolves around the Great Orme, first-time visitors are inevitably drawn to the **pier** (unrestricted access; free) jutting into Llandudno Bay, with views back to the limestone cliffs. Once the embodiment of Llandudno's ornate Victoriana, its neat wooden deck is overrun in summer with kids clamouring to board the modest fairground rides, and deckchair denizens cocking an ear to the taped sounds of some Wurlitzer maestro. Ice cream and candyfloss outlets abound, as a town ordinance bars the sale of such fripperies anywhere else on the waterfront.

If you're interested in Llandudno's past, don't miss the **Llandudno Town Trail**, with panels full of interesting nuggets scattered around town, which are mapped on a free leaflet from the tourist office.

South of the pier and a few-minutes' walk inland, the **Llandudno Museum**, 17 Gloddaeth St (Easter–Oct Tues–Sat 10.30am–1pm & 2–5pm, Sun 2.15–5pm; Nov–Easter Tues–Sat 1.30–4.30pm; £1.50), exhibits items unearthed in local copper mines (see opposite), Roman artefacts and a rural kitchen from Llanberis. Behind the museum on New Street, the **World War II Home Front Experience** (March–Oct Mon–Sat 10am–4.30pm, Sun 11am–3pm; £3.25) pays a nostalgic visit to early 1940s Britain, with wartime shopfronts, wardens' huts, bomb shelters and the like all packed into one small room, where ration books and children's toys are displayed alongside evocative treatment of the Women's Land Army.

From the pier, it's a leisurely ten-minute stroll along The Promenade, with its regal four-storey terraced hotels, to Vaughan Street and the region's premier contemporary art gallery at no. 12. **Oriel Mostyn** (Tues–Sat 10am–5pm; free; ⌨www.mostyn.org) is named after Lady Mostyn, for whom it was built in 1901. The gallery has no permanent collection, but its six yearly shows are usually worth seeing, with a particular leaning towards the current Welsh arts scene.

Otherwise, Llandudno is a supremely easy place in which to wander: on a sunny day, join the ranks of folk on the seafront deckchairs or head down to the beach, a sand and shingle affair where you might find a few sunbathers and the odd hardy swimmer.

The Great Orme

The views from the top of the **Great Orme** (Y Gogarth) are magical, stretching out over the seascapes all around: east towards Rhyl, west to the shores of Anglesey,

▲ Great Orme Tramway

and south beyond the sands of the Conwy estuary to the brooding, quarried northern limits of the Carneddau, where Snowdonia crashes into the sea.

Take a short walk across the rounded summit to escape from the crowds around the car park – it's easy to find somewhere to admire the view as fulmars wheel on the thermals, but less easy to see the feral goats which roam all over the mountain. Formed about 300 million years ago at the bottom of a tropical sea, this huge lump of carboniferous limestone was subsequently veined by mineral-bearing rock. Though there are a few minor Neolithic sites on the hill, it was in the Bronze Age that the settlement really developed, when the people began to smelt the contents of the malachite-rich veins, supplying copper throughout Europe, according to current thinking. The Celts further exploited the ore but there is no evidence of the mine being worked by Vikings who subsequently visited the area. Their legacy is the name: Orme derives from Old

Norse meaning "worm" or "sea serpent" – which is just how the Great Orme might have appeared in the mist to those approaching by sea.

Today the mountain is home to a profusion of rare or endangered maritime botanical species: goldilocks aster, spotted cats-ear and spiked speedwell. You can learn more about this intriguing place at the informative **Great Orme Country Park Visitor Centre** (Easter–Oct daily 10am–5pm; free) by the cafés and bar at the **Summit Complex** (Easter–Oct daily noon–11pm; Nov–Easter Sat & Sun only, same hours).

Apart from walking, there are three other ways to explore the Orme. The traditional favourite is **Marine Drive**, a four-mile circuit cut into the rock high above the coast. You can walk or cycle around Marine Drive (free), or make the anticlockwise circuit from near Llandudno's pier in your own car (£2.50 toll applies summer roughly 9am–8pm; winter 9am–4pm; access free at other times). A summit road leads off Marine Drive; with free parking at the top.

A separate route – Old Road – leads directly from Llandudno to the Summit Complex, running parallel to the mile-long route of the vintage, San Francisco-style **Great Orme Tramway** (Easter–Sept 10am–6pm; Oct 10am–5pm; £3.90 single, £5.20 return; Ⓦwww.greatormetramway.com), creaking up from the bottom of Old Road much as it has done since 1902. The third route starts at the base of the pier, close to the start of Marine Drive, where an Italianate colonnade flanks the short road to the **Happy Valley** formal gardens and the **Cable Car** (Easter–Oct daily roughly 10am–5pm, depending on the weather; £6.50), which lifts people up to the Summit Complex in open four-seater cabins. At the start it swings over **Llandudno Ski & Snowboard Centre** (variable hours, but generally daily 10am–10pm), where £17 gets you a couple of hours on the dry slopes (including all equipment), or for around a quarter of the price, you can make a couple of runs down the 700-yard-long, snow-free **Toboggan Run**.

The Great Orme Copper Mines

From the tramway's halfway station, it's a five-minute walk to the long-disused **Great Orme Copper Mines** (mid-March to Oct daily 9.30am–5pm; £6; ☏01492/870447, Ⓦwww.greatormemines.info). The earliest workings here were always assumed to be Roman, until excavations in the 1980s uncovered 4000-year-old animal bones that had been used as scrapers up to 200ft down. This is one of the few sites in Britain where mineral veins were accompanied by dolomitization, a rock-softening process which permitted copper to be extracted using the simple tools available in the Bronze Age, which led to Great Orme becoming the pre-eminent copper mine in Europe, if not the world.

After an explanatory video, the **self-guided tour** takes you down through a small portion of the four miles of tunnels so far uncovered – enough to get a feel for the cramped working conditions, and to see the burial site of one of three cats thought to have been sacrificed by superstitious miners. Topside, you can see some of the ongoing excavations and get a idea of how the copper ore was smelted to make tools.

Eating, drinking and entertainment

Llandudno is blessed with the best choice of **restaurants** in north Wales. Most cluster at the foot of the Great Orme around Mostyn Street, where numerous **pubs** cater to most tastes. The liveliest bars are along Upper Mostyn Street, which can be chaotically crowded at weekends.

Restaurants and cafés

Badgers Victoria Centre, Mostyn St. Slightly twee but excellent café and lunch spot, the higher prices justified by the food quality, attentive service and a range of five blends of cafetière coffee.

Bodysgallen Hall 3 miles south of town on the A470 ☏ 01492/584466. Top-notch traditional and modern British fare in one of Britain's best country hotels. Go for the full three-course dinner (£43; smart dress required) or a sumptuous lunch overlooking the gardens (£19–23). The afternoon teas (£14) and Sunday lunches (£27) are superb.

The Hambone Food Hall Lloyd St. Excellent deli producing great takeaway sandwiches to order along with a wide range of meat pies, pâtés, salads and tapas to go or eat in. Decent espresso, too.

Nineteen 19 Lloyd St. Casual café serving a range of panini, wraps and jacket potatoes along with a huge range of excellent juices and smoothies, plus wi-fi (extra charge).

Osborne's 17 North Parade ☏ 01492/860330, Ⓦ www.osbornehouse.co.uk. Opulent cream and white café and grill lit by candles and chandeliers with modern dishes such as lamb shanks with ratatouille (£12) and grilled sea bass with herb couscous. Or just pop in for coffee and cakes or a glass of wine.

The Seahorse 7 Church Walks ☏ 01492/875315, Ⓦ www.the-seahorse.co.uk. Intimate dinner-only restaurant with a bistro-style area downstairs and more formal seating upstairs. You're offered the same menu (£27 for 3 courses) in both areas, which might include seafood terrine followed by monkfish tail with a herb risotto. Closed Sun & Mon.

Bars and pubs

The Carlton 121 Mostyn St, corner of Gloddaeth St. Lively town-centre pub with a pool table, good beer and fine iron-and-glass verandas.

Cottage Loaf Market St. Flagstoned pub built from ships' timbers atop an old bakehouse. Popular for lunchtime eating and drinking all day.

Fat Cat 149 Upper Mostyn St. Frantic and fun café-bar with an eclectic clientele and heated outdoor section for year-round alfresco drinking and people-watching.

Fountains 114 Upper Mostyn St. Hugely popular early evening meeting point that's good for shots and cocktails.

King's Head Old Rd, by the bottom of the tramway. Llandudno's oldest pub, where Edward Mostyn and his surveyor mapped out the town, with some interesting photos and substantial, tasty bar meals, ranging from Welsh rarebit to noisettes of lamb.

Entertainment

Broadway Boulevard Grand Theatre, Mostyn Broadway, on the corner of Ty'n y Ffridd Rd ☏ 01492/879614. Llandudno's liveliest club, with a host of party nights.

Cineworld ☏ 0871/200 2000, Ⓦ www.cineworld.co.uk. Three miles south in Llandudno Junction, with nine screens.

Venue Cymru (Theatr Gogledd Cymru) The Promenade ☏ 01492/872000, Ⓦ www.venuecymru.co.uk. North Wales' premier live entertainment centre, this modern 1500-seat theatre lures touring companies and occasional international acts.

Conwy and around

Despite its small size, there's a huge amount to see and do in **CONWY**. Its complete belt of town walls enclose not just a stunning early-medieval castle but some fascinating glimpses into the past of north Wales. The town remains one of the highlights of the north coast, its setting on the Conwy estuary, backed by a forested fold of Snowdonia, irresistible to painters and photographers ever since Englishman Paul Sandby published his *Views of North Wales* in 1776. Even if you're a little weary of castle-hopping, Conwy is still worth a stop, whether for the wondrous Elizabethan town house, Plas Mawr, the three estuary bridges, or cutesy treats like Britain's smallest house and the Butterfly Jungle.

In Sandby's day, the Conwy estuary still produced a good living for the families who had held mussel-gathering rights on the sands for centuries, a heritage going back long before the foundation of the Cistercian monastery of Aberconwy here in 1172. The monastery, where Llywelyn ap Iorwerth ("the Great") died in 1240, was on the present site of the parish church of St Mary and All Saints, but a century later was moved eight miles upriver to Maenan, near Llanrwst, to make way for one of the doughtiest links in Edward I's chain of fortresses.

Arrival and information

Llandudno Junction, less than a mile across the river to the east, serves as the main **train station** for services from Chester to Holyhead, as well as for trains heading south to Betws-y-Coed and Blaenau Ffestiniog; only slow, regional services stop in Conwy itself (on request). National Express **buses** on the north coast run mostly stop in Llandudno, though usually one service a day pulls up outside the town walls on Town Ditch Road, as do open-top double-deckers to Llandudno. Local buses to Bangor and points west stop on Lancaster Square, while those to Betws-y-Coed, Llandudno and points east stop on Castle Street.

The **tourist office** (April–Oct daily 9am–5pm; Nov–March Mon–Sat 9.30am–4pm, Sun 11am–4pm; ☏01492/592248) shares the same building and hours as the castle ticket office. **Bikes** can be rented from Snowdonia Cycle Hire (☏01492/878771, ⓦ www.snowdoniacyclehire.co.uk; £17 a day, £12 half day), who deliver.

© Crown copyright

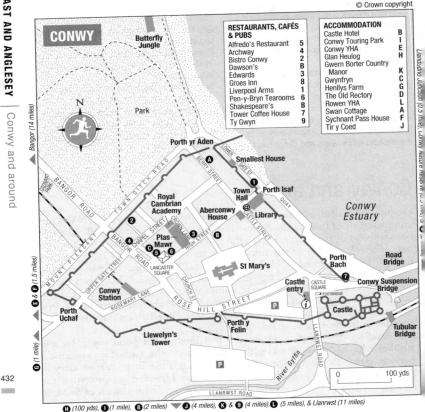

RESTAURANTS, CAFÉS & PUBS

Alfredo's Restaurant	5
Archway	4
Bistro Conwy	2
Dawson's	B
Edwards	3
Groes Inn	1
Liverpool Arms	8
Pen-y-Bryn Tearooms	6
Shakespeare's	B
Tower Coffee House	7
Ty Gwyn	9

ACCOMMODATION

Castle Hotel	B
Conwy Touring Park	I
Conwy YHA	H
Glan Heulog	K
Gwern Borter Country Manor	C
Gwynfryn	G
Henllys Farm	D
The Old Rectory	L
Rowen YHA	A
Swan Cottage	F
Sychnant Pass House	J
Tir y Coed	

Accommodation

Although the Conwy region offers a fair range of **accommodation** – including the only town-centre YHA hostel in the vicinity – the choice is a bit thin in the heart of town, and those without the transport to reach the less central places should book ahead in summer.

Hotels and guesthouses

Castle Hotel High St ☎01492/582800, ⓦwww .castlewales.co.uk. Former coaching inn in the heart of town, now restored to the exalted standard it deserves. There's also a very good restaurant where substantial breakfasts are served. ❼

Glan Heulog Llanrwst Rd ☎01492/593845, ⓦwww.snowdoniabandb.co.uk. One of Conwy's best small guesthouses, half a mile out on the B5106 Trefriw road with mostly en-suite rooms. ❸

Gwern Borter Country Manor Barker's Lane, Rowen ☎01492/650360, ⓦwww .snowdoniaholidays.co.uk. Comfortable manor house on a Conwy Valley farm just north of Rowen (bus #19), with sauna, gym and pony trekking available and easy access to walks into the nearby Carneddau range. ❹

Gwynfryn 4 York Place ☎01492/576733, ⓦwww .gwynfrynbandb.co.uk. B&B with five tastefully decorated rooms, each boasting a small fridge and DVD player, and access to a movie library. There's also free wi-fi and internet. The "superior" rooms have more space, views and bathtubs. ❸–❹

Henllys Farm Llechwedd, 1.5 miles west of Conwy ☎01492/593269. Appealing guesthouse on a working farm. Turn up Upper Gate St, bear left along St Agnes Rd, then follow signs for Llechwedd – Henllys is on the right. ❷

The Old Rectory Llansantffraid Glan Conwy ☎01492/580611, ⓦwww.oldrectorycountryhouse .co.uk. Georgian-style country house, opulently furnished with antiques and fine paintings, overlooking the Conwy estuary, a mile up the Conwy Valley. ❽

Swan Cottage 18 Berry St ☎01492/596840, ⓦswancottage.net. Central B&B with small but attractive en-suite rooms, two with great estuary views. ❷

Sychnant Pass House 1.5 miles up Sychnant Pass ☎01492/596868, ⓦwww .sychnant-pass-house.co.uk. More like a welcoming family home than a hotel, with comfortable rooms, an indoor pool, relaxing lounges stocked with games, books and cats, and extensive grounds where dogs play (guests' dogs are welcome). Five-course dinner (£30) is available nightly. ❻

Tir y Coed Rowen ☎01492 650219, ⓦwww .tirycoed.com. Very peaceful country house with landscaped grounds and views of the Carneddau range from some of the eight bold and eclectically decorated rooms, most with bathtubs. Dining (table d'hôte; £29) is part of the experience. ❻

Hostels and campsites

Conwy Touring Park ☎01492/592856, ⓦwww .conwytouringpark.com. A fully equipped campsite, just over a mile south along the B5106 (bus #19). It operates a strict "families and couples only" rule, so you'll have to look reasonably respectable to get in. Closed Nov–March. £9–17 per tent.

Conwy YHA Lark Hill ☎01492/593571 or 0870/770 5774, ⓔconwy@yha.org.uk. Spacious, modern hostel a 10min walk from town up the Sychnant Pass road with private rooms and small dorms (£17–22). The place is open all day, serves good-value meals (and is licensed), and also rents bikes to guests (£8 a half day). Open mid-Feb to Oct and winter weekends. ❶

Rowen YHA Rowen, half a mile up a steep hill above the village ☎0870/770 6012. Simple YHA hostel on the flanks of the Carneddau range, with superb views over the Conwy Valley. Bunks cost £13.50. Reached by turning right 200 yards past Rowen's pub, and served by bus #19 from Conwy. Open Easter & May–Aug.

The Town

Nothing within Conwy's core of medieval and Victorian buildings is more than two hundred yards from the irregular triangle of protective masonry formed by the town walls, which makes the town wonderfully easy to potter around. Though you'll get to see everything you want to in a day, you might want to stay longer.

Conwy Castle

During their incursions along Wales' north coast, Edward I's Anglo-Norman ancestors had all but destroyed the castle at Deganwy, near Llandudno, but

▲ Conwy Castle

maintaining a bridgehead west of the Conwy River had always eluded them. Accordingly, once over the river in 1283, Edward set about establishing another of his bastide towns. He chose a strategic knoll at the mouth of the Conwy River and set James of St George to fashion a castle to fit its contours. With the help of 1500 men, James took just five years to build **Conwy Castle** (April–Oct daily 9am–5pm; Nov–March Mon–Sat 9.30am–4pm, Sun 11am–4pm; last entry half an hour before closing; £4.70, joint ticket with Plas Mawr £7; CADW).

Overlooked by a low hill, the castle appears less easily defensible than others along the coast, but James constructed eight massive towers in a rectangle around the two wards, the inner one separated from the outer by a drawbridge and portcullis, and further protected by turrets atop the four eastern towers.

Barring a brief siege during the Welsh uprising of 1294, the castle saw little action until 1399, when Richard II stayed there on his return from Ireland, until lured from safety by the Earl of Northumberland, Bolingbroke's vassal. Northumberland swore in the castle's chapel to grant Richard safe passage, but imprisoned him at Flint, enabling Bolingbroke to become Henry IV. From the fifteenth century, the castle fell into disuse, and was bought in 1627 for £100 by Charles I's Secretary of State, Lord Conway of Ragley, who then had to refortify it for the Civil War. At the restoration of the monarchy in 1665, the castle was stripped of all its iron, wood and lead, and left substantially as it is today.

Strolling along the ramparts, you can look down onto something unique amongst the Iron Ring fortresses, a roofless but largely intact interior. The outer ward's 130-foot-long Great Hall and the King's Apartments are both well preserved, but the only part of the castle to have kept its roof is the **Chapel Tower**, named for the small room built into the wall whose semicircular apse still shows some heavily worn carving. On the floor below, there's a small exhibition on religious life in medieval castles.

The rest of the town

Anchored to the castle walls as if it were a drawbridge, Thomas Telford's slender **Conwy Suspension Bridge** (late March to Oct daily 11am–5pm; £1; NT) was part of the 1826 road improvement scheme, prompted by the need for better communications to Ireland after the Act of Union. Contemporary with his far greater effort spanning the Menai Strait (see p.444), it mimics the crenellations of the battlements above to compensate for spoiling the view of the castle immortalized by J.M.W. Turner. The bridge was used until 1958, was briefly threatened with demolition, and has now been restored to approximately its original state. It serves as a footbridge linking the town to a **tollhouse**, furnished as it would have been circa 1900, complete with period toll charges on a board outside.

The thirty-foot-high **town walls** branch out from the castle into a three-quarter-mile-long circuit, enclosing Conwy's ancient quarter. Inaccessible from the castle they were designed to protect, the walls are punctuated by 21 evenly spaced horseshoe towers, as well as twelve latrines bulging out from the wall-walk. Only half of the distance can be walked, the best section being from Porth Uchaf to Porth yr Aden (unrestricted access), with great views over the town to the castle and estuary beyond.

At Porth yr Aden you come down off the walls next to brightly rigged trawlers, mussel boats and the self-proclaimed **smallest house in Great Britain** (Easter to mid-Oct daily 10am–5pm, and often later in good weather; £1), which was built wedged between two terraces, one of them now demolished. The two tiny rooms combined are only nine feet high and six wide, the door taking up a quarter of the frontage. Most people will have to duck to get in, a problem that vexed the last resident, a six-foot-three fisherman, until he left around 1900.

Porth Isaf, the nearby gate in the town walls, leads up Lower High Street to the fourteenth-century timber and stone **Aberconwy House** on Castle Street (late March to Oct daily except Tues 11am–5pm; £3; NT), the oldest house in

The Iron Ring

Dotting the north Wales coast, a day's march from each other, Edward I's fearsome **Iron Ring** of castles represents Europe's most ambitious and concentrated medieval building project, designed to prevent the recurrence of two hugely expensive military campaigns (see Contexts, p.469). After Edward's first successful campaign in 1277, he was able to pin down his adversary, **Llywelyn ap Gruffydd** ("the Last") in Snowdonia and Anglesey, gaining space and time to build the now largely ruined castles at **Flint**, **Rhuddlan**, **Builth Wells** and **Aberystwyth**, and consolidate his grip by confiscating and upgrading several Welsh castles.

Although Llewellyn's second uprising (1282) also ultimately failed, Edward was determined not to have to fight a third time for the same land, and set about extending his Iron Ring in an immensely costly display of English might, which – together with the Treaty of Rhuddlan (1284) – effectively crushed Welsh resistance. **Harlech**, **Caernarfon** and **Conwy** are nearly contemporaneous, yet manifest a unique progression towards the later, highly evolved concentric design of **Beaumaris**, for all these castles (and the town walls of Caernarfon and Conwy) were built by **James of St George d'Espéranche** – the master military architect of his age – whose work at Conwy, Caernarfon, Harlech and Beaumaris is now recognized with **UN World Heritage Site** status.

Each castle was integrated with a **bastide town** – an idea borrowed from Gascony in France, where Edward I was duke – the town and castle being mutually reliant on each other for protection and trade. The bastides were always populated with English settlers, and the Welsh were only permitted to enter during the day, but not to trade and certainly not carrying arms. It wasn't until the eighteenth century that the Welsh would have towns they could truly call their own.

Conwy and its sole surviving medieval building, dating from about 1300. Built for a wealthy merchant, it saw service as a bakery, antique shop, sea captain's house and temperance hotel, somehow managing to survive numerous fires and Victorian improvements. Its various incarnations are re-created in rooms furnished with a simple yet elegant collection of rural furniture on loan from the Museum of Wales. Tours start with an introductory video in the attic, winding up in a kitchen complete with fireside settle, pewter plates and a few hunks of stale bread.

Conwy's grandest residence is the splendid **Plas Mawr**, or "great mansion" (April–Sept Tues–Sun 9am–5pm; Oct Tues–Sun 9.30am–4pm; £5.10, joint ticket with castle £7; CADW), just up the High Street at no. 20. One of the best-preserved Elizabethan town houses in Britain, it was built in a Dutch style for Robert Wynn of Gwydir Castle (see Llanrwst, p.365), who was one of the first native Welsh to live in the town, returning to the area after mixing at European courts. The main part of the house dates from 1576, with features such as the gatehouse added some ten years later to augment the grand effect. In the Great Hall, the impressive plaster over-mantel was designed to impress visitors with Wynn's noble credentials – especially his descent from the Princes of Gwynedd – and much of the superb plasterwork throughout the house relates to the Wynn dynasty, except in the Great Chamber, where he demurred, presumably so as not to upstage visiting royalty. The tour – aided by an excellent recorded commentary – concludes with an exhibition about Tudor and Stuart attitudes to disease and cleanliness that's compulsively gory, hilariously scatological and highly informative.

For over a century, Plas Mawr was home to the Royal Cambrian Academy, a group aiming to foster art in Wales. The **Royal Cambrian Academy Art Gallery** (Tues–Sat 11am–5pm, Sun 1–4.30pm; free; ⓦ www.rcaconwy.org) is now located just behind Plas Mawr in a converted chapel on Crown Lane. At their best during the annual summer exhibition, the airy, well-lit galleries display work by the Academy members, almost all Welsh or working in Wales.

There's more lightweight entertainment ten-minutes' walk north along Castle/Berry Street at the **Butterfly Jungle** (late March–Aug daily 10am–5.30pm; Sept & Oct daily 10am–4pm; £5; ⓦ www.conwy-butterfly .co.uk), a hothouse full of bougainvillea, hibiscus and oleander pollinated by some fifty breeds of tropical butterfly, most imported as chrysalises but several bred here.

If you're still stuck for something to do, short **river cruises** on the *Queen Victoria* or *Princess Christine* (£5) leave from the quay. Alternatively, try Conwy's best **short walk**. This heads onto the gorse-, bracken- and heather-covered slopes of **Conwy Mountain** (2 miles return; 1hr; 650ft ascent) and the 800-foot Penmaenbach and Alltwen peaks behind, all affording fantastic views right along the coast. The walk starts at a small car park on Mountain Road, reached by following Cadnant Park off Bangor Road just outside the town walls.

Eating and drinking

For a small town, Conwy has a reasonable range of **restaurants**, though if you want to sample some really great pubs, you've got to get a few miles out into the Conwy Valley. **Drinking** in town is fairly perfunctory, with nightlife being limited to the odd pub gig. Most people head into Llandudno or Bangor for anything more exciting.

Restaurants and cafés

Alfredo's Restaurant Lancaster Square
① 01492/592381. Good-value pizza and pasta dishes (£8–9) and respectable mains (£14–18) amongst the Chianti bottles. Evenings only.
Archway 12 Bangor Rd. Quality eat-in and take-out fish and chip restaurant also doing pizza and pies. On a fine evening take your haul to The Quay and wash it down with a pint from the *Liverpool Arms*.
🏃 **Bistro Conwy** Bishops Yard
① 01492/596326. Great casual restaurant tucked hard against the town walls and serving superbly prepared dinners. The spicy sage-crumbed pork with an apple and brandy cream sauce (£14) is excellent. Evening only.
Edwards 18 High St. A fine deli with a decent salad bar; the place to stock up for picnics.
Pen-y-Bryn Tearooms 28 High St. Slightly twee establishment in a sixteenth-century house, with delicious lunches and the best artery-hardening Welsh teas around.
Shakespeare's *Castle Hotel*, High St
① 01492/582800, ⓦ www.castlewales.co.uk. The more formal end of Conwy dining, where linen and

crystal prevail for lunch (£15 for 2 courses) and dinner (£23 for 3 courses). Closed Sat lunch.
Tower Coffee House Castle Square. Quality café set in one of the town wall towers with estuary views. Come for panini, stuffed baguettes, espresso and good cakes.

Bars and pubs

Dawson's *Castle Hotel*, High St. Refined lounge bar in an upmarket hotel with cask ales, good wine and superior bar meals (mains £11–17) which might be sea bass on grilled fennel or Gressingham duck leg with a leek and potato gratin.
Groes Inn Tyn-y-Groes, 2 miles south on B5106 to Llanrwst. Excellent bar meals (mostly using local produce) and cask ales at an atmospheric fifteenth-century pub which claims to be the oldest licensed house in Wales.
Liverpool Arms The Quay. Compact pub built into the town wall, whose dockside location makes it a hot venue on warm evenings.
Tŷ Gwyn Rowen, 4 miles south of Conwy. Village pub in an idyllic setting, with a friendly atmosphere, decent bar meals and a nice garden.

Around Conwy

With its marvellous setting and plentiful accommodation, Conwy is the ideal base for a few days spent exploring the Lower Conwy Valley and the coast around its estuary. It's easy to make a day-trip to Llandudno, and there's a smattering of other attractive diversions within a few miles' radius. Thousands come here specifically to see **Bodnant Garden**, and tiny **Rowen** has a low-key appeal. Conwy also acts as a base for the **Cambrian Way** long-distance walking path to Cardiff (see box, p.438).

Bodnant Garden and Rowen

During May and June, the 160-foot laburnum tunnel flourishes and banks of rhododendrons are in glorious bloom all over **Bodnant Garden**, eight miles south of Conwy (early March to Oct daily 10am–5pm; £7.20; NT), Wales' finest formal garden and one of the loveliest in Britain. Laid out in 1875 around Bodnant Hall (closed to the public) by its then owner, English industrialist Henry Pochin, the garden spreads over eighty acres of the Conwy Valley. Divided into an upper terraced garden and lower Pinetum and Wild Garden, shrubs and plants provide a blaze of colour throughout the opening season, but autumn is a perfect time to be here, with hydrangeas still in bloom and fruit trees shedding their leaves. You'll need a minimum of two hours to fully appreciate the place. The #25 bus runs here from Llandudno roughly every hour, calling at Llandudno Junction, or it's a two-mile walk from the Tal-y-Cafn train station on the Conwy Valley line.

Across the valley on the eastern slopes of the Carneddau range, the tiny mountainside hamlet of **ROWEN** is one of the prettiest in the area, composed of a few cottages, a post office, a chapel and the lovely *Tŷ Gwyn* pub (see above). If you don't mind the short drive into Conwy, it makes a great base for exploring the area. Try *Gwern Borter Country Manor, Tir y Coed*

The ultimate Welsh long-distance path, the **Cambrian Way** (sometimes dubbed "The Mountain Connoisseur's Walk") crosses the whole country, winding some 274 miles from Cardiff to Conwy through some of Wales' most spellbinding upland scenery – the Carneddau, the Glyderau, the Snowdon massif, Cadair Idris and the Brecon Beacons before dropping down through the Valleys to Cardiff. The walk requires a high degree of commitment and good route-finding skills (signposting is erratic en route), and while fit hikers might do the walk in one tough two-week push, most prefer to break it into manageable sections. The experience is undoubtedly heightened by spending nights under canvas atop the moors, but there are over a dozen YHA hostels and numerous B&Bs scattered along the route. Check out ⓦwww .cambrianway.org.uk for more details.

or the *Rowen YHA* hostel (all listed on p.433). The #19 bus links Rowen with Conwy and Llanrwst every hour or better.

Sychnant Pass and Penmaenmawr Mountain

Heading west towards Bangor it's worth taking a short detour inland along the Old Conwy Road (served by the very infrequent bus #75) and through the narrow cleft of **Sychnant Pass**, which separates Conwy Mountain from the Carneddau range. The road passes the *Conwy YHA* hostel (see p.433) and crosses the pass before dropping into the hamlet of **CAPELULO**, just over two miles west of Conwy, rejoining the A55 at workaday Penmaenmawr. If you have a decent map, Capelulo makes a good starting point for a walk across **Penmaenmawr Mountain**, an important source of stone for axe-making from around 3000 BC and still being quarried today. Not surprisingly, the area boasts several Neolithic remains, most notably the misnamed **Druid's Circle** (Y Meini Hirion) – marked on the map (grid reference 723746) simply as "Stone Circle".

Bangor and around

After a few days travelling through mid-Wales or in the mountains of Snowdonia, **BANGOR** makes a welcome change. It's not big; but, as the largest town in Gwynedd and home to the **University of Wales Bangor**, it passes in these parts for cosmopolitan. Students are the main reason for Bangor's vibrancy, and with only a trickle of summer visitors the city struggles to keep an active social life going outside term time. In contrast to the largely English-speaking north coast resorts, Bangor is overwhelmingly Welsh-speaking.

While the slate industry and road and rail projects brought some urbanization to Bangor in the nineteenth century, for well over a millennium before that the city was noted solely for its bishopric, founded as a monastic settlement by St Deiniol in 525 AD and thus the oldest continuous cathedral see in Britain, predating even Canterbury by some seventy years. At first, St Deiniol only cleared a space in the woods which became known as *Y Cae Onn* (The Ash Enclosure), later developing into the town's present name, a corruption of *bangori*, a type of interwoven wattle fence which presumably demarcated the monastic lands.

Arrival and information

All trains on the north coast line between Chester and Holyhead stop at Bangor's **train station** on Station Road, at the bottom of Holyhead Road. From here, Deiniol Road, Bangor's main street, runs along the bottom of the valley, changing its name to Garth Road and continuing almost to the pier. The long High Street runs one block parallel to the south; to the north, the grandiose university buildings dominate the skyline of Upper Bangor. National Express and local **buses** stop on a short spur of Garth Road, a few steps from the **tourist office** on Deiniol Road (April–Sept Mon–Fri 9.30am–4pm; ☎01248/352786). **Alternative information** on anything from the local green scene to women's and gay groups is best found at the redoubtable **Greenhouse/Tŷ Gwydr** resource centre, 1 Trevelyan Terrace (Mon–Fri 10am–4pm; ☎01248/355821, ⓔbangor.tic @gwynedd.gov.uk, ⓦwww.tygwydr.com), at the northern end of High Street. There's free **internet** access at the **library** (Mon, Tues, Thurs & Fri 9.30am–7pm, Wed & Sat 9.30am–1pm), opposite the tourist office on Ffordd Gwynedd.

Accommodation

Bangor doesn't have a huge choice of accommodation, particularly mid-range and fancy hotels. Most of the cheaper options are at the northern end of Garth Road, about twenty minutes' walk from the train station.

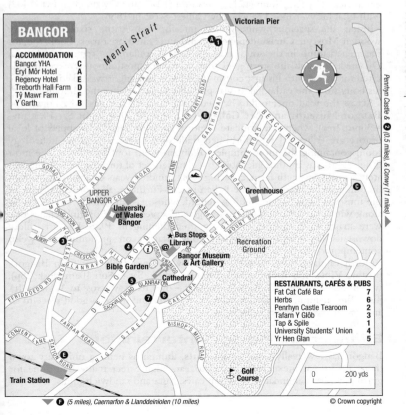

BANGOR

ACCOMMODATION
Bangor YHA	C
Eryl Môr Hotel	A
Regency Hotel	E
Treborth Hall Farm	D
Tŷ Mawr Farm	F
Y Garth	B

RESTAURANTS, CAFÉS & PUBS
Fat Cat Café Bar	7
Herbs	6
Penrhyn Castle Tearoom	2
Tafarn Y Glôb	3
Tap & Spile	1
University Students' Union	4
Yr Hen Glan	5

0   200 yds

© Crown copyright

Bangor YHA Tan-y-Bryn ☎ 0870/770 5686,
ⓔ bangor@yha.org.uk. A large house signposted on
the right of the A56, 10min east of the centre and
reached either by walking along High St or taking
bus #5, #6 or #7 along Garth Rd. Licensed and with
meals and internet available. £14–16
Eryl Môr Hotel 2 Upper Garth Rd
☎ 01248/353789, ⓦ www.erylmorhotel.co.uk.
Quiet, comfy, fully licensed hotel with its own
restaurant. The best rooms overlooking Bangor's
pier and the Menai Strait. ❹
Y Garth Garth Rd ☎ 01248/362277, ⓦ www
.thegarthguesthouse.co.uk. En-suite rooms in
marginally the best in a row of three serviceable,
low-cost B&Bs. ❷

Regency Hotel Holyhead Rd ☎ 01248/370819.
Good-value small hotel close to the train station. ❷
Treborth Hall Farm ☎ 01248/364104. Cheap and
cheerful campsite that's also the nearest to the
centre of Bangor: a mile or so out of town off the
A487 between the two Menai Strait bridges and
easily walkable from Upper Bangor (though #5
buses pass the entrance). £5–8 per pitch.
Tŷ Mawr Farm 5 miles southwest of Bangor (and
half a mile east of Llanddeiniolen) on the B4366
☎ 01286/670147, ⓦ www.tymawrfarm.co.uk. Cosy
B&B on a working farm with views of Snowdonia
and very good home-made food. Quality,
well-equipped self-catering cottages also available
for short lets outside the school holidays. ❸

The Town

Bangor's **cathedral** boasts the longest continuous use of any cathedral in
Britain. Little is recorded of the original buildings but a hint of the see's ancient
origins can be gleaned from the blocked-in window dating from the Norman
rebuilding of 1071. The rest of the structure is the result of reconstructions after
being sacked by King John (1211), Edward I (1277) and Owain Glyndŵr (1402)
with final heavy-handed touches by Gilbert Scott in 1866.

Inside, the spacious white-walled interior houses the sixteenth-century
wooden **Mostyn Christ**, depicted bound and seated on a rock. Look, too, for
the arched tomb in the south transept said to contain the remains of Owain
Gwynedd, though the story goes that after being posthumously excommuni-
cated for incest with his first cousin the Bishop of Bangor was asked to remove
his body from the cathedral. It was probably re-interred in the churchyard.

Across the road on Ffordd Gwynedd, the former Canonry now houses the
Bangor Museum and Art Gallery (Tues–Fri 12.30–4.30pm, Sat 10.30am–
4.30pm; free), where the standard regional museum fare and snippets of local
history are enlivened by refurbished traditional costumes and an archeology
room containing the most complete Roman sword found in Wales. The most
insightful rooms are those devoted to a complete set of furniture from a moderately wealthy Criccieth farm, covering three hundred years of acquisitions, from
brooding Welsh dressers to fine Italian pieces. Furniture also forms the basis of
the museum's homage to Thomas Telford, whose favourite chair can be found
along with a model of his Menai bridge and a piece of the original chains that
were stripped off the bridge during strengthening in 1935. The art gallery
downstairs has temporary displays concentrating on predominantly Welsh
contemporary works.

North of the centre, there's a fine view of Telford's bridge from Bangor's
pristine **Victorian Pier** (Mon–Fri 8.30am–dusk, Sat & Sun 10am–dusk; 25p),
which juts 1550 feet into the Menai Strait – over halfway across to Anglesey. It's
just a fifteen-minute walk from the town centre and makes a good place to sit
and watch the world drift idly by.

Eating, drinking and entertainment

Bangor has few really good **restaurants**, though as befits a university town
there are lots of inexpensive places to eat. High Street is the best zone for
grazing, with an abundance of cheap cafés, pasta and sandwich joints.

Fat Cat Café Bar 161 High St. Breezy modern decor and a moderately priced menu – from massive burgers to salmon-and-broccoli pasta quills – help pack this place out with students and locals.

Herbs 307–309 High St. Good daytime café serving sandwiches (£4), salads and meals (£5–9), with several vegetarian options. Closed Sun.

Penrhyn Castle Tearoom Penrhyn Castle (see below). When visiting Penrhyn be sure to leave time for lunch (or at least tea and cake) here. Dishes are based on recipes once used in the castle; the leek and cheese bread and butter pudding is very good, as is the lamb pie (both around £7).

Tafarn Y Glôb 7 Albert St, Upper Bangor. Good bar, popular with both students and locals, with real ales and occasional Welsh bands.

Tap & Spile Garth Rd. Another pub popular with students and locals, with great views of the pier and Menai Strait, plus meals and real ales at good prices.

University Students' Union Deiniol Rd ☎01248/353709. Venue for touring rock/pop bands, and home to the *Amser/Time* nightclub, which has cheap drinks, plus there's usually something happening on Mon and Wed nights, even over the quiet summer break. May close down for refurbishment in 2009.

Yr Hen Glan Glanrafon. Popular student bar notable for its budget meal deals. Often two-for-one offers for under £7.

Penrhyn Castle

There can hardly be a more vulgar testament to the Anglo-Welsh gentry's oppression of the rural Welsh than the nonetheless compelling **Penrhyn Castle** (late March–June, Sept & Oct daily except Tues noon–5pm; July & Aug daily except Tues 11am–5pm; £9, or £5.60 for grounds, kitchens & railway museum only; NT), two miles east of Bangor, which overlooks Port Penrhyn from its acres of isolating parkland. Built on the backs of slate miners for the benefit of their bosses, this monstrous nineteenth-century neo-Norman fancy, with over three hundred rooms dripping with luxurious fittings, was funded by the quarry's huge profits.

The responsibility falls ultimately on Caribbean sugar plantation owner, slave trader and vehement anti-abolitionist Richard Pennant, First Baron Penrhyn, who built a port on the northeastern edge of Bangor in order to ship his Bethesda slate to the world. But it was his self-aggrandizing great-great-nephew George Dawkins who inherited the 40,000-acre estate, added his ancestor's surname to his own, and with the aid of architect Thomas Hopper spent thirteen years from 1827 encasing the neo-Gothic hall in a Norman-style fortress complete with a monumental five-storey keep.

Vulgar though it may be, the decoration is impressive, and fairly true to the Romanesque, with its deeply cut chevrons, billets and double-cone ornamentation. Hopper even looked to Norman architecture for the design of the furniture, but abandoned historical authenticity when it came to installing the central heating system, which piped hot air through ornamental brass ducts at the cost of twenty tons of coal a month.

Everything is on a massive scale and no more so than in the Great Hall with its pair of stained-glass zodiac windows by Thomas Willement. Three-foot-thick oak doors separate subsequent rooms: the Library, with its full-size slate billiard table, and the oppressive Ebony Room, which leads onto the Grand Staircase. Upstairs, the lightness of the original William Morris wallpaper and drapes around the King's Bed are in marked contrast to the Slate Bed, designed for Queen Victoria but declined by her in favour of the Hopper-designed four-poster in the State Bedroom. The family managed to assemble the country's largest private **painting collection**. Much of this remains, especially in the two dining rooms, where there's a Gainsborough landscape, Canaletto's *The Thames at Westminster*, and a Rembrandt portrait. During the Blitz of 1940, some 1800 masterpieces from Britain's National Gallery were sent here for safekeeping, though Lord Penrhyn's drunken clumsiness and demands for rental payments forced the then Prime Minister, Winston Churchill, to have the treasures moved to a former slate mine at Manod for the rest of the war.

Away from the pomp you can visit the enormous **kitchens** convincingly laid out as if about to cater for the 1894 visit of the Prince and Princess of Wales, and the **Industrial Railway Museum** (same hours; entry with castle or grounds tickets), packed with gleaming examples of rolling stock once used on the estate's quarry-to-port rail line. Leave time too for the sumptuous gardens and the excellent café (see p.441). **Buses** #5, #6 and #7 run frequently from Bangor to Penrhyn's gates, a mile-long walk from the house.

Anglesey

The island of **Anglesey** (Ynys Môn) is a world apart from Wales, let alone the rest of Britain. After the mountains and hemmed-in settlements of Snowdonia, this green ripple of fields and farms comes as a bit of a shock. Seen from the four-lane A55 expressway which speeds across Anglesey towards Holyhead, the island can look dull, but take to the older A5, or the smaller roads, and you'll discover plenty to see and do.

Signs and slogans announce Anglesey as Mam Cymru, "The Mother of Wales", attesting to the island's former importance as the country's breadbasket. In the twelfth century, Giraldus Cambrensis noted that "When crops have failed in other regions, this island, from its soil and its abundant produce, has been able to supply all Wales". While feeding their less productive kin in Snowdonia is no longer a priority, the land remains predominantly agricultural, with small fields, stone walls and white houses reminiscent of parts of Ireland and England. Linguistically and politically, though, Anglesey is intensely Welsh, a Plaid Cymru stronghold with over seventy percent of its population using Welsh as their first language – one of the country's highest proportions of native speakers. Most residents will at least understand the lines of one of Anglesey's most famous poets, Goronwy Owen, whose eulogy on his homeland translates as "All hail to Anglesey/ The delight of all regions/ Bountiful as a second Eden/ Or an ancient paradise". Judging by the numbers who flock to the island's necklace of fine sandy coves and rocky headlands, many agree with Owen, but just as many charge straight through from Bangor to **Holyhead** and the Irish ferries, missing out on Wales' greatest concentration of pre-Christian sites and some superb coastal scenery.

The earliest people on Anglesey were Mesolithic hunters who arrived between 8000 and 4000 BC. Around 2500 BC, a new culture developed among the small farming communities, giving rise to the many henges and stone circles on the island, that held sway until the Celts swept across Europe in the seventh century BC, led by their priestly class, the druids. In the centuries prior to the Roman invasion, Anglesey – well positioned at the apex of Celtic sea traffic – became the most important druidic centre in Europe. The druids were so firmly established that Anglesey was the last place in Wales to fall to the Romans, in 61 AD.

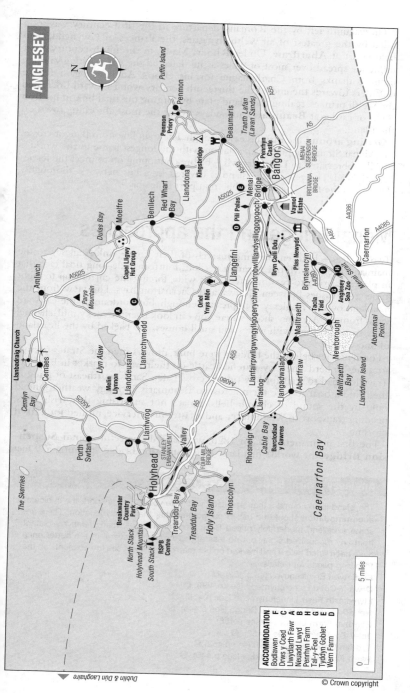

ANGLESEY

N

Dublin & Dún Laoghaire

The Skerries

Llanbadrig Church

Cemaes

Cemlyn Bay

Llyn Alaw

Porth Swtan

Melin Llynnon

Llanddeusant

Llanfflewyn

Llanfwrog

Valley

STANLEY EMBANKMENT

FOUR MILE BRIDGE

Holyhead

Breakwater Country Park

North Stack

South Stack

RSPB Centre

Holyhead Mountain

Treaddur Bay

Trearddur Bay

Holy Island

Rhoscolyn

Amlwch

Parys Mountain

A5025

Capel Lligwy Hut Group

C

A

Moelfre

Benllech

Red Wharf Bay

Dulas Bay

Llanddona

Llanerchymedd

Oriel Ynys Môn

Llangefni

A5

A55

A5025

Rhosneigr

Cable Bay

Barclodiad y Gawres

Llanfaelog

A4080

Malltraeth

Newborough

Malltraeth Bay

Llanddwyn Island

Aberffraw

Llangadwaladr

Llanfaelog

Llanfairpwllgwyngyllgogerychwyrndrobwllllantysiliogogogoch

Bryn Celli Ddu

Plas Newydd

Tacla Taid

Anglesey Sea Zoo

D Plas Pali

E

F

G

H

Brynsiencyn

Menai Strait

Abermenai Point

Caernarfon Bay

Menai Bridge

MENAI SUSPENSION BRIDGE

BRITANNIA BRIDGE

Bangor

Vaynol Estate

A55

A487

A4085

A4086

Caernarfon

Penmon

Penmon Priory

Puffin Island

Beaumaris

Traeth Lafan (Lavan Sands)

Kingsbridge

Penrhyn Castle

ACCOMMODATION

Bodlawen   F
Drws y Coed   C
Llwydiarth Fawr   A
Neuadd Lwyd   B
Penrhyn Farm   H
Tal-y-Foel   G
Tyddyn Goblet   E
Wern Farm   D

0   5 miles

The vacuum left by the Romans' departure in the fifth century was soon filled by the greatest of all Welsh dynasties, the Princes of Gwynedd, who held court at **Aberffraw**. Under Rhodri Mawr, in the ninth century, their influence spread over most of Wales as he defeated the encroaching Vikings, earning thanks from Charlemagne for his efforts. Anglesey again fell to outsiders towards the end of the thirteenth century when Edward I defeated the Welsh princes, sealing the island's fate by forging the final link in his Iron Ring of castles at **Beaumaris**, nowadays by far the most absorbing town on the island.

Getting around the island is easy enough. The train line from Bangor crosses the Menai Strait, stopping at the station with the longest name in the world – usually abbreviated to **Llanfairpwll** – before continuing on to meet the ferries at Holyhead. The rest of the island is covered by a bus network, thoroughly detailed in the free *Ynys Môn* public transport timetable.

Menai Bridge and the approaches

Two bridges – both engineering marvels of their time – link Anglesey to the mainland over the **Menai Strait**, a perilous fourteen-mile-long tidal race that in places narrows to two hundred yards wide, forcing the current up to eight knots as it rushes between Conwy and Caernarfon bays. The view from the mainland over to Anglesey is impressive enough, but outdone by the eastward vistas from the Anglesey shore, where you can look over the rocky mid-channel islets, some adorned with jetties and small houses, and backed by the heartland of Snowdonia.

For centuries before the bridges were built, drovers used the Strait's narrow stretches to herd Anglesey-fattened cattle on their way to market in England. Travellers had to wait for low tide to cross Lafan Sands, northeast of Bangor, then find a boat to take them across to Beaumaris, in foggy weather guided only by the sound of church bells. So it's not surprising that Irish MPs, needing transport to Westminster and a faster mail service, pushed for a fixed crossing.

The first permanent link, in 1826, was Telford's graceful **Menai Suspension Bridge**, the world's first large iron suspension bridge, spanning 579 feet

Anglesey's rural B&Bs

The island is so compact that, at least if you have your own transport, the choice of **accommodation** should be based on factors other than solely location. There are some excellent, moderately priced B&Bs and farmhouses, many relatively distant from any recognized sight, but no less appealing for it. Several of the better ones have been listed below and marked on our map of Anglesey; see the accounts on the following pages for details.

Bodlawen Brynsiencyn (see p.452). ❸
Drws-Y-Coed Llanerchymedd (see p.458). ❸
Llwydiarth Fawr Llanerchymedd (see p.458). ❹
Neuadd Lwyd Near Menai Bridge (see p.445). ❻
Penrhyn Farm Llanfwrog (see p.458). ❸
Tal-y-Foel Dwyran (see p.452). ❹
Tyddyn Goblet Brynsiencyn (see p.452) ❷
Wern Farm near Menai Bridge (see p.445). ❺

between piers and 100 feet above the water to allow high-masted sailing ships to pass. Almost everything about the project was novel, including the process of lifting the first 23-ton chain into place, which involved a pulley system and 150 men kept in time by a fife band. One man celebrated their achievement by running across the nine-inch-wide chain from Anglesey to the mainland.

In 1850, Robert Stephenson also made engineering history with his **Britannia Tubular Bridge**, which carried trains across the strait in twin wrought-iron tubes. It burned down in 1970, however, leaving only the limestone piers that now support the twin-deck A5/A55 road and rail bridge to Llanfairpwll and Holyhead.

You can learn more about both bridges and the men responsible for them at the **Thomas Telford Centre** (Easter & mid-June to Sept daily except Sat 10am–4pm; £3; ☎01248/715046, ⓦwww.menaibridges.co.uk), on Mona Road, 200 yards from the Anglesey end of the Menai Suspension Bridge. Among the architectural bridge drawings, pretty aquatints and explanatory panels you'll find a few intriguing hunks of grey iron – chain links, a huge rivet punch, capstan arms and a twelve-foot long spanner – plus the original pulleys used for hauling up the chains.

Nestling in the shadow of the older crossing, with a few private islands to break the view across the strait to the mainland, is the town of **MENAI BRIDGE** (Porthaethwy). A short bus ride (#53, #57 or #58) or just over half an hour's pleasant walk from Bangor affords views from the bridge over to the fourteenth-century **Church of St Tysilio** (open mid-July to Aug daily, and for Sunday services all year) on Church Island, where its patron saint founded his cell around 630 AD. Topped by a Celtic cross war memorial, the island has delightful views along the Strait and to both bridges. It can be reached through the woodland behind the car park on the approach to the Menai Bridge itself, or from the town along a causeway and waterside promenade named Belgian Walk (having been built by refugees during World War I).

If you have children to amuse, take the B5420 two miles northeast of the village to **Pili Palas** (Jan Sat & Sun 10am–dusk; Feb–March daily 10am–5pm; April–Oct daily 10am–5.30pm; Nov & Dec daily 10am–dusk; £6), a steamy walk-in butterfly house with up to seventy species, some as big as your hand. British butterflies that are becoming less common in the wild are bred for release here. An aviary and vivarium complete the setup.

Practicalities

If you plan to **stay** in Menai Bridge, be sure to book ahead at the amazingly hospitable *Wern Farm* (☎01248/712421, ⓦwww.angleseyfarms.com; ⑤), two miles north of town, off the A5025, whose farmhouse dates from the early seventeenth century. Alternatively, seek out 🍴 *Neuadd Lwyd*, four miles northwest (☎01248/715005, ⓦwww.neuaddlwyd.co.uk; ⑥), a superb country house which exudes informal elegance. The breakfasts are some of the finest anywhere, while the immaculate four-course table d'hôte dinner (£38) is an integral part of any visit.

Back in town, the choice of **places to eat** is surprisingly good, the best being *Tafarn y Bont* (☎01248/714864), right by the bridge on Telford Road, a quality brasserie with cosy rooms and an airy conservatory. The intimate *Liverpool Arms* on St George's Pier is a worthy alternative, serving pub grub and superb beer.

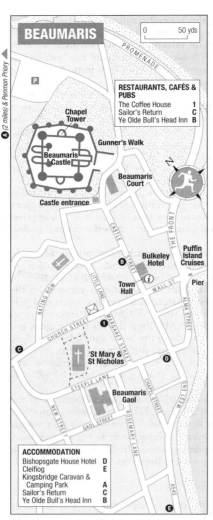

BEAUMARIS

0   50 yds

PROMENADE

2 miles & Penmon Priory

P

Chapel Tower

Gunner's Walk

Beaumaris Castle

Castle entrance

Beaumaris Court

RESTAURANTS, CAFÉS & PUBS
The Coffee House   1
Sailor's Return   C
Ye Olde Bull's Head Inn B

CASTLE STREET

THE FRONT

Bulkeley Hotel

Town Hall

Puffin Island Cruises

Pier

RATING ROW

LITTLE LANE

WALL ST

ALMA STREET

CHURCH STREET

MARGARET STREET

'St Mary & St Nicholas

STEEPLE LANE

Beaumaris Gaol

CHAPEL STREET

WEST END

NEW STREET

GAOL STREET

ROSEMARY LANE

A545

ACCOMMODATION
Bishopsgate House Hotel D
Cleifiog   E
Kingsbridge Caravan &
  Camping Park   A
Sailor's Return   C
Ye Olde Bull's Head Inn B

Beaumaris and around

The original inhabitants of **BEAUMARIS** (Biwmares) were evicted by Edward I to make way for the construction of his new castle and bastide town, dubbed "beautiful marsh" in a ploy to attract English settlers. Today the place can still seem like the small English outpost Edward intended, with a grand Georgian terrace (designed by Joseph Hansom, of cab fame) and more plummy English accents than you'll have heard for a while. Many of their owners belong with the flotilla of yachts, an echo of the port's fleet of merchant ships, which disappeared with the completion of the Menai bridges and subsequent growth of Holyhead.

Beaumaris is not only attractive, it boasts more sights than the rest of Anglesey put together. This inevitably brings the crowds here in summer, though even then the evenings are peaceful, with day-trippers gone and overnighters ensconced in their hotel restaurants.

The Town

While you can spend an hour or two mooching around Beaumaris's antique shops, enjoying the views across the Strait towards Bangor and along the coast to Llandudno's Great Orme from the stumpy pier, this shouldn't distract from the main attractions. The **castle** remains central to Beaumaris, its water-filled moat and loop-holed ramparts satisfying the British castle archetype more than any other in Wales. The law and order theme continues in the **court** and **jail**, both offering their own angle on Welsh subjugation. In good weather, a cruise out around **Puffin Island** or a wander along the nearby coastline close to **Penmon Priory** may suit better.

The Castle

Beaumaris Castle (April–Oct daily 9am–5pm; Nov–March Mon–Sat 9.30am–4pm, Sun 11am–4pm; £3.70; CADW) is the most picturesque of Edward's gargantuan fortresses, built in response to Madog ap Llywelyn's capture of Caernarfon in 1294. Its architect, James of St George, produced a symmetrical octagonal form, his finest and most highly evolved expression of concentric design. Lacking the domineering majesty of Caernarfon, Conwy or Harlech, its low outer walls seem almost welcoming – belying the deadly ingenuity of its design.

Sited on flat land at the edge of town, the castle is approached over a moat and through Moorish-influenced staggered entries at the huge towers of the Gate Next the Sea and the South Gatehouse. The moat originally linked the castle to the sea (now well over a hundred yards away), with a shipping channel allowing boats of up to forty tons to tie up at the iron rings hammered into a protective spur of the outer defences, **Gunner's Walk**. Supplies could be brought in, including the corn that was fed into a mill, still visible immediately below.

Despite over thirty years' work and plans for a lavish palace, the castle was never quite finished, leaving most of the inner ward empty, and the corbels and fireplaces unused. You can explore a disappointingly short section of the **wall walk**, from which archers could fire simultaneously from the inner and outer defences, and wander through miles of internal passages in the walls, finding your way to the first floor of the **Chapel Tower**, whose small but wonderfully resonant lime-washed chapel lies immediately above a modest "Castles of Edward I" exhibition.

▲ Beaumaris Castle and the Menai Strait

When put to the test, the castle failed to withstand Owain Glyndŵr – who took it in 1403 and held it for two years – but during the Civil War, its Royalist defenders held out against General Mytton and 1500 Parliamentarian troops until 1646. After Charles II's accession, the castle was returned to the Bulkeley family, only to be left to fall into ruin before twentieth-century restoration returned some of its glory.

The rest of the town

Fittingly, the castle overshadows the juridical instruments of English rule. Almost opposite, the Jacobean **Beaumaris Court** (Easter–Sept daily 10.30am–5pm; £3), was built in 1614 and, until 1971, hosted the quarterly Assize Courts. These were traditionally held in English, giving the jury little chance to follow the proceedings, and Welsh-speaking defendants none against judges notorious for slapping heavy penalties on relatively minor offences. Undoubtedly they sympathized with the sentiments embodied in *The Lawsuit*, a plaque in the main courtroom depicting two farmers pulling the horns and tail of a cow as a lawyer milks it.

Many citizens were transported from the court to the colonies for their felonies; others wound up in **Beaumaris Gaol**, on Steeple Lane (Easter–Sept daily 10.30am–5pm; £3.50). When it opened in 1829, this was considered a model prison, with running water and toilets in each cell, an infirmary and, eventually, heating. Women prisoners did the cooking and were allowed to rock their babies' cradles in the nursery above by means of a pulley system. Advanced perhaps, but nonetheless a gloomy place: witness the windowless punishment cell, the stone-breaking yard and the treadmill water pump. The least fortunate inmates were marched along a first-floor walkway through a door in the outer wall to the gibbet, where they were publicly hanged.

Nearby on Church Street is the **Church of St Mary and St Nicholas**, the only edifice in Beaumaris approaching the age of the castle. Though old enough – started in the twelfth century and rebuilt around 1500 – its chief interest is the coffin in the porch, used as a horse trough for years but originally holding Joan, wife of Llywelyn the Great and daughter of King John of England.

Interesting as Beaumaris is, a fine day might be better spent **cruising** with Puffin Island Cruises (Easter–Sept daily 10am–5pm; £6; ☎01248/810251), based in a kiosk at the foot of the pier. Numbers permitting, you can book an hour-long excursion around, but not onto, Puffin Island (see opposite), and also go fishing on cruises costing from £16 for two hours.

Practicalities

With no trains, long-distance coaches or proper tourist office, Beaumaris seems poorly served, but it has a regular **bus** service to Bangor (#53, #57 and #58), and the Town Hall, next to the *Bulkeley Hotel* on Castle Street, stocks leaflets and will advise on local amenities. Most **accommodation** is high standard and fairly pricey, though it's worth looking out for people offering ad hoc budget B&B in their houses over the summer. For a small place, Beaumaris has a good selection of daytime cafés and several more substantial **restaurants**.

Accommodation and camping

Bishopsgate House Hotel 54 Castle St ☎01248/810302, ⊛www.bishopsgatehousehotel .co.uk. High-standard, predominantly business-oriented nine-room hotel in an elegant Georgian town house with chintzy decor, all the expected facilities and a good restaurant. ❺

Cleifiog Townsend ☎01248/811507, ⊛www.cleifiogbandb.co.uk. There are just three rooms (plus a huge guest lounge) in this large mostly-Georgian town house with great views across Menai Strait to Snowdonia. The best room is on the corner with plenty of light, masses of wood panelling and a deep bath. A welcome tray with home-made biscuits and coffee, plus a great breakfast, round out the welcoming hospitality. ❹–❺

Kingsbridge Caravan & Camping Park
☎01248/490636, ⓦwww.kingsbridgecaravanpark .co.uk. Spacious campsite with a new shower block, two miles northeast towards Penmon. £16 per pitch.

Sailor's Return Church St ☎01248/811314, ⓦwww.sailorsreturn.co.uk. Simple en-suite rooms

above this good town pub, with decent food, and breakfast included in the price. ❸

Ye Olde Bull's Head Inn 18 Castle St ☎01248/810329, ⓦwww.bullsheadinn.co.uk. The best hotel in Beaumaris, this ancient coaching inn was used as General Mytton's headquarters during the Civil War and, in more peaceful circumstances, by Dr Johnson and Charles Dickens. It has a fantastic restaurant and a decent brasserie and bar (see below). They're also soon to open *The Townhouse*, across the street, done in modern contemporary style and a little cheaper. ❻

Eating and drinking

🏃 **The Coffee House** Margaret St. Cramped three-table daytime licenced café (with outside seating when clement) where everything is prepared and served with friendly care and attention. Nip in for espresso and cake or linger over French toast and bacon (£5) or an excellent Anglesey ploughman's (£7.50). Many of their best ingredients can be obtained at Sarah's Deli next door.

Sailor's Return Church St. Town pub best known for its hearty bar meals.

🏃 **Ye Olde Bull's Head Inn** 18 Castle St ☎01248/810329, ⓦwww.bullsheadinn.co.uk.

Beaumaris's top hotel doesn't disappoint when it comes to eating and drinking. There's a cosy old-fashioned bar but a more modern angle in the bare-boards conservatory brasserie, where you might expect seared coriander chicken and artichoke salad (£5.50) followed by lamb shank in redcurrant sauce (£11). The *Loft* restaurant is more formal, though no less contemporary, serving the likes of duck breast with a celeriac remoulade followed by halibut with a puy lentil, beetroot and pancetta reduction (two courses for £32, three for £39).

Penmon Priory and Puffin Island

One of the earliest monastic sites in Anglesey was on the now uninhabited Puffin Island, four miles northeast of Beaumaris. In Welsh it goes by the name Ynys Seiriol, recalling the sixth-century saint who, on becoming head of the Augustine **Penmon Priory** (unrestricted access; CADW), moved the island community the three-quarters of a mile to Penmon, on the mainland. St Seiriol soon became known as the White Saint, not for his unblemished purity, but because his weekly walk to Llanerchymedd to meet St Cybi involved journeying with his back to the sun in both directions. Cybi, journeying into the sun from present-day Holyhead, was dubbed the Tawny Saint.

While the priory's original wooden buildings were razed by the Danes in the tenth century, their replacements, the twelfth-century church and the thirteenth-century south range of the cloister, are still standing. Only the **church** is in good repair and still used, the serene, lime-washed nave housing an unusual Norman pillar-piscina – a font gouged from the plinth of a pre-Norman cross still used for Sunday services – and the Penmon Cross, moved here to prevent a thousand years of Welsh weather completely scouring off its plait and fret patterns. There's more patterned stonework in the south transept, approached through a magnificent chevron- and chequerboard-patterned arch. The church's site was chosen for its proximity to the refreshing waters of **St Seiriol's Well**, which now feeds a calm pool and is reached by either the path behind the church, or another opposite the distinctive domed dovecote, built around 1600 to house one thousand pairs of birds.

It cost £2 to park at Penmon, a fee that also covers you for the toll road which runs three-quarters of a mile beyond the dovecote to the easternmost point of Anglesey. A short strait separates you from **Puffin Island**, now a nesting point for razorbills, guillemots and puffins, all once permissible food during Lent. Take a walk past the quarries, where James of St George cut fossil-ridden limestone for Caernarfon and Beaumaris castles, and Telford and Stephenson found the footings for their bridges.

Getting here is no problem, as the frequent #57 Bangor–Beaumaris **buses** continue to Penmon roughly hourly every day except Sundays.

Llanfairpwllgwyngyllgogerychwyrndro bwllllandysiliogogogoch and the south coast

When Robert Louis Stephenson wrote "to travel hopefully is a better thing than to arrive" he might have been thinking of **LLANFAIRPWLL**, the village with the longest place name in Britain and little else but for a wool shop and a small train station (request stop only) bearing the famed sign **Llanfairpwllwyngyllgogerychwyrndrobwllllandysiliogogogoch**. Sadly, "St Mary's Church in the hollow of white hazel near a rapid whirlpool and the Church of St Tysilio near the red cave" is no authentic Welsh tongue twister, but simply the fabrication of a Menai Bridge tailor in the 1880s, who added to the original first five syllables in an attempt to draw tourists – as indeed it has.

Coming from Bangor, half a mile before the town you'll probably notice the bronze figure atop the 91-foot-high Doric **Marquess of Anglesey's Column** (daily 9am–5pm; £1.50). The apocryphal story has him declaring to Wellington, on having a leg blown off at Waterloo, "Begod, sir, there goes me leg", to which Wellington dryly replied, "Begod, sir, so it do". There hadn't been much love lost between them since the Marquess ran off with Wellington's sister-in-law some years previously. You can climb the 115 steps up to the Marquess to share his view across the strait to Snowdonia, and see his replacement leg at Plas Newydd, close to Bryn Celli Ddu: two good reasons to spend time in the area.

Practicalities

The main reason to stop in Llanfairpwll itself is to visit the **tourist office** by the station (Mon–Sat 9.30am–5.30pm, Sun 10am–5pm; closes 5pm Oct–Easter; ℡01248/713177, ✉llanfairpwll@nwtic.com), the only one worth its salt on the island. It is packed with free leaflets: look out for ones on "Historic Anglesey" and a series of "Circular Walks on the isle of Anglesey".

Trains continue from Llanfairpwll to Rhosneigr and Holyhead, but to visit the rest of the **south coast** you're reliant on **buses**. In high summer the handiest is the hourly #42 **bus** that passes Plas Newydd and Bryn Celli Ddu, Brynsiencyn and Newborough on its way to Aberffraw and Llangefni (see p.461). Services to Rhosneigr are limited to the infrequent #25 from Holyhead and the slightly more regular #45 from Llangefni.

Plas Newydd

A mile and a half along the A4080 southwest of Llanfairpwll is the approach to **Plas Newydd** (mid-March to Oct daily except Thurs & Fri noon–5pm;

gardens open an hour earlier; £7, garden only £5; NT). Though now owned by the National Trust, the house remains, as it has been since the eighteenth century, the home of the marquesses of Anglesey. A house had stood on this site since the sixteenth century, but it was the First Marquess's huge profits from Parys Mountain (see p.459) and other ventures that paid for its transformation by James Wyatt and Joseph Potter into a Gothic mansion in the late eighteenth century. Potter designed the pleasing, castellated stable block that almost upstages the modest-looking three-storey house with incongruous Tudor caps on slender octagonal turrets.

Inside, the Gothic Hall, with its Potter-designed fan-vaulted ceiling, leads to the longest and most finely decorated room in the house, the Music Room, originally the great hall. All available space is covered with oil paintings, including portraits of the First Marquess and Lady Paget, his first wife, both by John Hoppner. Despite the Gothic start, Wyatt was given free rein in the rest of the house, and there's a transition to the neoclassical on entering the Staircase Hall with its cantilevered staircase and deceptively solid-looking Doric columns, actually just painted wood. Predominantly dull paintings line the gallery, mainly portraits of monarchs and most family members, though those of the Sixth Marquess and his sister are the work of Rex Whistler, who spent two years here in the 1930s.

An exhibition in a former kitchen celebrates the artist, but it's in the **Rex Whistler Room** that you'll find Plas Newydd's glory and Whistler's masterwork: a whole 58-foot-long wall consumed by the magnificent trompe l'oeil painting of some imaginary seascape seen from a promenade. At first it seems utterly incongruous, but you are soon drawn into the fantasy, your position seeming to shift by over a mile as you walk along, altering your perspective on the mountains of Snowdonia and a whimsical composite of elements. Portmeirion is there, as are the Round Tower from Windsor Castle and the steeple from St Martin-in-the-Fields in London. Whistler himself appears as a gondolier, and again as a gardener in one of the two right-angled panels at either end, which appear to extend the room further.

The **Cavalry Museum**, a few rooms further on, exhibits the world's first articulated leg, a synthesis of wood, leather and springs, designed for the First Marquess, who lost his leg at Waterloo. By the time you've also visited the Neolithic **cromlech** located in grounds landscaped by Humphrey Repton in the early nineteenth century, you'll need to allow a couple of hours. Recover in the former milking parlour, now a fine tiled tearoom serving tasty snacks and light meals (open daily in summer).

Look out, too, for twenty-minute **cruises** from the house on Menai Strait, planned to take place throughout summer.

Bryn Celli Ddu

Almost a mile past Plas Newydd, a signposted side road leads half a mile north to **Bryn Celli Ddu** (unrestricted access; CADW), the "Mound of the Dark Chamber", one of the island's most significant prehistoric sites and an atmospheric spot, overlooked by a natural rock that may have been its precursor as a place of worship, and by the purple mountains of Snowdonia. Reached along a ten-minute path from the car park, it was built by Anglesey's late Neolithic inhabitants four thousand years ago. Several seasons of digs have shown it to be an extensive religious site, but today all you can see is a well-proportioned henge and stone circle, later built over to turn it into a passage grave beneath an earthen mound. The original entrance stone was whisked off to the National Museum in Cardiff, but a replica gives an idea of its carved spiral patterns. In the last chamber you'll find an impressive, smooth monolith under a rather less than impressive supporting concrete beam. The #42 **bus** passes within half a mile; otherwise it's an hour-long walk from Llanfairpwll.

Anglesey Sea Zoo and Brynsiencyn

Facing Caernarfon across the Menai Strait, seven miles southwest of Llanfairpwll, **Anglesey Sea Zoo** (Easter–Oct daily 10am–6pm; £7.25; ☎01248/430411, ⓦwww.angleseyseazoo.co.uk), is one of the most absorbing attractions on Anglesey. Local marine environments are simulated in wave tanks, and in shallow pools where plaice, turbot and dogfish, camouflaged against the shingle bottom, are barely visible from the catwalks above. They haven't entirely got away from glass-sided tanks, but most are large and the contents chosen to depict specific environments: tidal flats, quayside, wrecks and kelp forest amongst them. In keeping with the buildings' previous functions as an oyster hatchery and lobster breeding farm, the zoo uses aquaculture to give the lobsters a much greater chance of survival once released into the wild, and you can view an industrial-looking plant producing table salt from local seawater, which is sold in the shop and used in the zoo's café.

The only useful bus service (#42) stops in the unremarkable village of **BRYNSIENCYN**, two miles to the north. Between the Sea Zoo and Brynsiencyn there's **accommodation** at *Bodlawen* (☎01248/430379, ⓦwww.angleseyfarms.com; ❸), a large modern guesthouse overlooking the Menai Strait and Caernarfon with a relaxed atmosphere and an acclaimed opera-singing owner, Marian Roberts. Alternatively, try the bargain *Tyddyn Goblet* (☎01248/430296, ❷), a characterful farmhouse just off the A4080, or *Tal-y-Foel* (☎01248/430977, ⓦwww.tal-y-foel.co.uk; ❹), a particularly nice farmhouse B&B just north of Brynsiencyn at Dwyran.

Newborough and Malltraeth

Three miles southwest of the Sea Zoo, the end of the Menai Strait is marked by Abermenai Point, a huge sand bar backed by the 600-acre **Newborough Warren** (unrestricted access), one of the most important dune systems anywhere in Britain. Rabbits are common here, as are the otherwise rare thick-horned Soay sheep, Britain's oldest native breed. Since 1948, much of the land has been clad in pines which stabilize the ground and provide habitat for goldcrests, warblers and rare native red squirrels, justifying the Warren's designation as a national nature reserve.

Three main trails, all well marked and none more than an hour or two's stroll, weave through the pines to **Llanddwyn Island**, a glorious peninsula of rocky coves and sandy beaches. On it stands Tŷr Mawr (the Great Tower), built in 1800 to warn the ships in Caernarfon Bay, later supplanted by the disused lighthouse, built in 1873 in the style of an Anglesey windmill. There's also a row of restored cottages and a thirteenth-century church ruin dedicated to the patron saint of lovers in Wales, St Dwynwen. In the fifth century, after her abortive affair with Welsh prince Maelon, Dwynwen became a nun at Llanddwyn and requested that hopeful lovers who make a supplication to God in her name should receive divine assistance.

Access to the Newborough Warren section of the reserve is from a free car park down a short track from the roundabout where the A4080 bends north. The main walk from here is out to Abermenai Point (2 miles), but be careful as rapid tidal changes can quickly cover the broad sandy approach. To reach the reserve's main entrance (and Llanddwyn Island), continue north along the A4080 for half a mile to **NEWBOROUGH** (Niwbwrch), a town of limited appeal founded by Edward I to rehouse villagers displaced during the building of Beaumaris. From the village a road leads a mile down to a signposted toll barrier (£3 in coins) and a second car park. A third of a mile down this access road it is worth stopping briefly at **Llys Rhosyr** (unrestricted access), the ruined footings of several buildings which represent the partially excavated remains of the pre-thirteenth-century court of the Princes of Gwynedd.

Family entertainments around Newborough extend to the **Anglesey Model Village**, a mile south on the A4080 (Easter–Sept daily 10.30am–5pm; £2.50), with its 1:12 scale models of Anglesey landmarks and a model railway; and the **Tacla Taid**, signposted a mile east of Newborough (Easter–Sept daily 10.30am–5.30pm; £3.50), with several dozen classic and vintage vehicles in a big shed.

From 1945 until his death in 1979, the estuarine beaches to the north and around **MALLTRAETH** were the haunt of **Charles Tunnicliffe**, who spent much of his days producing beautifully detailed wildlife drawings, mainly birds. Examples of his work can be seen at Oriel Ynys Môn (see p.461).

Around Aberffraw

The area around Newborough and tiny **LLANGADWALADR**, three miles northwest, was once the seat of the great ruling dynasty of the Princes of Gwynedd who, from the seventh-century reign of Cadfan until Llywelyn ap Gruffydd's death in 1282, controlled northwest Wales, and often much of the rest of the country, from this now quiet corner of Anglesey. The most substantial evidence lies in **Llangadwaladr Church** (usually closed except Sun mornings), built in the thirteenth century with a memorial plaque, carved in Latin about 625, incorporated into an inside wall. It reads "Cadfan the King, wisest and most renowned of all kings". **CABLE BAY** (Porth Trecastell), two miles northwest of Aberffraw, was the eastern terminus of the first telegraph cable to Ireland, though it is now better known for its good sandy beach, popular with **surfers**. On the headland to the north, the heavily reconstructed remains of the 5000-year-old **Barclodiad y Gawres** burial chamber are more dramatic than nearby Bryn Celli Ddu, with chevrons and zigzag patterns, similar to Newgrange and other Boyne Valley sites seventy miles across the water in Ireland. CADW keep it locked, so to get inside you'll have to join one of the visits (Sat & Sun noon–4pm; free; ℡01407/810153) from the Wayside Stores, a mile north in Llanfaelog. Call a few minutes in advance so the guide can meet you either at the Wayside Stores or the burial chamber.

Rhosneigr

The weekday roar of fighter jets from the nearby RAF Valley airfield deafens you long before you reach the otherwise peaceful Edwardian seaside resort of **RHOSNEIGR**, two miles further north along the coast. Rambling over consolidated dunes behind a series of small bays, Rhosneigr remains justifiably popular with English holiday-makers, although space on the beach is these days contested by the dozens of devoted **windsurfers** and **kitesurfers** who flock here when the wind is right. It's the sort of low-key place you might feel like joining in: rent a board and rig from Funsport, 1 Beach Terrace (£15–25 per day, tuition £35 for 2hr; ℡01407/810899, ⓦwww.buckys.co.uk) and take to the sea or the small Maelog Lake, safer when the wind is offshore.

Rhosneigr has limited facilities, but you can **camp** at *Shoreside Camping* (℡01407/810279, ⓦwww.shoresidecamping.co.uk; £6 per person), by the train station a mile north of the town centre, and eat at *Sandy's Bistro* on the High Street, where mains cost around £9.

Holy Island

Just a few yards off the northwest coast of Anglesey, and connected by road and rail bridges, **Holy Island** (Ynys Gybi) is blessed with Anglesey's finest scenery, notably the spectacular sea cliffs around **South Stack**, and the Stone Age and Roman remains on **Holyhead Mountain**. It's also cursed with its most unattractive town, Holyhead, the ancient home of St Cybi, after whom the island gets its holiness. This is also the terminus for ferry routes to Ireland and good transport links mean you'll probably find your way there at some stage. In many respects, you can taste Ireland hereabouts without even getting on the ferry. The rough stone walls, prehistoric tumps (mounds) and stones, ragged bays and whitewashed farms that characterize Holy Island are all redolent of the west of Ireland, as is the laid-back atmosphere.

This hourglass of land all but joins up with Anglesey's west coast at two points. The more ancient and picturesque approach turns west at Valley (Dyffryn), and passes close to the fine beaches at **Rhoscolyn** and **Trearddur Bay** before reaching Holyhead. Most road traffic takes the fast A55 across a modern bridge into Holyhead, though rail and the older A5 still follow Thomas Telford's 1200-yard-long Stanley Embankment. Along the way Telford constructed distinctive octagonal tollhouses, used until 1895, when the A5 was Britain's last major toll road. A couple have been converted to houses and one, at the northern end of the Stanley Embankment, now operates as the *Tollhouse Tearooms*.

Getting to Holyhead itself isn't difficult, as trains and a fair number of Anglesey's buses go there. Rhoscolyn and South Stack can be reached from Holyhead by the #23 and the #22 respectively. The #4 bus to Holyhead from Bangor and Llangefni is the only really useful service to Trearddur Bay.

Holyhead

Drab **HOLYHEAD** (Caergybi; pronounced in English as "holly-head") isn't somewhere you'll want to spend much time in, and reasonably well-integrated train and ferry tables mean you shouldn't need to. Still, walking into town from the train and ferry terminals you get to experience the town's latest rejuvenation attempt, a pedestrian bridge known as the **Celtic Gateway**. With the footway slung on cables from two huge stainless steel arches it is an impressive sight, though it then deposits you on run-down Market Street.

The town's Welsh name indicates that this was the site of a Roman fort and home of the sixth-century saint Cybi. His hermit's cell was built in the protection of the Roman walls and is now marked by the partly thirteenth-century **Church of St Cybi** (June–Sept Mon–Sat 11am–3pm). Both walls and church have undergone substantial reconstruction, the church gaining stained glass by Edward Burne-Jones and William Morris.

North of here, the **Holyhead Maritime Museum** (March–Nov daily 10am–4pm; £2.50; ⓦ www.holyheadmaritimemuseum.co.uk) sits beside the Newry Beach seafront overlooking Britain's longest breakwater (nearly 1.5 miles long). Tucked into the old lifeboat station, the museum contains haunting memorabilia of local maritime disasters along with lovely models of lifeboats through the years, and the ferries that have plied the Ireland route over the

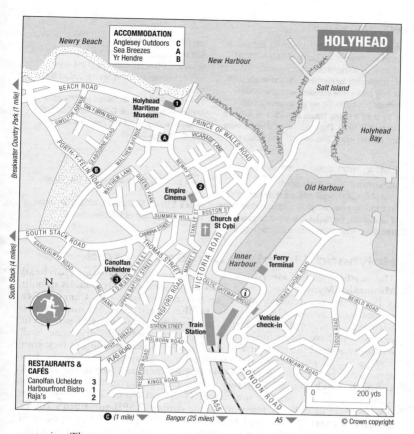

ACCOMMODATION
Anglesey Outdoors   C
Sea Breezes   A
Yr Hendre   B

RESTAURANTS & CAFÉS
Canolfan Ucheldre   3
Harbourfront Bistro   1
Raja's   2

centuries. There are even some whale's eardrums which show a passing resemblance to a human head and face. For no apparent reason, two on display here have been carved to portray Mussolini and Hitler.

Breakwater Country Park (daily 9am–dusk; free), a couple of miles west along Beach Road, is one of the better ways to pass the time if you miss your boat. An old brickworks marks the starting point for a bracing clifftop **walk** to the foghorn station on North Stack (an hour or so return), or on to South Stack, an hour's walk beyond (see below).

Practicalities

The A55 Expressway spills you into central Holyhead right by the **train station**, local and National Express **bus stops**, the passenger **ferry terminal** and **tourist office** (daily 8.30am–6pm; ☎01407/762622, ⓔholyhead@nwtic .com), which are all clustered together along with a Hertz **car rental** desk. Late-arriving ferry passengers are catered for at a small array of **B&Bs**, notably along Newry Street and Walthew Avenue, off Beach Road. Though fast food rules, you can still **eat** tolerably well in Holyhead. **Canolfan Ucheldre**, Mill Bank (☎01407/763361, ⓦwww.ucheldre.org) is Anglesey's premier centre for the performing arts and exhibitions, fashioned from a former convent chapel.

Accommodation

Anglesey Outdoors Porthdafarch Rd, just over a miles southwest of the centre ℡01407/769351, ⓦwww.angleseyoutdoors.com. Associate YHA (with no supplement for nonmembers) and independent activity centre with abundant accommodation including camping (£4 per person), bunk beds (£10; bring a towel), tepees (£60 for 4–6) and twin rooms (£32 for 2). There are self-catering facilities and bargain meals, plus all sorts of activities you can join, and gear to rent.

Sea Breezes 95 Newry St ℡01407/765682, ⓦwww.sea-breezes.com. One of the more homely and welcoming of several budget places on this street. ❶

Yr Hendre Porth-y-Felin Rd ℡01407/762929, ⓦwww.yr-hendre.co.uk. Comfy, floral B&B with a generous welcome, set in a charming ex-manse just off Walthew Ave. ❸

Eating and entertainment

Harbourfront Bistro Newry Beach ℡01407/763433. Small café and restaurant with good harbour views and some outdoor seating. Plenty of sandwiches, toasted baguettes and cakes plus the likes of pan-seared tiger prawns (£9) and veggie pasta bake (£8). Lunch daily except Mon; dinner Thurs–Sat.

Raja's 8 Newry St ℡01407/760333. Serves the tastiest Bengal curries for miles around.

Holyhead Mountain and South Stack

The northern half of Holy Island is ranged around the skirts of **Holyhead Mountain** (Mynydd Twr), rising 700ft to the west of Holyhead. Its summit is ringed by the remains of the seventeen-acre Iron Age **Caer y Twr** (unrestricted access; CADW), one of the largest sites in north Wales. Seemingly, it was only used during times of war, as no signs of permanent occupation have been unearthed, just a six-foot-high dry-stone wall enclosure around the ruins of a Roman beacon. Although you can pick your way up rough tracks from the Holyhead side in an hour or so, the best approach is by the infrequent bus #44 or your own transport to the car park at **South Stack** (Ynys Lawd), two miles west of Holyhead. A path (45min) leads from the car park to the top of Holyhead Mountain, though most people prefer to walk the few yards to the clifftop, RSPB-run **Ellin's Tower Seabird Centre** (Easter–Sept daily 10am–5.30pm; free). From April until the end of July, binoculars and closed-circuit TV give an unrivalled opportunity to watch up to 3000 birds – razorbills, guillemots and the odd puffin – nesting on the nearby sea cliffs while ravens and peregrines wheel outside the tower's windows.

A twisting path, with over four hundred steps, leads down from the South Stack car park to a suspension bridge over the surging waves, once the keeper's only access to the now fully automated pepper-pot **lighthouse** (Easter–Sept daily 10.30am–5.30pm; £4), built in 1809. Views on to the cliffs are stupendous as you climb down to the island and, once there, you'll find exhibitions on local wildlife and can take a tour of the lighthouse itself. Tickets are issued at the *South Stack Kitchen*, a café-cum-interpretive centre a hundred yards back along the lane.

William Stanley, who named Ellin's Tower (Twr Elin) after his wife, did most of the excavation work on the **Cytiau'r Gwyddelod** hut circles (CADW), across the road from the Seabird Centre car park. The name translates as the "huts of the Irish" – a common name for any ancient settlement – but evidence from excavations reveals little more than that the builders were late Neolithic or early Bronze Age people. The visible remains comprise nineteen low stone circles – some up to ten yards across – though there seem to have originally been fifty buildings, formed into eight distinct farmsteads separated by ploughed fields.

▲ Fast ferry leaving harbour for Ireland

Trearddur Bay and Rhoscolyn

At the waist of Holy Island's hourglass shape, a couple of miles south of Holyhead, the scattered settlement of **TREARDDUR BAY** (Bae Trearddur) shambles across low grassy hills, around a deeply indented bay punctuated by rocky coves. There's no centre to speak of, but it's a much nicer base than Holyhead and with a good, clean swimming beach.

If you can afford it, the best **place to stay** is the venerable, creaky *Trearddur Bay Hotel* (℡01407/860301, ⓦwww.trearddurbayhotel.co.uk; ❽), overlooking the main bay. It has a heated indoor pool, a good traditional restaurant and decent bar meals for those whose pockets aren't quite so deep. Apart from the *Trearddur Bay Hotel* and a couple of chippies, **eating** is restricted to the beachside *Waterfront Restaurant*, Lôn Isallt (℡01407/860006), which serves a broad spread of pub-style mains (£8–12) and has fab sea views. Under two miles further northwest, *Blackthorn Farm* (℡01407/765262, ⓦwww.blackthornleisure.co.uk; ❸) offers comfy B&B plus a nicely sited campsite (£16 per pitch) with a new shower block and even wi-fi.

At the southern tip of the island, a mile or so south of Trearddur Bay, a lane runs down to **RHOSCOLYN**, another scattered seaside settlement, even smaller and more appealing. With a couple of exquisite sandy beaches, lots of rocky outcrops and some delightful coastal walking, this is the ideal place to spend a few days chilling out.

The place to stay is *The Outdoor Alternative* (℡01407/860469, ⓦwww.outdooralternative.org), a relaxed, simple **campsite** (£5 per person) a few yards from the beach, which also runs a **self-catering hostel** with made-up bunks (£15); phone in advance for hostel bookings and for directions (you'll never find it otherwise). Meals are available on request, kayaks can be rented

(£20 a day) and staff can point you to some of the best walks. Just short of the beach car park, the pleasant *Glan Towyn* (T01407/860380; ❷) offers comfortable **B&B**. Nearby, the 🍴 *White Eagle Inn* (T01407/860267, Wwww .white-eagle.co.uk) gastropub offers some of the best eating on Holy Island, serving modern British cuisine (mains £8–14) and a bunch of excellent cask ales. The huge deck is a great spot for a pint of two before dinner.

Northern and inland Anglesey

The **northern and eastern sides of Anglesey** are quieter than the south and west; its settlements cluster behind sheltered coves that, with the odd rocky headland, form an appealing (if seldom dramatic) coastline. This is primarily family holiday country, though its thinner spread of caravan sites makes it much less oppressive than the north Welsh coast. None of the resorts is especially notable but all are well spaced, making cycling between them, or walking the coastal path, an ideal way to get around. Relying on **buses** is possible, though less rewarding.

Accommodation is detailed under the appropriate town accounts, but if you're exploring the coast with your own transport you may wish to head inland to stay at one of two farmhouses near Llanerchymedd, both of which serve wholesome, hearty dinners and are highly recommended. *Drws-Y-Coed* (T01248/470473, Wwww.angleseyfarms.com; ❸) is a comfy, B&B on a working farm a mile and a half east, while 🍴 *Llwydiarth Fawr* (T01248/470321, Wwww.angleseyfarms.com; ❹), is a spacious, agreeable Georgian mansion amid rolling hills half a mile north on the B5111.

The northwest coast to Cemaes

The main A5025 leaves Holyhead to follow the island's perimeter clockwise. There are plenty of nice sandy beaches around the village of **LLANFWROG**, where there's the lovely *Penrhyn Farm* farmhouse B&B (T01407/730134, Wwww.angleseyfarms.com; ❸).

A few miles inland, you might be tempted to swing off the main road for **LLANDDEUSANT**, where a signpost points to **Melin Llynnon** (Easter–Sept daily 11am–5pm; £2), Anglesey's sole remaining working windmill. At one time, fifty-odd mills all over Anglesey ground away to feed all of north

Wales; today, over thirty can still be seen, their sail-less stumps either rotting away in field corners or converted into barns and houses. Only Melin Llynnon survives in anything like its original form. Restored from dereliction under the guidance of Lincolnshire millwrights, it is now white-painted, canvas-sailed and once again producing flour. Everything in the mill is wind-powered, even the hoists that lift the grain through trapdoors, and almost extinct milling skills have been re-learnt by modern millers, who now demonstrate the process and sell the result – in bag and cake form – from a good café.

Back along the coastal drag, the highlight of the northwest coast is gently understated **PORTH SWTAN** (Church Bay), a diffuse settlement gathered loosely around a picturesque sweep of sand backed by yellow rocks dating from the pre-Cambrian era, some 570 million years ago. Just back from the beach, **Swtan** (Easter–Oct Fri–Sun noon–4pm; £3; Ⓦwww.swtan.co.uk) is the last thatched cottage on Anglesey, and has been restored and fitted with a small folk museum. Across the road, the wonderful *Lobster Pot* restaurant (℡01407/730241, Ⓦwww.lobster-pot.net; closed Sun evening, all day Mon, Dec & Jan) has live lobsters in tanks that are turned into just about every lobster dish imaginable (salad, Thermidor, Mornay; from £25). Nearby are a couple of low-key **campsites**, the church that gives the area its English name, and the friendly *Church Bay Inn*.

From here, the coast dives and ripples northwards to the harbourside village of **CEMAES**, wedged between the brooding bulk of the ageing **Wylfa Nuclear Power Station** and several dozen **windfarm** towers. It's a charming spot, with one of the most attractive harbours on the north coast, occupied by the odd trawler and boatloads of yachties. Tiny **Llanbadrig Church** (May–Sept daily 10am–noon & 2–4pm), on the headland at the eastern side of the bay, is one of only two Welsh churches dedicated to St Patrick. The present structure is mainly fourteenth century, but the church's origins go back to the fifth century, when Ireland's patron saint is supposed to have been shipwrecked on the small island offshore, and made his way to a cave below the site of the present church. The building was restored in the nineteenth century by Lord Stanley of Alderley, Bertrand Russell's grandfather, a Muslim who used Islamic imagery in the stained glass.

Amlwch and Parys Mountain

AMLWCH, five miles east of Cemaes, would be just another tiny fishing village but for **Parys Mountain** (Mynydd Parys) a mile or so inland, once the world's largest source of **copper**. The Ordovices, a great Celtic tribe who occupied north Wales in the Neolithic era, probably began to extract the ore, and the Romans certainly did so, but it wasn't until the eighteenth century that production reached industrial levels. Amlwch boomed in Wild West style, its population ballooning to six thousand by the late 1700s, making it Wales' second largest town. Pollution had become a problem, but people noticed that the iron hulls of ships didn't corrode in the copper-laced harbour waters, fuelling a demand for protective copper sheathing that boosted the market for Parys copper. International competition in the early nineteenth century saw the town sink back into its role of a fishing port, although copper has been mined on Parys ever since. You can reach the ruined pumping mill on top of Parys Mountain by a path from the car park on the B5111, a mile south of town, just next to the premises of the one company still trying to squeeze a profit from the exhausted mountain. The waymarked Industrial Heritage Trail (free leaflet available from the Amlwch Industrial Heritage

Centre; see below) leads around Parys' ravaged moonscape, made all the more bizarre by the derelict remains, multicoloured rocks, coppery pools of water and patches of scrubby heather and gorse.

Back in town, in the Watch House by the spruced-up Amlwch Port, locals have set up the **Amlwch Industrial Heritage Centre** (Easter–May daily 11am–2pm; June–Oct daily 11am–5pm; free), full of material on Amlwch's remarkable past, and with a café on the intentionally sloping floor of a former sail loft. The centre distributes a free *Porth Amlwch Heritage Trail* leaflet, but to explore the subterranean workings of Parys Mountain you'll have to join the Parys Underground Group on its weekly **underground tours** (Wed 6.30pm; £10; ℡01407/832255): you'll be supplied with helmet and lamp but should bring gumboots.

After visiting so many ancient churches in Wales, **Our Lady Star of the Sea**, a couple of hundred yards along the A5025, to the west of Main Street, comes as something of a novelty. Built in the 1930s of reinforced concrete, the great parabolic ribs of what could be a giant toast rack are supposed to represent an upturned boat, complete with portholes.

From Moelfre to Red Wharf Bay

MOELFRE has a reputation for shipwrecks, though wandering around the peaceful grey-pebbled cove on a sunny day it seems unlikely. An anchor behind the beach was salvaged from the *Hindlea*, which went down in October 1959, exactly a century after the 2700-ton *Royal Charter* foundered, with the loss of 450 lives and nearly £400,000-worth of gold. The dead are remembered by a memorial stone thirty minutes' walk north along the coastal path that starts at the end of the cove, past a small offshore cormorant colony.

Moelfre's only other point of interest lies a mile west off the A5025, where the late Neolithic **Din Lligwy Hut Group** (unrestricted access; CADW) forms the centrepiece of a site spanning three thousand years of human occupation. A five-sided walled enclosure contains the foundations of several circular and rectangular buildings dated to the second and fourth centuries which, along with the hut group on Holy Island, give the best indication of how these people actually lived, rather than how they buried their dead. To the northeast of the main enclosure stands **Capel Lligwy**, a forlorn-looking twelfth-century church, and a short distance to the south is the **Lligwy Burial Chamber** with its 28-ton capstone. All are just a short stroll from the road.

A few miles south of Moelfre, **Red Wharf Bay** (Traeth Coch), forms a broad, enticing sweep of golden sand which never gets too crowded. The most popular end is at Red Wharf Bay village: for more solitude and bigger views, go to the other end, reached down narrow hairpin lanes from the village of **LLANDDONA**.

Red Wharf Bay is backed by the atmospheric, wooden-beamed 🎋 *Ship Inn* (℡01248/852568, ⓦwww.shipinnredwharfbay.co.uk) where, on sunny days, the tables outside by the water are invariably packed with people supping real ales and tucking into the excellent meals (£8–13 mains). At such times you might want to wander down the road to *The Old Boathouse Café & Restaurant* which does comparably tasty meals for a pound or two less. If you want to **stay** hereabouts, try the welcoming *Hafod*, Amlwch Road, Benllech (℡01248/853092; ❸), in a large, comfortable Edwardian house.

Llangefni

About the only reason to venture inland is to visit **LLANGEFNI**, Anglesey's low-key county town, and the **Oriel Ynys Môn** gallery (daily 10.30am–5pm; free), half a mile along the B5111 from the town centre. Examining various aspects of Anglesey life, from pre-Christian sites and the dynastic lines of the Princes of Gwynedd to exhibits about conservation and the Welsh language, Oriel Ynys Môn provides an excellent overview of the sheer variety of factors in the island's turbulent history. A corner of the gallery is devoted to a mock-up of Charles Tunnicliffe's Malltraeth studio (see p.453), from where he made many of his wildlife paintings. Llangefni is five miles west of Llanfairpwll, and on the #4 bus route between Holyhead and Bangor.

Travel details

Unless otherwise stated frequencies for trains and buses are for Monday to Saturday services; Sunday averages 1–3 services, though the main routes are more frequent and some routes have no Sunday service at all.

Trains

Bangor to: Chester (27 daily; 1hr); Colwyn Bay (22 daily; 30min); Conwy (14 daily; 20min); Holyhead (27 daily; 30–40min); Llandudno Junction (27 daily; 20min); Rhosneigr (10 daily; 35min); Rhyl (22 daily; 40min).

Colwyn Bay to: Llandudno Junction (38 daily; 6min); Rhyl (38 daily; 15min).

Conwy to: Bangor (14 daily; 20min); Holyhead (14 daily; 1hr); Llandudno Junction (14 daily; 3min).

Holyhead to: Bangor (27 daily; 30–40min); Chester (27 daily; 1hr 30min–2hr); Conwy (14 daily; 1hr) ; Llandudno Junction (27 daily; 45min–1hr); Llanfairpwll (12 daily; 30min).

Llandudno to: Betws-y-Coed (6 daily; 45min); Blaenau Ffestiniog (4 daily; 1hr 10min); Chester (roughly hourly; 2hr 10min); Llandudno Junction (5 daily; 10min).

Llandudno Junction to: Bangor (27 daily; 20min); Betws-y-Coed (6 daily; 30min); Chester (roughly hourly; 2hr); Conwy (14 daily; 3min); Holyhead (27 daily; 45min–1hr); Llandudno (4 daily; 10min); Rhyl (38 daily; 20min).

Llanfairpwll to: Bangor (12 daily; 10min); Holyhead (12 daily; 30min).

Rhosneigr to: Holyhead (10 daily; 10min); Llanfairpwll (10 daily; 20min).

Rhyl to: Bangor (22 daily; 40min); Holyhead (20 daily; 1hr 10min–1hr 40min); Llandudno Junction (38 daily; 20min).

Buses

Bangor to: Beaumaris (every 30min; 30min); Bethesda (every 30min; 25min); Caernarfon (every 20min; 30min); Conwy (every 15min; 35min); Holyhead (every 30min; 1hr 15min); Llanberis (hourly; 45min); Llandudno (every 15min; 1hr); Llangefni (every 30min; 35min); Menai Bridge (every 30min; 12min).

Beaumaris to: Bangor (every 30min; 30min); Menai Bridge (every 30min; 15min); Penmon (6daily; 15min).

Conwy to: Bangor (every 15min; 35min); Llandudno (every 15min; 20min); Llanrwst (every 30min; 40min); Rowen (every 30min; 15min).

Holyhead to: Amlwch (7 daily; 50min); Bangor (every 30min; 1hr 15min); Cemaes (7 daily; 40min); Llanfairpwll (every 30min; 1hr); Llangefni (every 30min; 45min); Menai Bridge (every 30min; 1hr 5min); Rhoscolyn (3 daily; 15min); Trearddur Bay (hourly; 10min).

Llandudno to: Bangor (every 15min; 1hr); Blaenau Ffestiniog (7 daily; 1hr 10min); Conwy (every 15min; 20min); Llanrwst (every 30min; 1hr); Rhyl (every 10–20min; 1hr 10min).

Llanfairpwll to: Bangor (every 30min; 15min); Holyhead (every 30min; 1hr); Llangefni (every 30min; 15min); Newborough (11 daily; 20min).

Prestatyn to: Flint (every 30min; 50min); Rhyl (every 30min; 20min).

Rhyl to: Denbigh (every 20min; 45min); Llandudno (every 10–20min; 1hr 10min); Prestatyn (every

30min; 20min); Rhuddlan (every 20min; 10min); St Asaph (every 20min; 25min).

St Asaph to: Denbigh (every 20min; 20min); Rhuddlan (every 20min; 15min); Rhyl (every 20min; 25min).

Ferries

Holyhead to: Dublin (4 ferries daily; 3hr 15min; 2 catamarans daily; 2hr); Dun Laoghaire (2 catamarans daily; 2hr).

Contexts

Contexts

History

The beginnings

Before the end of the last Ice Age around ten thousand years ago, Wales and the rest of Britain formed part of the greater European whole and the early migrant inhabitants eked out a meagre existence on the tundra or a better one amongst the oak, beech and hazel forests in the warmer periods. Most lived in the southeast of Britain, but small groups foraged north and west, leaving 250,000-year-old evidence in the form of a human tooth in a cave near Denbigh in north Wales and a hand axe unearthed near Cardiff.

It wasn't until the early part of the **Upper Paleolithic age** that significant communities settled in Wales, those of the Gower peninsula interring the "Red Lady of Paviland" around 24,000 BC. This civilization remained on Europe's cultural fringe as the melting ice cut Britain off from mainland Europe around 5000 BC. Migrating Mesolithic peoples had already moved north from Central Europe and were followed by **Neolithic colonists**, whose mastery of stone and flint working found its expression in over a hundred and fifty cromlechs (turf-covered chambered tombs) dotted around Wales, primarily Pentre Ifan in Mynydd Preseli (see p.211), Bryn Celli Ddu (see p.451) and Barclodiad y Gawres on Anglesey (see p.453). Skilled in agriculture and animal husbandry, the Neolithic people also began to clear the lush forests covering Wales below 2000 feet, enclosing fields, constructing defensive ditches around their villages and mining for flint.

The earliest stone circles – more extensive meeting places than cromlechs – were built at this time and continued to spread over the country as the Neolithic period drifted into the **Bronze Age** around 2000 BC. Through their extensive trade networks, the inhabitants of Wales and the rest of Britain gradually changed to more sophisticated use of metals and developed a well-organized social structure. The established aristocracy engaged in much tribal warfare, as suggested by large numbers of earthwork forts built in this and the immediately succeeding period – the chief examples being at Holyhead Mountain on Anglesey and the Bulwalks at Chepstow.

The Celts

Celtic invaders spreading from their central European homeland settled in Wales in around 600 BC, imparting a great cultural influence. Familiar with Mediterranean civilization through trading routes, they introduced superior methods of metalworking that favoured iron rather than bronze, from which they forged not just weapons but also coins. Gold was used for ornamental works – the first recognizable Welsh art – heavily influenced by the symbolic, patterned **La Tène** style still thought of as quintessentially Celtic.

The Celts are credited with introducing the basis of modern Welsh. The original Celtic tongue was spoken over a wide area, gradually dividing into Goidelic (or Q-Celtic) now spoken in the Isle of Man, Ireland and

During Celtic times, the **druids** were a ritual priesthood with attendant poets, seers and warriors. Through a deep knowledge of ritual, legend and the mechanics of the heavens, the druids maintained their position between the people and a pantheon of over four thousand gods. Most of these were variations of a handful of chief gods worshipped by the great British tribes: the Silures and Demetae in the south of Wales, the Cornovii in mid-Wales and the Ordovices and Deceangli in the north.

Scotland, and **Brythonic** (P-Celtic) spoken in Wales and Cornwall, and later exported to Brittany. This highly developed language was emblematic of a sophisticated social hierarchy headed by **druids** (see above). Yet the Celts were unable to maintain an organized civic society to match that of their successors, the Romans.

The Romans in Wales

Life in Wales, unlike that in most of England, was never fully Romanized, the region remaining under legionary control throughout its three-hundred-year occupation. **Julius Caesar** made cross-Channel incursions in 55 and 54 BC, kicking off a lengthy but low-level infusion of Roman ideas which filtered across to Wales. This flow swelled a century later when the emperor **Claudius** took the death of the British king Cunobelin (Cynfelyn) as a signal to launch a full-scale invasion in 43 AD which in four years swept across southern England to the frontier of south Wales. Expansionism fomented anti-Roman feeling along the frontier between the Lowland Zone (southern and central England) and the Highland Zone (northern England, Scotland and Wales). Traditionally insular Welsh hill tribes united with their Brythonic cousins in northern England to oppose the Romans, who forced a wedge between them. The Roman historian **Tacitus** recorded the submission of the Deceangli near Chester, providing the oldest written mention of a Welsh land. The Romans, held back by troubles at home and with the East Anglian revolt of **Boudicca** (Boadicea), were limited to sending expeditionary forces against the Silures and the toughest nut, the druid stronghold of Anglesey. The Romans were kept at bay until around 75 AD, when legionary forts were built at Deva (Chester, England) and Isca Silurium (Caerleon) to act as platforms for incursions west along specially built military roads.

By 78 AD, Wales was under Roman control, its chief fortresses at Deva, Isca Silurium and Segontium (Caernarfon) boasting all the trappings of imperial Roman life: bath houses, temples, mosaics and underfloor heating. Through three centuries of occupation, the Celtic people sustained an independent existence, though elements of Roman life filtered into the Celtic culture: agrarian practices improved, a new religion was partly adopted from the newly Christianized Romans, the language adopted Latin words (pont for "bridge", ffenestr for "window") and the prevailing La Tène artistic style took on classical Roman elements.

The Roman Empire was already in decline when **Magnus Maximus** (Macsen Wledig) led a campaign to wrest control of the western empire from Emperor Gratian in 383 AD. Maximus' rule was short lived but Wales was effectively free of direct Roman control by 390.

The age of the saints

Historical orthodoxy views the departure of literate Latin historians, skilled stonemasons and an all-powerful army, as heralding the **Dark Ages**. In fact, a civic society probably flourished until a century later, when the collapse of trade routes was hastened by the dramatic spread of Islam around the Mediterranean, and Romanized society gave way to a structured form of **Celtic society**.

For the next few centuries, **Teutonic barbarian tribes** struggled for supremacy in the post-Roman power vacuum in southern and eastern England, having little influence in Wales, where the main dynastic kingdoms set to steer Wales' next seven hundred years were taking root. The confusion that surrounds the early years of these dynasties was further muddied in 1136, when Geoffrey of Monmouth published his *History of the Kings of Britain*, portraying **King Arthur** as a feudal king with his court at Caerleon. Victorian Romantics embellished subsequent histories, making it practically impossible to extract much truth from this period.

In the fifth century, the **Irish** (Gwyddyl), who had a long tradition of migrating to the Llŷn and parts of mid-Wales, attacked the coast and formed distinct colonies, but were soon expelled from the north by **Cunedda Wledig**, the leader of a Brythonic tribe from near Edinburgh, who went on to found the royal house of Gwynedd, consolidating the Brythonic language and naming regions of his kingdom – the modern Ceredigion and Meirionydd – after his sons. In the southwest, the Irish influence was sustained; the kingdom of Dyfed shows clear Irish origins.

These changes took place against a background of increasing religious energy. Between the fifth and the sixth centuries the **Celtic Saints**, ascetic evangelical missionaries, spread the gospel around Ireland and western Britain, promoting the Middle Eastern eremitical tradition of living a reclusive life. Where their message took root, they founded simple churches within a consecrated enclosure, or llan, which often took the saint's name, hence Llanberis (Saint Peris), Llandeilo (Saint Teilo) and numerous others. In south Wales, **Saint David** (Dewi Sant) was the most popular (and subsequently Wales' patron saint), dying around 589 after a miracle-filled life, during which he established the religious community at St Davids, which had become a place of pilgrimage by the twelfth century.

The Welsh kingdoms

Towards the end of the sixth century the **Angles** and **Saxons** in eastern Britain began to entertain designs on the western lands. The inability of the independent western peoples to unify against this threat left the most powerful kingdom, Gwynedd, as the centre of cultural and political resistance. The weaker groups were unable to hold the invaders, and after the battle at Dyrham, near Gloucester in 577, the Britons in Cornwall were separated from those in Wales, who became similarly cut off from their northern kin in Cumbria after the battle of Chester in 616.

Bonded by the people's resistance to the Saxons, the Welsh started to refer to themselves as **Cymry** (fellow-countrymen), rather than the Saxon term "Welsh", used by English-speakers today and which is generally thought to mean either foreigners or Romanized people. The construction of **Offa's Dyke**

(Clawdd Offa, see p.257) – a linear earthwork built in the middle of the eighth century to mark rather than defend the boundary between Wales and the kingdom of Mercia – gave the Welsh a firm eastern border and allowed them to concentrate on a gradual unification of the patchwork of kingdoms as their coasts were being harried by **Norse and Viking invaders**.

Rhodri Mawr (Rhodri the Great) killed the Viking leader off Anglesey, helping the country's rise towards statehood through his unification of most of Wales. By this stage, England had developed into a single powerful kingdom, and though the various branches of Rhodri's line went on to rule most of Wales down to the late thirteenth century, the princedoms were frequently forced to swear fealty to the English kings. Defensive problems were exacerbated by the practice of partible inheritance that left each of Rhodri's sons with an equal part of Wales to control.

Rhodri Mawr's grandson **Hywel Dda** (Hywel the Good) largely reunified the country from Deheubarth, his power base in southwest Wales. He added Powys and Gwynedd to his domain, but his most valuable legacy is his codification and promulgation of the medieval **Law of Wales** (Cyfraith Hywel Dda) in around 930 at modern-day Whitland (see p.174). Progressive and enlightened regional customs – such as women being allowed to initiate divorce proceedings, parity between children born in and out of wedlock, and non-punishment for theft of food that kept people alive – were fashioned into a single legal system that was forcibly abandoned under the 1536 Act of Union with England, though many elements of it survived in common-law practice.

After Hywel's death in 950, anarchy and internal turmoil reigned until his great-great-grandson, **Gruffydd ap Llywelyn**, seized power in Gwynedd in 1039. He unified all of Wales, taking the coronation of the weak English king, Edward the Confessor, as an opportunity to annex some of the Marches in Mercia. Edward's successor, Harold, wasn't having any of this and killed Gruffydd, heralding a new phase of political fragmentation.

The arrival of the Normans

In 1066, the **Normans** swept across the English Channel, killed Harold, the English king, and stormed England. Though Wales was unable to present a unified opposition to the invaders, the Norman king, William, didn't attempt to conquer Wales. The **Domesday Book** – his masterwork of subjugation commissioned in 1085 to record land ownership as a framework for taxation – indicates that he only nibbled at parts of Powys and Gwynedd. Instead, he installed a huge retinue of barons, the **Lords Marcher**, along the border to bring as much Welsh territory under their own jurisdiction as possible. Despite generations of squabbling, the barons managed to hold onto their privileges until Henry VIII's Act of Union over four hundred years later.

The payment of homage by **Rhys ap Tewdwr** (the king of Deheubarth), and **Gruffydd ap Cynan** (the king of Gwynedd) kept the Welsh borders safe until the death of William I in 1087. His son William Rufus made three unsuccessful invasions of Wales but finally left it to his Marcher lords to advance from their castles into south Wales, leaving only Powys and Gwynedd independent.

A lack of English commitment or resources allowed the Welsh to claw back their territory through years when distinctions between English, Normans and Welsh were beginning to blur, which helped form three stable political entities: Powys, Deheubarth and Gwynedd. The latter, led by **Owain Gwynedd** from his capital at Aberffraw on Anglesey, now extended beyond Offa's Dyke and progressively gained hegemony over the other two. Owain Gwynedd's grandson, **Llywelyn ap Iorwerth** (the Great), incorporated the weaker territories to the south into his kingdom and captured several Norman castles to reach the peak of the Welsh feudal pyramid. After tussling with England's King John, resulting in a degree of Welsh autonomy, Llywelyn engineered the smooth succession by commanding his princes to assemble at Strata Florida (see p.285) and pay homage not just to him but also to his son, Dafydd. This plan succeeded until after his death, when Wales began to disintegrate to the point where at Dafydd's death in 1246 the country had only nominal unity.

Most of the work of regrouping Wales around one standard fell to Llywelyn the Great's grandson and Dafydd's nephew, Llywelyn ap Gruffydd (Llewellyn the Last).

Edward I's conquest

By 1255, Llywelyn ap Iorwerth's grandson, **Llywelyn ap Gruffydd** (the Last), had won control of Gwynedd. During the next three years he pushed the English out of Gwynedd, then out of most of Wales. The English king Henry III was forced to respect Llywelyn's influence and ratified the **Treaty of Montgomery** in 1267, thereby recognizing Llywelyn as "Prince of Wales" in return for his homage. The English monarchy's war with the barons allowed Llywelyn time to politically consolidate his lands, which now stretched over all of modern Wales excepting Pembrokeshire and parts of the Marches.

The tables turned when Edward I succeeded Henry III and began a crusade to unify Britain. With effective use of sea power, Edward had little trouble forcing the already weakened Llywelyn back into Snowdonia. Peace was restored with the **Treaty of Aberconwy**, which deprived Llywelyn of almost all his land and stripped him of his financial tributes from the other Welsh princes, but left him with the hollow title of "Prince of Wales".

Edward now set about surrounding Llywelyn's land with castles at Aberystwyth, Builth Wells, Flint and Rhuddlan. After a relatively cordial four-year period,

Owain Glyndŵr, Welsh Hero

Still synonymous with Welsh pride today, renegade nationalist **Owain Glyndŵr** declared himself "Prince of Wales" in 1400. He and his crew of local supporters attacked the lands of nearby barons, slaughtering the English. Henry IV misjudged the political climate and imposed restrictions on Welsh land ownership, swelling the general support Glyndŵr needed to take Conwy Castle the following year. By 1404, Glyndŵr, who already had control over most of western Wales and sections of the Marches, took the castles at Harlech and Aberystwyth, summoned a parliament in Machynlleth, and had himself crowned Prince of Wales, with envoys of France, Scotland and Castile in attendance. He then demanded independence for the Welsh Church from Canterbury and set about securing alliances with English noblemen who had grievances with Henry IV. This last, ambitious move heralded Glyndŵr's downfall. A succession of defeats saw his allies desert him, and by 1408, when the castles at Harlech and Aberystwyth were retaken for the Crown, this last protest against Edward I's English conquest had lost its momentum. Little is known of Glyndŵr's final years, though it is thought he died in 1416, possibly in Herefordshire, leaving Wales territorially unchanged but the country's pride at an all-time high.

Llywelyn's brother Dafydd rose against Edward, inevitably dragging Llywelyn along with him. Edward didn't hesitate and swept through Gwynedd, crushing the revolt and laying the foundations for the remaining castles in his **Iron Ring**, those at Conwy, Caernarfon, Harlech and Beaumaris. Llywelyn, already battered by Edward's force, was captured and executed at Cilmeri (see p.249), after fleeing from the abortive Battle of Builth in December 1282.

Throughout the fourteenth century, famine and the Black Death plagued Wales. The Marcher lords appropriated the lands of defaulting debtors, while royal officials clawed in all the income they could from towns around the castles. These factors and the pent-up resentment of the English sowed seeds of a rebellion led by the tyrannical but charismatic **Owain Glyndŵr** (see p.301 & p.469).

The Tudors and union with England

During the latter half of the fifteenth century, the succession to the English throne was contested in the **Wars of the Roses** between the houses of York (white rose) and Lancaster (red rose). Welsh allegiance lay broadly with the Lancastrians, who had the support of the ascendant north Welsh Tewdwr (or Tudor) family. Henry Tudor escaped from besieged Harlech Castle to Brittany when Yorkist Richard III took the English throne in 1471. Fourteen years later, Henry returned to Wales, defeating Richard at the Battle of Bosworth Field, so becoming **Henry VII** and sealing the Lancastrian ascendancy.

For the most part Henry lived up to the high Welsh expectations, removing many of the restrictions on land ownership imposed at the start of Glyndŵr's uprising, and promoting many Welshmen to high office. Still, Wales had been largely controlled by the English monarch since the Statute of Rhuddlan (see box, p.472).

▲ Parliament House, Machynlleth

Sovereignty was finally fixed in Henry VIII's 1536 **Act of Union** (and a subsequent act of 1543). It's a misleading title, and one that was not used to describe the Act until the twentieth century, for it implies a level of equality between the two nations that did not in fact exist. Unlike the Acts of 1707 and 1800 that brought Scotland and Ireland into the Union – and were the decisions of independent parliaments in Edinburgh, Dublin and London to merge their identities – the 1536 Act was a unilateral decision by Westminster, a parliament that, at the time, had no Welsh representation. It decreed that English was to be the only language of the courts and other official bodies, effectively creating a two-tier Wales of English-speaking lords and masters and a Welsh-speaking proletariat. At the same time the Marches were replaced by shires (the equivalent of modern counties), the Welsh laws codified by Hywel Dda were voided, and partible inheritance (equal amongst all offspring) gave way to primogeniture, the eldest son becoming the sole heir. This period set in stone the struggles and the injustices that are still playing out nearly five hundred years later.

Just as Henry VIII's decision to convert his kingdom from Catholicism to Protestantism was born more from his desire to divorce his first wife, Catherine of Aragon, than from any religious conviction, it was his need for money, not recognition, which brought about the **Dissolution of the Monasteries** in 1536 – ultimately resulting in a more studied approach to religion and learning in general. Under the reign of Elizabeth I, Jesus College was founded in Oxford for Welsh scholars, and the Bible was translated into Welsh for the first time by a team led by Bishop **William Morgan** (see p.424).

The Dissolution hastened the emergence of the Anglo–Welsh gentry, a group eager to claim a Welsh pedigree while promoting the English language and the legal system.

The Civil War and the rise of Nonconformism

A direct descendant of the Tudors, **James I** came to the throne in 1603 to general popular approval in Wales. Many privileges granted to the Welsh during the Tudor reign came to an end, but the idea of common citizenship was retained, the Council of Wales remaining as a focus for Welsh nationalism. James, fearful of both Catholicism and the new threat of Puritanism – an extreme form of Protestantism – courted a staunchly Anglican Wales and curried the favour of Welsh ministers in the increasingly powerful Parliament. Though weak in Wales, Puritanism was gaining a foothold, especially in the Welsh borders, where William Wroth and Walter Cradock set up Wales' first dissenting church at Llanfaches in Monmouthshire in 1639.

The monarchy's relations with the Welsh were strained by **Charles I**, who was forced to levy heavy taxes and recruit troops, but the gentry were mostly loyal to the king at the outbreak of the **Civil War**, which saw the Parliamentary forces install **Oliver Cromwell** as the leader of the **Commonwealth**. The Puritan support for Parliament didn't go unnoticed, and after Charles' execution, they were rewarded with the livings of numerous parishes and the roots of Puritan Nonconformism spread in Wales.

The Statute of Rhuddlan

The **Statute of Rhuddlan** in 1284 set down the terms by which the English monarch was to rule Wales: much of it was given to the Marcher lords who had helped Edward I, the rest was divided into administrative and legal districts similar to those in England. Though the treaty is often seen as a symbol of English subjugation, it respected much of Welsh law and provided a basis for civil rights and privileges. Many Welsh were content to accept and exploit Edward's rule for their own benefit. In 1294, however, a rebellion led by Madog ap Llywelyn gripped Wales and was only halted by Edward's swift and devastating response. Most of the privileges enshrined in the Statute of Rhuddlan were rescinded.

As Cromwell's regime became more oppressive, the Anglican majority welcomed the successful return of the exiled **Charles II**, and the monarchy was restored, thereby suppressing Nonconformity. The Baptists, Independents and Quakers who made up the bulk of Nonconformists continued to worship in secret, until **James II** passed the **Toleration Act** in 1689, finally allowing open worship, but still banning the employment of dissenters in municipal government; a limitation which remained in force until 1828.

The rise of Methodism

The propagation of Nonconformism led to a welter of new religious books in Welsh in the late seventeenth century, but with most people still illiterate, religious observance remained an oral tradition. In 1699, the **Society for Promoting Christian Knowledge** established schools where the Bible, along with reading, writing and arithmetic, were taught in Welsh as well as English. This met with considerable success in middle-class anglicized towns, but failed to reach rural areas where children couldn't be spared from farm duties. The next big reformist push came in 1731, when **Griffith Jones** organized reading classes in the evenings and quieter winter season, so farmers and their families could attend. Within thirty years, half the Welsh population could read.

By the middle of the eighteenth century, a receptive and literate populace was ready for what became the **Methodist Revival**, driven by a strong belief in a resurgent Welsh nation. In contrast to the staid Anglican services, the Methodists held evangelical meetings. Meanwhile, improved schooling brought about a literary revolution, and Wales re-established itself as the language for a vast body of literature.

In 1811, the Calvinist Methodists broke from the framework of Anglicanism. As the gentry remained with the Established Church, the chapel became the focus of social life, discouraging folk traditions considered incompatible with puritanical thrift and temperance. Political radicalism was also discouraged, perpetuating the stranglehold on parliamentary power exercised by the powerful landed elite. Only property owners were eligible to vote and few were prepared to challenge established dynasties.

Human rights became an issue in 1776 with the publication of the American Declaration of Independence and a piece by the radical Welsh philosopher, **Richard Price**: *Observations on the Nature of Civil Liberty*. The subsequent calls for a greater degree of democracy – universal suffrage and annual parliaments – increased during the early days of the French

Revolution, but little was actually achieved until the next century, when radical Nonconformists were able to exploit the increasing political consciousness of the working class.

Wales and the Industrial Revolution

Small-scale mining and smelting had taken place in Wales since the Bronze Age, but agriculture remained the mainstay of an economy centred on meat, wool and butter. The enormous rise in grain prices in the early nineteenth century forced Welsh farmers to diversify and adopt the more advanced English farming practices of crop rotation, fertilizing and stock breeding. Around the same time, acts of Parliament allowed previously common land to be "enclosed", the grazing rights often being assigned solely to the largest landowner in the district. Inevitably, this forced smallholders to migrate to the towns where ever more workers were required to mine the seams and stoke the furnaces, fuelling the **Industrial Revolution**. In the north, **John Wilkinson** started his ironworks at Bersham (see p.327) and developed a new method of boring cylinders for steam engines; while in the south, foundries sprang up in the valleys around Merthyr Tydfil under English ironmasters. Gradually the under-educated, impoverished chapel-going Welsh began to be governed by rich, church-going, English industrial barons.

Improved materials and working methods enabled the exploitation of deeper coal seams, particularly in the south Wales valleys, not just to supply the iron smelters but for domestic fuel and to power locomotives and steamships. South Wales' rural valleys were ripped apart and quiet hamlets turned into long rows of attached houses snaking up the valley sides, roofed in north Wales slate.

Transportation of huge quantities of coal and steel was crucial for continued economic expansion, and the roads and canals built in the early nineteenth century were displaced around 1850 as the rail boom took hold. Great **engineers** made their names in Wales: **Thomas Telford** built canal aqueducts and successfully spanned the Menai Strait with one of Britain's earliest suspension bridges; **Isambard Kingdom Brunel** surveyed the Merthyr–Cardiff train line, then pushed his Great Western network almost to Fishguard; and **Robert Stephenson** speeded the passage of trains between London and Holyhead on Anglesey for the Irish ferry connection.

In mining towns, working conditions were atrocious, with men and women toiling incredibly long hours in dangerous conditions; children as young as six worked alongside them, until this was outlawed by the Mines Act in 1842. Pay was low and often in a currency redeemable only at the poorly stocked, expensive company (Truck) shop. The **Anti-Truck Act** of 1831 improved matters, but a combination of rising population, fluctuating prices and growing need for political change brought calls for reform. When it came in 1832, the **Reform Bill** fell far short of the demands for universal suffrage by ballot and the removal of property requirement for voters. This swelled the ranks of the Reformist Chartist movement, and when a petition with over a million signatures was rejected by Parliament, the **Chartist Riots** broke out in northern England and south Wales. The Newport demonstration was disastrous, the marchers walking straight into a trap laid by troops, who killed over twenty men and captured their leader, **John Frost**. Chartism continued in a weakened form for twenty years, buoyed by the **Rebecca Riots** in 1839–43 (see p.251), when guerrilla tactics put an end to tollgates on south Welsh turnpikes.

1850 to World War I

During the latter half of the nineteenth century the radical reformist movement and religion slowly became entwined, despite Nonconformist denial of political intentions. Due to the disparity of rights compared with Anglicans, the Nonconformists petitioned for **disestablishment** of the Church in Wales, politicizing their message.

Eventually, as a consequence of the 1867 Reform Act, industrial workers and small tenant farmers got the vote, giving a long-awaited strong working-class element to the electorate and seeing **Henry Richard** elected as Liberal MP for Merthyr Tydfil the following year, the first Welsh member of what soon became the dominant political force and bringing the ideas of Nonconformity – land reform, disestablishment and the preservation of the Welsh language – to Parliament for the first time.

The 1872 Secret Ballot Act and 1884 Reform Act, enfranchising farm labourers, further freed up the electoral system, although the Anglican church was only disestablished in 1920. The Nonconformist Sunday Schools offered primary education for the masses, supplemented by a number of secondary schools, as well as Wales' first major tertiary establishment in Aberystwyth in 1872 (the tiny St David's University College in Lampeter was already fifty years old by then); followed by colleges at Cardiff (1883) and Bangor (1884). Until they were federated into the University of Wales in 1893, voluntary contributions garnered by Nonconformist chapels supported the colleges. The apotheosis of "Chapel power" came in 1881 with the passing of the Welsh Sunday Closing Act, enshrining Nonconformism's three basic tenets: observance of the Sabbath, sobriety and Welshness.

The rise in Welsh consciousness

Immigration to the coal fields from England meant that English became the language of commerce and the route to advancement, Welsh being reserved for the home and chapel life of seventy percent of the population. Welsh was still being spoken in Nonconformist schools when, in 1846, they were inspected by three English barristers and seven Anglican assistants. The inspectors' report – known as **The Treason of the Blue Books** – declared the standards deplorable, largely due to the use of the Welsh tongue. The public defence of Welsh that ensued failed to prevent the introduction of the notorious "Welsh Not", effectively a ban on speaking Welsh in school.

As the nineteenth-century Romantic movement took hold throughout Britain, the London Welsh looked to their heritage. The ancient tales of The Mabinogion were translated into English, the **Welsh Language Society** was founded in 1885, eisteddfodau were reintroduced as part of rural life, and the ancient bardic order, the **Gorsedd**, was reinvented. But disestablishment remained the cause célèbre of Welsh nationalism. Perhaps the greatest advocate of both separatism and Welsh nationalism was **Michael D. Jones**, who helped establish a Welsh homeland in Patagonia.

By 1907 Wales had a national library at Aberystwyth, and a national museum was planned for Cardiff, by now the largest city in Wales.

Industry and the rise of trade unionism

The rise in Welsh consciousness paralleled the rise in importance of the **trade unions**. The 1850s were a prosperous time in the Welsh coal fields, but by the end of the 1860s the Amalgamated Union of Miners was forced to call a strike (1869–71), which resulted in higher wages.

A second strike in 1875 failed and the miners' agent, **William Abraham (Mabon)**, ushered in the notorious "sliding scale" which fixed wage levels according to the selling price of coal. This brought considerable hardship to the Valleys, which became insular worlds with strictly ordered social codes and a rich vibrancy born from the essential dichotomy of the chapel and the pub. Meanwhile, annual coal production doubled in twenty years to 57 million tons by 1913, when a quarter of a million people were employed. Similarly punitive pay schemes were implemented in the north Wales slate quarries where membership of **Undeb Chwarelwyr Gogledd Cymru** (The North Wales Quarrymen's Union) was all but outlawed by the slate barons. Things came to a head in 1900 when the workers at Lord Penrhyn's quarry at Bethesda started one of Britain's longest-ever industrial disputes, lasting three years.

From 1885, the vast majority of Welsh MPs were Liberals who helped end the sliding scale in 1902 and brought in an eight-hour day by 1908. The start of the twentieth century heralded the birth of a new political force when **Keir Hardie** became Britain's first Labour MP, for Merthyr Tydfil.

World Wars I and II

World War I (1914–18) was a watershed for Welsh society. The Welsh identified with the plight of defenceless European nations and rallied to fight alongside the English and Scots. At home, the state increasingly intervened in people's lives: agriculture was controlled by the state, rationing food, and industries, mines and railways were under public control. The need for Welsh food and coal boosted the economy and living standards rose dramatically. Many were proud to be led through the war by Welsh lawyer **David Lloyd George** (see p.401), who rose to the post of Minister of Munitions, then of War, becoming Prime Minister by 1916; but by the time conscription was introduced, patriotic fervour had waned. Many miners, reluctant to be slaughtered in the trenches and resentful of massive wartime profits, welcomed the 1917 Bolshevik Revolution, and though Communism never really took hold, the socialist Labour Party caught the postwar fallout.

Similar dramatic changes were taking place in rural areas, where Welsh farming was embracing new machinery and coming out of nearly a century of neglect. High wartime inflation of land prices and the fall in rents forced some landowners to sell off portions of major estates to their tenants in the so-called "green revolution".

The boom time of World War I continued for a few years after 1918, but soon the Depression came. All of Wales' mining and primary production industries suffered, and unemployment reached 27 percent, worse than in England and Scotland. The **Labour movement** ascended in step with the rise in unemployment, making south Wales its stronghold in Britain. This was challenged by Lloyd George's newly resurgent Liberal Party, but his Westminster-centred politics were no longer trusted in Wales and Labour held firm, seeking to improve workers' conditions: the state of housing was still desperate, and health care and welfare services needed boosting. The Labour Party effectively became the hope that had previously been entrusted to the chapels and later the Liberals.

A new sense of nationalism emerged and, in 1925, champions of Welsh national autonomy formed **Plaid Genedlaethol Cymru** (the National Party of Wales). In one of the first modern separatist protests, its president **Saunders Lewis** joined two other Plaid members and set fire to building materials at an RAF station on the Llŷn, was imprisoned, dismissed from his post and spent the rest of his life immersed in literary criticism, becoming one of Wales' greatest modern writers. Similar public displays and powerful nationalist rhetoric won over an intellectual majority, but the voting majority continued to fuel the Labour ascendancy in both local and national politics.

Some relief from the Depression came with re-armament in the lead-up to **World War II**, but by this stage vast numbers had migrated from south Wales to England, leaving the already insular communities banding together in self-reliant groups centred on local co-ops and welfare halls.

The demands of the war saw unemployment all but disappear and the Welsh economy gradually restructured, with more people switching from extractive industries to light manufacturing, a process which continues today.

Plaid Cymru were less enthusiastic about the war, remaining neutral and expressing unease at the large number of English evacuees potentially weakening the fabric of Welsh communities. However, the war saw the formation of a Welsh elementary school in Aberystwyth and Undeb Cymru Fydd, a committee designed to defend the welfare of Wales.

The postwar period

Any hopes for a greater national identity were dashed by the Attlee Labour government from 1945 to 1951, which nationalized transport and utilities with no regard for national boundaries, except for the Wales Gas Board. However, under the direction of Ebbw Vale MP, **Aneurin Bevan**, the postwar Labour government instituted the National Health Service, dramatically improving health care in Wales and the rest of Britain, and providing much-improved council housing.

The nationalized coal industry, now employing less than half the number of twenty years before, was still the most important employer at nationalization, but a gradual process of closing inefficient mines saw the number of pits drop from 212 in 1945 to 11 in 1989, and none today. Sadly, the same commitment wasn't directed at cleaning up the scars of over a century of mining until after 1966, when one of south Wales' most tragic accidents left a school and 116 children buried under a slag heap at **Aberfan** (see p.101).

After its postwar successes, the Labour Party remained in overwhelming control during the 1960s and 1970s, though Plaid Cymru became a serious opposition for the first time, partly due to Labour's reluctance to address nationalist issues. Attlee had thrown out the suggestion of a Welsh Secretary of State in 1946, and not until Plaid Cymru fielded numerous candidates in the 1959 election did the Labour manifesto promise a cabinet position for Wales.

The position of **Secretary of State for Wales** was finally created in 1964 by the Labour government, led by Harold Wilson, who also created the **Welsh Development Agency** and moved the Royal Mint to Llantrisant in south Wales. With Plaid Cymru's appeal considered to be restricted to rural areas, Labour was shocked by the 1966 Carmarthen by-election, when **Gwynfor Evans** became the first Plaid MP. It wasn't until 1974 that Plaid also won in the constituencies of Caernarfon and Meirionydd, and suddenly the party was a threat, forcing Labour to address the question of devolution.

By 1978 Labour had tabled the **Wales Act**, promising the country an elected assembly to act as a voice for Wales, but with no power to legislate or raise revenue. In the subsequent **referendum** in 1979, eighty percent of voters opposed the proposition, with even the nationalist stronghold of Gwynedd voting against.

Modern Wales

The Conservative (Tory) government of **Margaret Thatcher** came to power in 1979, achieving an unprecedented 31 percent of Welsh votes. The referendum that year effectively sidelined the home-rule issue and Thatcher was able to implement her free-market policies with an unstinting commitment to privatizing nationalized industries. With 43 percent of the Welsh workforce as government employees, privatization had a dramatic impact. The number of jobs in the steel industry, manufacturing and construction all plummeted, doubling unemployment in five years. Despite this, the Tories held their share of the vote and, because of changes to constituency boundaries, increased their tally of MPs at the 1983 election, while Labour saw their lowest percentage since 1918.

The resulting breakdown of traditional Valley communities and successive anti-union measures failed to break the solidarity of south Welsh workers during the year-long **Miners' Strike** (1984–85). As in many other countries, in the second half of the twentieth century, the Welsh turned away from the established religions in large numbers. The chapel has ceased to be the focal point of community life, and something like two-thirds of the country's six thousand chapels have closed.

During the 1980s, support for Plaid Cymru shifted back to the rural areas. At the same time, general enthusiasm for the Welsh language increased and a steady decline in numbers of Welsh-speakers was reversed: the number continues to climb today. New Welsh-only schools opened even in predominantly English-speaking areas, learners' classes sprouted everywhere and in 1982, S4C, the first **Welsh-language television channel**, began broadcasting.

The Tories landed the country with a succession of variously disinterested, and usually English, Secretaries of State who did little to further the Welsh cause. When Tony Blair and "New" Labour won a huge majority in 1997, one of the central policy proposals was the **devolution** of some degree of power from London to a parliament in Scotland and a **National Assembly for Wales** – the first all-Wales tier of government for six hundred years. The proposal was endorsed by the Welsh people only by the most slender of margins in a referendum. First elections to the Assembly took place in 1999, when a huge swing to Plaid Cymru denied the Labour party its assumed overall majority. To date, Labour still run the government in Cardiff Bay, with committed supporter of Welsh devolution, **Rhodri Morgan**, as First Minister.

In 2006 the Government of Wales Act gained Royal Assent, affirming that from May 2007 the Queen would have the new legal identity of "Her Majesty in Right of Wales", and would, for the first time, appoint Welsh Ministers and sign Welsh Orders in Council. The Act also made provision for a future referendum for Welsh people to vote on whether they would support the Welsh Assembly gaining the power to pass primary legislation (ie. "Welsh laws"). Now at home in its snazzy new building on the waterfront of Cardiff Bay, the Assembly is enmeshing itself into the fabric of Welsh life.

It's not just in the political arena that the country has grown up: there has been a significant surge of national confidence and self-expression, particularly in the cultural and sporting arenas. That is not to say that everything is rosy: the property market is at snapping point in many areas, farming lurches along in a state of semi-paralysis, and poverty and ill health still dog many old working-class communities. But these are interesting times in Wales: there is the undeniable feeling that this small country is facing a brighter future than many would have dared predict even one generation ago.

Chronology of Welsh history

250,000 BC ▶ Earliest evidence of human existence in Wales.

4000 BC ▶ Agriculturalism becomes widespread in Wales.

2000 BC ▶ Arrival of **Bronze Age** settlers from the Iberian peninsula.

600 BC ▶ **Celts** reach the British Isles.

43 AD ▶ **Romans** begin conquest of Britain.

78 ▶ Roman conquest of Wales completed as Agricola kills druids of Anglesey.

80–100 ▶ Caerleon amphitheatre built.

early 4thC ▶ Roman departure from Wales.

5th–6thC ▶ **Age of Saints**.

c.589 ▶ Saint David (Dewi Sant) dies.

616 ▶ Battle of Chester – Wales isolated from rest of Britain.

c.784 ▶ Offa's Dyke (Clawdd Offa) constructed.

c.900–50 ▶ Hywel Dda rules most of Wales.

1066 ▶ **Normans** invade Wales.

1067 ▶ Chepstow Castle started.

1180–93 ▶ St Davids Cathedral built.

1188 ▶ Archbishop Baldwin (accompanied by Giraldus Cambrensis) recruits for the Third Crusade.

1196–1240 ▶ **Llywelyn ap Iorwerth** (the Great) rules as Prince of Gwynedd and later most of Wales.

1246–82 ▶ **Llywelyn ap Gruffydd** (the Last) intermittently rules large parts of Wales.

1270–1320 ▶ Tintern Abbey built.

1276–77 ▶ **First War of Welsh Independence**.

1277 ▶ Llywelyn humiliated by signing **Treaty of Aberconwy**. Edward I begins Aberystwyth, Flint and Rhuddlan castles.

1282–83 ▶ **Second War of Welsh Independence**. Llywelyn's brother Dafydd rises up against Edward I.

1283 ▶ Caernarfon, Conwy and Harlech castles started.

1284 ▶ **Statute of Rhuddlan** signed by Edward I.

1301 ▶ Edward I revives title of "Prince of Wales" and bestows it on his son, Edward II.

1400–12 ▶ Third War of Welsh Independence. **Owain Glyndŵr**'s revolt.

c.1416 ▶ **Owain Glyndŵr** dies in hiding.

1485 ▶ Accession of **Henry VII** to the throne after landing from exile at Pembroke and beating Richard III at Bosworth.

1536–38 ▶ Henry VIII suppresses monasteries.

1536–43 ▶ **Acts of Union**: legislation forming the union of Wales and England. Equal rights but with a separate legal and administrative system conducted wholly in English.

1546 ▶ First book printed in Welsh: *Yn y Lhyvyr Hwnn*.

1571 ▶ Jesus College, Oxford (the Welsh college) founded.

1588 ▶ Translation of complete Bible into Welsh, chiefly by **William Morgan**.

1639 ▶ First Puritan congregation in Wales convened at Llanfaches, Gwent.

1646 ▶ Harlech and Raglan besieged during the **Civil War**. Harlech, the last Royalist castle, falls in 1647.

1660 ▶ Restoration of the monarchy.

1689 ▶ Toleration Act passed, allowing open, Nonconformist worship.

1743 ▶ Establishment of Welsh Calvinistic Methodist Church.

1759 ▶ Dowlais Ironworks started, followed by Merthyr Tydfil iron industry.

1782 ▶ Beginning of north Wales slate industry with the opening of Pennant's Penrhyn slate quarry at Bethesda.

1789 ▶ First **eisteddfod** for 200 years held at Corwen.

1793–94 ▶ Cardiff to Merthyr canal built.

1801 ▶ First census. Welsh population 587,000.

1839–43 ▶ **Rebecca Riots** close tollbooths on turnpikes.

1841 ▶ Taff Vale Railway built.

1845–50 ▶ Britannia Tubular Bridge built.

1865 ▶ Michael D. Jones founds Welsh colony in Patagonia.

1872 ▶ **University College of Wales** opens in Aberystwyth, followed by Cardiff (1883) and Bangor (1884).

1881 ▶ Passing of Welsh Sunday Closing Act.

1884 ▶ **Reform Act**. Farm labourers and small tenant farmers get the vote for the first time.

1900 ▶ Britain's first Labour MP, Kier Hardie, elected for Merthyr Tydfil.

1907 ▶ Founding of National Museum, Cardiff, and National Library, Aberystwyth.

1914–18 ▶ World War I.

1920 ▶ Disestablishment of Church of England in Wales.

1925 ▶ Plaid Genedlaethol Cymru (Welsh National Party) formed.

1926 ▶ **Miners' strike** and General Strike.

1929–34 ▶ Great Depression.

1936 ▶ Saunders Lewis and colleagues burn building materials on the Llŷn.

1939–45 ▶ World War II.

1951 ▶ Minister for Welsh Affairs appointed.

1955 ▶ Cardiff declared capital of Wales.

1963 ▶ Cymdeithas yr Iaith Gymraeg (Welsh Language Society) formed.

1964 ▶ James Griffith, first cabinet-level Secretary of State for Wales, appointed.

1966 ▶ **Gwynfor Evans**, first Plaid Cymru MP, elected for Carmarthen. Aberfan disaster.

1967 ▶ **Welsh Language Act** passed. Limited recognition of Welsh as a formal, legal language.

1979 ▶ Referendum on Welsh Assembly. Eighty percent of voters come out against a separate parliament.

1982 ▶ Welsh-language TV channel S4C begins broadcasting.

1984–85 ▶ **Miners' strike**.

1992 ▶ Welsh Language Bill gives Welsh equal status with English in public bodies.

1993 ▶ First Welsh film, *Hedd Wyn*, nominated for an Oscar.

1997 ▶ Referendum on Welsh Assembly. Only half the country votes, of whom 50.3 percent vote yes, a majority of just 6000 nationwide.

1999 ▶ First **Welsh Assembly** elections. Assembly begins sitting. Wales hosts the Rugby World Cup.

2006 ▶ The new Welsh Assembly building (the Senedd) opens on St David's Day. Government of Wales Act gains Royal Assent.

2008 ▶ Wales wins its tenth rugby Grand Slam, one hundred years after its inaugural win.

Modern Welsh nationalism

Although Plaid Cymru – the Welsh nationalist political party – was formed in 1925, the political impetus that gave birth to the new movement had been bubbling for decades, if not centuries.

The Welsh identity had always been culturally rich, but was politically expressed only as part of the great Liberal tradition: in the dying years of the nineteenth century, Welsh Liberal MPs organized themselves into a loose caucus roughly modelled on Parnell's Irish parliamentarians and, although the Welsh group was without the clout or number of the Irish MPs, 25 or 30 MPs voting en bloc was serious enough to be noticed. The fiery Welsh patriot **David Lloyd George** (1863–1945; prime minister 1916–22) had embodied many people's nationalist beliefs, although his espousal of greater independence for Wales came unstuck when, ever the expedient politician, he realized the potential difficulty of translating this ideal into hard votes in the industrialized, anglicized south of Wales. During Lloyd George's premiership, the Irish Free State was established, drawing inevitable comparisons with the Home Rule demands being less stridently articulated in Scotland and Wales. But the Liberal Party was in sharp decline, nowhere more markedly than in the industrialized Valleys, which had deserted them in favour of new socialist parties. With the urban slide of Liberalism, Welsh nationalism was gradually honed into the embryonic Plaid Cymru.

Initially, the party acted more as a pressure group, focused on the waning of the Welsh language. As war loomed over Europe in the latter half of the 1930s, Plaid maintained a controversially pacifist stance, winning few new converts. Most sensationally, in September 1936, Saunders Lewis and two other Plaid luminaries, the Rev. Lewis Valentine and D.J. Williams, set fire to the construction hut of a new aerodrome being built on the Llŷn as part of Britain's build-up to the war. They immediately reported themselves to the nearest police station, attracting huge publicity in the process. Interest in the ensuing trial electrified Wales, causing howls of outrage when the government decided to divert it from sympathetic Caernarfon to the Old Bailey in London. Even recalcitrant nationalist Lloyd George was outspokenly critical of the English decision. The three men were duly imprisoned for nine months, becoming Plaid Cymru's first heroes.

Postwar Wales

Despite dwindling support in the rest of Britain, the prewar Liberal tradition was still strong in rural Wales, though by the 1951 election this had become just three parliamentary seats out of 36. The **Labour party** was now the establishment in Wales, winning an average of around sixty percent of votes in elections from 1945 to 1966. Labour's 1945–51 administration had tinkered with a few institutions to give them a deliberately Welsh stance, but the subsequent Conservative government had little time for specifically Welsh demands. Two Welsh Labour MPs, Megan Lloyd George, daughter of the great Liberal premier, and S.O. Davies, spearheaded new parliamentary demands for greater Welsh independence, presenting a 1956 petition to parliament demanding a Welsh assembly which was signed by a quarter of a million people. Massive popular protests against the continued flooding of Welsh valleys and villages to provide water for England shook the establishment. The 1963 formation of the boisterous Cymdeithas yr Iaith Gymraeg – the **Welsh Language Society** – attracted a new youthful breed of cultural and linguistic nationalists to the fold. The ruling Conservatives offered the sop of nominating a part-time Welsh Minister, confirming Cardiff as the capital and making the red dragon the official Welsh flag. Meanwhile, the Labour party formed a Welsh Council where Labour MPs, trade unionists and ordinary party members began to articulate the need for greater independence. In the **general election of 1964**, the party stood on a more nationalistic platform than ever before. As usual, they swept the board in Wales, and finally won throughout the UK as a whole. As promised in their manifesto, the post of **Secretary of State for Wales**, backed by a separate Welsh Office, was created, although with fewer powers than the Scottish equivalent which had existed since just after the war.

Plaid Cymru starts to win

Plaid Cymru scored its first and most dramatic strike into Westminster when its president, Gwynfor Evans, won a by-election in Carmarthen in July 1966. In the heart of socialist south Wales, Plaid ran the Labour government astonishingly close in two by-elections: in Rhondda West (1967) and Caerphilly (1968), and the party saw swings of over 25 percent to cut Labour majorities of over twenty thousand to just a couple of thousand. From humble beginnings, it seemed that Plaid's time had come. Its traditional vote in the north and west was soaring and it appeared that the party had finally overcome its single-issue status around the Welsh language, while its membership ballooned to forty thousand. Welsh nationalism reached new heights at the time of the Prince of Wales' theatrical 1969 investiture at Caernarfon, a gesture resented by many. The cause also gained its first martyrs, when two extremist nationalists blew themselves up at Abergele in Clwyd whilst attempting to lay a bomb on the rail line where Prince Charles was due to travel. In many ways, such acts had a detrimental effect on Plaid's cause, wrongly linking extremism with the more moderate and constitutional methods of the party.

Despite amassing 176,000 votes (11 percent of the poll in Wales) in the **1970 general election**, Plaid failed to take any new seats and even lost their place in Carmarthen. The second 1974 election returned Gwynfor Evans in Carmarthen to join two other Plaid Cymru MPs elected in the February election, but Plaid's earlier success in the industrialized south had evaporated, and they lost their deposits in 26 of the 36 Welsh seats. Once again, they were a party geographically concentrated in the rural outposts of Wales.

The new Labour government now set up the **Wales Development Agency**, supported the new Wales TUC (Trades Union Congress), devolved the huge responsibilities of the Department of Trade and Industry in Wales to the Welsh Office in Cardiff, and even supported a referendum on devolution.

The 1979 referendum and beyond

On St David's Day 1979, the Welsh people made their feelings known, when on a massive four to one majority rejected the devolution proposal, and for many reasons. A large number of the eighty percent of the country who did not speak Welsh feared that a Welsh assembly would be the preserve of a new "Taffia", a *Cymraeg* elite. Both north and south Walians worried about potential domination by the other. People feared greater bureaucracy, particularly in the wake of the 1974 local government reorganization when a two-tier system of county and district councils had been imposed on Wales. A third tier, with few apparent powers, was not a terribly attractive proposition.

The shock waves were great. Weeks later, the Labour government fell and **Margaret Thatcher**'s first Conservative administration was ushered in. Political nationalism seemed to have gone off the boil, and Plaid Cymru were back to just two MPs representing the northwestern constituencies of Meirionydd and Caernarfon. The early 1980s were dominated by swiftly rising unemployment and a collapse in Britain's manufacturing base. Nowhere was this more evident than in south Wales, where mines and foundries closed and the jobless total soared. Welsh nationalism was suffering an identity crisis, typified by Plaid Cymru's controversial 1981 rewriting of its own constitution to fight for an avowedly "Welsh socialist state", causing some of its more conservative members to quit the party. Basing itself as a republican, left-wing party would, it was believed, bring greater fruit in the populated south. The nationalists suffered by implication from the activities of **Meibion Glyndŵr** (Sons of Glyndŵr), a shadowy organization dedicated to firebombing English holiday homes in Wales. Plaid continued to plough a firmly constitutional and peaceful route to national self-determination, but many people assumed that the bombers received covert support amongst the party's ranks.

Although Gwynfor Evans lost his Carmarthen seat in 1979, he was singlehand-edly responsible for the most high-profile activity of Welsh nationalism in the early 1980s. The Conservative party had fought the general election of 1979 on a manifesto that included a commitment to a Welsh-language TV channel. When plans for the new UK Channel 4 were drawn up, this promise had been dropped. The Plaid Cymru president decided to fast until death, if necessary, as a peaceful protest. It did not take long before this action, gaining enormous publicity in the media, forced the Thatcher government to make its first U-turn, and **Sianel Pedwar Cymru** (S4C) was born in 1982. Perhaps the Tories realized the political advantage of bringing Welsh nationalism into the legitimate fold, for the Welsh media industry, long accused of a nationalistic bent, dissipated many angry and impassioned arguments for national self-determination. Many of the most heartfelt radicals ended up in prominent positions within Wales' media.

Like so many other political affiliations and ideals in the 1980s, Welsh nationalism underwent something of a sea change during the decade. Plaid Cymru began to broaden its base as a radical and mature political force with a firmly socialist, internationalist outlook. The party developed serious policies on all aspects of Welsh life, from traditional rallying calls of language and media to sophisticated analyses of economic policy, the Welsh legal framework and the country's role in the European Union and the wider world. But Welsh devolution ceased to be the preserve of Plaid Cymru alone. Both Labour and the Liberal Democrats (inheri-tors of the great Liberal tradition), evolved devolutionary strategies for Wales and Scotland. Even the Conservatives reluctantly followed suit and, in government, continued to devolve more governmental decision-making out to the Welsh Office in Cardiff. This, ironically, strengthened the nationalist hand. Plaid and the other parties pointed out that a huge swath of government existed in Wales, not overseen by any all-Wales authority. The call for a Welsh assembly to oversee this vast array of public expenditure was consistently supported by huge majorities in opinion polls, and formed the basis of the Labour Party's manifesto for Wales throughout the 1990s.

Labour government and a new referendum

The **1997 general election** changed everything. The Conservatives were spectacularly swept from power, failing to keep any seats whatsoever in Wales. Labour – or "New" Labour as the party was styled under Tony Blair – won hugely, denting any further Plaid progress and keeping the nationalists firm in their northern and western strongholds and on little more than one tenth of the vote. However, as always, Plaid were better placed to do well under a Labour government than a Conservative one.

Within six months of Blair's election, referenda took place in Wales and Scotland on the devolution proposals. Scotland voted wholeheartedly for its parliament; in Wales, the proposals barely scraped through. Although this was potentially the first piece of self-government for Wales in 600 years, many nationalists felt that it fell far short of expectations and was not worth supporting. Plaid Cymru's own stance mirrored this ambivalence: initially unenthusiastic and only coming out for the Assembly in the latter stages of the campaign. Wales itself was split in half by the devolution vote. The border areas and Pembrokeshire, true to their historical anglicization, voted no, while Plaid's west coast strongholds and the "Old" Labour bastions of the industrial Valleys were enthusiastic enough – just – to swing the ballot.

The National Assembly for Wales

When it came to voting for the sixty-seat Welsh Assembly, Plaid Cymru achieved spectacular gains, taking Labour strongholds like Rhondda, Islwyn and Llanelli. The Plaid share of the vote was their highest ever, at nearly 30 percent, and it was enough to deny Labour – once the absolute party in Wales – an overall majority.

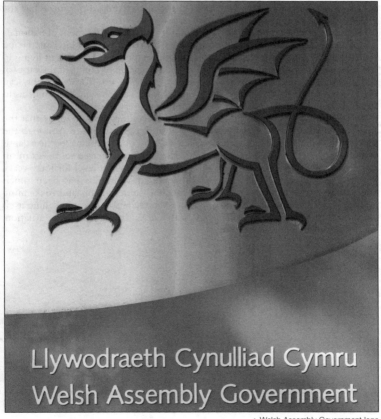

Llywodraeth Cynulliad Cymru
Welsh Assembly Government

▲ Welsh Assembly Government logo

So far, this has proven to be Plaid's high-water mark. The 2003 Assembly elections saw the party lose all of its Valleys seats and only just cling onto the status of largest opposition group. The party regained ground in the 2007 Assembly election but failed to dislodge Labour as the major party.

With Plaid Cymru having to play it as a sober democratic party, much of the more interesting aspects of Welsh nationalism are to be found away from party politics. Regular dust-ups over patronizing English attitudes still periodically ignite the media, while debates rage on about English in-migration and the purchase of second homes in the heartlands of the Welsh language and culture. In a journalistic atmosphere that has at times been decidedly febrile and ill-tempered, the first casualty has been proper debate, with everything reduced to hysterical soundbites. Out of this environment has come the pressure group **Cymuned** ("Community"; ⓦ www.cymuned.org), whose slogan "Dal dy dir!" ("Hold your ground!") is seen daubed all around Wales. Cymuned is slick, modern and thoughtful, and could well prove to be the intellectual driving force for modern Welsh nationalism, especially as Plaid Cymru continues to struggle with its wings clipped for electoral expediency. One of Plaid's main drawbacks has been confusion, and disillusion, over its leadership, particularly in the Assembly under the lacklustre Anglesey AM Ieuan Wyn Jones. There is, however, an impressive new generation emerging in Plaid, who, if given half the chance, should be able to restore some status to the party.

Since the arrival of the Assembly, it's hard for even the most ardent of nationalists to argue that Wales' system of government is the most pressing issue facing the nation. With farming in utter crisis, one of the poorest standards of living in the UK, and job opportunities limited to the low-wage old industrial sectors of the south, there are plenty of meatier matters to chew on. If the Assembly can be seen to make a difference to these issues, its reputation will soar, and this in itself is surely the best argument for according it greater power.

However, in the early years of the twenty-first century, it's safe to say that the majority of Welsh people are fairly happy with things as they are. Although the percentages of Welsh speakers have fallen slightly in the language's heartlands according to the 2001 census results, huge rises in the anglicized southeast mean that the number of Welsh speakers in Wales is at its highest level for forty years, and rising. Language aside, the general sense of Welshness has been much augmented in recent years, as much by sporting achievements and rock music as by any politician. Wales is more and more happily, and very easily, calling itself a nation. The question that still hangs in the air is simply this: to be a nation, does Wales really need to be a state?

Natural history of Wales

A comprehensive account of Wales' landscapes, land use, flora and fauna would take several books to cover. What follows is a general overview of the effects of geology, human activity and climate on the country's flora, fauna and land management.

Wales is covered with a wide array of sites deemed to be of national or international importance, all seemingly with different designations. The three **national parks** – Snowdonia, the Brecon Beacons and the Pembrokeshire Coast – comprise almost twenty percent of the country, with another couple of percent incorporated into the five **Areas of Outstanding Natural Beauty** (AONB): the Anglesey coast, the Llŷn coast, the Clwydian Range, the Gower peninsula and the Wye Valley. Smaller areas (from a few acres to large chunks of the Cambrian Mountains) with specific habitats such as lowland bogs or ancient woodlands are managed as **National Nature Reserves** (NNRs). Most are widely promoted, usually posted with information boards and threaded with easy, well-signed walking trails. All NNRs contain **Sites of Special Scientific Interest** (SSSIs; aka triple-SIs), a category including around another 700 locations in Wales singled out for special protection. Most are on private land with no right of access.

It must be remembered that nowhere in Wales is untouched, almost every patch of "wilderness" being partially the product of human intervention, thoroughly mapped, mined and farmed. Nor is anywhere free from pollution: the conurbations of England are too close, power stations and factories dot the countryside and some of the seas are in a poor state. That said, several clean-air-loving lichen species – found in few other places in Britain – abound in Wales.

Geology

Wales is packed with mountains, and the geological history of several areas deserve brief coverage. Between 600 and 400 million years ago, **Snowdonia** was twice submerged for long periods in some primordial ocean where molten rock from undersea volcanoes cooled to form igneous intrusions in the sedimentary ocean-floor layers. Snowdon, Cadair Idris and the Aran and

The rocks of Wales

Geologists puzzled over the forces that shaped the Welsh landscape for centuries before early nineteenth-century geologist **Adam Sedgwick** and his collaborator (and later rival) **Roderick Murchison** began to unravel their secrets. They explained the source of the shattered, contorted and eroded rocks that form the ancient peaks of Snowdonia and gave the rock types names associated with the land where their discoveries took place.

Silurian (400–440 million years ago) – named after the ancient south Welsh tribe, the Silures.

Ordovician (440–500 million years ago) – names after the Celtic Ordovices who occupied mid- and north Wales.

Cambrian (500–600 million years ago) – given the Roman name for Wales.

Anglesey, the Llŷn and Pembrokeshire all have older **pre-Cambrian** rocks, while those around St Davids are some of the most ancient in the world.

Arenig mountains are the product of these volcanoes, with fossils close to the summit of Snowdon, supporting the theory of its formation on the sea floor. After Silurian rocks had been laid down, immense lateral pressures forced the layers into concertina-like parallel folds with the sedimentary particles being rearranged at right angles to the pressure, giving today's vertically splitting sheets of **slate**, the classic metamorphosed product of these forces. It is known that the folded strata that rose above the sea bore no resemblance to today's mountains, the cliff face of Lliwedd on Snowdon showing that the summit was at the bottom of one of these great folds between two much higher mountains. In the very recent geological past from 80,000–10,000 years ago, these mountains were worked on by the latest series of **Ice Ages**, with glaciers scouring out hemispherical cirques divided by angular ridges, then scraping down the valleys, gouging them into U-shapes, with waterfalls plunging down their sides.

Snowdonia is linked by the long chain of the **Cambrian Mountains** to the dramatic north-facing scarp slope of the **Brecon Beacons**, south Wales' distinctive east–west range at the head of the south Wales coal field. Erosion of the ancient rocks which once covered what is now northern Britain washed down great river systems, depositing beds of old red sandstone from 350–400 million years ago. These **Devonian** rocks lay in a shallow sea where the molluscs and corals decayed to form limestone, which in turn was overlaid by more sediment forming millstone grit. Subsequent layers of shale and sandstone were interleaved with decayed vegetable matter, forming a band known as **coal measures**, from which the mines once extracted their wealth. The whole lot has since been tilted up in the north, giving a north to south sequence which runs over a steep sandstone ridge (the Brecon Beacons), then down a gentle sandstone dip-slope arriving at the pearl-grey limestone band where any rivers tend to dive underground into **swallow holes**. They reappear as you reach the gritstone, often tumbling over waterfalls into the coal valleys.

Land settlement and usage

After the last ice sheet drew back from Wales, the few plant species which had survived on the ice-free peaks were in a strong position to colonize, producing an open grassland community more than 10,000 years ago. Over several thousand years, forests of birch, juniper and hazel became mixed deciduous woodland with oak, elm and some pine, and in wetter areas damp-loving alder and birch. The Neolithic tribes began to settle on the upland areas, using their flint axes to clear the mountain slopes of their forests. The discovery of bronze and later iron hastened the process, especially since wood charcoal was required for smelting iron ore, and so began the spiralling devastation of Wales' native woodlands. As the domestication of sheep and goats put paid to any natural regeneration of saplings, more land became available for arable farming. Thin, acidic mountain soils and a damp climate made **oats** – fodder for cattle and horses – about the only viable cereal crop, except in Anglesey which, by the time the Romans arrived in the first century AD, was already recognized as Wales' most important wheat-growing land. Cattle rearing was increasingly important on the lusher pastures, and even as late as the twelfth century, Giraldus Cambrensis tells us that "the whole population lives almost entirely on oats and the produce of their herds, milk, cheese and butter".

Until the sixteenth century, Cistercian monasteries kept extensive lands, cleared woods and developed sheep and cattle farms which subsequently became part of the great estates which still take up large tracts of Wales.

By contrast, the less privileged were still smallholders living simple lives. In the 1770s the travel writer Thomas Pennant noted in his *Tours in Wales* that the ordinary people's houses on the Llŷn were "very mean, made with clay, thatched and destitute of chimneys". The poor state of housing had much to do with the practice of Tŷunnos.

In the eighteenth century, **droving** reached its peak. Welsh black cattle, fattened on Anglesey or the Cambrian coast, were driven to market in England, avoiding the valley-floor toll roads by taking highland routes that can still be traced. Nights were spent with the cattle corralled in a halfpenny field (so called because this was the nightly rate per animal) next to a lonely homestead heralded by three Scots pines, which operated as an inn. It was a tough journey for men and cattle, but easier than for geese, whose webbed feet were toughened for the long walk with tar and sand.

At home, women ground the wheat, aided by mills driven by the same fast-flowing streams that later provided power for textile mills, especially around Ruthin, Denbigh, Newtown, Llandeilo and along the Teifi Valley. The Cistercians had laid the foundations of the **textile industry** for both wool and flannel, but it had generally remained in the cottages, with nearly every smallholding keeping a spinning wheel next to their harp.

The next major shift in land use came with a wave of **enclosure acts** from 1760 to 1820, which effectively removed smallholders from upland common pasture and granted the land to holders of already large estates. The people were deprived of their livelihood, and access to open country was denied

The mountain building processes discussed above have left a broad spectrum of minerals under Wales. **Copper** had been mined since the Bronze Age and the Romans dabbled in **gold** extraction, but mining became big business in the latter half of the eighteenth century with the extraction of **slate** (see box, p.385) in North Wales and **coal** (see box, p.97) in the south.

Flora

Wales supports 1100 of Britain's 1600 native plants, with ferns and other moisture-loving species particularly well represented.

Until five thousand years ago, birch, juniper, hazel, oak and elm covered the mountainsides, but devastating forest clearances and a wetter climate have left only a few pockets of native woodland in the valleys, their regeneration threatened by sheep grazing on fresh seedlings. **Pengelli Forest** in Pembrokeshire represents one of Wales' largest blocks of ancient woodland, comprising **midland hawthorn** and **sessile oak**, the dominant tree in ancient Welsh forests. Parts of the Severn and lower Wye valleys are well wooded, as is the Teifi Valley, where oak, ash and sycamore predominate. You can still occasionally see evidence of coppicing – an important and ancient practice common a century ago – where trees are cut close to the base to produce numerous shoots harvested later as small-diameter timbers. Under the canopy, **bluebells** and **wood sorrel** are common, and in the autumn look out for the dozens of species of **mushroom**, especially the delicious but elusive **chantrelle**, found mainly under beech trees.

A far greater area of Wales is smothered in gloomy forests of planted **conifers** (predominantly sitka spruce) which are too shaded and acidic for wildflowers and are forbidding to most birds.

Perhaps the most celebrated of all Wales' plants are the **arctic alpines** that cling to small pockets of soil amongst the high crags and gullies of Snowdonia and the Brecon Beacons (their southernmost limit in Britain) away from grazing sheep and goats. Their range hasn't changed since they were discovered by seventeenth-century botanists such as Thomas Johnson and Welshman Edward Lhuyd, who found *Lloydia serotina*, a glacial relic more popularly known as the **Snowdon Lily**, actually a spiderwort that looks not unlike a small off-white tulip. In Britain, it is found only around Snowdon and then only rarely seen between late May and early June, when it blooms.

Cwm Idwal in the Ogwen Valley is a great place to spot some of the more common species, in particular the handsome **purple saxifrage**, whose tightly clustered flowers often push through the late winter snows, later followed by the starry and mossy saxifrages and spongy pink pads of **moss campion**. The star-shaped yellow flowers of **tormentil** are typical of high grassy slopes, and you may also find **mountain avens**, distinguished by its glossy oak-like leaves, and, when it blooms in June, by its eight white petals. From June to October, purple heads of **wild thyme** cover the ground, providing food for a small beetle unique to Snowdonia.

Poor acid soils on the igneous uplands foster the growth of lime-shy bracken, bilberry and purple **heather** – bell, ling, cross-leaved and Scottish are all found – which combine with decayed **sphagnum moss** in wetter areas to form peat bogs. These support the **bog asphodel**, which produces its brilliant yellow spikes in late summer, often in company with the **spotted orchid** and less frequently the tiny **bog orchid**. Insectivorous plants such as **butterwort** and **sundew** both gain nutrients that their poor surroundings cannot provide by digesting insects trapped on the sticky hairs of their leaves.

At sea level, the rivers spawn estuarine "meadows", which in summer are carpeted with bright violet **sea lavender**, followed by a mauve wash of **sea aster** after August. An unusual coastal feature is the dam-formed string of **Bosherston Lakes**, south of Pembroke, where the fresh water supports rafts of **white-water lilies**. Further west, the Pembrokeshire coast is a blaze of colour in early summer, with white-flowered **scurvy grass** and **sea campion**, yellow **kidney vetch** and **celandine**, and blue **spring squill**. **Water crowfoot** is found in fresh water near the coastal footpath, where you can also find the hemispherical lilac heads of **devil's bit scabious**. **Bluebells** and **red campion** cloak Pembrokeshire's islands, while the majority of species mentioned can be found in abundance in Newborough on Anglesey. Here, some of Wales' finest sand dunes are bound by **marram grass**, interspersed with **sea holly**, **sea bindweed** and the odd **marsh helleborine**.

Birds

With its long coastline, Wales, as you might expect, abounds in **sea birds**, and the profusion of islands and its position on the main north–south migratory route make several sites particularly noteworthy.

The Royal Society for the Protection of Birds (ⓦwww.rspb.org.uk), operates twelve sites throughout Wales, half of them on the coast. The islands off the Pembrokeshire coast are incomparable for sea-bird colonies, the granite pinnacle of **Grassholm** (see p.195), eight miles offshore, hosting the world's third-largest gannet colony with 32,000 pairs. Nearby, **Skokholm** and **Skomer** between them support 6000 pairs of **storm petrels** and an internationally significant population of 130,000 pairs of the mainly nocturnal **Manx shearwater**, which spend their winter off the coast of South America. Burrows vacated by rabbits on the islands also provide nests for puffins, while **razorbills, guillemots** and **kittiwakes** nest on the cliffs. Since the eradication of the rats that previously deterred burrow-nesting birds, Manx shearwaters are also now colonizing **Ramsey Island**, a few miles north. In the north, make for **Bardsey Island** off the Llŷn coast, and the wonderful **South Stack Cliffs** on Anglesey which, especially from May to July, are alive with breeding guillemots, razorbills and puffins.

The mud flats and saltings of Wales' estuaries provide rich pickings for wintering waders. The **Dee estuary**, on the northern border with England, plays host to Europe's largest concentration of **pintail** as well as **oystercatchers, knot, dunlin, redshank** and many others. Numerous terns replace them in the summer months.

Central Wales is celebrated for the recovery of the red kite (see box beow), while the high country supports large populations of **kestrels**, usually seen hovering motionless before plummeting onto an unsuspecting mouse or vole, and golden-brown **buzzards** gently wheeling on the thermals on the lookout for prey which can be as big as a rabbit. Buzzards and peregrine falcons are as happy picking at carrion, but have to compete with sinister black **ravens**, that inhabit the highest ridges and display their crazy acrobatics, often banding together to mob the bigger birds.

Acidic heather uplands between one and two thousand feet provide habitats for **grouse**, whose laboured flight is in complete contrast to the darting zigzag of its neighbour, the **snipe**. On softer grassland, expect to find the **ring ouzel**, a blackbird with a white cravat, and the **golden plover**, a bird still common, but being threatened, like many others, by the spread of conifer forests.

After the gloomy pines, it is a delight to wander in relict stands of the ancient oak woodlands, and along the streams where the **dipper** and **kingfishers**

Red kite recovery

Like many other raptors, fork-tailed **red kites** were traditionally persecuted by gamekeepers and suffered from the use of pesticides, which caused thinning of egg-shells. Before the banning of DDT in the 1960s Welsh red kite numbers were down to a handful of breeding pairs, mostly in the Elan Valley. But with careful management numbers have been on the increase for years and there are now around 250 pairs. Their once narrow range has expanded as far south as Pembrokeshire, and perhaps one day the heights of Snowdonia will again resound to the cry of the eagle which gives the mountains their Welsh name, Eryri.

flourish. On sheltered water you might also find shelduck, Canada geese and three species of swan.

Mammals

During the last interglacial period, Wales was warm enough to support hippos and lions, but humans, pressed for space by the expanding ice sheets, killed them off, leaving bears and boars which in turn were dispatched by human persecution. Some of the last beaver lodges in Britain dammed the Teifi in the twelfth century, while half a millennium later, wolves disappeared from the land. What remains is a restricted range of wild mammals topped up with semi-wild and feral beasts: shy herds of **ponies** on the Carneddau in Snowdonia and on the Brecon Beacons are rounded up annually, and the **goats** in Snowdonia and on the Great Orme at Llandudno are descendants of domesticated escapees. Generally welcomed by farmers, they forage on the precipitous ledges, thereby discouraging sheep from grazing ventures beyond their capabilities. About the only other large land mammals are the soft-fleeced **Soay sheep** at Newborough Warren on Anglesey.

Elusive, stoat-like **pine martens** thrive in sitka spruce forests where their diet of squirrels is readily available. Both pine martens and the more common **polecats** are found in wild corners throughout Wales. **Foxes** are widespread, along with the **brown hares**, **stoats** and **weasels**, though the **badger** is rarer and still the subject of persecution through the cruel sport of badger baiting. **Rabbits** seem to be everywhere, and the North American **grey squirrel** has all but dislodged the native red squirrel from its habitat, though it still hangs on around Lake Vyrnwy and at Newborough on Anglesey.

Otters almost became extinct in Wales some years back, but a concerted effort on the part of the Otter Haven Project has seen their numbers climbing in the Teifi and some of the rivers in Montgomeryshire, though they are seldom seen.

Fish, reptiles and insects

Wales' clean, fast-flowing rivers make ideal conditions for the **brown trout**, a fish managed for sport throughout the country. In Wales, the damming of rivers has seldom cut off spawning grounds, but the fishable limit of the Conwy in particular has been extended by the introduction of a fish ladder around the Conwy Falls. **Salmon** are less common, found mainly in the Usk and the Wye, the latter being the only river where it is important as game fish. Along with **roach**, **perch** and other coarse fish, the depths of Bala Lake (Llyn Tegid) claim the unique silver-white **gwyniad**, an Ice Age relic not dissimilar to a small herring, said never to take a lure. Llyn Padarn in Llanberis also notches up a rarity with the freshwater **char**. Conditions for successful fish farming do not exist in Wales, but commercially viable beds of **cockles** still exist on the north coast of the Gower and families still own rights to musselling the sands of the Conwy estuary.

With Welsh red dragons dying out along with King Arthur, much smaller lizards and two species of snake are all that remain of Wales' reptiles. The poisonous, triangular-headed **adder** is sometimes spotted sunning itself on dry south-facing rocks, but, except in early spring when it is roused from hibernation, it frequently slithers away unnoticed. The harmless **grass snake** prefers a wetter environment and is equally shy. Easily mistaken for a snake, the **slowworm** is actually a legless lizard and is common throughout Wales, as are **toads** and **frogs** – though the rare **natterjack toad** is only found in a few locations.

As for **butterflies**, southern British species – the common blue and red admiral – are abundant in sheltered spots, but aim for the woodland reserves, found dotted all over the country, to find the **dark green fritillary** and its pearl-bordered and silver-washed kin. South Wales is particularly good for insect life, with Pengelli Forest home to the rare **white-letter hairstreak** as well as one of Britain's rarest dragonflies, the bright blue **southern damselfly**, while the Gower peninsula harbours populations of **marbled white butterfly** and the **great green bush cricket**, uncommon anywhere else in Wales. Lastly, Snowdonia has the unique and aptly named **rainbow leaf beetle**.

Ecology and the future

With smokestack industries now largely absent from Wales, and the Valleys mostly devoid of working coal mines, nature is struggling to claw its way back. A verdure inconceivable forty years ago now cloaks the hillsides, and already the industrial remains are being cherished as cultural heritage; as much a valid part of the "natural" landscape as the mountain backdrops. If you need convincing, climb up to the disused slate workings behind Blaenau Ffestiniog or walk the old ironworks tramways around Blaenafon.

In other areas, much remains to be done to restore the ecological balance. The increasing commercialization of farming has led not just to the damaging application of pesticides and excessive use of nitrogen-rich fertilizers, but to the wholesale removal of **hedgerows** and **dry-stone walls**, ideal habitats for numerous species of flora and fauna. Conservation groups promote the skills needed to lay hedges and build dry-stone walls, but for every success, another chunk of farmland is paved over with a new bypass, or a meadow is turned over to **conifers**.

The tax incentives which formerly encouraged vast expanses of spruce no longer apply, but economics still favour clear-felling a single species every thirty years or so. The largest forest owner, the Forestry Commission, is keen to shake off its monoculture image and is bordering its forests with a mix of broad-leaved trees and conifers of different ages. As an extended public relations exercise they also welcome mountain bikers in some forests.

Far from being areas where nature is allowed to take its course, the **national parks** can be their own worst enemies, attracting thousands of people a day. Some attempt is being made to control the effects of tourism through path management and the limited promotion of public transport, but this is more than outweighed by the increasingly aggressive promotion of these regions.

Paradoxically, and for all the wrong reasons, **military zones** – Mynydd Eppynt and most of the Castlemartin peninsula, for example – have become wildlife havens away from the worst effects of human intervention.

Windfarms (see box, p.420) have become a contentious issue in recent years. Initial enthusiasm for this clean energy has waned as local people complain about the constant drone of the generators, and conservationists battle it out over the relative merits of a nuclear power station that will take 130 years to decommission (as well as several millennia for the fissile material to become safe) compared to several forests of elegant windmills on top of hills. Friends of the Earth: Cymru (@www.foe.org.uk/cymru) stand firmly in favour of wind power, but have come up against the Campaign for the Protection of Rural Wales (@www.cprw.org.uk), one of Wales' main independent environmental groups, which favours promotion of more efficient power usage.

Environmental groups are also keeping a weather eye on offshore **oil** and **gas** exploration, currently much under way off the Welsh coast, particularly in Cardigan Bay. Meanwhile in south Wales, there has been considerable resistance to developments in Milford Haven where huge liquefied natural gas-carrying ships from Qatar will soon be offloading their cargo and feeding it into Britain's gas network.

One success in recent years has been the decision not to press ahead with the **Usk Barrage**, which was planned to create a freshwater lake on the outskirts of Newport by damming the estuary, forcing otters and other protected species to abandon the river. Things aren't as rosy on the shores of the Severn estuary nearby, where the construction of the second Severn crossing has engendered a new stretch of motorway across the environmentally rich Caldicot Levels, destroying several SSSIs.

The Snowdonia National Park Authority has recognized that sustainable management of farmland is not only ecologically beneficial, but that the landscape, with its character largely defined by past farming practices, is worth maintaining in its own right. In response it has set up the **Tir Cymen** (which loosely translates as "well-crafted landscape") scheme, a ten-year government initiative which pays participating farmers to maintain stone walls, slate fences, earth banks, traditional stone buildings and archeological features. Trial schemes are in place in the southern Snowdonian region of Meirionydd, Dinefwr in Carmarthenshire, and around Swansea and the Gower peninsula.

Music in Wales

D ylan Thomas's observation that "We are a musical nation" is as relevant as ever. Despite the near-obliteration of the mining industry, male voice choirs remain a feature of Welsh life, with many choirs opening their practice sessions to the public. But Welsh music extends far beyond the dwindling chapels, into the country's village halls, clubs, festival sites and pubs. In quieter venues, harp players repay their musical debt to ancestors who accompanied the ancient bards (traditional poets and storytellers), while modern folk music draws directly from the broader Celtic musical tradition. Welsh-language rock musicians have traded commercial success for unabashed nationalism, spanning styles from punk to hip-hop. Some bands sing in both English and Welsh, and there is a fast-growing scene in English-language Welsh rock, building on the success of outfits like the Manic Street Preachers. These days, Wales continues to punch above its weight, churning out a huge amount of good music for a country its size.

Folk

In Welsh, the word "folk" translates as *gwerin*, which has a much wider meaning than its English counterpart, taking in popular culture as well as folklore. At a Welsh *gŵyl werin* (folk festival), you're as likely to encounter the local rock band as the local dance team – with the entire community turning out, too.

Welsh folk song has always remained close to the heart of popular culture, with contemporary folk songwriting conveying political messages and social protest, but traditional Welsh music and dance have fought back from near-extinction following centuries of political and religious suppression. Unlike their Celtic cousins in Ireland, Scotland and Brittany, many folk musicians in Wales have learnt their tunes from books and manuscripts rather than from older generations of players.

Where to get information

Cymdeithas Ddawns Werin Cymru (Welsh Folk Dance Society) is a useful source of events information, with an annual magazine and a twice-yearly newsletter, both bilingual. There's lots of information, details of events and further contacts on its comprehensive website ⓦ www.welshfolkdance.org.uk.

Taplas, the English-language bimonthly magazine of the folk scene in Wales, is a great source for current events, with back editions archived on its website, ⓦ www .taplas.co.uk.

The **St Fagans National History Museum**, near Cardiff (see p.130), is a vibrant museum and a vital centre for research and collecting work.

Scan **posters** for the word *twmpath* – the equivalent of a barn dance or ceilidh, and used when Welsh dances are the theme of the night. Calling (dance instructions) could be in Welsh or English, depending on where you are in the country. A *Noson Lawen*, literally "a happy night", usually offers a harpist, perhaps some dancers and a repertoire of Welsh standards.

For eisteddfodau, see *Festivals* colour section.

Cwlwm Celtaidd Porthcawl, near Bridgend ⓦ www.cwlwmceltaidd.com. Fantastic, increasingly high-profile long weekend at Trecco Bay caravan park of Celtic music and partying. Early March.

Tredegar House Festival Newport, Gwent ⓦ www.tredegarhousefolk.ik.com. A laid-back and enjoyable weekend at the eighteenth-century country house, good for session players and dancers. Mid-May.

Fishguard Folk Festival Pembrokeshire ⓦ www.pembrokeshire-folk-music.co.uk. Up-and-coming event with a good spread of international performers. Late May.

Gower Folk Festival Parkmill, Gower Peninsula ⓦ www.halfpennyfolkclub.com. Varied line-up in beautiful surroundings. Mid-June.

Gŵyl Ifan Cardiff ⓦ www.gwylifan.org. Wales' biggest and most spectacular dance festival, with hundreds of dancers giving displays in Cardiff city centre, the Bay, the Castle and St Fagans National History Museum. Late June.

Small Nations Festival Near Llandovery, Carmarthenshire ⓦ www.smallnations.co.uk. Lovely camping event on a farm, with global beats from Africa to home. Early July.

Sesiwn Fawr ("Big Session") Dolgellau ⓦ www.sesiwnfawr.co.uk. Events indoors and in the streets. Mid-July.

Swansea Shanty Festival Swansea ⓦ www.shanty.co.uk. Growing every year, the sea songs and music take place on and around a tall ship in the redeveloped marina. July.

Pontardawe International Festival Pontardawe ⓦ www.pontardawefestival.com. One of Britain's flagship folk events, with an ambitious line-up of international performers heading for the Swansea Valleys town each year. Mid-August.

The Greenman Festival Near Crickhowell ⓦ www.thegreenmanfestival.co.uk. Fantastic folk/music festival in the Brecon Beacons. Mid-August.

Tenby Folk Festival Tenby ⓦ http://gwylenaidyrenfys.co.uk/tenbyindex.html. Fast becoming a fixture of the Welsh folk festival scene. Late August.

A number of smaller dance festivals also take place around Wales, including the **Cadi Ha** in Holywell in early May and **Gŵyl Werin** in Caernarfon on the first weekend of October. See ⓦ www.welshfolkdance.org) for up-to-date details.

History

The bardic and **eisteddfod** traditions have played a key role in Welsh culture. Often the **bard**, who held an elevated position in Welsh society, was the non-performing composer, employing a harpist and a *datgeiniad*, whose role was to declaim the bard's words. The first eisteddfod appears to have been held in Cardigan in 1176, with contests between bards and poets and between harpers, *crwth*-players (see p.498) and pipers. Henry Vlll's **Act of Union** in 1536 was designed to anglicize the country by stamping out Welsh culture and language, and the eisteddfod tradition degenerated over the next two centuries.

The rise of **Nonconformist religion** in the eighteenth and nineteenth centuries, with its abhorrence of music, merry-making and dancing, almost sounded the death knell for Welsh traditions already battered by Henry VIII's assault. **Edward Jones**, *Bardd y Brenin* (Bard to the King), observed sorrowfully in the 1780s that Wales, which used to be one of the happiest of countries, "has now become one of the dullest". Folk music only gained some sort of respectability when London-based Welsh people, swept along in a romantic enthusiasm for all things Celtic, revived it at the end of the eighteenth century.

The **National Eisteddfod Society** was formed in the 1860s, and today, three major week-long events are held every year: the International Eisteddfod at Llangollen (@www.international-eisteddfod.co.uk) in July; the Royal National

Venues

In the Dyfed and Gwynedd heartland of the Welsh language, folk music can be heard in many of the same venues that stage rock events. The language is considered more important than musical categories, and the folk club concept is alien to Welsh-speakers, who never saw the need to segregate music that was a natural part of their cultural life. Folk clubs are found in the anglicized areas and only a few of them feature Welsh music. In the south, check for folk in the general programme at the **Welsh cultural clubs** in the area: Clwb Ifor Bach in Womanby Street, Cardiff (☎029/2023 2199); Clwb y Bont in Taff Street, Pontypridd (☎01443/491424) and Clwb Brynmenyn near Bridgend (☎01656/725323).

There are scores of weekly, fortnightly and monthly **sessions, gigs and jams** around Wales: for the latest round-up, check out @www.folkwales.org.uk/Regulars.html or @www.welshgigs.com. Below are a few of the best venues. All sessions are weekly on the specified day, unless otherwise stated.

South & West Wales
Barry Folk Club *Castle Hotel*, Jewel St, Barry. Informal session; all are welcome to perform. Wednesday.

Royal Oak Fishguard. Informal session; all welcome. Tues.

Halfpenny Folk Club *The Greyhound*, Llanrhidian, Gower ☎01792/850803. Designer-clad clientele rub shoulders with the chunky jumper brigade. Sun.

Llantrisant Folk Club *The Windsor Hotel*, Pontyclun (Club Secretary ☎01443/226892). International guest list mixed with local sessions centred on Welsh tunes. Wed.

Newport Folk Club *Lyceum Tavern*, Malpas Rd, Newport, Gwent. Weekly jams and monthly guests. Thursday.

Pontardawe Acoustic Club *Pontardawe Inn* (*Y Gwachel*), 123 Herbert St, Pontardawe (details ☎01792/865171). Mainstay of the Welsh folk scene, good for anything from very traditional stuff to modern folk-rock. Wed, plus live music Fri and Sat.

Y Mochyn Du Sophia Gardens, Cardiff. Great Welsh folk jam nights. Mon.

Mid-Wales
Black Lion Pontrhydfendigaid, Ceredigion. Monthly all-comers sessions alternated with Celtic and Welsh bands. Sat.

Gwerin Aber *Y Cŵps* (*Coopers Arms*), Llanbadarn Rd, Aberystwyth. Folk session, all instrumentalists welcome. Tues.

Live at the Talbot *Talbot Hotel*, Tregaron. Regarded as the best roots venue in Wales, with progammes posted online at @www.cambriaarts.org.uk.

Royal Head Shortbridge St, Llanidloes. Jam session; all welcome. Tues.

North Wales
See also @www.tony-franks.co.uk/northwalesfolk.htm.

Clwb Gwerin Conwy Folk Club The Malt Loaf, Rosehill St, Conwy. Session open to all. Mon.

Llangollen Folk Club *Sun Inn*, Regent St, Llangollen. Cheerful session. Wed.

Theatr Clwyd Cymru Mold, Flintshire ☎01352/755114. Regular live music.

The Nelson Beach Rd, Bangor. Irish sessions every Fri, plus monthly Welsh sessions (second Mon).

Y Mount Dinas Llanwnda, Gwynedd. Live sessions (usually first Mon each month).

Eisteddfod (⊕www.eisteddfod.org.uk) in the first week of August; and the Urdd Eisteddfod (⊕www.urdd.org), Europe's largest youth festival, at the end of May. The National and the Urdd alternate between north and south Wales.

The competitions' rules have meant that eisteddfodau have helped formalize Welsh culture. Such parameter-defining is naturally alien to the free evolution of traditional song and music, but, conversely, eisteddfodau have played a major role in keeping traditional music, song and dance at the heart of national expression.

The harp

Historically the most important instrument in the folk repertoire, the **harp** has been played in Wales since at least the eleventh century, although no instruments survive from the period before the 1700s, and little is really known about the intervening years. The only surviving music is the famous manuscript of **Robert ap Huw**, written about 1614 in a strange tablature that has intrigued music scholars: five scales were used, but no one has yet defined satisfactorily how they should sound. In recent years craftsmen have re-created the *cruth* (a stringed instrument which may have been either plucked or bowed), the *pibgorn* (a reed instrument with a cow's horn for a bell) and the *pibacwd* (a primitive Welsh bagpipe).

The simple early harps were ousted in the seventeenth century by the arrival of the **triple harp**, with its complicated string arrangement (two parallel rows sounding the same note, with a row of accidentals between them), giving it a unique, rich sound. The nineteenth-century swing towards classical concert music saw the invasion of the large **chromatic pedal harps** that still dominate today, but the triple, always regarded as the traditional Welsh harp, was kept alive by gypsy musicians who preferred to play something portable. A notable, and unique, Welsh harp performance that's well worth catching is the **Cerdd Dant**, where the harpist leads with one tune, accompanying soloists and groups take a counter-tune, and they all end up together on the final note.

Folk musicians

The country's foremost triple harpist, **Robin Huw Bowen**, has revived interest in the instrument with appearances throughout Europe and North America, and has done tremendous work making unpublished manuscripts of Welsh dance music widely available through his own publishing company. The lineage of North Wales triple harpist **Llio Rhydderch** stretches back centuries. For a more contemporary take on the instrument, poet/musician **Twm Morys** blends modern Welsh and Breton influences. One of Wales' most well-known harpists is **Elinor Bennett** (coincidentally the wife of Plaid Cymru's former leader Dafydd Wigley), who has accompanied some of Wales' biggest rock acts.

The father of Welsh folk, politician/songwriter **Dafydd Iwan**, remains as hugely popular and prolific as ever with charismatic performances and powerful albums

Record companies

Cob Records ☎01766/512170, ⊕www.cobrecords.com. Extensive mail-order business.
Cwmni Fflach ☎01239/614691, ⊕www.fflach.co.uk. Great label, with albums by KilBride and Llio Rhydderch among its folk releases. Its offshoot, Rasp, publishes indie, rock and dance music. See also p.90.
Sain ☎01286/831111, ⊕www.sainwales.com. The major Welsh recording company boasts a good number of folk albums and artists in its catalogue.

such as 2007's *Man Gwyn* (featuring songs about the early Welsh emigration to Patagonia and North America). Songwriter **Meic Stevens** (often referred to as the "Welsh Bob Dylan") straddles folk and acoustic rock: if you get the chance to see him live, grab it. Singer/harpist **Sian James**, from mid-Wales, has found fame for her spine-tingling voice and exquisite tunes. Other female pacesetters include the soulful **Julie Murphy**, born in Essex but now a fluent Welsh speaker, and Cardiff-born veteran singer **Heather Jones**.

The Hennessys, led by broadcaster, TV personality and songwriter Frank Hennessy, still have a huge and well-deserved middle-of-the-road following in the Cardiff area, twenty-odd years after joining the procession of Irish-influenced trios on the folk circuit. **Huw and Tony Williams**, from Brynmawr, are also popular names on the folk club circuit. Huw is perhaps best known in Wales for his eisteddfod-winning clog dancing.

One to watch is the young, high-energy **Mabon**, a seven-piece line-up of folk talent led by Celtic accordionist Jamie Smith. Likewise, **Elin and the Tribalites**, featuring a mix of Welsh and Irish traditions with a contemporary edge, are playing high-profile festivals and garnering attention nationwide.

Folk dance

Revived over the past half-century, **traditional dance** plays a big part in the folk culture of Wales. Dances written in recent years, often for eisteddfod competitions, have been quickly absorbed into the repertoire. **Cwmni Dawns Werin Caerdydd** (ⓦwww.cwmnidawns.com), Cardiff's official dance team, have taken their spectacular displays and musicians abroad to Texas, Japan and beyond. **Dawnswyr Nantgarw**, from the Taff Vale village that was the source of the country's romantic and raunchy fair dances, have turned Welsh dance into a theatrical art form: concise, perfectly drilled and very showy. Anglesey-based **Ffidl Ffadl** boast an excellent musician in well-known fiddler **Huw Roberts**. Also look out for **Dawnswyr Brynmawr**, and, in North Wales, **Dawnswyr Delyn**.

Pop music in Wales

The historic lack of international pop artists to emerge from Wales – long blamed on the music-industry dominance of London-based labels and media – has changed utterly in the last couple of decades, at least for English-language groups. It started with the **Manic Street Preachers** in the early 1990s, who spawned an unprecedented interest in contemporary Welsh rock. London A&R reps descended on Cardiff and Newport in search of the next big thing, accelerating the careers of bands like the **Super Furry Animals**, **Catatonia** and the **Stereophonics**. Their widespread success has meant bands from Wales no longer feel hampered by their provenance, and there is a wealth of fine new talent coming through.

These days there's also an increasingly thriving scene in Welsh-language rock, although as yet this remains largely outside the mainstream.

English-language Welsh pop

The biggest, most enduring name in English-language Welsh pop is 1960s sex symbol **Tom Jones**, still pulling crowds around the world. Similarly, Cardiff-born singer **Shirley Bassey** has carved out a hugely successful career since the mid-1950s, particularly with the immortal theme song to the 1964 James Bond

A great way to get the jump on the hottest new acts is to check posters for the following promoters who have carved a reputation for breaking new talent and mounting gigs, exhibitions, parties and events.

Canton Space Project Cardiff-based musician/DJ Owen Griffiths and friends promote a stellar line-up of dance, electronica, folk and acoustic acts.

Critical Mass Electronic/dance promoters.

The Family Indie rock specialist.

Forecast Promote an eclectic range of folk, experimental, rock and electronica acts.

Future Sounds More good indie rock.

Loose Another top indie rock talent-spotter and promoter.

Peaceful Progress Dub, Reggae, hip-hop and graffiti art.

Secret Garden Sound System Everything from acoustic to Balkan folk, ska, dance and legendarily wild, musically eclectic parties.

movie *Goldfinger*, and, in 1972, *Diamonds Are Forever*. More recently, in 2007, Bassey released *Get the Party Started*, featuring newly remixed and re-worked tracks by contemporary producers, which entered the UK charts at number six.

Cardiff musician-turned-record-producer **Dave Edmunds**, whose first band Love Sculpture scored a UK hit in 1968, has had his hands on many a hit record since then – both as a producer and a solo performer – during the 1970s and 1980s, and returned to touring in 2007. Classically trained pianist **John Cale**, born in Garnant near Ammanford, went to America in 1963 and found fame alongside Lou Reed with the **Velvet Underground**, one of the most influential avant-garde rock bands of the 1960s, managed by Andy Warhol. He has since recorded solo (including collaborative projects with other Welsh artistes).

In the 1980s, Welsh rock music was personified by Rhyl's rabble-rousing rock fundamentalists **The Alarm**, fronted by Mike Peters. Swansea's husky-toned rocker **Bonnie Tyler** (cousin by marriage to another Swansea native, actress Catherine Zeta Jones) achieved huge commercial success from the late 1970s onwards, and still tours. Possibly the most surprising Welsh success story of the 1980s was Fifties rock'n'roll impersonator **Shakin' Stevens**, who had a string of massive, nostalgia-driven hits.

It all changed in the 1990s. South Wales rock nihilists the **Manic Street Preachers**, hailing from the small town of Blackwood in the Sirhowy Valley, have become the most successful Welsh band ever. Few would have predicted this from their early career of bedsit-punk-meets-rock, topped with inflammatory statements such as "I laughed when John Lennon got shot", from the single *Motown Junk*. It was the mysterious 1995 disappearance, and presumed suicide, of fractured, anorexic guitarist Richey James Edwards, that changed everything for the Manics. They returned as a three-piece, storming the charts worldwide with their anthemic album, *Everything Must Go* (1996), which spawned huge hit singles, including the title track. Their follow-up album, *This Is My Truth, Tell Me Yours* (1998), continued their progress to megastardom, and included their first UK number one single, *If You Tolerate This, Then Your Children Will Be Next*.

The now legendary Welsh bands compilation album, *Dial M for Merthyr* (1995), showcased the Manics alongside many who subsequently became huge, all united by a tendency towards clever, zeitgeist lyrics and Welsh loquaciousness. Most exciting among them are the **Super Furry Animals**, whose fusion of Seventies psychedelia with new millennium clubland quirkiness and techno-geekery has created a niche all of their own: their seven albums to date, mixing both Welsh and English, are extraordinary. From poignant ballads to thumping, raw rock, they have proved to be masters of many genres and true innovators. The Super Furries' all-Welsh language album, *Mwng* (2000), became the best-selling work ever in Welsh, reaching number eleven in the UK album charts. Frontman Gruff Rhys also performs solo, releasing *Yr Atal Genhedlaeth* in 2005, and *Candylion* in 2007.

Now a successful solo artist, **Cerys Matthews**' lyrical talent had much to do with the success of the now-defunct **Catatonia**, the band that she fronted, and utterly dominated. Fine pop moments included their massive hits *Road Rage* and *Mulder and Scully*. Their pinnacle was one of the finest albums of the 1990s, *International Velvet* (1998), whose title track, with its verses in Welsh and roustabout English chorus of "every day, when I wake up, I thank the Lord I'm Welsh" is still something of an unofficial national anthem.

Another solo artist making their mark is **Euros Childs**, singer of the now split indie-psych band Gorky's Zygotic Mynci. Childs has released three albums including 2007's *Miracle Inn*, rich with piano, bass, drums and organ. The Gorky's have also since spawned the successful solo career of former bass player **Richard James**, whose debut album *Seven Sleepers Den* was released in 2006 to critical acclaim, with a follow-up album hitting the airwaves in 2009.

More lyrical dexterity, combined with clean-cut guitar chords, are the hallmarks of the **Stereophonics**, from Cwmaman in the Cynon Valley. Their sound is utterly distinctive, thanks largely to singer Kelly Jones' rasping voice, spawning massively successful albums and singles. Although not as identifiably Welsh as these acts, mega-group **Feeder** has increasingly taken on the national label, particularly since the suicide of drummer Jon Lee from Newport. Their diverse style encompasses haunting tunes of aching melancholy right through to bombastic rock blow-outs.

A new generation of bands whose influence has come more from the thrashier elements of post-millennial American rock. South Wales has been a particularly fertile breeding ground for this angst-ridden wall of noise, producing some of the genre's most celebrated protagonists: Swansea/Bridgend rockers **Funeral for a Friend** (aka FFAF), Rhondda nu-metal screamers **The Lostprophets** and Bridgend counterparts **Bullet For My Valentine**.

Storming the mainstream charts at home and abroad, **Duffy** (Aimee Anne Duffy) released her debut album *Rockferry* in 2008. Her big, soulful voice drew immediate comparisons with Amy Winehouse. The album's second single, *Mercy*, which featured on primetime US television programmes like *ER* and *Grey's Anatomy* as well as the *Sex and the City: The Movie* soundtrack, went straight to number one – making Duffy the first Welsh female to achieve a number one pop

Up-and-coming Welsh bands

Today's new wave of Welsh music is awash with talent. Keep a lookout for the following bands' recordings and gigs:

Attack + Defend Indie rock.

Cymbient Beautiful Sixties-influenced psychedelic pop.

Fortune Favours Edgy old-school rock; fronted by charismatic vocalist Pistol Pete Hurley.

Future of the Left Abrasive rock.

Los Campasinos Indie rock.

Slamfish Electronica/breakbeat.

Soft Hearted Scientists Folk/rock.

Truckers of Husk Instrumental alternative rock.

single in a quarter of a century, and the first-ever female from the Llŷn peninsula to top the UK music singles charts.

There's a thriving **dance music** scene, too, in all its fragmented glory. Tongue-in-cheek Newport rappers **Goldie Lookin' Chain** have a mammoth following. **Llwybr Llaethog** forged the way for later rap and hip-hop artists such as **MC Mabon** and **Pep Le Pew**, all of whom principally record in Welsh. Rural west Wales is the base for dub gurus **Zion Train**, doing spliffed-up remakes of classic new wave tracks. Big beatz'n'breaks come from Cardiff's **Phantom Beats**. **Vandal** is a local hero in the dance music realm, as are **Slamfish** and **Evora**.

Welsh-language rock

Established English-language artists like the Super Furry Animals' frontman Gruff Rhys are raising the profile of Welsh-language music to previously unscaled heights. But this is only a recent phenomenon. Whilst English-language Welsh bands have usually enjoyed success by making their nationality an irrelevance, Welsh-language bands have highlighted their strong national identity, fostering a unique, self-propagating Welsh-language rock scene. Boundaries are now increasingly blurred: many bands choose to sing in both Welsh and English, simply because it's the way most of their members use both languages.

The roots of this thriving, youthful and innovative scene owe much to a musical revolution whose shock waves emanated not from Cardiff or Newport, but from London. The **punk** explosion of 1976 kicked over many of rock's statues, partly thanks to the anarchic fervour of London bands like The Clash and the Sex Pistols, but also by virtue of its strong DIY ethic.

The home-grown Welsh-language pop scene consolidated when in 1983, Caernarfon punk band **Anhrefn** (Disorder) set up **Recordiau Anhrefn**, churning out what it called "dodgy compilations of up-and-coming left-field weirdo Welsh bands". Throughout the 1980s, any band that couldn't get some sort of record deal would simply press their own vinyl and sell their records at gigs. From this era, perhaps the most enduring legacy is the band **Datblygu**, most often described as a Welsh version of spectacularly misanthropic The Fall.

This DIY effort was boosted by the late Radio One DJ **John Peel** – to many, the standard-bearer for underground pop in the UK. Peel became aware of the growing number of Welsh-language bands and began playing their records on air and inviting them in for sessions. This introduced Welsh music to a Europe-wide audience and proved an important catalyst to new Welsh bands. By the 1990s, Welsh-language pop music had established a solid infrastructure of bands, labels and venues that continues to this day. One of the most prolific, eclectic and innovative of these labels is **Ankstmusik**, releasing Welsh-language pop of varied styles, best seen in some wonderful compilation albums, including *S4C Makes Me Want To Smoke Crack*, which contained tracks by Catatonia and professional Welsh weirdos **Rheinallt H. Rowlands** and **Ectogram**. On the same label, former Tystion rapper Gruff Meredith has metamorphosed to great acclaim into **MC Mabon**.

Other major promoters of Welsh-language pop are the Caernarfon-based **Crai Records**, a subsidiary of the more folk-oriented **Sain Records** and the **Fflach** label in Aberteifi (Cardigan), and their subsidiary **Rasp** for dancier artistes and projects. For a comprehensive list, click on "Record Labels" in the Directory section of the BBC's informative coverage of Welsh music at ⓦwww .bbc.co.uk/wales/music.

The grassroots Welsh **gig circuit** is also healthy, with a lively local pub and club scene. University student unions also regularly put on Welsh bands. Welsh-language pop bands can also be found at the **National Eisteddfod**, and local bars and clubs.

Books

S ome of the books listed here are published by small local presses, and you're unlikely to find them in bookshops outside Wales, though most can be ordered online. The Welsh Books Council website (🌐www.cllc .org.uk) sells a huge selection, and you'll often be able to pick up rare and out-of-print titles by scouring the many independent or secondhand bookshops in Wales – Hay-on-Wye is particularly good for the latter.

For information on readings and literary events throughout the year, check out the website of the Welsh National Literature Promotion Agency and Society for Authors at 🌐www.academi.org.

Welsh fiction is undergoing something of a renaissance; look out for works by the current leading crop of Welsh wordsmiths, spanning a wide range of styles and subject matters. Ones-to-watch include English-language writers such as Trezza Azzopardi, Kitti Harri and Dannie Abse, and Welsh-language authors including Tony Bianchi, Gwyn Jenkins, Ceri Wyn Jones and Alan Llwyd.

Travel and impressions

George Borrow *Wild Wales*. Highly entertaining and easy-to-read account of the author's walking tour of Wales in 1854.

Giraldus Cambrensis *The Journey Through Wales* and *The Description of Wales*. Two witty and frank books in one volume, written in Latin by the quarter-Welsh clergyman after his 1188 tour around Wales recruiting for the Third Crusade with Archbishop Baldwin of Canterbury. Both superb vehicles for Gerald of Wales' learned ruminations and unreserved opinions, *The Journey* breaks up the seven-week tour "through our rough, remote and inaccessible countryside" with anecdotes and ecclesiastical point-scoring, while *The Description* covers rural life.

Daniel Defoe *A Tour Through the Whole Island of Great Britain*. Classic travelogue opening a window onto Britain in the 1720s, with twenty pages on Wales.

🏃 **Gwynfor Evans** *Eternal Wales* (published as *Cymru o Hud* in Welsh). With magnificently moody photography by Marian Delyth, this is a passionate and erudite tour de

force through some of Wales' lesser-known corners.

🏃 **Peter Finch** *Real Cardiff* and *Real Cardiff Two*. Compelling ambles around the Welsh capital, full of oddball nuggets and with a terrific sense of context and place.

Ralph Maud *Guide to Welsh Wales*. Day tours around the country, highlighting places of historical significance for the Welsh patriot.

Jeremy Moore and Nigel Jenkins *Wales, The Lie of the Land*. A gorgeous, glossy tome that combines the luscious photography of Jeremy Moore and the musings of poet Nigel Jenkins. Spirited, passionate and a fine souvenir of contemporary Wales.

Jan Morris *Wales: Epic Views of a Small Country* (a rewrite of her earlier *The Matter of Wales*). Prolific half-Welsh travel writer Jan Morris immerses herself in the country that she evidently loves. Highly partisan and fiercely nationalistic, the book combs over the origins of the Welsh character and describes the people and places of Wales with precision and affection.

H.V. Morton *In Search of Wales*. Learned, lively and typically enthusiastic snapshots of Welsh life in the 1930s. A companion volume to his *In Search of England*.

Chris Musson *Wales from the Air*. Fascinating tour of the country via aerial photography and accompanying text, focusing on its historical development from pre-history to post-industry.

Thomas Pennant *A Tour in Wales*. First published in 1773, the stories from Pennant's horseback tour helped foster the Romantic enthusiasm for Wales' rugged landscapes.

Pamela Petro *Travels in an Old Tongue*. An American woman comes to Wales to study, is bewitched by the place, attempts to learn Welsh

and then sets off on a global pursuit of Welsh enclaves and speakers from Japan to Norway, Germany and Patagonia. Funny, informative and extremely perceptive about the language and its wider cultural significance.

Peter Sager *Wales*. A passionate and fabulously detailed 400-page celebratory essay on Wales, and especially its people, by a German convert to the cause of all things Welsh.

Meic Stephens *A Most Peculiar People: Quotations About Wales and the Welsh*. Varied volume of quotations going back to the century before Christ and up to 2000. As a portrait of the nation, with all of its frustrating idiosyncrasies and endearing foibles, it is a superb example.

History, society and culture

Jane Aaron et al (ed) *Our Sisters' Land: The Changing Identities of Women in Wales*. A series of challenging and well-written essays that delve deep into male-dominated Welsh society, from the home to the political system. Includes personal testimonies and some startling facts about just how entrenched bigotry still is within much of the Welsh establishment.

David Berry *Wales and Cinema: The First Hundred Years*. Thorough examination of this small country's contribution to the big screen, both in terms of stars, directors and writers and its frequent role as subject and setting. From the sublime – some of the superb recent young movies kick-started by S4C – to the ridiculous – Hollywood's take on Wales for blockbusters like *How Green Was My Valley*.

Richard Booth *My Kingdom of Books*. Typically bullish autobiography by the man who made Hay-on-Wye the world's biggest secondhand bookshop. Some interesting stuff on

his tussles with authority and his semi-serious declaration of Hay as an independent country.

Janet Davies *The Welsh Language*. Very readable history and assessment of one of Europe's oldest living languages. Packed full of maps showing the demographic and geographic spread of Welsh over the ages.

John Davies *A History of Wales*. Exhaustive run through Welsh history and culture from the earliest inhabitants to the late 1980s. Translated from the original 1990 Welsh-language edition, this is clearly written and very readable, but, at 700 pages, it's hardly concise.

Alice Thomas Ellis *A Welsh Childhood*. Whimsical reminiscences of growing up in north Wales. Welsh legends and folk tales form a large part of the backdrop, fermenting excitedly in the young imagination of the popular novelist.

Gwynfor Evans *Land of My Fathers* and *For the Sake of Wales*. Plaid

Cymru's late elder statesman first produced the former tome in Welsh, translating it into English for publication thirty years ago. It's a thorough and polemical history of the country. The latter work, his autobiography, covers Welsh political and social life from the war to the National Assembly. Hugely readable and inspirational.

Geoffrey of Monmouth *History of the Kings of Britain*. First published in 1136, this is the basis of almost all Arthurian legend. Writers throughout Europe and beyond used Geoffrey's unreliable history as the basis of a complex corpus of myth.

David Greenslade *Welsh Fever: Welsh Activities in the United States and Canada Today*. Essential companion for anyone searching out Welsh and Celtic roots in North America. Commentary on regions from Quebec to San Diego, along with accounts of a hundred individual sites of Welsh or Celtic interest.

Alan Llwyd *Cymru Ddu/Black Wales: a History*. A long and insightful look at the history of multi-racial Wales in both Welsh and English.

John Matthews *A Celtic Reader*. Selections of original texts, scholarly articles and stories on Celtic legend and scholarship. Sections on the druids, Celtic Britain and The Mabinogion. Assumes a deep interest on the part of the reader.

Elizabeth Mavor *The Ladies of Llangollen*. The best of the books on Wales' most notorious and celebrated lesbian couple. This volume traces the ladies' inauspicious beginnings in

Ireland, their spectacular elopement and the way that their Llangollen home, Plas Newydd, became a place of pilgrimage for dozens of influential eighteenth-century visitors.

Jan Morris and Twm Morys *A Machynlleth Triad/Triawd Machynlleth*. Three-part saga in Welsh and English about Machynlleth, Glyndŵr's capital. Jan Morris evokes the town at the time of Glyndŵr, looks at the place in the mid-1990s and imagines it "sometime in the 21st century" as the charmingly self-assured capital of an independent Wales. The book says much about Wales as a whole, is beautifully written and often very funny.

Trefor M. Owen *The Customs and Traditions of Wales*. Pocket guide to everything from outdoor prayer meetings to the curious Mari Lwyd, when men dress as grey mares and snap at all the young girls.

Mike Parker *Neighbours From Hell?* A light-hearted study of a thousand years of English attitudes – from lofty condescension to outright hostility – to Wales and the Welsh, written by one of the co-authors of this book.

Ned Thomas *The Welsh Extremist*. A good introduction to the political landscape that spawned the anti-English bombing campaigns of the 1970s. An evocative argument around the issues of oppression and emancipation.

Patrick Thomas *Candle in the Darkness: Celtic Spirituality from Wales*. Tales from the "Age of Saints" in Wales, with particular focus given to the numerous Celtic saints who originated here.

Art, architecture and archeology

Chris Barber and John Godfrey Williams *The Ancient Stones of Wales*. Comprehensive directory of standing stones and monoliths throughout Wales, together with

some of the most potent legends and stories associated with them. Exhaustively researched, if a little user-unfriendly.

Peter Lord *The Visual Culture of Wales*. Lavishly produced and beautifully illustrated three-volume overview of the art and architecture of Wales, from the early industrial society to the present day.

John Meirion Morris *The Celtic Vision*. Masterful examination by the superb Welsh sculptor of La Tène Celtic art and its religious meaning.

Literature

Enid Blyton *Five Get Into a Fix*. In this the seventeenth of Blyton's timeless series of kids' adventure novels, Julian, Dick, Anne, George and Timmy-the-dog unearth secret passageways to rescue an old woman from a sinister tower in the snowy Welsh mountains. Vintage "Famous Five".

Bruce Chatwin *On the Black Hill*. This entertaining and finely wrought novel follows the Jones twins' eighty-year tenure of a farm on the Radnorshire border with England. Chatwin casts his sharp eye for detail over both the minutiae of nature and the universal human condition, providing a gentle angle on Welsh–English antipathy.

Alexander Cordell *The Fire People*. Set against the backdrop of the Merthyr Tydfil riots of 1831, this is a feisty fictionalization of the life and unjust death of Dic Penderen, the "first Welsh Martyr of the working class". The same author's *Rape of the Fair Country*, *Hosts of Rebecca*, and *Song of the Earth* form a dramatic historical trilogy in the bestseller tradition, partly set in the cottages on the site of the Blaenafon ironworks during the lead-up to the Chartist Riots. *This Sweet and Bitter Earth* immortalizes Blaenau Ffestiniog in a lusty slate epic.

Lewis Davies *Work, Sex and Rugby*. Perennially popular novel that tells you all you need to know (and much you don't) about Valleys men.

Richard John Evans *Entertainment*. Scabrous roller-coaster ride through

Rhondda living and loving, guaranteed to offend and cause maximum hilarity.

Thomas Firbank *I Bought a Mountain*. One of the few popular books set in north Wales in which Anglo-Canadian Firbank spins an autobiographical yarn of his purchase of most of the Glyder range and subsequent life as a Snowdonian sheep farmer during the 1930s.

Iris Gower *Copper Kingdom*; *Proud Mary*; *Spinners' Wharf*; *Black Gold*; *Fiddler's Ferry*; *The Oyster Catchers* – the list goes on. Romantic novels by Wales' most popular author.

Niall Griffiths *Grits*; *Sheep-shagger*; *Kelly + Victor*; *Stump*; *Wreckage*. Arguably the best dissector of darkness, drugs, comradeship and hopelessness in modern Britain, Griffiths' panoply of novels set between Aberystwyth and Liverpool are suffused with a metaphysical sense of culture and landscape.

Emyr Humphreys *The Gift of a Daughter*. The mood and landscape of Anglesey is beautifully evoked by perhaps the greatest living Welsh novelist.

Siân James *Not Singing Exactly*. Dazzling and diverse short-story collection from one of Wales' premier romantic novelists.

Glyn Jones *The Island of Apples*. Set in south Wales and Carmarthen in the early years of the twentieth century, this is an artful portrayal of a sensitive Valleys youth's enthralment in the glamour of the district's new arrival.

Gwyn and Thomas Jones (trans) *The Mabinogion*. Welsh mythology's classic, these eleven orally developed heroic tales were finally transcribed into the *Book of Rhydderch* (around 1300–25) and the *Red Book of Hergest* (1375–1425). Originally translated by Lady Charlotte Guest between 1838 and 1849 at the beginning of the Celtic revival.

Lewis Jones *Cwmardy*. Longtime favourite socialist novel, written in 1937 and portraying life in a Rhondda Valley mining community in the early years of the twentieth century. Followed by its sequel, *We Live*.

Richard Llewellyn *How Green Was My Valley; Up into the Singing Mountain; Down Where the Moon is Small; Green, Green My Valley Now*. Vital tetralogy in eloquent and passionate prose, following the life of Huw Morgan from his youth in a south Wales mining valley through emigration to the Welsh community in Patagonia and back to 1970s Wales. A bestseller during World War II and still the best introduction to the vast canon of "valleys novels", *How Green Was My Valley* captured a longing for a simple, if tough, life, steering clear of cloying sentimentality.

Caradoc Pritchard *One Moonlit Night*. Dense, swirling tale of a young boy's emotional and sexual awakenings in an isolated north Wales village. Full-blooded Welsh prose at its most charged.

Malcolm Pryce *Aberystwyth Mon Amour*. Surprise bestseller in the shape of this furious, funny black comedy set in an Aberystwyth overlaid with film–noir surrealism and dastardly twists of plot.

Kate Roberts *The Living Sleep* and *Feet in Chains*, amongst others. Penned by one of the bestselling contemporary Welsh–language writers, these two novels, available in English translation, tell the tales of life in a north Wales slate village.

Ruth Janette Ruck *Hill Farm Story* and *Along Came a Llama*. Evocative stories about a farming area around Beddgelert.

Dylan Thomas *Collected Stories* and *Under Milk Wood*. The *Collected Stories* contains all of Thomas' classic prose pieces: *Quite Early One Morning*, which metamorphosed into *Under Milk Wood*, the magical *A Child's Christmas in Wales* and the compulsive, crackling autobiography of *Portrait of the Artist as a Young Dog*. In all of Thomas' works, the language still burns bright. *Under Milk Wood*, his most popular play, tells the story of a microcosmic Welsh seaside town (modelled on New Quay) over a 24-hour period. Ideally, obtain a recorded version of the play to absorb its rich poetry (or, as Thomas himself described it, "prose with blood pressure").

Gwyn Thomas *A Welsh Eye*. A partly autobiographical, partly anecdotal view of how it feels to grow up in a small Rhondda town; full of arcane and idiosyncratic wit and much more.

Alice Thomas Ellis (ed) *Wales – An Anthology*. A beautiful book, combining poetry, folklore and prose stories rooted in places throughout Wales. All subjects, from rugby and mountain climbing to contemporary descriptions of major events, are included in an enjoyably eclectic mixture of styles. Excellent introduction to Welsh writing.

Charlotte Williams *Sugar and Slate*. Humorous and unstintingly honest memoir of mixed identity: the author is the daughter of a black Guyanese father who grew up in a Welsh-speaking community.

John Williams *Five Pubs, Two Bars And A Nightclub; Cardiff Dead;*

Temperance Town. The first a very funny short-story collection, something of an inspiration for the E-culture hit film *Human Traffic*; the second a full-length novel that packs in the Welsh cultural references effortlessly and to great effect; and the third a novella in the same vein.

Raymond Williams *Border Country*. 1960 novel that perfectly captures the sense of change overwhelming rural Welsh life in that era. A timeless classic.

Poetry

Dannie Abse *Welsh Retrospective* and *Arcadia, One Mile*. Two superb collections from one of Wales' most prolific modern poets, showing his huge range of intellectual interests and warm, beguiling style of writing.

John Barnie *The City* and *The Confirmation*. One of Wales' best contemporary writers, notable mainly for his combination of poetry and prose styles, narration and description. Evocative tales of wartime childhood and stifling parenting, leading to a poignant search for love.

Ruth Bidgood *Lighting Candles*. Light, elegiac verse inspired by the Welsh landscape interweaving climate, scenery and emotion.

Gillian Clarke *Collected Poems*. A good introduction to the nature-inspired and homely poetry of one of Wales' leading contemporary writers.

Dafydd Johnston *Iolo Goch: poems*. All of the surviving poems of Owain Glyndŵr's court bard are shown in translation and context. A fascinating insight into courtly medieval Wales at a time of great national resurgence.

Gwyneth Lewis *Keeping Mum*. Wales' first-ever National Poet shows her verbal power and dexterity with this recent collection, especially when combing over the irregularities of bilingual existence.

Robert Minhinnick *Selected Poems*. Overview of the recent career of one of Wales' brightest young writers: best when picking over his English-speaking south Walian youth in rich, impassioned imagery.

Meic Stephens (ed) *New Companion to the Literature of Wales*. A customarily thorough volume of Welsh prose, spanning the centuries from the folk tales of The Mabinogion to modern-day writings.

Dylan Thomas *Collected Poems*. Thomas' poetry has always proved less popular than his prose- and play-writing, largely due to its density and difficulty. Many of his lighter poems resound with perfect metre and precise structure, including classics such as *Do Not Go Gentle Into That Good Night*, a passionate yet calm elegy to his dying father.

R.S. Thomas *Selected Poems 1946–1968*. The much-missed recluse, Thomas, wrote poetry that tugs at issues such as God (he was an Anglican priest), Wales ("brittle with relics") and the family. His passion shines throughout this book, probably the best overview of his prolific work.

Harri Webb (ed. Meic Stephens) *Collected Poems*. Fine collection of 350 works by a modern-day patriot and poet of biting satire and eloquent expression.

Wildlife and the environment

Douglas Botting *Wild Britain: A Traveller's Guide*. Not much use for species identification but plenty of information on access to the best sites and what to expect when you get there. Excellent photos.

Collins Field Guides Series of thorough, pocket-sized identification guides. Topics include insects, butterflies, wildflowers, mushrooms and toadstools, birds, mammals, reptiles and fossils.

🏃 **William Condry and Jeremy Moore** *Heart of the Country*. Jeremy Moore's gorgeous photography is the perfect accompaniment

to the late William Condry's Country Diary entries from *The Guardian*.

Michael Leach *The Secret Life of Snowdonia*. Beautifully photographed coffee-table tome delving into the least visible natural sights of Snowdonia – from feral goats to the Snowdon lily and a close-up of a raven in its nest.

David Saunders *Where to Watch Birds in Wales*. Enthusiasts' guide to Wales' prime birding locations, along with a bird-spotting calendar and a list of English–Welsh–Scientific bird names. Not an identification guide.

Outdoor pursuits

🏃 **Bob Allen** *On Foot in Snowdonia*. Inspirational and artfully photographed guide to the hundred best walks, from easy strolls to hard scrambles, in and around the Snowdonia National Park. Well-drawn maps, faultless instructions and a star rating for each walk help you to select your route.

Cicerone Guides *The Mountains of England and Wales*; *Wales, The Ridges of Snowdonia*; *Hill Walking in Snowdonia*; *Ascent of Snowdon*; *Welsh Winter Climbs*; *Scrambles in Snowdonia* and others, various authors. Clearly written pocket guides to the best aspects of Welsh mountain activities.

🏃 **Lawrence Main** *The Spirit Paths of Wales*. Wonderful guide to twenty Welsh walks, each along ley lines and other spiritually significant routes.

Terry Marsh *The Mountains of Wales*. A walker's guide to all 183 of the 600-metre peaks in Wales, giving step-by-step descriptions of one or more routes up them all with

additional historical references and local knowledge.

Ordnance Survey National Trail Guides Large, paperback editions full of instructive descriptions and additional side-walks from *Offa's Dyke North*, *Offa's Dyke South* and *Pembrokeshire Coastal Path*.

Stillwell's National Trail Companion Excellent big-pocket directory of reasonably priced accommodation close to some of the more popular UK long-distance paths. Welsh routes include the Cambrian Way, Glyndŵr's Way, the Offa's Dyke Path, the Pembrokeshire Coast Path and the Wye Valley Walk.

Shirley Toulson *The Drovers' Roads of Wales with Fay Godwin* and *The Drovers' Roads of Wales II: Pembrokeshire and the South with Caroline Forbes*. A pair of complementary photograph-enlivened books giving background material along with instructions on how to trace the routes along which Wales' characteristic black cattle were driven to market in England in the eighteenth and nineteenth centuries.

Film

Wales has formed the backdrop to many a movie, from low-budget local efforts to Hollywood (and even Bollywood) blockbusters. Few of the big films, however, have Welsh themes: more often than not, the country is either masquerading as somewhere else or just providing generic scenery. A vast new 12-sound-stage film studio near Bridgend (dubbed "Valleywood") commenced construction in 2007, but is currently plagued by financial problems and its future was not yet clear. Meanwhile, Wales' biggest current splash on screen – albeit the smaller one – is the revamp of *Dr Who*, made to startling effect by BBC Wales and featuring many prominent local landmarks, particularly around Cardiff, Barry and Pontypridd (for a list of locations, visit ⓦ www.doctorwholocations.net).

Movies with specifically Welsh stories have tended to be at the lower budget end of the spectrum, often playing on a slightly whimsical view of Wales, despite the huge success of Welsh film stars from Richard Burton through to Catherine Zeta Jones, Christian Bale, Rhys Ifans and Ioan Gruffudd. However, in 2006, the Film Agency for Wales was established with a charter "to ensure that the economic, cultural and educational aspects of film are effectively represented in Wales, the UK and the world". This commitment to a viable and sustainable Welsh film industry, combined with the output of talent from the International Film School Wales in Caerleon (such as Cannes- and BAFTA-winning writer/director Asif Kapadia), and star-powered films like 2008's *The Edge of Love* may herald the reversal of that trend.

An American Werewolf in London (1981). Cult-classic shlock-horror movie; the moor sequences at the beginning are the Brecon Beacons.

The Edge of Love (2008). Keira Knightley and Sienna Miller star as Vera Phillips and Caitlin MacNamara – the two great loves of Matthew Rhys's Dylan Thomas. Filmed in Thomas's old haunts on the Cambrian coast around New Quay.

The Englishman Who Went Up a Hill and Came Down a Mountain (1995). Bumbling comedy full of cod Welsh stereotypes and Hugh Grant as a similarly one-dimensional Englishman; filmed around Llanrhaeadr-ym-Mochnant and near Cardiff.

First Knight (1995). Sean Connery stars as King Arthur, with Richard Gere as Sir Lancelot, in this patchy action movie filmed largely in Snowdonia.

Happy Now (2001). Distinctly oddball thriller, filmed in and around Barmouth, which becomes the mysterious Welsh seaside town Pen-y-Wig.

Hedd Wyn (1993). First Oscar-nominated Welsh-language film, about the north Wales poet who went off to fight in World War I and never returned.

House of America (1997). Dark and depressing tale of secrets and yearning in one family stuck on a mouldering farm in west Wales.

How Green was my Valley (1941). None of it was filmed in Wales, but this Oscar-winning version of the classic Welsh book came to define the world image of Wales for generations.

Human Traffic (1999). Feelgood E-culture movie, with a star cameo by Welsh drug-trafficking guru Howard Marks. Filmed in Cardiff.

Inn of the Sixth Happiness (1958). Ingrid Bergman leads in this classic tale of self-discovery, where Snowdonia doubles as China.

King Arthur (2004). Big-screen epic, with huge battles and a rather less sensational account of the "real" king of the Britons than had gone before. Ioan Gruffudd shines as Sir Lancelot.

Kyun! Ho Gaya Na Pyaar (2004). Translating as "It has happened – love", this is a big-budget Bollywood production, with former Miss World, Aishwarya Rai, as the love interest. Large sections were filmed in mid-Wales and Snowdonia.

On the Black Hill (1987). Hauntingly beautiful adaptation of the downbeat Bruce Chatwin novel about twin brothers growing up in the Black Mountains.

Lawrence of Arabia (1962). The south Wales sand dunes of Merthyr Mawr doubled up as Arabia for Peter O'Toole, Omar Sharif and company.

The Prisoner (1971). Big-screen version of the enigmatic cult TV series, also filmed largely at the fantasy village of Portmeirion.

Solomon a Gaenor (1998). Filmed in both Welsh and English versions, this Oscar-nominated weepie is a *Romeo and Juliet* tale set in the Edwardian Valleys.

Twin Town (1997). Hilarious drug-fuelled romp set in Swansea that introduced Rhys Ifans to the world.

Under Milk Wood (1971). Phantasmagoric take on the classic Dylan Thomas "play for voices", with an all-star cast including Richard Burton and Elizabeth Taylor.

Very Annie Mary (2001). Offbeat tale of love and singing in the Valleys, with Ioan Gruffudd and Matthew Rhys camping it up to the nines as the only gays in the village.

Language

Language

Welsh

The Welsh language, *Cymraeg*, is spoken widely throughout the country and as a first language in many parts of the west and north. The language's survival, and resurgence, is a remarkable story, especially considering the fact that the heart of English culture and its language – the most expansionist the world has ever seen – lies right next door.

One of the most startling findings of the most recent British census was a significant increase in Welsh speakers throughout Wales, and the headline figure (around one in five people) is now higher than it's been in nearly half a century. From the sharp decline of the mid-twentieth century, it's a dramatic turnabout and testament to bold policies, particularly in education and mass media. National TV and radio stations broadcast in Welsh, road signs are written in both Welsh and English, Welsh-medium schools are everywhere, books in Welsh are published at a growing rate of around 400 every year and magazines, newspapers and websites in the old language are mushrooming.

In the families of Celtic languages, Welsh bears most similarity to the defiant Breton, the language of the northwestern corner of France, and the largely defunct Cornish. Scots and Irish Gaelic, together with defunct Manx, belong to a different branch of Celtic languages, and, although there are occasional similarities, they have little in common.

Some history

The Welsh language can be traced back to the sixth century. Celtic inscriptions on stones, a section of written Welsh in the eighth-century **Lichfield Gospels**,

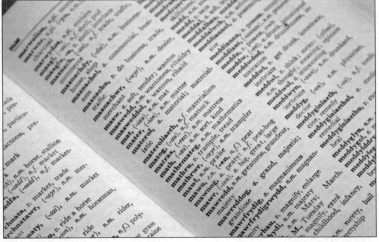

▲ Welsh-English dictionary

the tenth-century codified laws of Hywel Dda in neat Welsh prose, and the twelfth- and thirteenth-century **Mabinogion** folk tales (believed to have been collated from earlier Welsh writings) show that Welsh was a thriving language in the centuries up to the Norman invasion of 1066. Moreover, the early language is still identifiable and easily comprehensible for any modern-day Welsh speaker.

English domination since the Norman era has been mirrored in the fate of the Welsh tongue. The Norman lords were implanted in castles throughout Wales to subjugate the natives, with official business conducted in their native French. **Edward I** (1272–1307), who conquered Wales in 1284, was politically sensitive to the power of the language to define a nation, and is said to have promised the Welsh a prince, born in their own country who was unable to speak English. This promise was delivered when Edward had his pregnant wife take up residence in Caernarfon Castle, enabling the king to hold the newborn infant up as a non-English-speaking, Welsh-born prince.

Real linguistic warfare came with the 1536 **Act of Union** under Henry VIII (see box, p.471). This stated that "from henceforth no Person or Persons that use the Welsh Speech or Language shall have or enjoy any Manner, Office or Fees within this Realm of England, Wales or other of the King's Dominion, upon pain of forfeiting the same Office or Fees, unless he or they use and exercise the English Speech or Language". This only legitimized the growing practice of imposing English lords and churchmen on the restless, but effectively cowed, Welsh. Had it not been for William Morgan's 1588 **translation of the Bible** into Welsh, it is likely that the language would have died. As it was, bringing written Welsh into the ordinary, everyday public arena ultimately ensured its survival.

The fate of the language became inextricably linked with its religious use. Right up until the early part of the twentieth century, Welsh was actively, even forcefully, discouraged in educational and governmental establishments, but new and Nonconformist religious movements from the seventeenth century onwards embraced the language. The **Industrial Revolution** brought mine owners and capitalists from England into the rapidly urbanizing southeastern corner of Wales, further diluting the language – which was, nonetheless, upheld as the lingua franca in the growing numbers of chapels. In the first half of the nineteenth century, it is estimated that over ninety percent of the country's population spoke Welsh, with the remaining ten percent comprising those around the English border, in the small pocket of Pembrokeshire long known as "Little England Beyond Wales" and the wealthier classes of Wales for whom English was part of their badge of status.

In 1854, **George Borrow** undertook his marathon tour of Wales and noted the state of the native tongue throughout. As a natural linguist, he had mastered Welsh and fired questions at people he encountered as to their profi-ciency in both Welsh and English. The picture he paints is of poorer people tending to be monolingual Welsh speakers, wealthier people and those near the border bilingual. Discouragement of Welsh continued in many guises, most notably in it being forbidden in schools in the latter half of the nineteenth and early twentieth centuries. Anyone caught speaking in Welsh had to wear a "Welsh Not", a piece of wood on a leather strap that would only be passed on if someone else was heard using the language. At the end of the school day, the child still wearing the Welsh Not was soundly beaten. There are still older people in Wales who can remember this barbaric practice, and it is hardly surprising that use and proficiency of the language plummeted. Figures are borne out by the official British census, the first of which was undertaken in 1851, when 90 percent of the country are recorded as speaking the language. Every decade, the figures dipped quite spectacularly – 49.9 percent in 1901, 37.1 percent in 1921, 28.9 percent in 1951 and 18.9 percent in 1981. Then, in 1991, for the first time ever, and again in 2001, the percentage of Welsh speakers rose, still around the one-fifth mark but showing the most marked increase amongst the lower age groups, those most able to ensure its future.

Where Welsh is spoken

The figure of some twenty percent of fluent Welsh-speakers across Wales' population is best seen in its geographical context. Considering that nearly half of the nation's population lives in the anglicized regions of Gwent and around Cardiff, the spread of the language becomes clearer. Although it is unusual to hear it regularly in the border counties, it is commonly understood throughout most of West Glamorgan, Carmarthenshire, the northern half of Pembrokeshire, right around Cardigan Bay up to Caernarfon, the Llŷn peninsula and Anglesey and in parts of inland Denbighshire and Montgomeryshire. The northwestern corner, centred on Snowdonia, Anglesey and the Llŷn, is the real stronghold of Welsh, reflected in these areas' steadfast political affiliation to Welsh nationalism.

The politics of the language

That Welsh has a greater presence than could ever have been predicted a generation ago (when it was believed to be dying out) is largely due to those who campaigned to save it. The campaign dates back to the eisteddfod revivalists of the eighteenth century, although movements with a more political aim are a product solely of the twentieth century. The formation of **Plaid Cymru**, the Welsh National Party, in 1925 was largely around the issue of language, as indeed its politics have been ever since.

In the early 1960s, concerns about the language reached a zenith in the 1962 radio broadcast entitled *Tynged yr iaith* (The Fate of the Language) by the Plaid founder member, Saunders Lewis. This became a rallying cry that resulted in the formation of *Cymdeithas yr Iaith Gymraeg*, the **Welsh Language Society**, the following year. One of the most high-profile early campaigns was the daubing of monoglot English road signs with their Welsh translations, including any town sign written solely in the anglicized format. Nearly all signs are now in both languages. A 1967 Welsh Language Act allowed many forms of hitherto English officialdom to be conducted in either language, stating that Welsh, for the first time in over 400 years, had "equal validity" with English.

Still, bilingual road signs and tax forms weren't enough to stem the linguistic haemorrhage that threatened Wales. In the multinational, cross-media world of the late twentieth century, the keys to maintaining and promoting a language were in education and media, particularly television. Following the 1967 Act, **Welsh-medium education** blossomed, with bilingual teaching in all primary schools and for at least a year in all secondary schools. Many secondary schools, particularly in areas traditionally associated with the language, had Welsh as a compulsory subject for five years. Increasing numbers of schools all over the land educate their students in all subjects through the Welsh language. These trends drew objections from some non-Welsh-speaking parents that their children were being "forced" to learn a "dead" language. Although there are still periodic rumbles of discontent, most have come round to the well-founded view that a bilingual education (something sixty percent of the world's children

517

receive) actually helps children learn, increasing aptitude for other languages. At the other end of the educational spectrum, Welsh-language courses in the country's universities are growing in popularity and status, meaning that, for pretty much the first time in Wales' history, it is possible to be educated in Welsh from nursery to degree level.

Paralleling Welsh-medium education has been the other modern corner-stone for developing a language – a growth in **broadcast media**. The BBC Welsh-language Radio Cymru began in the late 1970s, to be joined – after a considerable battle (see p.49) by the Sianel Pedwar Cymru (S4C) TV station in 1982. Together, they have sponsored and programmed popular Welsh learners' programmes and given the old language greater space than it has ever enjoyed before.

The situation today

Welsh-language classes are now offered right across the country, including in some of the most anglicized of border towns, as well as outside the country in language centres across Britain, and universities in Europe and North America.

The Welsh language is both one of Wales' key strengths and its key drawbacks in the quest for some sort of national emancipation. There is still suspicion towards the Welsh-speaking "elite" who are seen to control the media and local government in the country. Welsh nationalism is so defined by the language that Plaid Cymru has nearly always had great difficulty in appealing to those who speak only English, particularly in the urban southeast. Nonetheless, the Welsh language continues to flourish. The **Welsh Language Board** was formed in 1994, and with the arrival of the **National Assembly** in 1999, with around half of its members proficient in Welsh, the language has gained a number of firm footholds in official life. Increasingly, Wales is developing as a model bilingual entity, in which there is room for both languages to thrive together.

Alphabet

Although Welsh words, place names in particular, can appear bewilderingly incomprehensible, the rules of the language are far more strictly adhered to than in English. Thus, mastering the basic constructions and breaking words down into their constituent parts means that pronunciation need not be anywhere near as difficult as first imagined.

The Welsh **alphabet** is similar to the English, although with seven vowels instead of five, and a different collection of consonants. As well as the same five vowels (a, e, i, o, u), Welsh also has y and w. Most vowels have two sounds, long and short: a is long as in c**a**r, short as in f**a**t; e long as in br**e**r, short as in p**e**t; i long as in s**ea**, short as an t**i**n; o long as in m**o**re, short as in d**o**g; u roughly like a Welsh i; w long as in s**oo**n, short as in l**oo**k; y long as in s**ea** and short as in b**u**n or p**i**n. A circumflex over any vowel lengthens its sound.

Adjoining vowels are common in Welsh. Ae, ai, aw, ew, iw, oe, oi, ou, wy and yw are the usual forms and are pronounced as the two separate sounds, with, generally, the stress on the first.

There are no letters j, k, v, x and z in Welsh, except in occasional words appro-priated and Cymrified from other languages. Additional Welsh consonants are ch, pronounced as in German or as in lo**ch**, dd, pronounced as a hard th as in **th**ose, ff and ph as a soft f as in **f**ive and si as in **sh**oe. The typically Welsh consonant that causes the most problem is the ll, featured in many place names such as **Ll**angoll**e**n. This has no direct parallel in English, although the tl sound in Ben**tl**ey comes close. The proper way to pronounce it is to place the tongue firmly behind the top row of teeth and breathe through it without consciously making a voiced sound. Single Welsh consonants are, for the most part, pronounced in similar ways to English. The exceptions are c and g, always hard as in **c**at and **g**ut (never soft as in ni**c**e or ra**g**e) and f, always pronounced as v as in **v**ine.

A further difficulty for those trying to recognize words is the Welsh system of word **mutation**, where a previous word can affect the beginning of a following one, principally to ease pronunciation. Prepositions commonly mutate the following word, turning an initial B into F or M, an initial C into G or Ngh, a D into Dd or N, F into B or M, G into Ngh or the initial letter being dropped altogether, Ll into L, M into F, P into B, Mh or Ph, T into Th, D or Nh. Thus, "in Cardiff (Caerdydd)" is "y**ng Ngh**aerdydd" (note that the "yn" also mutates to ease pronunciation) and "from Bangor" is "o **F**angor". Mutated words are extremely common in the component parts of place names.

Welsh vocabulary

Scotland	Alban	public	Cyhoeddus
museum	Amgeuddfa	society	Cymdeithas
son of	Ap (ab)	Welsh	Cymraeg
open	Ar Agor	a Welshwoman	Cymraes
closed	Ar Gau	Welshness	Cymreictod
for sale	Ar Werth	Welshman	Cymro
slow	Araf	Wales	Cymru
slow down (instruction)	Arafwch	the Welsh people	Cymry
		Assembly	Cynulliad
bread	Bara	good	Da
morning	Bore	Saint David	Dewi Sant
good morning	Bore da	no (as an instruction), nothing	Dim
breakfast	Brecwast		
table	Bwrdd	thank you	Diolch
bus	Bws	end	Diwedd
song	Cân	water	Dŵr
national	Cenedlaethol	day	Dydd
craft	Crefft	man (men)	Dyn (-ion)
welcome	Croeso	church	Eglwys
rood screen	Croglen	festival	Eisteddfod
literally "curved stone", generally used to refer to megalithic burial chambers	Cromlech	how much?	Faint?
		station	Gorsaf
		fair	Gweddol
		bed	Gwely
		hotel	Gwesty
glacially formed, cliff-backed and often lake-filled bowl in mountains. Also called cirque or corrie	Cwm	temporary summer-house	Hafod
		half	Hanner
		today	Heddiw

519

police	Heddlu	football	Pêl-droed
tonight	Heno	village	Pentre(f)
road	Heol	The Party of Wales	Plaid Cymru
longing, yearning	Hiraeth	good afternoon	P'nhawn da
spirit	Hwyl	buttress	Rhiniog
language	Laith	English language	Saesneg
fine, very	Lawn	Englishman	Sais
slate	Llech	saint	Sant
lodging place, B&B	Llety	causeway	Sarn
lion (often found in pub names)	Llew	Parliament	Senedd
		hello	Shwmae
England	Lloegr	shop	Siop
path	Llwybr	county, shire	Sir
book	Llyfr	street	Stryd
market	Marchnad	how are you?	Sut ydych chi? (formal) or Sut ywt ti? (informal)
woman	Menyw		
Michael, as in Llanfihangel	Mihangel		
		office	Swyddfa
mile	Milltir	post office	Swyddfa'r Post
hall	Neuadd	pub	Tafarn
town hall	Neuadd Y Dref	ticket	Tocyn
to swim	Nofio	the	Y, Yr or 'r
good night	Nos da	here	Yma
evening	Noson/noswaith	hospital	Ysbyty
good evening	Noswaith dda	school	Ysgol
last	Olaf		
please	Os gwelwch chi'n dda		

Welsh place names

The following list is of the most common words that you will see in town and village names.

mouth of a river; confluence of two rivers	Aber	home	Cartref
		castle	Castell
		meadow	Clun
river	Afon	gate, perch	Clwyd
small, lesser	Bach	red	Coch
neighbourhood	Bro	forest, woodland	Coed
slope of a hill	Bron	rock	Craig
hill	Bryn	artificial island on a lake	Crannog
mountain pass	Bwlch		
stronghold, chair	Cadair	valley	Cwm
fort	Caer	first	Cyntaf
centre	Canol	south	De
hundred	Cant	fort	Din or dinas
chapel	Capel	meadow	Dôl
stone	Carreg	over	Dros

black	Du	burial place of saint	Merthyr
east	Dwyrain	bare or rounded mountain	Moel
vale	Dyffryn		
ridge	Esgair	sea	Môr
small, lesser	Fach	coastal marsh	Morfa
big, greater	Fawr	mountain	Mynydd
farm	Fferm	valley, stream	Nant
road	Ffordd	new	Newydd
forest	Fforest	night	Nos
garden	Gardd	vale	Pant
blue	Glas	park	Parc
valley	Glyn	head, top (as of a valley)	Pen
north	Gogledd		
west	Gorllewin	village	Pentre(f)
white	Gwyn	hall, mansion	Plas
green	Gwyrdd	bridge	Pont
old	Hen	port, gateway	Porth
lower	Isaf	hill	Rhiw
sacred enclosure, early church	Llan	ford	Rhyd
		mound	Tomen
place	Lle	beach	Traeth
grey	Llwyd	town	Tref
lake	Llyn	tower	Tŵr
place, court	Llys	house	Tŷ
stone	Maen	uppermost, highest	Uchaf
field	Maes	higher	Uwch
big, greater	Mawr	near, by	Wrth
mill	Melin	island	Ynys
yellow	Melyn		

Welsh numbers

1	un	22	dau-ddeg-dau
2	dau (fem. dwy)	30	tri-deg
3	tri (fem. tair)	40	pedwar-deg
4	pedwar (fem. pedair)	50	pum-deg
5	pump	60	chwe-deg
6	chwech	70	saith-deg
7	saith	80	wyth-deg
8	wyth	90	naw-deg
9	naw	100	cant
10	deg	200	dau gant
11	un-deg-un	300	tri chant
12	un-deg-dau	400	pedwar cant
13	un-deg-tri	500	pum cant
20	dau-ddeg	600	chwe cant
21	dau-ddeg-un	700	saith cant

| 800 | wyth cant | 1000 | mil |
| 900 | naw cant | 1,000,000 | miliwn |

Resources for Welsh learners

Welsh-language classes are held throughout Wales – a list can be obtained from the Welsh for Adults Officer at the Welsh Language Board (see below). Otherwise, there are rafts of publications, on paper and electronically, as well as TV and radio programmes and support groups for the Welsh learner. The list below is by no means exhaustive.

Acen Tŷ Ifor, Bridge St, Cardiff CF10 2EE ☎029/20300800, Ⓦwww.acen .co.uk. S4C-originated company, now providing a multimedia Welsh course, together with a regular magazine and copious numbers of useful contacts.

Canolfan Iaith Nant Gwrtheyrn Llithfaen, Pwllheli, Gwynedd LL53 6PA ☎01758/750334, Ⓦwww.nantgwrtheyrn.org. Residential national language centre on the coast of the Llŷn.

Cymdeithas Madog (North American Welsh Studies Institute) Cymdeithas Madog, 2670 Glen Eagles Road, Lake Oswego, OR, 97034, USA Ⓦwww .madog.org. Annual residential language courses, plus a directory of resources.

Cymdeithas yr Iaith (Welsh Language Society) Pen Roc, Rhodfa'r Môr, Aberystwyth SY23 2AZ ☎01970/624501, Ⓦwww.cymdeithas.com. Campaigning and political organization dedicated to improving the status of the Welsh language.

National Language Unit of Wales Welsh for Adults Officer, Welsh Joint Education Committee, 245 Western Ave, Cardiff CF5 2YX ☎029/20265000, Ⓦwww.wjec.co.uk/nlu. Provides a comprehensive guide to Welsh teaching provision.

Welsh Language Board/Bwrdd yr Iaith Gymraeg 5–7 St Mary St, Cardiff CF10 1AT ☎029/20878000, Ⓦwww.bwrdd-yr-iaith.org.uk.

Small print and
Index

A Rough Guide to Rough Guides

Published in 1982, the first Rough Guide – to Greece – was a student scheme that became a publishing phenomenon. Mark Ellingham, a recent graduate in English from Bristol University, had been travelling in Greece the previous summer and couldn't find the right guidebook. With a small group of friends he wrote his own guide, combining a highly contemporary, journalistic style with a thoroughly practical approach to travellers' needs.

The immediate success of the book spawned a series that rapidly covered dozens of destinations. And, in addition to impecunious backpackers, Rough Guides soon acquired a much broader and older readership that relished the guides' wit and inquisitiveness as much as their enthusiastic, critical approach and value-for-money ethos.

These days, Rough Guides include recommendations from shoestring to luxury and cover more than 200 destinations around the globe, including almost every country in the Americas and Europe, more than half of Africa and most of Asia and Australasia. Our ever-growing team of authors and photographers is spread all over the world, particularly in Europe, the USA and Australia.

In the early 1990s, Rough Guides branched out of travel, with the publication of Rough Guides to World Music, Classical Music and the Internet. All three have become benchmark titles in their fields, spearheading the publication of a wide range of books under the Rough Guide name.

Including the travel series, Rough Guides now number more than 350 titles, covering: phrasebooks, waterproof maps, music guides from Opera to Heavy Metal, reference works as diverse as Conspiracy Theories and Shakespeare, and popular culture books from iPods to Poker. Rough Guides also produce a series of more than 120 World Music CDs in partnership with World Music Network.

Visit www.roughguides.com to see our latest publications.

Rough Guide travel images are available for commercial licensing at www.roughguidespictures.com

Rough Guide credits

Text editor: Gavin Thomas
Layout: Ankur Guha
Cartography: Ashutosh Bharti
Picture editor: Sarah Cummins
Production: Rebecca Short
Proofreader: Karen Parker
Cover design: Chloë Roberts
Photographers: Diana Jarvis and Scott Stickland
Editorial: **London** Ruth Blackmore, Andy Turner, Keith Drew, Edward Aves, Alice Park, Lucy White, Jo Kirby, James Smart, Natasha Foges, Róisín Cameron, Emma Traynor, James Rice, Emma Gibbs, Kathryn Lane, Christina Valhouli, Monica Woods, Mani Ramaswamy, Alison Roberts, Harry Wilson, Lucy Cowie, Helen Ochyra, Joe Staines, Peter Buckley, Matthew Milton, Tracy Hopkins, Ruth Tidball; **New York** Andrew Rosenberg, Steven Horak, AnneLise Sorensen, Ella Steim, Anna Owens, Sean Mahoney, Paula Neudorf; **Delhi** Madhavi Singh, Karen D'Souza, Lubna Shaheen
Design & Pictures: **London** Scott Stickland, Dan May, Diana Jarvis, Mark Thomas, Chloë Roberts, Nicole Newman, Emily Taylor; **Delhi** Umesh Aggarwal, Ajay Verma, Jessica Subramanian, Pradeep Thapliyal, Sachin Tanwar, Anita Singh, Nikhil Agarwal

Production: Vicky Baldwin
Cartography: **London** Maxine Repath, Ed Wright, Katie Lloyd-Jones; **Delhi** Rajesh Chhibber, Rajesh Mishra, Animesh Pathak, Jasbir Sandhu, Karobi Gogoi, Alakananda Roy, Swati Handoo, Deshpal Dabas
Online: **London** George Atwell, Faye Hellon, Jeanette Angell, Fergus Day, Justine Bright, Clare Bryson, Áine Fearon, Adrian Low, Ezgi Celebi, Amber Bloomfield; **Delhi** Amit Verma, Rahul Kumar, Narender Kumar, Ravi Yadav, Debojit Borah, Rakesh Kumar, Ganesh Sharma, Shisir Basumatari
Marketing & Publicity: **London** Liz Statham, Niki Hanmer, Louise Maher, Jess Carter, Vanessa Godden, Vivienne Watton, Anna Paynton, Rachel Sprackett, Libby Jellie, Laura Vipond; **New York** Geoff Colquitt, Nancy Lambert, Katy Ball; **Delhi** Ragini Govind
Manager India: Punita Singh
Reference Director: Andrew Lockett
Operations Manager: Helen Phillips
PA to Publishing Director: Nicola Henderson
Publishing Director: Martin Dunford
Commercial Manager: Gino Magnotta
Managing Director: John Duhigg

SMALL PRINT

Publishing information

This sixth edition published May 2009 by
Rough Guides Ltd,
80 Strand, London WC2R 0RL
345 Hudson St, 4th Floor,
New York, NY 10014, USA
14 Local Shopping Centre, Panchsheel Park,
New Delhi 110017, India
Distributed by the Penguin Group
Penguin Books Ltd,
80 Strand, London WC2R 0RL
Penguin Group (USA)
375 Hudson Street, NY 10014, USA
Penguin Group (Australia)
250 Camberwell Road, Camberwell,
Victoria 3124, Australia
Penguin Group (Canada)
195 Harry Walker Parkway N, Newmarket, ON,
L3Y 7B3 Canada
Penguin Group (NZ)
67 Apollo Drive, Mairangi Bay, Auckland 1310,
New Zealand
Cover concept by Peter Dyer.

Typeset in Bembo and Helvetica to an original design by Henry Iles.

Printed and bound in China

© Catherine Le Nevez, Mike Parker and Paul Whitfield 2009

536pp includes index

A catalogue record for this book is available from the British Library.

ISBN: 978-1-84836-050-1

1 3 5 7 9 8 6 4 2

Help us update

We've gone to a lot of effort to ensure that the sixth edition of **The Rough Guide to Wales** is accurate and up to date. However, things change – places get "discovered", opening hours are notoriously fickle, restaurants and rooms raise prices or lower standards. If you feel we've got it wrong or left something out, we'd like to know, and if you can remember the address, the price, the hours, the phone number, so much the better.

Please send your comments with the subject line "**Rough Guide Wales Update**" to ©mail@roughguides.com. We'll credit all contributions and send a copy of the next edition (or any other Rough Guide if you prefer) for the very best emails.

Have your questions answered and tell others about your trip at
⊛ community.roughguides.com

Acknowledgements

Catherine: The kind, insightful and fun-loving people who helped during my travels throughout Wales are too numerous to thank individually, so a heartfelt *diolch* to you all. In particular, thanks to the Cardiff crew (you know who you are!), the Bwlch crew (ditto!), and to the fantastic tourism professionals in Southeast Wales, Mid-Wales and the Cambrian Coast, as well as Glenda Lloyd Davies at Visit Wales. Thanks too to Dave Griffiths who came to the rescue when I was stranded the night I arrived. At Rough Guides, cheers to co-author Paul Whitfield and editor Gavin Thomas, and to Jo Kirby

and Monica Woods. As ever, thanks above all to my family.

Paul: Glenda Lloyd Davies and Lowri Jones at Visit Wales who helped make research trips much smoother, Sarah and Fraser for sharing mountain bike rides in the rain, Mike Parker for insights into Welsh life and an uplifting curry, Catherine for being a breeze to work with and Gavin Thomas for thorough editing and helping trim the fat. Lastly to Marion for enduring excessive eating, comfy beds and welcoming pubs beside windswept platforms.

SMALL PRINT

Readers' letters

Thanks to all the readers who have taken the time to write in with comments and suggestions (and apologies if we've inadvertently omitted or misspelt anyone's name):

Marc Albers, Bill Amos, Helen Clough, Jan and Geoff Cole, Michael Cooper, Tamzin Costello, Tony Evans, Bernard Gorman, M. Habberley, David and Barbara Hall, Rhiannon Humphreys, Rose James, Chris Jennings, Jens Kronborg, Benjamin Levy, Eric Lien, Richard Lysons, Pippa Marland, Kate Markham, Jacqui Mitchell, Dave Palmer, Neil Rowlands, Frans Schrijver, Claudia Senecal, Judith Smart, Gary Spinks, Stephen Spooner, John Trevitt, Barbara Wescombe, Brenda Wickham.

Photo credits

Index

Map entries are in colour.

N

O

P

INDEX

O

INDEX

Map symbols

▪▪▪▪	Welsh border	⅏	Archeological site
▬▬▬	Chapter division boundary	♦	Place of interest
▬▬▬	Motorway	⊠	Post office
═══	Major road	@	Internet access
═══	Minor road	ⓘ	Tourist office
▬▬▬	Pedestrianized road	⊞	Hospital
- - - -	Footpath	♦	Museum
▬•▬•▬	Railway	⏛	Monument
─────	River	⊙	Statue
─ ─ ─	Ferry route	⚐	Golf course
─────	Wall	🏊	Swimming pool
⋈	Bridge	△	Youth hostel
⊠	Gate	⚠	Campsite
⌐ⅼⅼⅼⅼⅼⅼ	Cliff	◉	Accommodation
▲	Mountain peak	✈	Airport
⌒	Cave	★	Bus stop
🕱	Waterfall	🅿	Parking
⥲	Marshland	⌂	Abbey
⬈	Viewpoint	ⵜ	Church (regional maps)
⼁	Wind farm	⬯	Stadium
🕯	Lighthouse	▬	Building
♔	Castle	⊞	Church/cathedral (town maps)
⏛	Stately home	▨	Park/forest
ⵝ	Gardens	▨	Beach
❀	Country park	⊡	Cemetery
∴	Ruins		

MAP SYMBOLS